INSPIRE / PLAN / DISCOVER / EXPERIENCE

ITALY

ITALY

CONTENTS

DISCOVER 6

EXPERIENCE 46

NEED TO KNOW 534

Left: Colosseum and Roman Forum; previous page: Matera at dusk; front cover: San Gimignano, Tuscany

DISCOVER

Lake Orta, Piedmont

WELCOME TO
ITALY

Magnificent piazzas, turquoise seas and rolling hills – Italy has it all. And that's before you add iconic art, more UNESCO World Heritage Sites than anywhere else on earth, and the Italian knack for *la dolce vita*. Whatever your dream trip to Italy entails, this DK Eyewitness travel guide is the perfect companion.

1 Flowers in bloom in Monti Sibillini national park, Umbria.

2 Traditional Italian food.

3 A picturesque canal in Venice lined with boats.

Italy only became a fully unified country in 1870 – before that it was a turbulent collection of rival city states. Happily for the visitor, their conflicting allegiances and histories resulted in a variety of architecture and art not seen anywhere else in Europe. From the mighty architecture of ancient Rome and Pompeii to the pretty Teutonic mountain villages of the north, and from the lacy Gothic palazzi of Venice to the refined Renaissance churches of Florence, a tour along the Italian peninsula is a roller-coaster ride through European history.

The landscape, too, is incredibly diverse. Ski the spectacular slopes of the Dolomites or witness volcanic pyrotechnics on the summit of Mount Stromboli. Lose yourself in the wilderness of the maquis-clad Sardinian mountains or spot wild ibex in the rocky valleys of the Gran Paradiso national park. Bask on the unspoiled beaches of Puglia or sip vintage wine in the vineyard-cloaked hills of Tuscany. However you choose to experience its natural beauty, Italy will not disappoint.

Italy can easily overwhelm with the sheer number of unmissable cities, towns, villages, archaeological and natural sites that pepper the peninsula. We've picked out themes and planned itineraries to whet your appetite, broken the country down into easily navigable chapters, and created colourful, comprehensive maps to help you plan the perfect visit. Whether you're staying for a weekend, a week, or longer, this DK Eyewitness guide will ensure that you see the very best the country has to offer. Enjoy the book, and enjoy Italy.

REASONS TO LOVE
ITALY

Evocative ruins, extravagant palaces, vineyards, strong espresso
and freshly baked pizza: there are so many reasons to love Italy.
Here, we pick some of our favourites.

THE APERITIVO *1*

There's no better way to
fill the hours before dinner.
Designed to whet your
appetite, this Italian tradition
consists of a cool sparkling
drink served with snacks
ranging from olives to
exquisite little antipasti.

CRUISING DOWN THE
GRAND CANAL *2*

Everyone should sail down
Venice's great waterway at
least once in their life. Take
the slow boat, Vaporetto 1,
and stand on the deck for
the best views – not only
of the lacy palace façades,
but of life in a city in which
everything happens by water.

3 PIZZA

Probably originating in Naples,
pizza is, of course, now available
all over Italy. Thick crusted in
Naples, thin in Rome, sold by the
slice, or folded over as a calzone,
pizza comes in endless varieties.
Wherever you eat it, you can be
sure it will be fresh from the oven.

4 THE PASSEGGIATA

In every town, village and city in Italy, locals put on their finery and head out for an evening stroll. They might do a little window shopping or stop for an aperitivo, but the main purpose of the passeggiata is to see, be seen and bump into friends.

THE PALAZZO 5

From the Gothic façades of Venice to Renaissance townhouses, *palazzi* give Italian cities and towns much of their beauty. Built by royalty, nobility and wealthy merchants, many have been turned into museums and hotels.

MARKETS 6

In a country that prides itself on its food, you'll find a colourful array of fresh produce in markets throughout Italy. Some are held in dedicated market buildings, others outside, but most have great street food stands nearby.

PIAZZA SAN PIETRO AT DAWN 7

Designed by Bernini, Piazza San Pietro is one of the most magnificent public spaces in the world. To see it at its best, get up at dawn and explore without the crowds.

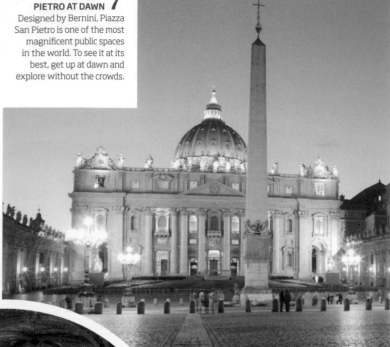

VESPAS 8

Launched in 1946 to meet the needs of a country crippled by war, the Vespa (wasp) became ubiquitous after Audrey Hepburn leapt on the back of one in *Roman Holiday* (1953).

9 THE DUOMO

The cathedrals (or *duomi*) of Italy are repositories for some of the world's greatest art. They cover every architectural style and era, from Byzantine to Baroque.

10 BEACHES

Italy has around 7,500 km (4,660 miles) of shoreline, and its coast is one of the most varied in Europe, with sandy beaches, volcanic bays, dramatic cliffs and rocky coves.

THE PIAZZA 11

From intimate squares to grand open-air drawing rooms, Italy's piazzas are an essential feature of everyday life. Some are lined with pavement cafés, while others host daily markets.

VISITING VINEYARDS 12

The best way to appreciate the complexities of Italian wine is to visit vineyards. Many welcome visitors, from tiny wineries to major producers who may have dedicated tasting rooms.

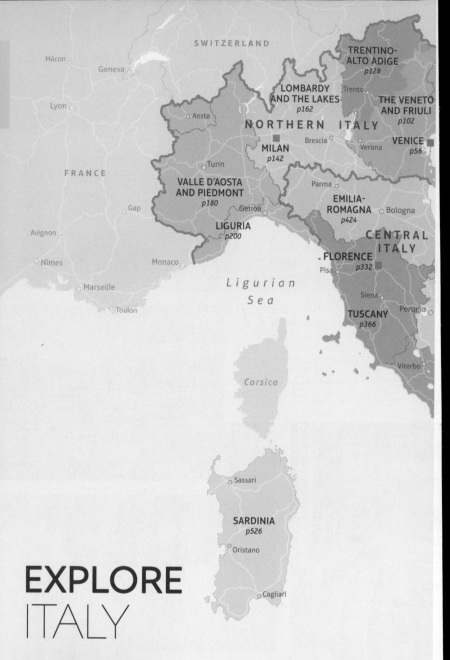

MâconGenevaLyonFRANCEGapAvignonNîmesMarseilleToulonSWITZERLAND

Aosta

NORTHERN ITALY

LOMBARDY AND THE LAKES
p162

Trento

TRENTINO-ALTO ADIGE
p128

THE VENETO AND FRIULI
p102

Brescia

MILAN
p142

Turin

Verona

VENICE
p56

VALLE D'AOSTA AND PIEDMONT
p180

Genoa

Parma

EMILIA-ROMAGNA
p424

Bologna

LIGURIA
p200

CENTRAL ITALY

FLORENCE
p332

Pisa

Siena

Perugia

TUSCANY
p366

Viterbo

Ligurian Sea

Corsica

Sassari

SARDINIA
p526

Oristano

Cagliari

Mediterranean Sea

EXPLORE
ITALY

This guide divides Italy into three distinct regions: northern Italy *(p48)*, central Italy *(p214)* and southern Italy *(p440)*. These regions have been divided into 20 colour-coded sightseeing areas, as shown on the map above.

AUSTRIA

SLOVENIA

Udine

Ljubljana

Zagreb

Trieste

Rijeka

CROATIA

Zadar

Ancona

EUROPE

North Sea

SWEDEN

DENMARK

UNITED KINGDOM

GERMANY

POLAND

CZECH REP.

FRANCE

SWITZ.

AUSTRIA

HUNGARY

CROATIA

ROMANIA

SERBIA

BULGARIA

ITALY

SPAIN

GREECE

ALGERIA

TUNISIA

Mediterranean Sea

LE MARCHE
p414

Adriatic Sea

UMBRIA
p400

Pescara

L'Aquila

Dubrovnik

■ **ROME**
p222

ABRUZZO, MOLISE AND PUGLIA
p476

LAZIO
p320

Foggia

Bari

Terracina

SOUTHERN ITALY

Brindisi

NAPLES
p448 ■

Salerno

Potenza

Taranto

CAMPANIA
p462

Tyrrhenian Sea

BASILICATA AND CALABRIA
p490

Cosenza

Ionian Sea

Messina

Reggio di Calabria

Palermo

SICILY
p500

Catania

Agrigento

Syracuse

0 kilometres   100

0 miles   100

N
↑

2 WEEKS
A Grand Tour of Italy

Day 1

Morning Kick off your two week tour in Como. Stroll the centre and visit the Duomo (p148), a melding of Renaissance and Gothic styles. Catch a hydrofoil service from the jetty to Lenno, the jumping off point for a trip to Villa del Balbianello (p167), a mansion featured in *Casino Royale*.

Afternoon Visit nearby Villa Carlotta (p166), one of the lake's grandest villas, with lush gardens tumbling to the shore.

Evening Soak up more lakeside views over dinner. For hearty dishes in a laidback setting, head to La Fagurida (lafagurida.it), or, if you're after something smarter, relax on the terrace of Al Veluu (www.alveluu.com).

Day 2

Morning Spend the morning wandering the cobbled streets of Varenna (p166). Stroll the gardens of Villa Monastero, then hike up to the Castello di Vezio, from where you can take in spectacular lake views. Back in town, grab a bite at one of the cafés.

Afternoon Zip across to Bellagio (p166) and enjoy a post-prandial walk in the park of Villa Serbelloni, which is owned by the Rockefeller Foundation. Spend the rest of the afternoon exploring town.

Evening For dinner, tuck into risotto with perch, a local speciality, at one of the town's many romantic little restaurants.

Day 3

Morning Arrive in Venice by train and start to explore on foot. Allow time to get lost and indulge in a little people-watching over a coffee while working out a walking route to Piazza San Marco. When you get there, sit on the terrace of Caffè Florian for a drink.

Afternoon Walk towards the Ponte dell'Accademia to cross the Grand Canal (p68), zigzagging across Dorsoduro to lively Campo Santa Margherita (p100).

Evening Have dinner at a nearby restaurant, such as Osteria Alla Bifora Venezia (Sestiere Dorsoduro 2930).

① Florence's Duomo.
② Villa Balbianello, Lake Como.
③ Pizza on a Venetian canal.
④ Picturesque street in Bellagio.
⑤ Ponte dell'Accademia, Venice.

Day 4

Morning Rise early for Mass at San Marco (p72) and drink in the atmosphere of the church. Weave north to the church of Santa Maria dei Miracoli (p85), then see the Giorgio Franchetti art collection in the Ca' d'Oro (p84). Take the gondola-ferry across to the Rialto (p82), and experience the market bustle over cicchetti (snacks) in a typical bar, or bacaro (p64).

Afternoon Plot a route to Ca' Rezzonico (p87) for an evocative taste of aristocratic Venetian life, then dive into the art collections of the Accademia (p90) and Peggy Guggenheim (p90).

Evening Head to Campo San Giacomo and watch the world go by in the unpretentious Al Prosecco wine bar.

Day 5

Morning Catch an early-morning train to Florence. Start with the Duomo, Baptistry and Campanile (p342), climbing the latter for a crow's-eye view of the city. Circuit the Romanesque Baptistry to see its east doors. Window-shop your way down Via dei Calzaiuoli to Piazza della Signoria (p346), dominated by the Palazzo Vecchio. Cross the medieval Ponte Vecchio (p356) for lunch on Piazza Santo Spirito (p361).

Afternoon Walk to the Cappella Brancacci (p362) then head back to the centre of town and visit the Uffizi (p344), which is at its least crowded after 4:30pm.

Evening Wind down with an aperitivo at Procacci 1885 on Via Tornabuoni.

Day 6

Morning Head to the Bargello (p354), a former prison now housing Renaissance sculptures. Devote the rest of the morning to ethereal frescoes by Fra Angelico in the convent of San Marco (p352).

Afternoon See Michelangelo's David at the Accademia (p348), then take the bus to the delicate church of San Miniato al Monte (p362), for splendid views.

Evening Walk downhill into town, ending up at the Ponte Vecchio, with time for an aperitivo along the Arno before dinner.

Day 7

Morning Make a day trip to Pisa (p378). Instead of heading straight to the Piazza dei Miracoli (p380), take in the atmosphere, with a visit to the market on Piazza delle Vettovaglie – a good place for lunch – and a walk along the Arno, lined with *palazzi*.

Afternoon Explore the sights on the Piazza dei Miracoli and climb the Leaning Tower.

Evening Head back to Florence for dinner at Il Latini (Via dei Palchetti 6R).

Day 8

Morning Take the Frecciarossa (high-speed train) to Rome, then get some ice cream in Piazza Navona (p258). After a visit to the Pantheon (p260), cross the Ponte Sisto to Trastevere (p298) for lunch in a trattoria.

Afternoon Catch a tram to the Colosseum (p242), then walk past the Roman Forum (p246) and Imperial Forum to the virtually-recreated villa of a wealthy patrician family at Palazzo Valentini (p253). Visit the Capitoline Museums (p250), and do not miss the bird's-eye view of the Forum from the museum café's terrace.

Evening Walk to the former Jewish ghetto (p264) for an aperitivo, then have dinner in a traditional kosher restaurant.

Day 9

Morning Start early to see St Peter's (p286) for Mass without the crowds then visit the Vatican Museums and Sistine Chapel (p288). Have lunch in a trattoria on Borgo Pio.

Afternoon Catch a tram to the Villa Borghese park, followed by visits to the Museo e Galleria Borghese (p314) and the Etruscan finds at Villa Giulia (p316).

Evening Have a drink on the stylish terrace of the Caffè delle Arti at Galleria Nazionale d'Arte Moderna, then take a tram to San Lorenzo for traditional Roman fare at Pommidoro (Piazza dei Sanniti 44/46).

Day 10

Morning Spend the morning at Ostia Antica (p326), returning in time for lunch in a trattoria in Testaccio.

Afternoon Head to Piazza del Popolo and Santa Maria del Popolo (p278), then explore

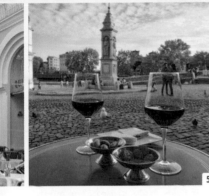

1. Staircase, Vatican Museums.
2. Historic streets of Naples.
3. Café on the island of Capri.
4. Piazza dei Miracoli, Pisa.
5. Aperitivo in a piazza in Rome.
6. Galleria Borghese, Rome.

the streets around the Piazza di Spagna *(p272)* and climb the Spanish Steps.

Evening Experience first-class seafood at Il Simposio *(p298)*, and then walk back to the centre via the Trevi Fountain *(p274)*, perhaps indulging in a final *gelato* at San Crispino *(Via della Panetteria 42)*.

Day 11

Morning Catch the Frecciarossa to Naples and take a hydrofoil to Capri *(p472)*. Head to the Grotta Azzurra *(p473)*, then take the funicular to Piazza Umberto I in Capri town.

Afternoon Enjoy a late lunch then climb up to the remains of Villa Jovis.

Evening Treat yourself to an aperitivo and dinner at Michelin-starred Il Riccio *(www. capripalace.com)*, a beach club in Anacapri.

Day 12

Morning Take the hydrofoil to Naples, then the Circumvesuviana train to Pompeii *(p466)*.

Afternoon Spend the afternoon exploring Pompeii and then move on to Sorrento, the starting point for the Amalfi Coast *(p470)*.

Evening Sip on a cocktail as you watch the sun set over Vesuvius, then enjoy a meal at one of the town's many restaurants.

Day 13

Morning Catch the bus to Positano *(p470)* for a stroll and early lunch in town.

Afternoon Walk the Sentiero degli Dei, which links the coast to the villages inland. Taking about three hours, it traces the cliffs of the Amalfi Coast, offering views of the Mediterranean Sea and the coastline.

Evening Hop on the bus to Amalfi *(p470)* and tuck into a traditional seafood dinner.

Day 14

Morning Explore Amalfi, making sure you don't miss the Duomo in the main square.

Afternoon Grab a *cuoppo* (fried seafood in a paper cone), then go via bus to Ravello *(p471)*. Stroll around Villa Rufolo and then take in sea views from Villa Cimbrone.

Evening Celebrate your tour with gorgeous sunset views and Campanian cuisine.

Camuni Carvings

The extraordinary rock carvings of the Val Camonica in Lombardy *(p175)* were created by people who settled in the valley during the Neolithic period (1000–400 BC). Known to the Romans as Camuni, these people produced some of the finest rock art in Europe. To see the best engravings, head for the Parco Nazionale delle Incisioni Rupestri.

Rock carving showing hunters and their horses at Val Camonica, Lombardy

ITALY FOR
ANCIENT ARCHAEOLOGY

From Etruscan painted tombs to prehistoric finds, Italy is one of the most astonishing destinations on earth for anyone interested in archaeology. Sicily and Southern Italy, once Magna Graecia, hold many ancient Greek ruins, while lovers of Roman civilization should target Rome, Pompeii and Herculaneum.

Etrucan Tombs

The Etruscans were Italy's first major civilization, living here from around 900 to 27 BC. Etruscan artifacts can be found in the Vatican Museums *(p288)* and Villa Giulia *(p316)*, but to best understand this culture, visit a necropolis. Decorated with feast scenes, the Tomb of the Leopards in the Museo Archeologico e Necropoli in Tarquinia is particularly beautiful *(p327)*.

Roman Life

Remnants of Ancient Rome can be found everywhere in Italy, from Aquileia *(p125)* and Aosta *(p195)* in the north to Herculaneum *(p468)* and Pompeii *(p466)* in the south. The latter were both preserved in a thick layer of ash when Vesuvius erupted in AD 79, and today present a vivid picture of Roman life. Of course, Rome has a glut of sites, which are best discovered on a walking tour of the city *(www.rome freewalkingtour.com)*.

→ The Colosseum in Rome, with its three tiers of arcades

Greece in Italy

In the 8th century BC, Greeks began to settle in Sicily and southern Italy. Several of the great intellectuals of Classical Greece, including Empedocles and Archimedes, were in fact Sicilian, and by the 4th century BC Siracusa was the most powerful city in the region. For a taste of the city's zenith, check out the summer festival of Greek drama at the Greek Theatre *(p510)*. It's easy to forget that you are not in Greece, when exploring the Valley of the Temples *(p514)* and its Museo Archeologico Pietro Griffo.

↑ Greek vase depicting Hephaestus and Dionysus from the Valley of the Temples, Agrigento

Nuraghic Giants

Sardinia is home to around 7,000 nuraghi, truncated stone structures dating from 1800 to 300 BC and built by a mysterious Mediterranean people. Start your journey into nuraghic history at the Museo Archeologico Nazionale G A Sanna in Sassari *(p530)*, then head for Mont'e Prama. This necropolis is guarded by an entire stone army of giants.

↑ Colourful Etruscan fresco at the Tomb of the Leopards, Lazio

→ Head of one of the Giants of Mont'e Prama, with its trademark spiral eyes

Did You Know?

Fresco means "fresh" in Italian. The process involves applying paint to wet plaster before it dries.

ITALY FOR RENAISSANCE
MASTERPIECES

The 14th to 16th centuries saw an explosion of the arts in Italy due to the wealth of Rome – the power-centre of the Christian Church – and the prosperity of the rest of the peninsula's city states. Cardinals, merchants and aristocrats alike flaunted their wealth and power through the patronage of artists, and left behind a cornucopia of Renaissance masterpieces.

Statuesque Sculptures

Renaissance sculptures were often executed on a large scale. Michelangelo's colossal statue of the young biblical hero David *(p348)* is the perfect example. The choice of subject was popular at the time, with David representing Florence as a warning to the Goliath of Rome. The influence of Classical Greek and Roman art is also evident in Pietro da Cortona's *Rape of the Sabine Women (p251)* and Ammannati's *Fountain of Neptune (p346)*.

Crowds admiring Michelangelo's *David* (1501–04) in Florence

The Creation of Adam on the Sistine Chapel ceiling, and *(inset)* Da Vinci's *The Last Supper* (c 1494-7)

Fabulous Frescos

Although this art form has existed since antiquity, fresco will forever be associated with the Renaissance and Michelangelo's Sistine Chapel ceiling *(p292)*. Michelangelo was initially reluctant to accept the commission from Pope Julius II in 1508, as he had little experience in fresco, but four years later, he had completed the 366 figures that can be seen on the ceiling today. Other Renaissance frescoes to seek out include Da Vinci's *The Last Supper* *(p154)*, Corregio's *Assumption (p435)* and Il Pordenone's *Adoration of the Magi (p119)*.

TOP 6 RENAISSANCE ARTISTS

Giotto (c 1270-1337)
Re-introduced realism into medieval art.

Botticelli (1445-1510)
Renowned for his mythological subjects.

Leonardo da Vinci (1452-1519)
An artist, inventor and architect.

Michelangelo (1475-1564)
Considered the best artist of his age.

Titian (1488-1576)
The first to paint for patrons all over Europe.

Artemisia (1593-1653)
Many of her paintings feature mythological and biblical women.

Perfect Paintings

The Renaissance saw a revival of Neoplatonism, which espouses that the contemplation of physical beauty leads to an understanding of spiritual beauty. This philosophy infuses *The Birth of Venus*, Botticelli's depiction of the Roman goddess of beauty, which hangs in the Uffizi Gallery *(p344)* alongside Raphael's *Madonna of the Goldfinch* and Michelangelo's *The Holy Family*. Feeling inspired to create your own masterpiece? Take a painting holiday *(www.paintingholidaysinitaly.com)*.

→

Detail of *The Birth of Venus* (c 1485), Sandro Botticelli's most famous work

▷ **Contemporary Construction**

In the 21st century, Italian architecture has taken on a sustainable and ethical bent. This is most visible in Milan's Bosco Verticale, which is covered in over 800 trees. Elsewhere, check out Zaha Hadid's Messner Mountain Museum Corones, which is carved into the mountainside.

 INSIDER TIP
Modern Venice

To see another side of Venice, away from the Gothic, Moorish and Renaissance buildings, take a tour with Viaggi di Architettura *(www. viaggidiarchitettura.it).*

ITALY'S INCREDIBLE
ARCHITECTURE

There is nowhere better than Italy to experience the glories of European architecture and the country's buildings speak of its tumultuous history. Of course, there are countless examples of ancient architecture *(p21)*, but the Romanesque and Gothic, Renaissance and Baroque, as well as Fascist and contemporary styles, are also well represented.

△ **Baroque Buildings**

In the Counter-Reformation, architecture aimed to inspire awe, with highly decorated features, including twisted columns and grand staircases. Turin was constructed by some of Baroque's biggest names; take a tour of the city to discover the work of Guarino Guarini and Filippo Juvarra *(www.somewhere.it).*

▷ Mussolini's Monuments

Fascist architecture is characterized by its simplicity, symmetry and scale – take Como's Casa del Fascio, which is a perfect rectangle, with a height half the length of its base. Milan was Mussolini's adopted city and has a huge number of Fascist buildings. Guiding Architects Milano run tours of the city *(www.ga-milano.it)*.

◁ Renaissance Symmetry

Bramante's masterpiece at San Pietro in Montorio in Rome *(p299)* is the embodiment of the Renaissance ideals of order, precision and symmetry, which were believed to reflect the perfection of God. Consisting of two concentric shells, the dome of Florence's Duomo *(p342)* also exemplifies the era's penchant for geometry.

▷ Glitzy Gothic

The pointed arches and intricate stonework of Gothic architecture were imported from France by the Cistercian monastic order, who sought to build taller and lighter buildings. Adopted by palace architects in Venice, it is exemplified in the delicate lacy stone embroidery of the Palazzo Ducale *(p76)*. Here, the style is combined with Byzantine and Moorish influences. Join a Hidden Doge's Treasure Tour to get under the skin of this wonderful building.

◁ Romanesque Landmarks

The rounded arches that typify the Romanesque style had their origins in ancient Roman basilicas, and re-emerged from the Dark Ages in buildings such as the Leaning Tower of Pisa *(p380)*. Interiors were usually simple, like those of their Roman predecessors, making great play of stone, geometry and light, elements clearly visible in Pisa's famous landmark. Florence's octagonal Baptistry *(p342)* also uses geometry to great effect and is thought to have been built on top of a Roman temple to Mars.

◁ Puglia and Sicily

Puglia is one of Italy's biggest producers of fresh produce, while Sicily's long history of invasions is reflected in its rich and varied cuisine. Order burrata (buffalo cheese with a creamy centre) in Puglia and accompany it with a glass of Salice Salentino wine. On Sicily, arancini (stuffed deep-fried rice balls) are perfect for lunch and Savia, in Catania, makes some of the best *(lnx.savia.it)*. In search of a sweet treat? Pasticceria Oscar in Palermo serves up classic Sicilian cannoli.

▷ Rome and Lazio

The traditional cuisine in this central region is based on cheap cuts of meat and offal, along with simple pasta dishes. Despite this simplicity, we guarantee that you won't be disappointed by the *pizza bianca* sandwiches (cooked pizza base, sliced and stuffed) or *spaghetti alla carbonara* at Lo Zozzone *(p263)*. It's not all meaty either – look out for *Carcio alla giudia* (deep-fried artichokes), which pair perfectly with a dry Frascati wine.

ITALY FOR
FOODIES

The gastronomic traditions of Italy are a vibrant mosaic, with specialities differing from one town to the next. Here, we talk you through the must-eats and must-drinks of each region, so you know what to order and where.

◁ Venice and the Veneto

Sipping a tart, orange Aperol spritz and grazing on *cicchetti e ombre* (traditional canapés), while over-looking a Venetian canal: bliss. These waterways are responsible for many of the local delicacies – the region's history as the nexus of trade between the east and the west lent it sweet-and-sour sauces and a penchant for seafood. *Risotto al nero di seppia* (squid-ink risotto) and *bigoli in salsa* (pasta with onion and anchovies) are the local must-eats.

◁ Florence and Tuscany

Rich bean soups, toasted bread topped with chicken liver pâté, and steaks from prized Chianina cattle dominate here. Start your evening chatting to regulars over *crostini* and a glass of Chianti at wine bar Fiaschetteria Nuvoli *(Piazza dell'Olio 15, Florence)*. Then, order *ribollita* (bread and vegetable soup) at Il Latini *(p370)* or Chianina steak at Trattoria Mario *(trattoriamario.com)*.

◁ Naples and Campania

This region is home to the classic Mediterranean diet, based on vegetables, tomatoes and olive oil. But this is also where pizza was born. The ideal Neapolitan dinner would encompass *mozzarella di bufala* (soft cheese made from buffalos' milk), a classic *pizza margherita* at Da Michele *(p454)*, washed down with a glass of Aglianico or Greco di Tufo, and then *sfogliatelle* (shell-shaped filled pastries) at Pasticceria Andrea Pansa *(www.pasticceriapansa.it)*.

TOP 3 BUDGET DINING TIPS

Stand for Coffee
Standing at the bar for a coffee can cost less, especially in Venice, than sitting at a table.

Menu Fisso
Fixed-price menus, including a glass of wine and water, can be extremely good value.

Aperitivo
When ordering a drink it may be offered as an "aperitivo". This will be more expensive but it will include antipasti, or items that can be selected from a menu, so you won't need to pay for dinner.

△ Milan and Northwest Italy

Risotto, truffles and polenta are popular inland, while coastal Liguria is famous for its seafood, olive oil and basil. Order pesto pasta in Genoa, risotto in Milan and *cacciucco* (seafood casserole) in Livorno. Earthy Barolo and rich Barbaresco grace local wine menus, while bitter-sweet Campari makes for the perfect apéritif. *Cin cin!*

Volcanoes and Mountains

With towering peaks peppering the country, Italy is a haven for mountain pursuits. Tackle the challenging Via Ferrata route through the Dolomites *(p132)*, hit the Alps' ski slopes or take a cable car up to the summit of Etna *(p522)* – the highest active volcano in Europe.

→

Snow-covered Mount Etna, looming over the city of Catania, Sicily

ITALY FOR
NATURAL
WONDERS

From erupting volcanoes to magnificent coastal scenery, Italy is rich in breathtaking natural wonders. Experience them by driving, hiking, sailing, skiing or simply lazing on a beach.

Valleys and Vineyards

Perhaps the most beautiful valley in Tuscany, the rolling cypress-spiked hills of Val d'Orcia to the south of Siena appear in the backgrounds of many Renaissance paintings. Lush and green in spring, crisp and golden in summer, this valley is captivating at any time of the year. Explore its sinuous country roads by bike, pausing at vineyards to sample Orcia wines.

←

Sunset over the picturesque hills of Val d'Orcia

TOP
5 **ITALIAN BEACHES**

Cala Goloritzé, Sardinia
A pebbled beach known for its turquoise waters.

Cala Bianca, Campania
This small beach has sand as white as snow.

Spiaggia delle Ghiaie, Tuscany
The perfect spot for snorkelling and diving.

Spiaggia dei Conigli, Sicily
Turtles come to lay their eggs on this beach.

Porto Miggiano, Puglia
A wild Adriatic spot.

Breathtaking Beaches

Italy has some fantastic beaches, especially in the south and on the islands of Elba, Sicily and Sardinia. Our top pick is Scala dei Turchi (p520), on the south coast of Sicily. Surrounded by blinding white cliffs, this stretch of glinting quartz is caressed by a crystalline turquoise sea. It's the perfect place for a dip.

→

The unique, white Scala dei Turchi cliffs in southern Sicily

Caves and Caverns

There is a hidden world beneath the Italian soil. Take a walk through the spectacular limestone formations of the Grotte di Frasassi (p421). One of Europe's largest cave-systems, over 15 km (9 miles) have been explored. Elsewhere, take a boat trip through the incredible Grotta Azzurra (p473).

→

The dramatic subterranean landscape of the Grotte di Frasassi

Hit the Slopes

In the north, the Alps *(p186)* and the Dolomites *(p132)* offer plenty of fun, with some of the continent's best ski resorts attracting both novice and advanced skiers. Here, cross-country trails wind through wooded landscapes, offering great off-piste opportunities. For something a bit different, head out on a snow-shoeing adventure with AIGAE *(www.aigae.org)* or try curling at the Palaghiaccio di Claut *(www.palaclaut.altervista.org)*.

People enjoying the snow on a ski slope in the Dolomites

ITALY FOR
OUTDOOR
ACTIVITIES

Thanks to its varied geography, Italy is a veritable haven for outdoor enthusiasts. The mountainous north offers some of Europe's best skiing and hiking, while the country's 7,000 km (4,350 miles) of coastline have their own appeal.

Take a Hike

Trails lace Italy from north to south, along dramatic mountain vistas, lake panoramas and seascapes. For Alpine scenery, make the most of the 750-km- (466-mile-) long Alpe Adria Trail *(alpe-adria-trail.com)*, which winds through Italy, Austria and Slovenia. In the south, don't miss the Sentiero degli Dei *(incampania.com)*, which hugs the cliffs of the Amalfi Coast *(p470)*. Trekking Italia organizes group treks to suit all abilities *(www.trekkingitalia.org)*.

←

Hikers walking through the gorgrous Dolomites in the summer

Take to the Water

Lake Garda *(p168)* attracts keen windsurfers, kite surfers and fly boarders who come to glide its wind-swept waters and perform old school tricks in the air. For water-skiing, wakeboarding and SUP, make for the Water Experience Centre *(waterexperience center.it)* on the calmer waters of nearby Lake Como *(p166)*. Bored of lakes? Head to Sardinia *(p527)* for some of the best snorkelling and diving in Europe with SubAquaDive *(www. subaquadive.it)* or, for a less energetic experience, cruise across Capri's deep blue waters *(p472)* with Capri Boat Experience *(www.capriboat experience.com)*.

→ Windsurfers riding the waves on Lake Garda

Wheelie Good Fun

Cyclists of all abilities will enjoy wheeling around Italy. Soak up lake and mountain scenery on a leisurely ride along the scenic Garda by Bike cycle path, a wooden and steel walkway hooked into the mountain walls 50 m (164 ft) above the lake. In Tuscany, the intermediate Giro del Chianti *(www. viaggiareinbici.it)* snakes up and down hills carpeted in vineyards and olive groves. The more adventurous should head to Sardinia's rugged interior *(p527)*, where a network of trails outside the city of Sinnai are sure to keep the adrenaline pumping.

 GREAT VIEW
Sky High

Linking the Alpine resorts of Courmayeur and Punta Hebronner, the 2,166-m (7,106-ft) Skyway Montebianco cable car grants vistas of Mont Blanc, Europe's highest peak *(www. montebianco.com)*.

↑ Cyclists take in the view from the Ponale trail in Riva del Garda

Dress the Part

The lively atmosphere and fun traditions of a festival make an exciting and kid-friendly introduction to local culture, food and history. Carnevale is a particularly great choice as it's celebrated all over Italy, with children dressing up to take part in processions or just to wander the town with their parents. The most famous celebrations are in Venice (p56) in the weeks leading up to Lent. On the 2nd and 3rd Sunday in August, the Volterra AD 1398 festival (www.volterra1398.it) sees the town (p392) return to the Middle Ages as locals dress up as knights, peasants, jugglers, musicians, friars and jesters.

↑ Masked revellers parading through the streets at the Venice Carnevale

ITALY FOR FAMILIES

Did You Know?

The orcs in J R R Tolkein's *Lord of the Rings* trilogy were reportedly inspired by Orcus.

Italy's broad mix of child-friendly attractions and activities means that you will never be short of ways to keep your kids entertained. Families are at the centre of Italian life so children will receive a warm welcome wherever they go, while an increasing number of museums and sites have dedicated tours for younger visitors.

Travel Back in Time

Italy's museums are always searching for new ways to entertain youngsters. Virtual reality installations at some sights – including the Palazzo Valentini (p253) and the Baths of Caracalla (p308) – do a great job of bringing history to life. The Vatican Museums' (p288) audio guide for children is so good that adults might wish to opt for it as well, while the Roman Gladiator School gives kids the chance to dress up as gladiators for the day and learn how to fight. All the gear is sanitized between each use.

←

Children admiring a sculpture in the courtyard of the Vatican Museums

↑ Sculpture of Orcus, god of the underworld, at the Bomarzo Monster Park

TOP 5 — BUDGET TIPS FOR FAMILIES

Free Travel
Children under a certain age or height can often travel for free. Check transport websites *(p540)* for details.

Family Passes
Save with family travel and museum passes in Rome, Florence and other major art cities.

Free Beaches
Look out for the *spiaggia libera* (free beach) signs.

Picnic Lunches
Italy is full of great delicatessens that let children pick their own sandwich fillings and charge a fraction of the price found in cafés. Most towns also have drinking water fountains and taps.

Hop-On, Hop-Off Tour Buses
In big cities these can be a cost-effective way to see as many sights as possible and keep tantrums to a minimum.

Weird and Wonderful

There are all kinds of quirky spots tucked away in this ancient and artistic country, and kids will love stumbling upon beautiful and bizarre surprises. Set off together and discover hidden gems like Bomarzo *(p325)* – a 16th century sculpture-filled wonderland scattered with monster statues – and the overgrown ruins of Valle dei Mulini *(p471)*.

Make Pizza and Gelato

Fancy having a budding chef in the family? Pizza and ice-cream-making classes for kids are becoming increasingly popular, especially in major cities. Italian Connection *(www. italian-connection.co.uk)* specializes in creating tailor-made experiences for families with children.

→
A lesson in making pizza, everyone's favourite Italian dish

Panoramic view of ↑
the amphitheatre in the
Vittoriale-degli-Italiani

ITALY FOR
INSPIRATION

With its gorgeous landscapes, romantic cityscapes and rich history, Italy
has inspired writers and poets for centuries. More recently, the country
has also become a favoured filming location, with many romantic comedies,
horror films and crime movies being set here.

On Screen

Hollywood loves Italy.
The troglodyte settlement
of Matera *(p494)* served as
the setting for *The Passion
of the Christ* (2004), while
scenes from Francis Ford
Coppola's classic *The
Godfather* (1972) were filmed
near Taormina *(p522)* in Sicily.
Head to Turin *(p190)* to relive
scenes from *The Italian Job*
(1969), in which a fleet of
Mini Coopers drive over the
test track of the Lingotto
building. Want to watch the
latest films? The Venice Film
Festival, the world's oldest
film festival, and the Turin
Film Festival both attract
big names in Italian and
international cinema.

→

Picturesque Matera
formed the backdrop for
The Passion of the Christ

On Page

Countless writers have sought inspiration in Italy, from William Shakespeare to Elena Ferrante. Get under the skin of your favourite piece of literature by visiting the creator's home. Alessandro Manzoni, author of historical novel *The Betrothed* (1827), lived in a stately house in Milan *(www.casadelmanzoni.it)*, while the decadent poet Gabriele D'Annunzi called Vittoriale degli Italiani, with its amphitheatre and warship, home *(www.vittoriale.it)*. As well as home-grown talent, Italy has beguiled visiting writers, from Lord Byron to Dan Brown. Don't miss the Keats-Shelley Memorial House *(p272)* in Rome. But you don't have to visit a writer's residence to get inspired. In Ferrante's novels, the city of Naples is as much a character as the people.

← Portrait of Italian poet and writer Gabriele D'Annunzio

SHOP

Libreria Acqua Alta
Books are displayed in boats, gondolas and bathtubs here.

◍ E3 🏠 Calle Lunga Santa Maria Formosa 5176/B, Venice
🌐 libreriaacquaalt avenezia.myadj.it

---

laFeltrinelli 3466
Europe's highest store at 3,466 m (11,371 ft).

🏔 A1 🏠 Punta Helbronner

Mercato Diaz
Milan's market has more than 100 stalls.

◍ E3 🏠 Piazza Armando Diaz, Milan 🌐 piazza diaz.com

In Music

Italy has long been known for its musical prowess and has been home to countless composers. The Casa Natale di Puccini in Lucca *(p382)* houses furniture, documents and memorabilia, as well as Puccini's treasured Steinway & Sons piano. Cremona is perhaps the most musical place in the country; take a tour of Stradivarius's hometown. Another famous Cremona resident was Giuseppe Verdi, whose villa is found nearby *(p178)*. Here, you can see the Fritz piano the composer used to create a number of his operas, including *Rigoletto* and *Aida*. Prefer to listen to the music? Book a ticket to the summer opera festival at the Arena di Verona *(www.arena.it)*.

→ Verdi's Fritz piano, placed in the villa's elegant dressing room

↑ The view down to the sea from the top of Taormina's Greek Theatre

Ancient Sites

Capture history on film at one of the country's countless ancient sites. Visit pretty Taormina's splendid Greek Theatre (p522) and photograph the ruins at sunset, making sure to capture both snowy Etna and the sparkling blue waters of the Mediterranean to the east. Frozen in time against the ominous backdrop of Mount Vesuvius, the ruins of Pompeii (p466) are equally photogenic, while Villa Jovis (p473) – Capri's Roman palace – has a magnificent setting atop Monte Tiberio.

ITALY FOR
PHOTOGRAPHERS

Each and every one of Italy's regions has its own distinctive physical and cultural identity, offering photographers boundless opportunities for capturing the country's many facets. While the crowds are flocking to Venice and Rome, these spots offer an alternative to Italy's most touristy places.

Valleys and Vineyards

With its undulating hills carpeted in vineyards and olive groves, Tuscany (p367) has natural beauty aplenty and the visitor numbers to prove it. To escape the crowds, head to Piedmont's Le Langhe (p199). These lesser-known vineyards easily rival those of Tuscany, with idyllic vine-clad hills set against the stunning backdrop of the snowy Alps.

Vineyards in the Chianti area of Tuscany, which is known for its red wines ↑

Art and Architecture

With more UNESCO World Heritage Sites than any other country in the world, Italy offers no shortage of artistic and architectural masterpieces to capture on camera. There's no need to battle the queues outside the Colosseum in Rome and Florence's Duomo. Instead, make a beeline for Italy's second cities, such as Turin and Siena, and head for the nearest church. Italy's religious buildings were designed to reflect the glory of God, with soaring ceilings and beautiful frescos. The secret is to seek out new perspectives – keep your eyes peeled, look up at ceilings and get off the beaten path.

→

The beautiful ceiling of Chiesa di Sant'Uberto, Turin

Hilltop Villages

In the early morning, the low-lying sun bathes Matera's cavernous dwellings in golden hues. Head to the Sassi district *(p494)* and put your camera on the floor to capture a unique view of this fascinating troglodyte settlement, with its hotchpotch of buildings. Other photogenic villages include Orvieto *(p410)* in Umbria and Pitigliano *(p398)* in southern Tuscany.

←

The jumble of buildings that make up the Sassi in Matera

Reflective Lakes

The Italian lakes are beguilingly beautiful. For unobstructed Lake Como views, climb up to the Castello di Vezio, a perfectly positioned medieval military outpost *(www. castellodivezio.it)*. At the viewpoint, a shrouded statue looks out over the water, making an eerie subject for your picture. To get the best shots of Lake Garda, take the cable car to the summit of Monte Baldo *(p169)*.

→

View over Lake Como from the Castello di Vezio

A YEAR IN
ITALY

Each of Italy's distinct regions has its own festivals and events, making the country's calendar as diverse as its landscapes. From gastronomic festivals to elaborate commemorations of every patron saint imaginable, there's always something going on.

Spring

The season kicks off with Easter, when the Pope's address draws massive crowds to Rome, fireworks light up Florence and re-enactments of The Passion are staged in Sicily. Sporting events include everything from rugby to cycling, while music festivals, such as Dolomiti Ski Jazz Festival and Florence's Maggio Musicale, bring diverse sounds. Foodies have much to look forward to too, with spring specialities, such as asparagus, spinach and rocket, featuring on menus.

1. Zubin Mehta conducting an orchestra at the Maggio Musicale Fiorentino

Summer

As temperatures climb, visitors flock to Italy, particularly for big-ticket events such as the Venice Art Biennale – the world's biggest contemporary art exhibition. Italians, however, head

SAN GENNARO MIRACLE

On the first Sunday in May, 19 September and 16 December, Neapolitans flock to the Duomo for one of Italy's most intriguing events. If the vial of San Gennaro's congealed blood liquifies, it is seen as a sign that Naples' patron saint has blessed the city.

for the coast, especially around Ferragosto (Assumption) on 15 August. During this national holiday, there are open-air concerts, dances and fireworks all over the country.

2. The Japan Pavilion at the 56th Venice Biennale, 2015

Autumn

The cooler months may seem slower and gentler than summer, but that doesn't mean that there are fewer festivals. Gastronomic events abound and celebrate whatever produce is local, be it chestnuts or truffles, cheeses or sausages. The highlight of any oenophile's calendar is La Vendemmia – the grape harvest – which is celebrated with riotous village festivities, when the latest wines flow freely.

3. Harvesting Nebbiolo grapes at the Travaglini winery in Gattinara, Piedmont

Winter

Fairs, markets and religious events are held up and down the country at this time of year. The Christmas holiday itself is low-key; more is made of other religious events such as Epiphany, where children receive stockings of gifts from La Befana – the Christmas witch – and Venice's Carnevale, when the streets mill with costumed and masked local "nobility" or crazily attired visitors.

4. Modelling Carnevale costumes in Venice, and (inset) La Befana figure sold at a Christmas market in Rome

TOP 5 SPORTING EVENTS

Six Nations
Italy's rugby team plays France, Ireland, Wales, England and Scotland in February and March.

Rome Masters
Famed clay-court tennis tournament in May.

Giro d'Italia
This cycle race takes place over several stages from May to June.

Calcio Storico
In June, Florence hosts historic football matches, with players dressed in authentic 16th-century costumes.

Italian Grand Prix
The Italian stage of the Formula One World Championship is held in September in Monza.

A BRIEF
HISTORY

Italy's history is one of discord and division. The only time Italy was united prior to the 19th century was under the Romans. For centuries, popes, emperors and warring states battled it out or fought against foreign invaders. The goal of a unified Italy was achieved in 1870.

The Age of the Etruscans

The Etruscans were Italy's first major civilization. Their origin is a mystery, as is their language, but from the 9th century BC they spread through central Italy, their chief rivals being the Greeks in the south. In the 6th century Etruscan kings ruled Rome, the city that would ultimately eclipse them.

From Republic to Empire

From the scores of tribes inhabiting ancient Italy, the Romans emerged to conquer the peninsula and impose their language, customs and laws on the other regions. Rome's success was due

1 Medieval map of the Roman Empire. ↑

2 Temple of Hercules Victor in the Forum Boarium, Rome.

3 Detail from Trajan's Column, Rome.

4 Mosaic of Emperor Justinian in San Vitale, Ravenna.

Timeline of Events

753 BC

Legendary date of the founding of Rome by demi-god brothers, Romulus and Remus

509 BC

Last Etruscan king, Tarquinius Superbus, expelled from Rome; establishment of Roman Republic

450 BC

Roman law codified in the Twelve Tables, purportedly based on a study of Greek legislature

265 BC

After an attempted uprising of enslaved people, the last Etruscan city, Volsinii, is destroyed by Romans; the inhabitants migrate and establish New Volsinii

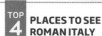

to superb skill in military and civil organization. The State was a republic ruled by two consuls but, as the extent of Rome's conquests grew, power passed to generals such as Julius Caesar. Caesar's heirs became the first Roman emperors.

The Golden Age of Rome

From the age of Augustus to the reign of Trajan, Rome grew until her empire stretched from Britain to the Red Sea. Despite the extravagance of emperors such as Nero, taxes and loot from military campaigns refilled the Imperial coffers, and Roman citizens enjoyed great wealth at the expense of conquered civilizations.

The Splitting of the Empire

A turning point in the history of the Roman Empire came with Emperor Constantine's decision to build a new capital at Constantinople (Byzantium). By the 5th century the Empire was split into two and Germanic invaders began migrating southwards. The Eastern Empire retained nominal control over parts of Italy from Ravenna, which became the most powerful city of the age, while Rome was reduced to ruins.

TOP 4 PLACES TO SEE ROMAN ITALY

Pantheon
Perfectly preserved temple (p260).

Pompeii
A city frozen in time by volcanic ash (p466).

Colosseum
Vast gladiatorial stadium (p242).

Hadrian's Villa
Emperor Hadrian's rural retreat (p328).

146 BC

Carthage falls to the Roman Republic in the Third Punic War; the city is redeveloped as Roman Carthage, the empire's major city in Africa

44 BC

Tensions between Julius Caesar and the Senate lead to his assassination and the breakdown of the Republic

79 AD

Eruption of Vesuvius destroys Pompeii and preserves its remains under a blanket of ash

161–80 AD

Reign of Marcus Aurelius; his death in 180 AD is considered the beginning of the eventual Fall of the Western Roman Empire

The Rise of Venice

Medieval Italy saw waves of foreign invaders joining the power-struggle between popes and emperors. In the confusion, many northern cities asserted their independence from feudal overlords. The most powerful was Venice, which grew rich through trade with the East and by shipping Crusaders to fight the Saracens in the Holy Land.

The Late Middle Ages

Old feuds between pope and emperor thrived throughout the 14th century, kept alive by two warring factions – the Guelphs, who backed the papacy, and the Ghibellines, who favoured Imperial power. Cities used the political chaos to consolidate their strength, building protective walls and towers and creating fortified public buildings such as the Palazzo Vecchio in Florence, Palazzo Pubblico in Siena and the Palazzo dei Priori in Viterbo. It was against this turbulent backdrop that a great new age in painting was inspired by artists such as Duccio and Giotto, while the Florentine poets Dante and Petrarch laid the foundations of Italian literature.

1. Leonardo Da Vinci's *Renaissance Man*.

2. Marco Polo departing from Venice.

3. Coronation of Charles V.

4. Guelphs fighting the Ghibellines.

Did You Know?

"Renaissance" is French for "*rinascita*", meaning rebirth, a term first used by Giorgio Vasari in the mid-1500s.

Timeline of Events

1204

Sacking of Constantinople in the 4th Crusade sees the power of Byzantium crushed

1239

Gregory IX excommunicates Holy Roman Emperor Frederick II for the second time; rivalry between Guelphs and Ghibellines intensifies

1320

Dante completes the *Divine Comedy*, reserving hell's worst punishments for corrupt popes

1378–1417

Period of Schism, with rival popes and antipopes in Rome and Avignon threatening the stability of Europe

1434

Super-wealthy banker and art patron Cosimo de' Medici comes to power in Florence

The Renaissance

Fifteenth-century Italy saw a flowering of the arts and scholarship unmatched in Europe since the Classical age. Architects turned to ancient Greek and Roman models for inspiration, while painting, with its new grasp of perspective and anatomy, produced a generation of artists that included such giants as Leonardo da Vinci, Raphael and Michelangelo. Patronage for this "rebirth" came from wealthy ruling dynasties, initiated by the Medici of Florence, with the papacy following their lead.

The Counter-Reformation

After the Sack of Rome by Imperial forces in 1527, Italy was at the mercy of Charles V, Holy Roman Emperor and King of Spain. In response to the growing threat from Protestantism, Charles V introduced a series of reforms, enforced by the might of the Spanish Inquistion, that imposed rigid orthodoxy and became known as the Counter Reformation. At the same time, the Catholic Church promoted Baroque architecture, art and music as part of a campaign to counter the simplicity and austerity of Protestantism.

TRIAL OF GALILEO

The great astronomer Galileo was frequently in trouble with the Inquisition. After being summoned to Rome for promoting heresy in 1633, he was forced to deny that the Earth and planets moved round the sun and was put under house arrest for the rest of his life.

1436
Brunelleschi completes dome of Florence cathedral commissioned by the Medici

1475
Birth of Michelangelo

1503
Giuliano della Rovere elected Pope Julius II, the most powerful of the Renaissance popes

1542
Inquisition established in Rome

1545–63
Council of Trent sets out agenda of Counter-Reformation

The Grand Tour

In the late 18th century Italy, with its great art treasures and Classical ruins, became Europe's first great tourist destination. Young English aristocrats visited Rome, Florence and Venice as part of the Grand Tour, while artists and poets sought inspiration in Rome's past. In 1800, Napoleon, who conquered and briefly united Italy, threatened to destroy the old order, but in 1815 the status quo was restored.

The Risorgimento

The word "Risorgimento" (resurgence) describes the five decades of struggle for liberation from foreign rule, culminating in the unification of Italy in 1870. In 1848, patriots rose up against the Austrians in Milan and Venice, the Bourbons in Naples, the South and Sicily, and the pope in Rome, where a republic was declared. Garibaldi valiantly defended the republic, but the uprisings were all too localized. By 1859, the movement was better organized, with Vittorio Emanuele II at its head. After just two years it had conquered all but Venice and Rome, both of which fell within a decade.

↑ Vittorio Emanuele II, the first king of a united Italy since the 6th century

Timeline of Events

1870
Rome falls to royalist troops and is made capital of new kingdom of Italy

1922
Fascists march on Rome; Mussolini invited to form government

1936
Italy conquers Abyssinia; pact with Germany, forming anti-Communist "Axis"

1943
Allies land in Sicily; Italy signs armistice and new Badoglio government declares war on Germany

1960
Olympic Games and first official Paralympic Games held in Rome

Fascism to Boomtime

In 1922, Fascist leader Benito Mussolini formed a government. By the 1930s, his party dominated virtually all aspects of life. Italy entered World War II with Nazi Germany, switching to the Allies after the invasion of Sicily by British and American troops. Disguised as a German soldier, Mussolini tried to flee to Switzerland in April 1945 but was found and shot by Communist partisans.

After the war, Italy's economic recovery was powered by great factories in the North, such as Fiat. Despite a series of unstable coalitions, terrorist outrages in the 1970s and corruption scandals of the 1990s (involving many government ministers and officials), the latter half of the 20th century was boomtime, with families enjoying a standard of living unthinkable a generation before.

Italy Today

In 2018, Italy swore in Western Europe's first populist government. The country still struggles due to a complex legal system, public debt, unemployment and a stagnant economy fuelled by the 2008 economic crisis. However, Italy continues to attract, with its history, superb cuisine, luxury industry and La Dolce Vita lifestyle.

1 Adolf Hitler and Benito Mussolini.

2 An 18th-century depiction of a gallery packed with art from Italy.

3 The Italian Senate in session.

4 The Fiat Factory in Turin in 1965.

1990
World Cup in Italy

1997
Earthquake in Assisi, severely damaging Giotto frescoes

2009
Earthquake in Abruzzo kills 308 and almost destroys town of L'Aquila

2013
Pope Francis elected

2019
Democratic Party forms a coalition government with populist Five Star Movement

2020
In March, Italy became the epicentre of the COVID-19 pandemic.

EXPERIENCE

Piazza Navona in Rome

NORTHERN
ITALY

Piazza San Marco at sunset

EXPLORE
NORTHERN ITALY

This section divides northern Italy
into seven colour-coded sightseeing
areas, as shown on the map below.
Find out more about each area
on the following pages.

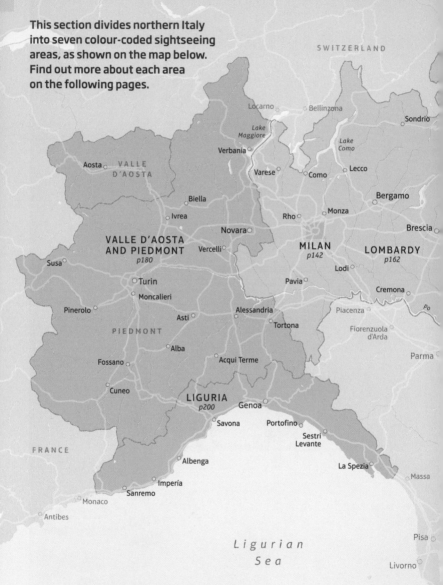

SWITZERLAND

Locarno
Bellinzona
Sondrio
Lake Maggiore
Verbania
Lake Como
Lecco
Aosta
VALLE D'AOSTA
Varese
Como
Bergamo
Biella
Rho
Monza
Brescia
Ivrea
Novara
MILAN
p142
LOMBARDY
p162
VALLE D'AOSTA
AND PIEDMONT
p180
Vercelli
Lodi
Cremona
Susa
Pavia
Po
Turin
Piacenza
Moncalieri
Fiorenzuola
d'Arda
Pinerolo
Asti
Alessandria
Parma
PIEDMONT
Tortona
Alba
Acqui Terme
Fossano
LIGURIA
p200
Genoa
Cuneo
Savona
Portofino
FRANCE
Sestri
Levante
Albenga
La Spezia
Massa
Imperia
Sanremo
Monaco
Antibes
Pisa

*Ligurian
Sea*

Livorno

0 kilometres   50
0 miles   50

N

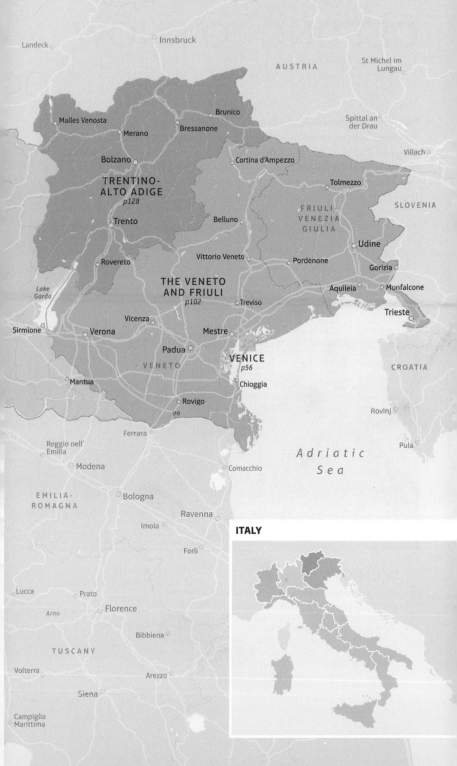

GETTING TO KNOW
NORTHERN ITALY

The economic powerhouse of the peninsula, northern Italy also encompasses an immense variety of landscapes, from the Alps, Dolomites and Italian Lakes, to the world-famous vineyards of Piedmont and the dramatic coast of Liguria. City-wise, Venice is the main focus, but historic towns such as Padua, Verona, Mantua and Trieste and bustling cities like Milan, Turin and Genoa also have their delights.

VENICE

PAGE 56

This improbable canal city of lacy Gothic palaces built on mudbanks amid the tidal waters of the Adriatic is totally unique. Once a powerful commercial and naval force in the Mediterranean, Venice has found a new role in the modern age. Her palazzi have become museums, shops, hotels and apartments, while her convents have been turned into centres for art restoration. These days there is barely an off-season, though visiting in winter, and taking the little alleyways that lead off the well-beaten tourist track, give a good chance of finding pockets of this magical city that still escape the crowds.

Best for
Getting lost and not caring

Home to
San Marco and the Doge's Palace

Experience
An ombra (glass of white wine) and cicchetti (bar snacks) in one of the traditional bars of the Rialto market

PAGE 102

THE VENETO AND FRIULI

Encompassing the natural beauty of the Dolomites and the rolling Euganean hills – along with magnificent ancient cities such as Verona, Vicenza and Padua – the Veneto is a region of extraordinary contrasts. Here, you can easily combine sightseeing with mountain hiking, skiing or wine-tasting in the region's many vineyards. Friuli-Venezia-Giulia is one of Italy's lesser-visited regions, producing some of Italy's finest white wines.

Best for
Romantic getaways and experiencing the unique east-meets-west atmosphere of Trieste

Home to
Juliet's Balcony in Verona and the Giotto-frescoed Scrovegni Chapel in Padua

Experience
An open-air opera performance at the Arena in Verona

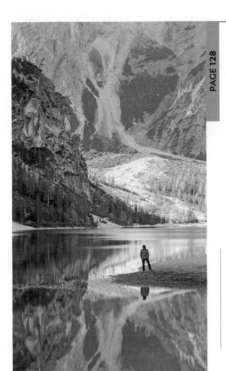

PAGE 128

TRENTINO-ALTO ADIGE

Dominated by the majestic peaks of the Dolomites, Italian-speaking Trentino and German-speaking Alto Adige (or Südtirol) make up Italy's northernmost region. Bordering Austria and Switzerland, it has long been a battle zone, witnessed by the string of medieval castles protecting the Adige valley. These days its dramatic mountains and unspoilt lakes, rivers, woodland and pastures make the region one of the best in Italy for skiing, hiking and mountain climbing.

Best for
Outdoor adventures in the Dolomites and indulging in the region's spas

Home to
The dramatic Vie Ferrate and the ski resort of Madonna di Campiglio

Experience
Craft beers created in Trento's many independent breweries

PAGE 142

MILAN

Italy's fashion capital, Milan is a slick, affluent and fast-moving international city. With a fabulous historic centre, dominated by Italy's most magnificent Gothic cathedral, it is the birthplace of numerous world-famous works of art, including Leonardo's *The Last Supper*, and is home to the renowned Teatro alla Scala opera company. Shopping is superb, the quality of places to eat and drink is world-class, and the regeneration of industrial buildings and formerly run-down parts of the city, such as the Navigli canal area, are providing ever-more places to drink and party.

Best for
Shopping and chic bars

Home to
Leonardo's The Last Supper *and the Castello Sforzesco.*

Experience
The buzzing nightlife of the Navigli canals

PAGE 162

LOMBARDY AND THE LAKES

Fringed by the Alps and carved out by glaciers, the Italian lakes are surrounded by pretty lakeside villages, exuberant villas and magnificent gardens. Of the three major lakes, only Como lies entirely within Lombardy – Maggiore shares a border with Piedmont and Garda with the Veneto. The historic cities of Bergamo, Pavia, Cremona and Mantua offer another aspect to the region, while the trails and peaks of the Parco Nazionale dello Stelvio provide perfect wild escapes.

Best for
Beautiful lakeside landscapes and watersports

Home to
Lake Como, Lake Garda and Mantua

Experience
A violin recital in Cremona

PAGE 180

VALLE D'AOSTA AND PIEDMONT

Abutting France, and bordered by the Alps, Valle d'Aosta and Piedmont were ruled by the royal House of Savoy until the 18th century, and the influence of French culture remains in the region's food and dialect. Valle d'Aosta is a largely rural region, a series of pretty Alpine valleys headed by dramatic peaks that offer some world-class skiing. Piedmont stretches from the industrial Po plain, dominated by the capital, Turin, to the rolling vineyards of Barolo and Le Langhe.

Best for
Skiing and mountain scenery

Home to
The Slow Food movement, Parco del Gran Paradiso and Turin

Experience
A truffle hunt or wine-tasting in the Barolo vineyards

PAGE 200

LIGURIA

Nestling at the foot of vine-covered mountains, Liguria has one of the prettiest and most dramatic coastlines in Italy, where pastel-coloured houses bask in the Mediterranean sun of the clement microclimate. The most attractive stretch of coast is the Riviera di Levante, to the south of the bustling regional capital and port of Genoa (Genova), and between Camogli and the five towns of the Cinque Terre. To the north of Genoa, the Riviera di Ponente is a thin strip of coastal plain stretching across to the French border that includes big resorts such as Sanremo.

Best for
Swimming, hiking and coastal walks

Home to
The pastel-painted coastal villages of Camogli and the Cinque Terre

Experience
Skinny twists of Ligurian trofie pasta smothered in freshly made pesto

Gondolas moored in the Grand Canal

VENICE

Lying in the extreme northeast of Italy, Venice became an independent Byzantine province in the 10th century. Exclusive trading links with the East and victory in the Crusade of 1204 brought wealth and power, which were only gradually eroded by European and Turkish rivals. Today, Venice's ties are with the local Veneto region that stretches from the flat river plains to the Dolomites.

Venice is one of the few cities in the world that can be truly described as unique. It survives against all the odds, built on a series of low mudbanks amid the tidal waters of the Adriatic, and regularly subject to floods. During the Middle Ages, under the leadership of successive doges (chief magistrates), Venice expanded its power and influence throughout the Mediterranean to Constantinople (modern Istanbul). Its immense wealth was celebrated in art and architecture throughout the city.

The riches of St Mark's alone bear witness to Venice's position as a world power from the 12th to 14th centuries. After slowly losing ground to the new states of Europe, however, it fell to Napoleon in 1797. Finally, Venice joined the Kingdom of Italy in 1866, so bringing unity to the country for the first time in its history.

More than 20 million visitors a year are welcomed by this magical city whose "streets are full of water". Little of the essential fabric of Venice has altered in 200 years, but beneath the surface, the city's foundations are changing. Venice rests on soft, alluvial soil, which – coupled with rising sea levels – means that the land is sinking over time. The city risks being entirely submerged by the year 2100.

VENICE

Must Sees
1 Basilica di San Marco
2 Palazzo Ducale
3 Santa Maria Gloriosa dei Frari
4 Rialto

Experience More
5 Ca' d'Oro
6 Madonna dell'Orto
7 San Giovanni Grisostomo
8 Santa Maria dei Miracoli
9 San Polo
10 Scuola Grande di San Rocco
11 Ca' Rezzonico
12 San Nicolò dei Mendicoli
13 San Sebastiano
14 Santa Maria della Salute
15 Punta della Dogana
16 Accademia
17 Peggy Guggenheim Collection
18 Santo Stefano
19 Torre dell'Orologio
20 Campanile
21 Museo Correr
22 San Zaccaria
23 Santa Maria Formosa
24 Santi Giovanni e Paolo
25 Statue of Colleoni
26 Scuola di San Giorgio degli Schiavoni
27 Arsenale
28 Torcello
29 Giudecca
30 San Giorgio Maggiore
31 Murano
32 Burano

Eat
① Osteria Alla Ciurma
② La Palanca
③ Osteria Santa Marina
④ La Zucca
⑤ Trattoria dalla Marisa

Drink
⑥ Bar Puppa
⑦ Al Timon
⑧ Bacarando in Corte dell'Orso
⑨ Skyline Rooftop Bar
⑩ Harry's Dolci

Shop
⑪ Ca' Macana
⑫ Papier Machè Venezia
⑬ Maschere di Guerrino Lovato

Canale delle Sacche
Canale Colombola
Rio del Riformati
Rio della Sensa
FOND. CARLO COLETTI
Rio di San Girolamo
FONDAMENTA DELLE CAPPUCCINE
Tre Archi
FOND. D. BATTELLO
CANNAREGIO
5
Crea
Canale di Cannaregio
FONDAMENTA SAVORGNAN
CAMPO DEL GHETTO NUOVO
San Giobbe
FONDAMENTA
CALLE RIELLO
Guglie
R. TERRA S. LEONARDO
CAMPO SAN GIOBBE
CAMPO S. GEREMIA
Parco Savorgnan
RIO TERRA LISTA DI SPAGNA
Palazzo Labia
PONTE DELLA LIBERTA
Scalzi
Riva di Biasio
Ponte degli Scalzi
LISTA DEI BARI
Stazione Ferrovie dello Stato Santa Lucia
FMTA. SANTA LUCIA
Ferrovia
CAMPO S. SIMEON PROFETA
S Simeòn Piccolo
CAMPO NAZARIO SAURO
Piazzale Roma
FMTA SAN SIMEON PICCOLO
SANTA CROCE
Ponte della Costituzione
Giardino Papadopoli
Piazzale Roma
PIAZZALE ROMA
San Nicolò da Tolentino
C DELLE CHIOVERE
Santa Maria Gloriosa dei Frari
Scuola Grande di San Rocco
10
3
Calle di Santa Maria Maggiore
Rio delle Burchielle
Rio Nuovo
RIO TERRA DEI PENSIERI
CALLE DEI PRETI
CAMPO SAN POLO
FONDAMENTA DELLE PROCURATIE
CAMPO SAN PANTALON
Rio di Ca' Foscari
Rio del Tintor
Rio Briati
CAMPO SANTA MARGHERITA
Scuola Grande dei Carmini
Ca' Rezzonico
FONDAMENTA SANTA MARTA
San Nicolò dei Mendicoli
12
Santa Maria dei Carmini
13
11
CAMPO SAN BARNABA
CAMPO ANGELO RAFFAELE
Rio di S. Nicolò
San Sebastiano
13
DORSODURO
FMTA ZATTERE PONTE LUNGO
Squero di San Trovaso
Rio di Ca' Trovaso
San Basilio
Zattere
Sacca Fisola
Canale
Molino Stucky
9
CAMPIELLO PRIULI
FMTA DELLE CONVERTITE
FMTA SANT'EUFEMIA
10
CAMPO SAN COSMO
CALLE ACCADEMIA DEI NOBILI

A
B
C

The Islands

Aeroporto di Venezia Marco Polo

Canale Osellino

Torcello 28

Mazzorbo

Burano 32

Laguna Veneto

Lazzaretto Nuovo

Area of main Venice map

Murano 31

Tronchetto

San Michele

Sant' Erasmo

Vignole

VENICE

Certosa

Santa Maria delle Grazie

San Servolo

Lido

0 km 3

0 miles 3

Parco Groggia

Canale delle Fondamenta Nuove

CAMPO DI SANT'ALVISE

Rio di Sant'Alvise

Sant'Alvise

FMTA DELLA SENSA

CAMPIELLO PIAVE

Orto

Madonna dell'Orto 6

FMTA D. ORMESINI

FMTA MADONNA DELL'ORTO

CAMPO DEI MORI

Palazzo Mastelli

Sacca della Misericordia

Museo Ebraico

FOND. DELLA MISERICORDIA

Santa Maria della Misericordia

FONDAMENTA NUOVE

Fondamente Nove

CAMPO SAN LEONARDO

RIO TERRA FARSETTI

Rio di Noale

Rio di S. Caterina

Gesuiti

CAMPO DEI GESUITI

CAMPO SAN MARCUOLA

RIO TERRA D. MADDALENA

CAMPO DELLA MADDALENA

San Marcuola

STRADA NOVA

CAMPO S. FELICE

CAMPO DEI SANTI APOSTOLI

CALLE DEL FUMO

FONDAMENTA NUOVE

Ospedale

CAMPO SAN ZAN DEGOLÀ

Fondaco dei Turchi

CAMPO SAN STAE

San Stae

STRADA NOVA

Ca' d'Oro 5

Rio dei Santi Apostoli

Campiello Widman

CAMPO SS. GIOVANNI E PAOLO

FOND. DEI MENDICANTI

Ospedale Civile

CAMPO S. GIACOMO DELL'ORIO

Palazzo Mocenigo

Ca' d'Oro

CAMPO SAN CASSIANO

Rialto Mercato

CAMPO D. PESCHERIA

Santa Maria dei Miracoli 8

San Giovanni Grisostomo 7

CAMPO S. MARIA NOVA

Statue of Colleoni 25 24

Santi Giovanni e Paolo

Celestia

RIOTERRA SECONDO

DELLA CHIESA

SAN POLO

CAMPO SAN STIN

RUGA VECCHIA S. GIOVANNI

Sant'Aponàl

CAMPO SAN POLO

CAMPO SAN SILVESTRO

4 Rialto

Rialto 8

CAMPO SAN MARINA

3

BARBARIA DELLE TOLE

San Francesco della Vigna

CAMPO D. CELESTIA

CAMPO S. TERNITA

San Lorenzo

CAMPO SAN STIN

CAMPO D. FRARI

9 San Polo

San Silvestro

RIVA DEL VIN

CALLE DELLA MADONNA

CAMPO S. BARTOLOMEO

SAL DEL VIN

CAMPO S. SALVADOR

CAMPO SANTA MARIA FORMOSA

12

CALLE DELLE CAPPUCCINE

CAMPO SS. GIOVANNI E PAOLO

Rio di San Giovanni Laterano

CASTELLO

Scuola di San Giorgio degli Schiavoni 26

Arsenale 27

CAMPO SAN LORENZO

SAL. DEI PRETI

Arsenale Vecchio

CAMPO SAN TOMA

San Tomà

Canal Grande

Sant'Angelo

Museo Fortuny

CAMPO SANT'ANGELO

SAN MARCO

RIVA DEL CARBON

CALLE DEI FABBRI

San Salvatore

MERCERIA

SPADARIA

San Zulian

SAL. S. LIO

RUGA GIUFFA

23 Santa Maria Formosa

San Zaccaria 22

SAL. DEI PRETI

CAMPO SAN ZACCARIA

San Giovanni in Bragora

CAMPO BANDIERA E MORO

SCHIAVONI

CAMPO S. BARTOLOMEO

11 San Samuele

SAL. SAN SAMUELE

18 Santo Stefano

CAMPO SANTO STEFANO

CAMPO SAN MAURIZIO

Teatro La Fenice

CAMPO S. FANTIN

Scala Contarini del Bovolo

CAMPO MANIN

CAMPO S. LUCA

Torre dell' Orologio 19

Campanile 20

Museo Correr 21

7

Basilica di San Marco 1

PIAZZA SAN MARCO

Palazzo Ducale 2

RIVA DEGLI SCHIAVONI

CAMPO S. ZACCARIA

San Zaccaria

Arsenale

RIVA CA DI DIO

CAMPO SAN BIAGIO

Ca' Rezzonico

Accademia

CAMPO SANT'ANGELO

CAMPO SANTO STEFANO

CALLE LARGA XXII MARZO

CAMPO SAN MOISE

San Marco-Vallaresso

San Marco-Giardinetti

Bacino di San Marco

Canale di San Marco

16 Accademia

Ponte dell'Accademia

CAMPO SAN VIDAL

CAMPO SAN VIO

Giglio

17 Peggy Guggenheim Collection

Santa Maria della Salute

Salute

RIO TERRA D. CATECUMENI

14

15 Punta della Dogana

RIO DI SAN VIO

CAMPO SAN GIORGIO

San Giorgio

San Giorgio Maggiore 30

FMTA ZATTERE AI GESUATI

FMTA ZATTERE ALLO SPIRITO SANTO

FMTA ZA TTERE AI SALONI

Spirito Santo

Hotel Cipriani

VENICE

della

Giudecca

Zitelle

FONDAMENTA D. ZITELLE

Le Zitelle

Palanca 2

Ponte Lungo

Redentore

FONDAMENTA SAN GIACOMO

FONDAMENTA DELLA CROCE

C. D. CROCE

29 Giudecca

LA GIUDECCA

0 metres 400

0 yards 400

N

→

1 Gondola ride under the Rialto Bridge.

2 Glass blowing in Murano.

3 Pastel-coloured houses lining the canal in Burano.

4 Coffee at Caffè Florian.

2 DAYS
A Weekend in Venice

Day 1

Morning Start the day at the bustling Rialto Market *(p82)*, stopping for mid-morning *cicchetti* (bar snacks) and prosecco in one of the market's wine bars. Afterwards, take a vaporetto along the Grand Canal. Not only is this one of the best (and fastest) ways to get around Venice, it's also one of the cheapest – a boon when staying in one of the world's most expensive cities. Line 1 zips you to San Marco in 25 minutes, and from there it's a short walk to Basilica di San Marco *(p72)*. English guided tours run daily at 11am, 2:30pm and 4pm, though it's best to see the mosaics in the morning light. Don't miss the Treasury, home to jewels, reliquaries, and Byzantine and Islamic art from the Crusades. Next, head to the adjacent Palazzo Ducale *(p76)* for paintings by Titian, Tintoretto and Veronese and a glimpse at the opulent Doge's restored apartments.

Afternoon After a hearty lunch, explore the district of San Polo *(p86)*, Venice's smallest *sestiere*, before heading to the magnificent Gothic Santa Maria Gloriosa dei Frari *(p80)* to see Titian's glorious *Assumption of the Virgin*.

Evening Finish the day with a campari spritz aperitivo in the ever-lively Campo Santa Margherita *(p100)*.

Day 2

Morning After breakfast, make for the Dorsoduro *sestiere* and visit the Ca' Rezzonico *(p87)*, a palace-turned-museum that traces the history of 18th-century Venice. Move on to the Accademia *(p90)*, which houses pre-19th-century art, then complete the triumvirate at the Peggy Guggenheim Collection *(p90)*, home to an exceptional selection of modern paintings and sculptures. Grab an espresso at the Guggenheim café before beginning a picturesque zig-zag across the city to Fondamente Nuove, where vaporetti depart for the northern section of the lagoon. On the way, stop at Venetian Renaissance church Santa Maria dei Miracoli *(p85)*, and then go for a bowl of spaghetti with clams at the canalside trattoria Da Rioba *(Fondamenta de la Misericordia 2553)* in Cannaregio.

Afternoon Stomach full, take the *traghetto* (ferry) to the small but pretty island of Torcello *(p96)*, where the church of Santa Maria Assunta houses some of the city's most stunning mosaics. Look out for depictions of angels, devils, beasts and hell-fire in the *Universal Judgment*, which covers the west wall.

Evening Head to Locanda Cipriani *(p64)* for dinner, and soak up the jaw-slackening views over Venice on the way.

Foundations of a Floating City

This breathtaking city is home to a dizzying array of architectural styles and influences, but don't lose sight of the bigger picture. Venetian builders made the impossible a reality by creating structures that float on water. The secret lies beneath the surface: layers of Istrian stone laid on top of closely packed wooden piles plunged deep into the ground. As you stroll through the city's ancient streets and navigate its intricate web of canals, be sure to take the time to appreciate this sheer feat of medieval engineering.

→

Placing the foundations for the new Campanile on Piazza San Marco, 1905

VENICE FOR
ASTOUNDING ARCHITECTURE

From Medieval to Neo-Classical, Venice's ostentatious palaces and opulent churches stand as testament to the Serenissima Republic's powerful reign. But the ever-growing number of contemporary marvels speak of a city that, although deeply rooted in its past, is very much focused on its future.

Building Bridges

Iron, wood or stone, bridges are vital links. The Bridge of Sighs (p79) is what many come to Venice to see and it does not disappoint, while the Rialto Bridge (p83) affords one of the most iconic views of the city. But perhaps most impressive is the Ponte della Libertà, which connects Venice to the mainland by train, car or bus. Nothing compares to the sense of wonder as hundreds of tiny Venetian islands come into view as you speed towards them.

→

A gondolier passing under the Rialto Bridge at sunset

Palazzos and Palladio

Admire the many palazzos that line Venice's Grand Canal *(p68)* for the price of a vaporetto ticket. Among them is the Venetian Gothic style Ca' d'Oro *(p84)*, named for its once shimmering, now faded, gold-leaf exterior. But lavish façades and ostentatious design are prevalent across the Veneto. Tread the boards at Andrea Palladio's Teatro Olimpico *(p116)* in Vicenza, a city defined by his signature style, or admire the many fine Palladian villas that line the Brenta Canal *(p118)*.

→

Ornate façade of Ca' d'Oro overlooking the Grand Canal

The World in One City

For centuries, Venice linked the Adriatic and the Mediterranean seas to Constantinople, Egypt and Syria, and the influence of these lands can be clearly seen in the city's ancient architecture. Take a tour of the Eastern Med as you explore the ground-floor arcades and open galleries of the Fondaco dei Turchi *(p68)*; gaze upon the crenellations of the Palazzo Ducale *(p76)* and pointed arches of the Basilica di San Marco *(p72)* that mirror those of Egyptian mosques; and lose yourself in the unmistakably Islamic tilework of many a canalside palazzo.

←

One of the magnificent colonnades that surround the Palazzo Ducale in Venice

Modern Marvels

Contemporary structures abound in Venice. Architects such as Tadao Ando, who designed the Teatrino of Palazzo Grassi *(p70)*, Santiago Calatrava, designer of metallic Ponte della Costituzione, and Carlo Scarpa who realised many of the Veneto's most iconic buildings, all left their mark on this ancient city. The Architecture Biennale showcases cutting-edge architectural works from around the globe. For anyone with a penchant for contemporary design and the latest architectural innovations, it's well worth a visit.

→

Bamboo Stalactite by VTN Architects at the Venice Architecture Biennale 2018

Bacari

Unique to Venice, *bacari* are bars where locals go for aperitivo and *chicchetti* (small plates of tapas-like bites). Venetians tend to head to their local *bacari* for drinks after work, or for a pre-dinner cocktail with friends. Try Al Bottegon *(Fondamenta Nani 992)*, Ai DiVini *(Fondamenta Trapolin 5905)* and Osteria al Squero *(Dorsoduro 943–4)* for a classic *bacari* experience.

A waiter preparing plates of *chicchetti* in one of Venice's *bacari*

VENICE FOR
FOODIES

Not far from Piazza San Marco lie a handful of neighbourhood trattorias, where locals huddle over plates of spaghetti. Stop by one of the city's ubiquitous *gelaterie* for an afternoon pick-me-up, or head to the outer *sestieri* (districts) for buzzy *bacari* (bars) serving Campari spritz and snacks.

RIALTO MARKET

Make like a Venetian and head to the tastebud-tantalizing Rialto market, where colourful stalls lining the Grand Canal in San Polo are piled high with fresh fruit and vegetables. The market is held every day apart from Sundays, and it is best to venture there in the early morning to get the best of the produce on offer. Next door is the Pescaria fish market; in the morning, fishermen sell the day's catch of octopus, squid, soft-shelled crabs and swordfish, much of which is caught locally. Don't leave your visit too late – few stalls are left in the afternoon.

Fine Dining

There are many fine-dining options in Venice, a favourite destination of the rich and famous. The charming Osteria Da Fiore *(www. ristorantedafiore.com)* has long been serving classic Venetian dishes with a twist, while the bucolic Venissa *(www.venissa.it)* has a thriving kitchen garden and even produces its own white wine.

Bars

These coffee-serving spots are where Venetians go for their breakfast coffee and brioche (sweet croissant). Drink orders change based on the time of day. If visiting before 11am, ask for a creamy cappuccino; any time after that calls for either an espresso or a macchiato (an espresso with an added spoonful of steamed milk). You can stop anywhere in Venice for a delicious caffeine fix, but Bar Puppa *(p85)* is one of the best.

↓ Coffee and romance next to the canals in Venice

↑ Venetian *gelato* on a sunny day by the canal

Gelaterie

Gelato is a way of life in Venice, with locals meeting for ice cream at any time of the day. Be sure to swing by Gelateria Alaska *(Calle Larga dei Bari)*, which serves unusual flavours such as ginger, rose, or orange, as well as the best chocolate ice cream in town.

Trattorias and Osterias

Trattorias are small, family-run places with short menus, while osterias traditionally focus on wines, with a few dishes on a daily-changing menu. To experience the intimate charm of these establishments for yourself, head to Al Timon *(p85)* or Alla Ciurma *(Calle Galiazza 406/A)*.

← Venissa, one of Venice's many fine-dining establishments

→ Chairs outside an osteria on a colourful Venetian street

Go Locavore

Support local business by shopping at local greengrocers, fishmongers and markets. The I & S stall at Santa Marta market (on Monday mornings) sells organic fruit and veg from Sant'Erasmo and has a delightful farm shop in Cannaregio *(www.iesfarm.it)*. The Natura Sì healthfood store *(www.naturasi.it)* satisfies all your eco-friendly desires, while Osteria Zanze XVI *(zanze.it)* meticulously sources local produce to create zero-kilometre cuisine.

→

Lemon trees and fresh produce for sale at a Venetian street market

SAVE VENICE!

Mass tourism, pollution, rising water levels and wave-induced erosion are just some of the issues that Venice has to contend with. A number of charities, grassroots movements and environmental scientists are searching for solutions to safeguard this most precious of cities. Here's how you can help.

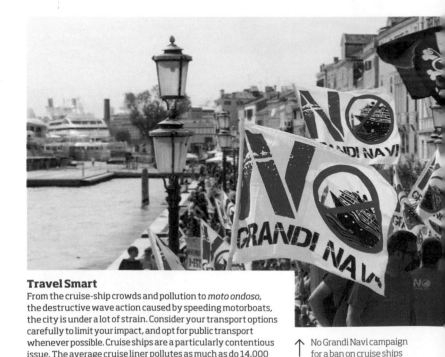

Travel Smart

From the cruise-ship crowds and pollution to *moto ondoso*, the destructive wave action caused by speeding motorboats, the city is under a lot of strain. Consider your transport options carefully to limit your impact, and opt for public transport whenever possible. Cruise ships are a particularly contentious issue. The average cruise liner pollutes as much as do 14,000 cars and damages the already fragile lagoon environment.

↑ No Grandi Navi campaign for a ban on cruise ships entering the lagoon

Shop Local

Whether you want to pick up some Murano glassware, a Venetian mask for Carnevale or some quirky souvenirs to take home, always try to buy the genuine article from a local vendor rather than an imported fake. Check out Gilberto Penzo's model boats *(www.veniceboats.com)*, try on Gondola-shaped shoes at Giovanna Zanella's workshop *(www.giovannazanella.com)*, or venture under the Rialto arches, where Daniele and Stefano Attombri *(www.attombri.com)* fashion antique Murano beads into stunning necklaces.

← An artisan carefully moulding molten glass into the shape of a horse at a Murano factory

TOP 6 EASY WAYS TO REDUCE YOUR IMPACT

Bring Your Own Bottle
Tap water is drinkable; top up at fountains.

Picnic Politely
Choose your spot wisely; don't sit on bridges or doorsteps.

Respect Local Life
Allow Venetians to go about their business and respect their space.

Follow Rubbish Rules
Be sure to put litter in the correct bins and recycle responsibly.

Avoid Rush Hour
Steer clear of public transport at busy times.

Say No to Plastic
Carry a shopper and avoid plastic bags.

PRESERVING THE CITY

There are multiple organizations working to protect Venetian heritage as well as its fauna and flora. The largest is Save Venice, whose dedicated team restores architecture and artworks, funded by the generosity of wealthy benefactors.

Get Your Hands Dirty

There are plenty of ways to get involved during your stay. Venice Calls *(www.venicecalls.com)* runs regular graffiti elimination days, as well as canal dredging and beach cleaning. The WWF *(www.wwf.it)* runs fun workshops, nature walks and rubbish collecting parties around the Alberoni dunes on the Lido. Further afield, dust off your binoculars and head to the Po Delta Park *(www.parcodeltapo.org)* to help count birds in one of the area's largest wetlands.

↑ A volunteer painting over unsightly graffiti on a city wall

THE GRAND CANAL
SANTA LUCIA TO THE RIALTO

The best way to view the Grand Canal as it winds through the heart of the city is from a vaporetto, or waterbus. Two lines travel the length of the canal. The palaces lining the waterway were built over a span of five centuries and present a panoramic survey of the city's history.

Shaped like a back-to-front "S", the Grand Canal snakes through the heart of Venice, connecting its various districts. From the earliest times it was a key trade and transport route, which is why the city's wealthy families built their palaces along its banks. The most spectacular palazzo on this stretch of the canal is the Gothic Ca' d'Oro, whose façade once glittered with gold. Santa Lucia, the city's railway station, links the city with the mainland.

View of the Ponte ↑ degli Scalzi and San Geremia beyond

| 0 metres | 100 | N |
| 0 yards | 100 | ↑ |

Canale di Cannaregio

The San Marcuola church was rebuilt in the 18th century, but the new façade was never completed.

San Geremia houses the relics of St Lucy.

The Palazzo Labia ballroom was decorated by Giambattista Tiepolo with scenes from the life of Cleopatra.

Ferrovia

Riva di Biasio

The Fondaco dei Turchi, the former Turkish warehouse, is now the Natural History Museum.

Ponte degli Scalzi

The 18th-century domed church of San Simeone Piccolo is based on the Pantheon in Rome.

→

The Baroque façade of San Stae, richly decorated with statues

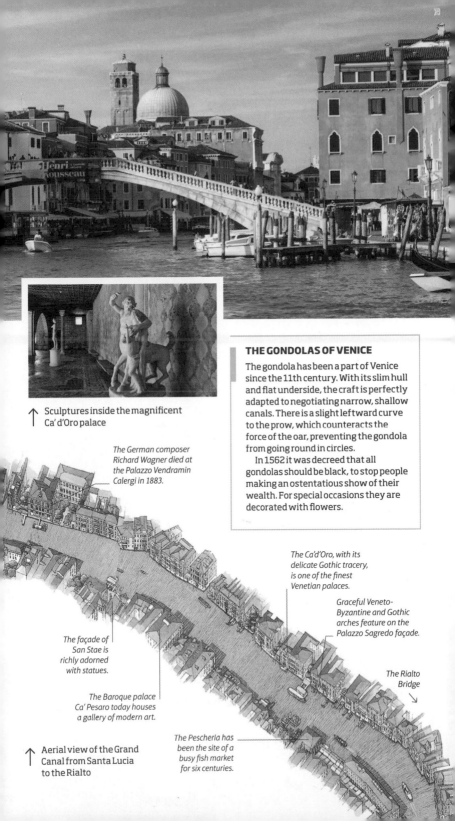

Sculptures inside the magnificent Ca' d'Oro palace

THE GONDOLAS OF VENICE

The gondola has been a part of Venice since the 11th century. With its slim hull and flat underside, the craft is perfectly adapted to negotiating narrow, shallow canals. There is a slight leftward curve to the prow, which counteracts the force of the oar, preventing the gondola from going round in circles.

In 1562 it was decreed that all gondolas should be black, to stop people making an ostentatious show of their wealth. For special occasions they are decorated with flowers.

The German composer Richard Wagner died at the Palazzo Vendramin Calergi in 1883.

The Ca'd'Oro, with its delicate Gothic tracery, is one of the finest Venetian palaces.

Graceful Veneto-Byzantine and Gothic arches feature on the Palazzo Sagredo façade.

The façade of San Stae is richly adorned with statues.

The Baroque palace Ca' Pesaro today houses a gallery of modern art.

The Rialto Bridge

The Pescheria has been the site of a busy fish market for six centuries.

Aerial view of the Grand Canal from Santa Lucia to the Rialto

THE GRAND CANAL
THE RIALTO TO SAN MARCO

After passing the Rialto, the canal doubles back on itself along a stretch known as La Volta (the bend). It then widens out and the views become more spectacular approaching San Marco. Façades may have faded and foundations battered with the tides, but the canal remains spectacularly beautiful.

The area around the Rialto Bridge is the oldest and busiest quarter of the city. Traditionally a centre of trade, crowded quaysides and colourful food markets still border the canal. Past the splendid curve known as La Volta, the view along the final stretch of the Grand Canal is one of the finest in Venice. Near the mouth rises the magnificent church of La Salute with busy St Mark's Basin beyond.

Lord Byron stayed in Palazzo Mocenigo in 1818.

Palazzo Grassi is now used for modern art exhibitions.

Now a museum of 18th-century Venice, Ca' Rezzonico was the last home of the poet Robert Browning.

Palazzo Capello Malipiero was rebuilt in 1622. Beside it stands the 12th-century campanile of San Samuele.

The world's greatest collection of Venetian paintings is housed in the Accademia.

← Majestic interior of the Ca' Rezzonico

Ponte dell'Accademia

Rialto

← Aerial view of the Grand Canal from the Rialto to San Marco

Palazzo Barzizza, rebuilt in the 17th century, preserves its early 13th-century façade.

The Riva del Vin is one of the few spots where you can sit on the banks of the Grand Canal.

 PICTURE PERFECT
Grand Canal

For an iconic shot of the Grand Canal there's no better place than the Ponte dell'Accademia. Get in position about half an hour before sunset and point your camera lens towards San Marco and Santa Maria della Salute.

↑ Crowds crossing the canal on the Ponte dell'Accademia

The Gritti Palace is now a luxury hotel.

Harry's Bar, founded in 1931 by Giuseppe Cipriani, is famous for its cocktails.

A one-storey palazzo houses Peggy Guggenheim's great modern art collection.

According to legend, the beautiful Palazzo Dario is cursed; many of its owners have died prematurely or lost their fortunes.

The Punta della Dogana customs house now contains a collection of contemporary art.

The vast weight of Baroque church Santa Maria della Salute is supported by over one million timber piles.

← Panoramic view of the Grand Canal towards Santa Maria della Salute

| 0 metres | 100 |
| 0 yards | 100 |

N ↑

❶ 🏛 🅜 🏛

BASILICA DI
SAN MARCO

📍 E3 🏛 Piazza San Marco 🚇 San Marco 🕐 Basilica: 9:30am–5pm Mon–Sat,
2–4:30pm Sun & hols; Museo Marciano: 10am–5:30pm daily 🌐 basilicasanmarco.it

Dark, mysterious and full of treasures, Venice's famous St Mark's Basilica blends the architectural and decorative styles of East and West to create one of Europe's greatest buildings. The extravagant Byzantine interior is embellished with golden mosaics, icons and ornate marble carvings.

Exterior of St Mark's

Built on a Greek cross plan and crowned with five huge domes, San Marco's owes its almost Asian-looking splendour to countless treasures from the Republic's overseas empire. Among these are copies of the famous bronze horses brought from Constantinople in 1204, and a wealth of columns, bas-reliefs and coloured marbles studded across the main façade. Mosaics from different epochs adorn the five doorways, while the main portal is framed by some of Italy's loveliest Romanesque carving (1240–65). Initially built in the 9th century, this is the third church to stand on the site.

↑ Romanesque carvings surrounding the arches of the main portal

San Marco's owes its Asian-looking splendour to countless treasures from the Republic's overseas empire.

←

Façade and campanile of the Basilica, seen from Piazza San Marco

Timeline

828–978	978–1117	1117–c 1300	1807
▲ A church is built to house relics of St Mark, stolen from Alexandria. It burns down in 976 and is rebuilt in 978	▲ The church is replaced by a grand basilica, "the House of St Mark", reflecting Venice's growing power	▲ 4,240 sq m (45,622 sq ft) of gleaming golden mosaics are added to the domes, walls and floors of the Basilica	▲ The doge's private chapel until 1807, San Marco succeeds San Pietro di Castello as the cathedral of Venice

↑ Ornate coloured marble panels on the exterior of the Basilica

Inside the Basilica

San Marco's magnificent interior is clad with dazzling mosaics, which begin in the narthex, or atrium, of the Basilica, and culminate in the glittering panels of the Pentecost and Ascension domes. The Genesis Cupola in the atrium has a stunning scene of the Creation of the World described in concentric circles. The *pavimento*, or floor, is also patterned with mosaics in marble and glass. Steps from the atrium lead to the Museo Marciano, home to the Basilica's famous horses. Other treasures include the jewel-encrusted Pala d'Oro, the Nicopeia icon and the precious hoards of silver, gold and glassware in the Treasury.

Statues of St Mark and angels, which crown the central arch, are additions from the early 15th century.

The Pentecost Dome was probably the first dome to be decorated with mosaics.

The four horses of St Mark are replicas of the gilded bronze originals, now protected inside the Basilica's museum.

> San Marco's magnificent interior is clad with dazzling mosaics, which culminate in the glittering panels of the Pentecost and Ascension domes.

↑ Section of San Marco's Basilica, with its many spires and cupolas

→ Stunning mosaic of Christ in Glory in the vast Ascension Dome

The Ascension Dome features a magnificent 13th-century mosaic of Christ surrounded by angels, the 12 Apostles and the Virgin Mary.

The alabaster columns of the altar canopy, or baldacchino, are adorned with New Testament scenes.

St Mark's body, believed lost in the fire of AD 976, reappeared when the new church was consecrated in 1094. The remains are housed in the altar.

The mosaic pavement shows beautiful pictures of birds and beasts.

The Treasury is a repository of precious artifacts from both Italy and Constantinople.

PALA D'ORO

Beyond the Cappella di San Clemente lies the entrance to San Marco's most valuable treasure: the Pala d'Oro. This bejewelled altarpiece consists of 250 enamel paintings on gold, enclosed within a gilded silver frame. Napoleon stole some of the precious stones in 1797, but the screen still gleams with rubies, pearls and sapphires.

Mosaics

The earliest of the Basilica's gleaming mosaics date from the 12th century, and were the work of mosaicists from the East. Their delicate techniques were soon adopted by Venetian craftsmen, who gradually took over the Basilica's decoration, combining Byzantine inspiration with Western influences. During the 16th century, many sketches by Tintoretto, Titian, Veronese and other leading artists were reproduced in mosaic.

Museo Marciano

Look out for signposts to the "Loggia dei Cavalli", which lead you up to the museum. Here, the gallery offers a splendid view into the Basilica. The star exhibits are gilded bronze horses, stolen from the top of Constantinople's Hippodrome (ancient racecourse) in 1204.

Gilded bronze horses housed in the Museo Marciano

② ⟨⟩ Ⓜ 💻 🏛

PALAZZO DUCALE

📍 E3 🏠 **Piazza San Marco 1** 🚤 **San Marco** 🕐 **Apr–Oct: 8:30am–9pm daily (to 11pm Fri & Sat); Nov–Mar: 8:30am–7pm daily; last adm: 30 mins before closing** 🚫 **1 Jan, 25 Dec** 🌐 **visitmuve.it**

A magnificent combination of Byzantine, Gothic and Renaissance architecture, the Palazzo Ducale (Doge's Palace) was the official residence of the 120 doges who ruled Venice from 697 to 1797. Artists such as Titian, Tintoretto and Bellini vied with each other to embellish the palace with painting and sculpture, not to mention architects Antonio Rizzo and Pietro Lombardo, the latter responsible for the ornate western façade.

The Palazzo Ducale was founded in the 9th century, when a fortress-like structure stood on this spot. The present palace owes its external appearance to the building work of the 14th and early 15th centuries, despite a string of fires in the 1500s. The designers broke with tradition by perching the bulk of the pink Verona marble palace on lace-like Istrian stone arcades, with a portico supported by columns below. The result is a light and airy masterpiece of Gothic architecture.

Sala del Senato

Sala delle Quattro Porte

Sala del Collegio

Anticollegio

The walls of the Sala dello Scudo, once part of the doge's private apartments, are covered with maps of the world. In the centre of the room are two giant 18th-century globes.

The Porta della Carta was once the main entrance to the palace.

New doges were crowned on the Giant's Staircase with the zogia or dogal cap.

> 💬 **INSIDER TIP**
> **Avoid Queues**
>
> Skip the huge queue for the Palazzo Ducale by buying your ticket online in advance. Failing that, head to the Correr Museum where you can buy a combined ticket without the wait.

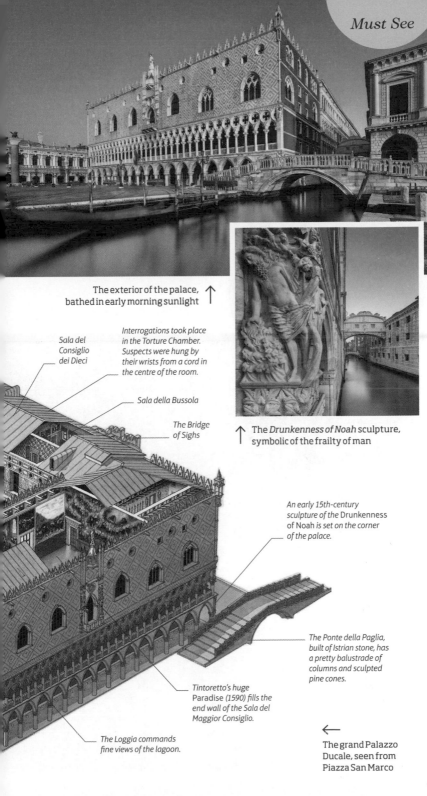

The exterior of the palace, ↑ bathed in early morning sunlight

Sala del Consiglio dei Dieci

Interrogations took place in the Torture Chamber. Suspects were hung by their wrists from a cord in the centre of the room.

Sala della Bussola

The Bridge of Sighs

↑ The *Drunkenness of Noah* sculpture, symbolic of the frailty of man

An early 15th-century sculpture of the Drunkenness of Noah *is set on the corner of the palace.*

The Ponte della Paglia, built of Istrian stone, has a pretty balustrade of columns and sculpted pine cones.

Tintoretto's huge Paradise (1590) fills the end wall of the Sala del Maggior Consiglio.

The Loggia commands fine views of the lagoon.

← The grand Palazzo Ducale, seen from Piazza San Marco

Exploring the Palazzo Ducale

A tour of the Palazzo Ducale takes visitors through a succession of richly decorated chambers and halls, arranged over four floors, culminating with the Bridge of Sighs, which links the palace to the prisons. The Secret Itineraries tour gives access to parts of the palace normally out of bounds, including the prison cell from which Casanova escaped.

State Apartments and Council Chambers

The doge's private State Apartments on the second floor were built after the fire of 1483. Looted under the orders of Napoleon, they are bare of furnishings, but the lavish ceilings and colossal carved chimneypieces in some of the rooms give an idea of the doges' lifestyle. The Sala dello Scudo, or map room, contains maps and charts, while the picture gallery features some incongruous wooden demoniac panels by Hieronymous Bosch.

The Scala d'Oro ("golden staircase") leads to the third floor and its Council Chambers. In the Sala del Consiglio dei Dieci, the awesomely powerful Council of Ten, set up in 1310, would meet to investigate and prosecute crimes concerning the security of the state. Napoleon pilfered some of the Veroneses from the ceiling

← Paintings by Tintoretto adorn the walls of the Sala del Collegio

→ The magnificent Sala del Maggior Consiglio, featuring Tintoretto's *Paradise* but two of the finest found their way back here in 1920: *Age and Youth* and *Juno Offering the Ducal Crown to Venice* (both 1553–4).

The magnificent Anticollegio chamber was the waiting room for those meeting with the Council. The end walls are decorated with mythological scenes by Tintoretto: *Vulcan's Forge, Mercury and the Graces, Bacchus and Ariadne* and *Minerva Dismissing Mars*, all

↑ Dank corridor leading to cells in the palace prisons

painted in 1578. Veronese's masterly *Rape of Europa* (1580), opposite the window, is one of the most eye-catching works in the palace.

In the Sala della Bussola were lions' heads, where citizens could post anonymous bills denouncing others for their crimes, real or imaginary. The wooden door in this room leads to the rooms of the Heads of the Ten, the State Inquisitors' Room and thence to the torture chamber and prisons.

The star attraction of the palace is the monumental Sala del Maggior Consiglio. It was here that the Great Council convened to vote on constitutional questions, to pass laws and elect the top officials of the Serene Republic. Tintoretto's huge *Paradise* (1587–90) occupies the eastern wall. Measuring 7.45 by 24.65 m (25 by 81 ft), it is one of the largest oil paintings in the world. A frieze along the walls illustrates 76 doges by Tintoretto's pupils. The portrait covered by a curtain is of Marin Falier, beheaded for treason in 1355.

Prisons

The Bridge of Sighs links the palace to what were known as the New Prisons, built between 1556 and 1595. Situated at the top of the palace, just below the leaded roof, are the *piombi* cells (*piombo* means lead). These cells are hardly inviting but prisoners here were far more comfortable than the criminals left to fester in the *pozzi* – the dark dank dungeons at ground level. The windowless cells of these ancient prisons are still covered with the graffiti of the convicts.

Did You Know?

Notorious womanizer Casanova escaped from the palace prisons through a hole in the roof of his cell.

3 ✍️

SANTA MARIA GLORIOSA DEI FRARI

📍C3 🏠Campo dei Frari 🚊San Tomà 🕐9am–6pm Mon–Sat, 1–6pm Sun & religious hols
🚫1 Jan, Easter, 15 Aug, 25 Dec & Mass 🌐basilicadeifrari.it

More commonly known as the Frari (a corruption of *frati*, meaning "brothers"), this vast Gothic church dwarfs the eastern area of San Polo. The airy interior is striking for the sheer size and quality of its works of art, including masterpieces by Titian and Giovanni Bellini, a statue by Donatello and several grandiose tombs.

The first church on this site was built by Franciscan friars in 1250–1338, but was replaced by a much larger building in the 15th century. The labyrinthine monastery and courtyards adjoining the church have been home to Venice's State Archives since the fall of the Republic. Its 300 rooms are loaded with precious records documenting the history of Venice right back to the 9th century.

Donatello's sculpture of St John the Baptist (1438) appears in the altar of the chapel immediately to the right of the apse.

The Monks' Choir consists of three-tiered stalls (1468), carved with bas-reliefs of saints and Venetian city scenes.

The campanile is 83 m (262 ft) high, the tallest in the city after that of San Marco.

Titian's spectacular work The Assumption of the Virgin (1518) draws the eye through the Monk's Choir, to the altar, and heavenwards.

Pietro Lombardo and Bartolomeo Bon carved this rood screen (1475) and its decorative marble figures.

The Madonna di Ca' Pesaro (1526) shows Titian's mastery of light and colour.

Canova's pyramidal tomb is based on a design he planned, but never constructed, as a monument for Titian.

The Gothic church of Santa Maria Gloriosa dei Frari ↑

1 The entrance to Santa Maria Gloriosa dei Frari faces the Rio dei Frari canal.

2 Titian's famous *Assumption of the Virgin* dominates the apse.

3 The sacristy's altarpiece, *Madonna and Child* (1488), by Bellini, is one of Venice's most beautiful Renaissance paintings.

4 The church's former monastery houses Venice's State Archives.

Courtyard and former monastery

④
RIALTO

📍 E3 🚏 Rialto

The commercial hub of Venice, the Rialto takes its name from *rivo alto* (high bank) and was one of the first areas of Venice to be inhabited. A financial and then a market district, it remains one of the city's busiest and most bustling areas. Locals and visitors alike jostle among the colourful stalls of the Erberia (fruit and vegetable market) and Pescheria (fish market), while people gather on the famous Rialto Bridge, browsing for souvenirs or taking a break to watch the swirl of activity on the Grand Canal below.

→
Boats cruising on the Grand Canal, with the Rialto bridge in the background

| 0 metres | 100 |
| 0 yards | 100 |

N ↑

Fondaco dei Tedeschi, originally a warehouse and lodgings for German traders, is now a luxury department store.

↑ The Grand Canal through the Rialto district

Palazzo Camerlenghi, built in 1528, was once the offices of the city treasurers (camerlenghi). The ground floor was the state prison.

Riva del Vin is one of the few spots to sit and relax on the banks of the Grand Canal.

Palazzo Barzizza, rebuilt in the 17th century, still preserves its early 13th-century façade.

Riva del Ferro is where barges unloaded iron (ferro).

Did You Know?

An early wooden Rialto Bridge collapsed under the weight of a wedding party in 1444.

① San Giacomo di Rialto

🏛 Campo San Giacomo, San Polo 📞 348 281 5492 🕐 9am–5pm Mon–Sat, 11am–7pm Sun 🚫 During Mass

The first church to be built on this site was allegedly founded in the 5th century, making it the oldest church in Venice. The present building dates from between the 11th and 12th centuries, while major restoration work took place in 1601. The original Gothic portico and huge 15th-century 24-hour clock on its façade are the church's most striking features.

The crouching stone figure on the far side of the square is the so-called Gobbo (hunchback) of the Rialto. In the 16th century this was a welcome sight for minor offenders who were forced to run the gauntlet from Piazza San Marco to this square at the Rialto.

② Rialto Market

🏛 San Polo 🕐 Fruit and vegetable market: dawn–12:30pm Mon–Sat; Fish market: dawn–12:30pm Tue–Sat

Venetians have come to the Erberia fruit and vegetable market to buy fresh produce for hundreds of years. Heavily laden barges arrive at dawn and offload their crates on to the quayside by the Grand Canal. Local produce includes red *radicchio* from Treviso, and succulent asparagus and baby artichokes from the islands of Sant'Erasmo and Vignole. In the adjoining Pescheria fish market are sole, sardines, skate, squid, crabs, clams and other species of seafood and fish for sale.

③ Rialto Bridge

Very few visitors leave Venice without crossing the iconic Rialto Bridge. The oldest of the four crossings over the Grand Canal, it is a wonderful place to watch the constant activity of boats on the water below. Stone bridges were built in Venice as early as the 12th century, but it was not until 1588, after the collapse, decay or sabotage of earlier wooden structures, that a competition was held for the design of a new Rialto bridge to be built in stone. Andrea Palladio, Jacopo Sansovino and Michelangelo were among the eminent contenders, but after months of deliberation it was the aptly named Antonio da Ponte who won the commission. Work was completed on the 48-m (157-ft) bridge in 1591. Until 1854, when the Accademia Bridge was constructed, the Rialto Bridge remained the only means of crossing the Grand Canal on foot.

> INSIDER TIP
> **Rialto Market**
>
> To see the market in full, bustling swing, visitors must arrive early in the morning – by noon the vendors are already starting to pack up.

EXPERIENCE MORE

⑤

Ca' d'Oro

📍 D2 🏛 Calle Ca' d'Oro
🚤 Ca' d'Oro 🕐 9am–2pm
Mon, 9am–7pm Tue–Sun
🚫 1 Jan, 1 May, 25 Dec
🌐 cadoro.org

In 1420 Marino Contarini, a wealthy patrician, commissioned the building of what he hoped would be the city's most magnificent palace. The building's intricate carving was entrusted to a team of Venetian and Lombard craftsmen, while the façade was adorned with the most expensive decorative finishes, including gold leaf, vermilion and ultramarine.

Over the years the palace was extensively remodelled, and by the 18th century it was in a state of semi-dereliction. In 1846 it was bought by the Russian Prince Troubetzkoy for the famous ballerina Marie Taglioni. Under her direction the palace went through heavy restoration, losing, among other things, its staircase and much of its original stonework. It was finally rescued by Baron Giorgio Franchetti, a wealthy patron of the arts, who bequeathed both the building and his private art collection to the state in 1915.

Pride of place on the first of the gallery's two floors goes to Andrea Mantegna's *St Sebastian* (1506), the artist's last work. The other main exhibits are ranged around the *portego* (entrance hall). This is largely dominated by the vivid 15th-century *Double Portrait* (c 1493) by the sculptor Tullio Lombardo and Sansovino's lunette of the *Madonna and Child* (c 1530). Rooms leading off the *portego* to the right contain numerous bronzes and medallions. Paintings here also include the famous *Madonna of the Beautiful Eyes*, attributed to Giovanni Bellini, a *Madonna and Child* attributed to Alvise Vivarini (both late 15th century), and Carpaccio's *Annunciation* (c 1504). A room to the left of the *portego* contains non-Venetian paintings, notably a *Flagellation* by Luca Signorelli (c 1480).

A lovely staircase leads to the second floor, which opens with a room hung with tapestries. It has bronzes by Alessandro Vittoria and paintings by Titian and Van Dyck. The *portego* displays frescoes (c 1532) by Pordenone from the cloister of Santo Stefano, while an anteroom contains damaged frescoes by Titian taken from the Fondaco dei Tedeschi.

---

⑥

Madonna dell'Orto

📍 D1 🏛 Campo Madonna dell'Orto 🚤 Madonna dell'Orto 🕐 10am–5pm Mon–Sat, noon–5pm Sun & pub hols 🚫 1 Jan, 25 Dec 🌐 madonnadellorto.org

Founded in the mid-14th century, this lovely Gothic church, founded was originally dedicated to St Christopher, patron saint of travellers, to protect the boatmen who ferried passengers to the islands in the northern lagoon. A 15th-century statue of the saint, restored by the

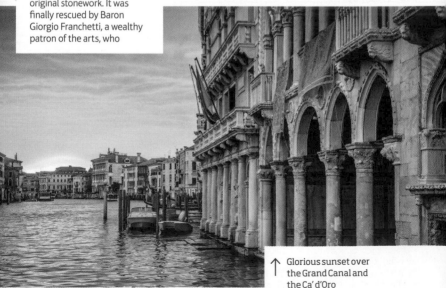

↑ Glorious sunset over the Grand Canal and the Ca' d'Oro

Venice in Peril fund, stands above the main portal. The dedication was changed and the church reconstructed in the early 15th century, after the discovery, in a nearby vegetable garden (*orto*), of a statue of the Virgin Mary said to have miraculous powers.

The interior features a magnificent painting by Cima da Conegliano, *St John the Baptist and Other Saints* (c 1493). The vacant space in the chapel opposite belongs to Giovanni Bellini's *Madonna with Child* (c 1478), stolen in 1993 for the third time.

The church's greatest remaining treasures are the works of art by Tintoretto, including the *Presentation of the Virgin in the Temple*, in the right nave. The most dramatic of his works are the towering masterpieces that decorate the chancel. On the right wall is the *Last Judgment*, whose turbulent content caused John Ruskin's wife, Effie, to flee the

church in horror. In *The Adoration of the Golden Calf* on the left wall, the figure carrying the calf, fourth from the left, is believed to be a portrait of the artist, who was a parishioner of the church.

DRINK

Bar Puppa
Best for local *cicchetti* (tapas) and glasses of house red and white.

📍E2 🏠Calle della Spezier 4800
📞041 476 14 54

Al Timon
A popular spot to stop by for an Aperol spritz next to the canal.

📍D2 🏠Fondamenta dei Ormesini, 2754
📞041 524 60 66

Bacarando in Corte dell'Orso
Enjoy a glass of wine or prosecco at this hidden bar just a minute's walk from the Rialto bridge.

📍E3 🏠Corte de l'Orso 5495 📞041 523 82 80

A RENAISSANCE MASTERPIECE

The Santa Maria dei Miracoli is one of the best examples of the early Venetian Renaissance. The façade is a harmonious tapestry of decorated panels and multi-coloured polished stone. Inside, the ceiling gleams with gilt miniatures.

The crowning lunette emphasizes the church's jewel-box appearance.

A false loggia is formed of Ionic arches, inset with windows.

The marble is fixed to the bricks in a way that prevents the build-up of damp.

7

San Giovanni Grisostomo

📍E3 🏠Campo San Giovanni Grisostomo
📞041 522 71 55 🚇Rialto
🕐8:15am-12:15pm & 3-7pm daily 🚫During Mass

This terracotta-coloured church is located near to the Rialto. Built between 1479 and 1504, it is a lovely Renaissance design, the last work of Mauro Coducci.

Inside, the light meter illuminates Giovanni Bellini's *St Jerome with Saints Christopher and Augustine* (1513) above the first altar on the right. This was most probably Bellini's last painting, executed when he was in his eighties.

Over the high altar hangs Sebastiano del Piombo's *St John Chrysostom and Six Saints* (1509–11).

8

Santa Maria dei Miracoli

📍E3 🏠Campo dei Miracoli
🚇Rialto or Fondamenta Nuove 🕐10:30am-4:30pm Mon-Sat 🚫1 Jan, 25 Dec
🌐chorusvenezia.org

This exquisite masterpiece of the early Renaissance was built in 1481–9 by the architect Pietro Lombardo to enshrine *The Virgin and Child* (1408), a painting believed to have miraculous powers. The picture, by Niccolò di Pietro, still hangs above the altar.

The interior, embellished by pink, white and grey marble, is crowned by a barrel-vaulted ceiling with portraits of saints and prophets. The balustrade, between the nave and the chancel, is decorated by Tullio Lombardo's carved figures of Archangel Gabriel, St Francis, the Virgin and St Clare.

The screen around the high altar and the medallions of the Evangelists in the cupola spandrels are also Lombardo's work. Overhead, above the main door, is a choir gallery that was once used as an entrance by nuns from the neighbouring convent.

San Polo

📍 D3 🏛 Campo San Polo
🚤 San Silvestro
🕐 10:30am–4:30pm
Mon–Sat 🗓 1 Jan, 25 Dec
🌐 chorusvenezia.org

This church is worth visiting for the Gothic portal and the Romanesque lions at the foot of the 14th-century campanile.

Inside, follow the signs for the *Via Crucis del Tiepolo* – 14 pictures of the Stations of the Cross (1749) by the painter Giandomenico Tiepolo; many of these works include vivid portraits of 18th-century Venetian life. The church also has paintings by Veronese and Palma il Giovane (the Younger), and a dramatic *Last Supper* by Tintoretto.

Scuola Grande di San Rocco

📍 C3 🏛 Campo San Rocco
🚤 San Tomà 🕐 9:30am–5:30pm daily 🗓 1 Jan, 25 Dec
🌐 scuolagrandesanrocco.it

Founded in honour of San Rocco (St Roch), a saint who dedicated his life to helping the sick, the Scuola started out as a charitable confraternity. Construction began in 1515 under Bartolomeo Bon and was continued by Scarpagnino until his death in 1549. The work was financed by donations from Venetians keen to invoke San Rocco's protection and the Scuola quickly became one of the wealthiest in Venice. In 1564 its members decided to commission Tintoretto to decorate its walls and ceilings.

The ground-floor cycle was executed in 1582–7, when Tintoretto was in his sixties, and consists of eight large paintings illustrating, among others, the life of Mary. The series starts with the *Annunciation* and ends with the *Assumption*.

The tranquil scenes of *The Flight into Egypt*, *St Mary Magdalene* and *St Mary of Egypt* are remarkable for their serenity. This is portrayed most lucidly by the repentant hermit's isolated spiritual contemplation in *St Mary of Egypt*. In all three paintings, the landscapes are rendered with noticeably rapid strokes, and are an important part of the final composition.

Scarpagnino's great staircase (1544–6), its upper flight decorated with two vast paintings commemorating the plague of 1630, leads to the Upper Hall. Here, biblical subjects decorate the ceiling and walls, painted by Tintoretto from 1575 to 1581.

The ceiling paintings portray scenes from the Old Testament. The three large and dynamic square paintings in the centre show episodes from the Book of Exodus: *Moses Strikes Water from the Rock*; *The Miracle of the Bronze Serpent*; and *The Fall of Manna in the Desert*. These all allude to the charitable aims of the Scuola in alleviating thirst, sickness and hunger. All three paintings are crowded compositions displaying much violent movement.

The vast wall paintings in the hall feature episodes from the New Testament, linking with the ceiling paintings. Two of the most striking are *The Temptation of Christ*, which shows a handsome young Satan offering Christ two loaves of bread, and *The Adoration of the Shepherds*. Like *The Temptation of Christ*, *The Adoration* is composed in two halves, with a female

The monumental Upper Hall in the Scuola Grande di San Rocco

Closely associated with the celebrated Scuola is the church of the same name, **San Rocco**. Designed by the sculptor and architect Bartolomeo Bon in 1489 and largely rebuilt in 1725, the exterior suffers from a mixture of styles. Inside, the chancel is decorated with a series of paintings by Tintoretto depicting scenes from the life of San Rocco.

San Rocco

🏛 Campo San Rocco 📞 041 523 48 64 🚊 San Tomà 🕐 9:30am-5:30pm daily (to 12:30pm 1 Jan, Easter & 25 Dec)

---

⑪

Ca' Rezzonico

📍 D4 🏛 Fondamenta Rezzonico 3136 🚊 Ca' Rezzonico 🕐 10am-5pm Wed-Mon (Apr-Oct: to 6pm); last adm: 30 mins before closing 🚫 1 Jan, 25 Dec 🌐 visitmuve.it

This palazzo houses the museum of 18th-century Venice, and its rooms are furnished with frescoes,

paintings and period pieces taken from other palaces or museums. The palazzo has an interesting history of its own. Building began with Longhena (architect of Santa Maria della Salute) in 1667, but the funds of the Bon family, who commissioned it, ran dry before the second floor was started. In 1712 the unfinished palace was bought by the Rezzonico family of Genoa, who spent a large portion of their fortune on its completion.

The Rezzonico family sold it on, in 1888, to the famous poet Robert Browning and his son, Pen. The outstanding attraction in the palace today is Giorgio Massari's ballroom, which occupies the entire breadth of the building. It is adorned with gilded chandeliers, carved furniture by Andrea Brustolon and a ceiling with *trompe l'oeil* frescoes. Other rooms have frescoes by Giambattista Tiepolo, including his lively *Nuptial Allegory* (1758), and one by his son, Giandomenico, originally in his villa at Zianigo. There are paintings by Longhi, Guardi and – rare in Venice – Canaletto. On the top floor is a reconstructed 18th-century apothecary's shop and the Pinacoteca Martini.

figure, shepherds and an ox below, and the Holy Family and onlookers above.

The splendid carvings below the paintings were added in the 17th century by sculptor Francesco Pianta. The figures are allegorical and include (near the altar) a caricature of Tintoretto with his palette and brushes, representing Painting. The easel painting *Christ Carrying the Cross* was once attributed to Giorgione, though many believe it to be by Titian.

Near the entrance to the Sala dell'Albergo is the *Annunciation* by Titian. The Sala dell'Albergo itself holds the most breathtaking of Tintoretto's works – the *Crucifixion* (1565). Henry James remarked of this painting: "No single picture contains more of human life; there is everything in it, including the most exquisite beauty." Tintoretto began the cycle of paintings in this room in 1564, when he won the commission with the ceiling painting *San Rocco in Glory*. On the wall opposite the *Crucifixion* are paintings of episodes from the Passion: *Christ before Pilate*; *The Crowning with Thorns*; and *The Ascent to Calvary*.

CARNEVALE

The Venetian gift for intrigue comes into its own during Carnevale, a vibrant, playful festival preceding the abstinence of Lent. Masks and costumes play a key role in this anonymous world; social divisions are dissolved, participants delight in playing practical jokes, and anything goes. The tradition of Carnevale in Venice began in the 11th century and reached its peak in popularity and outrageousness in the 18th century.

12 San Nicolò dei Mendicoli

📍 B4 **🏛 Campo San Nicolò** **📞 041 275 03 82** **🚤 San Basilio** **🕐 10am–noon & 3–5:30pm Mon–Sat, 9am–noon Sun & pub hols**

Contrasting with the remote and run-down area which surrounds it, this church still remains one of the most charming in Venice. Founded in the 7th century, it has been rebuilt extensively over the years. The little porch on the north flank was built in the 15th century and once sheltered the beggars, or *mendicanti*, who gave the church its name.

Thanks to the Venice in Peril fund, in the 1970s the church underwent one of the most comprehensive restoration programmes since the floods of 1966. Flooding had become such a problem that the priest often ferried himself around the church in a small wicker boat. The floor, which was 30 cm (1 ft) below the level of the canals, was rebuilt and raised slightly to prevent more flood damage. The roofs and lower walls were reconstructed, and the paintings and statues restored.

The interior is delightfully embellished, particularly the nave with its 16th-century gilded wooden statues. These include the figure of San Nicolò himself. On the upper walls is a series of paintings of the life of Christ (c 1553) by Alvise dal Friso and other pupils of Veronese.

Outside, a small column supports a stone lion, in a humbler echo of the Column of San Marco in the Piazzetta.

---

13 San Sebastiano

📍 C4 **🏛 Campo San Sebastiano** **🚤 San Basilio** **🕐 10:30am–1:30pm & 2:30–5pm Mon–Sat** **🚫 1 Jan, 15 Aug, 25 Dec** **🌐 chorus venezia.org**

This 16th-century church features one of the most colourful and homogeneous interiors in the whole of Venice. Much of its splendour is down to Veronese who, from 1555 to 1560 and again in the 1570s, was commissioned to decorate the sacristy ceiling, the nave ceiling, the frieze, the east end of the choir, the high altar, the doors of the organ panels and the chancel.

The paintings feature radiant colours and rich costumes. Those on the sacristy ceiling depict the *Coronation of the Virgin* and the *Four Evangelists*.

Of the other paintings, the finest are the three that tell the story of Esther, Queen

↑ Veronese ceiling painting in the church of San Sebastiano

of Xerxes I of Persia, famous for securing the deliverance of the Jewish people.

Veronese is buried here. His tomb is in front of the paved chapel to the left of the chancel.

---

14 Santa Maria della Salute

📍 D4–E4 **🏛 Campo della Salute** **🚤 Salute** **🕐 Main church: 9:30am–noon & 3–5:30pm daily; Sacristy: 10am–noon & 3–5pm Mon–Sat, 3–5pm Sun** **🚫 8 & 13 Jun** **🌐 basilicasalute venezia.it**

This great Baroque church standing at the entrance of the Grand Canal is one of the most imposing Venetian landmarks. Henry James likened it to "some great lady on the threshold of her salon".

Santa Maria della Salute was built in thanksgiving for the city's deliverance from the plague epidemic of 1630; hence the name *Salute*, which means "health and salvation".

Every 21 November, in celebration of the occasion, worshippers light candles and approach across a temporary bridge, resting on boats, which spans the mouth of the Grand Canal.

A BIT OF SPRITZ

The spritz is ubiquitous all over Italy, and no more so than in the Veneto, where the drink originated in the 1800s. The two most popular versions are made with either Aperol or Campari, depending on preference. The spirit is mixed with prosecco or sparkling water and white wine, and usually served with an olive or orange slice.

Baldassare Longhena started the church in 1630 at the age of 32, and worked on it for the rest of his life. It was completed in 1687, five years after his death.

The interior consists of a large octagonal space below the cupola and six chapels radiating from the ambulatory. The large domed chancel and grandiose high altar dominate the view from the main door.

The altar's sculptural group by Giusto Le Corte represents the Virgin and Child giving protection to Venice from the plague. The best of the paintings are in the sacristy to the left of the altar: Titian's early altarpiece *St Mark Enthroned with Saints Cosmas, Damian, Roch and Sebastian* (1511–12) and his dramatic ceiling paintings *Cain and Abel, The Sacrifice of Abraham and Isaac* and *David and Goliath* (1540–9). *The Wedding at Cana* (1551) on the wall opposite the entrance is by Jacopo Tintoretto.

⑮ ♦ 🖼 🛍

Punta della Dogana

📍E4 🏛Campo della Salute 🚤Salute ⏰10am-7pm Wed-Mon (ticket counter closes at 6pm) 🚫25 Dec 🌐palazzograssi.it

Formerly a customs house, where cargo ships were inspected before they entered Venice, the magnificent 17th-century Punta della Dogana was restored by the Japanese architect Tadao Ando and opened in 2009 as a contemporary art gallery. Together with the Palazzo Grassi, it houses the French billionaire François Pinault's large collection of contemporary art. It contains important works, including pieces by Jeff Koons, Takashi Murakami and British artists Rachel Whiteread and the Chapman Brothers. The building also has fantastic views towards St Mark's, San Giorgio and the two main canals of Venice.

SHOP

Here are the best places to buy Carnevale masks.

Ca' Macana
A wide range of masks, as well as in-store mask-making workshops.

📍C4 🏛Calle de le Botteghe 3172 🌐camacana.com

——————

Papier Machè Venezia
This is where locals buy their Carnevale masks.

📍E3 🏛Castello 5174/B/517 🌐papiermache.it

——————

Maschere di Guerrino Lovato
This boutique has supplied masks to films such as *Eyes Wide Shut*.

📍C4 🏛Canal Dorsoduro 3063 🌐mondonovo maschere.it

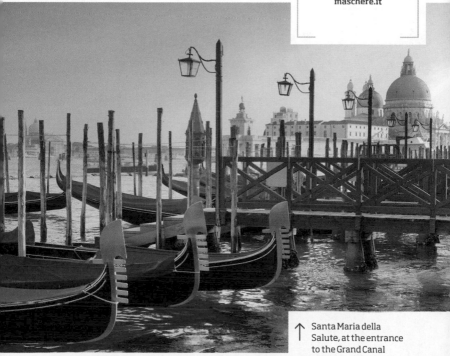

↑ Santa Maria della Salute, at the entrance to the Grand Canal

16

Accademia

D4 **Campo della Carità 1050** **Accademia** **8:15am-7:15pm Tue-Sun, 8:15-2pm Mon** **gallerie accademia.it**

Housing the largest collection of Venetian art in existence, the Accademia occupies three former religious buildings. The basis of the collection was the Accademia di Belle Arti, founded in 1750 by painter Giovanni Battisa Piazzetta. In 1807 Napoleon moved the collection to its current premises, enriching it with artworks removed from churches and monasteries.

Spanning five centuries, the paintings and altarpieces in the museum provide a complete spectrum of the Venetian school, from the Byzantine period through the Renaissance to the Baroque and the Rococo. Perhaps the highlight of the collection is Giorgione's famous *Tempest* (c 1507). In this enigmatic landscape, Giorgione was probably indulging in his imagination rather than portraying a specific subject.

The International Gothic collection shows the influence of Byzantine art on the early Venetian painters. Paolo Veneziano, the true founder of the Venetian school, displays a blend of both Western and Eastern influences in his sumptuous *Coronation of the Virgin* (1325). The linear rhythms are unmistakably Gothic, yet the glowing gold background and overall effect are distinctly Byzantine.

← Bellini's *Madonna and Child*, a star exhibit at the Accademia

Highlights of the Renaissance collection include Giovanni Bellini's *Madonna and Child between St John the Baptist and a Saint* (c 1504), Andrea Mantegna's *St George* (c 1460), Paolo Veronese's monumental *Feast in the House of the Levi* (1573) and Titian's haunting final painting, the *Pietà* (1575–6). Other must-see works include a view of Venice by Canaletto (dated 1763) and Vittore Carpaccio's ensemble of nine large wall paintings chronicling the tragic story of St Ursula (1495–1500).

 17

Peggy Guggenheim Collection

D4 **Palazzo Venier dei Leoni** **Accademia** **10am-6pm Wed-Mon** **25 Dec** **guggenheim-venice.it**

In 1949 the 18th-century Palazzo Venier dei Leoni was bought as a home by the American millionairess Peggy Guggenheim (1898–1979), a collector, dealer and patron of the arts who befriended, and

> Light-filled rooms and the large modern canvases provide a striking contrast to the Renaissance paintings in most Venetian churches and museums.

then furthered the careers of, many innovative abstract and Surrealist artists. One was Max Ernst, who became her second husband.

The Guggenheim is the best place in the city to see 20th-century art. Light-filled rooms and the large modern canvases provide a striking contrast to the Renaissance paintings in most Venetian churches and museums. The collection consists of 200 fine paintings and sculptures, each representing the 20th century's most influential modern art movements.

The dining room has notable Cubist works of art, including *The Poet* by Pablo Picasso, and an entire room is devoted to Jackson Pollock, who was "discovered" by Guggenheim.

Other artists represented are Braque, Chagall, de Chirico, Dalí, Duchamp, Léger, Kandinsky, Klee, Mondrian, Miró, Malevich, Rothko, Bacon and Magritte, whose Surreal *Empire of Light* (1953–4) shows a night scene of a darkened house in a wooded setting with a bright day sky above. The sculpture collection, which includes Constantin Brancusi's elegant *Maiastra* (1912), is laid out in the house and the picturesque paved garden.

Marino Marini's *Angelo della Città* (Angel of the Citadel, 1948), on the terrace overlooking the Grand Canal, is perhaps the most provocative piece. This shows a prominently displayed man sitting on a horse, erect in all respects.

There are presentations about Peggy Guggenheim and her collection given in several languages every day, and the museum holds special art workshops for children each Sunday.

Santo Stefano

 D4 Campo Santo Stefano Accademia or Sant'Angelo 11:30am–5pm Mon–Sat 1 Jan, Easter Sun, 15 Aug, 25 Dec chorusvenezia.org

Deconsecrated six times on account of the blood spilled within its walls, Santo Stefano – one of Venice's most beautiful churches – is now remarkably serene. Built in the 1300s, and altered in the 15th century, it has a carved portal by Bartolomeo Bon, and a campanile with a typical Venetian tilt. The interior has a splendid ship's keel ceiling with carved tie-beams, and the sacristy is crammed with valuable paintings.

←
Gallery filled with priceless works of art at the Accademia

↑ The Campanile, dominating the whole of the lagoon

19

Torre dell'Orologio

📍 E3 🏛 Piazza San Marco
🚤 San Marco 🕐 1 Jan, 25 Dec
🌐 visitmuve.it

This richly decorated clock tower on the north side of the piazza was built in the late 15th century, and Mauro Coducci is thought to have worked on the design. With its display of the phases of the moon and zodiac signs, the clock face was designed with seafarers in mind. According to legend, once the clock was completed, the two inventors had their eyes gouged out to prevent them from ever creating a replica.

On the upper level, the winged lion of St Mark stands against a star-spangled blue backdrop. At the very top, two huge bronze figures, known as the *Mori*, or Moors, strike the bell on the hour.

Guided tours to visit the clock tower must be booked in advance; they depart from the Museo Correr ticket office.

20

Campanile

📍 E3 🏛 Piazza San Marco
🚤 San Marco 🕐 Daily;
Apr: 9am–5:30pm;
May–Sep: 8:30am–9pm;
Oct: 9:30am–6pm;
Nov–Mar: 9:30am–4:30pm
🌐 basilicasanmarco.it

From the top of San Marco's campanile, high above the piazza, visitors can enjoy views of the city, the lagoon and, visibility permitting, the peaks of the Alps. It was from here that Galileo demonstrated his telescope to Doge Leonardo Donà in 1609. To do so he would have climbed the internal ramp, but access today is via a lift.

The first tower, completed in 1173, was built as a light-house to assist navigators in the lagoon. It took on a less benevolent role in the Middle Ages, when offenders were imprisoned – and in some cases left to die – in a cage hung near its summit. In July 1902, with little warning, the tower collapsed. The only casualties were the Loggetta at the foot of the tower and the custodian's cat. Donations flooded in, and in 1903 the foundation stone was laid for a new campanile *"dov'era e com'era"* ("where it was and as it was"). The new tower opened on 25 April (the Feast of St Mark), 1912.

21

Museo Correr

📍 E3–E4 🏛 Procuratie Nuove; entrance in Ala Napoleonica 🚤 San Marco
🕐 10:30am–6:30pm daily (Nov–Mar: to 5pm) 🕐 1 Jan, 25 Dec 🌐 visitmuve.it

Teodoro Correr bequeathed his extensive collection of works of art to Venice in 1830, thus forming the core of the city's fine civic museum.

Its first rooms form a suitably Neo-Classical back-drop for early statues by Antonio Canova (1757–1822). The rest of the floor covers the history of the Venetian

Republic, with maps, coins, armour and a host of doge-related exhibits.

The second floor contains a picture collection second only to that of the Accademia. The paintings, hung chronologically, trace the evolution of Venetian painting, and show the influence of Ferrarese, Paduan and Flemish artists.

The gallery's most famous works are by Carpaccio: *Portrait of a Young Man in a Red Hat* (c 1490) and *Two Venetian Ladies* (c 1507). The latter is traditionally, but probably incorrectly, known as *The Courtesans* because of the ladies' provocative low-cut dresses. The Museo del Risorgimento on the same floor looks at the history of Venice until unification with Italy in 1866.

22 San Zaccaria

🧭 F3 🏛 Campo San Zaccaria 📞 041 522 12 57 🚤 San Zaccaria 🕐 10am-noon & 4-6pm Mon-Sat; 4-6pm Sun & pub hols

Set in a quiet square just a stone's throw from the busy ferry terminals, the church of San Zaccaria is a successful blend of Flamboyant Gothic and Classical Renaissance styles. Founded in the 9th century, it was rebuilt between 1444 and 1515. Antonio Gambello began the façade in Gothic style and, when he died in 1481, Mauro Coducci added all the Classical detail.

Every Easter the doge came to San Zaccaria – a custom that started as an expression of gratitude to the nuns, who had relinquished part of their garden so that Piazza San Marco could be enlarged. The interior's artistic highlight is Giovanni Bellini's serene and

Torre dell' Orologio, with its winged lion sculpture *(inset)* →

sumptuously coloured *Madonna and Child with Four Saints* (1505) in the north aisle. A door off the right nave leads to the Chapel of St Athanasius, which in turn leads to the Chapel of San Tarasio. The chapel contains vault frescoes (1442) by Andrea del Castagno, and polyptychs (1443–4) by Antonio Vivarini and Giovanni d'Alemagna.

23 Santa Maria Formosa

🧭 E3 🏛 Campo Santa Maria Formosa 🚤 Rialto 🕐 10:30am-1:30pm & 2:30-5pm Mon-Sat 🔒 1 Jan, Easter Sun, 15 Aug, 25 Dec 🌐 chorusvenezia.org

Designed by Mauro Coducci in 1492, this church is most unusual in having two main façades – one overlooks the *campo,* the other the canal. The bell tower or campanile, added in 1688, is noted for the grotesque face at its base.

Two paintings stand out in the interior: a triptych (1473) by Bartolomeo Vivarini and Palma il Vecchio's *St Barbara* (c 1510).

↑ Imposing towers and wooden bridge at the Arsenale

Santi Giovanni e Paolo

📍E3 🏛️Campo Santi Giovanni e Paolo 🚤Fondamente Nuove or Ospedale Civile 🕐9am–6pm daily (from noon Sun & pub hols) 🚫1 Jan, Easter, 25 Dec 🌐basilicasanti giovanniepaolo.it

Known colloquially as San Zanipolo, Santi Giovanni e Paolo vies with the Frari as the city's greatest Gothic church. Located in the Castello area, it is slightly off the tourist track, meaning it is often very

↑ One of the stone lions guarding the entrance to Venice's Arsenale

quiet. Built by the Dominicans in the 14th century, the church is striking for its vast scale and architectural austerity. Known as the Pantheon of Venice, it houses monuments to no fewer than 25 doges. Among these are several fine works of art, executed by the Lombardi family and other leading sculptors.

Visitors enter through a doorway decorated with Byzantine reliefs and carvings by Italian sculptor Bartolomeo Bon. The doorway is thought to be one of Venice's earliest Renaissance architectural works. The commanding bronze statue at the opposite end of the church honours Doge Sebastiano Venier, who was Commander of the Fleet at Lepanto. A few steps away lies the tomb of Andrea Vendramin. Created by Pietro Lombardo in 1476–8, it takes the form of a Roman triumphal arch.

Highlights of the church include the Baroque high altar and the 16th-century frescoes attributed to Palma il Giovane. The tomb of Nicolò Marcello, a Renaissance tribute to Doge

🔍 HIDDEN GEM
Venice FC

For a local experience, book tickets to a Venice FC match, held from January to May at Stadio Pierluigi Penzo. Tickets are available from the club's website (*www. veneziafc.it*).

Nicolò Marcello by Pietro Lombardo, is another must-see masterpiece. Giovanni Bellini created the church's polyptych (1465), which shows St Vincent Ferrer, a Spanish cleric, flanked by St Sebastian and St Christopher. Nearby lies the tomb of Pietro Mocenigo, which commem-orates the doge's military pursuits when he was Grand Captain of the Venetian forces.

Further up on the right of the church is the grand Cappella di San Domenico, containing St Catherine of Siena's foot in a precious reliquary. Giovanni Battista Piazzetta frescoed the ceiling of this chapel. His *Glory of St Dominic* displays a mastery of colour, perspective and foreshortening that is said to have had a profound influence on the young Tiepolo.

㉕ Statue of Colleoni

♀E3 🏛 **Campo Santi Giovanni e Paolo** 🚉 **Ospedale Civile**

Bartolomeo Colleoni, the famous commander of mercenaries, left his fortune to the Republic on condition that his statue was placed in front of San Marco. A prominent statue in the piazza would have broken with precedent, so the Senate cunningly had Colleoni raised before the Scuola di San Marco instead of the basilica. A touchstone of early Renaissance sculpture, the equestrian statue of the proud warrior (1481–8) is by the Florentine Andrea Verrocchio, but was cast in bronze after his death by Alessandro Leopardi. The statue has a strong sense of power and movement.

㉖ Scuola di San Giorgio degli Schiavoni

♀F3 🏛 **Calle Furlani, Castello 3959a** 📞 **041 522 88 28** 🚉 **San Zaccaria** 🕐 **2:45–6pm Mon, 9:15am–1pm & 2:45–6pm Tue–Sat, 9:30am–1pm Sun** 🚫 **1 Jan, 1 May, 25 Dec and other religious hols**

This small gem houses some of Vittore Carpaccio's finest paintings, commissioned by the Schiavoni (or Dalmatian Slav) community in Venice.
The Scuola was established in 1451 and rebuilt in 1551. It has changed very little since.

→

Carpaccio's *Calling of St Matthew*, Scuola di San Giorgio degli Schiavoni

> **By the 16th century it had become the greatest naval shipyard in the world, capable of constructing a whole galley in 24 hours, using an assembly-line system.**

The exquisite frieze, executed between 1502 and 1508, shows scenes from the lives of patron saints St George, St Tryphone and St Jerome. Each episode of the narrative cycle is remarkable for its vivid colouring, minute detail and historic record of Venetian life. Outstanding among them are *St George Slaying the Dragon* and *St Jerome Leading the Tamed Lion to the Monastery*.

㉗ Arsenale

♀F3 🚉 **Arsenale**

The Arsenale was founded in the 12th century. By the 16th century it had become the greatest naval shipyard in the world, capable of constructing a whole galley in 24 hours, using an assembly-line system. Surrounded by crenellated walls, it was like a city within a city. Today the site is used as an exhibition space by the Biennale. Its impressive 15th-century gateway, twin towers and guardian lions can be viewed from the *campo* or bridge outside. The gateway was built by Antonio Gambello and is often cited as Venice's first Renaissance construction.
Around the corner, in Campo San Biago, the **Museo Storico Navale** charts Venetian naval history from the heyday of the Arsenale to the present. Exhibits include friezes from famous galleys of the past and a replica of the *Bucintoro*, the doge's ceremonial barge.

Museo Storico Navale
🌐 🏛 Campo San Biagio 🕐 10am–6pm daily (Nov–Mar: to 7pm) 🚫 Pub hols 🌐 visitmuve.it

EXPERIENCE Venice

Torcello

◉ 1F 🚌 12 from Fondamenta Nuove, then 9 from Burano

Established between the 5th and 6th centuries, Torcello was once a thriving colony with palaces, churches and a population that is said to have reached 20,000. But with the rise of Venice, the island went into decline. Today, the population is just 60, and all that remains of this once-bustling island are the Byzantine cathedral of Santa Maria Assunta, the church of Santa Fosca and the memory of its former glory.

Founded in 639 but radically restructured in 1008, **Santa Maria Assunta** retains its Romanesque form and arcaded 9th-century portico. The cathedral's campanile offers spectacular views. Inside, are breathtaking 12th- and 13th-century Doomsday Mosaics, which depict scenes of devils, angels, wild beasts and fires. The iconostasis is made up of exquisite marble panels showing peacocks drinking from the fountain of eternal life.

Alongside the cathedral is **Santa Fosca**, an elegant church based on a Greek cross design, encircled by a five-sided portico with columns and carved capitals.

The **Museo di Torcello**, in adjoining Gothic buildings, houses archaeological finds from the island and priceless treasures from the church.

Santa Maria Assunta
◈ ⊗ 🄲 041 73 01 19
🄲 10:30am–4:30pm daily
(Mar-Oct: to 5:30pm)
🄲 1 Jan, 25 Dec

Santa Fosca
🄲 For masses only

Museo di Torcello
◈ 🄰 Campo San Biagio
🄲 10am–5pm Tue–Sun (Mar-Oct: 10:30am–5:30pm) 🄲 21 Nov & pub hols 🆆 museodi torcello.provincia.venezia.it

Did You Know?

Daphne du Maurier came up with the plot for *Don't Look Now* during a visit to Torcello.

Giudecca

◉ D5 🚢 2, 4.1 or 4.2

In the days of the Republic, the island of Giudecca was a pleasure ground of palaces and gardens. Today it is very much a suburb of the city, its narrow alleys flanked by apartments, its squares overgrown and its palazzi neglected. Many of its old factories have been converted into modern housing. However, the long, wide quayside skirting the city side of the island makes a very pleasant promenade and provides stunning views of Venice across the water. The name Giudecca, once thought to have referred to the Jews, or *giudei*, who lived here in the 13th century, is more likely to have originated from the word

The campanile has great views over the lagoon.

The marble pulpit contains fragments of the first cathedral on the site.

Doomsday Mosaics cover the entire west wall.

Santa Fosca was built in the 11th and 12th centuries.

↓ Santa Maria Assunta in Torcello

↑ Palladio's church of San Giorgio Maggiore, on the island of the same name

giudicati, meaning "the judged". This referred to troublesome aristocrats who, as early as the 9th century, were banished to the island.

Hotel Cipriani, among the most luxurious places to stay in Venice, is discreetly located at the tip of the island. At the western end of Giudecca looms the massive Neo-Gothic Molino Stucky, a former flour mill that is now home to Venice's Hilton hotel.

Giudecca's main monument is Palladio's church of **Il Redentore** (The Redeemer). It was built in 1577–92 in thanksgiving for the end of the 1576 plague, which wiped out a third of the city's population. The Classical interior of the church presents a marked contrast to the ornate and elaborate style of most Venetian churches. The main

The Museo dell'Estuario contains archaeological finds.

paintings, by Paolo Veronese and Alvise Vivarini, are in the sacristy to the right of the choir.

Il Redentore

⊘ ⌂ Campo Redentore 🚆 Redentore ⏱ 10:30am-1:30pm & 2:30-5pm Mon-Sat 🚫 1 Jan, 25 Dec 🌐 chorus venezia.org

___

30

San Giorgio Maggiore

📍 F4 📞 041 522 78 27 🚆 San Giorgio ⏱ Apr-Oct: 9am-7pm daily; Nov-Mar: 8:30am-6pm daily

Appearing like a stage set across the water from the Piazzetta is the little island of San Giorgio Maggiore. The church and monastery, built between 1566 and 1610, are among architect Andrea Palladio's greatest achievements. The church's temple front and the spacious interior, with its perfect proportions, are typically Palladian.

On the chancel walls of San Giorgio Maggiore are two fine paintings by Tintoretto: *The Last Supper* and *Gathering of the Manna* (both 1594). In the Chapel of the Dead is his last work, *The Deposition* (1592–4), which was finished by his son Domenico.

The top of the campanile affords superb views of the

DRINK

Skyline Rooftop Bar
Skyline has a decidedly Miami vibe - think plush couches, white stools and, come nightfall, moody purple lighting. The views over Venice are the bar's main draw, but the cocktails aren't bad either.

📍 C4 ⌂ Molino Stucky, Giudecca 810 🌐 skylinebarvenice.it

___

Harry's Dolci
Part of the esteemed Cipriani chain, which first opened Harry's Bar in Venice in 1931. Expect white tablecloths, waiters in bow ties, panama hat-clad guests and Bellinis served on the quayside terrace.

📍 C5 ⌂ Fondamenta S Biagio 773 🌐 cipriani.com

city and lagoon. You can see the monastery cloisters below, now part of the **Fondazione Cini**, a cultural centre that hosts international exhibitions and events.

Fondazione Cini
⊘ ⌂ For guided tours only, check website 🌐 cini.it

31

Murano

F1 **4.1, 4.2 or 12 from Fondamenta Nuove; 3 from Piazzale Roma**

Much like Venice, Murano comprises a cluster of small islands connected by bridges. It has been the centre of the glassmaking industry since 1291, when the furnaces and glass craftsmen were moved here from the city, prompted by the risk of fire to the buildings and the unpleasant effects of the smoke.

Historically, Murano owes its prosperity entirely to glass. In the 15th and 16th centuries it was Europe's principal glass-producing centre. Murano's glass artisans were granted unprecedented privileges, but for those who left the island to find businesses elsewhere there were severe penalties – even death. Although a few of Murano's palazzi bear the hallmarks of its former splendour, and its basilica still survives, most tourists visit for the glass alone. Some are enticed by offers of free trips from

factory touts in San Marco; others go by excursion launch or independently on the public *vaporetti*.

Some of the factories are now derelict, but glass is still produced in vast quantities. Among the plethora of kitsch (including imports from the Far East) are some wonderful pieces, and it pays to seek out the top glass factories. Many furnaces, however, close at the weekend.

There is is also the **Museo del Vetro**, a glass museum housing a splendid collection of antique pieces. Its prize exhibit is the Barovier wedding cup (1470–80), with enamelwork by Angelo Barovier. There is also a section on modern glass.

The undisputed architectural highlight of Murano is the **Basilica dei Santi Maria e Donato**, whose magnificent colonnaded apse

---

MURANO GLASS

A main attraction of a trip to Murano is a demonstration of the glass-blowing technique. Visitors can watch while a glass-blower takes a blob of molten paste on the end of an iron rod and, by twisting, turning and blowing, transforms it into a vase, bird, lion, wine goblet or similar work of art. The display is followed by a tour of the showroom and some pressure from the salespeople. There is no obligation to buy, however.

↑ Vibrant colours in a Murano glass sphere

↑ Glass baubles in one of Murano's factories

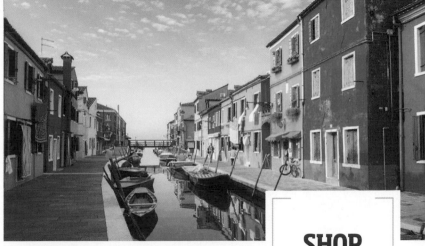

↑ Colourful fishermen's houses lining the waterways of Burano

is reflected in the waters of the San Donato canal. Despite some heavy-handed restoration undertaken in the 19th century, this 12th-century church still retains much of its original beauty. Visitors should note the Veneto-Byzantine columns and Gothic ship's keel roof. An enchantingly evocative mosaic portrait of the Madonna, portrayed standing alone against a gold background, decorates the apse. The church's floor is equally beautiful. With its medieval mosaics of geometric figures, exotic birds, mythical creatures and inexplicable symbols, it incorporates fragments of ancient glass from the island's foundries into its imagery.

Museo del Vetro
♿ 🏛 🏛 Palazzo Giustinian, Fondamenta Giustinian
🕐 10am–6pm daily (Nov–Mar: to 4:30pm) 🚫 1 Jan, 1 May, 25 Dec 🌐 museo vetro. visitmuve.it

Basilica dei Santi Maria e Donato
🏛 Campo San Donato
📞 041 73 90 56 🕐 8am–5:30pm daily 🚫 Sun am

32 🚇

Burano

📍 F1 🚤 12 from Fondamenta Nuove; 14 from San Zaccaria via Lido and Punta Sabbioni

Its canals fringed with brightly painted houses, Burano is the most colourful of the lagoon islands and can be recognized from a distance by the tilting tower of its church.

The main thoroughfare, Via Baldassare Galuppi, features traditional lace and linen stalls, plus open-air trattorias serving fresh fish.

The people of Burano are fishermen and lacemakers by tradition. You can still see fishermen scraping their boats or mending nets, but today lacemakers are rare. In the 16th century, the local lace was the most sought after in Europe. After a slump in the 18th century, the industry revived and a lacemaking school was set up here in 1872. You can watch authentic Burano lace being made at the school, now the **Museo del Merletto**, which displays fine examples of antique lace.

Museo del Merletto
♿ 🏛 Piazza Baldassare Galuppi 187 🕐 10:30am–5pm Tue–Sun (Nov–Mar: to 4:30pm) 🚫 1 Jan, 1 May, 25 Dec 🌐 visitmuve.it

SHOP

Here are the best places to buy Murano glassware.

Davide Penso
Watch a master craftsman create (affordable) necklaces and earrings by shaping portions of coloured glass over a flame.

📍 F1 🏛 Fondamenta Riva Longa 48, Murano 🌐 davidepenso.com

L'ISOLA – The Carlo Moretti Showroom
Founded by brothers Carlo and Giovanni, this glass factory creates exquisite homewares in vibrant patterns and colours.

📍 D3 🏛 Calle de le Botteghe 2970, Venice 🌐 lisola.com

Marina e Susanna Sent
The Sent sisters create glass jewellery and sculptures using traditional techniques passed down through their glassmaking family for generations.

📍 F1 🏛 Fondamenta Serenella 20, Murano 🌐 marinaesusanna sent.com

A SHORT WALK
DORSODURO

Distance 1.5 km (1 mile) **Time** 15 minutes
Nearest Vaporetto Ca' Rezzonico

Lively Campo Santa Margherita is at the heart of the *sestiere* of Dorsoduro. The square bustles with activity, particularly in the morning, when the market stalls are open, and in the evening when it is the haunt of students from nearby Ca' Foscari, now part of the University of Venice. The surrounding streets contain several spectacular buildings, most notably Ca' Rezzonico and the Scuola Grande dei Carmini, which has decorations by Tiepolo. Of the area's waterways, the delightful Rio San Barnaba is best appreciated from the Ponte dei Pugni, near the barge selling fruit and vegetables – itself a time-honoured Venetian sight. To discover the quieter part of the *sestiere*, travel east of the Peggy Guggenheim Collection for shaded squares and picturesque residences.

Campo Santa Margherita is an ideal place for relaxing in a café.

Scuola Grande dei Carmini contains nine ceiling panels (1739–44) in the hall on the upper floor, painted by Tiepolo for the Carmelite confraternity.

Palazzo Zenobio, built at the end of the 17th century, is now used for temporary exhibitions. With permission, visitors can see the fine 18th-century ballroom.

The church of Santa Maria dei Carmini has a Gothic side porch carved with Byzantine reliefs.

Fondamenta Gherardini runs beside the Rio San Barnaba, one of the prettiest canals in the sestiere.

Ponte dei Pugni was a traditional setting for fist fights between rival factions. They were finally banned in 1705 for being too violent.

↑ Barges lining the canal
by Campo San Barnaba

Locator Map
For more detail see p58

Did You Know?

Dorsoduro is built on solid subsoil, unlike much of Venice. This accounts for its name, meaning "hard backbone".

RIO DI CA' FOSCARI

Ca' Foscari was completed in 1437 for Doge Francesco.

C D ASEO

C SAONERI

C C FOSCARI

C DELLA VIDA

C D BOTTEGHE

CALLE BERNARDO

CANAL GRANDE

Palazzo Giustinian was home to Wagner in 1858.

The ballroom of Ca' Rezzonico covers the width of the palazzo.

CAMPO SAN BARNABA

○ **FINISH**

CALLE DEL TRAGHETTO

San Barnaba, a tiny islet within Venice, is a thriving community, with its own floating barge stall crammed with fresh produce.

| 0 metres | | 75 |
| 0 yards | | 75 |

N
↑

THE VENETO AND FRIULI

The Romans built frontier posts on this fertile land of silt deposits, and these survive today as the cities of Vicenza, Padua, Verona and Treviso. Strategically placed at the hub of the empire's road network, the cities prospered under Roman rule, but suffered in the wave of Germanic invasions of the 5th century AD.

The region's fortunes revived under the benign rule of the Venetian empire. The medieval cities of the Veneto lay on important trade routes such as the Serenissima, the road connecting the flourishing port cities of Venice and Genoa, and the Brenner Pass, used by commercial travellers crossing the Alps from northern Europe. Wealth from agriculture, commerce and the spoils of war paid for the beautification of these cities through the building of Renaissance palaces and public buildings, many designed by the Veneto's great architect, Andrea Palladio.

Today the Veneto is a thriving wine exporter, textile producer and agricultural centre, and Friuli is a focus for new technology while remaining largely agricultural. Both regions are popular tourist destinations, despite lying a little in the shadow of Venice, and boast an abundant and enchanting variety of attractions.

THE VENETO AND FRIULI

←

1 Vineyards in the Veneto's prosecco hills.

2 Harvesting the grapes.

3 Cured meat and cheese.

4 Bottle of Valdobbiadene prosecco and panettone.

2 DAYS

A Prosecco Tour of Veneto

Day 1

Morning Begin the tour in Valdobbiadene with a mid-morning glass of prosecco at Bar Alpino *(Via Mazzolini 14, Valdobbiadene)*, then move on to the restored farmhouse Osteria Senz'Oste *(Str. delle Treziese 4, Valdobbiadene)* for a simple self-service picnic-style lunch of bread, cured meats and olives in the grounds.

Afternoon A visit to Nino Franco vineyard *(Via Garibaldi 147, Valdobbiadene)*, one of the country's most esteemed prosecco producers, is a must but make sure you have called in advance to book your place. After a tour and an on-site tasting, move on to the ever-chic Bisol vineyard *(Via Follo 33, Santo Stefano di Valdobbiadene)* for further fizz tastings in their cool stone cellar.

Evening Check in to the utterly charming wine property Hotel Villa del Poggio *(Via dei Pascoli 8/a, San Pietro di Feletto)*, then journey high into the heart of prosecco country to Locanda Marinelli *(Via Castella 5, Farra di Soligo)* for beautifully presented plates of hyperlocal cuisine, matched with regional wines.

Day 2

Morning After a lazy hotel breakfast make for the Carpenè Malvolti vineyard *(Via Antonio Carpenè 1, Conegliano)*, one of the region's oldest family-run prosecco houses, in the centre of Conegliano. Next up, visit Zardetto vineyard, tucked away in the Conegliano hills *(Via Martiri delle Foibe, Scomigo)*, to see how they use modern techniques to create one of the most esteemed proseccos on the market.

Afternoon Book a table at the informal, family-run Trattoria Ristoro Fos de Marai *(Via Santo Stefano 20, Valdobbiadene, closed for dinner on Monday and all day Tuesday)*. The speciality here is meat cooked on an open grill and served at tables overlooking the vines.

Evening Head to Relais Dolce Vista *(Via Masare 4, Valdobbiadene)*, a quaint, family-run farmhouse with a swimming pool and extraordinary views over the prosecco hills. Owners Monica and Renato are very kind and generous, and will organize tours or day trips for you, book restaurants, or simply tell you about the region over a glass of wine.

↑ View over the River Adige towards the Duomo's bell tower

VERONA

🅰️ C2 ✈️ Villafranca 14 km (9 miles) SW 🚉 Piazzale 25 Aprile ℹ️ Via degli Alpini 9; www.veronatouristoffice.it

Verona is a vibrant trading centre, the largest city in the Veneto region (followed by Venice) and one of the most prosperous in northern Italy. Its ancient centre boasts many magnificent Roman ruins and fine palazzi built of *rosso di Verona*, the local pink-tinged limestone.

Castelvecchio

🏛️ Corso Castelvecchio 2
📞 045 80 62 611 🕐 11am-5pm Tue-Sun; last adm: 30 mins before closing
🚫 1 Jan, 25 Dec 🌐 museo dicastelvecchio.comune. verona.it

This impressive castle, built by Cangrande II between 1355 and 1375, houses one of the finest art galleries in the area outside Venice. The section on medieval and Renaissance art illustrates the influence of northern art on local painters. A walkway offers views of the Ponte Scaligero, a medieval bridge that leads to the Arsenal, fronted by gardens.

Teatro Romano and Museo Archeologico

🏛️ Regaste Redentore 2
📞 045 800 03 60 🕐 11am-5pm Tue-Sun; last adm:4:30pm 🚫 1 Jan & 25 Dec; early on performance days

This Roman theatre was built in the 1st century BC; little survives of the stage, but the seating area is largely intact. It offers great views of Verona.

A lift carries visitors from the Teatro up to the former monastery above, which is now an archaeological museum. The exhibits around the tiny cloister and in the monks' cells include mosaics, pottery and glass.

③ 🎨

Arena

🏛️ Piazza Brà 🕐 9am-6pm daily; last adm: 5:30pm
🚫 1 Jan, 25 Dec; early on performance days
🌐 museomaffeiano. comune.verona.it

Completed in AD 30, this is the world's third-largest Roman amphitheatre, after Rome's Colosseum (p242) and the amphitheatre at Santa Maria Capua Vetere (p474), near Naples. It could hold almost the entire population of Roman Verona, and visitors would come from across the Veneto to watch gladiatorial combats. Since then, the arena has seen executions, fairs, bullfights and opera.

④

San Lorenzo

🏛️ Corso Cavour 28
📞 045 805 00 00 🕐 10am-noon & 3-5:30pm Sat
🚫 During mass

San Lorenzo is one of Verona's lesser-known churches, but is one of the city's most beautiful. Built in 1117 on the remains of a Paleo-Christian basilica, the Romanesque exterior, with

1301
Dante is welcomed to the Scaligeri court, and dedicates the final part of his epic *Divine Comedy* to the ruler Cangrande I

1866
▼ The Veneto is reunited with Italy

1263
▲ The Scaligeri family begins their 124-year rule of Verona. They use ruthless tactics to rise to power but once established, the family brings peace to the city

1387
Verona falls to the Visconti of Milan, and then a succession of outsiders – Venice, France, and Austria – rule the city

1597
▲ Shakespeare sets *Romeo and Juliet* in Verona

alternate strips of stone and bricks, is typical of Veronese churches. The bell tower dates from the 15th century and inside there are 13th-century frescoes. The church has two unusual cylindrical towers.

---

⑤
Piazza delle Erbe
Once the site of the Roman forum, Piazza delle Erbe is named after the city's old herb market. Today's stalls, shaded by umbrellas, sell everything from herb-flavoured roast

suckling pig in bread rolls to succulent fresh-picked fruit.

---

⑥
Giardino Giusti

⌂ Via Giardino Giusti 2
☎ 045 803 40 29 ⏰ 9am–7pm daily; last adm: 6pm
🚫 25 Dec

This Renaissance garden was laid out in 1580. As in gardens of the period, there is a juxta-position of nature and artifice: the formal lower garden con-trasts with the woods above.

↑ The lower garden of the beautiful Giardino Giusti

The nave has a magnificent example of a ship's keel ceiling, so called because it resembles the inside of an upturned boat.

The plan of the church is modelled on an ancient Roman basilica, the Hall of Justice.

Andrea Mantegna's three-part altarpiece

Each of the wooden doors has 24 bronze plates nailed on to make the doors look like solid metal.

↑ The San Zeno Maggiore church complex

TOP 5 ROMANTIC THINGS TO DO

Verona in Love
Sign up to the citywide Verona in Love festival in February *(www. dolcementeinlove.com)*.

Wine Tasting
Hire a bicycle, pack a picnic, and go wine tasting in the emerald hills around Verona.

River Adige
Take a sunset stroll along the River Adige.

Giardino Giusti
Get lost among the statues, grottoes and clipped mazes of the Giardino Giusti.

Trattoria Dal Gal
Enjoy a romantic candlelit dinner at the Trattoria Dal Gal.

⑦ San Zeno Maggiore

🏠 Piazza Duomo 35
🕐 9:30am-1:30pm & 2:30-6pm Mon-Fri, 9am-6pm Sat, 1-6pm Sun 🕐 For mass
🌐 chieseverona.it

This magnificent church is brimming with trinkets, treasures and priceless artworks. One of the most spectacular examples of Romanesque architecture in Italy, San Zeno Maggiore is also the most revered in Verona, housing the shrine of the city's patron saint, San Zeno.

Built between 1120 and 1138, the façade is embellished with marble reliefs of biblical scenes, matched in vitality by bronze door panels showing the miracles of San Zeno. Beneath an impressive rose window, a graceful porch canopy rests on two slim columns. A brick campanile soars to the south, while a squat tower to the north is

said to cover the tomb of King Pepin of Italy (777–810).

⑧ Piazza dei Signori

🏠 Torre dei Lamberti
📞 045 927 30 27 🕐 10am-6pm Mon-Fri; 11am-7pm Sat, Sun & hols

In the centre of this elegant square is a 19th-century statue of Dante, whose gaze seems fixed on the forbidding Palazzo del Capitano, the former home of Verona's military commanders. Beside it is the equally intimidating Palazzo della Ragione (Palace of Reason) now the city's law courts. Stunning views of the Alps can be enjoyed from atop the Torre dei Lamberti, which rises from the west side of the courtyard.

⑨ Tombs of the Scaligeri

🏠 Via Santa Maria in Chiavica, 1a 🕐 10am-1pm & 2-5pm Tue-Sun

The tiny Romanesque church of Santa Maria Antica is almost swamped by the tombs built up against its entrance wall. Because it was their parish church, the Scaligeri rulers of Verona chose to be buried here, and their tombs speak of their military prowess. Perhaps the most notable is the tomb of Cangrande I (died 1329): the sarcophagus is surmounted by an equestrian statue of the ruler, a copy of the original which is now in Castelvecchio *(p108)*.

> **Stunning views of the Alps can be enjoyed from atop the Torre dei Lamberti, in the elegant Piazza dei Signori.**

↑ The western façade of Verona's Duomo, carved by Nicolò

Duomo

🏛 Piazza Duomo ⏰ 11am-5pm Mon-Fri, 11am-3:30pm Sat, 1:30-5:45pm Sun
🌐 chieseverona.it

Verona's cathedral was begun in 1139 and is fronted by a magnificent Romanesque portal carved by Nicolò, one of the two master masons responsible for the façade of San Zeno Maggiore. Here he sculpted the figures of Oliver and Roland, two of Charlemagne's knights. The highlight of the interior is Titian's lovely *Assumption* (1535–40). Outside is a Romanesque cloister in which the excavated ruins of earlier churches are visible. The 8th-century baptistry San Giovanni in Fonte (St John of the Spring) was built from Roman masonry; the marble font was carved in 1220.

Casa di Giulietta

🏛 Via Cappello 23 ⏰ Daily (pm only Mon)

The story of Romeo and Juliet has inspired countless dramas, films and ballets. At the Casa di Giulietta (Juliet's House), Romeo is said to have climbed to Juliet's balcony; in reality this is a restored 13th-century inn. Today, crowds throng to see the simple façade and stand on the small marble balcony. The run-down Casa di Romeo is a few streets away, in Via Arche Scaligeri. The so-called Tomba di Giulietta is in a crypt below the cloister of San Francesco al Corso on Via del Pontiere.

EAT

Casa Perbellini
Dining at this intimate, Michelin-starred trattoria is like stepping into a friend's kitchen - and that is exactly what the owners are after. The open kitchen is more a theatre stage than a food preparation area, and guests can interact with the chefs as they work.

🏛 Piazza San Zeno, 16
🕐 Mon & Sun

€€€

Trattoria Dal Gal
This welcoming neighbourhood local does plates of freshly made pastas matched with local wines. Choose from five daily-changing pasta dishes, then head straight for a dessert degustation, which can feature anything from tiramisu to fresh strawberries and sorbet.

🏛 Via Don Gregorio Segala, 39/B
🕐 Mon & Sun dinner

€€€

Visitors taking a photo on the famous balcony at Casa di Giulietta

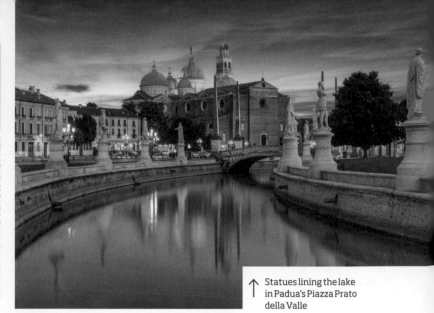

↑ Statues lining the lake in Padua's Piazza Prato della Valle

2

PADUA

🅰 D2 🚌 Piazza Boschetti 🚈 🛈 Vicolo Pedrocchi 9; www.turismopadova.it

Padua (Padova) is a university town with an illustrious academic history. Rich in art and architecture, it has two particularly outstanding sights. The magnificent Cappella degli Scrovegni (p114), north of the city centre, is famous for Giotto's lyrical frescoes, and forms part of the complex incorporating the Eremitani church and museums. The Basilica di Sant'Antonio is one of the most popular pilgrimage destinations in Italy.

①

Duomo and Baptistry

🅰 Piazza Duomo 📞 049 66 28 15 🕐 10am-6pm daily 🚫 1 Jan, Easter, 25 Dec

The Duomo was built in 1552 to designs partly drawn up by Michelangelo, on the site of an earlier 14th-century cathedral. Beside it stands a domed baptistry (c 1200). The interior is decorated with frescoes by Giusto de' Menabuoi. Dating from around 1378, they depict episodes from the Bible, including the Creation and the Crucifixion.

↑ Fresco of Christ by Giusto de' Menabuoi in Padua's Duomo

②

Palazzo della Ragione

🅰 Piazza delle Erbe (via the town hall) 📞 049 820 50 06 🕐 9am-7pm Tue-Sun (Nov-Jan: to 6pm) 🚫 1 May, 15 Aug

The "Palace of Reason" was built in 1218 to serve as Padua's law court and council chamber. The vast main hall was originally decorated with frescoes by Giotto, but fire destroyed his work in 1420. Frescoes painted by Nicola Miretto now cover its walls.

③

Chiesa degli Eremitani and Museo Civico Eremitani

🅰 Piazza Eremitani 8 🕐 Chapel: daily; Museum: 9am-7pm Tue-Sun 🚫 1 Jan, 1 May, 25 & 26 Dec 🌐 beniculturali.it

The Eremitani church, built from 1276 to 1306, contains magnificent roof and wall tombs and frescoes (1454–7) by Andrea Mantegna. The Museo Civico Eremitani holds a collection of rare Roman

EAT

Belle Parti

Tradition reigns at Belle Parti, from the candlelit, white-clothed tables to the sommelier on hand to match every dish with local wines.

🏠 Via Belle Parti 11
🕐 Sun

€€€

Osteria Dal Capo

The menu here truly delights, with seasonal dishes such as lasagne with radicchio, or black tagliatelle with chestnuts and pumpkin.

🏠 Via Obizzi 2
🕐 Lunch & dinner Sun, lunch Mon

€€€

---

medallions, a set of Venetian coinage, an archaeological section and an art gallery.

Basilica di Sant'Antonio

🏠 Piazza del Santo 📞 049 822 56 52 🕐 6:15am–7:30pm daily (winter: to 6:45pm)

This exotic church, with its Byzantine domes and minaret-like spires, is also known as Il Santo. It was built from 1232 to house the remains of St Anthony of Padua. Inside, the high altar features Donatello's magnificent reliefs (1444–5) on the miracles of St Anthony.

Statue of Gattamelata

Beside the entrance to the Basilica stands a great work of the Renaissance: a statue of the soldier Gattamelata by artist Donatello, made in 1452.

Orto Botanico

🏠 Via Orto Botanico 15
🕐 Tue–Sun (Apr–May: daily) 🕐 1 Jan, 25 Dec
🌐 ortobotanicopd.it

Padua's botanical garden is one of the oldest in Europe (1545). The gardens were used to grow Italy's first lilac trees, sunflowers and potatoes.

Scuola del Santo and Oratorio di San Giorgio

🏠 Piazza del Santo 📞 049 822 56 52 🕐 Tue–Sun

Five frescoes, including the earliest documented paintings

by Titian, are to be found here, including two scenes from the life of St Anthony, painted in 1511. The works in the San Giorgio oratory are by Altichiero da Zevio and Jacopo Avenzo, painted in 1378–84.

Palazzo del Bo

🏠 Via VIII Febbraio 2
🕐 For guided tours only (Mon–Sat) 🌐 unipd.it

The historic main university building originally housed the medical faculty, renowned throughout Europe. Guided tours include Galileo's pulpit and the oldest surviving medical lecture theatre in the world, built in 1594.

Giotto's frescoes
covering the walls of
the Scrovegni Chapel ↑

⑨ 🖽

CAPPELLA DEGLI SCROVEGNI

🅐 D2 🏛 Piazza Eremitani 🚌 Garibaldi-Giotto 🕐 9am–7pm daily; advance booking compulsory 📅 1 Jan, 25 & 26 Dec 🌐 cappelladegliscrovegni.it

Enrico Scrovegni built this chapel in 1303, hoping thereby to spare his dead father, a usurer, from the eternal damnation in hell described by the poet Dante in his *Inferno*. The interior of the chapel is covered with beautiful frescoes of scenes from the life of Christ, painted by Giotto between 1303 and 1305. As works of great narrative force, they exerted a powerful influence on the development of European art.

Giotto's Frescoes

The Florentine artist Giotto (1266–1337) is regarded as the father of the Renaissance, the great revival in the Classical traditions of Western art. His frescoes in this chapel – with their sense of pictorial space, naturalism and narrative drama – mark a decisive break with the Byzantine tradition of the preceding 1,000 years. In such scenes as *Lament over the Dead Christ* figures are naturalistic and three-dimensional, not stylized, and emotions are clearly expressed. Although Giotto was considered a great artist in his lifetime, few of the works attributed to him are fully documented. The frescoes in the Scrovegni Chapel are rare exceptions where his authorship is in no doubt.

↑ Exterior of the Cappella degli Scrovegni

← Giotto's *Mary is Presented at the Temple*

VISITING THE CHAPEL

It is compulsory to book your visit on the website in advance as there are strict limits on the number of visitors allowed in to the Scrovegni Chapel at any one time. Before entering, visitors must spend 15 minutes in a decontamination chamber, where an explanatory film on the chapel and its famous frescoes is provided. The visit itself is restricted to 15 minutes.

↑ Figures expressing grief in Giotto's *Lament over the Dead Christ*

3

VICENZA

 Piazza Stazione Piazza Matteotti 12; www.vicenzae.org

Vicenza is known as the adoptive city of Andrea Palladio (1508–80), who started out as a stonemason and became one of the most influential architects of all time. One of the wealthiest cities in the Veneto, Vicenza is celebrated the world over for its splendid and varied architecture, which shows the extraordinary evolution of Palladio's distinctive style. It also offers a dazzling array of elegant shops and cafés to visit.

① Piazza dei Signori

This square at the heart of Vicenza is dominated by the **Palazzo della Ragione**, its balustrade bristling with statues of Greek and Roman gods. Often referred to as the Basilica, the building is now an exhibition space. Beside it stands the 12th-century Torre di Piazza. The Loggia del Capitaniato, to the northwest, was built by Palladio in 1571.

Palazzo della Ragione
 Piazza dei Signori
044 42 22 28 50 For exhibitions, concerts and guided tours only Mon

② Teatro Olimpico

Piazza Matteotti 11
10am–6pm Tue–Sun (winter: 9am–5pm)
For performances
teatrolimpicovicenza.it

Palladio began work on the Teatro Olimpico, Europe's oldest surviving indoor theatre In 1579, but died the following year. His pupil Vicenzo Scamozzi took over the project, designing the scenery for the first production in 1585. Using wood and plaster painted to look like marble, he created the illusion of streets receding to a horizon through *trompe l'oeil* effects.

③ Museo Civico

Piazza Matteotti 37
Jul–Aug: 10am–6pm Tue–Sun; Sep–Jun: 9am–5pm Tue–Sun
museicivicivicenza.it

This museum is housed in Palazzo Chiericati, which was built by Palladio. Among the

→

The intricate stage design at the Teatro Olimpico

←

Palazzo della Ragione and the Torre di Piazza in Piazza dei Signori

Gothic altarpieces from Vicenza churches on display here is Hans Memling's *Crucifixion* (1468–70).

---

 ④ 🖼

Santa Corona

📍 Contrà Santa Corona ☎ 0444 22 28 11 🕐 Summer: 10am-6pm Tue-Sun (winter: 9am-7pm) 🚫 1 Jan, 25 Dec

This Gothic church was built in 1261 to house a thorn donated by Louis IX of France, and said to be from Christ's Crown of Thorns. Notable paintings include Giovanni Bellini's *Baptism of Christ* (c 1500) and the *Adoration of the Magi* (1573) by Paolo Veronese.

---

⑤

Monte Berico

📍 Viale X Giugno 87 🕐 Daily (only pm Sun) 🌐 monteberico.it

Monte Berico is the cypress-clad hill to which wealthy residents once escaped in the heat of summer to enjoy the cooler air and pastoral charms

of their country estates. The domed basilica honours the Virgin, who is said to have appeared here to announce that Vicenza would be spared from the 1426–8 plague.

---

 ⑥

San Lorenzo

📍 Piazza San Lorenzo 🕐 7am-7pm daily

The portal of this church is a fine example of Gothic stone carving, decorated with the figures of the Virgin and Child, and St Francis and St Clare.

---

 ⑦ 🖼

Villa Valmarana ai Nani

📍 Via dei Nani 8 🕐 10am-4pm (Mar-Oct: to 6pm) 🌐 villavalmarana.com

The wall alongside the Villa Valmarana, is topped by figures of dwarfs (*nani*), which give the building its name. The villa was built in 1688 by local architect Antonio Muttoni.

Inside, the walls are covered with frescoes by Tiepolo, in which the gods float on clouds, watching scenes from the epics of Homer and Virgil. In the separate Foresteria (guesthouse) are 18th-century frescoes painted by Tiepolo's son, Giandomenico.

⑧ 🖼 🏛

La Rotonda

📍 Via Rotonda 45 🕐 By appt only Tue-Thu, 10am-noon & 3-6pm Fri-Sun 🌐 villalarotonda.it

With its perfectly regular, symmetrical forms, this villa, is the epitome of Palladio's architecture. Also known as the Villa Capra Valmarana, it was built in 1550–52. The design, consisting of a dome rising above a cube, received immediate acclaim for the way it blends perfectly with its surroundings.

The villa has inspired many copies in cities around the world, including London, St Petersburg and Delhi.

PALLADIO

Andrea Palladio was perhaps the most sought-after architect of the 16th century. Inspired by the treatises of ancient authors such as Vitruvius and Virgil, Palladio designed elegant palaces and villas for his clients that harked back to the Classical Golden Age. His own architectural treatise *The Four Books of Architecture* gained him widespread international recognition.

EXPERIENCE MORE

④ Euganean Hills

C2 ⬛⬛ To Terme Euganee, Montegrotto Terme 🛈 Viale Stazione 60, Montegrotto Terme; www.turismopadova.it

The conical Euganean Hills, remnants of long-extinct volcanoes, rise abruptly out of the surrounding plain. Hot-water springs bubble up at Abano Terme and Montegrotto Terme, where scores of establishments offer thermal treatments.

The **Abbazia di Praglia**, 6 km (4 miles) west of Abano Terme, is a Benedictine monastery where the monks grow herbs and restore manuscripts. They also lead guided tours of parts of the abbey and the church (1490–1548), noted for its beautiful cloisters. There are carved stalls in both the choir and the refectory, and artworks by Zelotti, a 16th-century painter from Verona.

The charming town of Arquà Petrarca, on the southern edge of the Euganean Hills, is named after Francesco Petrarca (1304–74). This medieval poet, known in English as Petrarch, spent the final years of his life here. His house, the **Casa di Petrarca**, is frescoed with scenes from his lyrical poems. He lies buried in a simple sarcophagus in front of the church.

An 18th-century villa to the north of Arquà, **Villa Barbarigo** has fine Baroque gardens. Planned by Antonio Barbarigo in 1669, they are a grandiose mix of statuary, fountains, a maze, formal parterres, lakes and avenues of cypress trees.

Abbazia di Praglia
Ⓥ 🚹 Via Abbazia di Praglia 16, Bresseo di Teolo ⏲ Tue-Sun (pm only) 🚫 Religious holidays 🌐 praglia.it

Did You Know?
Petrarch's sonnets are often addressed to Laura, whose identity remains a mystery.

Casa di Petrarca
Ⓥ🚹 🚹 Via Valleselle 4, Arquà Petrarca 📞 0429 71 82 94 ⏲ Mar-Oct: 9am-12:30pm & 3-6:30pm Tue-Sun; Nov-Feb: 9am-12:30pm & 2:30-5pm Tue-Sun 🚫 1 & 8 Jan, 8, 25 & 26 Dec

Villa Barbarigo
🚹🚹🚹 🚹 Via Diana 2, Valsanzibio ⏲ Feb-Dec: daily 🌐 valsanzibiogiardino.it

⑤
Brenta Canal

D2 🚹 Padua & Venice ⬛ Venezia Santa Lucia, Padua 🚌 To Mira, Dolo & Strà

Over time, in order to prevent the Venetian lagoon silting up, the rivers flowing into it were diverted. The River Brenta was canalized in two sections: the older branch, between Padua and Fusina (just west of Venice), dates back to the 1500s and flows for 36 km (22 miles). Its potential as a transport route was quickly realized and villas were built along its length. Many of these buildings can still be admired today – the S11 road runs alongside most of the canal's length – and several of them are open to the public.

The 18th-century **Villa Pisani** at Strà has a frescoed ceiling by Tiepolo. The **Barchessa Valmarana** at Mira boasts 18th-century decorations. In Malcontenta is **Villa Foscari**, or Villa Malcontenta, one of Palladio's loveliest villas. It was built in 1560 and the interior features frescoes by Zelotti.

STAY

Maison Matilda
This hotel in a 19th-century palazzo in Treviso has six individually designed rooms. The "Charming" room has parquet floors and a four-poster bed. An all-day breakfast is served in a peaceful courtyard.

🚹 Via Jacopo Riccati, Treviso 🌐 maison matilda.com
€€€

→ Charming wooden bridge across the River Sile in Treviso

Villa Pisani

⊛ ⊛ ⊛ ◖ Via Pisani, Strà ⊙ 2:30am–8pm Tue & Thu, 8:30am–2pm Wed & Fri, 8:45am–2pm & 2:30–8pm Sat & Sun 🚫 1 Jan, 25 Dec 🌐 villa pisani.beniculturali.it

Barchessa Valmarana

⊛ ◖ Via Valmarana 11, Mira ⊙ 10am–4:30pm Tue–Sun (Mar–Oct: to 6pm) 🌐 villa valmarana.net

Villa Foscari

⊛ ◖ Via dei Turisti 9, Malcontenta ⊙ Tue & Wed, Fri–Sun am 🚫 Nov–Mar 🌐 lamalcontenta.com

---

Treviso

◖ D2 🚌 🚆 ℹ Via Fiumicelli 30, Piazza Borsa; www. visittreviso.it

A good place to start a tour of the fortified city of Treviso is Calmaggiore. The street links the 13th-century Palazzo dei Trecento town hall with the **Duomo**, which was founded in the 1100s but rebuilt several times. Inside the Duomo,

Titian's *Annunciation* (1570) vies for attention with the *Adoration of the Magi* fresco (1520) by Il Pordenone. More paintings by Titian and other Renaissance artists are in the **Museo Civico**.

Open mornings from Tuesday to Saturday, the city's bustling fish market is held on a picturesque island in the middle of Treviso's River Sile.

The church of **San Nicolò**, by the 16th-century city wall, contains interesting frescoes, including the first ever depiction of spectacles in art.

Duomo

◖ Piazza Duomo ⊙ Daily 🌐 parrocchietreviso.it

Museo Civico

⊛ ◖ Chiesa Santa Caterina, Piazzetta Mario Botter 1 ⊙ 10am–6pm Tue–Sun 🌐 museicivici treviso.it

San Nicolò

◖ Via San Nicolò 📞 0422 54 86 26 ⊙ Daily 🚫 Sun am

→

A boat moored by a small pier on a canal in Treviso

DRINK

Bar Beltrame

Piazza bars aren't to everyone's taste, but Bar Beltrame is so charming that it's impossible not to stop by. Wicker seats are crowded under cool stone arches, where stylish Treviso locals gather in the evening for a Campari spritz or glass of prosecco. Mini-sandwiches and bowls of crisps are complimentary.

◖ Piazza dei Signori, Treviso 📞 0422 54 07 89 🚫 Thu

7

Bassano del Grappa

🗺 D1 🚉 Vicenza 🚆🚌
ℹ Piazza Garibaldi 34; www.
comune.bassano.vi.it

This peaceful town lies at
the foot of Monte Grappa.
The River Brenta is straddled
by the graceful Ponte degli
Alpini, designed in 1569 by
Palladio. It is built of timber to
allow it to flex when hit by the
spring meltwaters. Bassano
is well known for its majolica
products (decorated and
glazed earthenware), some
of which are on display in
the **Palazzo Sturm**. The
town is also synonymous
with the popular Italian clear
spirit known as *grappa*. It is
produced from the lees
(*graspa*) left over from wine
production. Information
about the process, and also
about the impact of World
War I in the area, is given in
the **Museo degli Alpini**.

Palazzo Sturm

🕑🧵 🚪 Via Schiavonetti
🕐 Daily 🌐 museibassano.it

Museo degli Alpini

🕑🧵 🚪 Via Angarano 2
🕐 Tue–Sun 🌐 anamonte
grappa.it/index.php/
home/museo

8

Asolo

🗺 D1 🚉 Treviso 🚌
ℹ Piazza Garibaldi 73;
Mon–Wed; www.asolo.it

This tiny walled town was
once ruled by Queen Caterina
Cornaro (1454–1510), the
Venetian wife of the King of
Cyprus, who poisoned her
husband so that Venice would
gain Cyprus. Cardinal Pietro
Bembo, a poet, coined the
verb *asolare* to describe the
bittersweet life of enforced
idleness she endured in exile
here. Among others who fell
in love with the place was
poet Robert Browning, who
named a volume of poems
Asolanda (1889) after Asolo.

At Maser, 10 km (6 miles)
east of the town, stands the
magnificent **Villa Barbaro**. It
was designed by Palladio in
about 1555, in conjunction
with the artist Veronese, and
blends symmetry and light,
airy rooms with sumptuous
trompe l'oeil frescoes.

Villa Barbaro

 🚪 Maser 🕐 Apr–Oct:
10am–6pm Tue–Sat, 11am–
5pm Sun; Nov–Mar: 11am–
5pm Sat, Sun & pub hols
🗓 1 & 6 Jan, Easter Sun,
24–31 Dec 🌐 villadimaser.it

9

Castelfranco Veneto

🗺 D2 🚉 Treviso 🚆🚌
ℹ Via F M Preti 66; 0423
73 56 24; Wed–Sat am

The historic core of this town
lies within well-preserved
walls. The **Casa di Giorgione**,
said to be the birthplace of
the painter Giorgione (1478–
1511), houses a museum
devoted to his life. Giorgione
innovatively used landscape
to create mood, as can be
seen in his most famous work,
the broodingly mysterious
and evocative *Tempest (p90)*.

About 8 km (5 miles)
northeast of the town, at
Fanzolo, lies the pretty
Villa Emo (c 1555). Designed
by Palladio, it is a typical

←

Bassano del Grappa's Ponte
degli Alpini, designed by
Andrea Palladio

↑ Cypress-clad hills around the walled town of Asolo

example of his work: a cube flanked by two symmetrical wings. Inside there are lavish frescoes by Zelotti.

Casa di Giorgione

⊛ 📍 Piazza San Liberale
🕐 Tue–Sun am (& pm Fri–Sun)
🔗 museocasagiorgione.it

Villa Emo

⊛ 📷 📍 Via Stazione 5,
Fanzolo 🕐 Daily 🚫 1 Jan,
25 & 31 Dec 🔗 villaemo.org

Conegliano

📍 D1 🏛 Treviso FS 🚌
ℹ️ Via XX Settembre 61;
0438 212 30

Conegliano lies among prosecco-producing vineyards, and winemakers from all over Italy learn their craft at Conegliano's renowned wine school. Via XX Settembre, the arcaded main street, is lined with fine 15th- to 18th century palazzi, many in the Venetian Gothic style or decorated with fading frescoes. The Duomo contains the town's one great work of art, an altarpiece painted by local artist Cima da Conegliano (1460–1518) depicting the *Virgin and Child with Saints* (1493).

Reproductions of Cima's most famous works are on show in the **Casa di Cima**, the artist's birthplace. The detailed landscapes in the background of his paintings were based on the hills around the town; the same views can still be seen from the gardens surrounding the ruined battlements and towers of the 10th-century Castelvecchio (old castle).

Casa di Cima

⊛ 📍 Via Cima 24 📞 0438
224 94 🕐 Sat & Sun, pm
only and during temporary
exhibitions

THE DOLOMITE ROAD

The Strada delle Dolomiti, or Dolomite Road, is a feat of highway construction. It enters the Veneto region via the Passo Pordoi, which at 2,239 m (7,346 ft), is the most scenic of all the Dolomite passes. From here the route follows the winding S48 for another 35 km (22 miles) east to the resort of Cortina d'Ampezzo.

There are plenty of stopping places along the route where it is possible to pause and enjoy the spectacular views. In many of the ski resorts, cable cars will carry visitors up to Alpine refuges (some with cafés attached) that are open from mid-June to mid-September. These refuges mark the start of a series of signposted walks.

⓫ Cortina d'Ampezzo

🅐D1 🅐Belluno 🚌
ℹ️ Corso Italia 81;
www.infodolomiti.it

Italy's top ski resort is well supplied with restaurants and bars. Cortina is set amid the dramatic scenery of the Dolomites, which explains part of its attraction: all around, crags and spires thrust their distinctive weather-beaten shapes above the trees.

Cortina has above average sports facilities, thanks to hosting the 1956 Winter Olympics. In addition to downhill and cross-country skiing, there is also a ski jump and a bobsleigh run, as well as an Olympic ice stadium, swimming pools, tennis courts and riding facilities.

During the summer months, Cortina becomes an excellent base for walkers. Useful information on trails and guided walks is available from the tourist office or, during the summer, from the tour guides' office opposite.

STAY

Here are some of the best mid-range hotels in Cortina d'Ampezzo.

Villa Blu Cortina
Mountain chic at its best, with caramel Alpine-style furniture, plush carpets and great mountain views.

🅐Località Verocai 73
🆆hotelvillablu
cortina.it

€€€

Hotel Ambra Cortina
This hotel has 24 quaint Alpine rooms with wooden hues and floral drapes, some with whirlpools, spas and four-poster beds.

🅐Via XXIX Maggio 28
🆆hotelambracortina.it

€€€

Panda
A charming family-run hotel, Panda has simple but comfortable rooms. Those on the Balcony Floor have private terraces, and there's a self-contained apartment on the top floor.

🅐Via Roma 64
🆆cortinahotelpanda.it

€€€

⓬ Belluno

🅐D1 🚇🚌 ℹ️Piazza Duomo 2; www.info dolomiti.it

Picturesque Belluno serves as a bridge between the two different parts of the Veneto, with the flat plains to the south and the Dolomite peaks to the north. Both are encapsulated in the views to be seen from the 12th-century Porta Rugo at the southern end of Via Mezzaterra, the main street of the old town. More spectacular still are the views from the bell tower of the 16th-century Duomo (subsequently rebuilt). The nearby Baptistry houses a font cover with the figure of John the Baptist carved by Andrea Brustolon (1662–1732). Brustolon's works also grace the churches of San Pietro (on Via San Pietro) and Santo Stefano (Piazza Santo Stefano). North of Piazza del Duomo stands the elegant Palazzo dei Rettori (1491) – once home to the town's Venetian rulers – and the 12th-century Torre Civica, all that now survives of a medieval castle.

The **Museo Civico** contains paintings by Bartolomeo Montagna (1450–1523) and Sebastiano Ricci (1659–1734), and a notable archaeological section. North of the museum is Belluno's finest square, the Piazza del Mercato, with its arcaded Renaissance palaces and its fountain of 1410.

South of Belluno are the picturesque ski resorts of the Alpe del Nevegal; in the summer a chairlift operates from Faverghera up to a height of 1,600 m (5,250 ft), offering extensive views.

Museo Civico
⊘⊘⊘ 🅐Via Roma 28
🕘9am–noon Tue–Sun
(also 3–6pm Tue & Fri)
🆆mubel.comune.belluno.it

→
Snowy slopes around the fashionable resort of Cortina d'Ampezzo

WHERE TO GO IN CORTINA

Cortina is one of Italy's most fashionable resorts. Away from the slopes, days here are spent shopping on the town's main drag, Corso Italia, followed by cocktails at Bar Arnika *(Corso Italia 983)* or a local prosecco at wine bar Enoteca *(Via del Mercato 5)*. Anyone wanting something a bit more substantial will love wine-and-cured-meats bar Dok Dall'Ava LP 26 *(Largo delle Poste 26)*. The best city-centre après-ski happens at Birreria Hacker Pschorr *(Via Stazione 7)*, followed by dancing at VIP club *(Corso Italia 207)*.

Dramatic backdrop of the Dolomites in the charming ski resort of Cortina d'Ampezzo

⓭
Udine

⒜D1 ⎘ ℹ️ Piazza I Maggio 7; www.turismo fvg.it

Udine is a city of varied and surprising architecture. In the central Piazza della Libertà, the Loggia del Lionello (1448–56), built of pink stone in Venetian Gothic style, stands beside the Art Deco Caffè Contarena. Opposite, the Renaissance symmetry of the Porticato di San Giovanni is interrupted by the Torre dell'Orologio (Clock Tower, 1527), crowned by two bronze Moors that strike every hour. Note also the fountain of 1542, the two 18th-century statues, and the column supporting the Lion of St Mark.

Beyond the Arco Bollani, a gateway designed by Palladio in 1556, steps lead up to a 26-m (85-ft) hill that offers sweeping views over the city. On the hill is the 16th-century castle, now the **Musei Civici e Galleria di Storia e Arte Antica**, which houses fine art and archaeology collections.

Southeast of Piazza Matteotti, at the end of Via Savorgnana (where a small market is held), stands the Oratorio della Purità, and the Duomo with its octagonal bell tower. Both contain important paintings and frescoes by Giambattista Tiepolo (1696–1770). More of Tiepolo's work can be seen in the **Museo Diocesano e Galleria Tiepolo**, formerly the Palazzo Arcivescovile, which the artist decorated with frescoes.

Outside Codroipo, 24 km (15 miles) west, rises the imposing **Villa Manin**. A road passes through its grounds, so it can be seen even when the house – once the retreat of Ludovico Manin, the last doge of Venice (1725–1802) – and its gardens are closed.

Musei Civici e Galleria di Storia e Arte Antica

⊛ ⊛ ⒜ Piazzale del Castello ⒞ 0432 27 25 91 ⒪ Tue–Sun ⒞ 1 Jan, Easter, 1 May, 25 Dec

Museo Diocesano e Galleria Tiepolo

 ⒜ Piazza Patriarcato 1 ⒞ 0432 22 50 03 ⒪ Wed–Mon ⒞ 1 Jan, Easter, 25 Dec

Villa Manin

⊛ ⒜ Piazza Manin 10, Passariano ⒞ 0432 82 12 11 ⒪ Tue–Sun for exhibitions only ⒞ 1 Jan, 25 Dec

EAT

Rosenbar
This family-run place in Gorizia offers a great seasonal tasting menu. In summer you can eat on a terrace.

⒜ Via Duca d'Aosta 96, Gorizia ⓦ rosenbar.it

€€€

Al Piave
A homely trattoria in a town near Gorizia serving local dishes such as stewed beef.

⒜ Via Cormons 6, Mariano del Friuli ⓦ trattoriaalpiave.it

€€€

Ca' di Pieri
A popular eatery in Gorizia specializing in simple dishes such as gnocchi and minestrone.

⒜ Via Piero Antonio Codelli 5, Gorizia ⒞ 0481 53 33 08

€€€

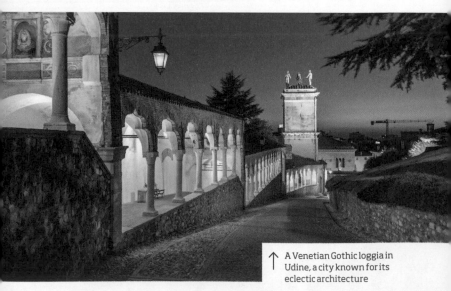

↑ A Venetian Gothic loggia in Udine, a city known for its eclectic architecture

SYMBOLISM IN EARLY CHRISTIAN ART

Christians were persecuted until AD 313, when their religion was granted official status by Constantine the Great. Prior to this they had developed a language of symbols - like the fish, or ICHTHUS (an acronym for Iesous CHristos THeou Uios Soter - Jesus Christ, Son of God, Saviour, in ancient Greek) to express their beliefs. Many of these symbols can be seen in the mosaics and marble tomb chests of Aquileia.

Aquileia

⚑ D2 🚌 🛈 Via Julia Augusta 11; www.turismo fvg.it

Aquileia, now little more than a village but encircled by the ruins of palatial villas, baths, temples and market buildings, provides a poignant reminder of the lost splendour of the Roman Empire.

It was here that Emperor Augustus received Herod the Great, King of Judea, in 10 BC, and it was here, too, in AD 381, that the early Christian church held a major council to settle doctrinal issues. In the 5th century, however, the town was abandoned following several sackings.

On a group of low islands in the Adriatic lagoon, attached to the mainland by a narrow causeway, Grado grew into a port for Aquileia in the 2nd century and was used as a haven during the barbarian invasions. Today, it is a popular seaside resort. At the centre of the old town is the Duomo, which contains 6th-century frescoes in the apse. Nearby, in the church of Santa Maria delle Grazie, there are more 6th-century mosaics.

Aquileia's **Basilica** was founded in about AD 313. Much of the original structure still survives, including the floor mosaics of the nave and Cripta degli Scavi below. The designs mix biblical stories, such as the tale of Jonah and the sea monster, and scenes from everyday life.

Mosaics and stone carvings from the 1st to 3rd centuries fill the **Museo Archeologico Nazionale**, along with glass, amber and a collection of flies, beautifully worked in gold, that formed the adornment of a Roman matron's veil.

The **Museo Paleocristiano**, not far from the ancient harbour, focuses on the development of art during the early Christian era.

Basilica

⊛ ⚑ Piazza Capitolo 1
📞 0431 91 067 🕐 Daily
🚫 During Mass

Museo Archeologico Nazionale

⊛ ⚑ Via Roma 1
🕐 10am-7pm Tue-Sun
🌐 museoarcheologico aquileia.beniculturali.it

Museo Paleocristiano

⚑ Piazza Pirano 1 📞 0431 91 76 19 🕐 8:30am-1:30pm Thu-Sat

Gorizia

⚑ E1 🚆🚌 🛈 Corso Italia 9; www.turismofvg.it

Gorizia was at the centre of fierce fighting during both world wars and was split in two by the 1947 Treaty of Paris, leaving part in Italy, part in Yugoslavia (now Slovenia).

The Museo Provinciale della Grande Guerra (Museum of the Great War), in the basement of the **Museo Provinciale di Storia e Arte**, has videos, photographs, and mock-ups of trenches, latrines and gun emplacements showing the waste, squalor and heroism of war.

On a mound nearby rises the castle, encircled by 16th-century fortifications. From here there are views over the town.

Southwest of Gorizia, scenic country roads pass through the foothills of the Carso (p126), a limestone plateau gouged with tunnels, caves and underground rivers.

Museo Provinciale di Storia e Arte

⊛ ⚑ Borgo Castello 13
📞 0481 53 39 26 🕐 9am-7pm Tue-Sun 🚫 25 Dec

Cividale del Friuli

🅰 D1 🚆 **ℹ Piazza Paolo Diacono 10; www.cividale.net**

A gate in the medieval walls of Cividale leads to the dramatic ravine of the River Natisone, which is spanned by the Ponte del Diavolo (Devil's Bridge). Above the river's north bank is the **Tempietto Longobardo** (Lombardic Chapel), an 8th-century church decorated with reliefs of saints, modelled in stucco. The town's history is traced in the excellent **Museo Archeologico Nazionale**, which contains the excavated remains of buildings from a Roman town, and a collection of Lombardic items including jewellery, ivory and weapons.

Next door is the Duomo, rebuilt in 1453 after a fire, with its beautiful silver altarpiece (13th century). The **Museo Cristiano**, off the south aisle, contains sculptures from the original church, like the altar donated by Ratchis, the Lombardic Duke of Friuli and later King of Italy (737–44), which is finely carved with scenes from the Life of Christ.

Tempietto Longobardo
🌐 🅰 Via Monastero Maggiore 34 📞 0432 70 08 67 🕐 Daily

↑ Cividale del Friuli, surrounded by forested mountains

Museo Archeologico Nazionale
🌐 🅰 Palazzo dei Provveditori Veneti, Piazza del Duomo 13 📞 0432 70 07 00 🕐 Daily (am only Mon) 🚫 1 Jan, 1 May, 25 Dec

Museo Cristiano
🌐 🅰 Via Condotti 1 🕐 Wed-Sun 🚫 1 Jan, 25 Dec 🌐 museocristiano.it

---

Grado

🅰 D2 🅰 Gorizia 🚌 ℹ Viale Dante Alighieri 72; www.turismofvg.it

An important port during the Roman Empire, this lagoon city became part of Austria in 1815, returning to Italy only after World War II. Today Grado is a pleasant resort, with a lively city centre. The **Basilica of Sant'Eufemia** features beautifully preserved 6th-century mosaics.

Grado is also a popular spa destination, and it offers outdoor activities such as tennis, sailing and golf.

Basilica of Sant'Eufemia
🅰 Campo Patriarca Elia 🕐 8am-7pm daily (winter: to 6pm)

Carso

🅰 E2

A limestone plateau cutting a swathe through northeastern Italy, the Carso region is utterly unique. Its features include a cliffside series of villages with some of the oldest and largest caves in the world, as well as forests, gorges, lakes, rivers and views to the Adriatic – all of them drawing keen hikers and cyclists to the region.

Heading north from Italy, country roads stretch into the Slovenian hills, past churches, wineries and farmhouses.

Trieste

🅰E2 ✈FS🚌
ℹ **Piazza Unità d'Italia 4b;
www.turismofvg.it**

Trieste is an atmospheric city with a long, bustling harbour lined with handsome buildings and lapped by the waves of the Adriatic Sea. From Villa Opicina, just to the north, there are sweeping views over the city, its bay and the coast of Slovenia.

The small **Acquario Marino** contains examples of the marine life in the Adriatic. On the upper floor is a vivarium filled with local and exotic reptiles and amphibians.

The **Castello di San Giusto**, built by Trieste's Venetian governors from 1368, is set on a terrace that offers views over the Gulf of Trieste. The castle houses two museums containing Roman mosaics and a collection of weapons and armour. Beside the castle lie the substantial ruins of the Roman **Basilica Paleocristiana** (or law court) built around AD 100. Note the stone magistrates' bench and throne.

Trieste's **Duomo** is built on the site of a 5th-century Christian basilica and two 9th-century churches. The churches were merged in the 14th century, leaving the cathedral with two apses and an asymmetrical façade. Highlights include the Gothic rose window, the bell tower and the two 13th-century Venetian-style apse mosaics.

The archaeological collection in the **Museo di Storia ed Arte e Orto Lapidario** documents Trieste's trade links with ancient Greece.

Beyond the city lies the **Grotta del Gigante**, a huge cavern filled with a series of tall stalagmites that resemble organ pipes in their formation.

At Grignano, 8 km (5 miles) northwest of the city, the **Castello di Miramare** is set in lush gardens. It was built as a summer retreat by the Archduke Maximilian in 1856–60, a few years before he was assassinated in Mexico.

Acquario Marino
⊘ 🏠 Molo Pescheria 2, Riva Nazario Sauro 1 📞 040 30 62 01 🕓 10am-7pm Thu-Tue

→
The 19th-century Castello di Miramare, at Grignano, near Trieste

Castello di San Giusto
⊘ 🏠 Piazza Cattedrale 3 📞 040 30 93 62 🕓 10am-7pm daily (Oct-Mar: Tue-Sun)

Basilica Paleocristiana
🏠 Via Madonna del Mare 11 📞 040 426 14 11 🕓 10am-noon Sun

Duomo
🏠 Piazza Cattedrale 2 📞 040 322 45 75 🕓 Daily

Museo di Storia ed Arte e Orto Lapidario
⊘ 🏠 Via della Cattedrale 1 📞 040 31 05 00 🕓 Tue-Sun

Grotta del Gigante
⊘⊘ 🏠 Borgo Grotta Gigante 42a 📞 040 327 312 🕓 10am-2:30pm Tue-Sun (Jul & Aug: 10am-4pm daily)

Castello di Miramare
⊘ 🏠 Viale Miramare, Grignano 📞 040 22 41 43 🕓 9am-7pm daily 🔒 1 Jan, 25 Dec

Elegant buildings lining the lively harbour of Trieste ↑

TRENTINO-ALTO ADIGE

The Italian-speaking Trentino – named after Trento, the regional capital – and the German-speaking Alto Adige or Südtirol (South Tyrol, the region bordering the upper reaches of the River Adige) differ dramatically in culture. However, they do share one feature in common: the majestic Dolomites, covered in snow for three months of every year and carpeted with exquisite Alpine plants for another three.

The region's mountains have been cut by glaciers into a series of deep, broad valleys. Travellers have passed up and down these valleys for generations – as confirmed by the extraordinary discovery of a 5,000-year-old man's body in 1991, found emerging from the surface of a melting glacier in Alto Adige. The frozen corpse wore leather boots, stuffed with hay for warmth, and was armed with an ice pick.

The paths once trodden by Neolithic man became major road networks under the Romans, when many of the region's cities were founded. By the Middle Ages, Alto Adige had established its very own distinctive culture under the Counts of Tyrol, whose land (later appropriated by the Habsburgs) straddled both sides of today's Italy-Austria border. The Tyrolean nobility built the castles that still line the valleys and the mountain passes, in order to protect travellers from brigands.

Another ancient legacy is the tradition of hospitality, found in the numerous guesthouses along the valleys. Many of these are built in the distinctive Tyrolean style, with beautiful timber balconies for making the most of the winter sun, and overhanging roof eaves to keep snow at a distance. Offering marvellous views, they make the ideal base from which to enjoy the region's mountain footpaths and ski slopes.

TRENTINO-ALTO ADIGE

Experience

1. Madonna di Campiglio
2. Malles Venosta
3. Merano
4. Castello di Avio
5. Rovereto
6. Trento
7. Cavalese
8. Bolzano
9. Canazei
10. Ortisei
11. San Martino di Castrozza
12. Brunico
13. Bressanone
14. Vipiteno

Skiing

From December through April, skiing in the Dolomites means gorgeous powdery slopes and some of the world's chicest resorts. Stop in for après-ski food at quaint restaurants offering hearty plates of dumplings, before retiring to one of the many cosy mountain huts dotted across the region.

→

Skiier on the slopes at the Madonna di Campiglio resort

THE DOLOMITES FOR
THRILLSEEKERS

A striking mountain range in northeastern Italy, the Dolomites are home to bubbling springs, thick tangles of forest, cool lakes and swathes of lush green fields. It's the perfect place for some adrenaline-pumping outdoor activities.

Via Ferrata

These well-marked climbing and scrambling routes are suitable for both beginners and experienced climbers from April to September. Following the metal rungs, steel cables, and cliff-top bridges, you can take the same route the military did during World War II, including the Pordoi pass.

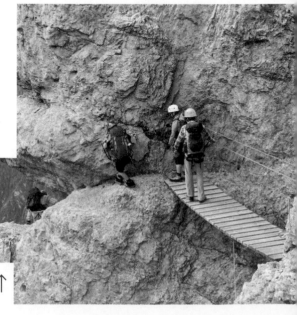

Scramblers on a small suspension bridge on the Via Ferrata ↑

Hot-Air Ballooning

One of the best ways to see the Dolomites is from a hot-air balloon. South Tyrol, in particular, is popular with balloon enthusiasts. The Dolomites Hot Air Balloon Festival runs every January in Dobbiaco, making it the best time to go.

→

Balloonists enjoying spectacular views of the Dolomites

Horseriding

Tackling the Dolomites' steep cliffs, high mountain plateaus and hair-raising ledges is a breeze when you're riding one of the region's local mountain horses. Riding holidays and organized treks are run throughout the year, taking advantage of the area's 300 annual days of sunshine. There's even the dedicated Eastern Trentino Riding Trail specifically for riding treks.

←

Horses roaming the land at the foot of the Dolomites

TOP 5 VIA FERRATA ROUTES

Ferrata Fausto Susatti
For beginners, this route goes through rocky terrain above Lake Garda.

Ferrata al Burrone Giovanelli
A family-friendly route that climbs ladders and metal brackets to a gorge.

Via delle Bocchette
This route crosses the peaks of the Dolomites along narrow ledges.

Ferrata delle Aquile
Expert hikers can walk along pillars overlooking the Adige Valley.

Ferrata di Punta Penia
This runs along the western ridge of Marmolada.

↑ Thrillseeker at the Adrenaline Centre Adventure Park

Tree Parks

Both the Adrenaline Centre Adventure Park in Ronco (*www.adrenalinecentre.it*) and the Adventure Park in Colfosco (*www.altabadia.org/it*) offer vertical challenges, fantastic outdoor adventures and tree-climbing activities for children and adults of all ages. There are also special play areas reserved for the tiniest tots.

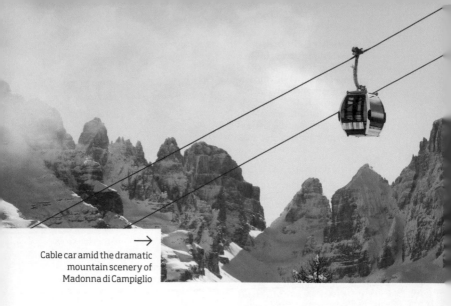

Cable car amid the dramatic mountain scenery of Madonna di Campiglio

EXPERIENCE

1

Madonna di Campiglio

 C1 ⬛ **i** Via Pradalago 4; www.campigliodolomiti.it

Madonna di Campiglio is the chief resort in the Val Meledrio. Nestling between the Brenta and Adamello groups of peaks, it makes the perfect base for walking or skiing amid the magnificent mountain terrain. Cableways radiate out from the town in every direction, giving easy access to the peaks.

The church at Pinzolo, 14 km (9 miles) south, has a well-preserved fresco depicting a *Dance of Death* (1539). The inevitable march of the figures, both rich and poor, is underlined by a text written in local dialect.

North of Pinzolo, the road west from Carisolo leads to the verdant and popular, yet unspoiled, Val Genova. About 4 km (2 miles) along the valley is the spectacular Cascate di Nardis, a waterfall that plunges down 90 m (300 ft). The two masses of rock at the bottom are said to be the forms of petrified demons.

2

Malles Venosta
Mals Im Vinschgau

 C1 🚆 **i** Via San Benedetto 1; www. vinschgau.net

Malles Venosta sits in high border country, close to Switzerland and Austria, and was a customs point during the Middle Ages. The town has several Gothic churches, whose spires and towers give an appealing skyline, mirroring the jagged peaks that rise all around. The oldest is the tiny church of San Benedetto, a 9th-century Carolingian building on Via San Benedetto, with frescoes of its patrons.

The medieval **Castel Coira** (Churburg) rises at Sluderno (Schluderns), 4 km (2 miles) southeast of Malles. It contains an excellent collection of weapons and armour.

CANEDERLI

Canederli are dumplings, traditionally made from stale bread, milk, eggs and flour. The name comes from the German word for dumplings, *knödel*, and they are served as a first course or in soups. *Canederli* can be flavoured with parsley, cheese, ham and spinach, and they are a common dish at most restaurants in Trentino-Alto Adige/Südtirol. They can also be purchased at local delis and supermarkets.

Clinging to the mountainside above the town of Burgusio (Burgeis), 5 km (3 miles) north of Malles, is the Benedictine **Abbazia di Monte Maria** (Marienberg), founded in the 12th century but enlarged in the 18th and 19th centuries. The church's crypt shelters an outstanding series of 12th-century frescoes.

The glorious medieval town of Glorenza lies just 2 km (1 mile) south of Malles.

Castel Coira
⊛⊛ 🅐 Churburg, Sluderno 📞 0473 61 52 41 ⏰ 20 Mar–Oct: Tue–Sun (& Mon if pub hol)

Abbazia di Monte Maria
⊛⊛⊛ 📞 0473 83 13 06 (abbey); 0473 84 39 80 (museum) ⏰ Mon–Sat (Nov–mid-Mar: groups by appt only) 🚫 Pub hols

---

Merano
Meran

🅐 C1 🚉🚌 🅸 Corso della Libertà 45; www.meran.eu

Merano is an attractive spa town popular with Austrians, Germans and Italians. On Corso della Libertà, a street of smart shops and hotels, stands the Kurhaus or Spa Hall built in 1914, now a concert venue. Furnished in period style, the 15th-century **Castello Principesco** was home to the Habsburg Archduke Sigismund.

Inviting gardens line the River Passirio, which winds its way through the town. The Passeggiata Lungo Passirio d'Inverno (Winter Walk) follows the north bank to the Roman bridge, Ponte Romano; the Passeggiata d'Estate (Summer Walk) on the south bank leads to the medieval Ponte Passirio.

The romantic 12th-century **Castel Tirolo** lies 4 km (2 miles) to the north of Merano. It hosts a fascinating museum of Tyrolean history.

↑ One of Merano's two beautiful promenades, skirting the River Passirio

The grounds of **Castel Trauttmansdorff** house a lovely botanical garden.

Castello Principesco
⊛⊛ 🅐 Via Galilei 📞 3290 18 63 90 ⏰ Tue–Sun & pub hols 🚫 7 Jan–Easter

Castel Tirolo
⊛⊛⊛⊛ 🅐 Via Castello 24, Tirolo ⏰ 10am–5pm Wed–Sun 🌐 schlosstirol.it

Castel Trauttmansdorff
⊛⊛⊛ 🅐 Via S Valentino 51a ⏰ 1 Apr–15 Nov: daily 🌐 trauttmansdorff.it

---

Castello di Avio

🅐 C1 🅐 Via Castello, Sabbionara d'Avio 📞 0464 68 44 53 🚌🚉 To Avio, then 3-km (2-mile) walk ⏰ Mar–Sep: 10am–6pm Wed–Sun (also Tue in Aug); Oct–Nov: 10am–5pm Wed–Sun; Mon & Tue if pub hol 🚫 3rd week of Nov–Feb

Castles line the Adige Valley to the Brenner Pass, but few are as accessible as the Castello di Avio. It was founded in the 11th century, extended in the 13th, and today offers far-reaching views. Among the many frescoes is a fantastic series depicting 13th-century battle scenes in the Casa delle Guardie (Sentry House).

WALK IN CEMBRA

A walk through the terraced slopes of the wine-producing town of Cembra, 20 km (12 miles) from Trento, takes you past pretty flower-filled villages and across scenic valleys. Some 6 km (4 miles) east of Cembra stand the Piramidi di Segonzano, a rare series of erosion pillars, some over 30 m (100 ft) high, each topped by a rock. Views encompass Cembra Valley and the Dolomites beyond.

5

Rovereto

🏛C1 🚆 ℹ️ **Corso Rosmini 21; www.visitrovereto.it**

Rovereto was at the centre of fierce fighting during World War I, after which the Venetian castle (built in 1416) that dominates the town was transformed into the **Museo Storico Italiano della Guerra**, a war museum. Near the museum entrance, stairs lead out on to the castle roof for a view of the imposing Ossario del Castel Dante.

Some distance away is the Campana dei Caduti (Bell of the Fallen), which was cast from melted-down cannons at the end of World War II; it is rung daily at sunset.

Below the war museum is the **Museo Civico**, with its collections on archaeology, art, natural history and folklore. The Mario Botta-designed **Museo di Arte**

> **The builders maintained architectural harmony by ignoring Gothic and Renaissance styles entirely.**

Contemporanea di Trento e Rovereto (MART) showcases 20th-century Italian art. A second site, in Via Portici, holds Italian Futurist art.

A little over 8 km (5 miles) north of Rovereto is **Castel Beseno**. This vast castle was built and rebuilt from the 12th to the 18th century to guard the junction of three valleys.

Just 5 km (3 miles) south of Rovereto, the main road passes through a valley littered with massive boulders: these are known as Lavini di Marco or Ruina Dantesca, because they are mentioned in Dante's *Inferno* (XII, 4–9). Fossilized dinosaur footprints have been discovered there.

Museo Storico Italiano della Guerra

🅿️ 🏛Via G Castelbarco 7 🕒Tue-Sun 🕒Pub hols 🌐museodellaguerra.it

Museo Civico

🅿️ 🏛Via Calcinari 18 🕒Tue-Sun 🕒1 Jan, 5 Aug, 1 Nov, 25 Dec 🌐fondazionemcr.it

MART

🅿️ 🏛Main museum: Corso Bettini 43; Casa d'Arte Futurista Depero: Via Portici 38 🕒Tue-Sun (Mon if pub hol) 🌐mart.trento.it

Castel Beseno

🅿️ 🏛Besenello 🕒Mar-Oct: Tue-Sun (Mon if pub hol); Nov-Feb: Sat & Sun 🌐buonconsiglio.it

6

Trento

🏛C1 🚆 ℹ️ **Piazza Dante 24; www.discovertrento.it**

Trento, the capital of the region to which it gave its name, has a fine cathedral, a castle and streets lined with Renaissance mansions. Trento is noted as the venue for the Council of Trent (1545–63), set up by the Catholic Church to consider reforms that might encourage breakaway groups like the German Protestants to return to the fold. The reforms were only partly successful.

The Duomo was begun in Romanesque style in the 1200s. It took three centuries to complete, in 1515, but the builders maintained architectural harmony by ignoring Gothic and Renaissance styles entirely. The result is a church of unusual integrity. Trento's Roman name, Tridentum, is

→

Hiking in the Val di Fiemme, near Cavalese

commemorated in the figure of Neptune, who stands at the top of the 18th-century fountain in Piazza Duomo. Immediately to the west of Trento a scenic round trip along a winding road leads up the north flank of Monte Bondone and back, via Vezzano, down the western slopes. The views along the route are magnificent, in particular from Vaneze and Vason. East of Trento, Pergine marks the start of the Val Sugana, a broad valley with lakes. In the hills north of Lake Levico lies the spa town of Levico Terme, distinguished by elegant Neo-Classical buildings set amid beautifully wooded parkland.

The **Museo Diocesano Tridentino** is housed in the Palazzo Pretorio, an imposing medieval building on Piazza Duomo. Its contents include early ivory reliquaries, Flemish tapestries and paintings depicting the Council of Trent.

Built in the 1200s and later enlarged with additional buildings, the vast **Castello del Buonconsiglio** is part of the defences of the town. The southern section of the castle consists of the magnificent Magno Palazzo (1530), built for the ruling prince-bishops of Trento, who were given extensive powers by the Holy Roman Emperor to foster loyalty to the pope. The lavish decoration (including frescoes of virile satyrs and nymphs by Gerolamo Romanino, 1531–2)

speaks of huge wealth and a luxurious lifestyle. The palazzo houses the Museo Provinciale, with paintings, ceramics and 15th-century wood carvings, and prehistoric, Etruscan and Roman items.

Museo Diocesano Tridentino
⊘ 🏛 Piazza Duomo 18
🕐 Wed-Mon 🚫 1 & 6 Jan, Easter, 26 Jun, 1 Nov, 25 Dec
🔵 museodiocesano tridentino.it

Castello del Buonconsiglio
⊘ 🏛 Via Bernardo Clesio 5
🕐 Tue-Sun (Jul & Aug: daily)
🚫 25 Dec 🔵 buon consiglio.it

---

❼
Cavalese
🅰 C1 🚌 🛈 Via Fratelli Bronzetti 60; www. visitfiemme.it

Cavalese is the chief town in the Val di Fiemme, a pretty region of flower-filled pastures, wooded valleys and Tyrolean architecture. At the centre of the town stands the **Palazzo della Magnifica Comunità**. Originally built in the 1200s, this was the seat of the medieval governing council which ruled the area as a semi-autonomous region. Today the panelled interiors contain medieval paintings by local artists and an archaeology collection.

Most visitors come for the excellent summer and winter resort facilities, and to climb, by cable car, to the 2,229-m (7,311-ft) top of Alpe Cermis.

At Predazzo, about 13 km (8 miles) east, the **Museo Geologico delle Dolomiti** explains the local geology.

Palazzo della Magnifica Comunità
⊘⊘ 🏛 Piazza Cesare Battisti 2 🕐 Jan-Mar: 2-6:30pm; Apr-Dec: 10am-2pm & 3-6:30pm Wed-Mon 🔵 palazzo magnifica.eu

Museo Geologico delle Dolomiti
⊘ 🏛 Piazza SS Filippo e Giacomo 1 🕐 10am-12:30pm & 4-7pm Tue-Sun (Oct-May: Tue-Sat) 🔵 muse.it

---

DRINK

Scrigno del Duomo
Every evening from 6pm this osteria serves one of the best aperitivi in Trento: plates of local cured meats and cheese, mini-sandwiches, quiches and dumplings, paired with excellent local red, white and rosé wines by the glass.

🅰 C1 🏛 Piazza Duomo 29, Trento 🔵 scrigno delduomo.com

Antica Birreria Pedavena
This enormous German-style Trento brewery serves jugs of their own beer, plus a decent selection of craft ales and beers.

🅰 C1 🏛 Piazza Fiera 13, Trento 🔵 birreria pedavena.com

Spectacular scenery in the Dolomites near Canazei

Duomo

 Piazza Walther **(** 0471 97 86 76 **(** 10am-noon & 2-5pm Mon-Sat

Museo Archeologico

⊘⊘⊙ **△** Via Museo 43 **○** Tue-Sun (Jul, Aug & Dec: daily) **W** iceman.it

---

9

Canazei

△ D1 **□** **i** Piazza Marconi 5; www.fassa.com

Canazei is a good base for exploring the Dolomites. In summer, chairlifts climb to viewpoints where the beauty of the encircling mountains can be appreciated to the full. The most popular panoramas are from Pecol and Col dei Rossi, reached by the Belvedere cableway from Via Pareda in Canazei: the cliffs of the Sella group are visible to the north, with Sasso Lungo to the west

BOLZANO DISHES

Canederli

In Bolzano these hearty bread dumplings are often mixed with cheese and speck, a type of smoked ham. **Find it at:** Restaurant Mauriz Keller *(Strada Rezia 32, Ortisei)*. The cheese and spinach version is fantastic.

Apple strudel

A real speciality of the region. Expect flaky pastry, sweet apples, pine nuts and dollops of whipped cream. **Find it at:** Restaurant Oberspeiser *(Klaus bei Terlan 15, Terlano)* or Café Lintner *(Via Leonardo da Vinci 8)*.

Goulash

This spicy, meaty Hungarian soup is exceptionally popular in Bolzano, no doubt thanks to its cool winter climes. The Italians serve it with lashings of runny polenta. **Find it at:** Wirtshaus Vögele *(Via Johann Wolfgang von Goethe 3, Bolzano)*.

8

Bolzano

Bozen

 △ C1 **FS** **□** **i** Via Alto Adige 60; www.bolzano-bozen.it

Bolzano, the capital of the Alto Adige, is the gateway between the Italian-speaking Trentino region and the German-speaking Alto Adige, or Südtirol, and has a marked Tyrolean atmosphere.

The old centre, Piazza Walther, is dominated by the imposing 15th-century Gothic **Duomo**, with its multicoloured mosaic-patterned roof and elaborate spire. The "wine door" inside the Duomo is carved with figures at work among vines and reflects the importance of wine to the local economy.

In the middle of Piazza Walther is a statue of Walther von der Vogelweide, the 13th-century troubadour – born, according to legend, in this area. North of the square, the streets are lined with houses adorned with intricate gables, balconies and oriel windows.

The modern **Museo Archeologico** houses impressive finds from the Stone Age, the Bronze Age, the Iron Age, Roman times and the time of Charlemagne. A key exhibit is Ötzi, the famous 5,000-year-old "Iceman".

and Marmolada, the highest of the Dolomites at 3,343 m (10,965 ft), to the south.

At Vigo di Fassa, 13 km (8 miles) southwest, the **Museo Ladino** focuses on the Ladin-speaking people of some of the valleys. Ladin – a Rhaeto-Romance language – is taught in local schools, and traditions thrive.

Museo Ladino

 🏛️Strada de Sèn Jan 5, Vigo di Fassa - Sèn Jan 🕐Times vary, check website 🗓️1 Jan, 16 Apr-9 Jun, mid Oct-Nov, 25 Dec 🌐istladin.net

---

10

Ortisei
Sankt Ulrich

🅰️C1 �æ 🈺Strada Rezia 1; www.valgardena.it

Ortisei is the prosperous main resort for the Val Gardena, and a major centre for wood carving; examples of local craftsmanship may be seen in local shops and in the **Museo della Val Gardena** (which also focuses on local archaeology).

To the south is the Alpe di Siusi (Seiser Alm) region, with Alpine meadows and onion-domed churches. The best way to explore this area is by cableway from Ortisei: to the

LANGUAGES IN ALTO ADIGE

Most residents in the autonomous region of Alto Adige/Südtirol speak German, followed by Italian, with a small sector of the population classing Ladin as their native dialect. The different languages reflect two different cultures that have lived side by side since the area - once part of the Austro-Hungarian Empire - became part of Italy after World War I. Road signs, train stations and restaurant menus feature both Italian and German. Schools teach the syllabus in two languages, and being bilingual is usually required for employment in the area.

---

northeast, a cable car runs to 2,518-m- (8,260-ft-) high Monte Seceda, and walks from here lead into the Odle Dolomites.

Museo della Val Gardena

 🏛️Via Rezia 83 🕐Dec-Mar: Tue-Fri; mid-May-Oct: Mon-Fri (Jul & Aug: Mon-Sat); 26 Dec-6 Jan: daily 🗓️31 Dec, 1 Jan 🌐museumgherdeina.it

---

11

San Martino di Castrozza

🅰️D1 �æ 🈺Via Passo Rolle 165; www.sanmartino.com

The resort of San Martino occupies one of the most

scenic and accessible valleys in the southern Dolomites, making it very popular with walkers and skiers. Cable cars rise to the peak of Alpe Tognola (2,163 m/7,095 ft), southwest of the town, and up the Cima della Rosetta (2,609 m/8,557 ft) to the east. Both offer views of the Pale di San Martino peaks, a stirring sight as the massive rock peaks, split by glaciers, rise above a sea of green meadows and woodland. San Martino is almost entirely surrounded by forest, which once supplied the Venetian Republic with timber for ships. The forest is now protected, and it is possible to see Alpine flowers, birds and other wildlife with relative ease.

Pretty Ortisei, with a Tyrolean onion-domed bell tower
↓

12 Brunico

Bruneck

🅐D1 🚋 *i* Via Municipio
7; www.bruneck.com

Overlooked by an imposing
medieval castle, this attractive town retains 14th-century
fortifications and a network
of narrow streets. The church
of St Ursula holds a series of
outstanding mid-15th-century
altar reliefs of the Nativity.
The **Museo Etnografico di
Teodone** offers displays of
traditional agricultural life
and local costumes; this
folklore museum also
provides an opportunity
to visit a 16th-century
farmhouse and barn.

Museo Etnografico di Teodone

⊛ ⑨ 🅐 Via Duca Diet 24,
Teodone 🅞 Easter–Oct:
Tue–Sat, Sun & pub hols pm
(Aug: also Mon) 🅦 volks
kundemuseum.it

13 Bressanone

Brixen

🅐D1 🚋 *i* Viale Ratisbona
9; www.brixen.org

The narrow medieval alleys
of Bressanone cluster around
the cathedral and the palace

↑ Players of the Alpine
horn in the historic
centre of Brunico

of the prince-bishops who
ruled the town for much of
its history.

The **Duomo** was rebuilt in
the 18th century but retains
its 12th-century cloister, which
is decorated with superb
15th-century frescoes. The
lavish interiors of Palazzo
Vescovile, the bishops'
Renaissance palace, house
the **Museo Diocesano**. It
contains precious items
from the Middle Ages, as
well as the **Museo dei
Presepi**, with its collection
of wooden crib figures that
are carved locally.

At Velturno (Feldthurns),
just 8 km (5 miles) to the
southwest, stands the
Renaissance **Castello di
Velturno**, the summer
retreat of the rulers of
Bressanone, noted for its
frescoed rooms. A little
over 3 km (2 miles) north of
Bressanone lies the **Abbazia
di Novacella**, a picturesque

← The richly decorated,
colourful cloister of
Bressanone Duomo

↑ The Torre dei Dodici in Vipiteno, with snowy peaks in the background

group of fortified monastic buildings with outstanding cloister frescoes. Further north up the valley, at Rio di Pusteria (Mühlbach), the remains of a 16th-century fortified barrier can be seen to the east of the town. The barrier funnelled ancient travellers through the customs post that divided Tyrol from the Görz district.

High above Rio di Pusteria, to the southeast, looms the massive outline of the **Castel Rodengo** (Rodeneck). The castle contains wonderful 13th-century frescoes showing battle scenes, the Last Judgment and courtly episodes from the *Iwein* romance by Hartmann von Aue, the medieval poet.

Duomo

 Piazza Palazzo Vescovile 1
🕐 6am-noon & 3-6pm daily
🚫 To visitors during mass
🌐 bz-bx.net

> **The castle contains wonderful 13th-century frescoes showing battle scenes, the Last Judgment and courtly episodes from the *Iwein* romance.**

Museo Diocesano & Museo dei Presepi

♿ 🅿 Piazza Palazzo Vescovile 2 🕐 10am-5pm Tue-Sun (Sep: daily) 🚫 6 Jan-mid-Mar, Nov, 24 & 25 Dec
🌐 hofburg.it

Castello di Velturno

♿✈ 🅿 Velturno 🕐 Mid-May-mid-Nov: Tue-Sun
🌐 castelvelturno.it

Abbazia di Novacella

♿✈ 🅿 Via Abbazia 1, Varna
📞 0472 836189 🕐 Mon-Sat
🚫 Pub hols

Castel Rodengo

♿✈ 🅿 Vill 1, Rodengo
📞 391 748 9492 🕐 Mid-May-mid-Oct: Sun-Fri

🔵 14

Vipiteno
Sterzing

🅰 C1 🚉 🔵 ℹ️ Piazza Città 3; 0472 76 53 25

Surrounded by mineral-rich valleys, Vipiteno is very Tyrolean in feel. On Via

Città Nuova, a street lined with fine mansions, rise the Gothic **Palazzo Comunale**, containing Renaissance sculpture and paintings, and the Torre dei Dodici clock tower, the symbol of the town. Wood carvings in the **Museo Multscher** are the work of Hans Multscher; this Bavarian sculptor came to Vipiteno in 1456–8 to carve the altar for the parish church, which lies just south of the town.

To the west, the charming Val di Racines includes waterfalls and a natural rock bridge.

Palazzo Comunale

🅿 Via Città Nuova 21
📞 0472 72 37 00
🕐 Mon-Fri 🚫 Fri pm & pub hols

Museo Multscher

♿ 🅿 Via della Commenda 11
📞 0472 76 64 64 🕐 Apr-Oct:
Tue-Sat 🚫 Pub hols

MILAN

Italy's economic powerhouse, a bustling city of finance and industry, media empires and fashion houses, Milan has an impressive cultural heritage. The buildings in the historic centre are perhaps more varied than in any other Italian city and the museums and galleries are among Italy's best.

The city was founded in the early 4th century BC when the Gallic Insubre tribes settled in the area where the Duomo now stands. It later became a flourishing commercial centre and was made the capital of the Western Empire by the Romans. Emperor Constantine, holding court here in 313, made Christianity the official religion, setting a new course for European history.

The 5th and 6th centuries marked a period of decline for Milan. After being invaded by numerous barbarian forces, the region was dissolved into a network of city-states. The 12th century saw the rise of the Lombard League, a band of forceful separatists founded to counter the imperialism of German emperors. Power was seized by the region's great families, most notably the Sforza family, which ruled from the 14th to the 16th centuries and commissioned many of the city's greatest palaces, churches and artworks. Ludovico "Il Moro" Sforza ushered in the Renaissance to Milan, inviting the likes of Leonardo da Vinci to his court, but ceded control to the French in 1499.

In the following centuries, the city repeatedly changed hands, eventually coming under Austrian control in 1706. The Milanese revolted in the Cinque Giornate, a five-day riot that triggered the end of foreign rule. King Vittorio Emanuele II, King of Sardinia, took control in 1858 and sent General Garibaldi to conquer the rest of the peninsula, forming the new kingdom of Italy.

MILAN

Must Sees

1. Duomo
2. Castello Sforzesco and Parco Sempione
3. Pinacoteca di Brera
4. Leonardo da Vinci's Last Supper

Experience More

5. Museo Poldi-Pezzoli
6. Teatro alla Scala
7. Palazzo Reale
8. Villa Belgiojoso Bonaparte and Galleria d'Arte Moderna (GAM)
9. Pinacoteca Ambrosiana
10. San Satiro
11. Navigli
12. Civico Museo Archeologico
13. Armani Silos
14. San Lorenzo Maggiore
15. MUDEC
16. Sant'Ambrogio
17. Museo Nazionale della Scienza
18. Fondazione Prada

Drink

1. Rita & Cocktails
2. Mag Café
3. Ugo
4. Morgante Cocktail and Soul
5. La Vineria

Stay

6. Camperio House
7. Hotel Viu
8. The Yard Milano

0 metres 400
0 yards 400
N

Hit the Arcades

Italy's oldest shopping centre, Galleria Vittorio Emanuele II was designed by architect Giuseppe Mengoni in 1865. The ceiling is glass-vaulted, while the floors have mosaics of the signs of the zodiac. Step on the genitals of Taurus for luck if you're on the hunt for a bargain (though you're unlikely to find one among the designer stores here). Steals are also rare at nearby department store La Rinascente *(www.rinascente.it)*, but it's still worth a browse for the views of the Duomo from the 7th floor food hall.

→

Stunning interior of the Galleria Vittorio Emanuele II

MILAN FOR
SHOPPERS

Shopping is practically a professional pastime in Milan, Italy's fashion and sartorial epicentre. A major textile production hub since the 19th century, the city today has boutiques, chains and department stores to suit every taste. If you're staying for a short time, these are the city's must-shop spots.

Mark This

On Saturday mornings, the historic Fiera di Sinigaglia flea market is held on Ripa di Porta Ticinese, displaying second hand items including jewellery and crafts *(www.fieradisinigaglia.it)*. On the last Sunday of the month, an antiques market takes over the same stretch of street, with hundreds of stands flogging silverware, antiques, clocks and furniture. For quirky items of clothing and accessories, head to Mercato San Marco in artistic Brera on a Monday or Thursday.

Fiera di Sinigaglia, an historic flea market held in Milan since the 1800s

TOP 3 MILANESE SOUVENIRS

Panettone
Pick up this sweet and fluffy dome-shaped bread, traditionally enjoyed at Christmas and New Year, in Milan.

Italian Design
Scout Italy's fashion capital for unique items of clothing and design.

Foodie Gift Box
w peck.it
Head to Peck, Milan's historic food hall, to stock up on carnaroli rice, hams, cheeses and much more.

Fashion Houses

Italy's most renowned fashion designers, such as Dolce & Gabbana, Roberto Cavalli and Versace, showcase their latest collections in the elegant boutiques that line the Fashion District. To gain an insight into the life of one of Italy's most celebrated designers, head to the Fornasetti Store, which displays all manner of Piero Fornasetti's whimsical creations, from items of furniture to accessories *(www.fornasetti.com)*.

→
Window-shoppers
outside Versace on
Via Montenapoleone

New Names

Milan is home to many new designers and Brera is the perfect place to discover them. Stella Jean is Italy's only world-renowned Black female fashion designer *(www.stellajean.it)* and is making waves in the industry. Emerging designer Chiara Andreatti creates furniture with subtle African accents *(chiaraandreatti.com)*.

←
A Stella Jean piece featured
at Milan Fashion Week

DUOMO

⊙E3 ⓐPiazza Duomo Ⓜ1,3 ⊞1,2,3,12,14,15,16,19, 24,27,54,73,60,61 ⓞMain cathedral: 8am–7pm daily; Museum: 10am–6pm Thu–Tue (to 10pm Thu & Sat); Baptistry: 9am–6pm daily; Roof terraces: 9am–7pm daily (May–Sep: to 10pm) ⓦduomomilano.it

Milan's massive Duomo has a forest of soaring marble spires dating back to 1386. In sheer figures it is impressive: it's the largest Gothic cathedral in the world, it has more than 3,500 exterior statues and it is supported by 52 massive columns inside.

From its inception to the finishing touches, Milan's cathedral took almost 430 years to complete. Construction began in 1386, with the city's bishop, Antonio da Saluzzo, as its patron. Duke Gian Galeazzo Visconti invited Lombard, German and French architects to supervise the works and insisted they use Candoglia marble, which was transported from Lake Maggiore along the Navigli canals. The official seal AUF (ad usum fabricae), stamped on the slabs, exempted them from customs duty. Over the centuries, some of Italy's best sculptors and architects worked on the cathedral, including Leonardo da Vinci. The cathedral was consecrated in 1418, yet remained unfinished until the 19th century, when Napoleon, who was crowned King of Italy here, had the façade completed. Its bronze doors were only fitted in 1965.

→ The lofty nave, supported by a thicket of 52 pilasters

← The Madonnina, a symbol of Milan, standing at the roof's highest point

ROOF TERRACES

The view of the city from the roof terraces is simply unforgettable. Take in a bird's-eye view of the city and the cathedral's remarkable Gothic crown of spires, gargoyles, statues and tracery.

↑ Intricate Gothic façade of Milan's Duomo

2 🗺️ Ⓜ️ 🛍️

CASTELLO SFORZESCO AND PARCO SEMPIONE

📍 C2 🏠 Piazza Castello Ⓜ️ Cairoli-Cadorna, 2 Lanza-Cadorna 🚋 1, 2, 3 🚌 50, 57, 58, 61, 94 🕐 Castello: 7am-7:30pm daily; Musei Civici: 9am-5:30pm Tue-Sun 🚫 1 Jan, 1 May, 25 Dec 🌐 milanocastello.it

The Sforza dukes of Milan ruled over one of the most cultured Renaissance courts in Europe from this complex of fortresses, castles and towers. Since 1896, the Castello Sforzesco has housed the Civic Museums, with a vast collection of art and decorative arts. The Parco Sempione, the old ducal hunting reserve, surrounds the castle.

Francesco Sforza, who became lord of Milan in 1450, and his son Lodovico il Moro made the Sforza castle the home of one of the most magnificent courts in Renaissance Italy, graced by Bramante and Leonardo da Vinci. Later, however, under Spanish, Austrian and French occupation the Castello went into decline and was used as barracks. Today, the Corte Ducale is home to the Raccolte di Arte Antica and the art and sculpture gallery, as well as the furniture collection, while the Rocchetta holds decorative arts and the Trivulzio Tapestries.

↑ Ornate frescoed ceiling in the Raccolte di Arte Antica

← Visitors enjoying a stroll in the Parco Sempione, the park surrounding the Castello Sforzesco

Furniture Collection and Pinacoteca

From 15th-century court furniture to 20th-century pieces by important designers such as Giò Ponti and Ettore Sottsass, the furniture collection showcases Milanese design through the ages.

The art gallery houses works from the mid-15th to the 18th centuries, with works by Mantegna, Antonello da Messina, Giovanni Bellini, Filippo Lippi, Titian, Tintoretto and Canaletto.

Applied Art Collection

The Rocchetta is perhaps best known for displaying Bramantino's splendid Trivulzio Tapestries. Other attractions here include a selection of old musical instruments, an array of medieval gold jewellery, and a large collection of fine Italian and European glass, ceramics, majolica and porcelain.

In the basement of the Corte Ducale are prehistoric and Egyptian displays featuring cult funerary objects, including a fascinating tomb from c 640 BC.

← Fountain lit up in the evening in front of the Castello Sforzesco

Raccolte d'Arte Antica

The collection of Ancient Art is arranged in broadly chronological order in rooms facing the Corte Ducale, while the 14th-century Pusterla dei Fabbri postern, rebuilt after being demolished in 1900, features 4th- to 6th-century sculpture.

Perhaps the highlight of this section is Michelangelo's masterpiece, the *Rondanini Pietà*. The artist was working on this until a few days before his death in 1564. Other star attractions include Agostino Busti's funerary monument to Gaston de Foix, which commemorates the death of the young captain on the battlefield in 1512, and the Sala delle Asse (1498), a room painted by Leonardo to look like an outdoor pergola.

Parco Sempione

This vast park occupies only a part of the old Visconti ducal garden and hunting reserve. The present-day layout was the work of Emilio Alemagna, who in 1890–93 designed it along the lines of an English garden.

Standing among the trees are monuments to Napoleon III, De Chirico's Metaphysical construction *Mysterious Baths*, a sulphur water fountain near the Arena and the Torre del Parco, a 108-m (354-ft) tower made of steel tubes in 1932 after a design by Giò Ponti.

TRIVULZIO TAPESTRIES

Named after General Gian Giacomo Trivulzio, who commissioned them in 1503, the stunning tapestries in the large Sala della Balla (ballroom) were designed by Bramantino. The 12 scenes in the cycle represent the 12 months of the year. The Trivulzio coat of arms (featuring a mermaid breaking a file on a diamond) frame each tapestry, along with an image of the sun and the relevant zodiac sign.

Sculpture of *Napoleon as Mars the Peacemaker* in the courtyard of the museum ↑

PINACOTECA DI BRERA

📍D2 🏛Via Brera 28 Ⓜ Lanza, Montenapoleone & Cairoli 🚋12, 14 🚌61 🕐8:30am–6:30pm Tue–Sat (from 2:30pm Sun) 🚫1 Jan, 25 Dec 🌐pinacotecabrera.org

The Brera holds one of Italy's most important art collections, featuring masterpieces by leading Italian artists from the 13th to the 20th centuries, including Raphael, Mantegna, Piero della Francesca and Caravaggio. The collection is unique among the country's major art galleries in that it isn't founded on the riches of the church or a noble family, but on the policies of Napoleon.

The museum is housed in the imposing 17th-century Palazzo di Brera, a grand palace built as a Jesuit college and later used as an art academy. In the early 19th century, Napoleon augmented the academy's collection with works stolen from churches across the region, opening a picture gallery here in 1809. Over the next two centuries, the collection grew to take in some of the finest examples of Italian Renaissance and Baroque painting.

13th–15th-Century Italian Painting

Rooms 2–4 feature frescoes from the *Oratory at Mocchirolo*, painted by an unknown Lombard master in around 1365–70. Other highlights include Ambrogio Lorenzetti's *Madonna and Child* and *Christ the Judge* by Giovanni da Milano.

↑ Gallery of Renaissance paintings in the Pinacoteca di Brera

Did You Know?

Next to the museum, just off Piazzetta di Brera, is a pretty botanical garden, a welcome retreat after gallery gazing.

15th-16th-Century Italian Painting

The Venetian section (rooms 5–9, 14 and 19) features works by 15th- and 16th-century artists active in the Veneto, including Giovanni and Gentile Bellini, Carpaccio, Titian and Veronese. Mantegna's *Dead Christ* (c 1480), a piece striking for its intense light and bold foreshortening, is a star attraction.

A large collection of 15th- to 16th-century Lombard paintings is exhibited in rooms 10–12, 14–16 and 19, including works by Bergognone, Luini, Bramantino and Vincenzo Foppa.

Rooms 20–23 illustrate artistic movements in the regions of Emilia and Marche. The Ferrara school is represented by leading artists Cosmè Tura, Francesco del Cossa and Ercole de' Roberti. In Room 24 is Raphael's altarpiece *The Marriage of the Virgin* (1504). Some scholars say the young man breaking the staff in the background to this painting is a self-portrait of the artist. Piero della Francesco's *Montefeltro Altarpiece* (c 1475) is in the same room. The egg suspended from the shell in this striking masterpiece is a symbol of the Immaculate Conception.

↑ Francesco Hayez's patriotic and sentimental painting *The Kiss*

17th-18th-Century Italian, Flemish and Dutch Painting

Among the non-Italian artists featured in rooms 31–32 are Rubens, Van Dyck, Rembrandt, El Greco and Brueghel the Elder. In room 38 is Francesco Hayez's *The Kiss* (1859), a frequently reproduced work epitomizing the optimism that prevailed after Italy's unification.

Jesi Collection

The 72 works of modern work donated by Emilio and Maria Jesi in 1976 and 1984 are on show in room 9. The collection, mostly by Italian artists, covers the 1910–40 period.

Leonardo's *Last Supper* fresco in the refectory of Santa Maria delle Grazie ↑

④ 🔁 🅜

LEONARDO DA VINCI'S LAST SUPPER

📍 B3 🏠 Santa Maria delle Grazie refectory, Piazza Santa Maria delle Grazie 2 Ⓜ 1, 2 Cadorna 🚋 16 🚌 18 🕐 8:15am–7pm Tue–Sun 🚫 Pub hols, 1 Jan, 1 May, 25 Dec 🌐 cenacolovinciano.net

This masterpiece was painted for Lodovico il Moro in the refectory of Santa Maria delle Grazie in 1495–7. Leonardo depicts the moment just after Christ has uttered the words, "One of you will betray me". The artist captures the stunned reactions of his disciples in a remarkably realistic and vivid representation of the Last Supper.

↑ Exterior of Santa Maria delle Grazie, where the *Last Supper* can be seen

Leonardo depicts Jesus composed in the centre, and all the disciples around the table shocked and protesting except Judas (fifth from the left) who drops his bread and recoils in guilty horror. Leonardo is reported to have wandered Milan in search of faces to use for the Apostles, and many of the sketches he produced survive in the Royal Library in Windsor, England. The painting is famous for the gesturing hands of the Apostles, so expressive that critics have said they "speak".

The fragility of the blotchy and faded image means that visits are limited to 15 minutes, but it is amazing there is anything left at all. Leonardo painted in tempera rather than the standard, longer-lasting fresco technique in which pigment is mixed with the plaster, and

↑ Judas cartoon, Royal
   Library, Windsor, UK

← Donato Montorfano's
   Crucifixion, on the opposite
   wall of the refectory

the painting started to deteriorate almost immediately. Later, a door was knocked through the bottom part of the picture, then Napoleon's troops used the wall for target practice and, in 1943, the rest of the monastery was destroyed by a bomb.

On the opposite wall of the refectory is Donato Montorfano's fresco of the *Crucifixion*, commissioned by the Dominican monks in 1495. In this dense composition the despairing Mary Magdalene hugs the cross while the soldiers on the right throw dice for Christ's robe. On either side of the work, under the cross, Leonardo added the portraits – now almost invisible – of Lodovico il Moro, his wife Beatrice and their children, which he signed and dated.

THE RESTORATION

It was not the humidity but the method used by Leonardo, *tempera forte,* that caused the immediate deterioration of the *Last Supper.* As early as 1550 the art historian Vasari called it "a dazzling blotch" and regarded it as a lost work. There have been many attempts to restore the *Last Supper,* but in retouching the picture further damage was often done. The seventh restoration ended in spring 1999: it lacks the vibrancy of the original, but it is at least authentic.

EXPERIENCE MORE

↑ Pollaiuolo's *Portrait of a Young Woman*, in the Museo Poldi-Pezzoli

 ⑤

Museo Poldi-Pezzoli

♀E2 **🏠Via Alessandro Manzoni 12** **🕐2:30-6pm Wed-Mon** **🚫Pub hols** **🌐museopoldipezzoli.it**

Giacomo Poldi-Pezzoli was a wealthy nobleman who, on his death in 1879, bequeathed his magnificent art collection to the state. Its most famous painting is the 15th-century Renaissance *Portrait of a Young Woman* by Antonio Pollaiuolo, though there are also works by Piero della Francesca, Botticelli and Mantegna, among others.

 ⑥

Teatro alla Scala

♀D2-E2 **🏠Piazza della Scala** **🌐teatroallascala.org**

This Neo-Classical theatre opened in 1778 and is one of the world's most prestigious opera houses. It has one of the largest stages in Europe and hosts sumptuous productions. Two hours before each performance the box office sells tickets at discount prices.

Located within the theatre, the **Museo Teatrale** houses sets and costumes of past productions and theatrical items dating back to Roman times. There is also a good view of the auditorium, with its gilded box galleries and huge chandelier.

Museo Teatrale

🏠Largo Ghiringhelli 1 (Piazza Scala) **🕐9am-5:30pm Tue-Sat** **🌐museoscala.org**

 ⑦

Palazzo Reale

♀E3 **🏠Piazza del Duomo** **🕐2:30-7:30 Mon; 9:30am-7:30pm Tue, Wed, Fri & Sun; 9:30-10:30pm Thu & Sat** **🌐palazzorealemilano.it**

The former royal palace, for centuries home to the Visconti

→ A room in the Museo Teatrale, located within the Scala Theatre

and other rulers of Milan, houses the Museo della Reggia. It displays the sumptuous interiors of the building and showcases the four historic phases of the palace, including the Neo-Classical era and the Restoration. The palace is also regularly used as a venue for prestigious temporary art exhibitions.

The building abutting the Palazzo Reale to the west (the Arengario) now houses a modern art museum, the **Museo del Novecento**. Works by international artists such as Braque, Kandinsky, Klee,

↑ Eclectic mix of old and new at the Museo Poldi-Pezzoli

Léger, Matisse, Mondrian and Picasso can be found alongside pieces by Italy's foremost 20th-century artists.

Museo del Novecento
 Piazza Duomo 8
🌐 museodelnovecento.org

8

Villa Belgiojoso Bonaparte and Galleria d'Arte Moderna (GAM)

📍 F2 🏛 Via Palestro 16
🕐 9am–5:30pm Tue–Sun
🌐 gam-milano.com

Milan's 19th-century and modern art collections are housed in a Neo-Classical villa built by Leopold Pollack

 HIDDEN GEM
Villa Necchi Campiglio

Just a 10-minute walk from GAM is this Art Deco villa-turned-museum. Here, you can see one-off artworks and wander the gardens for a glimpse of aristocratic life in the 1930s.

↑ Staircase at the Villa Belgiojoso Bonaparte and Gallerie d'Arte Moderna

in 1790 for Count Ludovico Barbiano di Belgiojoso. It was lived in by Napoleon in 1802 and later by Marshal Radetzky. The villa houses 19th-century Italian art, showing all the major art movements, as well as the Grassi and Vismara collections of 19th- and 20th-century Italian and international artists. Of particular note are works by Giorgio Morandi (1890–1964), Carlo Carrà (1881–1966), Modigliani (1884–1920) and De Chirico (1888–1978). Non-Italian artists include Van Gogh, Cézanne, Gauguin, Picasso, Matisse, Klee and Kandinsky.

STAY

Camperio House
This is a stylish, private, self-catering residence with an on-site restaurant, elegant Italian furnishings and ever-helpful staff.

📍 D3 🏛 Via Manfredo Camperio 9
🌐 camperio.com

 €€€

Hotel Viu
This chic hotel is set in an ecofriendly building covered with foliage. There are minimalist rooms and a stunning rooftop swimming pool.

📍 C1 🏛 Via Aristotile Fioravanti 6
🌐 hotelviumilan.com

 €€€

The Yard Milano
Boutique hipster hotel packed with objets d'art, plus 32 well-decorated suites.

📍 C5 🏛 Piazza XXIV Maggio 8 🌐 the-yard. hotels-milan.info

 €€€

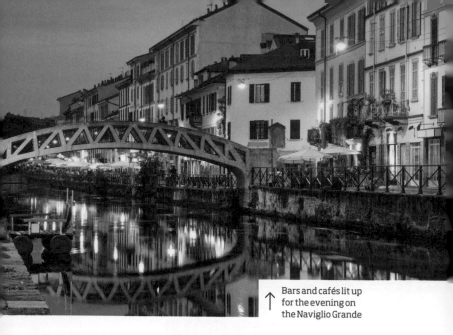

↑ Bars and cafés lit up for the evening on the Naviglio Grande

Pinacoteca Ambrosiana

9

📍 **D3** 🏠 **Piazza Pio XI 2**
🕐 **2-6pm Tue-Sun**
🌐 **ambrosiana.it**

The Ambrosiana is home to Cardinal Federico Borromeo's magnificent library of 36,000 manuscripts. These include a 5th-century illustrated *Iliad*, early manuscripts of Dante's *Divine Comedy* (1353) and the *Atlantic Codex* (1478–1519) by Leonardo da Vinci. In order to exhibit as much of the *Atlantic Codex* as possible, the pages on show are changed every three months.

The building also houses an art gallery, bequeathed by Borromeo in 1618. The collection ranges from 14th-century pieces to works of the early 19th century. Among the canvases are *Portrait of a Musician* by Leonardo, the *Madonna of the Canopy* by Botticelli (15th century), a cartoon version of Raphael's Vatican fresco, *The School of Athens* (16th century) and a reproduction of Caravaggio's *Fruit Basket*. There is also a strong collection of Venetian art, with paintings by Giorgione, Titian, Bassano and Tiepolo, and panel paintings by the late 15th-century Lombard painter Bergognone.

San Satiro

10

📍 **D3** 🏠 **Via Speronari 3**
📞 **02 87 46 83** 🕐 **9:30am-5:30pm Mon-Sat, 2-5:30pm Sun & pub hols**

Santa Maria presso San Satiro church is one of the most beautiful Renaissance buildings in Milan. It was built on the site of a 9th-century sanctuary, little of which remains apart from the Cappella della Pietà, beside an 11th-century bell tower.

The interior seems to be in the shape of a Greek cross, but this is an illusion created by *trompe-l'oeil* effects, since space restrictions led Bramante to choose a T-shaped plan. Above the altar is a 13th-century fresco. An octagonal baptistry lies off the right aisle. The church's façade was finished in the 19th century.

Navigli

11

📍 **C5** Ⓜ **2** 🚊 **2, 3, 9, 10, 14, 15**
🚌 **59, 71, 74**

Developed around a 90-km-(55-mile-) long series of artificial canals built between the 12th and 16th century, Milan's Navigli (canal) neighbourhood is one of the city's buzziest places. The area was historically designed to support Milan's growing trade routes, and it aimed to encourage the transport of merchandise such as marble to the city, from the Ticino and Adda rivers.

Despite being in construction from the 12th century, it wasn't until Leonardo da Vinci joined the project to design a new series of dams that the canal project really took hold. Leonardo then designed a second system of canals linking the Valtellina area with Milan, bringing further trade to the city, which was then Italy's industrial centre.

Today the Navigli area runs from Naviglio Pavese to Naviglio Grande, with a plethora of boutiques, cafés, restaurants and bars running alongside the waterways. It's one of Milan's most popular nightlife spots and is best visited in the early evening, when bars fling open their doors and welcome locals for aperitivo hour. There is very good furniture shopping in the area, too, with Italian artisans still working from small studios along the river. On the last Sunday of every month, a huge outdoor flea market takes place on Naviglio Grande.

Civic Museo Archeologico

📍C3 🏛Corso Magenta 15 📞02 88 44 52 08 Ⓜ1, 2 Cadorna 🚋1, 16, 19 🚌50, 58, 94 🕐9am-5:30pm Tue-Sun

At the entrance to this museum is a model of Roman Milan, which illustrates urban planning and architecture in Milan from the 1st to the 4th century AD. The exhibition begins in a hall on the right, containing clay objects and Roman sculpture. At the end of this room is a huge fragment of a torso of Hercules and 3rd-century-AD floor mosaics. Also in this room are two of the most important works in the museum: the Parabiago Patera and the Diatreta Cup. The Patera is a gilded silver plate with a relief of the

↑ The Parabiago Patera, in the Civico Museo Archeologico

goddess Cybele (4th century AD). The Diatreta Cup, which dates from the same period, is a single piece of coloured glass, with finely wrought, intricate decoration.

Armani Silos

📍A5 🏛Via Bergognone 40 📞02 91 63 00 10 Ⓜ2 Cadorna 🚋2, 9, 10, 14 🚌74 🕐11am-9pm Wed-Sun

Opened in 2015 by designer Giorgio Armani to mark 40 years of his career, this fashion-art museum offers a glimpse into the inimitable style created by the iconic Italian clothing brand. It runs across four floors in a former grain store, and visitors can view hundreds of outfits and accessories spanning Armani's collections from 1980 to the present day, under the themes of daywear, exoticism, colour schemes and light. The building is decidedly minimalist, with a pared-back design aesthetic: black ceilings, brushed-concrete floors and plenty of light. Visitors can also take a look at Armani's work-stations, with an archive of around 2,000 garment and accessory images, and prints of the most iconic Armani photo shoots of all time.

←

The brushed-concrete minimalist look of the Armani Silos

DRINK

Rita & Cocktails
An intimate neighbourhood locale doling out creative cocktails served in jam jars. Get there by 6pm for an aperitivo before it gets too busy.

📍B5 🏛Via Angelo Fumagalli 1 📞02 837 28 65

Mag Café
This popular bar is crammed with goodies - from coffee cups on the walls to wrought-iron lanterns and a bicycle hanging from the ceiling. Excellent cocktails, but it gets packed at happy hour.

📍B5 🏛Ripa di Porta Ticinese 43 📞02 39 56 28 75

Ugo
The bartenders at Ugo, one of the Navigli's best cocktail bars, magic up a mean *Negroni sbagliato*.

📍B5-C5 🏛Via Corsico 12 🚪Mon 🌐ugobar.it

Morgante Cocktail and Soul
This bar, in a private garden, offers potent Martinis and snacks.

📍C5 🏛Vicolo Privato Lavandai 2/a 🌐morgante cocktail.com

La Vineria
Choose from the long wine list here, and pair with charcuterie plates piled high with salami, *prosciutto di Parma* and local cheeses.

📍B5 🏛Via Casale 4 🌐la-vineria.it

San Lorenzo Maggiore

📍D4 🏛 Corso di Porta Ticinese 35 🕐 8:30am-6:30pm Mon-Fri, 9am-7pm Sat & Sun 🌐 san lorenzomaggiore.com

This grand church contains a vast collection of Roman and early Christian remains. The octagonal basilica was built in the 4th century, above what was probably a Roman amphitheatre, and rebuilt in the 12th and 16th centuries. In front of the church are 16 Roman columns and a statue of Emperor Constantine.

Don't miss the beautiful Cappella di Sant'Aquilino, a Romanesque chapel which is adorned with 4th-century mosaics and houses two early Christian sarcophagi. Other Roman architectural elements of this church are in a chamber below the chapel.

MUDEC

📍A5 🏛 Via Tortona 56 🕐 2:30pm-7:30pm Mon, 9:30am-7:30pm Tue-Sun (to 10:30pm Thu & Sat) 🌐 mudec.it

Milan's art and culture museum, MUDEC (Museo delle Culture di Milano) is set in the heart of the city's design district. It focuses on cultures of the world and their relationship with the city of Milan while also promoting local cultural activities. Inside, the permanent collection features everyday objects such as textiles and musical instruments donated to the city's missionaries, scholars and explorers during their travels in the Middle East, Asia and Africa. Check the website for an ever-changing series of excellent, innovative temporary exhibitions.

Sant'Ambrogio

📍C3 🏛 Piazza Sant' Ambrogio 15 🕐 10am-noon & 2:30-6pm Mon-Sat, 3-5pm Sun 🌐 basilica santambrogio.it

Sant'Ambrogio, or St Ambrose, Milan's patron saint and its bishop in the 4th century, was so eloquent that bees were said to fly into his mouth, attracted by his honeyed tongue. This is the basilica that he began in AD 379, though today most of it is 10th-century Romanesque. A gateway leads to the bronze doors of the entrance, flanked by two bell towers. Inside, note the fine rib vaulting and pulpit, as well as the 9th-century altar, which is decorated with gold, silver and gems. In a chapel off the south aisle, fine mosaics line a stunning cupola. In the crypt lies the tomb of Sant'Ambrogio himself.

Above the portico, **Sant' Ambrogio Museum** contains a fascinating collection of architectural fragments, tapestries and paintings relating to the church and its history.

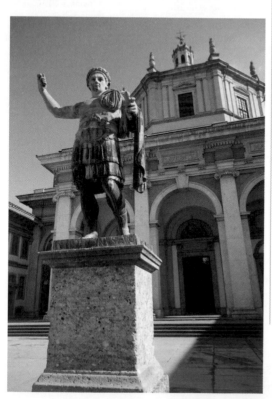

←

Statue of Constantine in front of the church of San Lorenzo Maggiore

Sant'Ambrogio Museum
C 0286 450 895 **O** 10am-noon & 2:30-5:30pm Mon-Sat, 3-5pm Sun

---

Museo Nazionale della Scienza

Q B3 **A** Via San Vittore 21 **O** 10am-6pm Tue-Fri (to 7pm Sat & Sun) **W** museoscienza.org

The largest science and technology museum in Italy, the Museo Nazione della Scienza covers transport, energy and communication, as well as art and science based on Leonardo da Vinci's work. Visitors get a glimpse into Italy's rich entrepreneurial and artisanal roots by way of some fascinating one-off objects.

Upon entering the museum, visitors are greeted by Italian military aircraft replicas, including a Farman 1909, plus modern aircraft such as the powerful Italian fighter jet the Fiat G.91. Train lovers can explore vintage railway façades and learn about Lombardy's public-transport history, while the submarine section looks at the Toti submarine S-506, built following World War II.

The Leonardo da Vinci section looks at completed versions of the artist's drawings, including the armoured fighting vehicle known as Leonardo's Tank and a spinning machine.

The cinema and photography rooms show how the claw device used for motion-picture film grew out of a sewing machine needle conceived by Singer in 1851. Among the exhibits in the fascinating television and telephone section is a pantelegraph, an early ancestor of the fax machine.

Elsewhere there are musical instruments dating from the 1600s onwards, and there is a fascinating 17th-century lute-makers workshop on display, too. Children will love the i.lab area, which allows hands-on interaction and participation.

↑ An astronaut's spacesuit in the Museo Nazionale della Scienza

↑ The colonnaded courtyard of the basilica of Sant'Ambrogio

Fondazione Prada

Q E5 **A** Largo Isarco 2 **O** 10am-7pm Wed-Mon (to 9pm Fri-Sun) **W** fondazioneprada.org

Set in a former grain distillery, this chic contemporary art museum is the brainchild of Prada duo Miuccia Prada and Patrizio Bertelli, who sought to bring a permanent cultural space to the city. The exhibitions here focus on literature, cinema, music, philosophy, art and science – but they also look at the ways in which these various disciplines interact.

Permanent exhibitions include the Processo Grottesco (a virtual-reality recreation of a Maiorcan grotto) and a room featuring works by artists Robert Gober and Louise Bourgeois. The museum's bar, Bar Luce, was designed by US film director Wes Anderson, who worked with the building's architectural details to create a space inspired by the 1950s and 60s, complete with vintage-style pinball machines.

LOMBARDY AND THE LAKES

Appreciated by the ancient Romans for their beautiful location and mild climate, the lakes of northern Italy – most of which are in Lombardy – are deservedly renowned for the fascinating and unique combination of magnificent scenery and historic and artistic heritage.

Besides Lake Maggiore, Lake Como and Lake Garda, there are smaller and less well-known bodies of water such as the lakes of Varese, Iseo and Idro. All are the result of glaciation in the Pleistocene era, which enlarged clefts already in the terrain. The lake shores were inhabited during the prehistoric period and were later colonized by the Romans, as can be seen in the grid street plans of many towns and in the villas at Lake Garda. Many churches, sanctuaries and castles were built here in the Middle Ages.

In the winter the shores of the lakes can be battered by winds from Central Europe, but the climate remains quite mild thanks to the water. Typical Mediterranean vegetation can be seen everywhere: vineyards, olive trees, oleanders and palm trees. The many splendid villa gardens along the lakes' shores enhance the environment.

In the 18th century a visit to the lake region was one of the stages on the Grand Tour, the trip to Europe considered essential for the education of young people of good birth. These shores were also favourites with writers, musicians and artists such as Goethe, Stendhal, Byron, Nietzsche, Toscanini, Hesse, Klee and Hemingway. In March 2020, the Lombardy region drew attention for an altogether different reason – when Italy became the epicentre of the COVID-19 pandemic, this area was hit the hardest.

LOMBARDY AND THE LAKES

Must Sees
1. Lake Como
2. Lake Garda
3. Certosa di Pavia

Experience More
4. Lake Maggiore
5. Monza
6. Bergamo
7. Lake Iseo
8. Val Camonica
9. Parco Nazionale dello Stelvio
10. Brescia
11. Mantua
12. Sabbioneta
13. Cremona
14. Pavia

TRENTINO-
ALTO ADIGE
p128

THE VENETO
AND FRIULI
p102

EMILIA-ROMAGNA
p424

①

LAKE COMO

A B1 **FS** Como, Lecco **i** Via Albertolli 7, Como; www.lakecomo.it

Set in an idyllic landscape of mountains and rugged hillsides, Lake Como has for centuries attracted visitors who come here to go boating, for walks in the hills, or for relaxation and inspiration. The northern stretches, in particular, are shrouded in an almost eerie calm. The long and narrow lake, shaped into a wishbone by glacial erosion, offers fine views up to the Alps and down to the towns of Como and Lecco.

①

Bellagio

This delightful resort on the cusp of the lake's two arms has everything: a harbourside arcade of cafés, sumptuous gardens surrounding stately villas, steep medieval alleys and hotels, restaurants and shops in all price ranges.

②

Varenna

Less touristy than Bellagio, Verenna has a pretty water-front promenade, two small churches with medieval frescoes and two spectacular villas with gardens to wander around. A 20-minute walk away is the medieval Vezio castle, which offers stunning panoramic views of the lake.

③

Villa Carlotta

A Via Regina Teodolinda 2b, Tremezzo **○** Mid-Mar-Sep: 9am-7pm daily; Oct: 9:30am-6:30pm daily **W** villacarlotta.it

Lake Como is famous for its extravagant villas, but while some gardens are open, few of the buildings themselves can be visited. At Villa Carlotta, however, it is possible to visit the exquisite landscaped gardens as well as the sumptuous late-Baroque villa.

④

Santa Maria del Tiglio

A Piazza XI Febbraio **C** 034 48 52 61 **○** Times vary, call ahead

This church in Gravedona is the most famous Lombard Romanesque construction in the Alto Lario region. Its main features are the black-and-white striped stone walls and the unusual octagonal bell tower set into its façade.

↑ The landscaped gardens of Villa Carlotta with Lake Como behind

Lake Como with the town of Gravedona in the foreground

EAT

Napule e'
A lakeside eatery, Napule e' does excellent pizzas and an even better seafood linguine.

🏠 Via Luigi Dottesio 22
🌐 napuleofficial.it

€€€

Cascina Respaù
Set in the hills above Como, this farmhouse serves a changing menu of dishes such as risotto and pastas washed down with local wines.

🏠 Via Santi Brigida e Respaù 📞 031 52 36 62

€€€

⑤

Como

The town that gave its name to the lake boasts a **Duomo** in mixed Gothic and Renaissance styles, with carvings on its façade. From the harbour, visitors can take a **funicular** to the hillside village of Brunate to take in views over the lake.

Duomo

🏠 Piazza del Duomo 📞 031 331 2275 🕐 10:45am-5:30pm Mon-Sat (to 4:30pm Sat), noon-5:30pm Sun

Brunate Funicular

🏠 Piazza A De Gasperi 📞 031 30 36 08 🕐 Every 15 min 6am-10:30pm daily

⑥

Villa Balbianello

🏠 Lenno 📞 034 45 61 10 🕐 Mid-Mar-mid-Jan: 10:30am-6:30pm Tue, Thu & Fri (to 7:30pm Sat & Sun)

The statue-lined balustrades that outline the gardens of this 1784 villa have caught the eye of many a film director.

⑦

Abbazia di Piona

🏠 Via Abbazia di Piona 55 📞 0341 94 03 31 🕐 9am-noon & 2:30-6pm daily

At the tip of the Ogliasca peninsula sits this Benedictine abbey. Founded in the 9th century, the abbey features some lovely Romanesque carvings. The monks distil and sell potent liqueur, too.

💬 INSIDER TIP
Flea Market

Each Saturday in the Piazza San Fedele in Como, the Mercato dell'Artigianato e Antiquariato sets up its stalls selling vintage clothing, art, furniture and homewares.

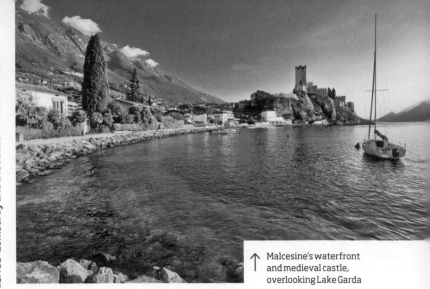

↑ Malcesine's waterfront and medieval castle, overlooking Lake Garda

2

LAKE GARDA

🗺️ C2 🚉 Peschiera del Garda, Desenzano del Garda 🚌⛴️ To all towns ℹ️ Viale Marconi 6, Sirmione; 0303 748 721

The largest and easternmost of the Italian lakes, Lake Garda borders three regions: Trentino to the north, Lombardy to the west and south, and the Veneto to the south and east. The lake is a favourite summer playground, its pristine waters and splendid scenery drawing swimmers, bikers, kitesurfers and boaters.

①

Gardone Riviera

This pleasant tourist resort is home to **Il Vittoriale**, an over-the-top Art Deco villa built for the poet and writer Gabriele D'Annunzio. Nearby is the **Giardino Botanico Hruska**, a small set of botanical gardens sitting on a terraced hillside.

Il Vittoriale

 🏠 Via del Vittoriale 12 📞 0365 296 511 🕐 9am-7pm daily (mid-Oct–mid-Mar: to 4pm) 🚫 Nov-Feb: Mon; 1 Jan, 24 & 25 Dec

Giardino Botanico Hruska

🏠 Via Roma 2 📞 336 410877 🕐 Mar-Oct: 9am-7pm daily

②

Isola del Garda

🎫 For guided tours mid-Apr-Oct: Tue-Fri & Sun 🌐 isoladelgarda.com

Garda's largest island once supported a monastery that attracted the great medieval saints: Bernardino of Siena, Francis of Assisi and Anthony of Padua. The monastery was destroyed by Napoleon and replaced with a Neo-Gothic villa with luxuriant gardens.

③

Desenzano del Garda

This is one the liveliest and most popular towns on Lake Garda. The **Villa Romana**, built in the 4th century, has beautiful polychrome floor mosaics.

Villa Romana

 🏠 Via Crocefisso 22 📞 030 914 3547 🕐 8:30am-5pm Tue-Sun (Mar-mid-Oct: 7pm)

④

Sirmione

A 13th-century castle, the Rocca Scaligera, dominates this town known for its thermal resorts. At the tip of the peninsula lies the **Grotte di Catullo**, the ruins of a villa thought to be the residence of the Roman poet Catullus.

Grotte di Catullo

 🏠 Via Catullo 📞 030 91 61 57 🕐 8:30am-5pm Wed-Sat & Mon (Jun-Sep: to 7:30pm), 2-7:20pm Sun

> 🔍 HIDDEN GEM
> ### Camaldolese Hermitage
>
> The Camaldolese Hermitage, located near Garda, offers panoramic views of the lake, but visitors must respect the sacred nature of the place.

DRINK

Villa Calicantus

Bardolino has long been famous for its light red wine, and this little winery in the Bardolino hills produces some of the best in the region. Booking is essential.

🏠 Via Concordia 13, Bardolino 🕐 Sun & Mon 🌐 villacalicantus.it

Gardaland

🏠 Via Derna 4 🕐 Nov, Jan–mid-Mar 🌐 gardaland.it

This popular theme park features roller coasters, carnival rides, a water park, a jungle safari and medieval shows.

Riva del Garda

This picturesque town at the northern tip of the lake is popular for outings on row boats and pedal crafts. Other pastimes include windsurfing, sailing, kayaking and mountain biking along the lake banks and into the Alpine foothills.

---

⑦

Malcesine

A fascinating lakeside town, Malcesine stands on a stretch of impervious rock, hence the name, *mala silex* (inaccessible rock). Its historic buildings are clustered below a medieval castle. A cable car climbs to the summit of Monte Baldo, offering far-reaching views.

→

View over Lake Garda from the Rocca Scaligera castle in Sirmione

CERTOSA DI PAVIA

B2 ⌂ Viale del Monumento 4, Pavia 📞 0382 92 56 13 🚌 From Pavia & Milan
🚇 Certosa, followed by 1 km (0.5 mile) walk 🕐 Apr-Sep: 9-11:30am & 2:30-6pm Tue-Sun
& hols (Apr: to 5:30pm); Oct-Mar: 9-11:30am & 2:30-4:30pm Tue-Sun (to 5pm Sun & hols)

The Charterhouse, 8 km (5 miles) north of Pavia, is the pinnacle of Renaissance architecture in Lombardy, a gloriously decorated Carthusian church and monastery built over 200 years.

Conceived as a monument to Gian Galeazzo Visconti, the Milanese ruler who founded the complex in 1396, the monastery and church were created by the great 15th-century craftsman Giovanni Antonio Amadeo, among others. The church was intended to be a kind of mausoleum housing the tombs of the Visconti family. The monastery gives a fascinating insight into the daily lives of Carthusian monks, who still live here under a strict vow of silence.

→
The grand Certosa di Pavia, seen from the side

The 15th-century choir stalls are beautifully carved and inlaid with intricate marquetry.

Several of the 17th-century altars in the chapels have lavish designs worked in semi-precious stones (pietra dura).

The tomb of Gian Galeazzo Visconti (1351–1402) is in the south transept.

The realistic tomb portraits of Ludovico and his child bride Beatrice d'Este were begun 11 years before Ludovico's death.

Bergognone's striking portrait of Christ (c 1488–93) is one of several frescoes and paintings by the artist in the transept and chapels.

1️⃣ The lower part of the façade, dating from the 15th century, is decorated with statues and carvings of Roman emperors, saints, apostles and prophets. The upper part of the façade dates from 1500.

2️⃣ This delightful arcaded Small Cloister, with fine terracotta ornamentation, contains a small garden, planted in formal designs.

3️⃣ The ceiling of the church is made up of a series of intricately decorated ribbed vaults.

The New Sacristy is painted with colourful ceiling frescoes.

PERUGINO'S ALTARPIECE

The church's six-panelled altarpiece was painted by Perugino in 1499 but now only one panel - that depicting *God the Father* (below) - is original; it is flanked by two paintings by Bergognone. The three original lower panels of Perugino's polyptych are on display in the National Gallery in London.

The monks' cells are attractive two-storey cottages with their own private gardens.

EXPERIENCE MORE

 4

Lake Maggiore

A B1 **A** Verbania **FS** 🚌
🚢 Stresa, Verbania, Baveno
& the islands **i** Piazza
Marconi 16, Stresa; www.
distrettolaghi.it

Lake Maggiore, the second-largest Italian lake after Lake Garda, is a long expanse of water nestling right against the mountains and stretching into Alpine Switzerland. The gently sloping shores are

Did You Know?

Ernest Hemingway, a fan of Lake Maggiore, spent time here to recover from his injuries in World War I.

dotted with camellias, azaleas and verbena.

A huge copper statue of Cardinal San Carlo Borromeo, the chief patron of the lake, stands in Arona, the town where he was born in 1538. It is possible to climb inside the statue and look out over the lake through his eyes and ears. Arona also has a ruined castle and a chapel dedicated to the Borromeo family.

Further up the western coast of the lake is Stresa, the chief resort and main jumping-off point for visits to the islands; the town boasts many grand hotels, handsome villas and pleasant gardens. Behind Stresa, a cable-car ride away, rises Monte Mottarone, a snow-capped peak offering spectacular panoramic views of the surrounding mountains, including Monte Rosa.

The Borromean islands, at the centre of the lake near

Stresa, are small jewels of natural beauty augmented by artificial grottoes, architectural follies and landscaped gardens. The Isola Bella is home to the 17th-century **Palazzo Borromeo** and its splendid gardens, while Isola Madre is largely given over to a botanical garden. The only island inhabited all year round is Isola dei Pescatori, with a population of 50. The private Isola di San Giovanni is the smallest of the isles, with a villa that once belonged to the great conductor Arturo Toscanini (1867–1957).

The lake becomes quieter towards the Swiss border, but continues to be lined with attractive villas. The **Villa Taranto**, located on the outskirts of Verbania, is home to one of Italy's finest botanic gardens.

About 3 km (2 miles) west of Cannobio, a market town

← Islands in beautiful Lake Maggiore, ringed by forested mountains

near Switzerland, is the dramatic gorge and tumbling waterfall of Orrido di Sant'Anna, which can be reached by boat.

Palazzo Borromeo
⊘ ▲Isola Bella ⛴From Stresa ◷Late Mar–Oct: 9am–5:30pm daily �🅦isole borromee.it

Villa Taranto
⊘ ▲Via Vittorio Veneto 111, Verbania, Pallanza 📞0323 40 45 55 ◷Apr–Sep: 9:30am–5:30pm daily (Oct: to 4:30pm daily)

---

❺
Monza

🅰B2 ▲Monza ⚏⛴
ℹPiazza Trento e Trieste; 039 67 91 488

These days Monza is mostly famous for its Formula One **Autodromo**, which lies inside a vast park that also has an elegant Rococo hunting lodge,

the Villa Reale, and a golf course. At one time, however, Monza was one of the most important towns in Lombardy. Theodolinda, the 6th-century Lombard queen, built its first cathedral and bequeathed her treasure to the town.

In the town centre is the **Duomo**, with its green and white façade and beautiful frescoes portraying Theodolinda's life. Behind the high altar is the Iron Crown, said to have belonged to Emperor Constantine. It is named after a small iron strip running around the inside of the crown, supposedly beaten from one of the nails used for the Crucifixion. More local treasures in the Duomo include a silver hen standing over seven tiny chicks – which symbolize Lombardy and the seven provinces it ruled – and a relic said to be John the Baptist's tooth.

Autodromo
⊘ ▲Parco di Monza ◷Daily 🗓Pub hols 🅦monzanet.it

Duomo
⊘ ▲Piazza Duomo ◷9am–1pm & 2–6pm Tue–Sun (Museo e Tesoro del Duomo) 🅦museoduomomonza.it

↓ Monza's elegant 12th century Romanesque Duomo

Elaborate carving

Rose window

Lions support columns and porch above

Alternating bands of marble

Sunrise over the charming old town of Bergamo Alta ↑

⑥

Bergamo

🅰B1 🚍🚌 **ℹ️ Via Gombito 13; www.visitbergamo.net**

Bergamo owes much of its artistic inspiration and architectural splendour to the influence of Venice, which ruled it from the 15th to the late 18th century. The town is divided into two distinct parts: Bergamo Alta, crowning the hill with its cluster of attractive medieval and Renaissance buildings, and the more modern Bergamo Bassa below.

The jewel of the upper town is Piazza Vecchia, containing one of the most appealing architectural ensembles in the region. Its buildings include the 12th-century Torre del Comune, with its fine clock and curfew bell that rings daily at 10pm; the late 16th-century Biblioteca Civica; and the attractive 12th-century Palazzo della Ragione, or law courts, adorned with a bas-relief of the Lion of Venice.

The arcades of the Palazzo della Ragione lead to Piazza del Duomo, which is domi-nated by the Cappella Colleoni, a chapel built in 1476 to house the tomb of Bergamo's famous political leader, Bartolomeo Colleoni. It is flanked by two 14th-century buildings: a baptistry and the porch leading to the Romanesque basilica of Santa Maria Maggiore. The Neo-Classical basilica's austere exterior contrasts with its Baroque interior, which contains the tomb of Bergamo-born composer Gaetano Donizetti (1797–1848).

One of the city's star attractions is the excellent **Galleria dell'Accademia Carrara**, a renowned picture gallery with works by Venetian masters and local artists, as well as paintings from the rest of Italy. Among the many famous masterpieces on display are 15th- and 16th-century works by Botticelli, Titian, Raphael and Perugino, 18th-century canvases by Tiepolo, Guardi and Canaletto, and paintings by Holbein, Dürer, Brueghel and Velázquez.

Bergamo and the neighbouring municipal-ities lost almost an entire generation to COVID-19.

Galleria dell'Accademia Carrara

♿ 🏛 Piazza Giacomo Carrara 82 📞 035 23 43 96 🕐 9:30am–5:30pm Wed-Mon

Octagonal drum influenced by the Duomo in Florence

Rose window

Patterned marble design

Highly ornate façade

← Bergamo's Capella Colleoni (1476), an early Renaissance masterpiece

Lake Iseo

🅐 C1 🅐 Bergamo & Brescia
🆂🅡🖼🚢 Iseo 🅘 Lungolago
Marconi 2/c, Iseo; www.
visitlakeiseo.info

This small glaciated lake is surrounded by tall mountains and waterfalls and boasts a mini-mountain of its own, in the form of the island of Monte Isola. Along the shores of the lake are a clutch of fishing villages such as Sale Marasino and Iseo itself. From Marone, on the east bank of the lake, a road leads to the village of Cislano, about 5 km (3 miles) away. Here, extraordinary spire-like rock formations rise from the ground, each topped by a boulder. These distinctive erosion pillars, one of the strangest natural wonders in Lombardy, are known as the "Fairies of the Forest".

8 Val Camonica

🅐 C1 🅐 Brescia 🆂🅡
🚌 Capo di Ponte 🅘 Via
Briscioli 42, Capo di Ponte;
www.turismovalle
camonica.it

This broad valley formed by a glacier is the setting for an extraordinary series of prehistoric rock carvings. These form an astonishing outdoor mural from Lake Iseo to Capo di Ponte and beyond, and the valley is an UNESCO cultural protection zone. More than 180,000 engravings from the Neolithic era until early Roman times have been found; the best are in the **Parco Nazionale delle Incisioni Rupestri**. Do not miss the Naquane rock, carved with nearly 1,000 figures from the Ice Age.

→
Village of Peschiera on Lake Iseo

Parco Nazionale delle Incisioni Rupestri

🅐 Capo di Ponte 🕒 8:30am-7pm Tue-Sun 🚫 1 Jan, 1 May, 25 Dec 🔳 parcoincisioni. capodiponte.beniculturali.it

9 Parco Nazionale dello Stelvio

🅐 C1 🅐 Trento, Bolzano, Sondrio & Brescia 🚌 From Bormio to Santa Caterina Valfurva & Madonna dei Monti 🅘 Via Roma 65, Peio (Trento); www. stelviopark.it

The Stelvio, Italy's largest national park, is the gateway from Lombardy to the glacier-strewn Dolomite mountains stretching into Trentino-Alto Adige. The glaciers are dotted with more than 50 lakes, and dominated by craggy peaks such as Gran Zebrù, Cevedale and Ortles – the tallest mountain here is 3,905 m (12,811 ft).

For walkers, the area offers excellent hiking, and access to remote areas populated by ibexes, marmots, chamois and eagles.

The only real population centre in the Lombardy part of the park is at Bormio, which boasts plenty of winter and summer sports facilities, and is a good base from which to explore the area. The town's **Giardino Botanico Alpino Rezia**, a 1 km (half a mile) walk from the centre, displays

some of the species of mountain plants found in the region.

Giardino Botanico Alpino Rezia

♿ 🅐 Via Sertorelli, Loc Rovinaccia, Bormio 🕒 Jun-Sep daily 🔳 ortobotanico italia.it

Brescia

**🅰C2 🚇 ⓘ Via Trieste 1;
030 306 12 00**

Lombardy's second city has a rich artistic heritage, ranging from Roman temples to the triumphalist Mussolini-era architecture of Piazza Vittoriale. The major sights include the Roman ruins around Piazza del Foro, consisting of the **Tempio Capitolino** (a temple incorporating the Museo di Santa Giulia, Brescia's main gallery) and a theatre. The **Pinacoteca Civica Tosio Martinengo** has masterpieces by Raphael, Lorenzo Lotto and Tintoretto.

The 11th-century **Duomo Vecchio** and 17th-century **Duomo Nuovo** are also star attractions. One of the relics in the Duomo Vecchio is the banner from the *Carroccio*, or sacred ox cart, which served as a symbol for the medieval Lega Lombarda.

Piazza della Loggia, where the market is held, is named after the Renaissance loggia, built in Palladian style. The 18th-century church of San Nazaro e San Celso on Via Bronzoni contains an altarpiece by Titian.

Tempio Capitolino
 🄰 Via Musei 55 🕒 Tue-Sun 🅦 bresciamusei.com

Pinacoteca Civica Tosio Martinengo
🄰 Via Musei 81/b 🄲 030 297 78 33 🕒 2–5:30pm Tue-Fri, 11am–6pm Sat & Sun

Duomo Vecchio & Nuovo
🄰 Piazza Paolo VI 🄲 030 42 714 🕒 9am–noon & 3–6pm daily

Mantua

🅰C2 🚇 ⓘ Piazza Andrea Mantegna 6; www.turismo. mantova.it

Mantua (Mantova in Italian) is a striking place of fine squares and aristocratic architecture, bordered on three sides by lakes formed by the River Mincio. The climate can be humid as a consequence, but the city more than makes up for it with its cultural history: it was the birthplace of the poet Virgil and the playground of the Gonzaga dukes for three centuries. Mantua was also the refuge where Shakespeare sent Romeo into exile from Verona, and the setting for Verdi's opera *Rigoletto*. These links are all celebrated in street names, signposts and monuments around the town. The theatrical connections are enhanced by the 18th-century Teatro Accademico Bibiena, on Via Accademia, which Mozart's father claimed was the finest he had ever seen.

The historic centre of Mantua is focused on three attractive main squares: Piazza delle Erbe; Piazza Broletto, named after the 13th-century building adorned with a statue of the poet Virgil; and the cobbled

> **Mantua was also the refuge where Shakespeare sent Romeo into exile from Verona, and the setting for Verdi's opera *Rigoletto*.**

Piazza Sordello. On one side of Piazza Sordello stands the Duomo, with an 18th-century façade and fine interior stuccoes by Giulio Romano (c 1492–1546); on another side is the forbidding façade of the Palazzo Bonacolsi, with its tall prison tower. Piazza delle Erbe is dominated by the Basilica di Sant'Andrea (15th century), designed largely by Leon Battista Alberti, the early Renaissance architect and theorist, and now flanked by an arcade of shops.

The square is also notable for the appealing 11th-century Rotonda di San Lorenzo, and the part-13th-century Palazzo della Ragione with its 15th-century clock tower.

The **Palazzo Ducale,** the vast, 500-room home of the Gonzaga family, covers the northeastern corner of the town and incorporates Castello San Giorgio (a 14th-century fortress), a basilica and the palace proper.

Works of art include a series of 15th-century frescoes by Pisanello, retelling episodes from the Arthurian legends; a large 17th-century portrait by Rubens of the ducal family in the Salone degli Arcieri; and – most absorbing of all – the frescoes by Mantegna in the Camera degli Sposi (1465–74). These portray Lodovico Gonzaga and members of his family and court in all their magnificence. The entire room is decorated with images of people, animals and fantastic landscapes, and completed by a light-hearted trompe-l'oeil ceiling of *putti* and a blue sky. Book ahead if you intend to visit the Camera degli Sposi.

At the other end of town stands the early 16th-century **Palazzo Tè**, built by Giulio Romano for the Gonzaga family as a base from which they could go horse riding. Here, the artworks conspire with the architecture to produce striking effects: in the Sala dei Giganti, for instance, the frescoed Titans seem to be tearing down the very pillars of the room. Also remarkable is the Sala di Amore e Psiche, decorated with erotic scenes from Apuleius' *Golden Ass* and said to celebrate Federico II's love for his mistress. Other rooms are lavishly painted with horses and signs of the zodiac.

Palazzo Ducale

♦♦ Piazza Sordello 40 8:45am-7:15pm Tue-Sun (last adm: 6pm) Pub hols ducalemantova.org

Palazzo Tè

♦ Viale Tè 13 1-6:30pm Mon, 9am-6:30pm Tue-Sun 25 Dec palazzote.it

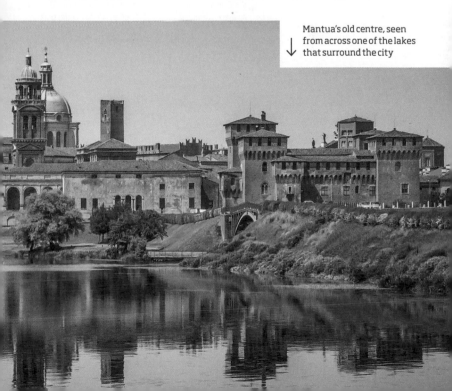

Mantua's old centre, seen from across one of the lakes that surround the city

12

Sabbioneta

C2 **Mantua** **From Mantua** **Piazza d'Armi 1; www.iatsabbioneta.org**

Sabbioneta is the result of a delightful experiment in the theory of Renaissance architecture. It was built by Vespasiano Gonzaga Colonna (1531–91) as an ideal city, and within its hexagonal walls is a perfect gridwork arrangement of streets and buildings designed on a human scale. The finest buildings include the splendid Teatro All'Antica designed by Scamozzi, the Palazzo Ducale, and the frescoed Palazzo del Giardino, which may be visited as part of a tour of the town.

13

Cremona

C2 **FS** **Piazza del Comune 5; www.turismo cremona.it**

Set in the Po Valley, the pretty city of Cremona is a major economic centre for agricultural production in the region. It is also famous for its rich musical heritage, thanks to former inhabitants such as the composer Claudio Monteverdi (1567–1643) and the violin-makers Andrea Amati (1505–77) and Antonio Stradivari, known as Stradivarius (1644–1737). The city's historic centre is dominated by the beautiful Piazza del Comune.

Cremona's main attraction is the exuberant part-Romanesque **Duomo**, and its bell tower – said to be the tallest medieval tower in Italy – known as the **Torrazzo**; the two are linked by a Renaissance loggia. The wonderful façade is dominated by the large 13th-century rose window and by a number of intricate touches, including a small portico with statues of the Virgin and saints. Inside, the Duomo is decorated with magnificent early 16th-century frescoes and Flemish tapestries, as well as paintings in the side chapels. The top of the Torrazzo tower offers sweeping views over the city. Outside the Duomo, note the pulpit where itinerant preachers, including San Bernardino of Siena, would address the crowd.

> **Did You Know?**
>
> Cremona is famous for *torrone*, a nougat eaten at Christmas time.

Next to the Duomo stands an octagonal 12th-century baptistry. On the other side of the piazza you can see the arcades of the late 13th-century Loggia dei Militi, where the town's lords once met. The Loggia is now a war memorial.

The **Palazzo del Comune** (town hall) is the other major building on the square. It was rebuilt in the 1200s.

The **Museo Civico**, in a 16th-century palazzo, houses the Pinacoteca, containing paintings, wood carvings, the cathedral's treasure and ceramics. The **Museo del Violino** has a large display of important historic instruments, including the Stradivari family collection of violins and masterpieces by Amati and Guarnieri. It also tells the history of the

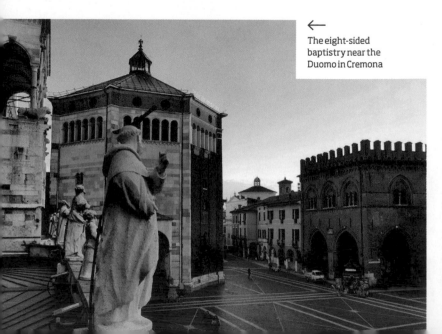

← The eight-sided baptistry near the Duomo in Cremona

violin and the importance of Cremona in the history of violin-making.

On the eastern outskirts of the town, on the road to Casalmaggiore, lies the Renaissance church of San Sigismondo (closed at lunchtime). It was here in a small chapel that Francesco Sforza married Bianca Visconti in 1441. The interior has 16th-century paintings, altarpieces and frescoes by artists of the Cremona school (Campi family, Gatti and Boccaccino).

Duomo & Torrazzo

⊛ ⌂ Piazza del Comune ☎ 0372 4071 🕘 8am-noon & 3:30-7pm Mon-Sat, 8am-noon & 3-7pm Sun

Palazzo del Comune

⌂ Piazza del Comune ☎ 0372 40 72 91 🕘 9am-6pm daily (to 5pm Sun) 🔒 For meetings, pub hols

Museo Civico

⊛ ⌂ Via Dati Ugolani 4 ☎ 0372 40 77 70 🕘 11am-6pm Wed, Thu & Sat, 4-10pm Fri 🔒 Pub hols

Museo del Violino

⊛ ⌂ Piazza Marconi 5 🕘 11am-5pm Wed-Sun 🔒 Pub hols 🌐 museodelviolino.org

Pavia

🅰 B2 🆎🚌 ℹ️ Piazza della Vittoria 21; www.vivipavia.it

During Pavia's golden age, the city was the Lombards' capital, and later witnessed coronations of Charlemagne and Frederick Barbarossa. Even after it lost its status to Milan in 1359, Pavia remained an important city, and great Romanesque churches, tall towers and other monuments still reflect this.

As well as the Charterhouse (Certosa) *(p170)*, there is the sandstone **Basilica di San Michele** off Corso Garibaldi. The building was founded in the 7th century but largely rebuilt in the 12th. Its façade is decorated with symbols and friezes of fantastic animals, and inside there are intricate carvings on the columns.

In the town centre, around Piazza della Vittoria, are such ancient monuments as the medieval Broletto (town hall), with its 16th-century façade, and the **Duomo**, begun in 1488 and worked on in turn by Giovanni Antonio Amadeo, Leonardo and Bramante. The dome was added in the 1880s. The 11th-century tower that stood next to it collapsed suddenly in 1989.

Crossing the river is the Ponte Coperto, a Renaissance covered bridge with a consecrated chapel halfway along it.

Pavia is also the site of one of Europe's oldest (1361) universities, now residing around a series of Neo-Classical courtyards off Strada Nuova. This road continues north to the 14th-century castle, now home to the **Museo Civico**.

Although the 12th-century church of **San Pietro in Ciel d'Oro** no longer boasts the fine gilded ceiling after which it is named, it does still contain a magnificent shrine to St Augustine, whose bones were allegedly brought to Pavia in the 8th century.

Basilica di San Michele

⌂ Piazza S Michele ☎ 0382 477691 🕘 8:30am-7pm Mon-Sat (from 3pm Sun)

Duomo

⌂ Piazza del Duomo ☎ 0382 386511 🕘 9am-noon & 3-7pm daily

Museo Civico

⊛ ⌂ Castello Visconteo, Viale XI Febbraio 35 🌐 museicivici.pavia.it

San Pietro in Ciel d'Oro

⌂ Piazza S Pietro in Ciel d'Oro 🕘 7am-noon & 3-7pm daily

↑ Tall towers in Pavia, reminders of the city's status in ancient times

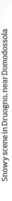

Snowy scene in Druogno, near Domodossola

VALLE D'AOSTA AND PIEDMONT

Piedmont and the neighbouring Valle d'Aosta are – apart from Turin and its cultural splendours – essentially countryside. To the north lie the Alps, with ski resorts such as Courmayeur, and the wild stretches of the Parco Nazionale del Gran Paradiso. To the south lie the vineyard-clad hills around Barolo, and seemingly endless fields of grain and rice, used in the local dish, risotto.

The northwest is also rich in culture. From the 11th century to the 18th, both the verdant Valle d'Aosta and Piedmont were part of the French-speaking principality of Savoy and enjoyed the influences of both sides of the Alpine divide. Even today, French and dialectal variants are still spoken in the remote valleys of Piedmont and in much of the Valle d'Aosta. It was only under Duke Emanuele Filiberto in the 16th century that the region was brought definitively into the Italian sphere of influence; and later it was to play the key role in the Risorgimento, the ambitious movement that united Italy under a king from Piedmont. The vestiges of this history are to be found in the medieval castles of the Valle d'Aosta and the clusters of chapels known as *sacri monti* (sacred mountains) built into the foothills of the Alps. The most impressive architecture in the northwest is undoubtedly to be found in Turin, a much underrated and surprisingly elegant Baroque city which boasts, among other things, one of the best Egyptian museums in the world.

Piedmont is also known for its industry – Fiat in Turin, Olivetti in Ivrea, Ferrero in Alba – but it has not forgotten its agricultural roots, and food and drink play an important role in the life of the region: the hills of southern Piedmont produce many of the great Italian red wines.

VALLE D'AOSTA AND PIEDMONT

Must Sees
1. Parco Nazionale Gran Paradiso
2. Turin

Experience More
3. Domodossola
4. Lake Orta
5. Varallo
6. Aosta
7. Sacra di San Michele
8. Avigliana
9. Vercelli
10. Novara
11. Asti
12. Alba
13. Bossea Caves
14. Garessio
15. Le Langhe
16. Cuneo

VALLE D'AOSTA
AND PIEDMONT

←

 Vineyards near Alba.

② Wine tasting.

③ Tagliatelle with truffle.

④ Local cheeses.

2 DAYS
A Gastronomic Tour of Piedmont

Day 1

Morning After breakfast, head out for a drive in the country, past vineyards and rolling hills. At Ca' del Baio *(Via Ferrere Sottano 33, Treiso)*, sample organic wines such a Barbaresco and Nebbiolo. After the tasting, purchase a bottle to enjoy later.

Afternoon Head to the pretty town of Alba *(p198)*, famed for its white truffles. Truffle season runs from September to January, during which you can join a truffle hunt *(www.italianna.com)*. Alba's food scene is one of the best in Italy; most restaurants offer truffle-based dishes, paired with local wines.

Evening Indulge your taste buds at Osteria del Boccondivino *(Via Mendicità Istruita 14, Bra)*, a member of the Slow Food Movement, a global organization dedicated to food cultures and traditions. Stay at the charming Hotel La Corte Albertina *(Via Amedeo di Savoia 8, Bra)*, and ask for a room with a view.

Day 2

Morning Grab a coffee and a still-warm custard-filled pastry at Bar Pasticceria Converso *(Via Vittorio Emanuele II 199, Bra)*, then drive to Marchesi di Barolo *(Via Roma 1, Barolo)*. This traditional estate has been run by five generations of the same family since 1929. Be sure to book ahead for tastings and a tour of the 16th-century cellars.

Afternoon Make the short drive to the family-run Cascina Meriame farmhouse *(Località Meriame 1, Serralunga d'Alba)*. Here, you'll use traditional recipes and local produce to create classic dishes. After, gather at the table to enjoy the fruits of your labour with some excellent wines, ranging from Barbera d'Alba to Nebbiolo d'Alba and Barolo.

Evening Plan on spending the night at the winery after a sublime dinner at Michelin-starred Guido *(Via Alba 15, Fontanafredda, Serralunga d'Alba)* nearby.

A Good Soak

Soothe aching muscles after a long day's skiing at a spa in the mountains. Sit back in steaming water as you enjoy Alpine scenery, then sweat out toxins in the saunas of the high-altitude spa at Pré-Saint-Didier (*www.qcterme.com*). The Saint Vincent thermal spa east of Aosta similarly offers steam baths, whirlpool tubs, indoor and outdoor pools, saunas and massages (*laviadelleterme.it*).

←

Guest relaxing in the outdoor baths at Pré-Saint-Didier

VALLE D'AOSTA AND PIEDMONT
IN WINTER

Fringed by the snowy Alps, the northwestern regions of Valle d'Aosta and Piedmont are a winter playground, with skiing, snowboarding, ice-skating and snowshoeing on offer. There's also plenty to delight those who prefer more sedate activities, such as lounging in a spa or indulging in a hearty meal.

TOP 5 REGIONAL SKI RESORTS

Cervinia
Ski bunnies come here, then take the lift to Zermatt in Switzerland.

La Thuile
La Thuile's facilities and slopes are ideal for skiers of all abilities.

Champoluc
Italy's best-kept secret is part of the Monterosa Ski area.

Courmayeur
This resort offers on- and off-piste skiing, plus great mountain eats.

Clavière
Clavière is best for beginners and families.

Snowboarding

From soft undulating pistes to challenging, steep corridors, the Alps offer some of the world's best riding for boarders of all abilities. Action-hungry freestylers can show off their latest tricks and enjoy some airborne fun at the region's many snowparks; Sestriere and Montgenèvre are home to two of the best.

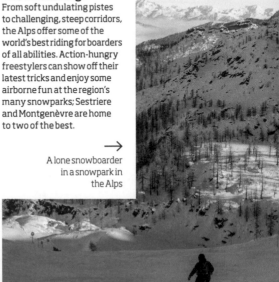

→

A lone snowboarder in a snowpark in the Alps

Hit the Slopes

Whether you love gliding on gentle slopes or mogul skiing on steep black runs, Italy offers pistes in spades. If that's still not enough to get your adrenaline pumping, there's plenty of off-piste and heli-skiing opportunities too, particularly around Mont Blanc – Europe's highest mountain. One of the biggest attractions of skiing in Valle d'Aosta and Piedmont is that you can cross over to France (from La Thuile) or Switzerland (from Cervinia) for a cosy chalet lunch without even having to show your passport.

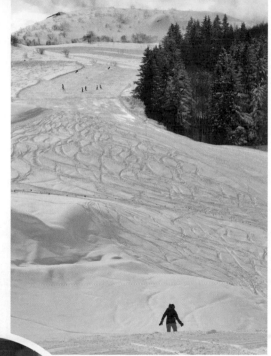

→

A skier at the foot of the slopes in La Thuile

Comfort Food

Piedmont specializes in hearty meat dishes such as *agnolotti* (pasta pockets stuffed with meat), *bollito misto* (boiled meat) and *brasato* (slow-cooked braised beef). *Bagna cauda*, a garlic and anchovy dip, is the Piedmontese alternative to fondue and is sure to warm you up. The cuisine of nearby Valle d'Aosta is equally comforting, with soups and stews, polenta and a fondue of Fontina, a local cheese.

←

Some *agnolotti* pasta, filled with a delicious mix of cheese and vegetables

Après It All

A skiing holiday is not just the time spent on the slopes. With bouji bars lining pedestrianized Via Roma, the resort at Courmayeur is the perfect spot to sip a cocktail by the fire after a day of skiing. Attracting a younger crowd, Sauze d'Oulx has a more laid-back approach, with many après-ski venues. In Sestriere and Bardonecchia, the action kicks off on the weekends.

→

Visitors enjoying an après-ski in Cervinia

1

PARCO NAZIONALE GRAN PARADISO

A1 Piedmont and Valle d'Aosta **FS** Aosta & Pont Canavese From Aosta or Pont Canavese to the different valleys **i** Parco Nazionale del Gran Paradiso visitor centre, Villaggio Minatori; www.pngp.it

A breathtaking wilderness of dramatic mountains and lush meadows, the Gran Paradiso is Italy's foremost national park, created in 1922 from part of a former royal hunting reserve of the House of Savoy.

The park is mainly a summer resort for walkers due to its unspoiled scenery, rare wildlife and unusual Alpine flowers, though there is also cross-country skiing during the winter months. It is home to the endangered ibex, as well as numerous chamois, marmots, ptarmigans and golden eagles. One of the main towns in the park is Cogne, beyond which is the hamlet of Lillaz. From here it is possible to walk through

←

Giardino Botanico Alpino
Paradisia at Valnontey

←

Bridge over a torrent in Cogne, set against the picturesque backdrop of the Aosta Valley

> **It is possible to walk through a stone garden - an open-air museum explaining the rocks in the area - and up to the Cascata di Lillaz, a fantastic waterfall.**

→

Dramatic rocky scenery surrounding the waterfall near the hamlet of Lillaz

a stone garden – an open-air museum explaining the rocks in the area – and up to the Cascata di Lillaz, a fantastic waterfall. At Valnontey, the other main town in the park, is the **Giardino Botanico Alpino Paradisia**, an Alpine botanical garden with a network of paths and grassy slopes set against the craggy backdrop of the mountains. Other highlights include the Castello di Aymavilles, an 18th-century castle framed by medieval corner towers, and the Val di Rhêmes Notre Dame, a broad valley offering magnificent scenery.

Giardino Botanico Alpino Paradisia
⌂ Frazione Valnontey 📞 0165 749 264
🕐 10am–5:30pm daily

IBEX

The endangered Alpine ibex is a species of wild goat that lives largely above the tree line of the Parco Nazionale Gran Paradiso. Ibexes tend to live in herds of around 10 to 20 individuals. The males, identifiable by their long curved horns, only join with female herds during breeding season, which starts in late autumn. Groups are often seen around Col Lauson at dawn and dusk, and also around Pont. Sightings are particularly common during the summer months.

②

TURIN

 A2 ✈ **Caselle 15 km (9 miles) N** 🚆 **Porta Nuova, Piazza Carlo Felice; Porta Susa, Piazza XVIII Dicembre** 🚌 **Corso Vittorio Emanuele II 131** ℹ️ **Piazza Castello/Via Garibaldi; www.turismotorino.org**

Mention Turin (Torino) and most people will think of industry and prosperity. It is certainly an economic powerhouse but it is also a town of grace and charm, with the Alps in the background, rolling hills close to the city centre, the River Po running through it, long tree-lined streets of Baroque architecture, elegant arcades of shops and excellent museums. Turin is also, of course, home to the famous Turin Shroud, the Fiat car company and the Juventus football team.

①

Duomo

🏛 **Via XX Settembre 87/ Piazza San Giovanni**
📞 **011 436 15 40** ⏰ **Daily**
🕐 **12:30–3pm**

The cathedral, built between 1491 and 1498 and dedicated to St John the Baptist, is the only example of Renaissance architecture in Turin. The sober square bell tower, which predates the rest of the church by 20 years, stands in refreshing contrast to Turin's sumptuous Baroque buildings; its top was designed by Filippo Juvarra in 1720. Inside, the Duomo is heavy with statuary and paintings. On the right side of the church is the Cappella della Sacra Sindone (Chapel of the Holy Shroud), which is incorporated into the Palazzo Reale (p193). The chapel is a remarkable feat, designed by Guarino Guarini (1624–83), with an extraordinary mesh-like cupola; the exterior is equally eccentric.

②

Palazzo Madama

🏛 **Piazza Castello 10**
⏰ **noon–7pm Thu & Fri, 10am–7pm Sat & Sun; last adm: 1 hour before closing**
🌐 **palazzo madamatorino.it**

Turin's main square once featured a medieval castle, which incorporated elements of the original Roman city walls. The castle was later enlarged and remodelled, and a new façade by Filippo Juvarra was added at the request of a royal widow in the 18th century. The castle was renamed Palazzo Madama and sits in the centre of the square with a stately façade. The interior, with its grand staircase and first floor, both designed by Juvarra, houses the Museo Civico d'Arte Antica.

This collection contains numerous treasures ranging from the Graeco-Roman era to the 19th century. The display includes *Portrait of an Unknown Man* by Antonello da Messina (15th-century) and reproductions of the Duc de Berry's Book of Hours, dating from around 1420. Furniture, glass, jewellery and textiles are also on display.

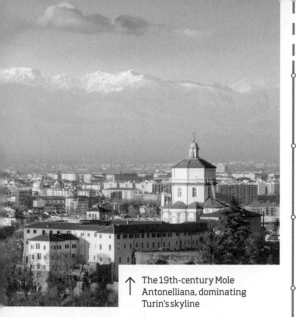

↑ The 19th-century Mole Antonelliana, dominating Turin's skyline

The map legend markers are:
- (4) Musei Reali Torino
- (1) Duomo
- (10) Palazzo Reale
- Armeria Reale / Giardini Reali
- (2) Palazzo Madama
- Teatro Regio
- (5) Palazzo Carignano
- (3) Museo Egizio
- (8) Piazza San Carlo
- (9) Mole Antonelliana/Museo del Cinema
- (6) Parco del Valentino
- Stazione Porta Nuova

↓ (7) Pinacoteca Giovanni e Marella Agnelli 3.5km (2 miles)

The sober square bell tower, which predates the rest of the church by 20 years, stands in refreshing contrast to Turin's sumptuous Baroque buildings.

Timeline

1st century BC
Turin is settled by the Romans

15th century
▷ University of Turin is established

1536
▷ Emanuele Filiberto of Savoy moves his capital to Turin

1861–5
Turin becomes the first capital of the newly unified Italy

1899
▷ The Agnelli family creates the car company Fiat (Fabbrica Italiana Automobili Torino)

1993
▷ Turin football team Juventus wins the UEFA cup for the third time

↑ Palazzo Madama, home to the Museo Civico d'Arte Antica

③

Museo Egizio

🏛 **Via Accademia delle Scienze 6** ⏰ **9am–2pm Mon, 9am–6:30pm Tue–Sun** 🌐 **museoegizio.it**

Turin owes its magnificent Egyptian Museum to the collection of Piedmont-born Bernardo Drovetti, who was stationed in Egypt as French Consul General at the time of the Napoleonic Wars. The items on display are arranged in chronological order, from 4000 BC to AD 700.

The ground floor hosts statues in rooms decorated by the Oscar-winning set designer Dante Ferretti, plus the reconstruction of the 15th-century-BC Rock Temple of Ellesija.

On the first floor is the Coffin Gallery, featuring very fine coffins, such as the 14th-century-BC Tomb of Kha and Merit, complete with the food, tools and ornaments buried with them for the afterlife.

The Papyrus Room holds a collection of enormous interest to scholars: one document, the Royal Papyrus, lists all the pharaohs up to the 17th dynasty, with their dates. The museum holds three different versions of the Book of the Dead, including the oldest known copy. On the second floor are artifacts from the Old Kingdom to the New Kingdom.

④

Musei Reali Torino

🏛 **Piazzetta Reale 1** ⏰ **9am–7pm Tue–Sun** 🌐 **museireali.beniculturali.it**

The collection of artworks that make up the Galleria Sabauda was originally started in the mid- to late 1400s, and it has been expanded over the centuries by the Savoy family.

The artworks are exhibited on four floors in chronological order, from medieval times to the 1700s, in large, bright rooms with self-explanatory labels and multimedia aids.

Among works of particular interest from the Italian schools are Antonio and Paolo Pollaiolo's 15th-century *Tobias and the Archangel Raphael*, the *Ritratto di Gentiluomo* by Bronzino and a *Madonna con Bambino* by Beato Angelico. Mantegna, Bellini and Veronese are among the other Italian artists represented here. Dutch and Flemish works include important paintings such as Jan Van Eyck's *St Francis* (15th century) and Rembrandt's *Old Man Sleeping* (17th century), as well as several portraits by Van Dyck. The fourth floor hosts the Gualino Collection, which contains Roman archaeological finds, Oriental artworks and a *Venere* (Venus) by Botticelli.

⑤

Palazzo Carignano

🏛 **Via Accademia delle Scienze 5** ⏰ **10am–6pm Tue–Sun (last adm: 5:30pm)** 🌐 **museorisorgimento torino.it**

This Baroque palazzo is not only Guarini's masterpiece; it is arguably the finest building in Turin, with its magnificent brick façade and ornate rotunda. It was built in 1679 for the Carignano family – an offshoot of the main House of Savoy and ancestors of the Italian kings – but came into its own in the 1800s. Italy's first king, Vittorio Emanuele II, was born here in 1820.

The palazzo is now home to the Museo Nazionale del Risorgimento Italiano, which, through paintings and a collection of artifacts, tells the story of Italy's unification. It introduces Mazzini, Cavour and Garibaldi – key figures in the Risorgimento.

⑥

Parco del Valentino

🏛 **Corso Massimo d'Azeglio** 📞 **011 443 17 01/02** ⏰ **Borgo Medioevale: 9am–7pm daily; Castle: 10am–7pm Tue–Sun; Orto Botanico: mid-Apr–mid-Oct: 9am–noon Mon–Fri, 3–7pm Sat, 10am–1pm, 3–7pm Sun**

This park contains the Borgo Medioevale, a complex of medieval buildings that was built for the General Italian exhibition of 1884. The edifices show different constructions and designs, based on traditional regional houses and castles.

The Orto Botanico, beside the castle, is an impressive botanical garden.

← Kha and his wife Merit adoring Osiris, from the Tomb of Kha, Museo Egizio

← Statue of Duke Emanuele Filiberto in the centre of Piazza San Carlo

Cinema Museum, which is widely believed to be the world's tallest museum.

Palazzo Reale/ Polo Reale

⌂ Piazzetta Reale
🕐 9am-7pm Tue–Sun; last adm: 6:30pm
🌐 museireali.beniculturali. it/palazzo-reale/

Behind this palace's austere façade, designed by Amedeo di Castellamonte, lie richly decorated state apartments; the ceilings were painted by Morello, Miel and Seyter in the 17th century. The splendid furnishings date from the 17th to the 19th centuries; they include the Chinese Cabinet, the Alcove Room, the lavish Throne Room, and the Scala delle Forbici, or Scissor Stairs, created by Juvarra in 1720.

Pinacoteca Giovanni e Marella Agnelli

⌂ Lingotto, Via Nizza 230/130 🕐 10am-7pm Tue–Sun (last adm: 6:15pm)
🌐 pinacoteca-agnelli.it

Located on the roof of the former Fiat factory (which has been redesigned by architect Renzo Piano), this museum displays art dating from between the 18th and 20th centuries, including works by Picasso, Matisse and Manet.

Piazza San Carlo

The ensemble of Baroque architecture on this square has earned it the nickname "Turin's drawing room". At its southern end are the twin churches of Santa Cristina and San Carlo; both were built in the 1630s, though the former has a Baroque façade, designed by Juvarra in the 18th century. At the centre of the square stands a 19th-century statue of Duke Emanuele Filiberto. The work, by Carlo Marocchetti, has become an emblem of the city. The Galleria San Federico, in the northwestern corner, is a stylish shopping arcade.

Mole Antonelliana/ Museo del Cinema

⌂ Via Montebello 20
🕐 10am-7pm Wed–Mon; last adm: 1 hour before closing 🌐 museocinema.it

This building is an unmissably tall landmark on Turin's skyline. It looks like a glorified lightning conductor: indeed, in 1953 an electrical storm damaged the top, which was replaced. The 167-m (550-ft) Mole, by Alessandro Antonelli (1798–1888), was meant to be a synagogue. On completion in 1889, the city left it for years without a use before it eventually housed the Risorgimento museum between 1908 and 1938. Today, the building provides panoramic views from its lift and houses the National

---

THE HOLY SHROUD

The most famous – and the most dubious – holy relic of them all is kept in the Duomo. The shroud, said to be the winding-sheet in which Christ was wrapped after His crucifixion, owes its fame to the fact that it bears the imprint of a crucified man.

Pretty Isola San Giulio, sitting in the middle of Lake Orta →

EXPERIENCE MORE

③
Domodossola

 B1 Verbania 🚉🚌
ℹ Piazza Matteotti 24;
www.comune.
domodossola.vb.it

At the centre of this mountain town lies the Piazza Mercato, or market square, framed by attractive arcades and houses from the 15th and 16th centuries. Pretty villages to the north include Crodo, with its cold-water mineral spas, and Baceno, where a 14th- to 16th-century church contains fine frescoes and wood carvings.

④
Lake Orta

 B1

Tiny Lake Orta snakes through mountains and woodlands. Orta San Giulio, a medieval village on a peninsula on the eastern coast, is known for Sacro Monte, a UNESCO-listed place of pilgrimage and worship on a hill overlooking the water. In the centre of the lake, Isola San Giulio, accessible by boat, is home to the 12th-century Basilica di San Giulio. There are good hiking routes around the lake.

⑤
Varallo

 B2 Vercelli 🚉🚌
ℹ Corso Roma 38; www.
atlvalsesiavercelli.it

The small town of Varallo is home to the remarkable **Santa Maria delle Grazie**. This late 15th-century church is notable for its beautiful frescoed wall depicting the *Life of Christ* and *trompe l'oeil* architectural elements, painted by Gaudenzio Ferrari (1484–1546).

A long stairway behind the church climbs up to the Sacro Monte, a religious community built at an altitude of about 610 m (2,000 ft) under the patronage of the Archbishop of Milan, San Carlo Borromeo.

The Basilica dell'Assunta is a riot of Baroque architecture. Dotted around it are over 40 chapels with statues and painted figures positioned in front of frescoed backdrops painted by Gaudenzio Ferrari, Tanzio da Varallo and others.

Santa Maria delle Grazie
🏛 Piazza Ferrari ⏰ Daily
🌐 sacromontedivarallo.com

> ### ALPINE TOWNS
>
> The smaller towns of the Val d'Aosta region are popular with Italians during the summer months for their lakes and cycling paths. Come winter, they draw skiers and snowboarders from around the world. Outside Turin, the town of Cuneo is popular with locals for its pretty medieval centre and proximity to the ski slopes. Similarly, the Alpine villages of Sestriere and Bardonecchia come alive in winter, as do the resorts of Courmayeur and Cervinia. Further off the beaten track is Macugnaga, a small mountain village popular with hikers and mountaineers.

⑥
Aosta

A1 FS 🚌 ℹ️ **Piazza Porta Pretoria 3; www.lovevda.it**

Surrounded by mountains, the town of Aosta combines ancient culture and spectacular scenery. The Romans captured it from the Gauls in 25 BC, and Aosta is still dotted with fine **Roman ruins** built in honour of Emperor Augustus.

In Roman times, entry to Aosta was through the Arch of Augustus, a triumphal arch now marred by a roof added in the 18th century. Ahead stands the Porta Pretoria, its double row of stone arches flanked by a medieval tower. Also worth a look is the 20-m- (65-ft-) high façade of the Roman Theatre. A little to the north is the amphitheatre, although this is almost completely buried apart from three columns. In the old town lies the Roman Forum, or marketplace.

To see the town's later architecture, start with a visit to the **Cattedrale**. This relatively modest shrine to St John the Baptist has a Gothic interior with floor mosaics and finely carved 15th-century choir stalls. Afterwards, head east of the town walls to the medieval church complex of **Sant'Orso**. The interior has 11th-century frescoes and a crypt holding the tomb of St Orso, patron saint of Aosta.

↑ Painted statues in a biblical scene decorating a chapel at the Sacro Monte

Exploring Aosta's surroundings will reward you with more stunning structures. 12 km (7 miles) east, **Castello di Fénis** has a well-preserved interior with frescoes and wooden galleries. To the southeast, the picturesque castle of **Castello di Issogne** has delightful decorative motifs, including a fountain with a centrepiece shaped like a pomegranate tree.

Roman Ruins
🏛️ Piazza Papa Giovanni XXIII (Roman Forum) 🕐 Daily

Cattedrale
⊘ 🏛️ Piazza Papa Giovanni XXIII 📞 0165 40413 🕐 6:30am–noon & 3-7pm daily 🚫 For mass

Sant'Orso
🏛️ Via Sant'Orso 🕐 Daily

EAT

Edera
A favourite among Lake Orta's residents.

B1 🏛️ Via Bersani 15, Orta San Giulio 🌐 ristorante ederaorta.com

€€€

Pizzeria La Campana
Simple, crisp-based pizzas in Orta San Giulio.

B1 🏛️ Via Giovanetti 43, Orta San Giulio 📞 0322 90 211

€€€

Ristorante Antico Agnello
Enjoy dishes such as pasta with rabbit ragout, near Lake Orta.

B1 🏛️ Via Solaroli 5, Miasino 🌐 ristorante anticoagnello.com

€€€

Castello di Fénis
⊘ 🏛️ Fénis 📞 0165 76 42 63 🕐 Daily 🚫 Oct-Mar: Mon

Castello di Issogne
⊘ 🏛️ Issogne 📞 0125 92 93 73 🕐 Daily 🚫 Oct-Mar: Mon

The 14th-century Castello di Fénis, near Aosta ↓

Wooden balcony

Few windows

Massive square tower

Pointed turret

Double row of defensive walls

Battlements

7

Sacra di San Michele

A A2 **Q** Via alla Sacra 14 **Q** From Avigliana & Turin **Q** Mar-Oct: 9:30am-5:30pm daily; Nov-Feb: 9:30am-noon & 2:30-4:30pm Mon-Fri, 9:30am-4:30pm Sat & Sun **W** sacradisan michele.com

This abbey complex is perched halfway up Monte Pirchiriano, at 962 m (3,156 ft). Its monastic community was founded around AD 1000. In its prime, the abbey attracted pilgrims on their way to Rome, and as a result it grew enormously powerful. It was subsequently looted several times, before falling into decline and eventually being suppressed in 1662.

The sanctuary is reached by climbing 154 steep steps hewn out of the rock. At the top of this stairway, known as the Scalone dei Morti (Stairway of the Dead), is the Romanesque Porta dello Zodiaco, a doorway carved with creatures and symbols relating to the signs of the zodiac. The church itself dates from the 12th–13th centuries. The interior houses 15th- and 16th-century paintings and frescoes, and a 16th-century triptych by the Piedmontese artist Defendente Ferrari.

8

Avigliana

A A2 **Q** Turin **FS** **Q** Corso Laghi 389; www.turismo avigliana.it

Perched beside two glacier-fed lakes and encircled by tall mountains, Avigliana looks breathtakingly beautiful. It is overlooked by the ruins of a castle, which was once the home of the Counts of Savoy.

The medieval houses here are largely unspoiled, particularly in the two main piazzas, Santa Maria and Conte Rosso. The church of San Giovanni (13th–14th century) contains early 16th-century paintings by Defendente Ferrari.

9

Vercelli

B B2 **FS** **Q** Viale Garibaldi 96; www.atlvalsesia vercelli.it

Set in a vast plain of paddy fields, Vercelli is the rice capital of Europe. The town also developed its own school of painting in the 1500s. The

Museo Borgogna is the best place to admire the town's Renaissance masterpieces.

The city's main architectural treasure is the 13th-century Basilica di Sant'Andrea, said to be the first example of Italian architecture to be influenced by the Gothic style of northern France – note the vaulted nave and flying buttresses. Overall, however, the Basilica, built from 1219 to 1227, remains a stunning achievement in Romanesque architecture. The façade changes colour halfway up, the blue-grey of the lower part turning to red and white in the twin towers. Off the north side is a 13th-century cloister framed by arcades.

The church of **San Cristoforo** houses frescoes and a fine *Madonna degli Aranci* (both c 1529) by Gaudenzio Ferrari.

Museo Borgogna

Q Via A Borgogna 4/6 **Q** 2:30-5:30pm Tue, Wed & Fri, 1:30-5:30pm Thu, 10am-1pm Sat, 11am-5pm Sun **W** museoborgogna.it

San Cristoforo

Q Via S Cristoforo 5 **C** 0161 25 80 00 **Q** Daily

Novara

A B2 **FS** **🚌** **i** Piazza Martiri della Libertà 3; www. turismonovara.it

Novara's arcaded streets, squares and historic buildings exude a quiet affluence. Many of the main buildings – like the Renaissance courtyard of the Broletto (town hall), with its graceful 15th-century red-brick arcades and covered stairway – stand around Piazza della Repubblica.

Across the piazza is the **Duomo**, rebuilt in around 1865 in Neo-Classical style. It contains Renaissance paintings of the Vercelli school and Flemish tapestries, as well as the remains of an earlier sanctuary on this site: these include the frescoed 12th-century chapel of San Siro and the 15th-century cloisters. The octagonal **Baptistry** next door is painted with medieval scenes of the Apocalypse. The **Museo della Canonica del Duomo**, beside the Duomo, has tombstones and inscriptions from the Roman and early Christian eras.

The forbidding abbey complex of Sacra di San Michele

DOUJA D'OR ASTI

On the second Sunday of September, Asti comes alive with a foodie festival that lasts three days and is said to be one of the truest representations of gastronomic country life in Italy. Farmers and producers from the province serve their best dishes and wines, including polenta, truffles, roasted meats and pastas. It's one of the region's most popular festivals, so it's advisable to book accommodation early.

A few streets away stands the **Basilica di San Gaudenzio**. It is crowned by an elongated four-tiered dome and spire. Designed by Alessandro Antonelli, it is reminiscent of his Mole Antonelliana in Turin *(p193)*. At the top of the spire, which is 121 m (400 ft) high, is a statue of San Gaudenzio himself. Inside, the late 16th-century church contains a fine collection of Renaissance and Baroque paintings by artists from Piedmont. These include a notable 17th-century battle scene by Tanzio da Varallo and a 16th-century altarpiece by Gaudenzio Ferrari.

Duomo & Baptistry
A Piazza della Repubblica **📞** 0321 66 16 35 **🕐** 7:30am-noon & 3-6pm daily

Museo della Canonica del Duomo
A Vicolo della Canonica 9 **🕐** 9am-6pm daily **🔒** Aug **🌐** museiduomonovara.it

Basilica di San Gaudenzio
A Via S Gaudenzio 22 **📞** 0321 62 98 94 **🕐** 8am-noon & 2:30-7pm daily

Asti

A B2 **FS** **🚌** **i** Piazza Alfieri 34; www.astiturismo.it

Renowned for its *spumante* (sparkling) wine, Asti is a noble city of medieval towers and elegant churches.

On Piazza Alfieri, a statue commemorates the local poet

↑ A bust of the 18th-century poet Vittorio Alfieri, born in Asti

and dramatist Vittorio Alfieri (1749–1803). Corso Alfieri runs the entire length of the old city centre. At its eastern end stands the 15th-century church of San Pietro in Consavia, with its terracotta decoration, 17th-century frescoes and attractive cloister. Beside it is the circular Romanesque Baptistry dating from the 10th to the 12th centuries.

West of Piazza Alfieri is the Collegiata di San Secondo (13th–15th century), which houses a Renaissance polyptych by Gandolfino d'Asti and 15th-century frescoes. The area around the western section of Corso Alfieri contains a few of the medieval towers for which the town was once famous. The nearby 14th-century Gothic Duomo holds 18th-century frescoes, and two 12th- to 13th-century carvings on the west corner of the transept.

12
Alba

A2 ◻ **Comune Cuneo**
ℹ **Piazza Risorgimento 2;**
www.langheroero.it

Piedmont's gastronomic capital, Alba is the home of Ferrero, Italy's most famous chocolate export, and of the precious white truffle. Grape lovers come to the region for the excellent Barbera d'Alba and Barolo wines. The town itself is charming, with cobbled streets leading to medieval buildings and palaces. The main drag of Via Cavour takes visitors to Piazza del Duomo, and the striking 11th-century Gothic Cathedral of San Lorenzo. From there, many choose to climb the Sineo, Bonino and Artesiano towers, with spectacular views over the city. Via Vittorio Emanuele snakes past local restaurants and cafés before arriving at the 15th-century Do House on Via Calissano, decorated with imprinted terracotta friezes.

Some excellent artwork can be found in the city, namely at the town hall, where the Caravaggio-style *Piccolo Concerto* by Mattia Preti stands, as well as a spectacular altarpiece by the avant-garde artist Pinot Gallizio. In nearby Piazza Savona, restaurants and bars do a roaring trade at lunch and in the evening, when locals gather for a pre-dinner cocktail under the arches.

13
Bossea Caves

A2 ◻ **Località Bossea,**
Comune Frabosa Soprana
FS **Mondovì** 🚌 **From**
Mondovì ◷ **Daily for**
guided tours only
W **grottadibossea.com**

Some 25 km (16 miles) south of Mondovì, near the end of a scenic route that follows the valley of the Torrente Corsaglia up into the Maritime Alps, are the caves of Bossea, some of the finest in Italy. The series of caves contains remarkable stalactite columns and shapes that have formed over many hundreds of thousands of years. Guided tours lead through different chambers – some of them surprisingly vast – following the underground rivers and lakes. The fascinating skeleton of a prehistoric bear

TRUFFLES

Alba's white truffle is among the world's most valuable fungi, often selling for thousands of euros at auction. These truffles are foraged in the woods around Alba, with dogs trained to sniff them out. The town's biggest event is the annual White Truffle Fair (October–November).

called *Ursus spelaeus*, which was discovered here, is also on display.

Bring a sweater – the temperature rarely rises above 9°C (50°F).

14
Garessio

A3 ◻ **Comune Cuneo**
FS 🚌 ℹ **Corso Statuto 1;**
www.garessio.net

One of the most attractive resorts of the Maritime Alps, Garessio is little more than a sprinkling of houses spread out over the hills, surrounded by woods of chestnut trees. It is also a very popular spa destination.

According to legend, the waters here have miraculous powers: in about AD 980 an octogenarian nobleman found

↑ Low sun in an autumnal landscape in the hills of Le Langhe

instant relief from his circulatory problems by drinking the mineral-rich water. Since then, the waters have been drunk for their remedial properties – linked in particular with the relief of diuretic and digestive problems – and for their refreshing taste.

The town of Ormea, 12 km (7 miles) southwest, is known for its ruined 11th-century castle, its church with late 14th-century Gothic frescoes and its attractive houses.

Le Langhe

 A2

Piedmont's Langhe hills are best known for their wines, cheese and white truffles, making it a gastronome's paradise. The region is listed by UNESCO as a World Heritage Site, thanks to unique winemaking traditions that combine historical methods with modern machinery. Hiking is popular here, thanks

←

The red rooftops of the town of Alba, famous for its truffles

to Le Langhe's rolling hills, topped with medieval towns such as Alba, Serralunga, Morra and Verduno.

16

Cuneo

A2 FS 🚌 ℹ Via Carlo Pascal 7; www.cuneo holiday.com

Cuneo in Italian means "wedge-shaped", and this perfectly describes the sliver of land that this town occupies at the confluence of two rivers, the Gesso and the Stura di Demonte. In early November the town hosts the regional cheese fair, with unusual local cheese varieties.

Cuneo centres on a large square, Piazza Galimberti, with its old arcades, where traders come to hawk their wares every Tuesday. Much of the town was rebuilt in the 18th and 19th centuries, providing Cuneo with wide, tree-lined boulevards, though the impressive viaduct that takes the railway line into town dates from the 1930s. The 18th-century church of Santa Croce has a pretty concave façade, designed by Francesco Gallo.

EAT

Restaurant Larossa
Expect a new spin on Piedmontese cuisine, including truffles, at this Alba restaurant.

📍 Via Giacomo Alberione 10d, Alba 🌐 ristorante larossa.it

€€€

Osteria dei Sognatori
Head to this Alba spot for roasted and stewed meats, fresh vegetables and truffle pasta.

📍 Via Macrino 8, Alba 📞 333 712 4121

€€€

La Piola
A small, buzzy bistro with a weekly changing menu of dishes made from local Alba produce. Truffles regularly feature in the fare.

📍 Piazza Risorgimento 4, Alba 🌐 lapiola-alba.it

€€€

LIGURIA

Backed by steep hillsides glittering with olive trees, Liguria looks out over the Tyrrhenian Sea. For centuries maritime trade was a mainstay, bringing sugar, salt and fish – the flavours of the region's cuisine – to the coast, along with prosperity. West of the bustling city of Genoa are sandy beaches, while the southeast offers walks between picturesque Cinque Terre fishing villages.

Genoa has a long history as a seafaring power, achieving greatness first as a trading post with ancient Greece and Phoenicia and, later, as the capital of a small commercial empire that at one stage eclipsed even Venice. The great sea admiral Andrea Doria came from Genoa, as did the 15th-century explorer Christopher Columbus.

Genoa's rise began in the 12th century, when it succeeded in beating the Saracen pirates that plagued the Ligurian coast. Thereafter, the maritime republic prospered, profiting from the Crusades to set up trading posts in the Middle East and marshalling its naval might to humble its rivals. The golden age lasted from the 16th to the mid-17th century. Factionalism among the ruling aristocracy and foreign conquest, by the French in 1668 and the Austrians in 1734, led to the region's decline. It was only in the early 19th century, with unification fervour spreading thanks to native son Giuseppe Mazzini and the revolutionary Garibaldi, that Liguria recaptured a glimpse of its former prominence.

Today, sheltered by the steep slopes that rise from the sea, faded, elegant mansions lie along the coast, particularly in Sanremo, where aristocrats came to spend the winter at the end of the 19th century.

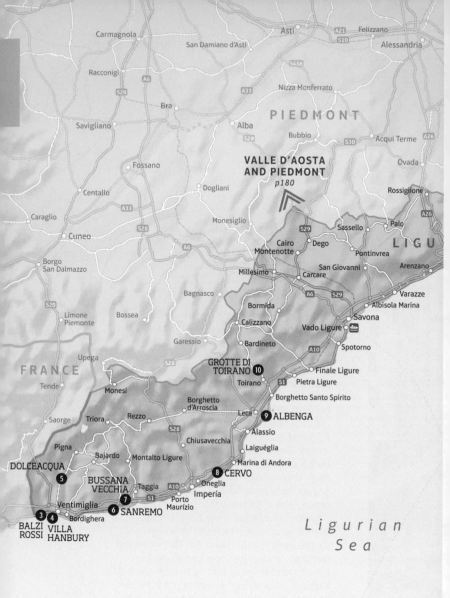

Carmagnola
Asti
Felizzano
San Damiano d'Asti
Alessandria
Racconigi
Nizza Monferrato
Savigliano
PIEDMONT
Bra
Acqui Terme
Alba
Bubbio
Ovada
VALLE D'AOSTA
AND PIEDMONT
Fossano
Dogliani
p180
Rossiglione
Centallo
Palo
Monesiglio
Sassello
LIGU
Caraglio
Cairo
Dego
Pontinvrea
Montenotte
San Giovanni
Arenzano
Cuneo
Borgo
San Dalmazzo
Millesimo
Carcare
Varazze
Bagnasco
A6
Albisola Marina
Bormida
Savona
Limone
Piemonte
Bossea
Calizzano
Vado Ligure
Garessio
Bardineto
Spotorno
Upega
FRANCE
GROTTE DI
TOIRANO
Finale Ligure
Tende
Toirano
Pietra Ligure
Monesi
Borghetto Santo Spirito
Borghetto
d'Arroscia
Saorge
Triora
Rezzo
Leca
ALBENGA
Pigna
Chiusavecchia
Alassio
Bajardo
Montalto Ligure
Laiguéglia
DOLCEACQUA
Marina di Andora
BUSSANA
VECCHIA
CERVO
Ventimiglia
Taggia
Oneglia
Bordighera
Imperia
BALZI
ROSSI
VILLA
HANBURY
SANREMO
Porto
Maurízio

Ligurian
Sea

LIGURIA

↓ Sardinia,
Tunisia

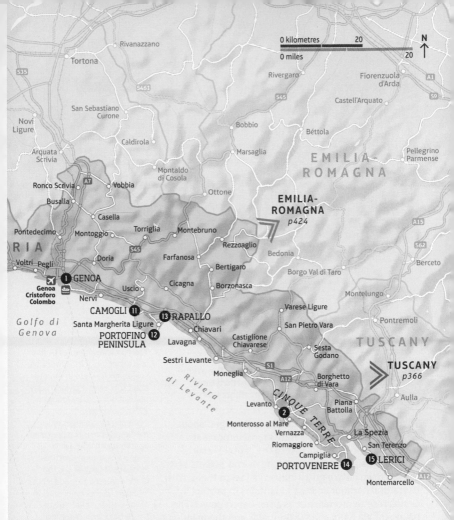

LIGURIA

Must Sees
1 Genoa
2 Cinque Terre

Experience More
3 Balzi Rossi
4 Villa Hanbury
5 Dolceacqua
6 Sanremo
7 Bussana Vecchia
8 Cervo
9 Albenga
10 Grotte di Toirano
11 Camogli
12 Portofino Peninsula
13 Rapallo
14 Portovenere
15 Lerici

The impressive fountain on Piazza de Ferrari in the heart of Genoa ↑

①
GENOA

 B2 ✈ **Cristoforo Colombo 6 km (4 miles) W** 🚆 **Stazione Principe, Piazza Acquaverde** ⛴ **Stazione Marittima, Ponte dei Mille** ℹ **Calata Falcone e Borsellino; www.visitgenoa.it**

There is something refreshingly rough-edged about Genoa (Genova in Italian), Italy's most important commercial port. In contrast to the genteel resorts along the neighbouring coast, the narrow streets of the old town have a gritty industrial feel to them. With its natural harbour and the mountains to protect it, Genoa rose to prominence as a sea-based power. The palazzi of Via Balbi and Via Garibaldi, and the paintings and sculptures dotted around the city in churches and museums, are among the finest in northwestern Italy.

① ⊘
San Lorenzo (Duomo)

🏛 **Piazza San Lorenzo** 📞 **010 26 57 86** 🕐 **Daily**

The Duomo, with its black-and-white-striped exterior, blends many architectural styles, from the 12th-century Romanesque side portal of San Giovanni to the Baroque touches of some of its chapels.

The most sumptuous of the chapels is dedicated to St John the Baptist, patron saint of the city; it includes a 13th-century sarcophagus that once held the venerated saint's relics.

Steps lead down from the sacristy to the **Museo del Tesoro di San Lorenzo**. It houses such treasures as a glass dish said to have been used at the Last Supper, and the plate on which the head of John the Baptist was allegedly served up to Salome.

Museo del Tesoro di San Lorenzo

📞 **010 209 18 63** 🕐 **9am-noon & 3-6pm Mon-Sat, 3-6pm Sun**

② ⊘ 🍴 🛍
The Port

The port is the heart of Genoa and the origin of its power as a seafaring city state in the 11th and 12th centuries. A workaday place, it is ringed by roads and 1960s buildings.

Among the vestiges of its medieval glory is the Lanterna lighthouse (restored in 1543) near the Stazione Marittima. Fires would be lit at the top of the Lanterna to guide ships into port. Today, regeneration of the port is in part due to the Renzo Piano-designed conference centre and the Aquarium, one of the largest in Europe. The port is now a lively area, home to shops, bars, restaurants and seasonal events. In summer, there's a swimming pool here, while an ice skating rink is erected in winter.

🔍 HIDDEN GEM
Sant'Andrea

On Via di Porta Soprana you can find a small quad of pretty 12th-century cloisters surrounding a garden. They are all that remain of the convent that once stood here.

- ← Stazione Principe 300 m (330 yd)
- (4) Palazzo Reale
- Palazzo Bianco (5)
- Palazzo Tursi
- Santissima Annunziata del Vastato
- (7) Pegli 6 km (4 miles)
- Darsena Ⓜ
- Ponte Morosini
- Staglieno Cemetery (6) ↑ 4 km (2.5 miles)
- PIAZZA VILLA GOFFREDO
- P.TTA CAMPO S. SABINA
- LARGO ZECCA
- Profumo di Rosa
- San Siro
- Palazzo Rosso
- Gelateria Profumo
- Aquarium
- Ponte Spinola
- The Port (2)
- Ponte Embriaco
- San Giorgio Ⓜ
- PIAZZA DELLE FESTE
- Palazzo S. Giorgio
- PIAZZA CARICAMENTO
- PIAZZA BANCHI
- Le Nuvole
- Santa Maria delle Vigne
- PIAZZETTA CAMBIASO
- CALATA CATTANEO
- San Lorenzo (Duomo) (1)
- Excelsa, Gelaterie Genovesi 2 km (1.2 miles)
- PIAZZA MATTEOTTI
- PIAZZA FERRARI
- S. Ambrogio o del Gesù
- PIAZZA DELLE ERBE
- S. Maria di Castello
- U Gelatu du Caruggiu
- Sant'Agostino (3)
- Sarzano Ⓜ
- Meliá Genova 750 m (800 yd)
- 0 metres 200
- 0 yards 200
- N ↑

(3)

Sant'Agostino

Piazza Sarzano 35

This Gothic church was begun in 1260, but destroyed in World War II. It is now deconsecrated and all that remains of the original building is the Gothic bell tower, decorated with coloured tiles. The monastery was also bombed. What remained were two ruined cloisters – one of which forms the only triangular building in Genoa. The cloisters have been converted into the **Museo di Sant'Agostino**, which houses the city's collection of architectural pieces, some dating back to the Roman era, along with fragments of sculpture and frescoes – all salvaged from Genoa's other destroyed churches. The finest piece is a fragment from the tomb of Margaret of Brabant, who died in 1311. She was the wife of Emperor Henry VII, who invaded Italy in 1310. The sculptures from her tomb were carved by Giovanni Pisano around 1313.

Museo di Sant'Agostino
📞 010 251 12 63 🕐 6 Oct–26 Mar: 9am-7pm Tue-Fri, 10am-7:30pm Sat & Sun; 27 Mar-5 Oct: 9am-6:30pm Tue-Fri, 9:30am-6:30pm Sat & Sun 🚫 Pub hols

EAT

Here are the best *gelaterie* in Genoa.

Gelateria Profumo

The decor is old-fashioned and so are the flavours but that's part of the magic. Make sure you try the pistachio and *crema* flavours.

 Vico Superiore del Ferro 14 🕒 Sun & Mon

€€€

Profumo di Rosa

At this ice-cream shop, Rosa prepares all the *gelato* herself. *Fragola* (strawberry) is the most popular flavour.

 Via Cairoli 13 🕒 Sun & Mon

€€€

Excelsa

This *gelateria* does *gelato* in tiny dessert cups, with interesting flavour combinations such as salted caramel and peanuts.

 Via Oreste de Gaspari 12-14 🕒 Mon am

€€€

U Gelatu du Caruggiu

Whipped cream and nuts will be added to every order here.

 Via di San Bernardo 91 🕒 Mon

€€€

Gelaterie Genovesi

Sorbets are the best pick here: choose from lemon, strawberry, raspberry or chocolate.

 Corso Sardegna 1 🕒 Mon

€€€

④ 🏛

Palazzo Reale

📍 Via Balbi 10 🕒 10am-7pm Thu & Fri, (from 10:30am Sat & Sun); last adm: 30 mins before closing 🕒 1 Jan, 25 Dec 🌐 palazzoreale genova.beniculturali.it

Used by members of the House of Savoy royal family from the 17th century onwards, this austere-looking residence has a highly ornate Rococo interior – most notably in its ballroom and its Hall of Mirrors. Among the collection of old master paintings is a *Crucifixion* by Van Dyck. The pretty garden, which slopes down towards the old port, includes an intriguing cobble-stone mosaic around the central fountain, depicting houses and animals.

Opposite the palace is the old university (1634), which was designed by Bartolomeo Bianco, as was much of Via Balbi. The large building brilliantly overcomes Genoa's hilly topography, and is constructed on four levels.

⑤ 🏛

Palazzo Bianco

📍 Via Garibaldi 11 📞 010 557 21 93 🕒 10am-2pm Tue-Thu (to 6pm Fri-Sun) 🕒 25 Dec

The Palazzo Bianco is situated on the most beautiful street in Genoa, Via Garibaldi, where there are numerous fine 16th-century mansions and palazzi. It houses the city's best collection of paintings, including some wonderful works by Filippino Lippi, Veronese and Caravaggio, as well as pieces by Dutch and Flemish masters Rubens, Van Dyck and Memling. Paintings by local Genoese artists such as Luca Cambiaso, Bernardo Strozzi and Domenico Piola are also on display. At No. 9 Via Garibaldi, **Palazzo Tursi** hosts the Lord Mayor's boardrooms, as well as an extension of the Palazzo Bianco Gallery. Across the street in the **Palazzo Rosso** is another great art collection, featuring

CHRISTOPHER COLUMBUS IN GENOA

The name of Cristoforo Colombo (c 1451–1506) - or Christopher Columbus, as English speakers know the explorer who first sailed from Europe to the Americas - is in evidence all over Genoa. A statue of Columbus greets those emerging into Piazza Acquaverde from Porta Principe railway station and various public buildings bear his name. In 17th-century Palazzo Belimbau, atop the old city walls, is a series of frescoes by the local artist Tavarone celebrating the explorer's life, and three of his letters are in the Sala del Sindaco in Palazzo Tursi (the city hall) on Via Garibaldi. Despite his frequent appearance, it is not certain whether Columbus was born in Genoa, in Savona, 15 km (9 miles) to the west, or outside Italy. However, city registers mention his father and various family homes within the city. The small ivy-clad house close to Porta Soprana may have been his childhood home.

works by Caravaggio and Dürer, as well as ceramics and furniture.

Palazzo Tursi

♿ 📞 010 557 21 93 🕐 10am–2pm Tue–Thu (to 6pm Fri–Sun)

Palazzo Rosso

♿ 📞 010 275 91 85 🕐 10am–2pm Tue–Thu (to 6pm Fri–Sun)

Staglieno Cemetery

🏠 Piazzale Resasco 📞 010 557 64 00 🕐 7:30am–5pm daily 🚫 Pub hols

Established in 1844, this grandiose cemetery is situated just over the hills northeast of Genoa along the Bisagno River, and is so large that it has its own bus system. The cemetery's tombs and monuments make up an eerie city of miniature cathedrals, Art Nouveau palaces and Egyptian temples. Its most famous resident is Giuseppe Mazzini, the Genoese revolutionary who died near Pisa in 1872.

Pegli

Until World War II, the town of Pegli, 6 km (4 miles) west of the city centre, was a popular weekend retreat for rich Genoese. Now it forms part of the city, but maintains an air of tranquillity thanks mainly

←

Cobblestone mosaic around the fountain at the Palazzo Reale

to its picturesque public parks and its two famous villas: the **Villa Durazzo-Pallavicini** and the **Villa Doria Centurione, Museo Navale**.

The 19th-century Villa Durazzo-Pallavicini houses an archaeological museum relating the pre-Roman history of the Ligurian coast. The villa's 19th-century garden is landscaped with romantic grottoes, pavilions and fountains. It also has a small botanical garden that contains a number of interesting specimens.

The 16th-century Villa Doria Centurione is now a naval history museum celebrating Genoa's glorious maritime past. Among the exhibits on display here are compasses, astrolabes, globes, model ships and a portrait of Columbus, ascribed to Ghirlandaio, probably dating from 1525.

Villa Durazzo-Pallavicini

🏠 Via Pallavicini 13, Pegli 🕐 9:30am–6pm Tue–Fri (from 10am Sat & Sun) 🚫 Nov–Feb 🌐 villadurazzopallavicini.it

Villa Doria Centurione, Museo Navale

🏠 Piazza Bonavino 7, Pegli 📞 010 696 98 85 🕐 9am–1:30pm Tue–Fri (to 6pm Sat, 1pm Sun) 🚫 Pub hols

↑ Pastel-coloured houses perched on the cliffside at Manarola

CINQUE TERRE

 B3 🚌 La Spezia, Lerici & Porto Venere 🚆 To all towns
📶 parconazionale5terre.it

The Cinque Terre are five villages – Monterosso al Mare, Vernazza, Corniglia, Manarola and Riomaggiore – located along the rocky coastline of the Riviera di Levante. Clinging dramatically to the steep cliffs, these villages are linked by an ancient footpath known as the Sentiero Azzurro (Blue Path), which offers some spectacular views of the rocky coastline and terraced vineyards that produce the local dry white wines. The footpath also provides access to secluded beaches. The best way to visit the villages is by boat or by train.

Monterosso al Mare

The largest of the five Cinque Terre villages, Monterosso al Mare, is situated to the northwest and overlooks a wide bay with its own sandy beach. Picturesque streets are lined with lemon trees and olive groves, and lead to a centre divided in two: the new development, Fegina, with bustling hotels and restaurants; and the old village of Monterosso, with narrow cobbled streets and pastel-coloured houses.

Vernazza

The fishing village of Vernazza is a warren of quaint, cobbled streets linked by *arpaie* (steep steps). Founded around 1000 AD, the village straddles a large rocky promontory. The main thoroughfare, Via Roma, stretches from the tiny harbour (Cinque Terre's only natural port) to Piazza Marconi, with plenty of cafés, bars and restaurants dotted along the way. Head further inland and wander up Vernazza's *caruggi* (narrow lanes) for sea views.

③

Corniglia

Perched at the pinnacle of rocky terraces and hemmed in by vineyards, Corniglia seems untouched by the passage of time. From the train station it is best to take a shuttle bus in, or, if you're feeling fit, head for the 377-step stairway that leads to the centre.

④

Manarola

Linked by the famous Via dell'Amore (Lovers' Lane) to Riomaggiore, a 15-minute walk away, Manarola is idyllic in every sense of the word. The oldest village of the

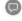 INSIDER TIP
Best Time to Visit the Villages

The best time to visit the Cinque Terre for hiking and swimming is from mid-April to mid-October. Avoid August, when hotel prices skyrocket and the hiking trails and beaches become very crowded.

STAY

Hotel Porto Roca

A charming hotel with an infinity pool, sea views and an excellent on-site restaurant.

⌂ Via Corone 1,
Monterosso al Mare
Ⓦ portoroca.it

€€€

La Malà

A lovely family-run B&B with stunning seaside views.

⌂ Via San Giovanni
Battista 29, Vernazza
Ⓦ lamala.it

€€€

Cinqueterre Residence

One of the more upmarket Cinque Terre hotels. Rooms come with a hot tub and a free minibar.

⌂ Via de Battè 67,
Riomaggiore Ⓦ cinque
terreresidence.it

€€€

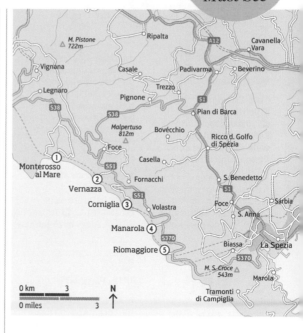

Cinque Terre, it thrives on winemaking, tourism and fishing – which means the seafood restaurants here are some of the best in Italy. The hamlet is divided by a road that was once a stream, Il Ponte, which connects the central church of San Lorenzo with the marina. Close by are hiking trails that cut through pretty vineyards with views down to the sea.

⑤
Riomaggiore

The pretty pastel-coloured houses of Riomaggiore cling to cliffs overlooking curved bays where colourful fishing boats bob on the water. The best known of the Cinque Terre villages, visitors flock here for its tiny beaches, excellent fish restaurants and buzzy bars.

↑ Sunbathers preparing for a swim off the coast of Corniglia

EXPERIENCE MORE

3

Balzi Rossi

A3 **Imperia**
Ventimiglia & Menton
**From Ventimiglia to Ponte
San Luigi, then a 10-min
walk** **soprintendenza.
liguria.beniculturali.it**

An unassuming promontory
is the setting for some of the
most important caves in
northern Italy. Guided tours
lead through the pre-Iron Age
dwellings, which contain
excavated burial sites where
the dead were adorned
with seashells. The **Museo
Nazionale dei Balzi Rossi**
contains tools, weapons
and stone-etched female
figures dating from
100,000 years ago.

**Museo Nazionale dei
Balzi Rossi**
 Via Balzi Rossi 9
0184 38113 **8:30am–
7:30pm Tue–Sun** **Pub hols**

4

Villa Hanbury

A3 **Corso Monte Carlo
43, Località La Mortola**
Ventimiglia **From
Ventimiglia** **Opening
hours vary; see website
for details** **Mon Nov–Feb**
giardinihanbury.com

In 1867, the English botanist
Sir Thomas Hanbury and his
brother bought this seaside
villa on a promontory. They
took full advantage of the
exceptionally mild Ligurian
climate to establish a garden
of exotic plants.

The collection, gathered
by Hanbury on trips to Africa
and Asia, has grown to
number more than 3,000
varieties of tropical flora,
including rubber trees,
palms and wild cacti.

5

Dolceacqua

A3 **Imperia** **FS**
**Via Patrioti Martiri 30;
www.dolceacqua.it**

This pretty village, 8 km
(5 miles) north of Ventimiglia,
is built on either side of the
River Nervia, its two halves
joined by an arching 33-m
(108-ft) medieval stone
bridge. The highlight is the
ruined 12th- to 15th-century
castle, inhabited for a while
in the 16th century by the
powerful Doria family from
Genoa. The two square towers
at the front dominate the
village. The terraced vineyards
in the surrounding hills
produce grapes for a robust
red wine known as Rossese
or vino di Dolceacqua.

6

Sanremo

A3 **Imperia** **FS**
**Corso Garibaldi 1; 0184
58 05 00**

Sanremo is a pleasant
resort of faded elegance.
The composer Tchaikovsky,
Alfred Nobel (the father of
modern explosives) and the
nonsense poet Edward Lear
all stayed in the stuccoed
mansions of the palm-lined
seafront avenue, the Corso
Imperatrice. The focus of the
town, then as now, is the
Casino. A little further down
the Corso stands the ornate
Russian Orthodox church of
San Borilio.

The old town, La Pigna (fir
cone), is a huddle of narrow
lanes with medieval houses
and pastel-coloured shutters.

←

Exotic plants in the elegant
Villa Hanbury gardens,
founded by an English botanist

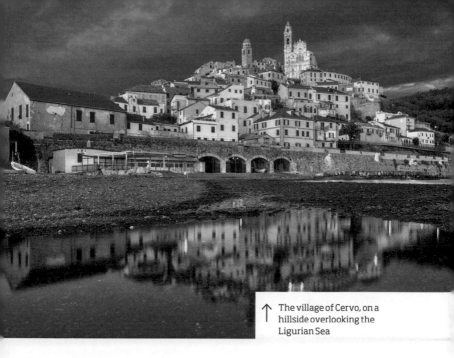

↑ The village of Cervo, on a hillside overlooking the Ligurian Sea

A coach service goes from Sanremo to San Romolo, a small village 786 m (2,579 ft) above sea level that offers beautiful views of the area.

Each February all eyes are locked on the town as the Festival di Sanremo singing competition is broadcast live from Teatro Ariston and watched by millions of fans.

 7

Bussana Vecchia

🅰A3 🅰Imperia, off Sanremo-Arma di Taggia road

Bussana Vecchia is a marvellously atmospheric ghost town. In February 1887 an earthquake shook the village, reducing its Baroque church and surrounding houses to ruins. (One survivor, Giovanni Torre del Merlo, went on to invent the ice-cream cone.)

The town was rebuilt closer to the sea and since then the original village has been taken over by artists, who have restored some interiors, providing a venue for summer concerts and exhibitions.

 8

Cervo

🅰A3 🅰Imperia 🆑🔲
ℹ Piazza Santa Caterina 2; www.cervo.com

Cervo is a seafront village with a narrow complex of streets and houses rising dramatically up from the shingle beach. At the top of the village is the concave Baroque façade of San Giovanni Battista. Chamber orchestra performances are held in front of the church in July and August. It is also known as the *"dei corallini"*, after the coral fishing that once brought prosperity to the local people.

 9

Albenga

🅰A3 🅰Savona 🆑🔲
ℹ Piazza San Michele; www.scoprialbenga.it

Until the Middle Ages, the Roman port of Albium Ingaunum played an important role. The sea, however, gradually moved further out, leaving the town, now called Albenga, stranded on the Centa River. Most striking now is its Romanesque brick architecture, in particular the three 13th-century towers clustered around the cathedral of San Michele. To the south is a 5th-century **Baptistry** with a ten-sided exterior and octagonal interior. Inside, the original 5th-century blue-and-white mosaics of doves represent the 12 Apostles.

Set in the medieval town hall, the **Museo Civico Ingauno** houses local archaeological finds, including pink and white Roman marbles from the 2nd century BC and various 1st-century funerary inscriptions. The main attraction is the *Crucifixion*, a 15th-century fresco by Giovanni Canavesio.

Baptistry
⊘ 🅰Piazza San Michele
📞347 808 58 11 🕐Tue–Sun (Oct–Apr: groups only Sun)
🗓1 Jan, Easter, 25 Dec

Museo Civico Ingauno
🅰Piazza San Michele
🕐9:30am–1pm Mon, Wed & Fri, 9:30am–1pm & 2:20–6pm Tue & Thu, 9:30am–1pm & 3:30–9pm Sat & Sun
🗓1 Jan, Easter, 25 Dec

Fascinating geological formations in the Grotte di Toirano ↑

Grotte di Toirano

A3 ⬛ Via alle Grotte, Toirano 🚌 From Albenga to Borghetto Santo Spirito 🚉 To Borghetto Santo Spirito or Loano 🕘 9am–12:30pm & 2–4:30pm daily 🚫 25 Dec–1 Jan 🌐 toirano grotte.it

Beneath the medieval town of Toirano lies a series of caves housing relics of Paleolithic life dating from 100,000 years ago.

The Grotta di Santa Lucia reveals the full beauty of the yellow and grey stalactites and stalagmites formed here over millennia.

The **Museo Etnografico della Val Varatella**, in the 16th-century stables of the Palazzo del Marchese, has a collection of agricultural and domestic tools.

Museo Etnografico della Val Varatella

⬙ ⬛ Via G Polla, Toirano 📞 0182 98 99 68 🕘 10am–1pm & 3–6pm daily

Camogli

B2 ⬛ Genoa 🚉🚌⛴ 🛈 Via XX Settembre 33; www.camogliturismo.it

Built on a pine-wooded slope, Camogli is a fishing village where seashells adorn the pastel-painted house walls.

Near the pebble beach and fishing port is the medieval Castello della Dragonara.

Camogli celebrates its famous Blessing of the Fish festival on the second Sunday of May. Sardines are fried in a huge pan and distributed free to everyone.

Portofino Peninsula

B2–B3 ⬛ Genoa ⛴ ⛴ Portofino 🛈 Via Roma 35; www.parcoportofino.com

Portofino is Italy's most exclusive resort and harbour town, crammed with the yachts of the wealthy. You can reach it by road (although cars are not allowed into the village), or by boat, from the resort of Santa Margherita Ligure. Above the town are the church of San Giorgio, containing relics said to be those of the dragon-slayer, and a castle.

On the other side of the peninsula, which you have to reach on foot (a 2-hour walk) or by boat, is the **Abbazia di San Fruttuoso**, named after a 3rd-century saint whose followers were shipwrecked here and, according to legend, protected by three lions. The white abbey buildings, set among pines and olive trees, date mostly from the 11th century, although the imposing Torre dei Doria was added some 500 years later.

Experienced divers can sign up for excursions to try to locate the Cristo degli Abissi, a bronze statue of Christ that sits 17-m (55-ft) deep on the sea bed near San Fruttuoso and is said to protect sailors.

Abbazia di San Fruttuoso

 ⬛ San Fruttuoso 📞 0185 77 27 03 🕘 Daily

Rapallo

B2 ⬛ Genoa 🚉🚌⛴ 🛈 Lungomare Vittorio Veneto 38; www.lamia liguria.it

Historians know Rapallo as the place where two post-World War I treaties were signed, while film buffs might recognize it from the 1954 movie *The Barefoot Contessa*, which was shot here. Rapallo was also a haven for writers such as D H Lawrence and Ezra Pound. The palm-lined esplanade ends in a 16th-century castle. A cable car from the centre of the town

Did You Know?

The Grotte di Toirano once provided shelter for cave bears during hibernation.

leads to the 16th-century **Santuario di Montallegro**, which houses a Byzantine icon said to possess miraculous powers.

Santuario di Montallegro

 Montallegro 📞 0185 23 90 00 🕐 Daily 🕐 Noon–2:30pm

---

⑭

Portovenere

🅰B3 🚉 La Spezia 🚌🚢
ℹ️ Piazza Bastreri 7; www.prolocoportovenere.com

Portovenere is one of the most romantic villages on the Ligurian coast, with its cluster of narrow streets lined with pastel-coloured houses. In the upper part of the village is the 12th-century church of San Lorenzo. A sculpture over the doorway here depicts the martyrdom of the saint who was roasted alive on a grill. On the stone promontory that curls out into the sea is the small, black-and-white, 13th-century church of San Pietro.

⑮

Lerici

🅰B3 🚉 La Spezia 🚌🚢
ℹ️ Via Biagini 35; www.lericicoast.it/en/lerici

The popular resort of Lerici sits on the edge of a beautiful bay overlooked by pastel-coloured houses. The forbidding medieval **Castello di Lerici** (13th century) was built by the Pisans and later passed to the Genoese. Today it houses a museum of geopaleontology and hosts art exhibitions and concerts.

The village of San Terenzo, across the bay, is where the poet Percy Bysshe Shelley spent his last years. It was from his home, the Casa Magni, that he set out in 1822 on a voyage to meet Leigh Hunt in Livorno. Tragically, he was shipwrecked near Viareggio and drowned.

Castello di Lerici

📲 Piazza San Giorgio
📞 0187 96 90 42 🕐 Tue–Sun

STAY

Hotel San Terenzo

Rooms here come with balconies and sea views. Guests can rent boats, plus there are ferry links to the Cinque Terre from San Terenzo.

🏠 Via S Biaggini 42, San Terenzo
🌐 hotelsanterenzo.it

€€€

Hotel Pino

Rooms at this stylish B&B, located just a short walk from San Terenzo's beach, have modern decor. Some offer beautiful sea views.

🏠 Via Garibaldi 12, San Terenzo
🌐 hotelpino.it

€€€

↑ The picturesque village of Portovenere, with colourful houses and a busy marina

CENTRAL ITALY

Vineyard-cloaked hills in Tuscany

EXPLORE
CENTRAL ITALY

This section divides central Italy into seven colour-coded sightseeing areas, as shown on the map above. Find out more about each area on the following pages.

VENETO

Rovigo

Po

Reno

Imola

Faenza

Forlì

Cesena

Ravenna

Rimini

San Marino

Pesaro

Fano

Bibbiena

Sansepolcro

Urbino

Arezzo

Città di Castello

Cagli

Ancona

LE MARCHE
p414

Gubbio

UMBRIA
p400

San Severino Marche

Macerata

*Adriatic
Sea*

Lago
Trasimeno

Perugia

Assisi

Foligno

Tevere

Orvieto

Spoleto

Ascoli
Piceno

Montefiascone

Terni

Teramo

Pescara

Viterbo

Nera

Rieti

L'Aquila

LAZIO
p320

ABRUZZO

Avezzano

Sulmona

Termoli

Tivoli

ROME
p222

Palestrina

Frosinone

Cassino

MOLISE

Campobasso

Anzio

Latina

Terracina

0 kilometres   50

0 miles   50

N

GETTING TO KNOW
CENTRAL ITALY

Stretching from the Adriatic to the Tyrrhenian Sea, and from the mists of the Po Valley to the Mediterranean, this is Italy's heartland. Rome and Florence – connected by frequent fast trains – are the main targets, closely followed by the hill towns of Tuscany and Umbria. There are, however, plenty of opportunities to leave the crowds behind, exploring the forgotten villages of Le Marche or walking in the Apennine Mountains.

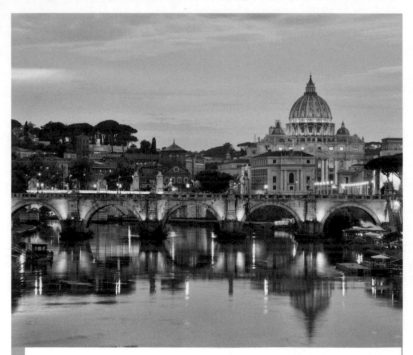

ROME

PAGE 222

Rome is an exuberant, noisy metropolis, where layers of history form an extraordinary stage for everyday life in a contemporary European capital. Yet in many ways, Rome remains a neighbourly city where the life of the community continues alongside its ancient monuments, medieval churches and picturesque piazzas. As well as sightseeing, Rome is a fabulous destination for more hedonistic pursuits, with a beguiling array of designer boutiques, tempting delicatessens, and wonderful places to eat, ranging from pavement cafés to chic, voguish restaurants.

Best for
Stumbling across amazing ancient sites by chance

Home to
The Colosseum and the Vatican

Experience
Opera at the Baths of Caracalla and Mass in St Peter's

PAGE 320

LAZIO

Lying between the Apennines and the Tyrrhenian sea, Lazio is a varied region of volcanic lakes, hot springs, mountains, ravines, vineyards and olive groves. The Etruscans, who flourished in the region in the 7th century BC, left behind cities and cemeteries, while traces of ancient Rome include Emperor Hadrian's magnificent villa at Tivoli, and the ruins of Ostia Antica. Lakes Bracciano, Bolsena and Albano are great for swimming and sailing; wine-lovers can tour the *cantinas* of the Castelli Romani; while the best beaches are on the shores of the Monte Circeo national park.

Best for
Days out and escapes from Rome

Home to
Bomarzo Monster Park, Tivoli and incredible volcanic lakes

Experience
Lunch on the shores of Lake Bracciano

PAGE 332

FLORENCE

Created in a whirlwind of artistic energy that can still be felt more than 500 years later, Florence is an exquisite monument to the Renaissance, the artistic and intellectual reawakening of the 15th century. But it is no museum piece: it is a lively place with bustling shops and markets, spirited street performers and a plethora of tempting *gelaterie*, markets, restaurants and cafés. With a compact historic centre bisected by the river Arno, it is an easy city to explore on foot. The north bank of the river is packed with art and architectural highlights, while to the south lies the more lived-in Oltrarno, with Ponte Vecchio connecting the two.

Best for
Sightseeing on foot, with plenty of coffee breaks

Home to
The Uffizi, the Duomo and Ponte Vecchio

Experience
Panoramic views of the city from San Miniato

→

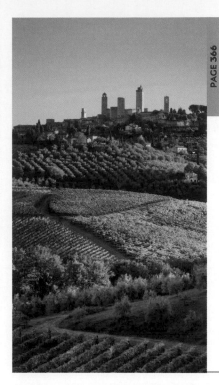

PAGE 366

TUSCANY

Famed for its art, history, wine and evocative landscapes, Tuscany offers the quintessential Italian experience, with its picturesque medieval hill-towns and vine-grooved hills. The towns of Siena, Pisa, Lucca, Cortona and Arezzo contain some of Italy's most familiar art treasures, while villages such as San Gimignano, with its iconic towers, or Pienza, a tiny Renaissance jewel, sit at the heart of the landscapes for which the region is renowned. The main targets for wine-lovers wanting to tour the region's wineries are Chianti, Montalcino and Montepulciano.

Best for
Rural scenery and picturesque hill-towns

Home to
Siena, the Leaning Tower of Pisa and Chianti wine

Experience
Wine-tasting in the ancient cellars of Montepulciano

PAGE 400

UMBRIA

With a profusion of exquisite medieval hill-towns surrounded by gentle pastures and high mountain wilderness, Umbria has been dubbed the "Green Heart of Italy". Famous for its truffles, mushrooms and cured meats, the region is a great destination for foodies. Walkers flock here for landscapes ranging from the eerie wastes of the Piano Grande to the mountainous splendours of Monti Sibillini national park. Assisi – birthplace of Saint Francis – and Spoleto are Umbria's loveliest towns, but there are many other gems, including Orvieto, Gubbio, Spello, Montefalco and Todi.

Best for
Hill-towns, food, country walks

Home to
Assisi, Spoleto and Lake Trasimeno

Experience
Truffle hunting and white-water rafting in the Valnerina

LE MARCHE

PAGE 414

The beach resorts of Le Marche buzz with activity all summer long, but the region's inland treasures remain almost undiscovered. Most of the countryside is a pretty mixture of woods and rolling hills peppered with fascinating little towns and villages. The cultural highlights are found in the walled city of Urbino – home to the Palazzo Ducale, the most famous court in Renaissance Italy – and medieval Ascoli Piceno, while the indented coast of the Conero peninsula provides respite from the uninterrupted sandy beaches that fringe the region's shoreline.

Best for
Driving around remote hill-towns

Home to
Urbino and the Conero peninsula

Experience
Macerata opera festival or coffee spiked with anice liqueur in Ascoli Piceno

PAGE 424

EMILIA-ROMAGNA

Stretching from the Adriatic coast inland across the hills and plains of the Po Valley, Emilia-Romagna marks the watershed between the cold north of the Alps and the hot Mediterranean south. The region is famous for its rich cuisine, and makes the perfect destination for foodies. Bologna, the regional capital, is a thriving medieval university city, while Modena is home to one of Italy's finest Romanesque cathedrals. Ravenna is perhaps Emilia-Romana's most extraordinary town, its churches glittering with mosaics.

Best for
Dining out and packing your suitcase with gastronomic delights to take home

Home to
The mosaics of Ravenna, long sandy beaches and historic towns filled with art

Experience
Mortadella, the original Dolognese sausage

ROME

The Tiber at dusk

VITTORIA

Tevere

Villa Giulia

Villa Ruffo

Santa Maria del Popolo

Il Pincio

PRATI

CAMPO MARZIO

Piazza di Spagna

Vatican Museums

BORGO

VATICAN CITY

Piazza S. Pietro

Castel Sant'Angelo

St Peters

PONTE

Piazza Navona

Pantheon

PIGNA

PARIONE

AROUND PIAZZA NAVONA
p254

Gesù

Campo de' Fiori

THE VATICAN AND TRASTEVERE
p282

Palazzo Farnese

Tevere

Musei Capitolini

Villa Farnesina

ANGELO

Palazzo dei Conservatori

Gianicolo

Piazza S. Apollonia

Piazza Bocca d. Verità

Villa Abamelek

Santa Maria in Trastevere

TRASTEVERE

Villa Sciarra

Santa Sabina

AVENTINE

TESTACCIO

Piazzale Ostiense

EXPLORE
ROME

This section divides Rome into
five sightseeing areas, as shown
above, and an area beyond the
city. Find out more about each
area on the following pages.

ITALY

Galleria
Nazionale d'Arte
Moderna

*Villa
Borghese*

Museo e Galleria
Borghese

LUDOVISI

Trinità dei
Monti

SALLUSTIANO

*Piazza
Barberini*

CASTRO
PRETORIO

*Piazza della
Repubblica*

TREVI

Trevi
Fountain

NORTHEAST ROME
p268

MONTI

Santa Maria
Maggiore

Mercati
Traianei

*Parco di
Traiano*

ESQUILINO

Palazzo
Nuovo

Roman
Forum

*Domus
Aurea*

**THE
ANCIENT
CENTRE**
p238

Colosseum

San
Clemente

LATERAN

*Pza. S. Giovanni
In Laterano*

PALATINE

*Parco
del Celio*

Santo Stefano
Rotondo

San Giovanni
in Laterano

*Parco del
Circo Massimo*

**AVENTINE
AND LATERAN**
p300

*Villa
Celimontana*

RIPA

CELIO

*Piazza
Albania*

*Parco di
Porta Capena*

*Parco
Egerio*

*Parco
San Sebastiano*

SAN
LORENZO

*Cimitero
Monumentale
del Verano*

GARBATELLA

0 metres   800
0 yards   800

N
↑

GETTING TO KNOW
ROME

Rome's *centro storico*, cradled within a great loop of the Tiber River, is a maze of cobbled streets and piazzas studded with fountains, palaces and churches. Peppering the city are the toothy remains of ancient Rome, shaded by green swathes of umbrella pines. Across the river, the dome of St Peter's dominates the horizon, rising high above Vatican City and the mellow façades and intimate piazzas of Trastevere.

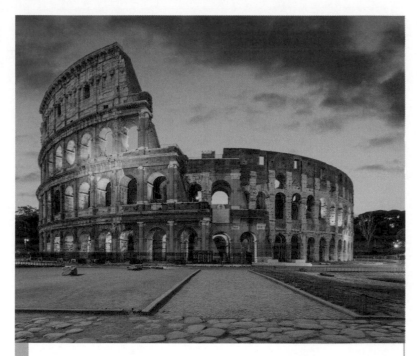

THE ANCIENT CENTRE

PAGE 238

Mussolini's Via dei Fori Imperiali slices above the ruins of the temples and basilicas that once formed the centre of political, commercial and judicial life in ancient Rome *(p41)*. By day, the area is filled with souvenir stands and coachloads of tourists following umbrella-toting guides around the Roman Forum, Colosseum and Capitoline Museums. The Forum is far quieter and more atmospheric at night, when the tour groups have left and the monuments are illuminated. Crowds are easier to avoid at all times in the green, pine-shaded expanses of the Palatine Hill.

Best for
Exploring the fascinating ruins of Ancient Rome

Home to
The Roman Forum, the Palatine and the Colosseum

Experience
Views of the Roman Forum from the terrace of the Caffè Capitolino

AROUND PIAZZA NAVONA

An extravagant Baroque oval dominated by the towering obelisk and cascading waters of Bernini's Four Rivers fountain, Piazza Navona is the social heart of Rome. An outdoor salon fringed with expensive pavement cafés, it is packed morning to night with buskers, mime-artists and street vendors. The tangle of narrow cobbled streets surrounding the square is home to extraordinary churches and palaces, enticing *gelaterie* and a string of busy cafés and restaurants.

Best for
People-watching in Piazza Navona

Home to
The Pantheon and the Gesù

Experience
Gelati from San Crispino or Grom

NORTHEAST ROME

The streets around Piazza di Spagna are studded with designer clothes and shoe boutiques, bijou cosmetics shops, art galleries, antiques shops and upmarket delicatessens. It is an area in which to wander and window-shop between some leisurely sightseeing. Via del Corso is full of chain stores, and at peak shopping times it transforms into a human river. Nearby are the Trevi Fountain, the imposing church of Santa Maria Maggiore, and the trendy Monti district, great for street food and alternative fashion shops.

Best for
Shopping

Home to
Piazza di Spagna, Santa Maria Maggiore and the Trevi Fountain

Experience
Lunch or a drink in Piazza Madonna dei Monti

→

PAGE 282

THE VATICAN AND TRASTEVERE

Home to St Peter's, the Sistine Chapel and the eclectic collections of the Vatican Museums, the Vatican is a must for both pilgrims and art lovers. The surrounding area is full of streets lined with souvenir shops and hawkers flogging Sistine Chapel T-shirts and plaster Pietàs. Nearby are the picturesque and higgledy-piggledy cobbled streets of Trastevere, where Piazza San Cosimato hosts a daily produce market, and shrines to the Madonna still protect the area's piazzas.

Best for
World-famous art and sculpture

Home to
St Peter's, the Vatican Museums and Castel Sant'Angelo

Experience
A Papal Audience on Piazza San Pietro

PAGE 300

AVENTINE AND LATERAN

Rising above the Tiber to the southwest of the Palatine, the twin-peaked Aventine Hill is a lush, leafy residential area with a handful of early Christian churches scattered among its secluded private villas. Although it is in the centre of Rome it is remarkably peaceful. Traditionally a working-class area, the adjacent Lateran retains an unpretentious feel. Its modern avenues open out onto beautiful churches and it is home to the huge Via Sannio clothes and shoes market.

Best for
Strolling through leafy parks

Home to
San Giovanni in Laterano and San Clemente

Experience
The spooky Mithraeum, hidden below the church of San Clemente

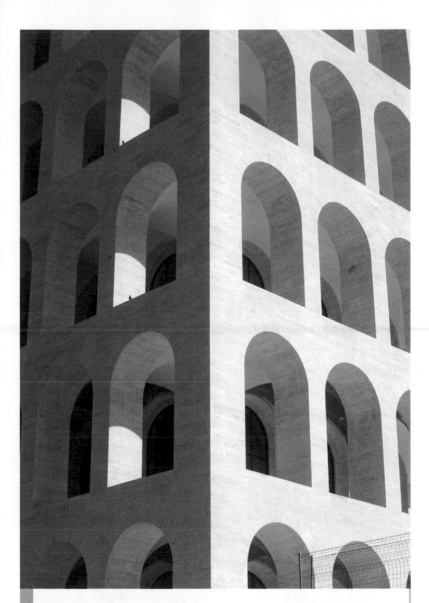

BEYOND THE CENTRE

Rome has a small, compact centre – you can walk across from one side to the other in only a couple of hours – and keen walkers can easily cover some of the city's peripheral sights on foot. Ranging from Roman catacombs to 21st-century MAXXI, and from the sumptuous Villa Borghese estate to the futuristic suburb of EUR, delving outside the centre not only brings you to sights off the beaten tourist track, but into residential neighbourhoods where you can get a real sense of everyday life in Rome.

Best for
Escaping the crowds and discovering Rome's hidden gems

Home to
Villa Giulia, Villa Borghese, MAXXI and EUR

Experience
A classical or jazz concert at the Auditorium Parco della Musica

→

1 The Colosseum

2 Fresco at the
Palazzo Massimo

3 Nuns in Piazza San Pietro

4 Enoteca Ferrara, Trastevere

3 DAYS
A Long Weekend in Rome

Day 1

Morning For an unforgettable experience, get up at dawn to see Piazza San Pietro almost empty, and enter St Peter's *(p286)* along with nuns, priests and pilgrims when it opens at 7am. The spiral steps that wind up to the cupola open at 8am, and having the amazing views to yourself is magical. Speed your entry into the Vatican Museums by booking a slot in advance on the website *(p289)*, and take in the glories of the Cortile della Pigna over breakfast in its café. With twelve museums and 7 km (4 miles) of corridors, there is too much to see in a single visit so select your highlights. Have lunch in the pizzeria outside the Carriage Pavilion.

Afternoon Take a bracing walk up the Janiculum Hill, with its great views over the city, winding down past the Tempietto *(p299)* into Trastevere *(p298)*.

Evening Enjoy a well-earned aperitivo in Piazza Santa Maria in Trastevere, followed by dinner at Enoteca Ferrara *(p297)*.

Day 2

Morning Explore the Colosseum *(p242)*, then walk to the entrance to the Palatine *(p248)* on Via di San Gregorio (which tends to be less busy than the main Forum entrance to the site). Do not miss the Flavian Palace or the surviving section of the Cryptoporticus tunnel. Head down to the Roman Forum, and spot the coins fused to the pavement of the Basilica Aemilia and the chequerboards in the steps of Basilica Julia. Treat yourself to lunch at La Bottega del Caffè, on Piazza Madonna dei Monti.

Afternoon Stroll up past the quirky boutiques of Via dei Serpenti to Trajan's Forum and Markets *(p250)*, an ancient Roman shopping mall, and admire the digitally reconstructed Roman villas below Palazzo Valentini. Afterwards see exquisite frescoes from a country villa belonging to Emperor Augustus's wife, Livia, at the Palazzo Massimo *(p281)*. You can book ahead to see some of the villa's other surviving frescoes in situ on the Palatine.

Evening Reflect on your busy day and collapse over a fine glass of wine at the Trimani II Wine Bar *(Via Cernaia 37/b)*.

Day 3

Morning Start with a leisurely caffè latte and *cornetto* at the Antico Caffè Vitti on pretty Piazza San Lorenzo in Lucina, then head across Piazza del Parlamento to Piazza del Montecitorio, where you can watch the politicians, lobby correspondents and protestors coming and going from the parliament building. Zigzag down to the Pantheon *(p260)*, taking in little Piazza delle Coppelle and Piazza Capranica. See Caravaggio canvases in the church of San Luigi dei Francesi and the courtyard of Sant'Ivo alla Sapienza *(p262)*, then cross Piazza Navona to lunch at the Chiostro Bramante Bistrot *(Arco della Pace 5)*.

Afternoon Enjoy the antiques shops along Via dei Coronari, then meander down Via Giulia to Campo de' Fiori *(p264)*, and into the Jewish Ghetto.

Evening Grab an aperitivo at one of the cafés on Via del Portico d'Ottavia and dinner at Piperno *(Via Monte dè Cenci 9)*.

Coffee

The average Italian visits simple café-bars at least twice a day – for breakfast and after lunch. Around Piazzas Navona, Spagna and Rotonda, ordinary café-bars are scarce, but there is one on almost every street corner elsewhere. Most Italians drink while standing up at the bar. For an authentic coffee experience, try Bar del Cappuccino on Via Arenula 50.

←

Traditional way of drinking coffee, standing at the bar

ROME FOR
FOODIES

There are few more enduring pleasures than lingering over a leisurely al fresco meal in a piazza in the Eternal City. Roman food is tasty, nutritious, simple and extremely varied. Menus tend to be seasonal and food is redolent of aromatic herbs, olive oil, garlic and onion.

INSIDER TIP
Gelato

Legend has it that the art of ice-cream making was brought to Sicily in the 16th century by its medieval Arab rulers who introduced the technique of blending fruit syrups and flower essences with snow taken from the slopes of Mount Etna. Gourmet ice creams made with organic ingredients have taken Rome by storm – try the delicious offerings at San Crispino *gelateria* on Via della Panetteria 42.

Traditional Roman Dishes

Originating in working-class areas such as Testaccio, traditional Roman food is based on cheap cuts of meat and offal and simple pasta dishes such as *cacio e pepe* (pecorino cheese and black pepper). *Carciofi alla giudia* (deep-fried artichokes) is a key delicacy introduced by the Jewish community of the Ghetto.

→

A traditional Roman restaurant on Via Arco di San Calisto in Trastevere

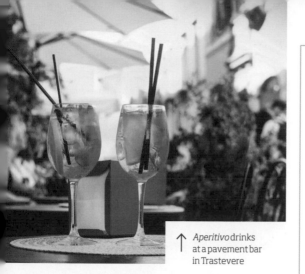

↑ *Aperitivo* drinks at a pavement bar in Trastevere

Aperitivo and Wine Bars

The *aperitivo*, a pre-dinner glass of wine, Aperol or Campari Spritz, served with snacks, is a tradition rooted in northern cities such as Turin and Milan, but is very popular in Rome too. At the very least there will be crisps, olives and peanuts to accompany the drinks, but often there are abundant buffets such as the one in Vin Allegro in Trastevere on Piazza Giuditta Tavani Arquati.

Food to Take Away

Hot takeaway food has been a feature of Italian life since Roman times. Taste hot focaccia dripping with Ligurian olive oil or a slice of pizza fresh from the oven (*pizza a taglio*), topped with anchovies and *puntarelle* (chicory shoots) or courgette flowers and ricotta, available at bakeries. Enjoy aubergine parmigiana (fried aubergines with cheese and tomato sauce) or herby roast chicken and golden-crusted savoury pies at a *rosticceria*.

↑ Antico Forno Roscioli on Via dei Chiavari 34, famous for *pizza a taglio*

EAT

Dine on creative dishes at one of Rome's chic new-wave eateries.

Casa Coppelle

This Franco-Roman restaurant offers a tempting range of dishes. The rack of lamb is a highlight.

🚇 U2 📍 Piazza delle Coppelle 49
🌐 casacoppelle.com

€€€

Bistrot64

One of the most affordable Michelin-starred restaurants in Italy, Bistrot64 specializes in flavours inspired by Italy and Japan.

📍 Via G Calderini 62/64
🌐 bistrot.it

€€€

Modern Rome

The 20th century opened in Rome with the Art Nouveau fantasies of the Coppodè Quarter, followed by Futuristic - even dystopian - EUR, founded by Mussolini *(p319)*. Watch out too for buildings designed by contemporary international architects, such as Renzo Piano's Auditorium Parco della Musica and Zaha Hadid's MAXXI *(p316)*. See ancient sculptures juxtaposed with the turbines of a former power plant at Centrale Montemartini *(p317)*.

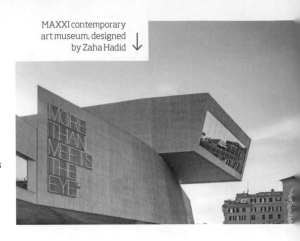

MAXXI contemporary art museum, designed by Zaha Hadid ↓

ROME FOR
ARCHITECTURE

Explore Rome on an incredible journey through the history of Western architecture. Ancient Roman relics are strewn throughout the city cheek-by-jowl with medieval basilicas, Renaissance palaces and extravagant Baroque piazzas, churches and fountains.

Ancient Rome

The architects of Imperial Rome combined the Classical styles of ancient Greece with innovative new forms such as the arch, the vault and the dome. Visit the Pantheon to see the world's largest unreinforced concrete dome. Note the three storeys of Doric, Ionic and Corinthian columns on the Colosseum, imitated in façades of palaces and churches throughout the world.

The Colosseum, a prime example of ↓ ancient architecture

Christian Rome

The first places of worship were simply houses belonging to Christians or sites of martyrdoms. Visit San Crisogono *(Piazza Sidney Sonnino)* to see the excavations of a private home that was used as an early Christian church. The first purpose-built churches were based on the Roman basilica, with three naves and an apse. To see Rome's main basilicas, visit St Peter's *(p286)*, San Giovanni in Laterano *(p304)* and Santa Maria Maggiore *(p276)*. More flamboyant Baroque innovations are Sant'Ivo alla Sapienza *(p262)* and San Carlo alle Quattro Fontane *(p279)*, designed by Borromini, and Bernini's Sant' Andrea al Quirinale *(p279)*.

THE LAYERS OF SAN CLEMENTE

Around 200 AD an aristrocrat built a temple to the god Mithras in the central room of his house. In the 4th century the temple and house were filled in, and a church dedicated to Christian martyr San Clemente was built on top. In the 12th century this was filled with rubble to form the foundation for yet another church.

↑ St Peter's, one of the world's most iconic churches

Renaissance and Baroque Rome

Rome is an extravaganza of Baroque piazzas, fountains and stairways, and enticing glimpses of frescoed ceilings through the windows of vast noble palaces. For spectacular views of Rome's buildings and piazzas, take a walk at night to see them lit up in the dark. The interiors of Palazzo Doria Pamphilj *(p266)*, Galleria Borghese *(p314)* and Villa Farnesina *(p296)* give a wonderful taste of glamour.

↑ Baroque Palazzo Doria Pamphilj and its entrance *(inset)*

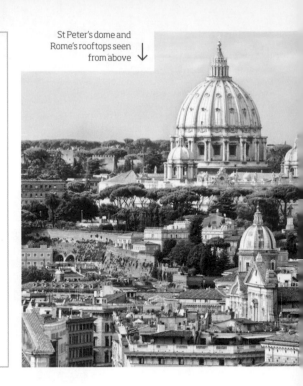

St Peter's dome and Rome's rooftops seen from above ↓

ROME
ON A SHOESTRING

Although expensive, Rome's historic centre is compact, so it can mostly be seen on foot. Ancient sites, piazzas, palace façades and beautiful parks can be enjoyed without spending any money, while the city's churches are free to enter.

Food and Drink

Rome is full of marvellous delicatessens, bakeries and takeaway pizzerias where you can get fabulous food for a fraction of the prices charged in cafés and restaurants. Parks make good locations for picnics. Look out for bars advertising *aperitivo* or "happy hours", where you pay a set price for a drink and can help yourself from an ample buffet. To save money at other times, order and drink at the bar to avoid paying for table service.

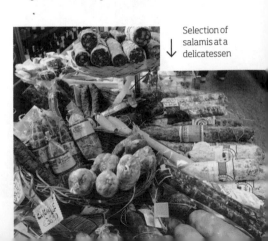

Selection of salamis at a delicatessen ↓

Sights and Views

The Pantheon is the only one of Rome's ancient monuments to which entry is free, thanks to having been converted into a church in the Byzantine era. Many visitors find the Colosseum more impressive from without than within. Entry to the Victor Emmanuel Monument – with some of the best views in Rome – is free, though to see the view from the very top you have to pay a small fee for the lift. There are other great city views from the Pincio Gardens and Janiculum Hill. There is no charge to get close to Trajan's Column – use the zoom on your phone or camera to see details of the marble carving up close. Access to St Peter's is free, allowing you to see famous works such as Michelangelo's *Pietà* and Bernini's Baldacchino.

> 💬 INSIDER TIP
> **Free Entry to Museums**
>
> State and city museums are free for all visitors who are under the age of 18. The Vatican Museums are free for everybody on the last Sunday of every month.

↑ Mosaics of a blue-and-gold-walled heaven in the apse of Santa Prassede

Art

See Michelangelo's muscular *Moses* masterpiece for free at San Pietro in Vincoli. Marvel at magnificent Byzantine mosaics in Santa Prassede. Entering the church's tiny Chapel of St Zeno is akin to walking into a jewel box. Although entry is charged for exhibitions at MAXXI and MACRO, there are usually free video presentations, and large parts of the buildings, such as MACRO Peroni's roof terrace, can be entered for no charge.

↑ MACRO contemporary art gallery, converted from a former Peroni beer factory

ROME:
THE ANCIENT
CENTRE

The Capitol, the southern summit of the Capitoline Hill, was the symbolic centre of the Roman world and home to the city's three most important temples. These were dedicated to the god Jupiter Optimus Maximus, protector of Rome, Minerva, goddess of wisdom and war, and Juno Moneta, a guardian goddess. Below the Capitol lies the Forum, once the focus of political, social, legal and commercial life; the Imperial Fora, built when Rome's population grew; and the Colosseum, the centre of entertainment. Overlooking the Forum is the Palatine Hill, where Romulus is said to have founded Rome in the 8th century BC and where emperors made their home for over 400 years.

This part of the city has always been a study of contrasts. In Roman times the emperors' palaces on the Palatine were located just a stone's throw from the docks where roustabouts heaved goods imported from around the world. Today, the area Is again an enclave of smart houses and greenery, studded with hidden art treasures and some of the world's finest ancient monuments and priceless archaeological finds.

ROME: THE ANCIENT CENTRE

Must Sees
1 The Colosseum
2 Capitoline Hill
3 Roman Forum
4 Palatine

Experience More
5 Trajan's Forum and Markets
6 Capitoline Museums
7 Forum of Augustus
8 Forum of Caesar
9 Arch of Constantine
10 Mamertine Prison
11 Santa Maria in Aracoeli
12 Palazzo Valentini

Eat
1 Caffè Capitolino

Drink
2 American Bar

COLOSSEUM

1 🏛 Ⓜ 🛍

📍 K6 🏛 Piazza del Colosseo 1 🚌 75, 81, 85, 87, 117, 673, 810 🚋 3 to Piazza del Colosseo
🕐 10:30am–approx 1 hour before sunset daily (last adm: 1 hour before closing) 📅 1 Jan, 25 Dec 🌐 coopculture.it

Rome's greatest amphitheatre was commissioned by the Emperor Vespasian in AD 72. Deadly gladiatorial combats and wild animal fights were staged by the emperor and wealthy citizens, largely to gain popularity. Slaughter was on a huge scale: at the inaugural games in AD 80, over 9,000 wild animals were killed. The Colosseum could hold up to 55,000 people, who were seated according to rank.

The Colosseum was built to a practical design, with its 80 arched entrances allowing easy access to the spectators, but it is also a building of great beauty. The drawing here shows how it looked at the time of its opening in AD 80. It was one of several similar amphitheatres built in the Roman Empire – other surviving examples are at El Djem in North Africa, Nîmes and Arles in France, and Verona in northern Italy. Despite being damaged over the years by neglect and theft, the Roman Colosseum remains a majestic sight.

The velarium was a huge awning which shaded spectators from the sun.

↑ An arched corridor in the Colosseum

Stone plundered from the façade during the Renaissance was used to build several palaces and bridges, and also parts of St Peter's.

Timeline

72
◀ Emperor Vespasian begins work on the Colosseum

80
Vespasian's son, Titus, stages the inaugural festival here

404
◀ Gladiatorial combats are banned

442
Building damaged in an earthquake

523
◀ Wild animal fights are banned

1200s
Frangipane family turns Colosseum into a fortress

1312
◀ Emperor Henry VII gives Colosseum to the people of Rome

💬 INSIDER TIP
How to Handle the Colosseum

The quietest time to visit this ever-popular sight is early morning – be sure to arrive at least 30 minutes before the scheduled opening time to avoid the crowds. Be aware that the costumed "gladiators" charge for photos.

→
Illustration of the Colosseum as it was in AD 80

↑ The interior of the Colosseum as it looks today

The podium was a large terrace where the emperor and the wealthy upper classes had their seats.

The vomitorium was the exit used from each numbered section.

Internal corridors were designed to allow the crowds to move freely.

Corinthian columns

Ionic columns

Doric columns

Spectators reached their seats by means of staircases to the various levels of the amphitheatre.

Arched entrances were all numbered to speed up the entry of the vast crowds.

CAPITOLINE HILL

9 H6 **△** Piazza del Campidoglio **🚌** 40, 63, 70, 81, 87 & other routes through Piazza Venezia

One of the seven hills of Rome, the Capitoline Hill was first the fortified centre of ancient Rome and later home to its most important temples. The broad flight of steps leading up the hill and the Piazza del Campidoglio at its head were designed in the 16th century by Michelangelo.

The Piazza del Campidoglio is flanked by Palazzo Nuovo and Palazzo dei Conservatori, which house the Capitoline Museums (p250) with their fine collections of sculpture and paintings. It is well worth walking behind the museums to the Tarpeian Rock, for a superb view of the Forum lying below. At the centre of the piazza is a gilded bronze statue of Marcus Aurelius, the original of which is in the Capitoline Museums. Legend has it that when the last gold leaf flakes off the statue the world will end. Another major highlight of the area is the Victor Emmanuel Monument, which was begun in 1885 and inaugurated in 1911 in honour of Victor Emmanuel II, the first king of unified Italy (p44).

↑ Hall of the Philosophers in Palazzo Nuovo at the Capitoline Museums

→ The imposing Vittorio Emanuele II Monument

Did You Know?

The nearby Roman Ghetto and the trendy Monti district are home to a great selection of cafés and bars.

San Marco has splendid 9th-century mosaics in the apse.

Victor Emmanuel Monument

Santa Maria in Aracoeli

Palazzo Nuovo was made into a public museum in 1734.

Palazzo Senatorio, the splendid Renaissance seat of the city government.

Palazzo dei Conservatori

Palazzo Venezia, once the home of Mussolini, now holds a museum of fine and decorative arts.

The Cordonata, Michelangelo's broad steps, are presided over by the colossal statues of Castor and Pollux.

The Temple of Jupiter

→ Illustrated map of the sights on the Capitoline Hill

The Tarpeian Rock is a cliff from which traitors were believed to have been thrown to their death in ancient Rome.

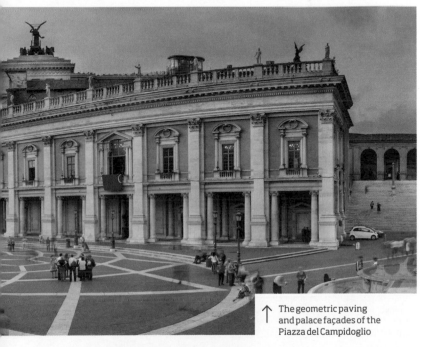

↑ The geometric paving and palace façades of the Piazza del Campidoglio

↑ Visitors exploring the dramatic ruins of the Roman Forum

③ ⊘ Ⓜ 🏛

ROMAN FORUM

📍 J6 🏠 Via della Salara Vecchia 5/6 🚌 85, 87, 117, 175, 186, 810 Ⓜ Colosseo 🚋 3 🕐 10:30am–1 hour before sunset 🚫 1 Jan, 25 Dec 🌐 coopculture.it

Gazing on the picturesque ruins today, you would hardly guess that the Forum was the symbol of civic pride for 1,000 years. Its beginning, more than 3,000 years ago, was as a cemetery for the village on the Palatine Hill. When the marshy land was drained in the 6th century BC, the Forum took on a more central role.

In the early days of the Republic, the Forum was a chaotic place, containing food stalls and brothels as well as temples and the Senate House. By the 2nd century BC, Rome controlled not only Italy, but also Greece, Spain and North Africa, and the need for a more dignified centre arose. Food stalls and street hawkers were replaced by business centres, monuments and law courts. As the population expanded, the Forum became too small. However, it remained the ceremonial centre of the city under the Empire, with emperors renovating old buildings, erecting new temples and monuments, and celebrating military victories here. To appreciate the layout of the Forum before attempting to wander through its confusing patchwork of ruined temples, triumphal arches and basilicas, it is best to view the whole area from the Capitoline Hill above.

↑ Arch of Septimius Severus, a triumphal arch celebrating military victories

THE VESTAL VIRGINS

The cult of Vesta, the goddess of fire, dates back to at least the 8th century BC. Romulus and Remus were allegedly born of the Vestal priestess Rhea and the god Mars. Six virgins kept the sacred flame of Vesta burning in her circular temple. The girls, who came from noble families, were selected when they were between 6 and 10 years old, and served for 30 years. They had high status and financial security, but were buried alive if they lost their virginity and whipped by the high priest if the sacred flame died out. Although they were permitted to marry after finishing their service, few did so.

Arch of Septimius Severus

The Rostra was the orator's tribune from which speeches were made.

Reconstructed Curia, or ancient Roman Senate House

The Basilica Aemilia was a meeting hall for business.

Temple of Romulus, now part of the church of Santi Cosma e Damiano

Three vast barrel vaults are all that remain of the Basilica of Constantine and Maxentius.

Romanesque bell tower of Santa Francesca Romana

This small museum contains finds from the Forum.

Temple of Saturn

Temple of Castor and Pollux

Basilica Julia, named after Julius Caesar, was the seat of the civil magistrates court.

Temple of Vesta

House of the Vestal Virgins

Arch of Titus

Temple of Venus and Rome

↑ Aerial view of the ruins in the Roman Forum

④ 🥾 🏛 🏢

PALATINE

📍 J7 🏠 Via di San Gregorio 30 🚌 75, 80, 81, 175, 673, 850 Ⓜ Colosseo
🚋 3 🕐 10:30am–1 hour before sunset 🚫 1 Jan, 25 Dec 🌐 coopculture.it

Shaded on its lower slopes with pines, and scattered in spring with wild flowers, the Palatine is the most pleasant and relaxing of Rome's ancient sites. Once the residence of emperors and aristocrats, the ruins range from the simple house in which Augustus is thought to have lived, to the Domus Flavia and Domus Augustana, the public and private wings of a luxurious palace built by Domitian at the end of the 1st century AD.

Most European languages derive their word for palace from the name of this hill. All-important in the history of early Rome, first as its birthplace and then as the site of its leaders' houses, it became the home of the glitterati of the late Republic and the Imperial family. Today the remains of elaborate fountains, colourful marble floors, fine stone carvings, columns, stuccoes and frescoes can be seen within the magnificent walls of the Imperial palaces.

A History of the Palatine Hill

The Founding

According to legend the twins Romulus and Remus were brought up on the Palatine by a wolf. Here Romulus, having killed his brother, is said to have founded the village that was destined to become Rome. Traces of mud huts dating back to the 8th century BC have been found here, lending archaeological support to the legend.

The Republic

By the 1st century BC the Palatine was Rome's most desirable address, home to the leading citizens of the Republic. Its residents, including the erotic poet Catullus and the orator Cicero, were notoriously indulgent, their villas magnificent with doors of ivory, floors of bronze and frescoed walls.

↑ The Palatine Hill, seen from inside an arch of the Colosseum

The Empire

Augustus was born on the Palatine in 63 BC, and lived there after becoming emperor. The hill was therefore an obvious choice of abode for all future emperors. Domitian's palace, the Domus Flavia, and its private quarters, the Domus Augustana, remained the official residence of emperors for more than 300 years.

Many of the wall paintings have survived in the private quarters of the House of Livia, where Augustus is believed to have lived with his wife.

The courtyard of the Domus Flavia was lined by Domitian with mirror-like marble, so he could spot would-be assassins.

The Cryptoporticus, an underground gallery decorated with stuccoed walls, was built by Emperor Nero.

The Temple of Cybele honours the goddess of fertility.

The Domus Flavia was the public and official portion of Domitian's palace. The Roman poets praised this villa as the most splendid.

The House of Augustus features four rooms with magnificent frescoes.

Domus Augustana was the private home of the emperors.

Known as the Stadium, this sunken oval garden probably held a box from which emperors could watch the wealthy strolling by or riding in sedans and carriages.

The Palace of Septimius Severus, an extension of the Domus Augustana, projected beyond the hillside, and was supported by giant arches.

Illustration of the ruins on the Palatine Hill, seen from above ↑

EXPERIENCE MORE

5

Trajan's Forum and Markets

J5 **Forum: Via dei Fori Imperiali; Markets: Via IV Novembre** **06 06 08** **9:30am-7:30pm daily (last adm: 6:30pm)**

Originally considered among the wonders of the Classical world, Trajan's Forum and Markets now show only a hint of their former splendour.

Trajan began to build his forum in AD 107 to commemorate his final conquest of Dacia (present-day Romania) after campaigns in AD 101–2 and 105–6. It was his most ambitious project yet, with a vast colonnaded open space centring on an equestrian statue of the emperor, a huge basilica and two big libraries. Dominating the ruins today

is Trajan's Column, which originally stood between the two libraries. Spiralling up its 30-m- (98-ft-) high stem are minutely detailed scenes from the Dacian campaigns, beginning with the Romans preparing for war and ending with the Dacians being ousted from their homeland. The subtly modelled reliefs were designed to be seen from viewing platforms on the libraries, and are consequently difficult to interpret from ground level.

The market complex, which is situated directly behind the Forum, was begun slightly earlier. Like the Forum, it was probably designed by Apollodorus of Damascus, and was the ancient Roman equivalent of the shopping centre. There were around 150 shops laid out on five levels, selling everything from

> ### Did You Know?
>
> Palazzo Valentini runs screenings of a brilliant animation of the bas-reliefs of Trajan's Column. Book in advance.

oriental silks and spices to fruit, fresh fish (sold alive from salt-water tanks), wine, oil, fabrics and flowers. It was also here that the *annone*, or corn dole, was distributed. This was a free ration of corn given to Roman men, a practice which was introduced in the Republic by politicians who wanted to buy votes and prevent unrest during periods of famine. The markets now host a series of contemporary art exhibitions.

6

Capitoline Museums

H6 **Piazza del Campidoglio** **40, 63, 70, 81, 87 & many other routes through Piazza Venezia** **9:30am-7:30pm daily** **1 Jan, 1 May, 25 Dec** **museicapitolini.org**

There has been a collection of Classical sculptures on the Capitoline Hill since Pope Sixtus IV, a patron of the arts and sciences, donated a group of bronze statues to the city in 1471. Paintings, as well as sculpture, are now housed in two palaces designed by Michelangelo: Palazzo Nuovo and Palazzo dei Conservatori.

The former contains a fine selection of Greek and Roman sculptures. Star exhibits include the *Discobolus*, a Greek statue showing the twisted form of a discus thrower (later transformed by an 18th-century sculptor into a wounded warrior), and

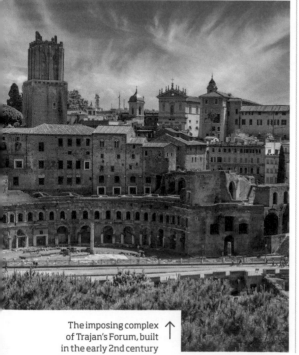

The imposing complex of Trajan's Forum, built in the early 2nd century ↑

←

Antique statuary
adorning the halls of the
Capitoline Museums

Caravaggio, Van Dyck and
Titian. Highlights here include
Caravaggio's sensual and
highly unorthodox portrait
of a young *St John the Baptist*
caressing a sheep (1595–6),
Bernini's bust of the mythological, snake-haired monster
Medusa (1640s) and Pietro
da Cortona's *The Rape of
the Sabine Women* (1629),
a glamorization of the
mass abduction of Sabine
women by the Romans.

7

Forum of Augustus

H5 **Piazza del Grillo 1**
06 06 08 **87, 186**
**To the public, but
viewable from above**

The Forum of Augustus, which
once stretched from the foot
of sleazy Suburra to the edge
of Caesar's Forum, was built to
celebrate Augustus's victory in
41 BC over Brutus and Cassius,
the assassins of Julius Caesar.
Consequentially, the temple
in its centre was dedicated to
Mars the Avenger. The temple,
with its cracked steps and four
Corinthian columns, is easily
identified. Originally it had
a statue of Mars that looked
very like Augustus, but in case
anyone failed to notice the
resemblance, a colossal statue
of the emperor himself was
placed against the wall of
the Suburra quarter.

HIDDEN GEM
Villa Aldobrandini

High above Via IV
Novembre is this walled
garden planted with
palms and orange trees,
with plenty of benches
for a quiet picnic.

EAT

Caffè Capitolino
The big draw of this
café-restaurant on
the top floor of the
Capitoline Museums
is its vast terrace, with
a panoramic view that
takes in rooftops and
assorted ruins. Go for
superior coffee and cake
rather than a full meal.

H6 **Piazzale
Caffarelli 4** **musei
capitolini.org/it/oltre_
il_museo/cafeteria**

---

the *Dying Galatian*, a Roman
sculpture of a wounded
Celtic soldier that has been
frequently copied by artists
since its rediscovery in the
17th century. There are also
antique copies of works by

the famous Greek sculptor
Praxiteles, including his *Faun*
and *Venus of Cnidus*. Other
highlights include the *Mosaic
of the Doves*, a 1st-century-AD
mosaic that once decorated
the floor of Hadrian's Villa at
Tivoli *(p328)*, and the Hall of
the Philosophers, featuring
Roman copies of busts of
Greek politicians, scientists
and poets that once adorned
the homes of wealthy Romans.

The Palazzo dei Conservatori
was the seat of the city's
magistrates during the late
Middle Ages. Its frescoed halls
are still used occasionally for
political meetings, and the
ground floor houses the
municipal registry office.
Much of the palazzo is given
over to sculpture, including
the iconic bronze she-wolf
suckling the baby twins
Romulus and Remus, frag-
ments of a huge statue of
Constantine, and the *Spinario*,
a charming 1st-century-BC
bronze sculpture of a boy
trying to remove a thorn from
his foot. The art galleries on
the second floor hold works
by Veronese, Tintoretto,

Ruins of temples and scattered columns at the Forum of Caesar

8 Forum of Caesar

 J5 🅰 Clivo Argentario 1
☎ 06 06 08 🚌 80, 85, 87, 175, 186, 810 ⏱ To research scholars by appointment only

The first of Rome's Imperial fora was built by Julius Caesar to relieve congestion in the Roman Forum when Rome's population boomed. He spent a fortune buying up and demolishing houses on the site. Pride of place went to a temple dedicated in 46 BC to Venus Genetrix (Venus the Ancestor), as Caesar claimed to be descended from the goddess. The temple contained statues of Caesar and Cleopatra as well as of Venus, but all that remains today is a platform and three Corinthian columns. The forum was once enclosed by a double colonnade, under which was sheltered a row of shops. However, this burned down in AD 80 and was rebuilt by Domitian and Trajan. The latter also added the Basilica Argentaria – which became an important financial exchange – as well as shops and a heated public lavatory.

9 Arch of Constantine

📍 K7 🅰 Between Via di San Gregorio & Piazza del Colosseo 🚌 75, 85, 87, 175, 673, 810 🚋 3 🚇 Colosseo

This arch was built in AD 315 to mark Constantine's victory three years before over his co-emperor Maxentius at the Battle of the Milvian Bridge. Constantine attributed the victory to a vision of Christ, but there is nothing Christian about the arch: most of the reliefs were scavenged from earlier pagan monuments.

10   Mamertine Prison

📍 H6 🅰 Clivo Argentario 1
☎ 06 69 89 63 75 🚌 80, 85, 87, 175, 186 🔒 Closed due to COVID-19, with no date for reopening

Below the 16th-century church of San Giuseppe dei Falegnami is a dank

 The Arch of Constantine, one of Imperial Rome's last monuments

dungeon in which, according to Christian legend, St Peter and St Paul were imprisoned. They are said to have caused a spring to bubble up into the cell, and to have used the water to baptize two prison guards. The prison was in an old cistern with access to the city's main sewer (the Cloaca Maxima). The lower cell was used for executions, and corpses were thrown into the sewer. However, the inmates, who received no food, often died of starvation.

 11

Santa Maria in Aracoeli

📍 H5 🏛 Scala dell'Arce Capitolina 14 📞 06 69 76 38 37 🚌 63, 70, 81 🕐 9am–6:30pm daily (winter: 9:30am–5:30pm)

This church stands on the site of the temple of Juno on the northern summit of the Capitoline Hill, and dates back to at least the 6th century. The church is famous for its ornate gilded ceiling and a series of frescoes by Pinturicchio, dating from the 1480s. They depict scenes from the life of San Bernardino of Siena. The miracle-working *Santo Bambino* figure, stolen in 1994, has been replaced by a replica.

 12

Palazzo Valentini

📍 H5 🏛 Via Foro Traiano 85 🕐 Closed due to COVID-19, with no date for reopening 🌐 palazzovalentini.it

During maintenance work in the basement of Palazzo Valentini in 2005, the remains of two houses belonging to

a leading patrician family of Imperial Rome were discovered. Elegant living rooms, courtyards, a kitchen and a private baths complex were revealed, complete with fascinating traces of their original decorations.

Using digital technology, light and sound effects, film and projections, the houses have been "reconstructed", creating a virtual-reality museum that brings ancient Rome vividly to life. Tours take visitors through the rooms. It is an incredible experience – as you watch, mosaic floors, marble decorations, statues and frescoed walls are restored to their former glory, while sound effects are used to recreate an earthquake that buckled the floors in AD 38.

→

Pinturicchio's frescoes in the church of Santa Maria in Aracoeli

DRINK

American Bar

Nestled in greenery and offering stunning views of the Imperial Forums, this old-time rooftop bar is a lovely spot for a cocktail in the summer. There's also a smart restaurant attached, if you want to make a night of it.

📍 J5 🏛 Hotel Forum, Via Tor de' Conti 25 🌐 hotelforum.com

ROME: AROUND PIAZZA NAVONA

The area around Piazza Navona, known as the *centro storico*, has been inhabited for at least 2,000 years. Piazza Navona stands above an ancient stadium; the Pantheon has been a temple since AD 27; and the ruins of the Curia of Pompey remain in the Area Sacra di Largo Argentina. The area's heyday began in the 15th century, when the papacy returned to Rome. Throughout the 16th, 17th and 18th centuries, princes, popes and cardinals settled here, as did the artists and artisans they commissioned to build and adorn lavish palaces, churches and fountains.

The area showcases Baroque Rome in all its glory, with curvaceous architecture and elaborate fountains by the era's two greatest architects, Bernini and Borromini, and churches filled with works by Caravaggio and Rubens. These days Piazza Navona is a centre of Roman nightlife, but the area's artistic heritage lives on in the workshops of craftsmen and antiques restorers, while some of its ancient buildings, such as the Theatre of Marcellus in the Ghetto, have been converted into exclusive flats.

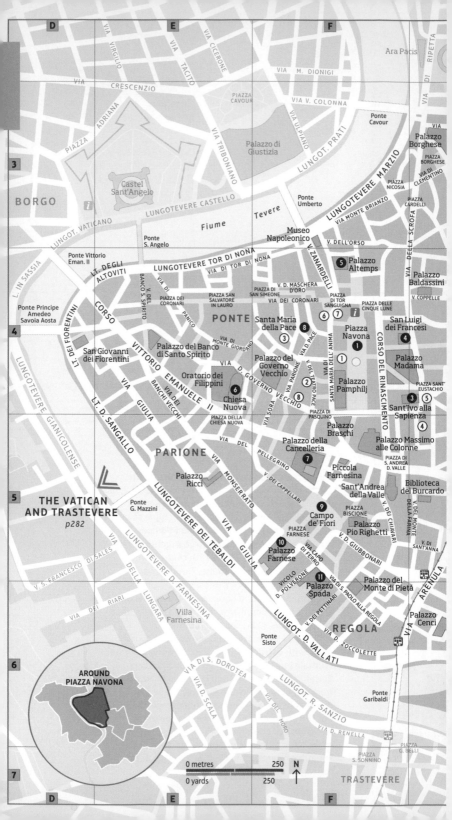

AROUND PIAZZA NAVONA

D	**E**	**F**

VIA DI RIPETTA

Ara Pacis

VIA M. DIONIGI

PIAZZA CAVOUR

VIA V. COLONNA

VIA CICERONE

VIA TACITO

VIA VIRGILIO

VIA CRESCENZIO

PIAZZA ADRIANA

Palazzo di Giustizia

VIA ULPIANO

VIA TRIBONIANO

LUNGOT. PRATI

Ponte Cavour

Palazzo Borghese

PIAZZA BORGHESE

VIA DI CLEMENTINO

PIAZZA NICOSIA

PIAZZA CARDELLI

3

Castel Sant'Angelo

LUNGOTEVERE CASTELLO

Ponte Umberto

LUNGOTEVERE MARZIO

VIA MONTE BRIANZO

VIA DELLA SCROFA

BORGO

LUNGOT. VATICANO

Fiume Tevere

Ponte S. Angelo

Museo Napoleonico

V. DELL'ORSO

V. ZANARDELLI

5 Palazzo Altemps

Palazzo Baldassini

V. COPPELLE

Ponte Vittorio Eman. II

LT. DEGLI ALTOVITI

LUNGOTEVERE TOR DI NONA

VIA DI TOR DI NONA

VIA DEL BANCO S. SPIRITO

VIA DEI CORONARI

PIAZZA SAN SALVATORE IN LAURO

VIA DEI CORONARI

V. D. MASCHERA D'ORO

PIAZZA DI SAN SIMEONE

PIAZZA DI TOR SANGUIGNA

PIAZZA DELLE CINQUE LUNE

L. IN SASSIA

Ponte Principe Amedeo Savoia Aosta

LT. DEI FIORENTINI

CORSO

PANICO

PONTE

VIA DI MONTE GIORDANO

6 **7** **i**

San Luigi dei Francesi **4**

4

San Giovanni dei Fiorentini

VIA GIULIA

VITTORIO EMANUELE II

Palazzo del Banco di Santo Spirito

Santa Maria della Pace **3** **8**

V. D. PACE

Piazza Navona **1**

CORSO DEL RINASCIMENTO

Palazzo Madama

4

Oratorio dei Filippini

VIA DEI BANCHI VECCHI

Palazzo del Governo Vecchio

2

1

Palazzo Pamphilj

PIAZZA SANT' EUSTACHIO

LT. D. SANGALLO

VIA GIULIA

VIA D. GOVERNO VECCHIO

Chiesa Nuova **6**

VIA SORA

8

VIA PARIONE

VIA DEL TEATRO PACE

VIA DI SANTA MARIA DELL'ANIMA

Sant'Ivo alla Sapienza **3** **5**

4

LUNGOTEVERE GIANICOLENSE

PIAZZA DELLA CHIESA NUOVA

VIA DEL

Palazzo Braschi

PIAZZA DI PASQUINO

Palazzo Massimo alle Colonne

PIAZZA DI S. ANDREA D. VALLE

4

THE VATICAN AND TRASTEVERE
p282

PARIONE

VIA MONSERRATO

Palazzo della Cancelleria **7**

PELLEGRINO

Piccola Farnesina

Sant'Andrea della Valle

Biblioteca del Burcardo

VIA DEL MONTE DELLA FARINA

5

Palazzo Ricci

Ponte G. Mazzini

LUNGOTEVERE DEI TEBALDI

VIA DEI CAPPELLARI

V. DEI CAPPELLARI

9 Campo de' Fiori

PIAZZA BISCIONE

Palazzo Pio Righetti

V. DEI CHIAVARI

V. DI SANT'ANNA

Ponte Sisto

V. S. FRANCESCO DI SALES

VIA DEI RIARI

DELLA LUNGARA

Villa Farnesina

LUNGOTEVERE D. FARNESINA

PIAZZA FARNESE

10 Palazzo Farnese

VIA CAPO DI FERRO

V. D. GIUBBONARI

VICOLO D. POLVERONE

11 Palazzo Spada

VIA DI S. PAOLO ALLA REGOLA

Palazzo del Monte di Pietà

ARENULA

Palazzo Cenci

6

AROUND PIAZZA NAVONA

V. DEI PETTINARI

V. D. ZOCCOLETTE

REGOLA

LUNGOT. D. VALLATI

VIA DI S. DOROTEA

VIA D. SCALA

VIA DEL MORO

Ponte Sisto

LUNGOT. R. SANZIO

Ponte Garibaldi

V. D. RENELLA

PIAZZA G. BELLI

7

PIAZZA S. SONNINO

TRASTEVERE

0 metres 250
0 yards 250

N ↑

| **D** | **E** | **F** |

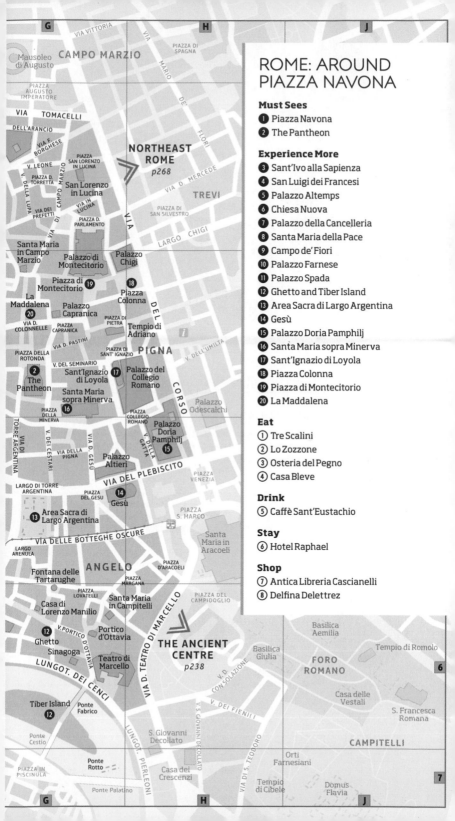

ROME: AROUND PIAZZA NAVONA

Must Sees
1. Piazza Navona
2. The Pantheon

Experience More
3. Sant'Ivo alla Sapienza
4. San Luigi dei Francesi
5. Palazzo Altemps
6. Chiesa Nuova
7. Palazzo della Cancelleria
8. Santa Maria della Pace
9. Campo de' Fiori
10. Palazzo Farnese
11. Palazzo Spada
12. Ghetto and Tiber Island
13. Area Sacra di Largo Argentina
14. Gesù
15. Palazzo Doria Pamphilj
16. Santa Maria sopra Minerva
17. Sant'Ignazio di Loyola
18. Piazza Colonna
19. Piazza di Montecitorio
20. La Maddalena

Eat
1. Tre Scalini
2. Lo Zozzone
3. Osteria del Pegno
4. Casa Bleve

Drink
5. Caffè Sant'Eustachio

Stay
6. Hotel Raphael

Shop
7. Antica Libreria Cascianelli
8. Delfina Delettrez

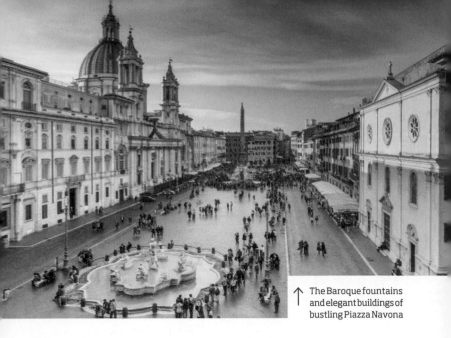

↑ The Baroque fountains and elegant buildings of bustling Piazza Navona

①

PIAZZA NAVONA

📍 F4　🚌 46, 62, 64, 70, 81, 87, 116, 492, 628

No other piazza in Rome can rival the theatricality of Piazza Navona. The luxurious cafés are the social centre of the city, and day and night there is always something going on in the pedestrian area around the three flamboyant Baroque fountains.

Piazza Navona is dominated by the Egyptian obelisk, cascading waters and gleaming marble figures of Bernini's Fontana dei Quattro Fiumi (1651), which features representations of the four great rivers of the time (the Nile, the Plate, the Ganges and the Danube). Bernini also sculpted a Moor wrestling a dolphin at the centre of the Fontana del Moro to the south of

the square. At the north of the square is the 19th-century Fontana di Nettuno, showing the sea god Neptune struggling with a sea monster. Looming over the centre of the square is Sant'Agnese in Agone, a church dedicated to a virgin martyred on the site in AD 304 for refusing to marry a pagan. Borromini designed the church's startling concave façade (1652–7).

Timeline

1500–1600
Rome's city market is transferred from the Campidoglio to Piazza Navona

1655–1866
Every August, the fountains are plugged and the piazza flooded. The lower classes swim while the aristocrats watch from their carriages

1–100 AD
△ A stadium is built for athletic contests (*agones*), chariot races and other sports. Piazza Navona is later built to follow the shape of this stadium

1644–55
△ Pope Innocent X, whose family palazzo is on the piazza, commissions a new church, palace and fountain for the square

1869
Rome's city market moves to the nearby Campo de' Fiori

Sant'Agnese in Agone

Fontana del Nettuno

Piazza Navona

Fontana dei Quattro Fiumi

Palazzo Madama, the seat of the Italian Senate, was originally built for the Medici family in the 16th century.

The tiny domed church of Sant'Ivo alla Sapienza (1642–50) is one of Borromini's most original creations.

Fontana del Moro

Palazzo Braschi, a late 18th-century building designed by Cosimo Morelli, has a splendid balcony overlooking the piazza.

Sant'Andrea della Valle, begun in 1591, has a flamboyant Baroque façade by Ercole Ferrata.

Piazza Navona and the surrounding streets ↑

1 Bernini's elaborate Fontana dei Quattro Fiumi forms the centrepiece of Piazza Navona.

2 The square is lined with art stalls in the daytime, while buskers and mime artists perform after dark.

3 Dotted around Piazza Navona are numerous places to dine al fresco.

THE LEGEND OF THE FOUNTAIN

The rivalry between Bernini and Borromini has given rise to the legend that the veiled head of the river Nile in the Fontana dei Quattro Fiumi was Bernini's way of conveying his disgust at Borromini's façade for Sant'Agnese in Agone, while the figure of the river Plate, with his arm upraised, expresses Bernini's fear that the church is so badly constructed it might collapse. In fact, the fountain was completed a year before construction on the church began.

PANTHEON

📍U3 🏛Piazza della Rotonda 🚌116 and routes along Via del Corso, Corso Vittorio Emanuele II and Corso del Rinascimento 🕐9am–7pm daily
🌐pantheonroma.com

With its awe-inspiring domed interior, the Pantheon – the Roman temple of "all the gods" – is the best-preserved ancient building in Rome. Unlike many other Roman structures that fell into disrepair, it became a church in the 7th century, ensuring its continued use and conservation.

↑ The immense portico, built on the foundations of Agrippa's temple

Inside the Pantheon

The interior of the church is dominated by the vast hemispherical dome, which has both a height and diameter of 43 m (142 ft). The hole at the top of the dome, the oculus, provides the only light; we owe this marvel of engineering to the Emperor Hadrian, who designed the structure (AD 118–125) to replace an earlier temple built by Marcus Agrippa, son-in-law of Augustus. The shrines that line the wall of the Pantheon range from the Tomb of Raphael to those of the kings of Italy.

Did You Know?

The Pantheon's dome remains the largest unreinforced concrete dome in the world.

The walls of the drum supporting the dome are 6 m (19 ft) thick.

118–25
Hadrian builds new Pantheon

609
▽ Pope Boniface IV consecrates Pantheon as church of Santa Maria ad Martyres

1309–77
While the papal seat is in Avignon, the Pantheon is used as a poultry market

27–25 BC
▲ Marcus Agrippa builds first Pantheon

663
Byzantine Emperor Constans II strips gilded tiles from the roof

1632
▲ Urban VIII melts bronze from the portico for the baldacchino

Oculus

Oculus and coffered interior of the Pantheon's dome ↑

The dome was cast by pouring concrete mixed with tufa and pumice over a temporary wooden framework.

The Tomb of Raphael rests below a Madonna sculpture by Lorenzetto (1520).

← Illustration of the Pantheon

Ornate Baroque interior of the church of San Luigi dei Francesi

5 Palazzo Altemps

⬤F4 **⬤Via di Sant'
Apollinare 46** **⬤70, 81, 87,
115, 280, 628** **⬤2–7:45pm
Tue–Fri (from 10:30am Sat
& Sun)** **⬤1 Jan, 25 Dec**
⬤coopculture.it

An extraordinary collection of Classical sculpture is housed in this branch of the Museo Nazionale Romano *(p281)*. Restored as a museum during the 1990s, the palazzo was originally built for Girolamo Riario, nephew of Pope Sixtus IV in 1480. In the popular uprising that followed the pope's death in 1484, the building was sacked and Girolamo fled the city. In 1568 Cardinal Marco Sittico Altemps bought the palazzo; it was renovated in the 1570s by Martino Longhi the Elder, who added the obelisk-crowned belvedere and marble unicorn.

The Altemps family were avid collectors; the courtyard and its staircase are lined with ancient sculptures, which complement the Ludovisi sculptures. One of the highlights is the marble statue *Galata's Suicide*, a copy of the original in the Salone del Camino. On the first floor is the Greek, 5th-century-BC Ludovisi Throne, with a panel depicting Aphrodite.

EXPERIENCE MORE

3 Sant'Ivo alla Sapienza

⬤G4 **⬤Corso del
Rinascimento 40** **⬤06 06
08 (tourist information)**
**⬤30, 70, 81, 87, 116, 186,
492, 628** **⬤9am–noon Sun**

Hidden in the courtyard of Palazzo della Sapienza, seat of the old University of Rome, Sant'Ivo's spiral belfry is nevertheless a distinctive landmark on Rome's skyline. Built by Borromini in 1642–60, the church is astonishingly complex, an ingenious combination of concave and convex surfaces. The work spanned the reigns of three popes, and incorporated in the design are their emblems: Urban VIII's bee, Innocent X's dove and olive branch, and the star and hills of Alexander VII.

4 San Luigi dei Francesi

⬤F4 **⬤Piazza di San Luigi
de' Francesi 5** **⬤06 68 82 71**
**⬤70, 81, 87, 116, 186, 492,
628** **⬤Opening times vary,
check website** **⬤saintlouis-
rome.net**

The French national church in Rome, San Luigi is a 16th-century building that is best known for three magnificent canvases by Caravaggio in the Cerasi chapel. Painted between 1597 and 1602, these were Caravaggio's first significant religious works: *The Calling of St Matthew*, *Martyrdom of St Matthew* and *St Matthew and the Angel*. The first version of this last was initially rejected because it depicted the saint as an old man with dirty feet.

6 Chiesa Nuova

⬤E4 **⬤Via del Governo
Vecchio 134** **⬤06 687 52
89** **⬤46, 64** **⬤7:30am–
noon & 4:30–7pm daily**

San Filippo Neri commissioned this church in 1575 to replace the dilapidated one given to his Order by Pope Gregory XIII. Neri required his followers to humble themselves, and he set aristocratic young men to work as labourers on the church.

Against his wishes, the nave, apse and dome were richly frescoed after his death by Pietro da Cortona. There are three paintings by Rubens around the altar. The first versions were rejected, so Rubens repainted them on slate, placing the originals above his mother's tomb.

Palazzo della Cancelleria

♥F5 **⌂Piazza della Cancelleria** **☎0669 88 75 66** **🚌46, 62, 64, 116, 916** **🕐7:30am–8pm Mon–Sat, 9:30am–7:30pm Sun & hols**

A supreme example of early Renaissance architecture, this palazzo, begun in 1485, was allegedly financed by the gambling proceeds of Raffaele Riario, Pope Sixtus I's nephew.

In 1478 Riario was involved in the Pazzi conspiracy against the Medici, and when Giovanni de' Medici became Pope Leo XIII in 1513, he took belated revenge, turning the palace into the papal chancellery.

Santa Maria della Pace

♥F4 **⌂Vicolo del Arco della Pace 5** **🚌70, 81, 87, 116, 492, 628** **🕐9:30am–6:30pm daily**

Named by Pope Sixtus IV to celebrate the peace he hoped to bring to Italy, this church dates from the 1480s and contains a beautiful fresco by Raphael. Bramante's refined cloister was added in 1504, while the façade was designed in 1656 by Pietro da Cortona.

One of three Rubens paintings near the altar in the Chiesa Nuova ↓

EAT

Tre Scalini
This terrace café is famous for its *tartufo* – dark-chocolate ice cream studded with shards of bitter chocolate and served with a wafer and smear of whipped cream.

♥F4 **⌂Piazza Navona 28** **🕐Wed** **☎0668 80 19 96**

 €€€

Lo Zozzone
A Roman institution, this homely place on a cobbled side street near Piazza Navona serves *pizza bianca* stuffed with an array of fillings from mozzarella to artichoke.

♥F4 **⌂Via del Teatro Pace** **☎0668 80 85 75**

 €€€

Osteria del Pegno
This romantic restaurant offers a menu of perfectly executed Italian dishes. Complimentary limoncello and homemade biscuits round off a meal nicely.

♥F4 **⌂Vicolo Montevecchio 8** **☎0668 80 70 25**

 €€€

Casa Bleve
In a grand vaulted dining room, this *enoteca*-restaurant has an impressive wine list and gourmet offerings.

♥G5 **⌂Via del Teatro Valle 48** **🌐casa bleve.com**

 €€€

9 Campo de' Fiori

F5 **116 & routes to Corso Vittorio Emanuele II**

Campo de' Fiori (Field of Flowers) was one of the liveliest and roughest areas of medieval and Renaissance Rome. Cardinals and nobles mingled with fishmongers and foreigners in the piazza's market; Caravaggio killed his opponent after losing a game of tennis on the square; and the goldsmith Cellini murdered a business rival nearby. Today, the area continues to be a hub of secular activity, with a colourful morning market (Monday to Saturday), and numerous bars and trattorias.

In the Renaissance the piazza was surrounded by inns, many of which were owned by the 15th-century courtesan Vannozza Catanei, mistress of Pope Alexander VI.

The square was also a place of execution. The statue in its centre is the philosopher Giordano Bruno, burned at the stake for heresy on this spot in 1600 for suggesting the earth moved around the sun.

10 Palazzo Farnese

F5 **Piazza Farnese** **23, 116, 280 & routes to Corso Vittorio Emanuele II** **For guided tours only (Mon, Wed & Fri, times vary); book online at least one week ahead** **inventerrome.com**

Originally constructed for Cardinal Alessandro Farnese, who became Pope Paul III in 1534, this palazzo was started by Antonio da Sangallo the Younger, and continued after his death by Michelangelo.

The palace, now the French Embassy, can be seen only as part of a private tour.

11 Palazzo Spada

F5 **Piazza Capo di Ferro 13** **06 683 24 09** **23, 116, 280 & routes to Largo di Torre Argentina** **8:30am-7:30pm Wed-Mon**

A stucco studded with reliefs of illustrious Romans, this palazzo was built in 1550, but bought in 1637 by Cardinal Bernardino Spada. A keen patron of the arts, Spada commissioned Borromini to create an illusionistic tunnel that appears four times longer than it is. The cardinal's art collection, in the Galleria Spada, includes works by Guercino, Dürer and Artemisia Gentileschi.

12 Ghetto and Tiber Island

G6 **23, 63, 280, 780 & routes to Largo di Torre Argentina**

The first Jews came to Rome as traders in the 2nd century BC and were greatly appreciated for their financial and medical skills during the Roman Empire. Persecution began in the 16th century, when Pope

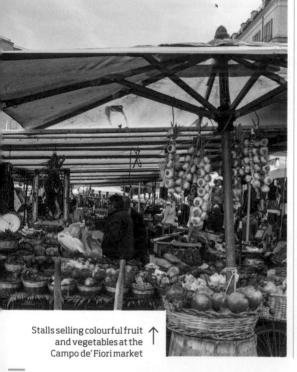

Stalls selling colourful fruit and vegetables at the Campo de' Fiori market

Lush gardens on Tiber Island, home to a hospital nowadays

Paul IV forced all of the Jews to live within a walled enclosure, an area later to form the hub of the present-day Ghetto.

Today Via del Portico d'Ottavia, the district's main street, leads to Rome's central synagogue. Ponte Fabricio links the Ghetto with Tiber Island, a centre of healing since 293 BC, when a temple to Aesculapius was founded. The island is now home to a hospital.

13

Area Sacra di Largo Argentina

📍 G5 🏛 Largo di Torre Argentina 🚌 40, 46, 62, 64, 70, 81, 87, 186, 492 🚫 To the public

The remains of four temples were discovered here in the 1920s. Dating from the Republican era, they are among the oldest in Rome, and are known as temples A, B, C and D. The oldest (temple C) dates from the early 3rd century BC. It was placed on a high platform preceded by an altar and is typical of Italic temple plans. Temple A is from the 3rd century BC, but in medieval times the small church of San Nicola di Cesarini was built over its podium. The column stumps to the north belonged to a great portico, known as the Hecatostylum (portico of 100 columns). Behind temples B and C, near Via di Torre Argentina, are the remains of a great platform of tufa blocks. These have been identified as part of the Curia of Pompey, a building where the Senate met, and where Julius Caesar was assassinated by Brutus, Cassius and their followers on 15 March 44 BC.

Gesù

📍 G5 🏛 Piazza del Gesù 📞 06 69 70 01 🚌 H, 46, 62, 64, 70, 81, 87, 186, 492, 628 🕐 7am–12:30pm & 5–7:30pm (to 8pm Sun)

Built between 1568 and 1584, the Gesù was Rome's first Jesuit church. The Jesuit order was founded in 1537 by a Basque soldier, Ignatius Loyola, who became a Christian after being wounded in battle. The order was heavily engaged in missionary activity.

The much-imitated design of the Gesù typifies Counter-Reformation architecture, with a large nave with side pulpits for preaching to crowds, and a main altar as the centrepiece for the Mass. The illusionistic decoration on the nave ceiling and dome was added by Il Baciccia in the 17th century.

> ### Did You Know?
> Michelangelo offered to design the Gesù church for free, but died before it reached the planning stages.

The nave depicts the *Triumph of the Name of Jesus* and its message is clear: faithful, Catholic worshippers will be joyfully uplifted to Heaven while Protestants and heretics are flung into the fires of Hell. The message is reiterated in the Cappella di Sant'Ignazio, a rich display of lapis lazuli, silver and gold. The Baroque marble by Legros, *Triumph of Faith over Idolatry*, shows a female "Religion" trampling on the head of the serpent Idolatry, while in Théudon's *Barbarians Adoring the Faith*, an angel aims a kick towards a decrepit old barbarian couple entangled with a snake.

SHOP

Antica Libreria Cascianelli

Located opposite the Hotel Raphael, this wonderful shop (in business since 1837) is an Aladdin's cave of antiquarian books, vintage posters, postcards and maps, as well as antiques. It's a very rewarding place for a browse.

📍 F4 🏛 Largo Febo 14 📞 348 863 0220 🕐 Sun am

Delfina Delettrez

A scion of the Fendi dynasty, Delettrez is a jeweller whose bold and distinctive creations are beautifully arrayed in this sparkling little boutique made to resemble a jewellery box.

📍 F4 🏛 Via del Governo Vecchio 67 🕐 Sun & Mon am 🌐 delfinadelettrez.com

15

Palazzo Doria Pamphilj

⊙ H5 **⌂** Via del Corso 305 **🚌** 64, 81, 119, 492 **⊙** 9am–7pm daily, by appt only **⊘** 1 Jan, Easter Sun, 1 May, 25 Dec **⊚** doriapamphilj.it

Palazzo Doria Pamphilj is a vast edifice whose oldest parts date from 1435. When the Pamphilj family took over in 1647 they built a new wing, a splendid chapel and a theatre.

The family art collection has over 400 paintings dating from the 15th to 18th centuries, including a portrait of Pope Innocent X by Velázquez and works by Titian, Guercino, Caravaggio and Claude Lorrain. The opulent rooms of the private apartments retain many of their original furnishings, including Brussels and Gobelins tapestries, Murano chandeliers and a gilded crib.

16

Santa Maria sopra Minerva

⊙ G4 **⌂** Piazza della Minerva 42 **☎** 06 6793926 **🚌** 116 & many other routes **⊙** 10:30am–12:30pm & 3–7pm daily

One of Rome's rare Gothic buildings, this church was built in the 13th century over what were thought to be the ruins of a Temple of Minerva. It was a stronghold of the Dominicans, who produced some of the Church's most infamous inquisitors and tried the scientist Galileo

 →

Marble sculpture in the church of Santa Maria sopra Minerva

in the adjoining monastery. Inside, the church has a superb collection of art and sculpture, ranging from 13th-century Cosmatesque tombs to a bust by Bernini. Highlights include Antoniazzo Romano's *Annunciation* (featuring Cardinal Juan de Torquemada, uncle of the vicious Spanish Inquisitor), and the Carafa Chapel's frescoes by Filippino Lippi.

In the Aldobrandini Chapel are the tombs of the 16th-century Medici popes, Leo X and his cousin Clement VII, and near the steps of the choir is a stocky *Risen Christ*, begun by Michelangelo.

The church also contains the tombs of many famous Italians, such as St Catherine of Siena who died in 1380, and Fra Angelico, the Dominican friar and painter, who died in 1455. Outside, Bernini's spectacular sculpture of an elephant holds an obelisk on its back.

17

Sant'Ignazio di Loyola

⊙ G4 **⌂** Piazza di Sant' Ignazio **☎** 06 679 44 06 **🚌** 117, 119, 492 **⊙** 7:30am–7pm Mon–Sat, 9am–7pm Sun

This church was built by Pope Gregory XV in 1626 in honour of St Ignatius of Loyola, founder of the Society of Jesus (Jesuits)

and the man who most embodied the zeal of the Counter-Reformation. Along with the Gesù (p265), Sant'Ignazio forms the nucleus of the Jesuit area of Rome. It is one of the city's most extravagant Baroque churches and its vast interior is plated with precious stones, marble, stucco and gilt, creating a thrilling sense of theatre. The church has a Latin-cross plan, with an apse and many side chapels.

A cupola was planned but never built, as the nuns from a nearby convent objected that it would obscure the view from their roof garden. Instead the space was filled by a perspective painting of a dome on a flat disc.

Even more striking is the ceiling created by Andrea Pozzo in 1685, a propagandist extravaganza extolling the success of Jesuit missionaries throughout the world. Above four women, representing Europe, Africa, Asia and America, lithe angels and beautiful youths are sucked into a heaven of fluffy clouds.

↑ Night time in Piazza di Montecitorio, with its Egyptian obelisk

 18

Piazza Colonna

📍H4 🚌116, 117, 492

Home to Palazzo Chigi, official residence of the prime minister, Piazza Colonna is dominated by the Column of Marcus Aurelius. This was erected after the death of Marcus Aurelius in AD 180 to commemorate his victories over the barbarian tribes of the Danube. It is an imitation of Trajan's Column *(p250)*, but the style of the relief sculptures is different. The wars of Marcus Aurelius are rendered with simplified pictures in stronger relief – Classical proportions have been sacrificed for clarity.

 19

Piazza di Montecitorio

📍G4 📞06 676 01 🚌116
🕐1st Sun Oct-Jun

The obelisk in the centre of Piazza di Montecitorio formed the spine of a giant sundial brought back from Egypt by Augustus. It vanished in the 9th century, and was rediscovered under medieval houses during the reign of Julius II (1503–13).

The piazza is dominated by the Palazzo di Montecitorio, designed by Bernini and completed in 1697, after his death, by Carlo Fontana.

DRINK

Caffè Sant'Eustachio
Many Romans believe that this tiny bar serves the city's best coffee – hence the hordes of locals that throng it from morning till late. There's a tempting selection of coffee-flavoured cakes too.

📍G4
📍Via Sant'Eustachio 82
🌐santeustachio ilcaffe.com

It has been the seat of Italy's Chamber of Deputies since the late 19th century.

 20

La Maddalena

📍G4 📍Piazza della Maddalena 53 📞06 899 281 🚌116 & many other routes 🕐7am-noon & 5-8pm Mon-Fri, 9:30am-noon & 5-8pm Sat & Sun

Situated in a small piazza near the Pantheon, the Maddalena's façade, constructed in 1735, epitomizes the dynamism of the late Baroque. Its curves recall Borromini's San Carlo alle Quattro Fontane *(p279)*. The façade has been restored, despite the protests of Neo-Classicists who dismissed its painted stucco as icing sugar.

The diminutive dimensions of the church did not deter 17th- and 18th-century decorators from filling the interior with paintings and ornaments from the floor to the top of the elegant cupola.

The magnificent Trevi Fountain

ROME: NORTHEAST

This area stretches from the exclusive shopping streets around Piazza di Spagna to the Esquiline Hill, a once bourgeois but now run-down area full of early Christian churches, their interiors mosaicked like jewellery boxes. The Piazza di Spagna and Piazza del Popolo district grew up in the 16th century, when the increase in the influx of pilgrims was such that a road was built to channel them as quickly as possible to the Vatican. About the same time, the Quirinal Hill became the site of a papal palace. When Rome became the capital of Italy in 1870, Via Veneto grew into a lavish residential area, and the Esquiline was covered with apartments for the new civil servants.

One of the busiest parts of the city, Northeast Rome offers plenty of opportunities for window-shopping, sightseeing and dining. The city's most fashionable *passeggiata* unfolds down the length of the Via del Corso, while tourists flock to Rome's most famous fountain, the Trevi. The trendy Monti district offers an array of hip shops, restaurants and bars, and Rome's most multicultural quarter, the Esquiline, is the city's best spot for ethnic dining options.

ROME: NORTHEAST

Must Sees

1. Piazza di Spagna
2. Trevi Fountain
3. Santa Maria Maggiore

Experience More

4. Villa Medici
5. Santa Maria del Popolo
6. Ara Pacis
7. Mausoleum of Augustus
8. Sant'Andrea al Quirinale
9. San Carlo alle Quattro Fontane
10. Palazzo Barberini
11. Santa Maria della Concezione
12. Santa Maria della Vittoria
13. Palazzo Massimo alle Terme
14. Santa Prassede
15. San Pietro in Vincoli

Eat

1. Gelateria Cecere

Drink

2. Antico Caffè Greco
3. Doney Café

❶

PIAZZA DI SPAGNA

🔲 H2 🚌 116, 117, 119 Ⓜ Spagna

Shaped like a crooked bow tie and surrounded by tall, shuttered houses painted in muted shades of ochre, pink and cream, Piazza di Spagna is crowded all day and (in summer) most of the night. It is the most famous square in Rome, long the haunt of expatriates and foreign visitors.

↑ View from outside the Trinità dei Monti, at the top of the Spanish Steps

History of Piazza di Spagna

In the 17th century the Spanish embassy was on the square, and the area around it was deemed to be Spanish territory – anyone who unwittingly trespassed was in danger of being dragooned into the Spanish army. In the 18th and 19th centuries the square stood at the heart of the main hotel district, attracting aristocrats doing the Grand Tour (p44), as well as artists, writers and composers.

Spanish Steps

In 1700, the Bourbon royal family became the rulers of Spain as well as France. It was decided to symbolize their power by linking the French church of Trinità dei Monti with the Spanish Embassy by building the steps.

←

Frescoes by Daniele di Volterra inside the Trinità dei Monti

Babington's Tea Rooms, founded in 1896, serves English teas.

The Fontana della Barcaccia, designed by Bernini's father Pietro, represents a sinking boat.

Trinità dei Monti

The Keats-Shelley Memorial House, where the poet Keats died in 1821, is now a museum.

The Collegio di Propaganda Fide, built in 1662, has a superb façade by Borromini.

Sant'Andrea delle Fratte contains two angels by Bernini (1669) made for Ponte Sant'Angelo.

Did You Know?

According to legend, the Fontana della Barcaccia was built after Tiber floods beached a boat in the piazza in 1598.

←

Illustration of the Piazza di Spagna and surrounding streets

The Fontana della Barcaccia at ↑
the foot of the Spanish Steps

②
TREVI FOUNTAIN

📍H4 🚌52, 53, 61, 62, 63, 71, 80, 116, 119 and other routes along Via del Corso and Via del Tritone

Tucked away on a tiny piazza, this is the most famous – and the largest – fountain in Rome. Built in 1762 by Italian architect Nicola Salvi, in the flamboyant Rococo style, the Trevi Fountain is a creamy travertine extravaganza of rearing sea-horses, conch-blowing Tritons, craggy rocks and flimsy palm trees built into the side of the Palazzo Poli.

Trevi Water

Legend has it that the fountain is named after a young virgin named Trivia who showed Roman engineers the location of a freshwater spring. The water now comes from the Acqua Vergine, a Roman aqueduct built in 19 BC and fed by springs some 22 km (14 miles) from the city.

In the 19th century, Trevi water was considered the sweetest in Rome, and English residents are said to have kept supplies at home for making tea. These days chemicals are added to the water to keep algae at bay. A long-standing tradition states that anyone who wants to guarantee their return to the city should throw a coin in the water – around €3,000 is thrown into the fountain daily.

→

Relief depicting Trivia revealing the location of the freshwater spring

EAT

Gelateria Cecere

The simple, long-established Cecere has a loyal following among Romans for its ice cream, made to an old (and secret) family recipe. It is famous for its rich marsala-spiked *zabaglione* flavour, but the pistachio and chocolate are fabulous too.

📍H4 🏠Via del Lavatore 84
📞06 679 2060

€€€

LA DOLCE VITA

Federico Fellini's 1960 film is about a *paparazzo* (played by Marcello Mastroianni) drifting through the decadent nightlife of Rome, and meeting a beautiful Swedish actress played by Anita Ekberg. The well-known scene – Ekberg taking a shower in the Trevi Fountain – may be largely responsible for making the Trevi the most famous and photographed fountain in the city.

Sculptures

The central statue of Neptune, Roman God of the Sea, was executed by Pietro Bracci, who took over work on the fountain after the death of Nicola Salvi, his long-time friend, in 1751. The theme of the work, ingeniously grafted onto the back of a palazzo, is the taming of the waters.

Neptune's conch-shell chariot is powered by two sea-horses steered by Tritons. One Triton struggles to master an unruly beast, while the other leads a far more docile animal. The horses symbolize the different moods of the sea. In the niches next to Neptune are figures representing Abundance (to his left), with her cornocopia of fruit, and Salubrity (on his right), who holds a cup from which a snake drinks.

$\longrightarrow$ Detail of a conch-blowing Triton leading a *hippocampo* (sea-horse)

$\downarrow$ The Trevi Fountain, set against the façade of the Palazzo Poli

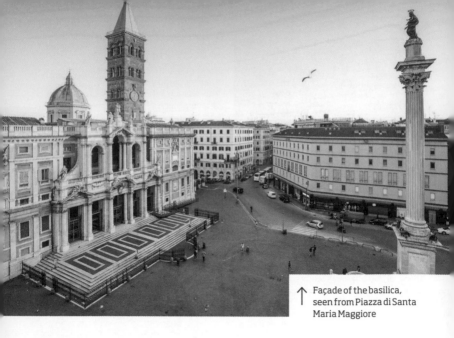

↑ Façade of the basilica, seen from Piazza di Santa Maria Maggiore

3 🛍️

SANTA MARIA MAGGIORE

📍L4 🏠Piazza di Santa Maria Maggiore 📞06 69 88 68 00 🚌16, 70, 71, 714
🚋14 Ⓜ️Termini, Cavour 🕐7am–6:45pm daily

The biggest among the 26 churches in Rome dedicated to the Virgin Mary, Santa Maria Maggiore was originally built in the 5th century. It was adapted by many popes over the centuries, giving it an unusual mix of different architectural styles.

Legend has it that Pope Liberius had Santa Maria Maggiore built after he dreamt the Virgin told him to construct a church on the spot where he found snow. When it fell on the Esquiline in the middle of a baking hot August day, he set to work. Santa Maria Maggiore's colonnaded nave is part of the original 5th-century building. The Cosmatesque marble floor and Romanesque bell tower are medieval. The Renaissance saw a new coffered ceiling, and the Baroque gave the church twin domes and its imposing front and rear façades. The mosaics are Santa Maria's most famous feature.

The biblical scenes in the aisle and the mosaics on the triumphal arch date from the 5th century. Medieval highlights include a 13th-century enthroned Christ in the loggia.

← Virgin and Child sculpture in Piazza di Santa Maria Maggiore

↑ Mosaics and baldacchino inside Santa Maria Maggiore

The Cappella Paolina (1611) is packed with spectacular works of art.

The Coronation of the Virgin is the central image in a series of stunning apse mosaics.

The Tomb of Cardinal Rodriguez (1299) contains wonderful Cosmatesque marblework.

The Cappella Sistina houses the tomb of Pope Sixtus V (1584–7).

The gold used for the gilded ceiling (inside) was some of the first brought from America by Columbus.

↑ Santa Maria Maggiore, seen from above

Timeline

356
▲ Virgin appears to Pope Liberius

420
Probable founding date

432–40
Sixtus III completes church

1075
▼ Pope Gregory VII kidnapped while saying Christmas Mass here

1288–92
Nicholas IV adds apse and transepts

1347
Cola di Rienzo crowned Tribune of Rome in Santa Maria Maggiore

1673
▲ Carlo Rainaldi rebuilds apse

The elegant location of the 16th-century Villa Medici

EXPERIENCE MORE

Villa Medici

📍 H2 🏛 Accademia di Francia a Roma, Viale Trinità dei Monti 1 🚌 117 Ⓜ Spagna ⏰ For tours 9:30am & 6:30pm Tue–Sun (booking recommended) 🌐 villamedici.it

Superbly positioned on the Pincio Hill, above Piazza di Spagna, this 16th-century villa has retained the name that it assumed when Cardinal Ferdinando de' Medici bought it in 1576. From the terrace you can look across the city to Castel Sant'Angelo. It is now home to the French Academy, founded by Louis XIV in 1666 to give artists the chance to study in Rome. From 1803 musicians were also allowed to study here: both Berlioz and Debussy were students.

The villa is only open for exhibitions and guided tours. Tours include the formal gardens, which feature a gorgeously frescoed pavilion and copies of ancient statues.

⑤ Santa Maria del Popolo

📍 G1 🏛 Piazza del Popolo 12 🚌 117, 119, 490, 495, 926 Ⓜ Flaminio ⏰ 8:30am–noon & 4–6pm Mon–Fri, 4:30–6pm Sat & Sun 🌐 smariadelpopolo.com

Santa Maria del Popolo, one of the first Renaissance churches in Rome, was commissioned by Pope Sixtus IV in 1472.

↑ *Trompe l'oeil* cupola in the church of Santa Maria del Popolo

Lavish endowments have made it one of Rome's greatest artistic treasures.

Shortly after Sixtus died in 1484, Pinturicchio and his pupils frescoed two chapels (first and third right) for the della Rovere family. On the altar of the first chapel there is a lovely *Nativity* from 1490 that depicts a stable at the foot of a Classical column.

In 1503 Sixtus IV's nephew Giuliano became Pope Julius II and had Bramante build a new apse. Pinturicchio was called in again to paint its vaults with Sibyls and Apostles framed in an intricate tracery of freakish beasts.

In 1513 Raphael created the Chigi chapel (second left) for the wealthy banker Agostino Chigi. The design combines sacred and profane; there are pyramid-like tombs and a ceiling mosaic of God holding the signs of the zodiac describing Chigi's horoscope. Raphael died before the chapel was finished and it was completed by Bernini, who added the dynamic statues of Daniel and Habakkuk. In the Cerasi chapel, left of the altar, there are two realistic works painted by Caravaggio in 1601: the *Conversion of St Paul* and the *Crucifixion of St Peter*. The artist uses daringly exaggerated lighting and foreshortening techniques to intensify the dramatic effect.

 6

Ara Pacis

G2 **Lungotevere in Augusta** 70, 81, 117, 119, 186, 628 9am-7:30pm daily (last adm: 6:30pm) 1 Jan, 25 Dec arapacis.it

Painstakingly reconstructed over many years from its scattered fragments, the exquisitely carved Ara Pacis (Altar of Peace) celebrates the peace created by Emperor Augustus throughout the Mediterranean. Commissioned in 13 BC and completed four years later, the altar stands in a square enclosure of Carrara marble, carved with realistic reliefs of such quality that experts think the craftsmen may have been Greek.

The reliefs on the north and south walls depict a procession that took place on 4 July 13 BC, in which the members of the emperor's family can be identified, including Augustus's grandson, Lucius, clutching at the skirt of his mother, Antonia. The site is housed in a building by architect Richard Meier.

DRINK

Antico Caffè Greco

Founded in 1760, this café was once a meeting place for artists and intellectuals, including Keats and Byron, and it still retains the feel of a refined salon. Coffee and cake here is a (pricey) treat.

H2 **Via dei Condotti 862** anticocaffegreco.eu

 7

Mausoleum of Augustus

G2 **Piazza Augusto Imperatore** 06 06 08 81, 117, 492, 628, 926 For events; call for info

Now just a weedy mound ringed with cypresses, this was once the most prestigious burial place in Rome. Augustus had the mausoleum built in 28 BC as a tomb for himself and his descendants. The circular building was 87 m (270 ft) in diameter with two obelisks. Inside were four concentric passageways linked by corridors where urns holding the ashes of the Imperial family were placed, including those of Augustus who died in AD 14.

 8

Sant'Andrea al Quirinale

J4 **Via del Quirinale 29** 06 487 45 65 116, 117 9am-noon & 3-6pm Tue-Sun

Sant'Andrea was designed for the Jesuits by Bernini and executed between 1658 and 1670. The site was wide but shallow, so Bernini took the radical step of pointing the long axis of his oval plan towards the sides. At the altar he combined sculpture and painting to create a theatrical crucifixion of Sant'Andrea (St Andrew); the diagonally crucified saint on the altarpiece looks up at a stucco effigy of himself ascending to the lantern, where the Holy Spirit and cherubs await him in heaven.

9

San Carlo alle Quattro Fontane

K3 **Via del Quirinale 23** 06 488 32 61 116 & routes to Piazza Barberini Barberini 10am-1pm Mon-Sat, noon-1pm Sun

In 1638, Borromini was commissioned by the Trinitarians to design a church and convent on a tiny cramped site at the Quattro Fontane crossroads. The church, so small that it is said it would fit inside one of the piers of St Peter's, is designed with bold, fluid curves on both the façade and interior.

In a small room off the sacristy hangs a portrait of Borromini. He committed suicide in 1667, and a chapel that was reserved for him in the crypt remains empty.

 ←

Detail of the reliefs on the Ara Pacis, a marble altar created in 9 BC

10

Palazzo Barberini

📍K3 🏛Via delle Quattro Fontane 13 🚌52, 53, 61, 62, 63, 80, 116, 175, 492, 590 Ⓜ️Barberini 🕙10am–6pm Thu–Sun (booking recommended) 🔒1 Jan, 25 Dec 🌐barberini corsini.org

When Maffeo Barberini became Pope Urban VIII in 1623, he decided to build a grand family palazzo. Designed by Carlo Maderno as a typical country villa on the fringes of the city, it now overlooks Piazza Barberini, where traffic hurtles around Bernini's Triton fountain. Maderno died shortly after the foundations had been laid, and Bernini and Borromini took over.

Of the many sumptuously decorated rooms, the most striking is the Gran Salone, with an illusionistic ceiling frescoed by Pietro da Cortona in 1633–9. The palazzo also houses part of the Galleria Nazionale d'Arte Antica, with works by Titian, Filippo Lippi, Caravaggio and Artemisia Gentileschi. The most famous is a portrait of a courtesan, reputedly Raphael's lover, *La Fornarina*, although not painted by the artist himself.

11

Santa Maria della Concezione

📍J3 🏛Via Veneto 27 🚌52, 53, 61, 62, 63, 80, 116, 175 Ⓜ️Barberini 🕙Church: 7am–1pm & 3–6pm daily; Crypt: 9am–7pm daily 🌐cappuccini viaveneto.it

Below this unassuming church is a crypt decked with the dearticulated skeletons of 4,000 Capuchin monks. They form a macabre reminder of the transience of life, with vertebrae wired together to make sacred hearts and crowns of thorns, and, in one chapel, the skeleton of a tiny Barberini princess.

12

Santa Maria della Vittoria

📍K3 🏛Via XX Settembre 17 📞06 42 74 05 71 🚌61, 62, 175, 910 Ⓜ️Repubblica 🕙8:30am–noon & 3:30–6pm daily

Santa Maria della Vittoria is an intimate Baroque church with a lavish, candlelit interior. Inside the Cornaro chapel you will find one of Bernini's most ambitious sculptures, the *Ecstasy of St Teresa* (1646). The physical nature of St Teresa's ecstasy is apparent as she appears collapsed on a cloud with her mouth half open and eyes closed, struck by the arrow of a smiling angel. On either side, past and present ecclesiastical members of the Venetian Cornaro family, who

↑ The crypt of Santa Maria della Concezione, decorated with thousands of human bones

commissioned the chapel, sit in boxes as if watching and discussing the scene being played out in front of them.

Palazzo Massimo alle Terme

Q L4 **A** Largo di Villa Peretti 1 **🚌** All routes to Termini **M** Repubblica **🕐** 2–7:45pm Tue–Fri (from 10:30am Sat & Sun), by appt only **W** coopculture.it

Founded in 1899, the Museo Nazionale Romano – one of the world's leading museums of Classical art – houses most of the antiquities found in Rome since 1870, as well as important older collections. During the 1990s it underwent a major reorganization and now has five branches: the Palazzo Altemps (p262); the Baths of Diocletian; the Aula Ottagona; the Crypta Balbi; and the Palazzo Massimo alle Terme. One ticket is valid for all sites. In the Palazzo Massimo alle Terme, exhibits dating from the 2nd century BC to the late 4th century AD

↑ Classical statuary on display in the Palazzo Massimo alle Terme, Museo Nazional Romano

are displayed in a series of rooms over three floors. Highlights include the *Quattro Aurighe* mosaics from a villa in northern Rome, the breath-taking series of frescoes from Livia's summer villa, and the famous statue of her husband, the Emperor Augustus.

DRINK

Doney Café
Located right in the heart of Via Veneto, the Doney recreates *Dolce Vita*-era glamour with enormous chandeliers and retro furnishings. There's a rather pricey restaurant here, or you can come at aperitivo time for a cocktail and a spot of people-watching.

Q K2 **A** Via Veneto 125 **W** restaurant doney.com

Santa Prassede

Q L5 **A** Via Santa Prassede 9a **📞** 06 488 24 56 **🚌** 16, 70, 71, 75, 714 **M** Vittorio Emanuele **🕐** 7am–noon & 4–6:30pm daily

The church was founded by Pope Paschal II in the 9th century and decorated by Byzantine artists with the most important glittering mosaics in Rome. In the apse Christ stands between Santa Prassede and her sister, dressed as Byzantine empresses, among white-robed elders, lambs, feather-mop palms and bright red poppies. The Cappella di San Zeno is even lovelier, a jewel-box of a mausoleum, built by Pope Paschal II for his mother, Theodora. Her square halo shows that she was still alive when the mosaic was created.

San Pietro in Vincoli

Q K5 **A** Piazza di San Pietro in Vincoli **📞** 06 97 84 49 50 **🚌** 75, 85, 117 **M** Colosseo **🕐** 8am–12:30pm & 3–7pm daily (Oct–Mar: to 6pm)

This church's name means "St Peter in Chains", so called because it houses what are said to be the chains with which St Peter was shackled in the Mamertine Prison (p252).

San Pietro is now best known for the Tomb of Julius II, commissioned by the pope from Michelangelo in 1505. Much to the artist's chagrin, Julius soon became more interested in the build-ing of a new St Peter's and the tomb project was laid to one side. After the pope died in 1513, Michelangelo resumed work on the tomb, but had only completed the statues of the *Dying Slaves* (now found in Paris and Florence) and *Moses* when he was called away to paint the *The Last Judgment* in the Sistine Chapel.

ROME: THE VATICAN AND TRASTEVERE

Vatican City, the world capital of Catholicism, is the world's smallest state. It occupies 43 ha (106 acres) within high walls watched over by the Vatican guard. It was the site where St Peter was martyred (c AD 64) and buried, and it became the residence of the popes who succeeded him. The papal palaces, next to the great basilica of St Peter's, are home to the Sistine Chapel and the eclectic collections of the Vatican Museums, as well as being the residence of the pope. Neighbouring Trastevere, the area "across the Tiber", is quite different. The proud and independent inhabitants of Trastevere consider themselves the most authentic Romans. In one of the most picturesque old quarters of the city, it is still possible to glimpse scenes of everyday life that seem to belong to bygone centuries despite the proliferation of fashionable boutiques, cafés and restaurants characteristic of the area today. Some of Rome's most fascinating medieval churches lie hidden in the patchwork of narrow, cobbled back-streets, the only clue to their location an occasional glimpse of a Romanesque bell tower. Of these, Santa Cecilia was built on the site of the martyrdom of the patron saint of music, San Francesco a Ripa commemorates St Francis of Assisi's visit to Rome, and Santa Maria in Trastevere is the traditional centre of the spiritual and social life of the area.

ROME: THE VATICAN AND TRASTEVERE

Must Sees
① St Peter's
② Vatican Museums

Experience More
③ Castel Sant'Angelo
④ Villa Farnesina
⑤ Galleria Corsini
⑥ Botanical Gardens
⑦ Santa Maria in Trastevere
⑧ Santa Cecilia in Trastevere
⑨ San Pietro in Montorio and the Tempietto

Eat
① Dal Toscano
② Franchi
③ Il Simposio

Drink
④ Enoteca Ferrara
⑤ Ombre Rosse

↑ ② 150 m
(165 yd)

2

THE VATICAN
AND TRASTEVERE

CRESCENZIO

③

PIAZZA
CAVOUR

VIA V. COLONNA

VIA ALBERICO II

VIA
ADRIANA

VIA
GIOVANNI
VITELLESCHI

PIAZZA
ADRIANA

VIA
TRIBONIANO

VIA
ULPIANO

Palazzo di
Giustizia

3

Castel
Sant'Angelo

③

Santa Maria in
Traspontina

ⓘ

PIAZZA
PIA

LUNGOT. VATICANO

LUNGOTEVERE
CASTELLO

Ponte
Umberto

Ponte
S. Angelo

Fiume Tevere

Ponte Vittorio
Eman. II

LUNGOT. TOR DI NONA

Ponte
Principe Amedeo
Savoia Aosta

PONTE

VIA ZANARDELLI

Palazzo
Altemps

Palazzo
Baldassini

PIAZZA DI
MONTECITORIO

4

AROUND
PIAZZA NAVONA
p254

VIA D. GOVERNO VECCHIO

CORSO DEL RINASCIMENTO

PIAZZA
NAVONA

PIGNA

PIAZZA DELLA
ROTONDA

V. DEL SEMINARIO

LUNGOTEVERE GIANICOLENSE

V. DELLA LUNGARA

CORSO VITTORIO EMANUELE II

VIA GIULIA

LT. D. SANGALLO

Chiesa
Nuova

VIA DI
SANTA MARIA DELL'ANIMA

Palazzo
Pamphilj

The Pantheon

PARIONE

VIA MONSERRATO

Sant'Andrea
della Valle

PIAZZA DI
S. ANDREA
D. VALLE

V. DEI CESTARI

LARGO DI
TORRE
ARGENTINA

5

Ponte
G. Mazzini

LUNGOTEVERE DEI TEBALDI

CAMPO
DE' FIORI

PIAZZA
FARNESE

VIA DELLE BOTTEGHE OSCURE

Carcere
di Regina
Coeli

V. S. FRANCESCO
DI SALES

Fiume Tevere

VIA DELLA LUNGARA

LUNGOTEVERE D. FARNESINA

Palazzo
Spada

LUNGOT. D. VALLATI

ANGELO

VIA ARENULA

Casa di
Lorenzo Manilio

6

VIA DEI RIARI

Galleria Corsini ⑤

④ Villa
Farnesina

Casa della
Fornarina

Porta
Settimiana

VIA DI S.
DOROTEA

PIAZZA
TRILUSSA

Ponte
Sisto

LUNGOT. DEI CENCI

⑥
Botanical
Gardens

VIA
GARIBALDI

VICOLO
BOLOGNA

VIC. DEL CEDRO

VIA D. SCALA

V. D. MATTONATO

V. D.
PANIERI

VIA DEL MORO

V. DELLA PELLICCIA

④ LUNGOT. R. SANZIO

VIA D. RENELLA

Ponte
Garibaldi

LUNGOT.
D. ANGUILLARA

ISOLA
TIBERINA

Ponte
Cestio

7

GIANICOLO

San Pietro in Montorio
and the Tempietto

⑨

Fontana dell'
Acqua Paola

VIA GIACOMO MEDICI

VIALE TRENTA APRILE

VIA G.
GARIBALDI

VIA GOFFREDO MAMELI

VIA DELLA PAGLIA

Museo de Roma
in Trastevere

⑤

⑦

Santa
Maria in
Trastevere

PIAZZA S.
APOLLONIA

V. D. ARCO
D. S. CALISTO

VIA
DELLA

PIAZZA
S. SONNINO

TRASTEVERE

PIAZZA
G. BELLI

LUNGARETTA

PIAZZA IN
PISCINULA

Caserma dei Vigili
della VII Coorte

V. DEI
SALUMI

LUNGOT. RIPA

VIA LUCIANO MANARA

V. DELLE FRATTE
DI TRASTEVERE

VIA S.
FRANCESCO A

VIA
FIENAROLI

V. D.
RENELLA

V. S.
GALLICANO

VIA S.
SANTINI

TRASTEVERE

Santa Cecilia
in Trastevere ⑧

VIA
ANICIA

VIA DEI GENOVESI

PIAZZA
S. CECILIA

V. P.
PERETTI

A. Bertani

PIAZZA S.
COSIMATO

V. L. SANTINI

V. NATALE
DEL GRANDE

VIA
ROMA
LIBERA

PIAZZA
MASTAI

VIA
DELLA
LUCE

VIA
MADONNA
DELL'ORTO

PIAZZA DEI
MERCANTI

San Michele a
Ripa Grande

VIA FABRIZI

VIA NICOLA FABRIZI

VIA E. MOROSINI

VIALE DI TRASTEVERE

VIA A RIPA

San Francesco
a Ripa

PORTO DI RIPA
GRANDE

8

VIA SENI

VIALE TRENTA APRILE

VIA CALANDRELLI

Villa
Sciarra

VIALE

VIA DANDOLO

VIALE
LORIOSO

V. SACCHI

V. G. INDUNO

VIA TAVOLACCI

PORTA
PORTESE

D   E   F   G

ST PETER'S

📍 B3 🏛 Piazza San Pietro 🚌 23, 49, 70, 180, 492 Ⓜ Ottaviano San
Pietro 🕐 Basilica: Apr-Sep: 7am-6pm daily (mid-Oct-Mar: to 6:30pm);
Treasury: Apr-Sep: 8am-6:30pm daily (Oct-Mar: to 5:30pm); Grottoes:
Apr-Sep: 8am-6pm daily (Oct-Mar: to 5pm); Dome: Apr-Sep: 8am-6pm
daily (Oct-Mar: to 5pm) 🌐 vatican.va

Catholicism's most sacred shrine, the sumptuous basilica of
St Peter's draws pilgrims and tourists from all over the world.

Inside St Peter's

Marking the site where St Peter was martyred and buried, the
basilica holds hundreds of precious works of art, some salvaged
from the original 4th-century basilica built by Constantine,
others commissioned from Renaissance and Baroque artists.
The dominant tone is set by Bernini, who created the
baldacchino twisting up below Michelangelo's huge dome.
He also created the *cathedra* in the apse, with four saints
supporting a throne that contains fragments once
thought to be relics of the chair from which St Peter
delivered his first sermon. From the basilica you can
visit the Grottoes, where the late Pope John Paul II
is buried, the Treasury and St Peter's Sacristy, or
the terrace for panoramic views. You
can can also book in advance
(*www.papalaudience.org*) for
an audience with the pope,
which takes place at 10am
every Wednesday in Piazza
San Pietro or in the Papal
Audience Chamber.

The 136.5-m-
(448-ft-) high
dome, designed
by Michelangelo,
was not finished
in his lifetime.

The Monument to Pope
Alexander VII (inside)
was Bernini's last work
in St Peter's.

Pope Urban VIII commissioned
Bernini's extravagant
baldacchino in 1624.

The Papal Altar
stands over the
crypt where
St Peter is buried.

The foot of St Peter,
sculpted in the 13th
century, has worn thin
from pilgrims touching
it over the centuries.

←

Michelangelo's dome
and the top of the
baldacchino

Timeline

AD 61
▽ Burial of St Peter

200
Altar built marking grave of St Peter

1452
Nicholas V plans restoration

1547
Michelangelo named as chief architect of St Peter's

324
Constantine builds basilica

800
△ Charlemagne crowned Emperor of the Romans in St Peter's

1514
Raphael named director of works

1626
New basilica of St Peter's consecrated

→ Piazza San Pietro, the grand oval plaza surrounding the basilica

Protected by glass since an attack in 1972, Michelangelo's Pietà (1499), located in the first chapel on the right, was created when the sculptor was only 25.

POPE'S BLESSING

On Sundays (at noon), religious festivals and special occasions such as canonizations, the pope stands on the balcony at the Library window and blesses the faithful crowds gathered in Piazza San Pietro below.

These bronze doors from the old basilica were decorated with biblical reliefs by Filarete between 1439 and 1445.

From this Library window, the pope blesses the faithful.

← St Peter's, centre of the Catholic faith

→

The monumental spiral staircase designed by Giuseppe Momo in 1932

2 ⊘ ⊗ 🍴 🖥 🛍

VATICAN MUSEUMS

📍 C3 🏛 Città del Vaticano (entrance in Viale Vaticano) 🚌 49 to entrance, 23, 81, 492, 990
Ⓜ Ottaviano San Pietro, Cipro 🕐 9am–6pm Mon–Sat (last admission 4pm), 9am–2pm last
Sun of month (last admission 12:30pm; free entry); low-cut or sleeveless clothing, shorts,
mini-skirts and hats are not allowed 🚫 Religious and pub hols 🌐 museivaticani.va

Home to the Sistine Chapel and Raphael Rooms as well as to one of the world's
most important art collections, the Vatican Museums are housed in palaces originally
built for Renaissance popes Julius II, Innocent VIII and Sixtus IV. Most of the later
additions were made in the 18th century, when priceless works of art accumulated
by earlier popes were first put on show. Strung along 7 km (over 4 miles) of
corridors, these incredible collections form one of the world's largest museums.

Among the Vatican's greatest treasures are
its superlative Greek and Roman antiquities,
together with the magnificent artifacts
excavated from Egyptian and Etruscan
tombs during the 19th century. Some of
Italy's leading artists, such as Raphael,
Michelangelo and Leonardo da Vinci, are
represented in the Pinacoteca (art gallery)
and parts of the former palaces, where
they were employed by popes to decorate
sumptuous apartments and galleries.
The absolute highlights of this complex of
museums are the Sistine Chapel and the
Raphael Rooms, which should not be missed.

↑ The Cortile della Pigna, with a spherical
bronze sculpture by Arnaldo Pomodoro

INSIDER TIP
Skipping the Queue

Book a ticket for the first slot of the day online. You can head straight to the Sistine Chapel, then make your way slowly backwards. For an extra fee, book a Breakfast Visit, which gives entry from 7:15am and includes breakfast and an audio guide.

Gregorian Profane Museum

Spiral staircase designed by Giuseppe Momo

Entrance

Belvedere Palace

Cortile della Pigna

Pio Clementino Museum

Pinacoteca

Egyptian Museum

Gallery of the Candelabra

Gallery of the Tapestries

Bramante Staircase

Gallery of the Maps

Sistine Chapel

Octagonal Courtyard

↑ Highlights of the Vatican Museums complex

Borgia Apartment

Raphael Rooms

Timeline

1473
△ Pope Sixtus IV builds Sistine Chapel

1503-13
Pope Julius II starts Classical sculpture collection

1508
▽ Raphael begins work on Rooms; Michelangelo begins painting the Sistine Chapel ceiling

1541
Michelangelo's Last Judgment is unveiled

1655
△ Bernini designs Royal Staircase

1758
Founding of Gregorian Profane Museum

1771
△ Founding of Pio Clementino Museum

HIGHLIGHTS OF THE VATICAN COLLECTION

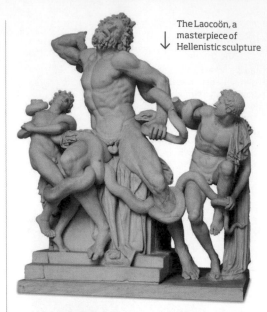

The Laocoön, a masterpiece of Hellenistic sculpture ↓

Pio Clementino Museum

The Vatican's prize pieces of Greek and Roman sculpture form the nucleus of this museum. Most of the works are Roman copies of lost ancient Greek originals, notably *The Laocoön*, a violently contorted Hellenistic work showing the Trojan priest Laocoön and his two sons struggling to escape from the writhing coils of a sea serpent. Also here is the *Apollo Belvedere*, considered a paragon of physical perfection by Renaissance artists, and the muscular, contorted Belvedere Torso, whose influence can be seen on Michelangelo's *ignudi* (male nudes) in the Sistine Chapel. A menagerie of animal-themed sculptures and mosaics are gathered together in the Room of the Animals.

On either side of the museum are two staircases. The original spiral stairway designed by Bramante in 1505 is open only to special tours. The modern double helix stairway, commonly called the Snail or Momo Staircase, was designed by Giuseppe Momo in 1932. It was inspired by Bramante's original.

Did You Know?
Bramante designed the spiral staircase so that it could be ridden up on horseback.

Gregorian Profane Museum

In a space infused with natural light, the Gregorian Profane museum spans Classical antiquity and includes large marble fragments from the Athens Parthenon, Roman copies of Greek sculptures and a striking mosaic from the Baths of Caracalla portraying full-length figures of athletes.

Egyptian Museum

Egyptian culture and mythology became extremely fashionable in Imperial Rome, and the collection here consists chiefly of Egyptian antiquities brought to the city to adorn buildings such as the Temple of Isis (which once stood near the Pantheon), Villa Adriana at Tivoli, and the Gardens of Sallust to the southeast of the Villa Borghese park. Also on display are painted mummy cases and tomb finds.

Galleries of Maps, Tapestries and Candelabra

A long corridor is divided into three contiguous galleries. The Gallery of the Maps displays 16th-century maps of Italy's regions and papal territories painted as if Rome were literally at the centre of the world, with areas south

← Classical sculptures gallery in the Pio Clementino Museum

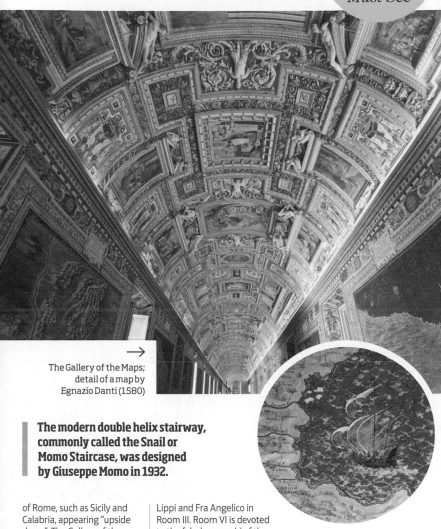

→

The Gallery of the Maps;
detail of a map by
Egnazio Danti (1580)

The modern double helix stairway, commonly called the Snail or Momo Staircase, was designed by Giuseppe Momo in 1932.

of Rome, such as Sicily and Calabria, appearing "upside down". The Gallery of the Tapestries has early 16th-century silk, gold and wool tapestries woven in Brussels to designs inspired by Raphael, while the Gallery of the Candelabra has immense marble candle holders.

Pinacoteca

There are some splendid Renaissance works from all over Italy in the 18 rooms of the art gallery. Don't miss the fragments of frescoes of apostles and angel musicians in Room IV by Melozzo da Forlì or the exquisitely romantic Madonna paintings by Filippo Lippi and Fra Angelico in Room III. Room VI is devoted to the fabulous world of the Crivelli brothers, 16th-century Venetian artists who depicted fragile doll-like Madonnas enclosed within elaborate painted frames of fruit and flowers. Raphael has an entire room (VIII) devoted to his work, notably *The Transfiguration*, which includes a woman with red-gold hair, who is thought to have been his lover, La Fornarina. Next door in Room IX is a single, rare work by Leonardo da Vinci depicting St Jerome in the desert. There are also notable paintings by Titian, Crespi, Veronese and Caravaggio.

GALLERY GUIDE

The museum complex is vast: the Sistine Chapel is 20 to 30 minutes' walk from the entrance, so allow plenty of time. There is a strict one-way system. It is best to be selective or choose one of four colour-coded itineraries, which vary from 90 minutes to a five-hour marathon.

Michelangelo's
breathtaking
ceiling frescoes ↑

SISTINE CHAPEL: THE CEILING

Although Michelangelo had studied fresco-painting under Ghirlandaio, until 1508 he had mainly gained fame through his work as a sculptor. Nonetheless, Pope Julius II commissioned him to paint the ceiling of the Sistine Chapel, which would result in one of the greatest masterpieces of Western art.

At the time, the ceiling was painted simply blue, with golden stars. Michelangelo frescoed over the old ceiling painting between 1508 and 1512, working on specially designed scaffolding. He persuaded the pope to give him a free hand, and spent four years painting 366 figures from the Old and New Testaments, illustrating the bibilical stories of the Creation of the World, the Fall of Man and the Coming of Christ. *Ignudi* (male nudes) are depicted around these frescoes. In the spandrels surrounding the vault are sibyls, prophetesses from pagan mythology, which, in the Renaissance, were adopted by Christian artists as figures who could foresee the Coming of Christ. The central painting, *The Creation of Adam*, portraying God reaching down from a cloudy heaven to create Adam, is one of the most reproduced religious paintings of all time.

RESTORATION OF THE CEILING

From 1979 until 1994 a huge restoration programme was carried out. Five hundred years of soot, candle smoke and glue – along with breadcrumbs and retsina used by earlier restorers, and brush hairs and fingerprints left behind by Michelangelo – were removed. The faded, eggshell-cracked figures were discovered to have rose-petal skin, lustrous hair and to be wearing luscious strawberry-pink, lime-green, lemon and orange shot-silk robes. Critics were surprised that Michelangelo's palette was so bright.

The Last Judgment by Michelangelo, showing souls meeting the wrath of Christ

SISTINE CHAPEL: THE WALLS

Wall Frescoes

The massive walls of the Sistine Chapel were frescoed by some of the finest artists of the 15th and 16th centuries. The twelve paintings by artists, including Perugino, Ghirlandaio, Botticelli and Signorelli, show parallel episodes from the lives of Moses and Christ. The decoration of the walls was completed between 1534 and 1541 by Michelangelo.

The Last Judgment

Twenty-four years after he had finished the Sistine ceiling, Michelangelo was commissioned by Pope Paul III Farnese to cover the altar wall of the chapel with a fresco of The Last Judgment. Michelangelo drew on Dante's Inferno. The painting is a bleak, harrowing work, showing the damned hurtling towards a putrid hell, the blessed being dragged up to heaven, and saints demanding vengeance for their martyrdoms, a theme chosen by the Pope to warn Catholics to adhere to their faith in the turmoil of the Reformation.

Did You Know?

Michelangelo's self-portrait is seen on the flayed skin held by St Bartholomew in *The Last Judgment*.

RAPHAEL ROOMS

In 1508, Pope Julius II asked Bramante to recommend an artist to redecorate his private suite of four rooms. Bramante suggested a young artist named Raphael. The resulting frescoes swiftly established Raphael as one of the leading artists in Rome, putting him on a par with Michelangelo. Raphael and his pupils took over 16 years to fresco the rooms.

Hall of Constantine

The frescoes here, started in 1517, were executed mainly by Raphael's pupils and show the triumph of Christianity over paganism, focusing on key moments in the life of Emperor Constantine.

Room of Heliodorus

The theme here is divine intervention and includes *The Expulsion of Heliodorus from the Temple* and the dazzling *Liberation of St Peter*, in which an angel frees St Peter (a portrait of Julius II) from prison.

Room of the Segnatura

The frescoes here celebrate the Renaissance ideal – the ability of the intellect to discover the truth. The key work is *The School of Athens* in which Raphael painted leading Greek philosophers in a vaulted hall.

Room of the Fire in the Borgo

This celebrates a miracle in 847, when Pope Leo IV is said to have extinguished a fire in the quarter around the Vatican by making the sign of the cross.

→ Detail of *The School of Athens*, with Plato and Aristotle in the centre

←
Hall of Constantine, a
celebration of the triumph of
Christianity over paganism

EXPERIENCE MORE

3

Castel Sant'Angelo

📍E3 🏛Lungotevere Castello 🚌34, 280 🕐9am–7:30pm daily 🚫1 Jan, 25 Dec 🌐castelsant angelo.beniculturali.it

This massive fortress takes its name from the vision of the Archangel Michael by Pope Gregory the Great in the 6th century as he led a procession across the bridge, praying for the end of the plague.

The castle began life in AD 139 as the Emperor Hadrian's mausoleum. Since then it has been a bridgehead in the Emperor Aurelian's city wall, a medieval citadel and prison, and a place of safety for popes during times of political unrest. A corridor links it with the Vatican Palace, providing an escape route for the pope.

From dank cells to fine apartments of Renaissance popes, the museums cover all aspects of the castle's history, including the Sala Paolina, with illusionistic frescoes (1546–8) by Pellegrino Tibaldi and Perin del Vaga, and the Courtyard of Honour.

4

Villa Farnesina

📍E6 🏛Via della Lungara 230 🚌23, 280 🕐9am–2pm Mon–Sat & every 2nd Sun 🌐villafarnesina.it

The fabulously wealthy Sienese banker Agostino Chigi commissioned this villa in 1508 from his fellow Sienese Baldassare Peruzzi. Chigi's main home was across the Tiber, and the villa was designed purely for lavish banquets. Artists, poets, cardinals, princes and the pope himself were entertained here in magnificent style. Chigi also used the villa for sojourns with the courtesan Imperia, who allegedly inspired one of the *Three Graces* painted by Raphael in the Loggia of Cupid and Psyche.

The simple, harmonious design of the Farnesina, with a central block and projecting wings, made it one of the first true villas of the Renaissance. Peruzzi decorated some of the interiors himself, such as the Sala della Prospettiva upstairs, in which the illusionistic frescoes create the impression of looking out over 16th-century Rome through a marble colonnade.

Other frescoes, by Sebastiano del Piombo and Raphael and his pupils, depict Classical myths, while the vault of the main hall, the Sala di Galatea, is adorned with astrological scenes showing the position of the stars at the time of Chigi's birth. After his death in 1520 the banking business collapsed, and in 1577 the villa was sold off to the Farnese family.

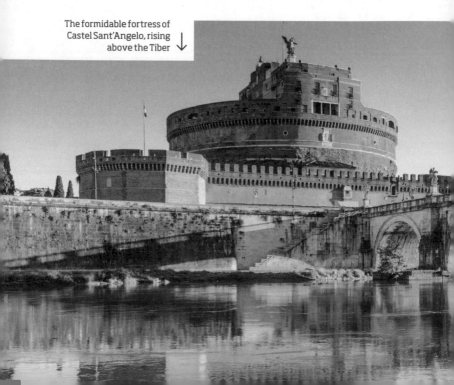

The formidable fortress of Castel Sant'Angelo, rising above the Tiber ↓

⑤ Galleria Corsini

📍 E6 🏠 Via della Lungara 10 🚌 23, 280 🕙 10am–6pm Thu–Sun 🚫 1 Jan, 25 Dec, 31 Dec Ⓦ barberini corsini.org

The history of Palazzo Corsini is intimately entwined with that of Rome. Built for Cardinal Domenico Riario in 1510–12, it has boasted among its many distinguished guests Bramante, the young Michelangelo, Erasmus, the mother of Napoleon and Queen Christina of Sweden, who died here in 1689. The palazzo was rebuilt by Ferdinando Fuga, who planned the façade to be viewed from an angle, as Via della Lungara is too narrow for a full-frontal view.

When the palazzo was purchased by the state in 1893, the Corsini family donated their collection of paintings, which formed the core of the national art collection, and was soon augmented. The collection

↑ Raphael's *Triumph of Galatea* fresco in Villa Farnesina

is now split between Palazzo Barberini and Galleria Corsini. Although the best works are in the Barberini, there are paintings by Van Dyck, Rubens, Murillo and, notably, an androgynous *St John the Baptist* (c 1604) by Caravaggio and a *Salome* (1638) by Reni. The strangest work is a portrait of the rotund Queen Christina as the goddess Diana by J Van Egmont.

⑥ Botanical Gardens

📍 D6 🏠 Largo Cristina di Svezia 24 ☎ 06 49 91 71 16 🚌 23, 280 🕙 9:30am–6:30pm (Nov–Mar: 5:30pm) Mon–Sat 🚫 Pub hols

Sequoias, palm trees and splendid collections of orchids are among the 7,000 plants represented in the Botanical Gardens. Species are grouped to illustrate their botanical families and their adaptation to different climates. There are also some curious plants like the ginkgo that have survived virtually unchanged from prehistoric eras. Now owned by the University of Rome, the gardens were originally part of the Palazzo Corsini.

DRINK

Enoteca Ferrara

This cosy *enoteca* has a vast wine list with a good selection of wines by the glass and helpful staff. There's a smart restaurant attached, although the aperitivo buffet might leave you with little room for dinner.

📍 F6 🏠 Piazza Trilussa 41 Ⓦ enotecaferrara.it

Ombre Rosse

This friendly bar's pleasant terrace on little Piazza di Sant' Egidio is a great spot for a prosecco as you take in the predinner Trastevere whirl. There's live music – from rock 'n' roll to blues – several nights a week.

📍 E7 🏠 Piazza di Sant'Egidio 12 Ⓦ ombre rosseintrastevere.it

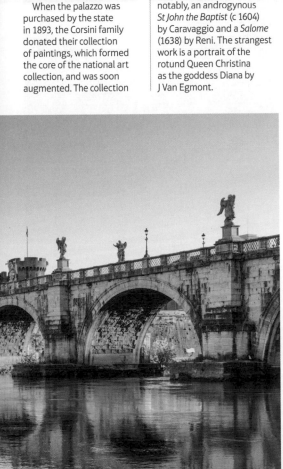

EAT

Dal Toscano
This classic trattoria specializes in steak, but it also offers a superb thick Tuscan soup and a great range of pasta dishes.

 C2 Via Germanico 58 Mon ristorante daltoscano.it

€€€

Franchi
A first-class delicatessen with a tantalizing array of lunchtime snacks.

 D2 Via Cola di Rienzo 200 06 686 55 64

€€€

Il Simposio
A fine-dining restaurant specializing in fish.

 E3 Piazza Cavour 16 ilsimposioroma.it

€€€

7

Santa Maria in Trastevere

 E7 Piazza Santa Maria in Trastevere 06 581 48 02 H, 23, 280 7:30am–9pm daily

Santa Maria in Trastevere was probably the first Christian place of worship in Rome, founded by Pope Callixtus I in the 3rd century, when emperors were still pagan and Christianity a minority cult. According to legend,

→

Remarkably brilliant mosaics in the church of Santa Maria in Trastevere

it was built on the site where a fountain of oil had miraculously sprung up on the day that Christ was born. The basilica became the focus of devotion to the Madonna and, although today's church and its mosaics date largely from the 12th and 13th centuries, images of the Virgin continue to dominate. The façade mosaics probably date from the 12th century, and show Mary, Christ and ten lamp-bearing women. Inside in the apse is a stylized 12th-century *Coronation of the Virgin* and, below, a 13th-century series of realistic scenes from the life of the Virgin by Pietro Cavallini. The oldest image of the Virgin is a 7th-century icon, the *Madonna di Clemenza*, which depicts her as a Byzantine empress flanked by a guard of angels. It sits above the altar in the Cappella Altemps.

8

Santa Cecilia in Trastevere

G7 Piazza di Santa Cecilia 06 589 92 89 H, 23, 44, 280 Main church: 10am–1pm & 4–7pm daily; Cavallini fresco: 10am–12:30pm Mon–Fri

St Cecilia, aristocrat and patron saint of music, was martyred here in AD 230. After an unsuccessful attempt to suffocate her by locking her in the hot steam bath of her

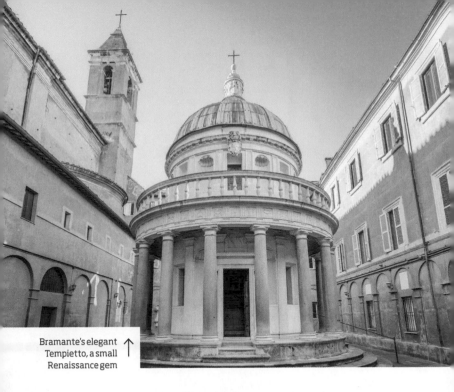

Bramante's elegant Tempietto, a small Renaissance gem ↑

house for three days, she was beheaded. A church was built, possibly in the 4th century, on the site of her house (still to be seen beneath the church). Her body was lost, but it turned up again in the Catacombs of San Callisto (p317). In the 9th century it was reburied here by Pope Paschal I, who rebuilt the church. A fine apse mosaic survives from this period. The altar canopy by Arnolfo di Cambio and the fresco of *The Last Judgment* by Pietro Cavallini can be reached through the adjoining convent; they date from the 13th century, one of the few periods when Rome had a distinctive artistic style.

In front of the altar is a delicate statue of St Cecilia by Stefano Maderno, which is based on sketches made of her perfectly preserved relics when they were briefly disinterred in 1599.

SAN COSIMATO MARKET

In the heart of Trastevere, this lively market in Piazza San Cosimato has abundant fruit and vegetables along with some excellent cheeses and cured meats. There's also a fantastic playground to keep the kids entertained while you browse for bargains.

San Pietro in Montorio and the Tempietto

📍E7 🏛Piazza di San Pietro in Montorio 2 📞06 581 39 40 🚌44, 75, 115 🕐Main church: 8am–noon & 3–4pm daily; Tempietto: 10am–6pm Tue–Sun

The Tempietto, a diminutive masterpiece of Renaissance architecture completed by Bramante in 1502, stands in the courtyard of San Pietro in Montorio. Its circular shape is an echo of early Christian *martyria*, chapels built on the site of a saint's martyrdom. This was erroneously thought to be the spot where St Peter was crucified. Bramante ringed the chapel with Doric columns, a Classical frieze and a fine balustrade.

ROME: AVENTINE AND LATERAN

The southernmost of the seven hills in Rome and, according to legend, Remus's preferred spot for the foundation of the city, the Aventine stood outside the city walls for centuries after Romulus set up camp at the Palatine Hill. During the Imperial period, this former working-class suburb gained in prestige and became one of the more affluent parts of the city. The nearby Lateran was the residence of the popes in the Middle Ages, and the Basilica of San Giovanni beside it rivalled St Peter's in splendour. After the return of the popes from Avignon at the end of the 14th century , the area declined in importance.

This is one of the greenest parts of the city, taking in the Celian and Aventine Hills, as well as the very congested area around San Giovanni in Laterano. The Celian, now scattered with churches, was a fashionable place to live in Imperial Rome. Some of the era's splendour is still apparent in the ruins of the Baths of Caracalla. Behind the Baths rises the Aventine Hill, a peaceful, leafy area, with the superb basilica of Santa Sabina, and lovely views across the river to Trastevere and St Peter's. By contrast, in the valley below, cars and Vespas skim around the Circus Maximus, following the ancient charioteering track, while to the south lies Testaccio, a lively working-class district.

ROME: AVENTINE AND LATERAN

Must See

① San Giovanni in Laterano

Experience More

② Santa Maria in Cosmedin
③ Temples of the Forum Boarium
④ Santa Maria in Domnica
⑤ Santi Quattro Coronati
⑥ Santo Stefano Rotondo
⑦ San Clemente
⑧ Baths of Caracalla
⑨ Pyramid of Caius Cestius
⑩ Protestant Cemetery
⑪ Santa Sabina

Shop

① Mercato di Testaccio

1

SAN GIOVANNI IN LATERANO

📍M7 🏛 Piazza di San Giovanni in Laterano 🚌16, 81, 85, 87, 650 🚊3 Ⓜ San Giovanni
☎ 06 69 88 64 33 🕐 Cathedral: 7am-6:30pm daily; Cloisters: 9am-6pm daily; Museum:
10am-5:30pm daily; Baptistry: 7am-12:30pm & 4-6:30pm daily

Until the Middle Ages, this basilica was the most important religious building in Rome. Popes resided in the adjacent Lateran Palace and were crowned here. After the papacy moved to Avignon in 1309, the basilica declined in importance, but it continues to house the *cathedra* of the Bishop of Rome, the pope.

Early in the 4th century, the Laterani family were disgraced and their land taken by Emperor Constantine to build Rome's first Christian basilica. Today's church retains the original shape, but has been rebuilt several times, most notably in 1646 when Borromini restyled the interior. Until 1870 all popes were crowned in the basilica. It still remains the city's main cathedral, and the seat of the Bishop of Rome, the pope, who celebrates Maundy Thursday Mass here and attends the annual blessing of the people.

TRIAL OF A CORPSE

Fear of rival factions led the early popes to extraordinary lengths. An absurd case took place at the Lateran Palace in 897 when Pope Stephen VI tried the corpse of his predecessor, Formosus, for disloyalty to the Church. The corpse was found guilty; its right hand was mutilated and it was thrown into the Tiber.

↓ Grand façade of the basilica on Piazza di San Giovanni in Laterano, and *(inset)* Borromini's restyled interior

Timeline

AD 313
▲ Constantine gives Laterani site to Pope Melchiades for a church

314–18
Five-aisled basilical church is built

324
Basilica consecrated by Pope Sylvester I and dedicated to the Redeemer

1144
Church dedicated to San Giovanni in Laterano

1308–9
Church destroyed by fire; papacy moves to Avignon

1646
Borromini rebuilds interior

1730–40
▼ Alessandro Galilei constructs main façade

The domed baptistry dates back to Constantine's time. Its octagonal shape has served as the model for baptistries throughout the Christian world.

The Chapel of San Venanzio is decorated with 7th-century mosaics.

The pope gives his annual blessing from the upper loggia of the North Façade.

Only the pope can celebrate mass at this altar.

Apse

Possibly by Giotto, the Boniface VIII Fresco shows the pope announcing the Holy Year of 1300.

Museum entrance

Built by the Vassalletto family in about 1220, the cloisters are remarkable for their inlaid marble mosaics.

The altarpiece in the Corsini Chapel is a mosaic copy of Guido Reni's painting of Sant'Andrea Corsini.

The main entrance, on the East Façade (1735), is adorned with statues of Christ and the Apostles.

Basilica of San Giovanni in Laterano ↑

EXPERIENCE MORE

2

Santa Maria in Cosmedin

📍 H7 🏛 Piazza della Bocca della Verità 📞 06 678 77 59 🚌 23, 44, 81, 160, 170, 280, 628, 715, 716 🕐 9am–7pm Sat & Sun 🌐 cosmedin.org

This church was built in the 6th century, but the Romanesque bell tower and portico were added in the 12th century. In the 1800s a Baroque façade was removed and the church restored to its original simplicity. It contains many fine examples of Cosmati work, in particular the mosaic pavement, the raised choir, the bishop's throne, and the canopy over the main altar.

Set into the wall of the portico is the Bocca della Verità (Mouth of Truth), a grotesque marble face, thought to have been an ancient drain cover. Medieval tradition had it that the jaws would snap shut on liars – a way of testing the faithfulness of spouses.

 HIDDEN GEM
Aventine Orange Garden

Take a break from sightseeing in a pretty orange garden just off Via di Santa Sabina, on the Aventine Hill. It has some truly spectacular views of the Tiber.

3

Temples of the Forum Boarium

📍 H7 🏛 Piazza della Bocca della Verità 🚌 23, 44, 81, 160, 170, 280, 628, 715, 716 🕐 1st & 3rd Sun of month for guided tours only 🌐 coopculture.it

These wonderfully well-preserved Republican-era temples are at their best in moonlight, standing in their grassy enclave beside the Tiber sheltered by umbrella pines. During the day, they look less romantic, stranded in a sea of traffic. They date from the 2nd century BC, and were saved from ruin by being consecrated as Christian churches in the Middle Ages by the Greek community then living in the area. The rectangular temple, formerly known as the Temple of Fortuna Virilis, was probably dedicated to Portunus, the god of rivers and ports. Set on a podium, it has four Ionic travertine columns fluted at the front and 12 half-columns embedded in the tufa wall of the *cella* – the room that housed the image of the god. In the 9th century the temple was converted into the church of Santa Maria Egiziaca, after a 5th-century prostitute who reformed and became a hermit.

The smaller circular temple, made of solid marble and

Santa Maria in Cosmedin, with its distinctive Romanesque bell tower ↓

The circular Temple of Hercules Victor, one of the Temples of the Forum Boarium

surrounded by 20 fluted columns, was dedicated to Hercules but was long thought to be a Temple of Vesta because of its similarity to the one in the Forum.

 4

Santa Maria in Domnica

L8 **Piazza della Navicella 12** **06 77 20 26 85** **81, 117, 673** **Colosseo** **For church services only**

Santa Maria in Domnica was probably founded in the 7th century, and renovated in the 9th century. By this time the Romans had lost the art of making mosaics, so Pope Paschal I imported mosaicists from Byzantium. They created an exquisite apse mosaic showing the Virgin, Child and angels in a garden of paradise. Paschal I is kneeling at the Virgin's feet wearing a square halo, indicating that he was alive when it was made.

In 1513 Andrea Sansovino added a portico decorated with lions' heads, a punning homage to Pope Leo X.

5

Santi Quattro Coronati

L7 **Via dei Santi Quattro Coronati 20** **06 70 47 54 27** **85, 117, 810** **3** **10–11:45am Mon-Sat, 4–5:45pm daily**

The name of this fortified convent (Four Crowned Saints) refers to four Christian soldiers martyred after refusing to worship a pagan god. For centuries it was the bastion of the pope's residence, the

 The Bocca della Verità, in the portico of Santa Maria in Cosmedin

Lateran Palace. Erected in the 4th century AD, it was rebuilt after invading Normans set fire to it in 1084.

Highlights are a delightful garden cloister and the Chapel of St Sylvester, where 12th-century frescoes tell the story of Emperor Constantine's conversion to Christianity.

6

Santo Stefano Rotondo

L8 **Via di Santo Stefano Rotondo 7** **06 421 199** **81, 117, 673** **10am–1pm & 3:30–6:30pm Tue-Sat (winter: 9:30am–12:30pm & 2–5pm)**

Santo Stefano Rotondo was built between 468 and 483 on a circular plan with four chapels in a cruciform shape. Its circular inner area is enclosed by two concentric corridors. A third, outer corridor was demolished on the orders of Leon Battista Alberti. In the 1500s Niccolò Pomarancio, Antonio Tempesta and others covered the walls with 34 frescoes detailing the martyrdoms of saints.

San Clemente

7 🔗 🏛

♀ L7 ⛪ **Via di Labicana 95** 🚌 **85, 87, 117, 186, 810** Ⓜ **Colosseo** 🚋 **3** 📞 **06 774 00 21** 🕐 **9am-12:30pm, 3-6pm Mon-Sat, noon-6pm Sun & bank hols; last adm: 20 mins before closing**

In 1857 Father Mullooly, the Irish Dominican prior of San Clemente, began excavations beneath the existing 12th-century basilica. He and his successors discovered a 4th-century church and, below that, a number of ancient Roman buildings. On the lowest level is a temple devoted to the cult of Mithras, a mystical all-male religion that was imported from Persia and rivalled Christianity for popularity in the 2nd and 3rd centuries AD.

The centrepiece of the upper church is the 12th-century apse mosaic *Triumph of the Cross*, in which the crucified Christ is represented as the tree of life, nourished by the rivers of Paradise and surrounded by foliage and animals. Also worth seeing is the splendid 12th-century spiral paschal candlestick, striped with glittering Cosmati mosaics, and the 8th-century *scola cantorum* (choir enclosure), salvaged from the church below.

It took 40 years to shovel out the rubble from the lower church, revealing a three-aisled basilica with traces of frescoes, including one of Byzantine Empress Theodora converted into a *Madonna and Child* by the later addition of a haloed baby. From this level, steps lead down to the foundations of a Roman apartment block with the temple to Mithras – complete with sacrificial altar – in what was once its courtyard.

↑ Sumptuous interior of the church of San Clemente

Baths of Caracalla

8   🔗 🏛

♀ K9 ⛪ **Viale delle Terme di Caracalla 52** 🚌 **160, 628** 🚋 **3** 🕐 **9am-2pm Mon, 9am to 1 hour before sunset Tue-Sun** 🚫 **1 Jan, 25 Dec** 🌐 **coopculture.it**

Rearing up at the foot of the Aventine Hill are the red-brick ruins of the Baths of Caracalla. Begun by Emperor Septimius Severus in AD 206, and completed by his son Caracalla in AD 217, they remained in use until the 6th century, when the Goths sabotaged the city's aqueducts.

→

The monolithic remains of the vast Baths of Caracalla complex

Going for a bath was a social event in ancient Rome, and complexes such as Caracalla offered an impressive array of facilities: art galleries, gymnasia, gardens, libraries, lecture rooms and shops selling food and drink.

A Roman bath was a long and complicated business, beginning with a form of Turkish bath, followed by a spell in the *caldarium,* a large hot room with pools of water to moisten the atmosphere. Then came the lukewarm *tepidarium,* followed by a visit to the large central meeting place known as the *frigidarium,* and finally a plunge into the *natatio,* an open-air swimming pool. For the wealthy, this was followed by a rub-down with scented woollen cloth.

Most of the rich marble decorations of the baths were scavenged by the Farnese family in the 16th century to adorn the rooms of Palazzo Farnese *(p264).* There are, however, statues and mosaics from the Baths in the Museo Archeologico Nazionale in Naples *(p452)* and in the Vatican's Gregorian Profane Museum *(p290).*

So dramatic is the setting that it is the regular venue for the open-air opera season.

Pyramid of Caius Cestius

📍 H10 🏛 Piazzale Ostiense
☎ 06 39 96 77 02 (for tours on 3rd & 4th w/end of month) 🚌 23, 280 🚋 3
Ⓜ Piramide

Caius Cestius was a wealthy but unimportant 1st-century BC *praetor,* or senior magistrate. At the time, inspired by the Cleopatra scandals, there was a craze for all things Egyptian, and Caius decided to commission himself a pyramid as a tomb. Set into the Aurelian Wall near Porta San Paolo, it is built of brick and faced with white marble; according to an inscription, it took just 330 days to build in 12 BC.

🔟 Protestant Cemetery

📍 G10 🏛 Cimitero Acattolico, Via di Caio Cestio ☎ 06 574 19 00 🚌 23, 280 🚋 3
🕐 9am–5pm Mon–Sat, 9am–1pm Sun; last adm: 30 mins before closing

Non-Catholics have been buried in this cemetery behind the Aurelian Wall since 1738. In the oldest part (on the left as you enter) is the grave of the poet John Keats, who died in 1821 in a house on Piazza di Spagna *(p272).* He wrote his own epitaph: "Here lies one whose name was writ in water". Close by rest the ashes of Percy Bysshe Shelley, who drowned in 1822.

🔟 Santa Sabina

📍 G8 🏛 Piazza Pietro d'Illiria 1 ☎ 06 57 94 01
🚌 23, 44, 170, 781
🕐 7:15am–8pm daily

High on the Aventine stands an early Christian basilica, founded by Peter of Illyria in AD 425 and later given to the Dominican order. It was restored to its original simplicity in the early 20th century. Light filters through 9th-century windows onto a nave framed by pale Corinthian columns. Above the main door is a blue and gold 5th-century mosaic inscription to Peter. In the side portico outside is a 5th-century panelled door carved with biblical scenes, notably one of the oldest images of the Crucifixion (top left-hand corner).

SHOP

Mercato di Testaccio
This is a must for anyone who takes food seriously – as well as the market stalls, there are takeaway food stands offering everything from assorted tasty morsels to freshly squeezed juices.

📍 G10 🏛 Via Lorenzo Ghiberti
🌐 mercatoditestaccio.it

↑ Weeping angel statue at the Protestant Cemetery

A SHORT WALK
PIAZZA DELLA BOCCA DELLA VERITÀ

Distance 1 km (0.5 miles) **Time** 10 minutes
Nearest bus stops 23, 44, 81, 160, 170, 280, 628, 715, 716, 780

A quiet corner of the city, this area beside the Tiber is great for escaping the crowds. It was ancient Rome's first port and its busy cattle market. Substantial Classical remains include two small temples from the Republican age and the Arch of Janus from the later Empire. In the 6th century the area became home to a Greek community from Byzantium, who founded the churches of San Giorgio in Velabro and Santa Maria in Cosmedin. Follow tradition and place your hand inside the Bocca della Verità (the Mouth of Truth), a mythological stone sculpture in the portico of Santa Maria in Cosmedin.

Sant'Omobono, dating to the 16th-century, stands in isolation in the middle of an important archaeological site where the remains of sacrificial altars and two temples from the 6th century BC have been discovered.

START

The 11th-century Casa dei Crescenzi features columns and capitals from ancient Roman temples

The Temples of the Forum Boarium are the best preserved of Rome's Republican temples (p306).

Ponte Rotto, as this forlorn ruined arch in the Tiber is called, means simply "broken bridge". Built in the 2nd century BC, its original name was Pons Aemilius.

LUNGOTEVERE DEI PIERLEONI

Tevere

PONTE PALATINO

↑ The well-preserved Temple of Hercules in the Forum Boarium

The Fontana dei Tritoni, by Carlo Bizzaccheri, was built here in 1715. The style shows the powerful influence of Bernini.

Locator Map
For more detail see p302

Medieval interior
of Santa Maria
in Cosmedin ↑

*Santa Maria della
Consolazione is named
after an icon that
consoled criminals at
Tarpeian Rock (p245).*

FINISH

VIA DEI FIENILI

GIOVANNI DECOLLATO

VIA DI SAN TEODORO

VIA DI SAN TEODORO

PIAZZA DELLA
BOCCA DELLA
VERITA

VIA DEI CERCHI

VIA DELLA
GRECA

*The 15th-century portal
of the ancient round
San Teodoro church is
decorated with the insignia
of Pope Nicholas V.*

*The plain Renaissance façade
of San Giovanni Decollato was
completed in about 1504.*

*San Giorgio in Velabro's simple
12th-century portico of Ionic
columns was destroyed by a bomb
in 1993 but has been restored.*

*The Arco degli Argentari,
dedicated to Emperor
Septimius Severus in
AD 204, is decorated with
scenes of religion and war.*

*The square Arch of
Janus with arches on
each side dates from
the 4th century AD.*

*The medieval church of Santa
Maria in Cosmedin has a fine
marble mosaic floor and a
Gothic baldacchino (p306).*

0 metres	100
0 yards	100

N ↑

ROME: BEYOND THE CENTRE

Must See

❶ Museo e Galleria Borghese

Experience More

❷ MAXXI (National Museum of 21st Century Arts)

❸ Villa Giulia

❹ Catacombs

❺ Centrale Montemartini

❻ Mattatoio

❼ EUR

❽ Cinecittà Si Mostra

It is well worth making the effort to see some of Rome's outlying sights. Just outside the centre are the Villa Giulia, home to a magnificent Etruscan museum, and the Museo Borghese on the splendid Villa Borghese estate, with its extraordinary collection of virtuoso statues by Bernini. South of the city, follow the atmospheric Via Appia Antica to the outskirts of the modern city and discover the evocative ruins of ancient churches and early Christian catacombs. Further north, MAXXI gives a tantalising taste of the Rome of the future.

❶ MUSEO E GALLERIA BORGHESE

📍D4 🏛Villa Borghese, Piazzale Scipione Borghese 🚌52, 53, 116, 910 🚋3, 19
🕐9am–7pm Tue–Sun; advance booking essential; limited time slots for entry
📅1 Jan, 25 Dec 🌐galleriaborghese.beniculturali.it

There are few places in the world where it is possible to weave together a day in a park with high culture as easily as at the Villa Borghese. Some of Bernini's best sculptures and paintings by Caravaggio, Titian and Raphael sit alongside Classical works in this beautiful frescoed 17th-century villa set in extensive grounds.

The villa and park were laid out by Cardinal Scipione Borghese, favourite nephew of Pope Paul V, who had the estate designed for pleasure. The hedonistic cardinal was a patron of the arts and commissioned sculptures from Bernini which now rank among the artist's most famous works. Today the villa houses the private Borghese Collection. Online booking is essential.

Sculpture

The sculpture collection is on the ground floor of the villa. Among the highlights is one of Bernini's finest works, *Apollo and Daphne* (1624) in room 3, which shows the nymph Daphne metamorphosing into a laurel tree in order to escape abduction by Apollo. Abduction is also the theme of *The Rape of Proserpina*, again by

Bernini's marble sculpture of David, completed in 1624 ↓

THE BORGHESE COLLECTORS

Scipione used this villa to display the antiquities collection given to him by his uncle, Pope Paul V, to which he added sculptures by Bernini. When later heir Camillo Borghese married Pauline Bonaparte, he gave the bulk of the Classical sculpture collection to his brother-in-law, Napoleon. They now form the core of the Louvre's antiquities wing.

← Bust of Cardinal Scipione Borghese

Bernini, in room 4. Here, muscular Hades throws his head back with laughter, his strong fingers pressing into the maiden's soft flesh as she struggles to break free of his grasp.

Paintings

The upper floor, of the villa is devoted to Baroque and Renaissance paintings. Works on display include Raphael's masterpiece *Deposition*, Titian's *Sacred and Profane Love*, and various works by Caravaggio, including the sensuous *Boy with a Basket of Fruit*.

The Park

The estates of the Villa Borghese, Villa Giulia and the Pincio gardens form one vast park, with the Giardino del Lago, at its centre, named after an artificial boating lake. Dotted around it are an array of attractions, including artificial ponds, mock temples, a children's play centre, a zoo, an outdoor theatre, the world's smallest purpose-built cinema and a horse-riding track.

↑ Exterior of the villa, now the Museo e Galleria Borghese

↑ Raphael's bold and moving masterpiece *Deposition*

EXPERIENCE MORE

2

MAXXI (National Museum of 21st Century Arts)

 D4   Villa Guido Reni 4A
53, 217, 910   2   11am-8pm Tue-Sun (to 7pm Wed, Thu & Sun)   1 May, 25 Dec
maxxi.art

Along with the nearby Parco della Musica, MAXXI has put Rome on the contemporary arts map. Completed in 2009, it is located in a building designed by the late architect Zaha Hadid. The museum showcases emerging Italian and international artists. An impressive amount of space is also given over to architecture.

3

Villa Giulia

D4   Piazzale di Villa Giulia 9   06 322 65 71
52   3, 19   9am-8pm Tue-Sun   1 Jan, 25 Dec
museoetru.it

Villa Giulia was built in the mid-16th century as a country retreat and pleasure palace for Pope Julius III, who would regularly float up the River Tiber from the Vatican on a flower-decked barge to check on its progress. The gardens were planted with 36,000 trees and studded with statues, grottoes, pavilions and fountains. The house was filled with an outstanding collection of sculptures: 160 boats packed with statues and ornaments were sent to the Vatican after the Pope died in 1555.

Since 1889 the villa has been home to the Museo Nazionale Etrusco, devoted to the ancient Etruscan civilization that lived in central Italy before the Romans and traded metals for ceramics and luxury objects made by the Greeks and Phoenicians (p40). The museum's collection includes several important pieces that were repatriated to Italy after being illegally excavated and sold to collectors and museums across the globe. Included among these is the 6th-century-BC *Euphronius Vase*, painted with spectacular images of Hypnos, god of sleep, and Thanatos, god of death; it was returned to Italy from the Metropolitan Museum in New York in 2008. Other highlights include the *Ficoroni Cist*, an exquisitely engraved 4th-century-BC bronze marriage coffer designed to hold mirrors

---

EAT

Eataly

As well as a bewildering range of niche producers of everything from artisanal cheese to craft beer, this cathedral to gastronomy houses bars, restaurants and cookery schools. There's a packed calendar of tastings and other food-related events.

D4   Piazzale 12 Ottobre 1492
eataly.net

316

Futuristic MAXXI museum, designed by Zaha Hadid

and cosmetics; the spiral-handled *Faliscan Crater*, a beautifully painted vase used to hold wine or oil, dating back to the 4th century BC; and the famous *Husband and Wife Sarcophagus*, a 6th-century-BC tomb on which the deceased couple are shown banqueting in the afterlife.

Catacombs

D4 **Via Appia Antica 126** 118, 218

The first part of the Via Appia was built in 312 BC by Appius Claudius Caecus. In 190 BC, when it was extended to the southern ports of Taranto and Brindisi, the road became Rome's link with its empire in the East. It was also the route taken by the funeral processions of the dictator Sulla (78 BC) and Emperor Augustus (AD 14), and it was along this road that St Paul was led as a prisoner to

Rome in AD 56. The church of Domine Quo Vadis marks the spot where St Peter is said to have met Christ when fleeing Rome. The road is lined with ruined family tombs, decaying monuments and collective burial places (*columbaria*). Beneath the fields on either side lies a maze of catacombs.

In burying their dead in underground cemeteries outside the city walls, the early Christians were simply obeying the laws of the time. They were not forced to use them because of persecution, as later popular myth has suggested. Many saints were buried here, and the catacombs later became shrines and places of pilgrimage.

Today several catacombs are open to the public. The vast **Catacombs of San Callisto**, hewn from volcanic tufa, contain niches, or *loculi*, which held two or three bodies, as well as the burial places of several early popes. Close by, walls in the Catacombs of San Sebastiano are covered in graffiti invoking St Peter and St Paul, whose remains may once have been moved here.

Catacombs of San Callisto
06 513 01 580 9am-noon, 2-5pm Thu-Tue 1 Jan, late Jan-late Feb, Easter Sun, 25 Dec

Centrale Montemartini

D4 **Via Ostiense 106** 23, 769 9am-7pm Tue-Sun 1 Jan, 1 May, 25 Dec centrale montemartini.org

An enormous former industrial site, originally housing Rome's first power station, has been restored and turned into a fascinating art centre. Two enormous generators still occupy the central machine room, creating quite an intriguing contrast to the artifacts and exhibitions on display.

On display at Centrale Montemartini are Roman statues and artifacts belonging to the Capitoline Museums (*p250*). Many of the statues were discovered during excavations in the late 19th and early 20th centuries, including some from the Area Sacra di Largo Argentina (*p265*).

Ruins of a Roman-era aqueduct along the Via Appia Antica ↓

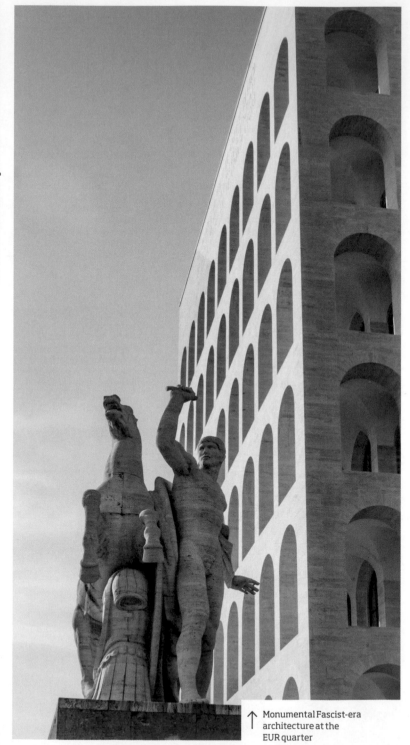

↑ Monumental Fascist-era architecture at the EUR quarter

6

Mattatoio

D4 **Piazza Orazio Giustiniani 4** **For events and exhibitions only** **mattatoioroma.it**

For much of the 20th century, the Testaccio neighbourhood was a working-class quarter, dominated by its vast 19th-century slaughterhouse, the Mattatoio. The district has now become one of the city's trendiest areas, and the Mattatoio itself, considered an important industrial architectural landmark, has been transformed into a centre for contemporary art hosting temporary exhibitions and art-related events.

7

EUR

D4 **170, 671, 714** **EUR Fermi, EUR Palasport**

The Esposizione Universale di Roma (EUR), a suburb to the south of the city, was originally built for an international exhibition, a kind of "Work Olympics", that was planned for 1942, but never took place because of the outbreak of war. The architecture was intended to glorify Fascism (*p45*), and as a result the bombastic style of the buildings can look overblown and rhetorical to modern eyes. Of all the buildings the best known is probably the Palazzo della Civiltà del Lavoro (the Palace of the Civilization of Work), an unmistakable landmark for people arriving from Fiumicino airport.

Despite the area's dubious architecture, EUR has been a planning success, and

→

Entrance to the film studios at Cinecittà, now open to the public

---

EAT

Sibilla

The location - a wisteria-clad terrace with a view of a Greek temple - can hardly be beaten, and the food at Sibilla is pretty special too: expect refined versions of traditional Italian cuisine.

D4 **Via della Sibilla 50, Tivoli** **ristorantesibilla.com**

€€€

---

people are keen to live here. As well as residential housing, the vast marble halls along the wide boulevards are also home to a number of government offices and museums. Best among the latter is the small **Museo dell'Alto Medioevo** (Museum of the Early Middle Ages), which houses a spectacular reconstruction of a highly decorated marble clad room from Ostia Antica.

A visit is well worth the journey and the ticket price for that alone.

Museo dell'Alto Medioevo

Viale Lincoln 3 **8am-7pm Tue, Sat & Sun** **altomedioevo.beniculturali.it**

8

Cinecittà Si Mostra

D4 **Via Tuscolana 1055** **10am-6:30pm Wed-Mon** **cinecittasimostra.it**

Cinecittà Si Mostra (literally translating as Cinecittà Shows Off) offers the chance to step behind the scenes of Italy's most famous film studio. Costumes and props are exhibited, including the dress worn by Elizabeth Taylor in *Cleopatra* (1963). Visits include tours of film sets, such as a replica Broadway created for the Martin Scorsese film *Gangs of New York* (2002) and a mock ancient Rome (which stood in for ancient Pompeii in a 2008 episode of *Doctor Who*), along with a visit to the working film studio.

The hill-town of Civita di Bagnoregio, near Montefiascone

LAZIO

With its ancient forests, volcanic lakes, wetlands, mountains and beaches, Lazio is a region of fascinating contrasts. In addition to its many archaeological sites, Lazio today offers skiing, swimming and watersports.

Lazio was inhabited at least 60,000 years ago, although the first signs of a civilization date back to the 10th century BC. By the 7th century BC a flourishing Etruscan and Sabine civilization based on trade and agriculture existed in the north, while the region's southern margins were colonized by the Latins, Volsci and Hernici. History mingles with myth in the writings of Virgil, who describes how Aeneas landed in Lazio, where he married the daughter of the king of the Latins. Romulus and Remus (legendary founders of Rome) were descendants of this alliance.

With the rise of Rome as a power, the Etruscan and Latin peoples were, in time, overwhelmed and the focus of the region turned to the city of Rome. Great roads and aqueducts extended out of the city like spokes of a wheel, and wealthy patricians built lavish villas in the surrounding countryside.

The early Middle Ages saw the rise of the Church's temporal power and, with the foundation of monasteries at Subiaco and Montecassino, Lazio became the cradle of western monasticism, and eventually part of the Papal States. In the 16th and 17th centuries, wealthy papal families competed with one another to build luxurious villas and gardens.

Throughout its history, however, Lazio has been eclipsed and neglected by Rome. The Pontine marshes were a malaria-ridden swamp until the 1920s, when Mussolini had them drained and brought new roads and agricultural improvements.

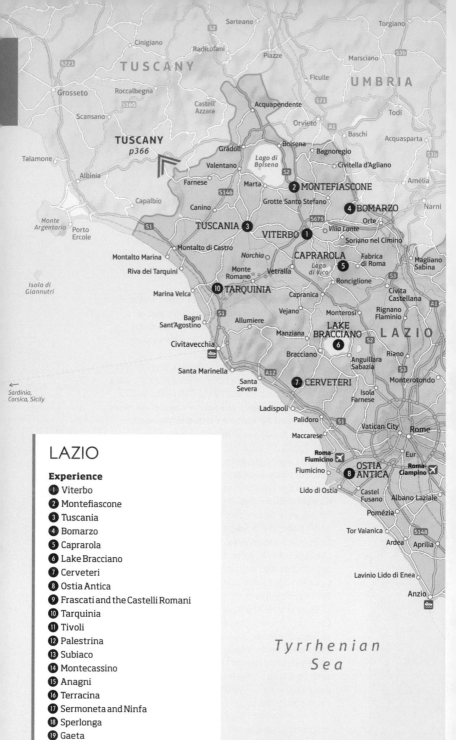

LAZIO

Experience

0 kilometres 20

0 miles 20

N

EXPERIENCE

Viterbo

🅰D4 FS🚌 ℹ️ Via Ascenzi 1;
www.visit.viterbo.it

Viterbo was an important Etruscan centre before falling to the Romans in the 4th century BC. Its heyday came when it briefly became the papal seat (1257–81). It was devastated in World War II, but the medieval core has been carefully restored.

In San Pellegrino, Viterbo's oldest and best-preserved quarter, medieval houses with towers, arches and external staircases line narrow streets.

On Piazza San Lorenzo the 12th-century Duomo boasts a striped bell tower, a solemn 16th-century façade and a stark Romanesque interior. The adjacent 13th-century Palazzo Papale, with a finely carved loggia, was built for popes on their visits to the city.

The town's civic buildings border Piazza del Plebiscito. The most interesting is the 15th-century **Palazzo dei Priori**, frescoed inside by Baldassare Croce with scenes from the town's history and mythological past.

The **Villa Lante**, northeast of Viterbo, was begun in 1562 by Vignola for Cardinal Gambara. The main attractions are the Renaissance gardens and fountains. Be aware that many of the fountains will spray people without warning.

Palazzo dei Priori

 🅰Piazza Plebiscito
📞0761 30 47 95 🕐Daily

Villa Lante

 🅰Bagnaia 📞0761 28 80 08 🕐8:30am to 1 hour before sunset Tue–Sun
🚫1 Jan, 25 Dec

---

❷
Montefiascone

🅰D4 🅰Viterbo FS🚌
ℹ️Piazza V. Emanuele;
0761 64 79 41

This pretty town sits on the edge of a defunct volcanic crater between the shores of Lake Bolsena and the Via Cassia. It is dominated by the bulk of its cathedral, Santa Margherita, whose 1670s dome is second in size only to St Peter's.

On the town's outskirts, towards Orvieto, lies San Flaviano, a lovely building with a 12th-century church oriented east over an 11th-century church pointing west. Inside are some fine 14th-century frescoes and freely carved capitals.

The popular lakeside resort of Bolsena, 15 km (9 miles) north on Lake Bolsena, has a medieval castle, as well as boats to the islands of Bisentina and Martana.

---

❸
Tuscania

🅰D4 🅰Viterbo
🚌 ℹ️Piazzale Trieste;
0761 445 42 59

Tuscania's trim walls and towers are visible from afar

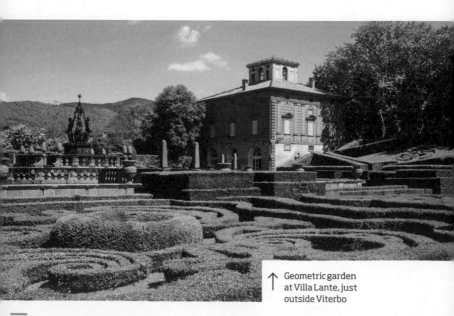

↑ Geometric garden at Villa Lante, just outside Viterbo

→ View across the city of Tuscania, with its towers visible

on the empty low-lying plains between Viterbo and Tarquinia. Although shaken by an earthquake in 1971, its medieval and Renaissance buildings have been carefully reconstructed. Just outside the city walls, on the rocky Colle San Pietro, two remarkable churches of the Lombard-Romanesque period occupy the site of Tuscana, a major Etruscan centre conquered by Rome in 300 BC.

Santa Maria Maggiore, at the foot of the hill, has a Lombard-Romanesque asymmetric façade with blind arcades and a bold rose window. Over the central door lies a simple marble Madonna and Child, framed by abstract motifs and biblical scenes.

The Lombard-Romanesque church of San Pietro, on top of the hill, is a striking building of ochre-hued tufa and white marble details. It stands on a grassy piazza, along with two medieval towers and a bishop's palace. The façade features an intricately inlaid rose window flanked by strange reliefs, including three-headed bearded demons.

4

Bomarzo

⬛D4 **🏛Parco dei Mostri, Bomarzo** **🚉To Viterbo** **🚌From Viterbo (not Sun or pub hols)** **🕐9am–7pm (winter: to sunset)** **🌐sacrobosco.it**

The Monster Park beneath the town of Bomarzo was created between 1522 and 1580 by Duke Vicino Orsini as a bizarre memorial to his late wife, and is essentially the world's first theme park. Orsini embraced the artificiality and distortion of the Mannerist period by creating lopsided buildings and sculpting huge boulders of stone into fantastic creatures and vast allegorical monsters. Most famous of all is a huge screaming face, but there is also a giant ripping a man in two, a life-size elephant crushing a Roman soldier, and a series of dragons, nymphs, mermaids and sphinxes.

5

Caprarola

⬛D4 **🚉Viterbo** **🚌** **ℹVia Filippo Nicolai 2; www.caprarola.com**

Perhaps the grandest of the country villas created during the 17th century by the wealthy families of Rome, **Palazzo Farnese** is the focal point of the medieval village of Caprarola. Designed by Vignola, it was built between 1559 and 1575 and takes its star shape from the foundations of a large pentagonal fortress designed by Antonio da Sangallo the Younger half a century earlier.

Created, according to legend, by Hercules ramming his club into the ground, Lago di Vico, 5 km (3 miles) west of Caprarola, occupies the remnants of a volcanic crater. An idyllic enclave, the lake is encircled by the wooded slopes of the Cimini Hills.

Palazzo Farnese
⊘ 🏛Caprarola 📞0761 64 60 52 🕐Tue–Sun 🚫1 Jan, 25 Dec

EAT

Hostaria del Ponte da Lorena

Set inside an 18th-century palace near Montefiascone, this restaurant has a lovely courtyard and a terraced garden.

⬛D4 **🏛Piazza G Battista 1, Lubriano** **🚫Tue** **🌐hostaria delponte.it**

€€€

La Piazzetta del Sole

This little spot is tucked into a tiny hamlet, a short drive from Tuscania, and run by two visionary women.

⬛C4 **🏛Via XX Settembre 129, Farnese** **🚫Lunch Mon-Fri** **🌐piazzettadelsole.com**

€€€

Trattoria Zi Maria

First-rate traditional regional food is served in this trattoria, near Cerveteri. The venison with wild berries is exceptional.

⬛C4 **🏛Via Sasso Manziana 2, Sasso-Cerveteri** **🚫Tue** **🌐trattoriazimaria.com**

€€€

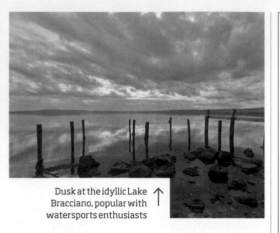

Dusk at the idyllic Lake Bracciano, popular with watersports enthusiasts

6
Lake Bracciano

D4 **Roma**
Bracciano **Piazza IV Novembre, Bracciano; 06 99 81 61**

Bracciano is a large lake famous for its fish, and popular for watersports and lakeside lunches.

Medieval Anguillara, to the south, is the prettiest of the lakeside towns with romantic views over the water. The main town, Bracciano, on the east shore, is dominated by **Castello Orsini-Odescalchi**, a pentagonal 15th-century structure with frescoes by Antoniazzo Romano and other Tuscan and Umbrian artists.

Castello Orsini-Odescalchi
Piazza Mazzini 14 **06 99 80 23 79** **10am-5pm daily** **1 Jan, 25 Dec**

> **HIDDEN GEM**
> **Calcata**
>
> For some 30 years, the town of Calcata, to the north of Lake Bracciano, was left to ruin. But in the late 1960s, a group of artists, musicians and intellectuals established a creative colony here that continues to thrive to this day.

7
Cerveteri

D4 **Roma**
Piazza A. Moro, 1; 06 99 55 26 37

In the 6th century BC Cerveteri (ancient Kysry) was one of the largest and most culturally rich towns of the Mediterranean. The Etruscan **necropolis**, 2 km (1 mile) outside town, is a network of streets lined with tombs dating from the 7th to the 1st century BC. The Tomba dei Rilievi is decorated with plaster reliefs of tools, pets and mythological figures. While the best finds are now in museums, such as the Vatican Museums and Villa Giulia, some can be seen in the small **Museo Nazionale Archeologico Cerite**.

There are more traces of the Etruscans to be seen at Norchia, where the tombs are carved out of a rock face, and Sutri, whose amphitheatre is one of the few relics of the living Etruscans.

Necropolis
Via della Necropoli 43/45 **06 994 00 01** **Tue-Sun** **Some pub hols**

Museo Nazionale Archeologico Cerite
Piazza Santa Maria **06 994 13 54** **8:30am-7:30pm Fri-Sun** **Pub hols**

8
Ostia Antica

D5 **Viale dei Romagnoli 717, Ostia** **06 56 35 80 99** **Piramide, then train from Porta San Paolo** **8:30am to 1 hour before sunset Tue-Sun** **1 Jan, 1 May, 25 Dec**

For more than 600 years Ostia was Rome's main port and a busy trading centre, until the 5th century AD when a disastrous combination of malaria and commercial competition sent the town into decline. Silt preserved its buildings and it now lies 5 km (3 miles) inland.

The ruins of Ostia give a vivid idea of life in Classical times. The main thoroughfare, the Decumanus Maximus, runs through the Forum, which houses Ostia's largest temple, the Capitol, and past the restored theatre, still used for open-air concerts in the summer. The road is lined with baths, shops and multistorey buildings. There is even a Thermopolium, or bar, with a marble counter and paintings advertising food and drink.

Frascati and the Castelli Romani

D4 **Roma** **FS** **Frascati**

The Alban hills have long been a country retreat for Romans. In Classical times they were scattered with villas; during the Middle Ages with fortified castles (hence the name); and in the 16th and 17th centuries with luxurious residences. During World War II German defences were based in the Alban hills and many Castelli towns were damaged by Allied bombs. Partly protected by a nature reserve, the hilltop towns are popular day-trip destinations and famous for their white wine. Frascati's central piazza is a belvedere overlooked by the **Villa Aldobrandini**, a majestic 17th-century building in a splendid park of grottoes and fountains.

The fortified **Abbazia di San Nilo** in Grottaferrata, 3 km (2 miles) south, was founded in 1004 and contains some lovely 17th-century frescoes by Domenichino in the chapel. Overlooking Lake Albano,

6 km (4 miles) south, Castel Gandolfo is the site of the pope's summer palace.

Villa Aldobrandini

06 91 01 41 40 **Gardens only: call ahead**

Abbazia di San Nilo

Corso del Popolo 128, Grottaferrata **By appt, Mon-Sat** **abbaziagreca.it**

10

Tarquinia

C4 **Viterbo** **FS**
Largo Barriera di San Giusto; 0766 84 92 82

Ancient Tarquinia (Tarxuna) was one of Etruria's most important centres. It occupied a strategic position on a ridge to the northeast of the present town until the 4th century BC, when it fell to Rome.

The highlight of Tarquinia is the **Museo Archeologico e Necropoli**, which has one of Italy's best collections of Etruscan finds, including a group of terracotta winged horses from the 4th century BC.

↑ A decorative jug in the Museo Archeologico in Tarquinia

On a hilltop 2 km (1 mile) southeast of town are the frescoed tombs of the necropolis dug into the soft volcanic tufa. There are almost 6,000 tombs but only about 15 can be visited at a time. The frescoes that decorate them, designed to remind the dead of life, range from frenetic dancing figures in the Tomb of the Triclinium to diners reclining in the Tomb of the Leopards.

Museo Archeologico e Necropoli

Piazza Cavour **0766 85 6036** **Tue-Sun** **1 Jan, 1 May, 25 Dec**

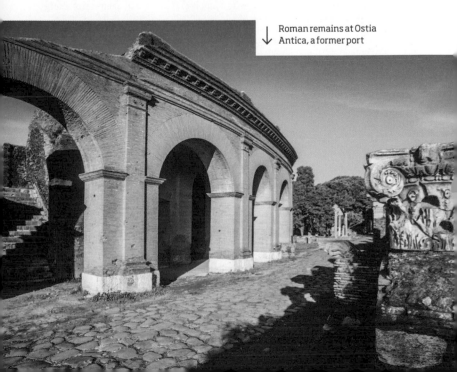

↓ Roman remains at Ostia Antica, a former port

⑪ Tivoli

Ⓐ D4 🚉 Roma 🚆📧
ℹ️ Piazzale Nazioni Unite;
www.visittivoli.eu

Hill-town Tivoli, a popular excursion from Rome, was a favoured resort of the ancient Romans, attracted by its fresh water and sulphur springs, and beautiful countryside. The temples that once covered Tivoli's hilltop are still visible in places. Some are half buried in medieval buildings, others, such as the temples of Sibyl and Vesta, are relatively intact.

The town's most famous sight is the **Villa d'Este**, a sumptuous country residence created in the 16th century by Pirro Ligorio for Cardinal Ippolito d'Este from the shell of a Benedictine monastery. It is known primarily for its gardens, steeply raked on terraces, and studded with spectacular, if somewhat faded and moss-hung, fountains. Although suffering from reduced water pressure and polluted water due to centuries of neglect, the gardens give a vivid impression of the frivolous luxury enjoyed by the papal families. Highlights include the Viale delle Cento Fontane and the Fontana dell'Organo Idraulico, which, thanks to a hydraulic

↑ A waterfall within the gardens of the famed Villa d'Este, Tivoli

system, can play music. At the other end of town, the **Villa Gregoriana**, now a hotel, is set in a lush wooded valley where paths wind down into a deep ravine.

About 5 km (3 miles) west of Tivoli are the ruins of **Hadrian's Villa**. Easily seen in conjunction with a visit to the town, this is one of the largest and most spectacular villas ever built in the Roman Empire (it once covered an area greater than the centre of Imperial Rome).

Hadrian was an inveterate traveller and his aim in creating the villa was to reproduce some of the wonders he had seen around the world. The Stoa Poikile, for example, a walkway around a rectangular pool and garden, recalls the painted colonnade of the Stoic

philosophers in Athens, while the Canopus evokes the grand sanctuary of Serapis in Alexandria. There are also ruins of two bath complexes, a Latin and a Greek library, a Greek theatre, and a private study on a little island known as the Teatro Marittimo.

Today the rambling ruins make a lovely place to relax, picnic or explore.

Villa d'Este
⊗ 🏠 Piazza Trento 1
📞 0774 33 29 20 🕐 Tue–Sun
🚫 1 Jan, 25 Dec

Villa Gregoriana
🏠 Largo Sant'Angelo
📞 0774 33 26 50 🕐 Mar–mid-Dec: daily 🚫 Mid-Dec–Feb

Hadrian's Villa
⊗ 🏠 Largo Marguerite Yourcenar 🚫 Pub hols
🌐 villaadriana.beniculturali.it

⑫ Palestrina

Ⓐ D4 🚉 Roma 🚌

Medieval Palestrina grew up over the terraces of a huge temple dedicated to the goddess Fortuna Primigenia, the mother of all gods. The temple, founded in the 8th century BC and rebuilt in the 2nd century BC by Sulla, housed one of the most important oracles of ancient times. The terraces of the sanctuary, littered with fragments of columns and porticoes, lead up to the curved Palazzo Barberini. Built over the site of a circular temple, the Palazzo now houses the **Museo Nazionale Prenestino**, best known for a 1st-century-BC mosaic of the Nile in flood. This museum also boasts a famous sculpture of the Capitoline Triad.

Museo Nazionale Prenestino
⊗ 🏠 Via Barberini 📞 06 953 81 00 🕐 9am–8pm daily; archaeological area until dusk

LAZIO MONASTERIES

St Benedict founded the Abbey of Montecassino around 529 and there wrote his famous *Rule*, which became the fundamental monastic code of western Europe. The Cistercians, an offshoot of the Benedictines, were followers of St Bernard, whose creed was based on austerity and self-sufficiency. Cistercian abbeys in Lazio include Valvisciolo and San Martino in Cimino.

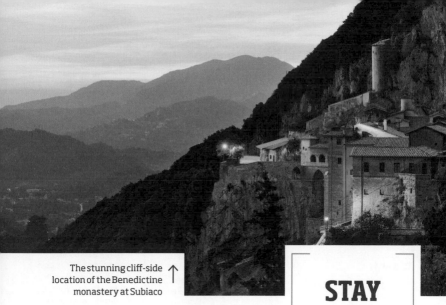

The stunning cliff-side location of the Benedictine monastery at Subiaco ↑

⑬ Subiaco

 D4 🚗 Roma 🚌 ℹ️ Town Library, Viale della Repubblica 26; 0774 85 050

In the 6th century, weary of the decadence of Rome, St Benedict left the city to become a hermit in a cave above Subiaco. Others joined him, and eventually there were 12 monasteries in the area.

Only two of these now survive: **Santa Scolastica**, dedicated to Benedict's sister, is organized around three cloisters, one Renaissance, one early Gothic and the third Cosmatesque. Higher up, the 12th-century **San Benedetto** is a more rewarding destination. Overhanging a deep gorge, it comprises two churches built on top of each other. The upper is decorated with 14th-century Sienese frescoes; the lower, built over several levels, incorporates the original cave where Benedict spent three years after fleeing Rome.

Santa Scolastica

🏠 3 km (2 miles) E of Subiaco 📞 0774 85 569 🕐 Daily

San Benedetto

🏠 3 km (2 miles) E of Subiaco 📞 0774 85 039 🕐 Daily

⑭ Montecassino

 E5 🚗 Cassino 📞 0776 31 15 29 🚆 Cassino, then bus 🕐 Apr–Oct: 9am–7pm daily; Nov–Mar: 9am–12:30pm & 3:30–7pm daily

The Abbey of Montecassino, the mother church of the Benedictine Order and an important centre of medieval art, was founded in 529 by St Benedict. By the 8th century it was an important centre of learning, and by the 11th century it had become one of the richest monasteries in Europe.

In 1944 Montecassino was a German stronghold and therefore a target for Allied bombing campaigns. Most of the complex was devastated, including the lavish Baroque church, but the walls remained intact and the abbey withstood for three months before falling to the Allies. The adjoining war cemeteries commemorate the 30,000 soldiers killed.

↑ Interior of the nave of Anagni's imposing Romanesque Duomo

 Anagni

D5 **Frosinone** FS⊟
Via Vittorio Emanuele 187; www.visitanagni.com

According to legend, Saturn founded five towns in south-east Lazio, including Anagni, Alatri and Arpino. This area is now known as La Ciociaria, from *ciocie*, the bark clogs worn in the area until about 30 years ago.

Before the Romans conquered this part of Lazio it was inhabited by several different tribes: the Volsci, the Sanniti, and the Hernici. Little is known of them, apart from the extraordinary walls with which they protected their settlements. In later years these were believed to have been built by the Cyclops, a mythical giant, which gave them their present name of Cyclopean walls.

Anagni was the most sacred Hernician centre until its destruction by the Romans in 306 BC. In the Middle Ages it was the birthplace and family seat of several popes, an era from which many buildings survive, most notably Boniface VIII's 13th-century mullion-windowed palace.

The beautiful Romanesque Duomo, Santa Maria, built over the ancient Hernician acropolis, boasts a fine Cosmati mosaic floor from the 13th century as well as 14th-century Sienese frescoes.

The crypt of San Magno is frescoed with one of the most complete surviving cycles of the 12th and 13th centuries.

Alatri, perched on an olive-covered slope 28 km (17 miles) east of Anagni, was an important Hernician town. It has an impressive double set of Cyclopean walls, 2 km (1 mile) long and 3 m (10 ft) high, from its 7th-century-BC acropolis.

The bustling town of Arpino, 40 km (25 miles) east of Alatri, was the birthplace of the Roman orator Cicero. About 3 km (2 miles) above Arpino, at the site of the ancient town of Civitavecchia, is a tremendous stretch of Cyclopean walls with a rare gateway with a pointed arch.

 Terracina

D5 **Latina** FS⊟
Piazza Municipio 1; 0773 70 77 02

Roman Terracina was an important commercial centre on the historic Roman road, the Via Appia *(p317)*. Today it is a popular seaside resort, with fascinating medieval buildings and Roman ruins in its historic centre. The more modern part of town by the sea is full of restaurants, bars and hotels.

Bombing in World War II uncovered many of the town's ancient structures, notably a stretch of the Appian Way and the original paving of the Roman Forum in Piazza del Municipio. The 11th-century Duomo was built in the shell of a Roman temple, and is still entered by the temple's steps. The medieval portico is adorned with a lovely 12th-century mosaic. Next door, the modern town hall is home to the **Museo Archeologico**, devoted to local Greek and Roman finds.

About 3 km (2 miles) above the town are the podium and foundations that once supported the Temple of Jove Anxur, dating back to the 1st century BC. This huge arcaded platform offers vertiginous views of Terracina and its bay.

Museo Archeologico
⊗ **Piazza Municipio**
0773 70 73 13 **Daily**

 Sermoneta and Ninfa

D5 **Latina** FS**Latina Scalo** **From Latina**
Piazza del Comune 1; 0773 30312

Sermoneta is a lovely hilltop town overlooking the Pontine Plains, with narrow cobbled streets winding around medieval houses, palaces and churches. The Duomo has a fine 15th-century panel by

→

Wisteria in bloom in the picturesque gardens of Ninfa

Benozzo Gozzoli showing the Virgin cradling Sermoneta in her hands. At the top of the town is the fairy-tale Castello Caetani, frescoed by a pupil of Pinturicchio.

In the valley below lies the abandoned medieval village of Ninfa, converted into lush **Gardens of Ninfa** by the Caetani family in 1921.

Gardens of Ninfa

  Via Provinciale Ninfina 68, Cisterna di Latina
Sat & Sun, by appt only
giardinodininfa.eu

18

Sperlonga

D5 Latina Corso San Leone 22; 0771 55 70 00

Sperlonga is a seaside resort surrounded by beautiful sandy beaches. The old town sits on a rocky promontory, a picturesque labyrinth of narrow alleyways and piazzettas offering an occasional glimpse of the sea below. It is full of bars, restaurants and boutiques.

The area around Sperlonga was a summer retreat for the ancient Romans. They built villas along the coast, and converted natural caves into places to dine and relax.

In 1957, archaeologists excavating the complex of Tiberius's luxury villa, just outside the town, found some 2nd-century-BC Hellenistic sculptures in a cave open to the sea. These sculptures, depicting Homer's *Odyssey*, are thought to be by the same artists from Rhodes responsible for *The Laocoön (p290)*. They are displayed in the **Zona Archeologica**'s Museo Archeologico Nazionale.

Zona Archeologica

 Via Flacca 0771 54 80 28 Summer: daily (winter: Thu–Sun) 1 Jan, 25 Dec

---

19

Gaeta

D5 Latina Piazza Traniello 18; 320 038 0413

According to Virgil, Gaeta was named after Aeneas's wet nurse Caieta, who was allegedly buried here. The town sits on the southern headland of the gulf of Gaeta, under Monte Orlando. The historic centre is dominated by a mighty Aragonese castle and the pinnacles of mock-Gothic San Francesco. To the north, the modern quarter links Gaeta to the picturesque bay of Serapo.

↑ A bright, sunny day on the beautiful sandy beach at Sperlonga

TOP 5 **BEACHES IN LAZIO**

Sperlonga
D5
Beach resort village with charming alleyways, ancient stone houses and the famed Cave of Tiberius.

Gaeta
D5
With seven sandy beaches to choose from, Gaeta is a popular summertime getaway.

Tor Caldara (Anzio)
D5
Opposite a nature reserve, this beach has golden sands and blue, crystal-clear waters.

San Felice Al Circeo
D5
With underwater coves and grottoes ideal for diving, this seaside town is also a surfer's paradise.

Cala Feola
D5
In a beautiful cove on Ponza, this is the only sandy beach to be found on the island.

FLORENCE

The cradle of the Renaissance, Florence was at the centre of a cultural and artistic revolution during the 15th century. Inspired by the rediscovery of Classical culture, and under the lavish patronage of the Medici – then the richest family in Europe – artists like Michelangelo, Botticelli and Donatello, and architects such as Brunelleschi and Leon Battista Alberti, created a city that remains one of the world's greatest artistic capitals.

While the Etruscans had long settled in the hills around Fiesole, Florence first sprang to life as a Roman colony in 59 BC. Captured by the Lombards in the 6th century, the city later emerged from the Dark Ages as an independent city state. By the 13th century a burgeoning trade in wool and textiles, backed by a powerful banking sector, had turned the city into one of Italy's leading powers. Political control was wielded first by the guilds, and later by the Florentine Republic. In time, power passed to leading noble families, of which the most influential were the Medici, a hugely wealthy banking dynasty. Florence, and later Tuscany, remained under the family's almost unbroken sway for three centuries. During this time the city was at the cultural and intellectual heart of Europe, its cosmopolitan atmosphere and wealthy patrons providing the impetus for a period of unparalleled artistic growth. By 1737 the Medici had died out, leaving the city under Austrian (and briefly Napoleonic) control until Italian Unification in 1860.

FLORENCE

Must Sees

① Duomo and Baptistry
② Uffizi
③ Piazza della Signoria
④ Galleria dell'Accademia
⑤ Palazzo Pitti

Experience More

⑥ Basilica di San Marco
⑦ Santissima Annunziata
⑧ Museo Archeologico
⑨ Spedale degli Innocenti
⑩ Museo dell'Opera del Duomo
⑪ Bargello
⑫ Santa Croce
⑬ Museo Galileo
⑭ Ponte Vecchio
⑮ Palazzo Vecchio
⑯ Orsanmichele
⑰ Palazzo Davanzati
⑱ Palazzo Strozzi
⑲ San Lorenzo
⑳ Cappelle Medicee
㉑ Mercato Centrale
㉒ Palazzo Antinori
㉓ Palazzo Rucellai
㉔ Santa Maria Novella
㉕ Ognissanti
㉖ Santo Spirito
㉗ Santa Felicita
㉘ Piazzale Michelangelo
㉙ San Miniato al Monte
㉚ Cappella Brancacci

Eat

① Osteria Antica Mescita San Niccolò
② Il Rifrullo
③ Enoteca Fuori Porta
④ I Bastioni di San Niccolò

Drink

⑤ Cantinetta Antinori
⑥ Casa del Vino
⑦ Fratelli Zanobini

Stay

⑧ Hotel Brunelleschi

Shop

⑨ Scuola del Cuoio
⑩ SIGNUM
⑪ Officina Profumo Farmaceutica di Santa Maria Novella

→

1 The Duomo dominating Florence's skyline.

2 Designer shop on Via Tornabuoni.

3 Piazza Santo Spirito.

4 Interior of Palazzo Pitti.

2 DAYS

A Tour of Florence

Day 1

Morning Start the day at the Piazza del Duomo (p342); climb Brunelleschi's enormous dome and admire the famous bronze Baptistry doors before strolling to Piazza della Signoria (p346), where a replica of Michelangelo's *David* and an array other statues can be seen. Just around the corner, Mercato Nuovo sells exquisite Florentine souvenirs, including leather goods and speciality paper. After crossing Ponte Vecchio (p356), turn left and walk along the river for lunch at Osteria Antica Mescita San Niccolò (p362).

Afternoon Refuelled and refreshed, you will be ready for the walk up to Piazzale Michelangelo (p362) for awe-inspiring views. Carry on to San Miniato al Monte before taking the shorter – but steeper – Salita al Monte back down the hill, stopping at the rose garden. Cross the Ponte alle Grazie bridge to reach Santa Croce (p355). Explore the interior of this awe-inspiring church – paying your respects to the tombs of Michelangelo, Machiavelli and Galileo – and visit the leather school at the rear.

Evening Have dinner at the excellent Gucci Garden (Piazza della Signoria 10).

Day 2

Morning Make the San Lorenzo complex, including the startling Cappelle Medicee (p358), today's first stop, followed by a look around the adjacent Mercato Centrale. See the frescoes at Santa Maria Novella (p360) nearby before making a tiny detour to the extraordinary Officina Profumo Farmaceutica historic perfumery (p361). For a tasty lunch and a glass of wine, try Cantinetta Antinori (p359), just beyond Santa Maria Novella.

Afternoon After lunch, stroll past the designer stores of Via Tornabuoni, stopping just before the river at the Museo Ferragamo (p358) to see shoes worn by some of Hollywood's classic stars. Cross the bridge to the Oltrarno district where the shopping theme changes to antiques on the way to Palazzo Pitti (p350). After visiting the rich interiors and galleries of this incredible 15th-century palace, end the afternoon with a relaxing stroll around the Boboli Gardens (p351).

Evening Reward yourself with an aperitivo in Piazza Santo Spirito (p361) before dining at one of the Oltrarno's authentic eateries, such as L'Brindellone (Piazza Piattellina 10).

Colourful Street Art

In between the galleries and museums, keep an eye out for art of a less classical kind. Pisa is home to the colourful *Tuttomondo* mural *(p379)* by Keith Haring, the American artist's last public work, while central Florence is dotted with Italian artist Blub's reimaginings of famous portraits, in which the subjects are depicted underwater wearing a snorkel and mask. Clet, a French artist whose works adorn numerous street signs, has a studio in Florence's San Niccolò district. Explore the latest street art with the city's map of spaces available for approved open-air works *(www.firenzestreetart.com)*.

→

Street artists re-creating a Renaissance masterpiece on the pavements of Florence

Did You Know?
—
Copies of Michelangelo's *David* can be seen in Florence's Piazza della Signoria and Piazzale Michelangelo.

FLORENCE FOR
ART LOVERS

Tuscany is a paradise for art lovers, with countless world-famous masterpieces, a multitude of stunning cities of art – including Florence, the undisputed home of the Renaissance – and a thriving contemporary art scene. With the region's inspiring landscapes, it's no wonder that so many top artists were drawn to work here.

The Uffizi

This museum *(p344)* is the ultimate Renaissance primer, with masterpieces by some of Italy's greats: Giotto, Botticelli, Leonardo da Vinci, Michelangelo, Raphael, Titian, Caravaggio and beyond. Choose your favourite from the 1,700 artworks on display – just beware of overload and an attack of Stendhal, or Florence Syndrome, a psychosomatic illness triggered by viewing lots of beautiful works of art quick succession.

→

Paintings and sculpture on display in one of the Uffizi's elegant galleries

Stunning Sculptures

Tuscany's white Carrara marble has been popular with sculptors since Roman times. It was a favourite of Michelangelo, who used it for his famous *David*, and is still greatly prized by modern artists - the town of Pietrasanta has numerous contemporary works on display.

← Michelangelo's *David* in Florence's Galleria dell'Accademia

Renaissance Frescoes

The fresco (literally "fresh") technique was popular in the Renaissance and results in remarkably vivid colours. Those in Florence's Brancacci Chapel *(p362)* are exceptional, as is the series by Piero della Francesca at San Francesco in Arezzo *(p384)*.

→ The striking frescoes in the Brancacci Chapel in Florence

Flavourful Festivals

Tuscany's countless food festivals *(sagre)* provide a fantastic opportunity to try local specialities. Highlights include the traditional steak festival held in Cortona (mid-August), the Lari cherry festival (last weekend May and first weekend June) and the *cacciucco* (hearty seafood soup) festival in Livorno (mid-June). The San Miniato truffle and Pienza cheese festivals (November and September respectively) celebrate some of the region's most prestigious produce.

→
Sampling the wares at a food festival in Livorno

FLORENCE FOR
FOODIES

Traditionally hearty and flavoursome, Tuscany's largely simple specialities allow the character and taste of the region's excellent ingredients to shine through. Popular favourites include the chunky T-bone steaks, while vegetarians are well catered for with innumerable pasta and pizza options.

Tuscan Staples

The traditional salt-free Tuscan bread, *pane toscano* – which originated in the 12th century when Pisa placed a blockade on the trade of salt to Florence – is the perfect partner for the tasty local cold cuts and cheeses. Be sure to try *finocchiona* (the region's speciality salami flavoured with fennel seeds) and *lardo di colonnata* (pork aged with herbs and spices in marble vats), as well as the fabulous pecorino sheep's cheese from Pienza. A glass of Chianti or one of Tuscany's other red wines makes the ideal accompaniment.

←
Cold cuts and *pane toscano*, traditional Tuscan staples

Where to Eat

From three-star Michelin fine dining in Florence's Enoteca Pinchiorri *(www.enotecapinchiorri.it)* to street food, the choice of where to eat couldn't be more varied. For quality local produce in a relaxed environment, seek out delis like Gino Cacino (Siena) and butcher-eateries such as Macelleria Stiaccini (Castellina in Chianti) and Falorni (Greve in Chianti).

$\longrightarrow$

One of the gourmet dishes at Florence's Enoteca Pinchiorri

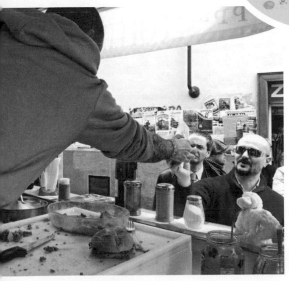

Florentine Street Food

Central Florence is peppered with kiosks laden with steaming pans of *lampredotto*, made from tripe and the city's most traditional and popular street food. The top stalls in the city include Nencioni (Piazza Mercato Nuovo), Nerbone (Mercato Centrale) and L'Antico Trippaio (Piazza de' Cimatori).

$\longleftarrow$

Ordering a *panino con lampredotto* from a stall in Florence

❶ 🔁

DUOMO AND BAPTISTRY

📍 C2 🏠 Piazza del Duomo 🚌 1, 6, 14, 23 🕐 Times vary, check website 🚫 15 Aug, 25 Dec & religious hols
🌐 duomo.firenze.it

Rising above the heart of the city, the richly decorated Duomo – Santa Maria del Fiore – and its orange-tiled dome have become Florence's most famous symbols.

Typical of the Florentine determination to lead in all things, the cathedral is Europe's fourth-largest church. It can hold 20,000 people and to this day remains the city's tallest building. One of the great Renaissance structures, its foundation stone was laid in 1296, but the Neo-Gothic patterned marble façade, inspired by the decoration of the Campanile alongside, was not completed until 1887. Clad in white, green and pink Tuscan marble, the Campanile was designed by Giotto in 1334 and completed after the artist's death. Opposite the Duomo stands the Baptistry of San Giovanni; with its celebrated bronze doors and precious mosaics, it holds the octagonal font where many famous Florentines, including Dante, were baptized. The Baptistry may date back to the 4th century, making it one of Florence's oldest buildings.

↑ Mosaics in the interior of the Baptistry

Colourful 13th-century mosaics illustrating *the Last Judgment* decorate the ceiling of the Baptistry.

→ Florence's octagonal Baptistry

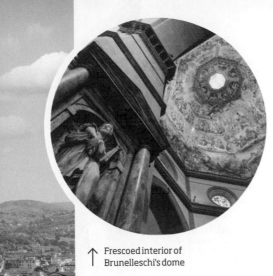

↑ Frescoed interior of Brunelleschi's dome

BAPTISTRY DOORS

In 1401, Lorenzo Ghiberti won a competition to design the north Baptistry doors. In 1425–52 he designed the east doors, which Michelangelo dubbed the "Gate of Paradise". The original ten relief panels are in the Museo dell'Opera del Duomo (p354); those on the Baptistry are copies.

← The Duomo's enormous dome and Campanile towering above Florence's skyline

The top of the dome offers spectacular views over the city.

Bricks in the dome were set between marble ribs in a self-supporting herringbone pattern.

The dome, designed by Brunelleschi (1420–36), was the largest of its time to be built without scaffolding.

Domenico di Michelino's Dante Explaining the Divine Comedy (1465) painting shows the poet outside Florence against a backdrop of Purgatory, Hell and Paradise.

The colourful, intricately inlaid pavement dates from the 16th century.

Copies of reliefs by Andrea Pisano on the Campanile's first storey depict the Creation of Man, and the Arts and the Industries.

The Duomo, seen from ↑ the Piazza del Duomo

② ⊘ Ⓜ ▣ 🛍

UFFIZI

📍 C3 🏛 Piazzale degli Uffizi 6 🚌 1, 3, D ⏰ 8:15am–6:50pm Tue–Sun 🚫 1 Jan & 25 Dec 🌐 uffizi.it

The Uffizi is one of Italy's greatest art galleries. It covers the whole sweep of Florentine art, from stylized Byzantine icons to the flowing lines of early medieval works, through Renaissance masterpieces to the colourful complexities of Mannerist paintings.

The Uffizi was built in 1560–80 to house offices (*uffici*) for Cosimo I dei Medici, the Grand Duke of Tuscany. The architect, Giorgio Vasari, used iron as reinforcement, enabling his successor, Buontalenti, to create an almost continuous wall of glass on the upper storey. From 1581, the Medicis used this well-lit space to display the family art treasures, creating what is now the oldest gallery in the world. Today, the paintings are hung chronologically to show the development of Florentine art from Gothic to Renaissance and beyond.

Gothic Art

Rooms 2 to 6 of the gallery are devoted to Tuscan Gothic art from the 12th to the 14th century. Giotto (1266–1337) introduced a degree of naturalism that was new in Tuscan art. The angels and saints in his *Ognissanti Madonna* (1310), in room 2, express a range of emotions, from awe and reverence to puzzlement.

Early Renaissance

The Botticelli paintings in rooms 10–14 are the highlight of the Uffizi's collection. The brilliant colours of *Primavera* (c 1482) are a reminder that Renaissance artists often experimented with new pigments to achieve striking effects. A celebration

Elegant exterior of ↑ the Uffizi, designed by Vasari and Buontalenti

GALLERY GUIDE

Book your ticket in advance to avoid queues. The earliest works are on the second floor – start here to explore the collection. There are many well-known Early Renaissance paintings in rooms 7–18. Ancient Greek and Roman sculptures are in the second-floor corridor, as well as room 56 on the first floor. Some familiar High Renaissance masterpieces are hung on the first floor, and masters from other European countries are in rooms 46–55.

← Visitors marvelling at Botticelli's famous masterpiece *Primavera*

of spring, the painting is populated with goddesses and over 500 species of plant. Zephyrus, the west wind, blows in from the right, while Mercury dispels clouds on the left.

Room 15 contains works attributed to the young Leonardo. Still under the influence of his tutor Andrea del Verrocchio, he was already developing his own highly naturalistic style in *The Annunciation* (1472–5) and in his first independent commission, the unfinished *Adoration of the Magi* (1481).

Michelangelo's vibrant and expressive *Holy Family* tondo ↑

High Renaissance

Michelangelo's *The Holy Family* (1506–8), in room 35, is striking for its bright colours and the unusually twisted pose of the Virgin. Room 66 on the first floor is dedicated to Raphael. The tender *Madonna of the Goldfinch* (1506) shows signs of earthquake damage dating from 1547. Works by Titian (1488–1576) are in room 83, including *The Venus of Urbino* (1538), said to be one of the most beautiful nudes ever painted.

Later Paintings

Rooms 90 to 93 are dedicated to Caravaggio (1571–1610) and his legacy in the 17th century. There are works by several of his followers, including Gerard van Honthorst (1592–1656), a Dutch artist renowned for his artificially lit scenes, and Artemisia Gentileschi (1593–1656), a female painter best known for her brutal masterpiece *Judith Slaying Holofernes* (1611–12).

↑ Raphael's serene *Madonna of the Goldfinch*

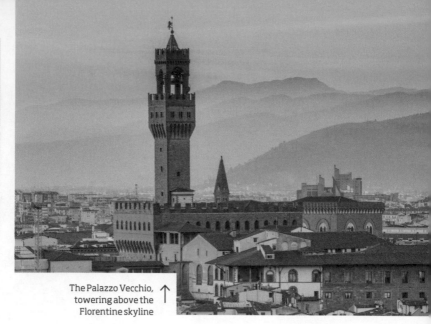

The Palazzo Vecchio, towering above the Florentine skyline ↑

The Salone dei Cinquecento (1495) contains a statue of Victory by Michelangelo.

The crossed keys on this heraldic shield represent Medici papal rule.

The frieze over the palace entrance says "Christ is King", implying that no mortal ruler has absolute power.

The Uffizi

Michelangelo called the Fontana di Nettuno, created by Ammannati (1575), a "waste of good marble".

The Marzocco is a copy of the lion of Florence, carved by Donatello in 1420.

This bronze statue (1554) of Perseus beheading Medusa was intended to warn Cosimo I's enemies of their probable fate.

Copy of David

3

PIAZZA DELLA SIGNORIA

📍 C3 🕐 Palazzo Vecchio: 9am–7pm Mon–Wed & Fri–Sun (to 2pm Thu) 🌐 museicivicifiorentin.comune.fi.it/en/palazzovecchio

Florence's public living room and outdoor sculpture gallery, the Piazza della Signoria has been at the heart of the city's political and social life for centuries.

The great bell of the Palazzo Vecchio, the city's town hall, once used to summon citizens to *parlamento* (public meetings) here, and the square has long been a popular promenade for both visitors and Florentines. The piazza's statues (some are copies), sheltered by the 14th-century Loggia dei Lanzi, commemorate the city's major historical events, though its most famous episode is celebrated by a simple pavement plaque near the Loggia: the execution of the fanatical religious leader Girolamo Savonarola.

↓ The Palazzo Vecchio, seen from the Piazza della Signoria

← Tourists admiring the many marble statues in the Loggia dei Lanzi

The Loggia dei Lanzi, designed by Orcagna (1382), is named after the Lancers, the bodyguards of Cosimo I.

Roman statues, possibly of emperors, line the Loggia.

→ The beautifully decorated first courtyard of the Palazzo Vecchio

Giambologna's Rape of the Sabine Women *(1583) was carved from a single block of marble.*

DAVID

The famous Michelangelo statue symbolizes triumph over tyranny. The original sculpture stood in the piazza until 1873. Damaged during an anti-Medici riot, it was wheeled over to the Accademia for safe-keeping (*p348*) and replaced with a replica.

Michelangelo's monumental masterpiece *David* (1501–4), in the Galleria dell'Accademia

GALLERIA DELL' ACCADEMIA

D1 **Via Ricasoli 58/60** **9am–6pm Tue–Sun**
galleriaaccademiafirenze.beniculturali.it

Michelangelo's proud *David* (1501–4) towers over visitors in the Accademia, Europe's first art school. A spectacular collection of art was amassed here for students to copy, including paintings by Botticelli, Lorenzo di Credi, Orcagna, Perugino and del Sarto.

Founded in 1563, the Academy of Fine Arts was the first school established in Europe specifically to teach the techniques of drawing, painting and sculpture. The art collection displayed here was formed in 1784 to provide material for students to study and copy.

Michelangelo's Sculptures

The Accademia's most treasured sculpture is Michelangelo's *David*, a colossal 5.2-m- (17-ft-)tall nude of the biblical hero who killed the giant Goliath. The sculpture which originally stood in Piazza della Signoria, established Michelangelo, at the age of 29, as the foremost sculptor of his time.

The gallery is also home to Michelangelo's *Quattro Prigionieri (Four Prisoners)*, sculpted between 1521 and 1523 and intended to adorn the tomb of Pope Julius II. The muscular figures struggling to free themselves from the stone are among the artist's most dramatic works.

↑ Visitors gathering on the street outside the Galleria dell'Accademia

Florentine Paintings

Among the Accademia's collection of 15th- and 16th-century Florentine paintings are important works by Filippino Lippi, Fra Bartolomeo, Bronzino and Ridolfo Ghirlandaio. Star pieces include the *Madonna del Mare (Madonna of the Sea)*, attributed to Botticelli (1445–1510), and *Venus and Cupid* by Jacopo Pontormo (1494–1556), based on a preparatory drawing by Michelangelo.

Did You Know?

David's hands and head are exaggerated because he was originally meant to be placed high up on the Duomo.

CASSONE ADIMARI

One of the highlights of the Accademia's collection is an elaborately painted wooden chest, the *Cassone Adimari* (1440–45), by Lo Scheggia, the stepbrother of the painter Masaccio. Originally part of a wealthy bride's trousseau, it is decorated with details of Florentine life, clothing and architecture. A scene of the bridal party appears on the chest in front of the Baptistry.

5

PALAZZO PITTI

B4 **Piazza de' Pitti** **11, C3, D** **8:30am–6:30pm Tue–Sun**
uffizi.it/en/pitti-palace

This one-time residence of the Medici family is a treasure trove, with its lavish royal apartments and galleries of modern art, costume, silverware and porcelain. The palace's true jewel is the Galleria Palatina: frescoed by Pietro da Cortona, it holds one of the best collections of Raphaels and Titians in the world, second only to the Uffizi.

Galleria Palatina

The Palatine Gallery, which forms the heart of the Pitti museum complex, contains countless masterpieces by artists such as Botticelli, Titian, Perugino, Andrea del Sarto, Tintoretto, Veronese, Giorgione and Gentileschi. The works of art, accumulated by the Medici family and the house of Habsburg-Lorraine, are still hung much as the grand dukes wished, regardless of subject or chronology. Highlights of the collection include Antonio Canova's statue of the *Venus Italica* (1810), Titian's *Portrait of a Gentleman* (1540), Raphael's *Madonna della Seggiola* or *"Madonna of the*

Chair" (c 1513–14) and Caravaggio's *The Sleeping Cupid* (1608). The gallery consists of eleven main salons, the first five of which are painted with allegorical ceiling frescoes glorifying the Medici.

Appartamenti Reali

The Royal Apartments on the first floor of the south wing of the Palazzo were built in the 17th century. They are decorated with frescoes by various Florentine artists, a series of portraits of the Medici by the Flemish painter Justus Sustermans, and a group of 18th-century Gobelins tapestries. In the late

Palazzo Pitti's façade, thought to be the work of Brunelleschi ↓

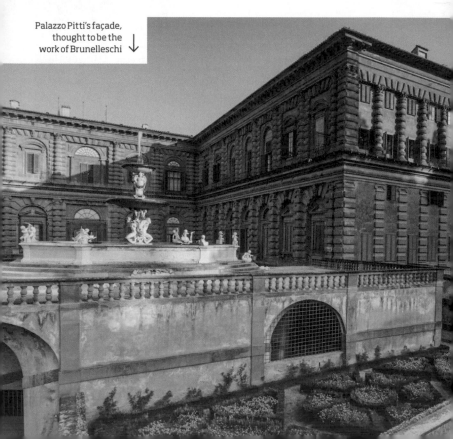

18th and early 19th centuries, the apartments were revamped in Neo-Classical style by the Dukes of Lorraine when they succeeded the Medici dynasty as the rulers of Florence.

The apartments are lavishly appointed with ornate gold-and-white stuccoed ceilings and rich decoration, notably the walls of the Parrot Room, which are covered with an opulent crimson fabric detailed with a bird design. The Tapestry Rooms are hung with 17th- and 18th-century tapestries made by French, Belgian and Italian workshops.

Other Collections

The Museo degli Argenti (Silverware Museum) is housed in rooms formerly used by the Medici as summer apartments. The family's lavish taste is reflected in the vast array of precious objects on display: Roman glassware, ivory, carpets, crystal, amber and fine works by Florentine and German goldsmiths. The Galleria del Costume, which opened in 1983, reflects changing tastes in courtly fashion from the late 18th century up to the 1920s. Highlights of the Galleria d'Arte Moderna (Modern Art Gallery) are the wonderful paintings of the Macchiaioli (spot-makers), a group of Tuscan artists with a style similar to that of the French Impressionists.

↑ Masterpieces and frescoes adorning the Galleria Palatina

THE BOBOLI GARDENS

The Boboli Gardens are a lovely place to escape the rigours of sightseeing. Laid out for the Medici in 1549, they were opened to the public in 1766 and present an excellent example of stylized Renaissance gardening. The neatly clipped box hedges of the formal gardens lead to wilder groves of ilex and cypress trees, planted to create a contrast between artifice and nature. Baroque and Rococo influences are evident in the gardens' burbling fountains, cypress avenues and countless hidden statues.

EXPERIENCE MORE

Basilica di San Marco

D1 Piazza di San Marco 055 28 76 28
4:30-7pm daily, 10am-12:30pm Thu-Tue

The Basilica of St Mark, which comprises a church and convent, was founded in the 13th century and enlarged in 1437, when Dominican monks from nearby Fiesole moved to Florence at the invitation of Cosimo il Vecchio. He had the convent rebuilt by his favourite architect, Michelozzo, whose simple cloisters and cells provide the setting for a remarkable series of devotional frescoes (c 1438–45) by Florentine painter and Dominican friar Fra Angelico. The convent and art collections form the **Museo di San Marco**.

Michelozzo's magnificent Chiostro di Sant'Antonino was named after the church's first prior, Antonino Pierozzi (1389–1459). Most of the faded frescoes in this cloister describe scenes from the saint's life by Bernardino Poccetti. The panels in the corner are by Fra Angelico. A door in the right side of the cloister leads to the Ospizio dei Pellegrini (Pilgrims' Hospice). Today it houses the museum's freestanding paintings, including three famous masterpieces: Fra Angelico's *Deposition* (c 1432–4), an altarpiece painted for the church of Santa Trinità; the *Madonna dei Linaiuoli*, commissioned by the Linaiuoli (flaxworkers' guild) in 1433; and the moving *Lamentation over Christ* (c 1436–41).

In the courtyard, right of the convent's former bell, is the vaulted Sala Capitolare (Chapterhouse), decorated with an over-restored *Crucifixion and Saints* (1440) painted by Fra Angelico.

Covering one wall of the small Refettorio (refectory) is a fresco of the *Last Supper* (c 1480) by Domenico Ghirlandaio. Stairs from the courtyard lead to the first floor, where you suddenly see Fra Angelico's *Annunciation* (c 1440). Beyond, ranged around three sides of the cloister, are the Dormitory Cells. These 44 tiny monastic cells are frescoed with scenes from *The Life of Christ* (1439–45) by Fra Angelico and his assistants. The cells numbered 1 to 11 are generally attributed to Fra Angelico personally, as is the lovely fresco of the *Madonna and Saints* on the right of the corridor.

Cells 12–14 were once occupied by Savonarola, the zealous Dominican monk who became Prior of San Marco in 1491.

On the opposite side of the courtyard, cells 38 and 39 were reserved for Cosimo il Vecchio when he retreated to the convent to find spiritual sustenance and peace.

Along the third corridor lies a colonnaded hall displaying a series of priceless illuminated manuscripts. This was Europe's first public library, designed by Michelozzo in 1441 for Cosimo il Vecchio.

Did You Know?

San Marco is home to Europe's first public library, which opened in 1441 and contained 400 books.

Museo di San Marco

055 088 20 00 (reservations) 8:15am-1:50pm Mon-Sat & 2nd & 4th Sun of month 1st & 3rd Mon & last Sun of month

---

Santissima Annunziata

D1 Piazza della Santissima Annunziata 055 26 61 81 7:30am-12:30pm & 4-6:30pm daily

Founded in 1250, the church of the Holy Annunciation was

THE "MAD MONK"

Girolamo Savonarola (1452-98), Prior of San Marco, became popular for his calls for Christian renewal. When France threatened invasion in 1494, Florence expelled the ruling Medici family, installing a republic with the friar at the helm. He led campaigns against the excesses of the Renaissance, burning priceless works of art, but his radical approach enflamed Pope Alexander VI, and he was executed in 1498. At San Marco you can see several relics of the "Mad Monk", including his cloak and a part of the wooden beam he was hanged from.

← Detail of Fra Angelico's *Annunciation*

rebuilt by Michelozzo between 1444 and 1481. Its atrium contains frescoes by the Mannerist artists Rosso Fiorentino, Andrea del Sarto and Jacopo Pontormo. Perhaps the finest of its panels are *The Journey of the Magi* (1511) and *The Birth of the Virgin* (1514) by del Sarto.

The heavily decorated, dark interior has a frescoed ceiling completed by Pietro Giambelli in 1669. Here is one of the city's most revered shrines: a painting of the Virgin Mary that, according to devout Florentines, was begun by a monk in 1252 but completed by an angel. Newlywed couples traditionally visit the shrine (on the left as you enter the church) to present a bouquet of flowers to the Virgin and to pray for a happy marriage.

A door from the north transept leads to the Chiostrino dei Morti (Cloister of the Dead), so called because it was originally used as a burial ground. Today it is best known for del Sarto's beautiful fresco *The Madonna del Sacco* (1525).

The church is situated on the northern flank of Piazza della Santissima Annunziata, one of the finest Renaissance squares in Florence. Designed by Brunelleschi, the delicate nine-bay arcade fronts the Spedale degli Innocenti to its right, while at the centre of the square stands a bronze equestrian statue of Duke Ferdinando I. Started by Giambologna, it was finished in 1608 by his assistant Pietro Tacca (who designed the square's bronze fountains).

8
Museo Archeologico

🔲 D1 🏛 Piazza Santissima Annunziata 9B 📞 055 235 75 🕐 2-7pm Thu, 8:30am-2pm Fri, Sat & 1st Sun of month 🚫 1 Jan, 1 May, 25 Dec

The Archaeological Museum is in a palazzo built by Giulio Parigi for the Princess Maria Maddalena de' Medici in 1620.

The first floor contains a splendid series of Etruscan bronzes as well as the famous *Chimera* (4th century BC), a mythical lion with a goat's head imposed on its body and a serpent for a tail. Equally impressive is the 1st-century *Arringatore* bronze found near Lake Trasimeno in Umbria.

A large section on the second floor is dedicated to Greek vases, notably the famed François Vase, found in an Etruscan tomb near Chiusi.

9
Spedale degli Innocenti

🔲 D1 🏛 Piazza della Santissima Annunziata 12 📞 055 203 71 🚫 1 Jan, Easter, 25 Dec

Named after Herod's biblical Massacre of the Innocents, the "Hospital" opened in 1444 as Europe's first orphanage. Part of the building is still used for this purpose. Brunelleschi's arcaded loggia is decorated with glazed terracotta roundels, added by Andrea della Robbia in around 1498, showing babies wrapped in swaddling bands. At the left end of the portico you can see the *rota*, a rotating stone cylinder on which mothers could anonymously place their unwanted children and ring the bell for them to be admitted to the orphanage.

Within the building lie two elegant cloisters: the Chiostro degli Uomini (Men's Cloister), built between 1422 and 1445 and decorated with *sgraffito* roosters and cherubs; and the smaller Women's Cloister (1438). The upstairs gallery contains a handful of fine works, including terracottas by della Robbia and pictures by Botticelli, Piero di Cosimo and Domenico Ghirlandaio.

10

Museo dell'Opera del Duomo

📍 D2 🏠 Via della Canonica 1
🕐 Mon, Sat & Sun, by
appt only; check website
for opening times and
bookings 🌐 duomo.
firenze.it/en/59/opera-
duomo-museum

The Cathedral Works Museum
is dedicated to the history of
the Duomo. The main ground-
floor room holds statues from
Arnolfo di Cambio's workshop
which were once placed in the
cathedral's niches. Nearby is
Donatello's *St John*. Another
room contains 14th- and
15th-century religious
paintings and reliquaries.

Michelangelo's *Pietà* has
pride of place on the staircase.
The hooded figure of Nico-
demus is widely believed
to be a self-portrait.

The first room on the upper
floor contains two choir lofts,
dating to the 1430s, by Luca
della Robbia and Donatello.
Carved in crisp white marble
and decorated with coloured
glass and mosaic, both depict
children playing musical

instruments and dancing.
Among a number of other
works by Donatello in this room
are his statue of *La Maddalena*
(1455) and several Old
Testament figures, including
the prophet Abakuk (1423–5).

11

Bargello

📍 D3 🏠 Via del Proconsolo 4
📞 055 064 94 40 🚌 14, A
🕐 8:45am-1:30pm Mon-Sat

Florence's second-ranking
museum after the Uffizi, the
Bargello contains a wonderful
medley of applied arts and
Italy's finest collection of
Renaissance sculpture. Begun
in 1255, the fortress-like
building was initially the town
hall, but it later became a
prison and home to the chief
of police (the *Bargello*). It
also became known for its
executions, which took place in
the main courtyard until 1786,
when the death sentence was
abolished by Grand Duke
Pietro Leopoldo. The building
opened as one of Italy's first
national museums in 1865.
The key exhibits range over

↑ Pietro Francavilla's
statue *Jason with
the Golden Fleece*,
in the Bargello

three floors, beginning with
the Michelangelo Room,
with three contrasting works
by this artist, the most famous
a tipsy-looking *Bacchus* (1497).
Close by are a powerful bust
of *Brutus* (1539–40) and
a circular relief depicting the
Madonna and Child (1503–5).
Countless works by other
sculptors occupy the same
room. Among them is an
exquisite *Mercury* (1564) by
the Mannerist genius, Giambologna, as well as several
virtuoso bronzes by the
sculptor and goldsmith
Benvenuto Cellini (1500–71).

The courtyard's external
staircase leads to the first floor,
which opens with a wonderfully
eccentric bronze menagerie
by Giambologna, and Pietro
Francavilla's marble sculpture
Jason with the Golden Fleece
(late 1580s). To the right is the
Salone del Consiglio Generale,
a cavernous former courtroom
that contains the cream of the
museum's Early Renaissance
sculpture. Foremost among its
highlights is Donatello's heroic
St George (1416) – the epitome
of "youth, courage and valour
of arms" in the words of
Vasari. Commissioned by the
Armourers' Guild, the statue

> **Michelangelo's *Pietà* has pride of place
> on the staircase. The hooded figure of
> Nicodemus is widely believed to be a
> self-portrait.**

was brought here from Orsanmichele in 1892. At the centre of the room, in direct contrast, is Donatello's androgynous *David* (c 1430), famous as the first free-standing nude by a Western artist since antiquity. Among the room's more easily missed works, tucked away on the right wall, are two reliefs depicting *The Sacrifice of Isaac* (1402). Created by Brunelleschi and Lorenzo Ghiberti respectively, both were entries in the competition to design the Baptistry doors.

Beyond the Salone, the Bargello's emphasis shifts to the applied arts, with room after room devoted to decorative rugs, ceramics, silverware and a host of other beautiful *objets d'art*. The most celebrated of these rooms is the Salone del Camino on the second floor, which features the finest collection of small bronzes in Italy. Some are painstakingly accurate reproductions of antique models, others are copies of Renaissance statues. Giambologna, Cellini and Antonio del Pollaiuolo are represented here.

12 Santa Croce

📍 D3 🏠 Piazza di Santa Croce 16 ☎ 055 246 61 05 🚌 C1, C2, C3 🕐 11am-5pm Mon-Wed, Fri & Sat, 7-10pm Thu, 1-5pm Sun

Dating from 1295, the Gothic church of Santa Croce features a magnificent Neo-Gothic façade by Niccolò Mattas, added in 1863. The campanile

---

SHOP

Scuola del Cuoio

Buy handmade leather goods or simply watch leather crafters at work in frescoed rooms to the rear of the Santa Croce church. This school was founded in 1949 by a local firm to teach war orphans a profession.

📍 E3 🏠 Via San Giuseppe 5R 🌐 leather school.biz

---

was built in 1842 to replace the original, destroyed by lightning in 1512.

Inside the church are tombs of famous Tuscans, including Galileo and Machiavelli, plus a grand tomb for Michelangelo sculpted by Vasari and a monument to Dante, who was buried in Ravenna, where he died in exile *(p432)*. Among rich collection of the artworks, Cimabue's 13th-century *Crucifixion* is a highlight, as are the magnificent *Last Supper* and *Tree of Life* frescoes by Taddeo Gaddi (c 1355–60) in the refectory. Fresco cycles by Giotto feature the life of St Francis in the Bardi Chapel and, in the Peruzzi Chapel, the life of St John the Baptist (on the left) and St John the Evangelist (right). The Baroncelli Chapel is frescoed by Taddeo Gaddi (1332–8) with scenes from the life of the Virgin. The Cappella de' Pazzi, a spectacular domed chapel with classical proportions begun in 1441 by Brunelleschi, has terracotta roundels created by Luca della Robbia (c 1442–52).

↑ The distinctive Neo-Gothic façade of the church of Santa Croce

Museo Galileo

📍 C3 🏛 Piazza dei Giudici 1 📞 055 26 53 11 🕐 9:30am–6pm Fri–Mon 🚫 1 Jan & 25 Dec

This lively and superbly presented museum devotes two floors to various scientific themes, illustrating each with countless fine displays and a panoply of old and beautifully made scientific instruments. It is also something of a shrine to the celebrated Pisa-born scientist Galileo Galilei (*p43*). The Museo Galileo houses the only surviving instruments he designed and built, including two telescopes and the objective lens from the telescope with which he discovered Jupiter's moons on a winter's night in 1610.

Some of the best exhibits on display here are the early maps, globes and astrolabes, antique microscopes, thermometers and barometers. There are also some fine old clocks, mathematical instruments, calculators, a horrifying collection of 19th-century surgical instruments, and some graphic anatomical models. The museum has installed a large bronze sundial outside the entrance that can be used to read the hour and the date.

Ponte Vecchio

📍 C3

Ponte Vecchio, the oldest surviving bridge in the city, was built in 1345, the last in a succession of bridges and fords on the site that dated back to Roman times. Designed by Giotto's pupil Taddeo Gaddi, it was originally the domain of blacksmiths, butchers and tanners, who used the river for disposing of waste. They were reviled for their noise and stench and were evicted in 1593 by Duke Ferdinando I – replaced by jewellers and goldsmiths who were deemed less offensive on the nose. The elevated Corridoio Vasariano runs along the eastern side of the bridge, above the shops. Giorgio Vasari designed the corridor in 1565 to allow the Medici family to move about their residences without having to mix with the public. This was the city's only bridge to escape destruction during World War II, and visitors today come as much to admire the views as to browse among the antiques and jewellery shops. A bust of the famed goldsmith Benvenuto Cellini stands in the middle of the bridge.

Palazzo Vecchio

📍 C3 🏛 Piazza della Signoria (entrance on via della Ninna) 📞 055 276 83 25 🚌 C1, C2, D 🕐 9am–7pm Mon–Wed & Fri–Sun (to 2pm Thu) 🚫 25 Dec

The "Old Palace" still fulfils its original role as town hall. It was completed in 1322 when a huge bell, used to call citizens to meetings or warn of fire, flood or enemy attack, was hauled to the top of the imposing bell tower. While retaining much of its medieval appearance, the interior was remodelled for Duke Cosimo I in 1540. The redecoration was undertaken by Vasari, who incorporated bombastic

The Ponte Vecchio, a popular spot for jewellery hunters

frescoes (1563–5) depicting Florentine achievements. Michelangelo's *Victory* statue (1525) graces the Salone dei Cinquecento, which also has a tiny study decorated by Florence's leading Mannerist painters in 1569–73. Other highlights include the Cappella di Eleonora, painted by Bronzino (1540–45); the loggia, with its views over the city; the Sala dei Gigli (Room of Lilies) with Donatello's *Judith and Holofernes* (c 1455) and frescoes of Roman heroes by Ghirlandaio (1485). The excellent museum for children and the Secret Itineraries (a series of private rooms and hidden passageways) can be toured by reservation.

Orsanmichele

🚩 C3 🏛 Via dell'Arte della Lana 📞 055 064 94 50 ⏰ By appt only; church: 10am-4:50pm daily; Museum: 2:15pm, 3:20pm & 4:30pm Mon & Sat

Built in 1337 as a grain market, Orsanmichele was later converted into a church which took its name from Orto di San Michele, a monastic garden long since

INSIDER TIP
Fontana del Porcellino

Head to Mercato Nuovo to perform a popular good luck ritual: stroke the shiny snout of the bronze wild boar statue while dropping a coin into the fountain. It's said that if your coin passes through the grating, your wish will come true.

vanished. The arcades of the market became windows, which are today bricked in, but the original Gothic tracery can still be seen. The decoration was entrusted to Florence's major *Arti* (guilds). Over 60 years they commissioned sculptures of their patron saints to adorn the 14 exterior niches; however, today many of the figures on display are copies. Among the sculptors were Lorenzo Ghiberti, Donatello and Verrocchio.

The beautifully tranquil interior contains an opulent 14th-century altar by Andrea Orcagna, a *Virgin and Child* by Bernardo Daddi (1348) and a statue of the *Madonna and Child with St Anne* by Francesco da Sangallo (1522). Upstairs is a small museum dedicated to statuary.

Palazzo Davanzati

🚩 C3 🏛 Via Porta Rossa 13 📞 055 064 94 60 ⏰ 2-6:30pm Mon & Wed-Sat

This wonderful museum makes use of original fittings and furniture to recreate a typical well-to-do 14th-century townhouse. Among the highlights is the *Sala dei Pappagalli* (Parrots Room), with its beautiful frescoes and rich tapestries.

In one corner of the inner courtyard is a well and a pulley system to raise pails of water to each floor – a real luxury, since most medieval households had to fetch water from a public fountain.

↑ The elegant inner courtyard of Palazzo Vecchio

18 Palazzo Strozzi

📍 B3 🏛 Piazza Strozzi
🕐 2-8pm Mon-Fri (to 11pm
Thu), 10am-8pm Sat & Sun
🌐 palazzo strozzi.org

Sheer size accounts for the impact of the Palazzo Strozzi and, although it is only three storeys high, each floor exceeds the height of a normal palazzo. It was commissioned by the wealthy banker Filippo Strozzi, who had 15 buildings demolished to make way for the palazzo. He hoped it would rival the Medici palaces elsewhere in the city.

Work on the building continued until 1536, with three major architects contributing to its design – Giuliano da Sangallo, Benedetto da Maiano and Simone del Pollaiuolo. Look out for the original Renaissance torch-holders, lamps and rings for tethering horses that still adorn the corners and façades. The palace is now primarily used as an exhibition venue.

19   San Lorenzo

📍 C2 🏛 Piazza San Lorenzo 9
☎ 055 21 40 42 🕐 10:30am-5:30pm Mon-Sat 🚫 1 & 6 Jan, 10 Aug

Built on the site of the city's former cathedral, consecrated in 393, San Lorenzo was the parish church of the Medici

> HIDDEN GEM
> **Museo Ferragamo**
>
> On Via Tornabuoni, inside Palazzo Spini Feroni, the Museo Ferragamo honours shoe designer Salvatore Ferragamo. On display are shoes made for such stars as Marilyn Monroe and Sophia Loren.

family. In 1419 Brunelleschi was commissioned to rebuild it in Classical style, with three naves separated by rows of Corinthian columns. Almost a century later, Michelangelo submitted plans for the façade, but the work was never carried out. Michelangelo did, however, work on the Medici tombs and the Biblioteca Laurenziana (library), which features an unusual triple staircase and a carved wooden ceiling. The Old Sacristy presents a harmonious combination of Brunelleschi's classical architecture and a series of reliefs by Donatello, whose last works were the church's two bronze pulpits. Situated in the nave, these were completed by his pupils in 1460 and feature reliefs capturing the flinching pain of Christ's Passion and the glory of the Resurrection. Although accessed by a separate entrance, the Cappelle Medicee are a continuation of the San Lorenzo complex.

20 Cappelle Medicee

📍 C2 🏛 Piazza di Madonna degli Aldobrandini 6
🚌 Many routes 🕐 8:45am-1:30pm Sat-Mon, 2-6:30pm Wed-Fri 🌐 bargellomusei. beni culturali.it

The Medici Chapels divide into three distinct areas. Beyond the entrance hall lies a low-vaulted crypt, a suitably subdued space for the brass-railed tombs of many lesser members of the Medici family. From here steps lead to the octagonal Cappella dei Principi (Chapel of Princes), a vast family mausoleum begun by Cosimo I in 1604. The ceiling is garishly frescoed and the walls are smothered in huge swathes of semi-precious *pietre dure* (inlaid stone). Spaced around the walls are the tombs of six Medici Grand Dukes. A corridor leads to Michelangelo's

New Sacristy, designed as a counterpoint to Brunelleschi's Old Sacristy in San Lorenzo. Three groups of statues, all carved by Michelangelo between 1520 and 1534, stand around the walls: that on the near left-hand wall is *The Tomb of the Duke of Urbino* (grandson of Lorenzo the Magnificent). Opposite is *The Tomb of the Duke of Nemours* (Lorenzo's third son). Close to the unfinished *Madonna and Child* (1521) is the simple tomb containing Lorenzo the Magnificent and his murdered brother, Giuliano (died 1478).

21 Mercato Centrale

📍 C1 🏛 Piazza del Mercato Centrale
🕐 8am-midnight daily

At the heart of the San Lorenzo street market is the bustling Mercato Centrale, Florence's busiest food market. It is housed in a vast two-storey building of cast-iron and glass, built in 1874 by Italian architect Giuseppe

→

Corinthian columns lining San Lorenzo's elegant interior

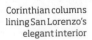

Mengoni, who also designed the Galleria Vittorio Emanuele II in Milan (p147).

The ground-floor stalls sell meat, poultry, fish, hams, oils and cheeses. There are also Tuscan takeaway foods such as *porchetta* (roast suckling pig), *lampredotto* (cow's stomach) and *trippa* (tripe). The first floor functions as a large bar/restaurant, with seating. There are food stalls, a bank, a bookshop and a cooking school. On the mezzanine you will find a pizzeria and a restaurant.

Palazzo Antinori

⊙ D2 ⊙ Piazza Antinori 3 ⊘ To the public

Palazzo Antinori, originally named the Palazzo Boni e Martelli, was constructed in 1461–6 and, with its elegant courtyard, is one of the finest small Renaissance palazzi in Florence. It was acquired by the Antinoris in 1506 and has remained with the same family ever since.

The dynasty owns large estates all over Tuscany and in the neighbouring region of Umbria, producing a range of well-regarded wines, olive oils and liqueurs. You can sample these in the frescoed wine bar to the right of the courtyard, Cantinetta Antinori.

Palazzo Rucellai

⊙ B2 ⊙ Via della Vigna Nuova 18 ⊘ To the public

Built in 1446–51, this is one of the most ornate Renaissance palaces in the city. It was commissioned by Giovanni Rucellai, whose enormous wealth derived from the import of a rare and costly red dye made from lichen, found only on the Spanish island of Mallorca. The precious dye was called *oricello*, from which the name Rucellai is derived.

Giovanni commissioned several buildings from the architect Leon Battista Alberti, who designed this palace as a virtual textbook illustration of the major Classical orders.

DRINK

Cantinetta Antinori
Enjoy prestigious Antinori wines by the glass, a meal of Tuscan fare or just see the Chianti cart in the courtyard.

⊙ B2 ⊙ Piazza Antinori 3 ⊘ Sun ⓦ cantinetta-antinori.com

Casa del Vino
Lined with wooden shelves full of bottles, this place is ideal for a glass of Chianti and a *panino*.

⊙ C1 ⊙ Via dell'Ariento 16R ⊘ Sun ⓦ casadelvino.it

Fratelli Zanobini
An atmospheric wine-bar with standing room only.

⊙ B1 ⊙ Via Sant'Antonino 47R ⊘ Sun ⓦ lelame.com

Santa Maria Novella

◉ B2 ⌂ Piazza di Santa Maria Novella 🚌 Many routes ◷ Times vary, check website ☎ 1 & 6 Jan, Easter, 15 Aug, 1 Nov, 8 & 25 Dec 🔳 smn.it

Part monastery and part museum, this basilica is fronted by a spectacular green-and-white marble façade. The original church was built by the Dominicans between 1279 and 1357, with the eye-catching Romanesque façade added in the mid-15th century by pioneering Renaissance architect Leon Battista Alberti.

The Gothic interior is no less striking, and houses some of

HIDDEN GEM
Wine Windows

As the bubonic plague took over Europe in the Middle Ages, Florentines used wine windows (*buchette del vino*) to avoid contact with patrons. Today, these portals are making a comeback - serving wine, coffee and gelato.

---

the most important works of art in Florence. The illusion of perspective is a running theme in many of the works you'll see here. A crucifix by Giotto at the centre of the nave appears exceptionally long due to a trick of perspective, created by the piers being closer together at the altar end. The superb *Holy Trinity* fresco (c 1427) is especially renowned as one of the Renaissance's first masterpieces of perspective. It was painted by Masaccio, who used architectural illusion and clever compositions to create a three-dimensional effect in this work.

There are more extra-ordinary frescoes to be found elsewhere in the chapels. Works by brothers Nardo di Cione and Andrea Orcagni depict scenes from Dante's *Divine Comedy* in the Cappella Strozzi, and scenes from *The Life of John the Baptist* in the Cappella Tornabuoni – showing Florentine aristocrats in contemporary dress – were painted by Ghirlandaio, who was probably assisted by the young Michelangelo. Perspective paintings of the *Genesis* by Paolo Uccello adorn the walls of the Green Cloister,

while the Cappellone degli Spagnoli features frescoes of salvation and damnation by Andrea di Bonaiuto.

㉕

Ognissanti

◉ A2 ⌂ Borgo Ognissanti 42 ☎ 375 565 20 13 ◷ Church: 9:30am–12:30pm & 4-7:30pm Thu-Tue; Ghirlandaio's *Last Supper* fresco: 9am–1pm Mon & Sat

Ognissanti, or All Saints, used to be the parish church of the Vespucci, one of whose members – the 15th-century navigator Amerigo – gave his name to the New World. The young Amerigo is depicted in Ghirlandaio's fresco of the *Madonna della Misericordia* (1472) in the second chapel on the right. Ghirlandaio's *The Last Supper* (1480) can be seen in the convent next door. The major artwork here, however, is Giotto's *Crucifix*, painted on wood with vibrantly colourful accents.

The church of Santo Spirito, with its ornate Baroque baldacchino

↑ Splendid façade of the church of Santa Maria Novella

㉖
Santo Spirito

📍B3 🏠Piazza Santo Spirito 30 📞055 21 00 30 🚌D 🕐10am–1pm & 3–6pm Mon & Tue, Thu–Sat, 11:30am–1:30pm & 3–6pm Sun & pub hols

The Augustinian foundation of this church dates from 1250. The present building was designed by the architect Brunelleschi in 1435, but not completed until the late 15th century. The unfinished, modest façade was added in the 18th century.

Inside, the harmony of the proportions has been somewhat spoiled by the elaborate Baroque baldacchino and the High Altar, which was finished in 1607 by Giovanni Caccini. The church has 38 side altars, decorated with 15th- and 16th-century Renaissance paintings and sculpture, among them works by Cosimo Rosselli, Filippino Lippi and Domenico Ghirlandaio. The latter painted a magnificent *Madonna and Child* (1466) for the Nerli Chapel in the south transept.

In the north aisle, a door beneath the organ leads to a vestibule with an ornate coffered ceiling. It was designed by Simone del Pollaiuolo in 1491. The sacristy adjoining the vestibule, in which 12 huge columns are crammed into a tiny space, was designed by Giuliano da Sangallo in 1489.

㉗
Santa Felìcita

📍B4 🏠Piazza di Santa Felìcita 📞055 21 30 18 🚌D 🕐9:30am–12:30pm & 3:30–5:30pm Mon–Sat

There has been a church on this site since the 4th century. The present structure, begun in the 11th century, was remodelled in 1736–9 by Ferdinando Ruggieri, who retained Giorgio Vasari's earlier porch (added in 1564) as well as many of the church's original Gothic features.

The Capponi family chapel to the right of the entrance contains two important works by the Tuscan artist Jacopo da Pontormo: *The Deposition* and *The Annunciation* (1525–8). Their strange composition and remarkable colouring make them two of Mannerism's greatest masterpieces.

28

Piazzale Michelangelo

⊙ E5 ⌂ Piazzale Michelangelo 🚌 12, 13

Of all the great Florentine viewpoints – such as the Duomo and Campanile – none offers such a magnificent panorama of the city as Piazzale Michelangelo. Laid out in the 1860s by Giuseppe Poggi, and dotted with copies of Michelangelo's statues, its balconies attract many visitors and the inevitable massed ranks of souvenir sellers. However, this square remains an evocative spot, especially when the sun sets over the Arno and distant Tuscan hills.

29

San Miniato al Monte

⊙ E5 ⌂ Via della Porte Sante 34 📞 055 234 27 31 🚌 12, 13 ⏱ 9:30am-1pm & 3-7pm daily (from 8:15am Sun)

San Miniato is one of the most beautiful Romanesque churches in Italy. Begun in 1018, it was built over the shrine of San Miniato (St Minias), a rich Armenian merchant beheaded for his beliefs in the 3rd century. The façade, begun around 1090, has the geometric marble patterning typical of Pisan-Romanesque architecture. The statue on the gable shows an eagle carrying a bale of cloth, the symbol of the Arte di Calimala (guild of wool importers), who financed the church in the Middle Ages. The 13th-century mosaic shows Christ, the Virgin and St Minias. The same protagonists appear in the apse mosaic inside the church, which sits above a crypt supported by columns salvaged from ancient Roman buildings. The floor of the nave is covered with seven mosaic panels of animals and signs of the zodiac.

Other highlights include Michelozzo's free-standing Cappella del Crocifisso (1448) and the Renaissance Cappella del Cardinale del Portogallo (1480) with terracotta ceiling roundels (1461) by Luca della Robbia. There is a fresco cycle of *Scenes from the Life of St Benedict* by Spinello Aretino in the sacristy, which was completed in 1387.

30

Cappella Brancacci

⊙ A3 ⌂ Piazza del Carmine 📞 055 238 21 95 🚌 D ⏱ By appt only, 10am-5pm Fri, Sat & Mon (from 1pm Sun) 🔒 Pub hols

The Cappella Brancacci, a chapel within the Church of Santa Maria del Carmine, contains the famous frescoes on *The Life of St Peter*, which were commissioned by the Florentine merchant Felice Brancacci around 1424. Although the paintings were begun by Masolino in 1425, many of the scenes are by his more famous pupil Masaccio (who died before completing the cycle) and by Filippino Lippi, who finished the work from 1480.

Masaccio's powerful works were pioneering for the Renaissance, and they were later studied by great artists including Michelangelo. Noteworthy features include the tragic realism he portrayed in scenes such as *The Expulsion of Adam and Eve* and his life-like depiction of beggars in the scene of *St Peter Healing the Sick*, something considered revolutionary at the time.

While Masolino's scenes may appear less immediate and animated in contrast, they do demonstrate a remarkably delicate use of colour. Filippino Lippi contributed such emotional episodes as the *Proconsul Sentencing St Peter to Death*, a scene that includes a self-portrait (on the far right) and a portrayal of Botticelli

→

View across Florence at dusk, as seen from Piazzale Michelangelo

(to the right of the crucifixion, looking out of the painting). St Peter is distinguished from the crowds in every scene by his orange cloak.

EAT

Osteria Antica Mescita San Niccolò

Historic trattoria serving a range of Florentine dishes, including *lampredotto*.

⊙ D4 ⌂ Via San Niccolò 60R 🌐 osteriasanniccolo.it

Il Rifrullo

Contemporary place with bar service, a lunchtime buffet, Sunday brunch and a garden.

⊙ D4 ⌂ Via San Niccolò 55R 🌐 ilrifrullo.com

Enoteca Fuori Porta

Popular restaurant dishing up good contemporary and traditional cuisine.

⊙ D4 ⌂ Via Monte alle Croci 10R 🌐 fuoriporta.it

I Bastioni di San Niccolò

This place serves really exceptional pizzas.

⊙ D4 ⌂ Via dei Bastioni 9R 📞 055 247 67 60

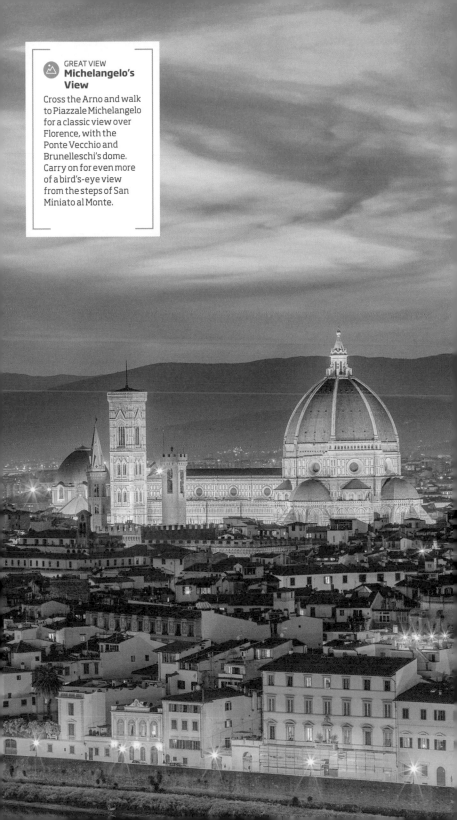

GREAT VIEW
Michelangelo's View

Cross the Arno and walk to Piazzale Michelangelo for a classic view over Florence, with the Ponte Vecchio and Brunelleschi's dome. Carry on for even more of a bird's-eye view from the steps of San Miniato al Monte.

A SHORT WALK
OLTRARNO

Distance 1.5 km (1 miles) **Time** 15 minutes
Buses 11, C3 & D

For the most part, the Oltrarno is a homely area of small houses, quiet squares and shops selling antiques, bric-a-brac and foodstuffs. The Via Maggio, a busy thoroughfare, breaks this pattern, but step into the side streets and you can escape the bustle. The restaurants serve authentic, reasonably priced food, and the area is full of studios and workshops restoring antique furniture. Among the things to see are Santo Spirito and Palazzo Pitti, one of the city's largest palaces, which contains an art collection second only to that of the Uffizi.

The 16th-century fountain and gargoyle in Piazza de' Frescobaldi were designed by Buontalenti, as was the façade (1593–4) of the nearby church of Santa Trinità.

Ponte Santa Trinità

START

Simplicity is the keynote of Santo Spirito, Brunelleschi's last church. It was completed after his death in 1446.

The Cenacolo di Santo Spirito was the refectory of a monastery that once stood here. It contains a dramatic fresco attributed to Orcagna (c 1360).

The Palazzo di Bianca Cappello (1579) is covered in ornate sgraffito.

Between 1846 and 1861, Casa Guidi was the home of the poets Robert Browning and Elizabeth Barrett Browning.

Traditional inlaid mosaics can be purchased at this shop, Pitti Mosaici.

↑ Elaborate fountain on the corner of Piazza de' Frescobaldi

Locator Map
For more detail see p334

Ponte Vecchio (p356)

FINISH

BORGO SAN JACOPO

VIA TOSCANELLA

V. DI RAMAGLIANTI

VIA DE' GUICCIARDINI

Did You Know?

The nearby San Niccolò district is home to lots of great-value bars and restaurants.

| 0 metres | 100 |
| 0 yards | 100 |

N ↑

Palazzo Guicciardini was the birthplace of historian Francesco Guicciardini, a friend and contemporary of Niccolò Machiavelli.

Several museums are contained within the Palazzo Pitti (p350), including an outstanding collection of paintings.

→ Exterior of Palazzo Pitti, seen from the Boboli Gardens

San Gimignano surrounded by vineyards

TUSCANY

Tuscany has long held a special place in the hearts of visitors. Its picturesque hill-towns gaze across the countryside, many encircled by Etruscan walls and slender cypress trees. Handsome palaces testify to the region's wealth, while medieval town halls indicate a long-standing tradition of democracy and self-government. In the countryside, among the vineyards and olive groves, there are hamlets and farmhouses, as well as fortified villas and castles – reminders of the violence and strife that tore Tuscany apart during the Middle Ages. Several imposing castles and villas were built for the Medici family, the great patrons of the Renaissance who supported eminent scientists, such as Galileo.

Northern Tuscany, and the heavily populated plain between Florence and Lucca, is dominated by industry, with intensively cultivated land between the cities and the wild mountainous areas. The area centred around Livorno and Pisa is now the region's economic hub. Pisa, at the height of its powers, dominated the western Mediterranean from the 11th to the 13th centuries. Its navy opened up extensive trading routes with North Africa, and brought to Italy the benefits of Arabic scientific and artistic achievement. During the 16th century the Arno estuary began to silt up, ending Pisan power.

At the heart of central Tuscany lies Siena, which was involved in a long feud with Florence. Its finest hour came with its victory in the Battle of Montaperti in 1260, but it was devastated by the Black Death in the 14th century and finally suffered a crushing defeat by Florence in the siege of 1554–5. Northeastern Tuscany, with its mountain peaks and woodland, provided refuge for hermits and saints, while the east was home to Piero della Francesca, the early Renaissance painter whose timeless and serene works are imbued with an almost spiritual perfection.

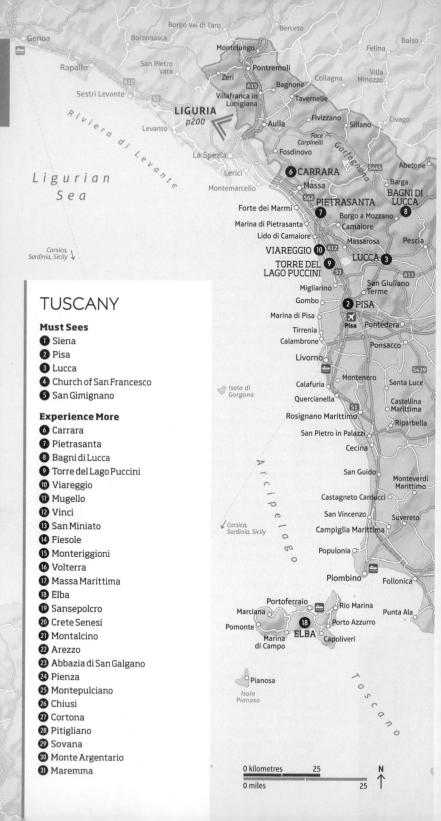

TUSCANY

Must Sees

1. Siena
2. Pisa
3. Lucca
4. Church of San Francesco
5. San Gimignano

Experience More

6. Carrara
7. Pietrasanta
8. Bagni di Lucca
9. Torre del Lago Puccini
10. Viareggio
11. Mugello
12. Vinci
13. San Miniato
14. Fiesole
15. Monteriggioni
16. Volterra
17. Massa Marittima
18. Elba
19. Sansepolcro
20. Crete Senesi
21. Montalcino
22. Arezzo
23. Abbazia di San Galgano
24. Pienza
25. Montepulciano
26. Chiusi
27. Cortona
28. Pitigliano
29. Sovana
30. Monte Argentario
31. Maremma

7 DAYS

A Week in Tuscany

Day 1

Morning Begin your week in Pisa at the celebrated Leaning Tower and the Piazza dei Miracoli *(p380)*. Climb the tower and explore the impressive Duomo and Baptistry before tucking into a traditional *cecina* (chickpea fritter) for lunch at Il Montino *(Via del Monte 1)*.

Afternoon Wander around the historic streets of central Pisa *(p378)* and then take the train to Florence.

Evening End the day with a stroll by the Arno river and a hearty Tuscan dinner at Il Latini *(Via dei Palchetti 6R)*.

Day 2

Morning Dedicate the morning to the Uffizi *(p344)* followed by a *panino* and a glass of wine at I Fratellini *(p340)*, just off Piazza della Signoria.

Afternoon Wander from Piazza del Duomo *(p342)* to Ponte Vecchio *(p356)* and explore the antiques shops and quiet backstreets

of the Oltrarno *(p364)*. Afterwards, visit the Cappella Brancacci to see the famous *Life of St Peter* frescoes *(p362)*.

Evening Walk to Piazzale Michelangelo *(p362)* for panoramic views of the city at sunset before dining at Enoteca Fuori Porta *(p362)* at the bottom of the hill.

Day 3

Morning Drive from Florence along the Strada Chiantigiana, through the picturesque vine-covered hills of Chianti *(p391)*. Stop at Casa del Chianti Classico in Radda, and have lunch at the bistro.

Afternoon Drive to San Gimignano *(p386)* to see its towers, then head for Siena.

Evening En route to Siena, stop in at the walled village of Monteriggioni *(p392)* for dinner at Il Pozzo *(Piazza Roma 20)*.

Day 4

Morning Start your day at Siena's striking tiger-striped Duomo *(p376)* and, after

1. Pisa's Leaning Tower.
2. Cyclists crossing the Arno.
3. San Gimignano.
4. Pecorino cheese.
5. Pitigliano centre.

coffee on Piazza del Campo, climb Torre del Mangia (p372). Nearby Osteria Il Grattacielo (p375) is ideal for lunch.

Afternoon Explore the narrow medieval streets of central Siena, visit the serene Santuario e Casa di Santa Caterina (p374) and stroll in the nearby Orto de' Pecci, a green oasis in the heart of Siena.

Evening For a tasty fresh pasta dinner, head to Osteria da Cice (Via S. Pietro 32).

Day 5

Morning Dedicate today to the region's best food and wine, starting at the hill town of Montalcino (p394), some 40 km (25 miles) from Siena. Enjoy a tasting of Brunello at the Fattoria dei Barbi winery (p394) and settle down for a leisurely lunch at their bistro.

Afternoon Nearby Pienza (p396) is famous for its Pecorino (sheep's cheese). To buy some of the best, stop into local delicatessen Bindi Enzo (Località il Borgo 55).

Evening End the day by visiting the ancient wine cellars and trying the Vino Nobile in Montepulciano (p396).

Day 6

Morning Continue south to reach Pitigliano (p398), a picturesque medieval town clamped to a tufa ridge. Explore the narrow streets and take in the dizzying views before grabbing lunch at Trattoria Il Grillo (Via Cavour 18).

Afternoon From here it is a 5-km (3-mile) walk along Vie Cave to pretty Sovana (p398). Walk or take the bus back to Pitigliano and drive to Saturnia (p399).

Evening Spend the evening dining and using the spa at Terme di Saturnia (p399).

Day 7

Spend a leisurely final day at the fishing village of Porto Ercole (p399). Enjoy a meal at one of the many seafood restaurants before making the journey home.

❶

SIENA

🅰C3 🆁 Piazzale Rosselli 🚍 Piazza Grasmci 🛈 Piazza del Campo 56; www.terresiena.it

Siena's principal sights cluster in the maze of narrow streets and alleys around the fan-shaped Piazza del Campo. One of Europe's greatest medieval squares, the piazza sits at the heart of the city's 17 *contrade*, a series of parishes whose ancient rivalries are still acted out in the twice-yearly Palio (p375). Loyalty to the *contrada* of one's birth is fierce, and as you wander the streets you will see each parish's animal symbols repeated on flags, plaques and carvings. Siena's hilly position also means that city walks offer delightful hidden corners and countless stunning views.

①

Piazza del Campo

Italy's loveliest piazza occupies the site of the old Roman forum, and for much of Siena's early history it was the city's principal marketplace. It began to assume its present shape in 1293, when the Council of Nine, Siena's ruling body at the time, began to acquire land with a view to creating a grand civic piazza. The red-brick paving was begun in 1327 and completed in 1349, its distinctive nine segments designed to reflect the author-ity of the Council of Nine and to symbolize the protective folds of the Madonna's cloak. The piazza has been the focus of city life ever since, a setting for executions, bullfights and the drama of the Palio (p375), a festival centred around a bareback horse race. Cafés, restaurants and fine medieval palazzi now line the Campo's fringes, dominated by the Palazzo Pubblico (1297–1342) and Torre del Mangia, built in 1348 (p374). This imposing ensemble tends to over-shadow the Fonte Gaia on the piazza's northern edge. The fountain is a 19th-century copy of an original carved by Jacopo della Quercia in 1409–19. Its reliefs depict the *Virtues, Adam and Eve* and the *Madonna and Child*. The fountain's water is still supplied by a 500-year-old aqueduct.

← ③ Santuario e Casa di Santa Caterina (50m)

← ⑥ San Domenico (400m)

Striped black-and-white marble pillars support the Duomo's vaulted ceiling.

VIA DI FONTEBRANDA

VIA FRANCIOSA

PIAZZA SAN GIOVANNI

VIA DEL FUSARI

PIAZZA DEL DUOMO

VIA DEL CAPITANO

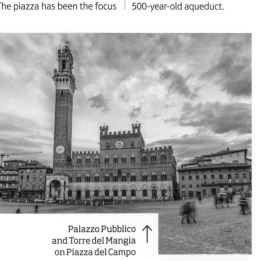

↑ Palazzo Pubblico and Torre del Mangia on Piazza del Campo

Via della Galluzza leads to the Casa di Santa Caterina.

Siena's skyline, dominated by the Duomo's bell tower and the Torre del Mangia ↑

The Loggia della Mercanzia is where Siena's medieval merchants did business.

The Logge del Papa was built in honour of Pius II in 1462.

Tourist information

The reliefs of the Fonte Gaia are 19th-century copies of originals by Jacopo della Quercia.

⑤ Pinacoteca Nazionale (500m) ↓

↑ Siena's historic core, centred around Piazza del Campo

PIAZZA INDIPENDENZA

VIA DI DIACCETO

VIA DI CITTÀ

VIA DI PANTANETO

VIA DEL PORRIONE

VIA DI SALICOTTO

VIA DI CITTÀ

VIA DEL POGGIO

VIA DI CITTÀ

PIAZZA DEL MERCATO

VIA DUPRÈ

↑ Siena's vast, medieval San Domenico basilica, dedicated to St Catherine

Palazzo Pubblico

🏛 Piazza del Campo 1
📞 0577 29 22 32 🕐 Palazzo: 10am-7pm daily (winter: to 6pm); Tower: 10am-7pm (winter: to 4pm)

Although it continues in its ancient role as Siena's town hall, the Palazzo Pubblico's medieval rooms, some decorated with paintings of the Sienese school, are open to the public as the Museo Civico.

The main council chamber, or Sala del Mappamondo, is named after a map of the world painted by Ambrogio Lorenzetti in the early 1300s. One wall is covered by Simone Martini's fresco of the *Maestà* (1315), depicting the Virgin in Majesty as the Queen of Heaven, attended by the Apostles, saints and angels. Opposite is a fresco (attributed to Simone Martini, but possibly later) of the mercenary *Guidoriccio da Fogliano* (1330). The walls of the chapel are covered with frescoes of the *Life of the Virgin* (1407) by Taddeo di Bartolo, and the choir stalls are decorated with wooden panels inlaid with biblical scenes. The Sala della Pace contains the *Allegory of Good and Bad Government*

(c 1338–40), a pair of frescoes by Ambrogio Lorenzetti. They form one of the most important series of medieval secular paintings. In the *Good Government* fresco civic life flourishes, while the *Bad Government* reveals rubbish-strewn streets and ruins.

The Sala del Risorgimento is covered with late 19th-century frescoes illustrating the events leading up to the unification of Italy under King Vittorio Emanuele II (*p44*).

In the palace courtyard is the entrance to the Torre del Mangia, the palace's huge 102-m (330-ft) bell tower. Built by the brothers Muccio and Francesco di Rinaldo between 1338 and 1348, it was named after the first bell-ringer, whose idleness led to the nickname Mangiaguadagni (literally "eat the profits").

GREAT VIEW
Bird's-Eye View

The small balcony of the San Paolo pub (*Vicolo San Paolo 2*), directly opposite the Torre del Mangia, is the very best place to go for views over the Campo. Come for a drink or panino.

---

③

Santuario e Casa di Santa Caterina

🏛 Costa di Sant'Antonio
📞 0577 28 81 75 🕐 8:30am-1:30pm Fri-Mon, 1:15-6:45pm Tue-Thu

Siena's patron saint, Catherine Benincasa (1347–80), was the daughter of a tradesman. At the age of eight she devoted herself to God and had many visions, and later received the stigmata (wounds of Christ). Like St Catherine of Alexandria, her namesake, she was said to have been betrothed to the Christ child in a vision – a scene that inspired many artists. Her eloquence persuaded Pope Gregory XI to return the seat of the papacy to Rome in 1376, after 67 years of exile in Avignon. She died in Rome and was canonized in 1461.

Today Catherine's house is surrounded by chapels and cloisters. Among them is the Church of the Crucifixion, built in 1623 to house the 12th-century crucifix, in front of which she received the stigmata in 1375. The house is decorated with paintings of events from Catherine's life by artists including her contemporaries Francesco Vanni and Pietro Sorri.

④ Palazzo Piccolomini

🏛 Via Banchi di Sotto 52
📞 0577 24 71 45 🕐 8am–1:45pm Mon, Thu–Sat (to 5:15pm Tue & Wed) 🚫 Sun & pub hols

Siena's most imposing private palazzo was built in the 1460s for the wealthy Piccolomini family by Florentine architect Bernardo Rossellino. It contains the Sienese state archives, account books and taxation documents dating back to the 13th century. Some of the leading artists of their day painted the wooden bindings used to enclose the tax and account records. The paintings, now displayed in the Sala di Congresso, often show scenes of Siena or episodes from the city's past.

Other records include a will attributed to Boccaccio and the council's contract with Jacopo della Quercia for the Fonte Gaia (*p372*).

⑤ Pinacoteca Nazionale

🏛 Via San Pietro 29 📞 0577 28 11 61 🕐 8:30am–1:30pm Fri–Mon, 1:15–6:45pm Tue–Thu 🕐 2nd & 4th Sun of month, 1 Jan, 25 Dec

This fine gallery, housed in the 14th-century Palazzo Buonsignori, contains an unsurpassed collection of paintings by artists of the Sienese school. Arranged in chronological order, from the 13th century through to the Mannerist period (1520–1600), highlights include Duccio's *Madonna dei Francescani* (1285), Simone Martini's masterpiece *The Blessed Agostino Novello and Four of His Miracles* (c 1330) and Domenico di Pace Beccafumi's Mannerist *Christ Descending into Limbo* (1536). Pietro Lorenzetti's *Two Views*, from the 14th century, are early examples of landscape painting, and Pietro da Domenico's *Adoration of the Shepherds* (1510) shows how the art of Siena remained visibly influenced by its Byzantine roots long after the naturalism of the Renaissance had reached across the rest of Europe.

⑥ San Domenico

🏛 Piazza San Domenico
🕐 7am–6:30pm daily (winter: 8:30am–6pm)

The preserved head of the city's patroness, St Catherine of Siena, can be seen in a gilded tabernacle on the altar of a chapel dedicated to her in the huge, barn-like Gothic church of San Domenico (begun 1226). The chapel itself was built in 1460 for this purpose and is dominated by Sodoma's frescoes (1526), to the right and left of the altar, which show Catherine in states of religious fervour and her early life. The church has the only portrait of St Catherine considered authentic, painted by her friend Andrea Vanni. The fresco by Vanni can be found in the Chapel of the Vaults.

EAT

Osteria Il Grattacielo

This tiny restaurant specializes in local cheeses, cold cuts and vegetable dishes.

🏛 Via Pontani 8
📞 331 742 2835

€€€

Bagoga

A charming trattoria run by a one-time Palio jockey.

🏛 Via della Galluzza 26 🚫 Mon 🌐 ristorante bagoga.it

€€€

THE PALIO OF SIENA

The Palio is Tuscany's most famous festival and it occurs in the Campo each year on 2 July and 16 August at 7pm. This historic event is a bareback horse race first recorded in 1283. The jockeys represent 10 of Siena's 17 *contrade* (districts); the horses are chosen by the drawing of lots. Preceded by days of colourful pageantry, processions and heavy betting, the races themselves last only 90 seconds. Thousands watch the race, and rivalry is intense. Animal rights campaigners have long lobbied to put an end to the Palio, claiming the horses suffer unduly from the summer heat and uproarious crowds.

⑦ 🛠

SIENA DUOMO

🅰C3 🏛Piazza del Duomo 🚌Pollicino 🕐Times vary, check website
🌐operaduomo.siena.it

Siena's hulking Duomo (1136–1382) is a treasure house of late Gothic sculpture, early Renaissance painting and Baroque design. The early architects dressed the cathedral in striking Romanesque stripes, but the form is firmly Gothic and one of the best examples of the style in Italy.

Had 14th-century plans to create a new nave come to fruition, this spectacular building would have become the largest church in Christendom. In the event the plan came to nothing, abandoned when the plague of 1348 virtually halved the city's population. Among the Duomo's treasures are sculptural masterpieces by Nicola Pisano, Donatello and Michelangelo, a fine inlaid pavement and a magnificent fresco cycle by Pinturicchio. Equally fascinating are the cathedral out-buildings: the Baptistry, the Museo dell'Opera Metropolitana (housed in the side aisle of the uncompleted nave) and the Santa Maria della Scala hospital across the square, where 1440s frescoes in the wards depict a series of fascinating medieval hospital scenes.

↑ Coffered vaulting inside the dome of Siena Duomo

Black-and-white marble pillars support the nave vault.

Della Quercia, Ghiberti and Donatello sculpted the font in the Baptistry.

The Campanile was added in 1313.

The pulpit panels were carved by Nicola Pisano in 1265–8.

The inlaid marble floor is usually uncovered in September and October.

Pinturicchio's frescoes (1509) in the Piccolomini Library portray the life of the Pope Pius II.

The north aisle contains sculptures by Michelangelo.

Many façade statues have been replaced by copies; the originals are in the cathedral museum.

← Exterior of Siena Duomo, seen from the Piazza del Duomo

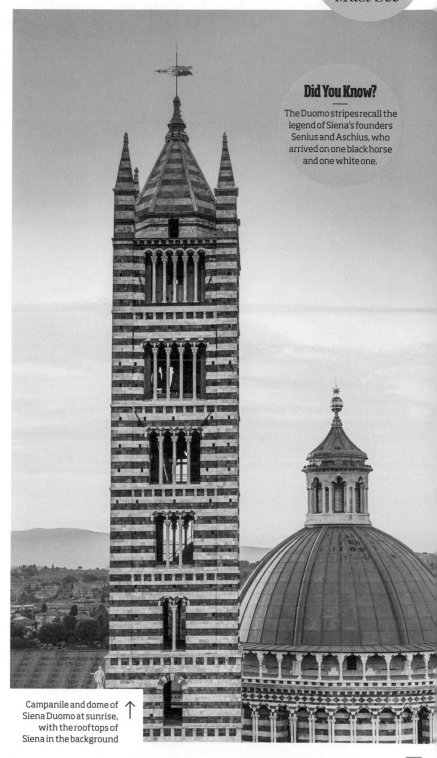

Did You Know?

The Duomo stripes recall the legend of Siena's founders Senius and Aschius, who arrived on one black horse and one white one.

Campanile and dome of ↑ Siena Duomo at sunrise, with the rooftops of Siena in the background

↑ Elegant palazzos lining the banks of the River Arno in central Pisa

②

PISA

 C3 ✈ Galileo Galilei 4 km (2 miles) S 🚆 Pisa Centrale, Pza della Stazione 🚌 Viale Gramsci ℹ Piazza Duomo 7; www.turismo.pisa.it

There is more to Pisa than the Leaning Tower. Instead of heading straight to the Piazza dei Miracoli, first take in the lively ambience of the historic centre. Stroll its piazzas, explore its museums and take in its many churches and palazzos. The city's medieval buildings hark back to the Golden Age in the 12th and 13th centuries, when the powerful navy ensured dominance of the seas and brought back vast mercantile riches.

①

Museo Nazionale di San Matteo

🏠 Lungarno Mediceo, Piazza San Matteo 1 📞 050 541865 🕐 8:30am-6pm Tue-Sat, 8am-1pm Sun

Housed in an elegantly fronted medieval convent, this museum, though a little disorganized, has a good selection of Pisan and Florentine art from the 12th to the 17th centuries. Highlights include Gentile da Fabriano's 15th-century *Madonna of Humility*, Masaccio's *St Paul* (1426) and Donatello's bust of San Rossore (1424–7).

②

Santa Maria della Spina

🏠 Lungarno Gambacorti 📞 055 121919 🕐 10am-1pm Mon, 3-7pm Tue-Thu, 10am-1pm & 3-7pm Fri-Sun

The roofline of this tiny church, just beyond the Ponte Solferino, bristles with spiky Gothic pinnacles, spires and niches sheltering statues of saints and apostles. The decoration reflects the history of the church, which was built between 1230 and 1323 to house a thorn *(spinas)* from Christ's Crown of Thorns.

③

Palazzo Blu

🏠 Lungarno Gambacorti 9 🕐 10am-7pm daily (to 8pm Sat & Sun) 🌐 palazzoblu.it

The striking sky-blue colour of this palazzo, which overlooks the River Arno, dates from the late 18th century, a time when numerous visitors from St Petersburg stayed here. The palazzo regularly hosts world-class temporary exhibitions, while the collection focuses on Pisan art from the 14th to 20th centuries and the beautifully decorated rooms include period furnishings.

④

Tenuta San Rossore

🏠 Località Cascine Vecchie 🚌 Bus 6 from Pisa 🌐 parco sanrossore.org

The San Rossore estate, just outside Pisa, is at the heart of a vast area of parkland that stretches along the coast from Viareggio to Livorno. Hire a bicycle at the Cascine Vecchie visitor centre, join a horse trek or take a tour by a horse-drawn carriage or road-train. There are picnic spots as well as bars and restaurants on the estate.

Map labels:
- Tenuta San Rossore 4.5 km (3 miles)
- VIA CONTESSA MATILDE
- VIA PIAVE
- VIA ROSMINI
- VIA S. STEFANO
- VIA LUIGI BIANCHI
- VIA FRANCESCO RISMONDO
- Battistero
- Duomo
- ⑦ The Leaning Tower of Pisa
- PIAZZA DEL DUOMO
- Museo delle Sinopie
- Museo dell' Opera del Duomo
- VIA DON G. BOSCHI
- V. MARIA
- V. CAPPONI
- VIA DEL BRENNERO
- VIA SAN ZENO
- PIAZZA SANTA CATERINA
- Santa Caterina
- VIA ROMA
- VIA SALVI
- Orto Botanico
- V. DEI MILLE
- VIA S. DON G. BOSCHI
- V. DA FAGGIOLA
- V. DEI MARTIRI
- V. CARDUCCI
- PIAZZA SANTA CATERINA
- VIA SAN LORENZO
- VIA FILIPPO BUONARROTI
- Piazza dei Cavalieri ⑤
- Santo Stefano
- VRENZO FUCINI
- San Francesco
- VIA N. PISANO
- VIA DERNA
- VIA SANTA
- VIA PAOLI
- V. SAN FREDIANO
- PIAZZA S. FELICE
- VIA SAN FRANCESCO
- V. S. ANDREA
- V. LALLI
- VIA RESORGIMENTO
- VIA ROMA
- PIAZZA DANTE
- Tattoria Sant'Omobono
- BORGO STRETTO
- Alle Bandierine
- VIA DEL GIARDINO
- VIA TRIESTE
- VIA TRENTO
- San Nicola
- PIAZZA VETTOVAGLIE
- Teatro Verdi
- VIA E. FERMI
- LUNGARNO PACINOTTI
- PIAZZA GARIBALDI
- V. PALESTRO
- PIAZZA SOLFERINO
- Ponte di Mezzo
- Museo Nazionale di San Matteo ①
- LUNG. SIMONELLI
- Ponte Solferino
- ② Santa Maria della Spina
- LUNG. GAMBACORTI
- VIA GIUSEPPE MAZZINI
- PIAZZA XX SETTEMBRE
- ③ Palazzo Blu
- LUNGARNO MEDICEO
- Arno
- LUNGARNO GALILEO GALILEI
- LUNG. SONNINO
- VIA A. MARIO
- CORSO ITALIA
- VIA VINCIA DEI SISMONDI
- VIA SAN MARTINO
- VIALE FINTA
- Ponte d. Fortezza
- VIA SAN PAOLO
- VIA FRANCESCO CRISPI
- VIA SANT'ANTONIO
- San Martino
- VIA G. BRUNO
- LUNG. FIBONACCI
- San Paolo a Ripa d'Arno
- PIAZZA S. ANTONIO
- Santa Maria del Carmine
- Tuttomondo mural ⑥
- Giardino Scotto
- VIA F. TURATI
- PIAZZA VITTORIO EMANUELE II
- Bastione Sangallo
- VIA NINO BIXIO
- VIA CESARE BATTISTI
- VIALE BENEDETTO CROCE
- VIALE FRANCESCO BONAINI
- PIAZZA DOMENICO GUERRAZZI
- Ponte d. Vittoria
- PIAZZA DELLA STAZIONE
- VIA VESPUCCI
- VIA CORRIDONI
- Stazione Pisa Centrale
- 0 metres 400
- 0 yards 400
- N

EAT

Ristorante Poldino

At the heart of the San Rossore park, this restaurant serves tasty Tuscan dishes made largely with produce from the estate.

🏠 Località Cascine Vecchie 13, Parco San Rossore 🌐 poldino.com

€ € €

Trattoria Sant'Omobono

Enjoy local flavours – rabbit with olives, tripe, and baby octopus with potatoes – at this simple trattoria.

🏠 Piazza Sant'Omobono 6 📞 050 540 847

€ € €

Alle Bandierine

This popular family-run eatery is the perfect place for delicious spaghetti and plenty of fresh seafood. The house wine is excellent.

🏠 Via Mercanti 4 🌐 ristorante allebandierine.it

€ € €

---

⑤

Piazza dei Cavalieri

The building on the north side of this square is home to Italy's prestigious university the Scuola Normale Superiore. Designed by Giorgio Vasari in 1562, the building was headquarters of the Cavalieri di Santo Stefano, an order of knights created by Cosimo I.

MUSEO PIAGGIO

Visitors staying in Pisa should not miss the opportunity to visit this great museum in Pontedera, just a 15-minute train ride away. Vespa scooters have been made in Piaggio since the 1940s. The collection, open Monday to Saturday, includes custom and race versions of the iconic motorbikes (www. museopiaggio.it).

⑥

Tuttomondo mural

🏠 Piazza Vittorio Emanuele II 17

The last of Keith Haring's colourful murals decorates the back wall of the 14th-century church of Sant'Antonio Abate. The American artist took four days to complete the mural, which features 30 figures in representing peace in the world. The Keith Art Shop Café opposite is an ideal spot to admire the work.

THE LEANING TOWER OF PISA AND THE PIAZZA DEI MIRACOLI

🅐 C3 🏛 Piazza dei Miracoli 🚌 4, 21 🕐 Opening times vary, check website 🌐 opapisa.it

Pisa's Leaning Tower (Torre Pedente) is just one of the religious buildings that rise from the emerald lawns of the Piazza dei Miracoli, or "Square of Miracles", sometimes incorrectly called Campo dei Miracoli – the magical land referred to in Carlo Collodi's novel *The Adventures of Pinocchio* (1883). Located to the northwest of the city centre, the complex also features Pisa's Duomo, the cathedral Baptistry and the Camposanto.

Piazza dei Miracoli

The famous Leaning Tower started life as a campanile for Pisa's Duomo, begun in 1063, with its four-tiered façade of creamy colonnades. The Baptistry was begun on Romanesque lines in 1152, and completed in a more ornate Gothic style in 1278. The fourth building on the square, the arcaded cemetery, is said to enclose soil brought by the Crusaders from the Holy Land.

and the sandy silt subsoil, but none tilts so famously as the Leaning Tower. Begun in 1173, the tower began to tip sideways before the third storey was completed, but construction continued until its completion in 1350. More than ten years of engineering work stabilized the tower in 2008, and visitors can now safely climb to the top.

The Leaning Tower

All the buildings of the Piazza dei Miracoli lean because of their shallow foundations

The domed Cappella del Pozzo was added to Camposanto in 1594.

The late 14th-century Triumph of Death *frescoes depict various allegorical scenes on death and the need to live a good Christian life.*

The monument contains earth from the Holy Land and carved Roman sarcophagi.

Nicola Pisano's great marble pulpit, completed in 1260, is carved with lively scenes from the life of Christ.

Pisa's Piazza dei Miracoli ↑ cathedral complex, seen from outside the Baptistry

↑ The Piazza dei Miracoli, featuring the Leaning Tower and Duomo

Frescoes were added to the dome's interior after a fire in 1595.

Seven bells hang from the top of the Leaning Tower.

The bronze panels for the south transept door depicts The Life of Christ.

A frieze shows that work began on the tower in 1173.

The carved supports for Giovanni Pisano's pulpit (1302–11) symbolize the Arts and Virtues.

Coloured sandstone, glass and majolica plates decorate the 12th-century façade.

Buscheto, the Duomo's original architect, is commemorated in a 12th-century wall tomb.

↑ The colonnaded interior of the nave in Pisa's Duomo

↑ Market stalls line
Piazza Anfiteatro
in central Lucca

③

LUCCA

🅰C3 🚉Piazza Ricasoli 🚌Piazzale Verdi ℹ️Piazza
Curtatone; www.turismo.lucca.it

Lucca's picturesque cobbled streets still follow the
grid pattern of the Roman colony founded in 180 BC.
The centre is surrounded by imposing 16th- and
17th-century city walls, topped by a wide, tree-lined
promenade – a pleasant and popular place to walk.
The town has a number of splendid Pisan-Romanesque
churches and attractive squares, including the Piazza
Anfiteatro, an unusual oval-shaped piazza edged by
buildings that retain the shape of the ancient Roman
amphitheatre that once stood here.

①

Duomo di San Martino

🅰Piazza Antelminelli
📞0583 49 05 30
🕐9:30am-6:30pm
Mon-Sat, noon-6:30 Sun

Dedicated to San Martino,
Lucca's cathedral dates from
the 11th century. Decorated
with Romanesque sculptures
and colonnades, the façade
(1204) was built after the campanile (begun in 1060), which
was originally intended as a
defence tower and explains
the asymmetric appearance.

The main portals contain
remarkable carvings by
Guidetto da Como and Nicola
Pisano. Notable works in the
interior include Ghirlandaio's
painting *The Madonna and
Saints* (c 1479) in the sacristy,
a *Last Supper* by Tintoretto
and the tomb of Ilaria del
Carretto (1405–6), a beautiful
marble sarcophagus by Jacopo
della Quercia. The Volto Santo is
a venerated crucifix said to be
a medieval copy of one carved
at the time of the Crucifixion.
Ornaments used to adorn
the crucifix during religious
festivals are on display in the
Museo Dell'Opera del Duomo,
along with other treasures.

②

Museo Nazionale di Villa Guinigi

🅰Via della Quarquonia
📞0583 49 60 33 🕐Noon-
7:30pm Tue-Sat 🕐1 Jan,
1 May, 25 Dec

This sprawling Renaissance
villa is home to a collection of
artifacts dating from the 8th
century BC to the 18th century
AD. Exhibits include ancient
Etruscan and Roman objects,
paintings and sculptures by
Fra Bartolomeo, and some
fine Romanesque reliefs
from Lucca's churches.

③ 🏛️

Casa Natale di Puccini

🅰Corte San Lorenzo 9
🕐10am-7:30pm daily
🌐puccinimuseum.org

The 15th-century house,
where the great composer
Giacomo Puccini (1858–1924)
was born, contains some of
his furniture and costumes
used for his operas, as well
as the piano he used to
compose many works.

→

Marble statues in the
formal gardens of
Palazzo Pfanner

④
Torre Guinigi

🏠 Via Sant'Andrea 45
🕐 9:30am-7:30pm daily
(winter: to 4:30pm)

Dating from the 1300s, this
tower is one of the many
structures built by the Guinigi
family. The holm oaks growing
at the top of the tower make
this a popular attraction.

⑤
Via Fillungo

Lucca's main shopping street
winds its way through the old
town towards the Anfiteatro
Romano. The deconsecrated

🔍 HIDDEN GEM
**Santa Maria
Forisportam**

Beyond the Roman walls
of Lucca (Forisportam
meaning "outside the
gate"), this 12th-century
church (*Piazza Santa
Maria Forisportam*)
contains two great
paintings by Guercino.

13th-century church of San
Cristoforo lies halfway down.

⑥
Palazzo Pfanner

🏠 Via degli Asili 33 🕐 Apr-
Nov: 10am-6pm daily
🌐 palazzopfanner.it
This elegant villa (1667) is best
known for its formal 18th-
century gardens, which feature
statues of classical gods.

⑦
San Michele in Foro

🏠 Piazza San Michele
🕐 7:40am-noon &
3-6pm daily

The towering façade of the
Romanesque church of
San Michele is topped by

Did You Know?

Parts of *Portrait of
a Lady*, starring John
Malkovich and Nicole
Kidman, were filmed at
Palazzo Pfanner.

the huge winged figure
of the Archangel Michael
slaying a dragon.

⑧
San Frediano

🏠 Piazza San Frediano
📞 05 83 53 57 6 🕐 9am-
6:30pm daily

San Frediano's striking façade
features a colourful 13th-
century mosaic, *The Ascension*.
Inside, pride of place goes to a
Romanesque font carved with
scenes from the life of Christ
and the story of Moses.

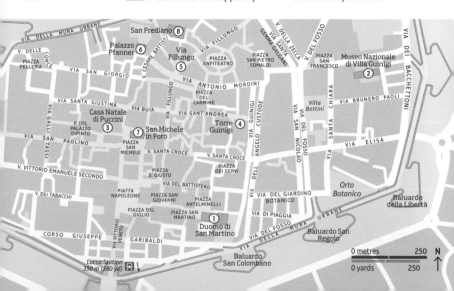

CHURCH OF SAN FRANCESCO

⌂C3 🏛 Piazza San Francesco, Arezzo 🕒9am–7pm Mon–Fri, 9am–6pm Sat, 1–6pm Sun (winter: closes an hour earlier) 🌐 pierodellafrancesca.it

The 13th-century Church of San Francesco in Arezzo *(p395)* houses one of Italy's greatest fresco cycles, Piero della Francesca's *Legend of the True Cross* (1452–66). The cycle tells the tale of the cross that Christ was crucified on, the True Cross, in 12 episodes. The paintings combine robust realism, vivid figures and lively battle scenes.

Narrative of the Fresco Cycle

Della Francesca presents the story of the True Cross in dramatic detail. The narrative begins on the right-hand wall with a scene showing a sprig from the Tree of Knowledge being planted over Adam's grave. The Queen of Sheba then visits Solomon and foresees that a bridge made from the Tree will be used to crucify the world's greatest king. Solomon, assuming he is that king, orders the bridge to be buried. We then see the Annunciation and Christ on the Cross at the centre of the fresco cycle. Centuries later, Constantine has a vision of the Cross and hears a voice saying "in this sign you shall conquer". Constantine goes on to defeat his rival Maxentius, while Judas Kyriakos is tortured into revealing the location of the True Cross. Three crosses are then dug up and Constantine's mother Helena recognizes the True Cross. The Persian king Chosroes is defeated after stealing the Cross and the True Cross is finally returned to Jerusalem.

↑ Exterior of the Church of San Francesco in Arezzo

1️⃣ A sprig from the Tree of Knowledge is planted over Adam's grave; The Queen of Sheba visits Solomon; Constantine defeats Maxentius.

2️⃣ The true Cross is returned to Jerusalem; Helena recognizes the True Cross; the Persian king Chosroes is defeated after stealing the Cross.

3️⃣ Judas Kyriakos reveals the location of the True Cross; the Annunciation; Solomon buries the bridge; Constantine has a vision about the Cross.

3

San Gimignano's skyline, bristling with medieval towers ↑

5

SAN GIMIGNANO

🅐 C3 🚌 Porta San Giovanni 🅸 Piazza del Duomo 1; www.sangimignano.com

The 13 towers that dominate San Gimignano's skyline were built by noble families in the 12th and 13th centuries, when the town's position – on the main pilgrim route from northern Europe to Rome – brought it great prosperity. The plague of 1348, and the diversion of the pilgrim route, led to its decline, as well as its preservation. San Gimignano is rich in works of art, and has lots of good shops and restaurants, although many close from November to March.

①

Museo Civico

🏠 Palazzo Comunale, Piazza del Duomo
📞 0577 28 63 00
🕐 11am-7pm daily

Frescoes in the courtyard of this museum feature the coats of arms of city mayors, as well as a 14th-century *Virgin and Child* by Taddeo di Bartolo. The first room you'll come to is the Sala di Dante, where an inscription recalls a visit by the poet to this palace in 1300. The floor above has an art collection, which includes excellent works by Bartolo di Fredi, Benozzo Gozzoli, Pinturicchio and Filippino Lippi.

②

Sant'Agostino

🏠 Piazza Sant'Agostino
🕐 10am-noon & 3-6pm Tue-Sun

Consecrated in 1298, this church has a simple façade and a Rococo interior (c 1740) by Vanvitelli. Above the main altar is the *Coronation of the Virgin* (1483) by Piero del Pollaiuolo.

③

Collegiata

🏠 Piazza del Duomo
🕐 10:30am-6:30pm Mon-Wed & Fri (to 6pm Sat & Sun)

This 12th-century Romanesque church contains a feast of frescoes, including 26 episodes from the Old Testament (1367) by Bartolo di Fredi.

④

Museo San Gimignano 1300

🏠 Via Costarella 3 🕐 10am-5pm daily (May-Nov: to 6pm) 🌐 sangimignano 1300.com

A reconstruction of San Gimignano as it was in the 13th and 14th centuries is the main highlight of this museum. The exhibits – all handmade – include 72 "tower houses", a symbol of the city's power in the Middle Ages.

DRINK

Vernaccia di San Gimignano Wine Museum

Try San Gimignano's famous white wine and its lesser known reds, rosé and Vin Santo, at this regional wine museum. A fascinating multimedia experience also recounts the history and culture surrounding the wines.

🏠 Via della Rocca 1
🌐 sangimignanomuseo vernaccia.com

② Sant' Agostino (270 m/ 295 yd)

VIA SAN MATTEO

VIA CAPASSI

VIA DIACCETO

VIA CAPASSI

PIAZZA DELL' ERBE

③

①

④

VIA DEL CASTELLO

VIA DI QUERCECCHIO

VIA DEGLI INNOCENTI

VIA BERINANO

VIA PIANDORNELLA

On the Piazza del Duomo is the Palazzo Vecchio del Podestà (1239), whose tower is probably the town's oldest.

The Palazzo Comunale (1288–1323) features a large Maestà (1317) by Lippo Memmi.

The Piazza della Cisterna, the heart of the old town, is named after the well at its centre.

The Annunciation by Ghirlandaio, completed in 1482, is in a courtyard loggia alongside the Collegiata.

Illustrated map of the centre of San Gimignano

Via San Giovanni is lined with shops selling local goods.

EXPERIENCE MORE

Carrara

C3 **Massa Carrara**
Lungomare Vespucci 24;
www.visitacarrara.it

Carrara's white stone has been prized for centuries by famous sculptors from Michelangelo to Henry Moore. The region's 300 or more quarries date back to Roman times, making this one of the world's oldest industrial sites in continuous use. Many of the town's marble-sawing mills and workshops offer visitors the chance to see the ways in which marble and quartz are worked. These techniques – along with marble artifacts old and new – can be seen at the **Museo Civico del Marmo**.

Local marble is put to good use in the town's Duomo on Piazza del Duomo, particularly in the fine Pisan-Romanesque façade with its delicate rose window. The cathedral square also contains Michelangelo's house, used by the sculptor during his visits to select blocks of marble. The town has some lovely corners to explore, in particular the elegant Piazza Alberica. Most visitors head for the stone quarries at nearby Colonnata and at Fantiscritti (take a bus or follow the signs to the "Cave di Marmo").

Museo Civico del Marmo
Viale XX Settembre
0585 84 57 46 9:30am–1pm & 3:30–6pm Tue–Sun

Pietrasanta

C3 **Piazza Statuto**

This medieval town has long been a draw for sculptors, thanks to the white marble quarried from the Alpi Apuane mountains that form the town's backdrop.

MICHELANGELO'S QUARRY

Michelangelo discovered exceptional marble on Monte Altissimo, and he even began his own access road to the precious stone following his commission to decorate the façade of Florence's San Lorenzo *(p358)*. Although the project was abandoned (and San Lorenzo remains unadorned), the quarry is still in use today.

More recently, artistic metal-casting foundries have been established here alongside the many marble workshops. The **Museo dei Bozzetti**, in a former monastery, contains a fascinating collection of maquettes and scale models that have been used in preparation for artworks, including César's famous thumb sculpture. The town's Piazza Duomo is dominated by the 13th-century Duomo di San Martino, with its splendid 14th-century façade. Inside the adjacent brick campanile is a spectacular helical staircase by Donato Benti, a Florentine sculptor and architect.

Dotted around the town are over 70 sculptures by contemporary artists. Among them are works by Fernando Botero (born 1932) and Igor Mitoraj (1944–2014), both of whom had studios here.

Museo dei Bozzetti
Via Sant'Agostino 1
Opening times vary, check website museo deibozzetti.it

A white-marble quarry in the vicinity of Carrara

→ Sandy beach at Viareggio, on the Versilia coast

8 Bagni di Lucca

 C3 Lucca 🚌 ℹ Viale Umberto I, inside the town hall; 0583 80 57 45

All over Tuscany there are hot springs of volcanic origin, like Bagni di Lucca. The Romans first exploited the springs and built bath complexes where army veterans who settled in the area could relax. More spas came into prominence in the Middle Ages and the Renaissance, and they continue to be recommended for relieving a variety of ailments, such as arthritis.

Tuscan spas really came into their own in the early 19th century, when Bagni di Lucca reached its heyday as one of Europe's most fashionable spas, frequented by emperors, kings and aristocrats. Visitors came not only for thermal cures, but also for the Casino (1837), one of Europe's first licensed gambling houses. These days the town is rather sleepy, and its main sights are the 19th-century monuments, including the Neo-Gothic English Church (1839) on Via Crawford and the Cimitero Anglicano (Protestant Cemetery) on Via Letizia.

Southeast of Bagni di Lucca lies another popular spa town, Montecatini Terme. Developed in the 18th century, this town features a wide range of spa architecture, from Neo-Classical to Art Nouveau establishments.

9 Torre del Lago Puccini

C3 Lucca 🚆🚌 ℹ Viale Kennedy 2; 0584 35 98 93

A glorious avenue of lime trees, the Via dei Tigli, links Viareggio with Torre del Lago Puccini, once the home of the opera composer Giacomo Puccini (1858–1924). He and his wife are buried in their former home, now the **Museo Villa Puccini**, which houses the piano on which the maestro composed many of his most famous works. Lago Massaciuccoli, a nature reserve for rare and migrant birds, provides a pretty backdrop for open-air performances of Puccini's works.

Museo Villa Puccini

 🚪 Viale Giacomo Puccini 266 🕐 Tue–Sun; times vary, check website 🚫 Nov, 25 Dec 🌐 giacomopuccini.it

💬 INSIDER TIP
Scottish Barga

Take a trip from Bagni di Lucca to Barga. A depression in the 1800s saw many locals of this medieval town move to Glasgow. Look for signs of links with Scotland, such as tartans, and the annual fish and chips festival in August.

10 Viareggio

C3 Lucca 🚆🚌 ℹ Piazza Nieri e Paolini 2; 0584 96 67 63

Known for its carnival, held in January and early February, this is the most popular of the resorts on the Versilia coast. Its famous "Liberty" (Art Nouveau) style of architecture can be seen in the grand hotels, villas and cafés built in the 1920s after the original boardwalk and timber chalets went up in flames in 1917. The finest example of Liberty architecture is the Gran Caffè Margherita at the end of Passeggiata Margherita, designed by the prolific father of Italian Art Nouveau, Galileo Chini.

A pretty square in the hilltop town of San Miniato

semi-derelict Rocca (castle), built for Frederick II, German Holy Roman Emperor, in the 13th century. Close by stands the **Museo Diocesano**, which is home to a *Crucifixion* (c 1430) attributed to Filippo Lippi, a terracotta bust of Christ attributed to Verrocchio (1435–88), and the *Virgin of the Holy Girdle* by Andrea del Castagno (c 1417–57). Next door, the red-brick Romanesque façade of the Duomo dates from the 12th century. Its inset majolica plates, evidence of trade with Spain or North Africa, probably represent the North Star and the constellations of Ursa Major and Minor (all three were key points of reference for early navigators).

Museo Diocesano
🅰 🅰 Piazza Duomo ⏰ Times vary, check website 🆆 san miniato.chiesacattolica.it

⑪ Mugello

🅰 C3 🅰 Florence 🚌 ℹ Via Togliatti, Borgo San Lorenzo; www.mugellotoscana.it

Mugello is an area of wooded hillsides, Renaissance villas and villages. The **Parco Mediceo di Pratolino** has fountains, grottoes and statues, including Giambologna's imposing *Apennine Colossus*.

In Scarperia, the 14th-century **Palazzo dei Vicari** has a curious façade decorated with the heraldic shields of successive governors, and a Brunelleschi clock that was used for the panoramic bell-tower timepiece.

Parco Mediceo di Pratolino
🅰 🅰 🅰 Via Fiorentina 276, Vaglia ⏰ Apr–Oct: 10am–8pm Fri–Sun

Palazzo dei Vicari
🅰 🅰 🅰 🅰 🅰 Piazza dei Vicari, Scarperia 📞 055 846 81 65 ⏰ 10am–1pm & 3:30–7:30pm Wed–Sun (winter: to 6:30pm)

⑫ Vinci

🅰 C3 🅰 Florence 🚌 ℹ Via Montalbano 1; 0571 93 32 85

The birthplace of Leonardo da Vinci (1452–1519), this hilltop town celebrates its most famous resident in the **Museo Leonardiano**. On display are wooden models of Leonardo's machines and inventions, including a bicycle, a car, an armoured tank and even a machine-gun.

Museo Leonardiano
🅰 🅰 Castello dei Conti Guidi 📞 0571 93 32 51 ⏰ 10am–7pm daily

⑬ San Miniato

🅰 C3 🅰 Pisa 🚌 ℹ Piazza del Popolo; 0571 422 33

This hill-top town manages to remain aloof from the vast industrial sprawl of the Arno Valley. Its key building is the

14

Fiesole

⚠ C3 🏛 Florence 🚌
ℹ Via Portigiani 3;
055 596 13 11

Fiesole stands in rolling hilly countryside 8 km (5 miles) north of Florence. It is a popular retreat from the city thanks to its hilltop position which attracts cool breezes. Founded in the 7th century BC, the original Etruscan colony was a powerful force in central Italy, only surrendering its supremacy following the foundation of Florence (1st century BC).

The restored Duomo of San Romolo in Piazza Mino da Fiesole was begun in 1028. It has a massive bell tower and a bare Romanesque interior. Behind the Duomo, an archaeological area contains the remains of a 1st-century-BC Roman theatre, traces of Etruscan walls from the 4th century BC and the **Museo Civico Archeologico**, with a collection of bronzes, ceramics and jewellery.

Via di San Francesco, a steep lane offering lovely views, leads to the Franciscan friary of San Francesco (14th century) and the interesting 9th-century church of Sant'Alessandro, with a Neo-Classical façade.

Via Vecchia Fiesolana leads to the hamlet of San Domenico, where the 15th-century church of the same name contains a painting of the *Madonna with Angels and Saints* (c 1430) by Fra Angelico and the Chapter House

contains a fresco of *The Crucifixion* (c 1430), by the same artist. Close by, on the Via della Badia dei Roccettini, is the Badia Fiesolana, a pretty Romanesque church with a striped marble façade and interior of local grey sandstone, *pietra serena*.

Museo Civico Archeologico
⊕ ⚑ Via Portigiani 1
⏰ Times vary, check website
🌐 museidifiesole.it

CHIANTI

With its vine-covered hillsides, pretty villages and grand villas and castles, Chianti is a lovely place to explore. The panoramic SS 222 Strada Chiantigiana runs the length of the Chianti winemaking zone, a large area between Florence and Siena; the best wines, however, are from the much more restricted Chianti Classico territory - look for the Chianti Classico black cockerel (Gallo Nero) symbol. For the very best, opt for a Chianti Classico Riserva or Chianti Classico Gran Selezione.

↑ A panorama of Florence from the hill of Fiesole

15

Monteriggioni

🅰 C3 🅰 Siena
🅸 Piazza Roma 23; www.
monteriggioniturismo.it

This medieval hilltop town was built in 1203 and ten years later became a garrison town. It is completely encircled by high walls with 14 heavily fortified towers, built to guard the northern borders of Siena's territory against invasion by Florentine armies.

Dante used Monteriggioni as a simile for the deepest abyss at the heart of his *Inferno*, which compares the town's "ring-shaped citadel… crowned with towers" with giants standing in a moat. The perfectly preserved walls are best viewed from the Colle di Val d'Elsa road. Within the walls, the sleepy town consists of a large piazza, a pretty Romanesque church (on the piazza), a few houses, a couple of craft shops, restaurants, and shops selling many of the locally produced Castello di Monteriggioni wines.

West of Monteriggioni by 3 km (2 miles) lies the former Cistercian abbey of **Abbadia Isola** (12th century).

This Romanesque church was largely rebuilt in the 18th century. It contains frescoes by Taddeo di Bartolo and Vincenzo Tamagni.

Abbadia Isola

📞 335 665 1581 🕘 9am–1pm Mon–Fri, 3–6pm Sat & Sun

16

Volterra

🅰 C3 🅰 Pisa 🅸 Piazza
dei Priori 20; www.
volterratur.it

The Etruscan city of Volterra sits on a high plateau, offering fine views over the surrounding hills. In many places the ancient Etruscan walls still survive. The **Museo Etrusco Guarnacci** has one of Italy's best collections of Etruscan artifacts, including the group of over 600 cinerary urns, made from alabaster or terracotta, many of which were gathered from local tombs.

The Palazzo dei Priori, the medieval seat of government on Piazza dei Priori, is the oldest of its kind in Tuscany. It was Begun in 1208 and houses 14th-century frescoes. The Pisan-Romanesque Duomo, on Piazza San Giovanni, has a fine 13th-century pulpit with sculptured panels.

Volterra's art gallery and museum, the **Pinacoteca e Museo Civico**, features works by Florentine artists. *Christ in Majesty* (1492) by Ghirlandaio shows Christ hovering above an idealized Tuscan landscape. Luca Signorelli's *Virgin and Child with Saints* (1491) states his debt to Roman art through the reliefs on the base of the Virgin's throne. Painted in the same year, his *Annunciation* is a well-balanced composition. Another highlight is Rosso Fiorentino's Mannerist painting, *The Deposition* (1521).

←

View over the hills
and rooftops of
Massa Marittima

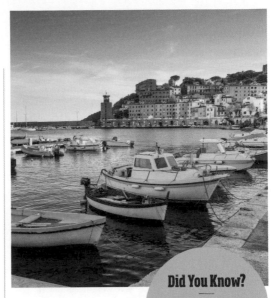

→ Charming marina on Elba's east coast

Volterra is famous for its craftsmen, who have been carving elaborate statues and objets d'art from locally mined alabaster for 2,500 years.

Museo Etrusco Guarnacci

 🏛 Via Don Minzoni 15 📞 0588 863 47 🕐 9am-7pm daily 🚫 1 Jan, 25 Dec

Pinacoteca e Museo Civico

🏛 Via dei Sarti 1 📞 0588 875 80 🕐 9am-7pm daily 🚫 1 Jan, 25 Dec

---

17
Massa Marittima

🅰 C4 🚏 Grosseto 🚌 ℹ Piazza Garibaldi; www.turismo massamarittima.it

Set in the Colline Metallifere (metal-bearing hills) where lead, copper and silver ores have been mined for centuries, Massa Marittima is far from being a grimy industrial town. Many Romanesque buildings still survive from the time when the town became an independent republic (1225–1335). The Romanesque-Gothic **Cattedrale di San Cerbone** is dedicated to St Cerbone, a 6th-century saint whose story is sculpted in stone above the main portal.

The **Museo della Miniera** (Museum of Mining), located partially inside a former mine shaft, explores this important local industry with exhibits explaining mining techniques, tools and minerals. Housed in a former convent, the **Museo di San Pietro all'Orto** displays sculptures, statues and paintings from the cathedral.

Dominated by the 1,000-year-old Castello della Gherardesca, the hilltop town of Castagneto Carducci is ringed by a number of vineyards producing award-winning wines. **MuSeM** traces the evolution of wine within the territory and includes an area dedicated to tastings.

Cattedrale di San Cerbone

🏛 Piazza Garibaldi 🕐 8am-noon & 3-5pm daily

Museo della Miniera

🏛 Via F Corridoni 📞 0566 90 22 89 🕐 For guided tours (2:30pm & 6:30pm Fri, 10am, 2:30pm & 6:30pm Sat & Sun)

Museo di San Pietro all'Orto

🏛 Palazzo del Podestà, Piazza Garibaldi 📞 0566 90 65 25 🕐 Tue–Sun

MuSeM

🏛 Via Casone di Ugolino 24 📞 0565 77 51 10 🕐 10am-8pm Tue–Sun

---

18
Elba

🅰 C4 🚏 Livorno 🚌 Portoferraio 🚌 ℹ Viale Elba 4; www.visitelba.info

Elba's most famous resident was Napoleon, who was exiled for nine months here after the

> ### Did You Know?
>
> During his exile, Napoleon oversaw a series of major infrastructure reforms on Elba.

fall of Paris in 1814. Today Italy's third-largest island is mainly populated by holiday-makers, who come by ferry from Piombino, 10 km (6 miles) away on the mainland. The main town is Portoferraio, with an old port, and a modern seafront of hotels and fish restaurants.

The landscape of the island is varied. On the west coast, which tends to be a little less touristy, there are sandy beaches suitable for all watersports. The east coast, centred on the town of Porto Azzurro, the island's second port, is more rugged, with high cliffs and stony beaches. Inland, olive groves and vineyards line hillsides, and vegetation covers the mountains. A good way to see the interior is to take the road from Marciana Marina to the medieval village of Marciana Alta. Close by, a minor road leads to a cable car that runs to the viewpoint on Monte Capanne (1,018 m/3,300 ft).

19 Sansepolcro

🅐D3 🅐Arezzo 🚌 🅘Via Giacomo Matteotti 8; www. prolocosansepolcro.it

Sansepolcro is the birthplace of Piero della Francesca (1410–92). The town's **Museo Civico** contains two of his masterpieces: *The Resurrection* (1463) and the *Madonna della Misericordia* (1462). It also has a 15th-century *Crucifixion* by Luca Signorelli. In the church of San Lorenzo on Via Santa Croce there is a *Deposition* in the Mannerist style by Rosso Fiorentino (1494–1541).

Museo Civico

🎨 🅐 Via N Aggiunti 65 📞 0575 73 22 18 ⏱10am–1:30pm & 2:30-7pm (winter: to 6pm) daily ☒Pub hols

20 Crete Senesi

🅐C3 🅐Asciano 🚊🚌 🅘Corso Matteotti 124; 0577 71 44 50

To the south of Siena and central Tuscany is the area known as the Crete Senesi, which is characterized by round clay hillocks eroded by heavy rain over the centuries. Dubbed the "Tuscan desert", it is almost completely barren. Cypress and pine trees, planted to provide windbreaks along roads and around isolated farmhouses, are an important feature in this empty, primeval landscape. Shepherds tend to flocks of sheep here; the milk is used to produce the strongly flavoured pecorino cheese that is popular throughout Tuscany.

21 Montalcino

🅐C4 🅐Siena 🚌 🅘Piazza del Popolo; www.montalcino.net

Hilltop Montalcino sits at the heart of the vineyards that produce Brunello, one of Italy's finest red wines. It can be sampled in the **Enoteca La Fortezza di Montalcino** (a wine shop) situated in the 14th-century Fortezza with its impressive ramparts. On the way from the fortress into town is the monastery of Sant' Agostino and its 14th-century church and, just beyond, the Palazzo Vescovile. On Piazza del Popolo the slim tower of the 13th-century Palazzo Comunale, stands tall above the town.

Enoteca La Fortezza di Montalcino

🅐Piazzale Fortezza ⏱Daily ☒enotecalafortezza.com

TOP 3 MONTALCINO WINERIES

Castello di Banfi
🅐C4 🅐Poggio alle Mura, Montalcino ☒castellobanfi.com
Based around a hilltop castle, this winery runs tours and tastings.

Fattoria dei Barbi
🅐C4 🅐Località Pordernovi 170, Montalcino ☒fattoriadeibarbi.it
Cellar tours, a wine museum and a delight-ful tavern draw the crowds here.

Podere Le Ripi
🅐C4 🅐Località Le Ripi ☒podereleripi.it
Biodynamic winery with tastings and tours.

↑ The typically desert-like landscape of the Crete Senesi

→
Market stalls on
a picturesque
square in Arezzo

Arezzo

C3 🚌 **ℹ** Piazza Libertà 1

Arezzo is one of Tuscany's wealthiest cities, its prosperity based on a thriving jewellery industry. Although much of its medieval centre was unfortunately destroyed during World War II, the city preserves some outstanding sights: foremost are Piero della Francesca's famous frescoes in the church of San Francesco (p384). Nearby, the Pieve di Santa Maria boasts an ornate Romanesque façade. To its rear stretches the steeply sloping Piazza Grande, flanked by an arcade (1573) by Vasari, and by the Palazzo della Fraternità dei Laici (1377–1552).

The huge **Duomo** to the north is best known for its 16th-century stained glass and a small fresco of *Mary Magdalene* by Piero della Francesca (1416–92).

The **Museo Diocesano (Mudas)** features three wooden crucifixes, dating from the 12th and 13th centuries, a bas-relief of *The Annunciation* (1434) by Rossellino and paintings by Vasari. More works by Vasari can be seen in the **Museo Casa di Vasari**, a house built by the artist in 1540.

Still more of Vasari's frescoes are displayed in the **Museo d'Arte Medioevale e Moderna**, a museum famed for its excellent collection of majolica pottery.

The **Fortezza Medicea**, a ruined Medici castle built by Antonio da Sangallo in the 16th century, has fine views.

Duomo

🏛 Piazza Duomo 1 📞 0575 402 72 26 🕐 Daily

Museo Diocesano (Mudas)

♿ 🏛 Piazza del Duomo 1 📞 0575 402 72 68 🕐 Apr-Jun: 10am-6pm Wed-Mon

Museo Casa di Vasari

♿ 🏛 Via XX Settembre 55 📞 0575 35 44 49 🕐 Wed-Mon

Museo d'Arte Medioevale e Moderna

♿ 🏛 Via di San Lorentino 8 📞 0575 40 90 50 🕐 Tue-Sat

Fortezza Medicea

🏛 Parco il Prato 📞 0575 37 76 78 🕐 Tue-Sun

Abbazia di San Galgano

C3 🏛 Siena 🚌 🕐 Times vary, check website 🌐 abbazia-san-galgano. business.site

This Cistercian abbey lies in a superb setting. San Galgano (1148–81) was a brave but dissolute knight who turned to God, renouncing the material world. When he tried to break his sword against a rock as a symbol of his rejection of war, it was swallowed by the stone. This he saw as a sign of God's approval. He built a hut on a hill above the abbey (the site of today's beehive-shaped chapel at Montesiepi, built c 1185).

The abbey, begun in 1218, is Gothic in style, reflecting the French origins of the Cistercian monks who designed it. They divided their lives between prayer and labour. Despite an emphasis on poverty, the monks became very wealthy thanks to the sale of wood. By the mid-1300s, the abbey was corruptly administered and gradually fell into decline, until its dissolution in 1652.

St Galgano's sword stands embedded in a stone just inside the door of the circular oratory. The 14th-century stone walls of the side chapel are frescoed with depictions from Galgano's life by Italian painter Ambrogio Lorenzetti (1290–1348).

24
Pienza

 C4 ⬛ **Siena** 🚌 ℹ️ **Via delle Case Nuove 4; www. prolocopienza.it**

Pienza is a delightful village whose intimate centre was almost completely redesigned in the 15th century by Pope Pius II. Born as Aeneas Sylvius Piccolomini in 1405, when the village was known as Corsignano, he became a leading Humanist scholar and philosopher. Elected pope in 1458, he rebuilt his birthplace, renaming it Pienza in his own honour. Florentine architect and sculptor Bernardo Rossellino was commissioned to build a cathedral, papal palace and town hall (all completed 1459–62), but a planned model Renaissance town was never realized. Some idea of what might have been, however, can still be gained from the **Palazzo Piccolomini**, the former papal palace, home to Pius's descendants until 1968.

The airy Duomo next door contains six altarpieces of the *Madonna and Child*, each commissioned from leading Sienese painters of the day. Rossellino was forced to build the Duomo on a cramped site with poor foundations, and cracks started to appear in the building before it was

even completed. Today, the church's eastern end suffers from severe subsidence.

Palazzo Piccolomini
♿️🕐 **Piazza Pio II** 📞 **0577 286300** 🕙 **10:30am–6:30pm Wed-Mon** 🚫 **25 Dec & 1 Jan**

25
Montepulciano

 C4 ⬛ **Siena** 🚌 ℹ️ **Piazza Don Minzoni 1; www. prolocomontepulciano.it**

This is one of Tuscany's highest hill-towns, its walls and fortifications offering broad views over Umbria and southern Tuscany, and over the vineyards providing the Vino Nobile wine that has made its name famous. The streets are brimming with Renaissance palazzi.

🔍 HIDDEN GEM
Ancient Cellars

Below Montepulciano's town centre is a network of ancient cellars, many of which are open to the public, accessed from several restaurants, shops and wine stores, including the historic winemaker Contucci *(Via del Teatro 1)*.

 Verdant rolling hills in the countryside around Pienza

The main street, the Corso, climbs to the Duomo (1592–1630), the setting for one of the masterpieces of the Sienese School, the *Assumption* (1401), created by Taddeo di Bartolo. The High Renaissance church, Tempio di San Biagio (1518–34), lies off the road to Pienza.

26
Chiusi

 D4 ⬛ **Siena** 🚃🚌 ℹ️ **Via Porsenna 79; www.prolocochiusi.it**

Chiusi used to be one of the most powerful cities in the Etruscan league, reaching the height of its influence in the 7th and 6th centuries BC. Many Etruscan tombs dot the surrounding countryside, the source of exhibits like vases and urns in the town's **Museo Archeologico Nazionale**.

The Romanesque **Duomo** includes recycled Roman pillars and capitals. The wall decorations in the nave were painted by Arturo Viligiardi in 1887. There is a Roman mosaic underneath the high altar. Visits can be made to several Etruscan tombs under the town from the **Museo della Cattedrale**, a museum in the cloister of the Duomo.

Museo Archeologico Nazionale
⊘ ⊘ ⌂ Via Porsenna 93 ☏ 0578 201 77 ⏱ 9:30am–8pm daily

Duomo & Museo della Cattedrale
⊘ ⌂ Piazza Duomo ⏱ Times vary, check website ⓦ museodella cattedrale.it

---

㉗

Cortona

⒜D3 ⌂ Arezzo 🚆🚌
ⓘ Piazza Signorelli 9; 0575 63 72 23

One of the oldest hill-towns in Tuscany, Cortona, founded by the Etruscans, is also one of the most scenic. A major power in the Middle Ages, it was able to hold its own against Siena and Arezzo. Today it is a charming maze of old streets and medieval buildings. The town's early history is traced in the **Museo dell'Accademia Etrusca**, which contains Etruscan artifacts as well as Egyptian and Roman remains. The small **Museo Diocesano** features several fine paintings, in particular a *Deposition* (1502) by Luca Signorelli and a sublime *Annunciation* (c 1434) by Fra Angelico. Signorelli, born in Cortona, is buried in the church of San Francesco (built in 1245), which contains an *Annunciation* painted in Baroque style by Pietro da Cortona, another native artist.

Museo dell'Accademia Etrusca
⊘ ⌂ Palazzo Casali, Piazza Signorelli 9 ☏ 0575 63 72 35 ⏱ Summer: 10am–7pm daily (winter: to 5pm Tue–Sun) ⊗ 25 Dec

Museo Diocesano
⊘ ⌂ Piazza del Duomo 1 ☏ 0575 628 30 ⏱ 10:30am–6:30pm Fri–Mon

---

PECORINO DI PIENZA

Pienza is famous for its delicious sheep's cheese, which is aged for at least 90 days in oak barrels. Try some of the variously aged cheeses and other produce at the Taverna del Pecorino *(Via Condotti 1)*.

→

Wheel of pecorino di Pienza cheese

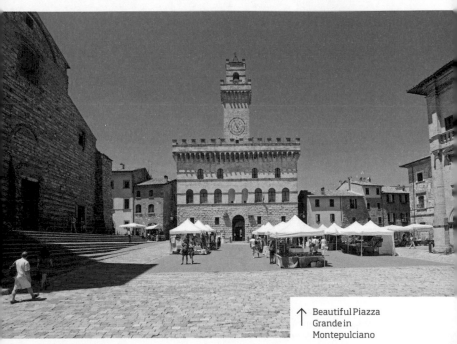

↑ Beautiful Piazza Grande in Montepulciano

28
Pitigliano

C4 🏛Grosseto ▣
i Piazza Garibaldi;
0564 61 71 11

Perched on a plateau, high above cliffs carved out by the river Lente, Pitigliano looks spectacular. The houses seem to grow out of the cliffs, which are riddled with caves cut out of the soft limestone. Its maze of tiny medieval streets includes a small Jewish ghetto, formed in the 1600s by Jews fleeing persecution in the papal states.

The **Museo di Palazzo Orsini** displays a small exhibition of work by local artist Francesco Zuccarelli (1702–88). He also painted two of the altarpieces in the medieval Duomo in Piazza San Gregorio.

The **Museo Civico Archeologico** contains finds from ancient local settlements.

Museo di Palazzo Orsini
⊛ 🏛Piazza Fortezza
Orsini 25 📞0564 61 60 74
🕐10am–1pm & 3–5pm Tue–Sun (Aug: 10am–8pm daily)

Museo Civico Archeologico
⊛ 🏛Piazza Fortezza
Orsini, 59c 📞0564 61 40 67
🕐Summer: 10am–6pm daily (winter: to 4pm daily)

29
Sovana

C4 🏛Grosseto *i* Via del Pretorio 9; 338 86 188 56

Sovana's single street ends in Piazza del Pretorio, home to the church of Santa Maria, which contains frescoes and a 9th-century altar canopy. A lane beyond leads through olive groves to the Duomo, filled with reliefs and carvings from an earlier church on the site. Some Etruscan tombs lie in the surrounding countryside.

 INSIDER TIP
Tuscia's Etruscan Footpaths

Bordering Tuscany, Lazio and Umbria, the area known as Tuscia is rich in Etruscan remains such as the Vie Cave, walled footpaths carved into the rock. There are several examples of these near Pitigliano.

30
Monte Argentario

🏛C4 🏛Grosseto ▣
i Piazzale del Valle,
Porto Santo Stefano;
0564 33 20 75

Monte Argentario was an island until the early 1700s, when the shallow waters separating it from the mainland began to silt up, creating two sandy spits of land, known as

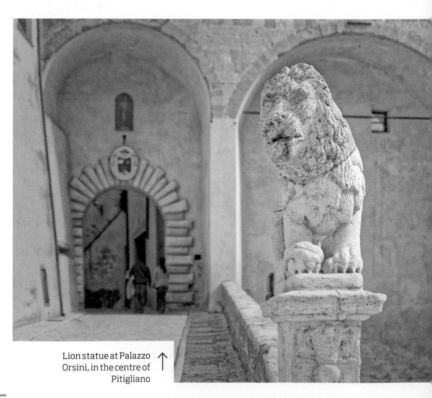

↑ Lion statue at Palazzo Orsini, in the centre of Pitigliano

→ Sunset at the Cala Violina beach in Maremma

tomboli, which enclose the Orbetello lagoon. Today the lagoon is host to a beautiful nature reserve that is well worth visiting. Orbetello itself, a lively and relatively unspoilt little town, was linked to the island in 1842, when a dyke was constructed from the mainland.

Porto Ercole and Porto Santo Stefano, the main harbour towns on the peninsula, are upmarket resorts that are favoured by wealthy yacht owners and become busy in peak season. In the summer, ferries from Porto Santo Stefano call at Giannutri, a privately owned island. Interior roads – notably the Strada Panoramica – offer peaceful drives past rocky coves and bays.

Maremma

Ⓐ C4 Ⓖ Grosseto Ⓒ Daily ⊟ From Alberese to entrances & to tour departure point for Inner Park Areas 𝒊 Piazza del Popolo 3, Grosseto; www. parco-maremma.it

The Etruscans, followed by the Romans, were the first to cultivate the marshes and low hills of the Maremma. Following the collapse of the Roman Empire, however, the area fell prey to flooding and malaria and was left virtually uninhabited until the 1700s. Since then the land has been reclaimed, the irrigation canals unblocked and farming developed on the fertile soil.

Did You Know?

Traditional *butteri*, Tuscan cowboys, are still employed in the Maremma.

The Parco Naturale della Maremma was set up in 1975 to preserve the native flora and fauna, and to prevent development on the coastline. Entrance to much of the park is restricted to access on foot or by a park bus from Alberese. Other more marginal areas, however, such as the excellent beach at Marina di Alberese, are easier to see.

SATURNIA'S SPA WATER

Holiday-makers come to Saturnia, a town to the west of Sovana and Pitigliano, for the water. The Cascate del Mulino consists of a series of natural pools, with rocks stained coppery green, on the Gorello river just outside Saturnia. It is possible to bathe in the warm (37°C/98°F) sulphur water here at any time, all year round, free of charge.

The Terme di Saturnia, on the other hand, is a resort hotel that provides spa facilities, health treatments and even an 18-hole golf course (*Località Follonata*).

UMBRIA

Long dismissed as Tuscany's "gentler sister", Umbria has finally emerged from the shadow of its more famous western neighbour. Forming an expanse of gentle pastoral countryside and high mountain wilderness, this picturesque region is full of historic hill-towns. With its dramatic landscapes, it is a popular destination for walkers, while the beach-fringed shores of Lake Trasimeno offer great swimming and sailing opportunities.

The region was inhabited in the 8th century BC by the Umbrians, a peaceable farming tribe, and later colonized by the Etruscans and Romans. In the Middle Ages, the Lombards established a dukedom centred around Spoleto. By the 13th century much of the region was scattered with independent city-states, most of them eventually absorbed by the Papal States, where they remained until Italian unification in 1860.

Today the old towns are Umbria's chief glory. In Perugia, the region's capital, and the smaller centres of Gubbio, Montefalco and Todi, there are numerous Romanesque churches, civic palaces, vivid fresco cycles and endless medieval nooks and crannies. Spoleto, renowned for its summer arts festival, blends grandiose medieval monuments with Roman remains and some of Italy's oldest churches. Assisi, the birthplace of St Francis, contains the Basilica di San Francesco, frescoed in part by Giotto. At Orvieto, magnificently situated on its volcanic crag, there are Etruscan remains and one of Italy's finest Romanesque-Gothic cathedrals.

Umbria's oak woods, ice-clear streams and rich soils yield many delicacies. Chief among these are trout and truffles, olive oils to rival those of Tuscany, prized lentils from Castelluccio, cured meats from Norcia and tangy mountain cheeses. Sadly, this beautiful area is also frequently hit by earthquakes, which cause considerable damage to its many artistic monuments.

UMBRIA

Must See
① Basilica di San Francesco

Experience More
② Gubbio
③ Perugia
④ Lake Trasimeno
⑤ Assisi
⑥ Spello
⑦ Montefalco
⑧ Cascata delle Marmore
⑨ Orvieto
⑩ Todi
⑪ Spoleto
⑫ Monti Sibillini
⑬ Valnerina

LE MARCHE
p414

❶
BASILICA DI SAN FRANCESCO

🅰D4 🏠Piazza San Francesco, Assisi 🚌🚆 🕐Lower Church: 8:30am–5:45pm Mon–Fri (from noon Sun & pub hols); Upper Church: 8:30am–6:45pm Mon–Fri, 1–4:45pm Sun & pub hols 🌐sanfrancescoassisi.org

The burial place of St Francis, this basilica was begun in 1228, two years after his death. This Basilica remains among the most influential monuments of Western art today.

Over the 13th and 14th centuries, the Basilica's Upper and Lower Churches were decorated by the foremost artists of their day, among them Cimabue, Simone Martini, Pietro Lorenzetti and Giotto, whose frescoes on the *Life of St Francis* are some of the most renowned in Italy. The pictorial style was reproduced in many new Franciscan churches across the country. The Basilica, which dominates the town of Assisi (*p408*), is one of the world's great Christian shrines and receives vast numbers of pilgrims.

↑ Lower Church entrance, seen from the Lower Plaza

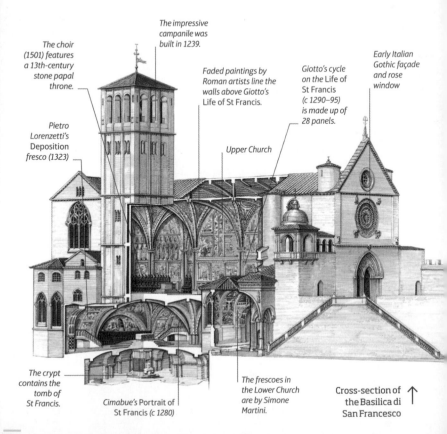

The choir (1501) features a 13th-century stone papal throne.

The impressive campanile was built in 1239.

Faded paintings by Roman artists line the walls above Giotto's Life of St Francis.

Giotto's cycle on the Life of St Francis (c 1290–95) is made up of 28 panels.

Early Italian Gothic façade and rose window

Pietro Lorenzetti's Deposition fresco (1323)

Upper Church

The crypt contains the tomb of St Francis.

Cimabue's Portrait of St Francis (c 1280)

The frescoes in the Lower Church are by Simone Martini.

Cross-section of the Basilica di San Francesco ↑

Gothic arches soaring above the
13th-century Upper Church ↑

EXPERIENCE MORE

② Gubbio

 D3 🚊 Perugia 🚆 Fossato di Vico-Gubbio 🚌 🛈 Via della Repubblica 15; 075 922 06 93

Founded by the Umbrians in the 3rd century BC, Gubbio assumed greater prominence in the 1st century AD as a Roman colony (Eugubium). It emerged as an independent commune in the 11th century then, from 1387 to 1508, it was ruled from Urbino by the Dukes of Montefeltro.

The 13th-century Duomo is distinguished by a wagon-vaulted ceiling whose curved arches symbolize hands in prayer. Medieval Via dei Consoli leads to the 13th-century Palazzo del Bargello – a stone-faced building formerly the headquarters of the chief of police. Also here is the Fontana dei Matti (Fountain of the Mad), named after the belief that anyone who walks around it three times will go insane.

In the lower town, the church of San Francesco (1259–82) is known for 17 faded frescoes showing scenes from the *Life of the Virgin* (1408–13) by Ottaviano Nelli.

The **Palazzo dei Consoli**, a mighty civic palace begun in 1332 by Gattapone, houses the Museo Civico, known for the Eugubine Tablets (250–150 BC). These seven bronze slabs are inscribed with Etruscan and Roman characters, likely a phonetic translation of prayers from the ancient Umbrian and Etruscan languages.

Attributed to Francesco di Giorgio Martini, the **Palazzo Ducale** was built in 1470 for the Montefeltro as a copy of the family home in Urbino *(p418)*. It also has a pretty Renaissance courtyard.

Palazzo dei Consoli

⊗ 🏛 Piazza Grande 📞 075 927 42 98 🕐 10am-1pm & 3-6pm daily (Nov-Mar: 10am-1pm & 2:30-5:30pm) 🔒 13-15 May, 25 Dec

Palazzo Ducale

⊗ 🏛 Via Federico da Montefeltro 📞 075 927 58 72 🕐 1:30-7:30pm Mon (from 8:30am Tue-Sun) 🔒 1 Jan, 25 Dec

③ Perugia

 D4 🚆🚌 Piazza Vittorio Veneto 🛈 Piazza Matteotti 18; turismo.comune. perugia.it

Perugia's old centre hinges around the pedestrianized Corso Vannucci, named after the local painter Pietro Vannucci (Perugino). At its northern end is Piazza IV Novembre, dominated by the Fontana Maggiore, a 13th-century fountain by Nicola and Giovanni Pisano. To the rear rises the 15th-century Duomo. Its Cappella del Santo Anello contains the Virgin's "wedding ring", a weighty piece of agate said to change colour according to the character of the person wearing it. The third pillar in the south nave holds a Renaissance painting of the *Madonna delle Grazie* by Gian Nicola di Paolo. The figure is credited with miraculous powers, and mothers bring newly baptized children and kneel before it.

Away from the Corso is the Oratorio di San Bernardino

↑ The historic centre of the medieval town of Gubbio

→ Perugia's old centre, home to the medieval Palazzo dei Priori *(inset)*

(1457–61) on Piazza San Francesco, with a colourful façade by Agostino di Duccio.

On Piazza Giordano Bruno is San Domenico (1304–1632), with decoration by Agostino di Duccio and the Gothic tomb of Benedict XI (c 1304). Housed in the cloisters of San Domenico, the fascinating **Museo Archeologico Nazionale dell'Umbria** exhibits prehistoric, Etruscan and ancient Roman artifacts.

The monumental walls and bristling crenellations of the **Palazzo dei Priori** mark it as Umbria's finest public building. Among its fine rooms is the Sala dei Notari (c 1295), the former lawyers' hall, vividly frescoed with scenes from the Old Testament – the work of a follower of Pietro Cavallini.

> **HIDDEN GEM**
> ### Perugina Chocolate Factory
> Visit the Perugina Chocolate Museum and Factory *(Viale San Sisto 207/C)* and enjoy tastings or a chocolate-making course. Every October, chocoholics gather here for the Eurochocolate festival.

The doorway is guarded by a pair of large bronzes made in 1274: a Guelph lion and a griffin, the medieval emblem of Perugia. The Sala di Udienza del Collegio della Mercanzia, built around 1390, was formerly used by the Merchants' Guild. This room is late Gothic in style, with exquisite panelling and 15th-century inlaid wood.

Also in the palace is the Collegio del Cambio, Perugia's former money exchange, which was begun in 1452. Its walls are covered with superlative frescoes (1498–1500) by Perugino, works devoted to Classical and religious scenes. A glum self-portrait scowls down from the centre of the left wall, while the hand of Perugino's pupil Raphael may be evident in some panels on the right wall.

Most of the works in the fine collection of the **Galleria Nazionale dell'Umbria** are 13th- to 18th-century paintings by local artists, but the highlights are altarpieces by Piero della Francesca and Fra Angelico.

Museo Archeologico Nazionale dell'Umbria
✦ ⌂ Piazza Giordano Bruno 10 ☎ 075 572 71 41 🕐 8:30am-7:30pm Tue-Sun

Palazzo dei Priori
⌂ Corso Vannucci 19 ☎ 075 573 64 58 🕐 9am-1pm & 3-7pm daily

Galleria Nazionale dell'Umbria
✦ ⌂ Palazzo dei Priori, Corso Vannucci 19 ☎ 075 58 66 84 15 🕐 2-7:30pm Wed-Fri, 8:30am-7:30pm Sat & Sun 🔒 1 Jan, 25 Dec

---

④
Lake Trasimeno

🅰 D3 ⌂ Perugia 🚉 Castiglione del Lago 🛈 Piazza Mazzini 10, Castiglione del Lago; www.umbriatourism.it

Edged with low hills, this is Italy's fourth-largest lake. The town of Castiglione del Lago has small sandy beaches and a 16th-century castle used for summer concerts. The church of Santa Maria Maddalena has a *Madonna and Child* (c 1500) by Eusebio di San Giorgio.

The town of Passignano sul Trasimeno offers boat trips to Isola Maggiore. The island's charming village is known for lace-making.

At the foot of the town, near the station, the 16th-century church of Santa Maria degli Angeli was built around the Porziuncola, a tiny frescoed chapel where both St Francis and St Clare founded their religious orders. The church grounds also include a rose garden and the Cappella del Transito, the infirmary where St Francis died.

About 4 km (2 miles) out of Assisi, towards Monte Subasio, is the Eremo delle Carceri, a stone-built monastery surrounded by peaceful woodland. Here you can see the grottoes where St Francis and his companions used to withdraw to contemplate.

→

The Fontana dei Tre Leoni, in Assisi's main square

6

Spello

🅐D4 🅐Perugia 🄵🄵 ▣
🄸Piazza Matteotti 3; 0742 30 10 09

Spello is one of the better-known villages in the Vale of Spoleto. Although not badly damaged in the 2016 earthquake, some sites may remain closed in 2019 to rule out structural damage. Spello is renowned for a fresco cycle by Pinturicchio in the Cappella Baglioni of the church of Santa Maria Maggiore (12th–13th century), on Via Consolare. Painted around 1500, the frescoes depict scenes from the New Testament. Towards the centre of the village is the Gothic church of Sant'Andrea (13th century), on Via Cavour. This road becomes Via Garibaldi, which leads to San Lorenzo, a Baroque gem of a church dating from the 12th century.

Spello also boasts Roman ruins from the age of Augustus, including the Porta Consolare at the end of Via Consolare, and the twin-towered Porta Venere by Via Torri di Properzio.

The road to Assisi over Monte Subasio offers stunning views from the top of the mountain above Spello.

5

Assisi

🅐D4 🅐Perugia 🄵🄵 ▣
🄸Piazza del Comune; www.visit-assisi.it

This medieval town, with its geranium-hung streets and fountain-splashed piazzas, is heir to the legacy of St Francis (c 1181–1226), who is buried in the Basilica di San Francesco (p404).

Piazza del Comune, Assisi's main square, is dominated by the columns of the Tempio di Minerva, a Roman temple front from the Augustan age. The Palazzo Comunale, opposite, is home to the Pinacoteca Comunale, an art gallery with works by local medieval artists. Also on the square, the Fontana dei Tre Leoni incorporates three lion statues representing the three city districts.

Down Corso Mazzini lies the Basilica di Santa Chiara, the burial place of St Clare – Francis's companion and the founder of the Poor Clares (an order of nuns). One of its chapels contains the crucifix that is said to have bowed its head and ordered Francis to "repair God's church". The crucifix originally came from San Damiano, a sublime church set amid olive groves south of Porta Nuova.

The Abbazia di San Pietro, on Piazza San Pietro, has a Romanesque façade and 13th-century frescoes in the chapel on the left. The nearby Oratorio dei Pellegrini, a 15th-century pilgrims' hospice, contains well-preserved frescoes by Matteo da Gualdo.

Assisi's Duomo (San Rufino) dates from the 12th and 13th centuries and has a superb Romanesque façade. Inside, archaeological items are displayed in the attractive crypt, and there is a small museum of paintings. You can also see the font where St Clare and St Francis were baptized. From the Duomo, head up to Rocca Maggiore, an imposing castle with wide-reaching views across the Umbrian countryside.

> The 16th-century church of Santa Maria degli Angeli was built around the Porziuncola, a tiny frescoed chapel where both St Francis and St Clare founded their religious orders.

Like Spello, the nearby village of Bevagna sprang to life as a way station on the Via Flaminia (the Roman road that ran through this part of Umbria). The medieval Piazza Silvestri is the setting for two Romanesque churches. San Silvestro (1195) is the more atmospheric of the pair, thanks to its ancient crypt, but San Michele (late 12th century) has an elegant portal, famed for the little gargoyles on either side.

Montefalco

 D4 🅰 Perugia 🚌
🛈 Via Ringhiera Umbra 25; 0742 37 92 43

Montefalco, whose name (Falcon's Mount) draws inspiration from its lofty position and sweeping views, is the best of the villages in the Vale of Spoleto. You might happily spend a morning here, most of it in the polished **Complesso Museale di San Francesco** housed in the former church of San Francesco. Its highlight is Benozzo Gozzoli's *Life of St Francis* (1452), a radiant fresco cycle that borrows heavily from Giotto's cycle in Assisi (*p404*). Other painters represented here are Perugino, Tiberio d'Assisi and Niccolò Alunno, all leading medieval Umbrian artists.

Just outside the town walls, the church of Sant'Illuminata is covered with frescoes by the local 16th-century artist Francesco Melanzio. About 2 km (1 mile) beyond, the prettily situated church of San Fortunato is decorated with frescoes by Gozzoli and Tiberio d'Assisi.

The village with the most spectacular setting in the Vale of Spoleto is Trevi. The churches of San Martino (16th century), on Passeggiata di San Martino, and Madonna delle Lacrime (1487–1522), south of Trevi on the road into the village, contain paintings by Perugino and Tiberio d'Assisi, among others.

Complesso Museale di San Francesco

⊘ 🅰 Via Ringhiera Umbra 6
📞 0742 37 95 98 🕐 10:30am–1pm & 2:30–5pm Wed–Sun
🚫 1 Jan

Cascata delle Marmore

 D4 🅰 Terni; Voc Cascata 30 (Belvedere Superiore) & Piazzale F Fatati 6 (Belvedere Inferiore)
🕐 Times vary, see website 🌐 cascata dellemarmore.info

 Created by the Romans during works to link the Nera and Velino rivers in 271 BC, this spectacular 165-m- (540-ft-)

high waterfall is located near the town of Terni. Its powerful flow is diverted for hydroelectric power for much of the time, so you can only view it during certain periods (check online). The park has two main viewpoints, with a shuttle bus running between them. At the Belvedere Superiore, the Specola viewing tower, built in 1781 by Pope Pius VI, is the ideal spot to witness the falls' rainbow phenomenon. There's also a series of footpaths between the viewpoints and through woodland.

←

The Romanesque façade of Bevagna's San Michele church, designed by Maestro Binello

9 Orvieto

A D4 **Q** Terni **F**S ☐
i Piazza Duomo 24;
www.inorvieto.it

Set on a huge slab of tufa, Orvieto was colonized nine centuries before Christ and flourished in the Etruscan period as Velzna. You can explore this era of the town's history at **Necropoli Etrusca – Crocifisso del Tufo**. This Etruscan necropolis has burial chambers built of blocks of tufa. Etruscan letters, thought to be the names of the deceased, are inscribed on some of the tombs.

After the Romans destroyed it in 264 BC, the town didn't revive until the medieval period, when it became the residence of the popes. The main highlight from this prosperous period of Orvieto's history is the **Duomo**. Begun in 1290, and some 300 years in the making, this is one of Italy's greatest cathedrals. It was inspired by the Miracle of Bolsena in which real blood from a consecrated host supposedly fell on the altar cloth of a church in nearby Bolsena. Its breathtaking façade, is characterized by horizontal bands of white travertine and lue-grey basalt. The **Museo dell'Opera del Duomo** is an interesting little museum containing an eclectic collection of treasures given to the Duomo.

Cappella Nuova

14th-century rose window

Carved choir stalls

→
The Duomo of Orvieto

💬 INSIDER TIP
Orvieto Underground

Book yourself onto a fascinating tour through the numerous caves and chambers carved into the rock below Orvieto since Etruscan times. Tours leave from Piazza Duomo 23 *(www. orvietounderground.it)*.

Among the highlights here are paintings by Lorenzo Maitani (c 1275–1330) and sculptures by Andrea Pisano (c 1270–1348). Connected to this museum is the **Museo d'Arte Moderna "Emilio Greco"**. It is devoted to the modern Sicilian sculptor Emilio Greco (1913–95), who is responsible for the bronze doors of the Duomo.

Another pair of mueums well worth visiting are the **Museo Claudio Faina** and **Museo Civico**. The first of these two museums has a well-known, low-key collection of Etruscan remains, including a large number of Greek vases that were found in Etruscan tombs in the surrounding area. The Museo Civico contains ancient Greek artifacts and Etruscan copies of Greek works.

One of the more obscure attractions in Orvieto is the **Pozzo di San Patrizo**. This well was commissioned in 1527 by Pope Clement VII and designed by the Florentine architect Antonio da Sangallo to provide the town with a water supply in case of attack. Two 248-step staircases drop into its dank interior, cleverly arranged as a double helix (spiral) so as not to intersect. The 62 m (203 ft) shaft took ten years to complete.

Necropoli Etrusca - Crocifisso del Tufo

⊘ **A** Loc Le Conce **C** 0763 34 36 11 ⏰ 10am-7pm Wed-Sat & 1st and 2nd Sun of month

Duomo

A Piazza Duomo ⏰ Times vary, check website **w** opsm. it/duomo-di-orvieto-visite-e-orari/

Museo dell'Opera del Duomo and Museo d'Arte Moderna "Emilio Greco"

⊘ **A** Piazza Duomo ⏰ Tue-Sun; times vary, check website **w** opsm.it

Museo Claudio Faina and Museo Civico

⊘ ⊘ **A** Piazza Duomo 29 **C** 0763 34 15 11 ⏰ 9:30am-6pm daily (Oct-Mar: to 5pm) 🚫 Nov-Feb: Mon

Pozzo di San Patrizio

⊘ **A** Viale Sangallo **C** 0763 34 37 68 ⏰ Daily

Todi

⚑ D4 ⌂ Perugia 🚉➡ ℹ️

An ancient Etruscan, and then Roman, settlement, the hill-town of Todi still preserves a picturesque medieval centre.

The main square, Piazza del Popolo, is flanked by the lovely plain-faced Duomo. Built in the 13th century on the site of a Roman temple to Apollo, it has a dusky interior and one of Umbria's finest choirs (1521–30). Note the altarpiece at the end of the right aisle by Giannicola di Paolo (a follower of Perugino).

Also flanking the piazza are the Palazzo dei Priori (1293–1337) and the linked Palazzo del Capitano (1290) and Palazzo del Popolo (1213). Inside the Palazzo del Capitano, distinguished by its redoubtable medieval interior, lies the **Museo Civico**, with a collection of local Etruscan and Roman artifacts. There are altarpieces and sacred objects in the **Pinacoteca Comunale**, also housed in the palace.

A few steps from the piazza rises San Fortunato (1292–1462), named after Todi's first bishop, with a florid Gothic doorway (1415–58). The choir (1590) is superb, but the church's most famous work is *Madonna and Child* (1432) by Masolino da Panicale (fourth chapel on the right). The crypt contains the tomb of Jacopone da Todi (c 1228–1306), a noted medieval poet and mystic.

To the right of the church are some shady gardens, from which a path (past the tiny castle) drops through the trees to emerge just in front of Santa Maria della Consolazione (1508–1607), near the N79. One of central Italy's finest Renaissance churches, and based on a Greek cross, it may have been built to a plan by Bramante.

Museo Civico e Pinacoteca Comunale

♿ ⌂ Piazza del Popolo 29/30 📞 0758 95 62 27 🕐 10am–1pm & 3-6pm Wed-Sun

MONTEFALCO SAGRANTINO WINERIES

Scacciadiavoli
⚑ D4 ⌂ Località Cantinone 31, Montefalco 🌐 cantina scacciadiavoli.it
Visit to see how Sagrantino and other local wines are made. Founded in 1884, this is one of Montefalco's oldest wineries.

Tenuta Bellafonte
⚑ D4 ⌂ Via Colle Nottolo 2, Bevagna 🌐 tenuta bellafonte.it
As well as tours of the winery, accommodation is on offer here.

Lungarotti
⚑ D4 ⌂ Viale Lungarotti 2, Torgiano 🌐 lungarotti.it
The main cellar of this winery is at Torgiano, along with fascinating wine and olive oil museums.

↑ The town of Todi, dominated by the church of San Fortunato

→

Approach to Spoleto's Duomo

Spoleto

🅐 D4 🅐 Perugia 🚆🚌
ℹ Largo Ferrer 6; www. spoletocard.it

Within its wooded setting, Spoleto is the loveliest of the Umbrian hill-towns. Founded by the Umbrians, it was one of central Italy's main Roman colonies, a prominence maintained by the Lombards, who in the 7th century made it the capital of one of their three Italian dukedoms. After a spell as an independent city state, in 1354 Spoleto fell to the papacy.

The church of San Pietro was founded in 419 AD and built on an ancient necropolis. Its façade is covered in Romanesque relief sculptures, considered some of the finest examples in Umbria. From here, head north towards the town centre on Viale Giacomo Matteotti and Via San Carlo.

At the southern end of Piazza del Mercato is the Arco di Druso, a 1st-century-AD Roman arch. Via Aurelio Saffi, at the piazza's northern end, leads to Romanesque church Sant'Eufemia.

A short way beyond, the fan-shaped Piazza del Duomo opens out to reveal Spoleto's 12th-century Duomo, graced with an elegant Romanesque façade. Filling the apse of the Baroque interior is a great fresco cycle. The final work of Fra Lippo Lippi, from 1467–9, it describes episodes from the *Life of the Virgin*. The Cappella Erioli is adorned with Pinturicchio's unfinished *Madonna and Child* (1497).

The best of the exceptional churches in the lower town is 4th-century San Salvatore, located in the main cemetery. Nearby stands San Ponziano, fronted by a captivating three-tiered Romanesque façade. Its crypt is decorated with Byzantine frescoes.

ROMANESQUE CHURCHES IN UMBRIA

Umbria's church-building tradition had its roots in ancient Roman basilicas. The region's Romanesque façades are usually divided into three tiers, often with three rose windows arranged above a trio of arched portals. The three doors usually correspond to the interior's nave and two aisles, which derive from the simple barn-like plan of Roman basilicas. Inside, the presbytery is often raised in order to allow for the building of a crypt, which usually contained the relics of a saint or martyr. Many of the churches took centuries to build, or were repeatedly modified over time, often acquiring elements of Gothic, Baroque or Renaissance styles.

① Spoleto's Duomo (1198) has eight rose windows, a mosaic (1207) and a Renaissance portico (1491).

② The Duomo (1253) in Assisi is a fine example of a three-tiered façade (p408). It also has a pointed arch.

③ Todi's Duomo was begun in the 13th century, but construction work continued until the 17th century (p411).

The church of **San Gregorio** dates from 1069, but its façade and campanile incorporate fragments of Roman buildings. Some 10,000 Christian martyrs are supposedly buried near the church. They were reputedly slaughtered in the town's Roman amphitheatre, traces of which can be seen in the barracks on Via del Anfiteatro.

A magnificent 14th-century aqueduct, the **Ponte delle Torri** ("bridge of towers") is 80 m (262 ft) high and was designed by Gattapone (from Gubbio). From the bridge, there are views of the bastions of the Rocca Albornoz, a huge papal fortress built in 1359–64, also by Gattapone.

A Roman patrician's dwelling, the **Casa Romana** dates from the 1st century AD and was believed to be owned by Emperor Vespasian's mother. Among the museum's treasures are intricate mosaic floors and well-preserved frescoes.

San Gregorio
🅐 Piazza Giuseppe Garibaldi, 34 📞 0743 441 40

Ponte delle Torri
🅐 Via Giro del Ponte

Casa Romana
🅐 Via Visiale 📞 90743 23 42 50 🕐 10:30am-1:30pm & 2-7pm Thu-Tue

⑫
Monti Sibillini

🅐 D4 🅐 Macerata 🚆 Spoleto 🚌 Visso 🅘 Via Paolo da Visso; www.sibillini.net

The national park of the Monti Sibillini in eastern Umbria provides the region's wildest and most spectacular scenery. A range 40 km (25 miles) long, the mountains form part of the Apennines, a chain that runs the length of the Italian peninsula. Monte Vettore is the loftiest point, and the peninsula's third highest; it stands at 2,476 m (8,123 ft), a great whale-backed peak close to the cave of the mythical sybil that gave the region its name.

Good maps and trails make this a superb walking area, while drivers can follow hairpin roads to some of Italy's most magical landscapes. Chief of these is the Piano Grande, a huge upland plain surrounded by a vast amphitheatre of mountains. Bare but for flocks of sheep and bedraggled haystacks, the plain blazes with wild flowers in spring and lentils grow later in the year. The only habitation was Castelluccio, a beautiful, neglected mountain village that was sadly nearly destroyed by the November 2016 earthquake.

SPOLETO FESTIVAL
Each year, Spoleto becomes one big stage for 17 days between late June and mid-July during the Spoleto Festival, held since 1958. Operas, concerts, plays, dance shows, talks and visual art displays are held at venues throughout this medieval town.

⑬
Valnerina

🅐 D4 🅐 Perugia 🚆 Spoleto, then bus 🅘 Via Giovanni da Chiavano 1, Cascia; 0743 711 47

The Valnerina (Valley of the River Nera) curves through a broad swathe of eastern Umbria before emptying into the Tiber. It is edged with craggy, tree-covered slopes and dotted with upland villages and fortified hamlets.

The star attraction is **San Pietro in Valle**, an 8th-century monastery. Its nave walls are covered in 12th-century frescoes. Some of the best Romanesque carvings in Umbria can be found here.

San Pietro in Valle
🅐 Località Ferentillo, Terni 📞 0744 78 01 29 🕐 Apr-Oct: daily

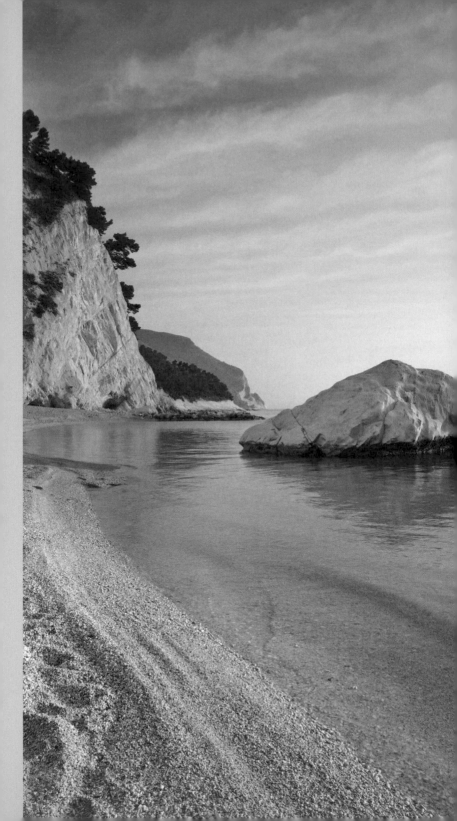

LE MARCHE

Tucked away in a remote corner between
the Adriatic Sea and the Apennine mountains,
Le Marche (the Marches) is an enchanting rural
patchwork of old towns, hill country and long, sandy
beaches. In pre-Christian times the area was settled
by the Piceni, a tribe eventually assimilated by the
Romans. In the 4th century BC, exiles from Magna
Graecia colonized much of the region. The most
notable town was Ancona, also the northernmost
point of Greek influence on the Italian peninsula.
During the early Middle Ages the region marked the
edge of the Holy Roman Empire, giving rise to its
present name (march meant "border area").

The region's historical peak was reached in the
15th century under Federico da Montefeltro, whose
court at Urbino became one of Europe's leading
cultural centres. Much of Urbino's former grandeur
survives, particularly in Federico's magnificent
Renaissance Palazzo Ducale, now home to a regional
art collection. Ascoli Piceno is almost as enchanting
as Urbino, its central Piazza del Popolo among the
most evocative old squares in Italy. Smaller towns
like San Leo and Urbania and the republic of San
Marino also boast fine medieval monuments.

Today, probably as many people come to
Le Marche for its beaches and towns as for its hilly,
unspoiled interior. Especially beautiful are the
snow-capped peaks of the Monti Sibillini, situated
in magnificent walking and skiing country.

Regional cuisine encompasses the truffles and
robust cheeses of the mountains, tender hams and
salamis, olive *ascolane* (olives stuffed with meat
and herbs) and *brodetto*, fish soup made in several
versions up and down the coast. Dry, white
Verdicchio is the best-known wine, although more
unusual names, such as Bianchello del Metauro,
are gaining in popularity.

LE MARCHE

Must See

1. Urbino

Experience More

2. San Marino
3. Pèsaro
4. Fano
5. Macerata
6. Urbania
7. Grotte di Frasassi
8. Senigallia
9. Ancona
10. Conero Peninsula
11. Loreto
12. Ascoli Piceno

Adriatic Sea

Marotta

8 **SENIGALLIA**
Marzocca
Montemarciano
Rocca Priora
Falconara Marittima
Ostra
Chiaravalle
9 **ANCONA**
Portonovo
10 **CONERO PENINSULA**
S76
A14
Jesi
Camerano
Santa Maria Nuova
Numana
Osimo
Filottrano
LORETO 11
Porto Recanati
Cingoli
Montefano
Recanati
LE MARCHE
Potenza Picena
Porto Potenza Picena
S361
S16
Civitanova Alta
Civitanova Marche
MACERATA 5
Sforzacosta
Sant 'Elpidio a Mare
Porto Sant'Elpidio
San Severino Marche
S77
Abbazia di Fiastra
A14
Montegranaro
Lido di Fermo
Tolentino
Porto San Giorgio
S78
Mogliano
S239
Santa Maria a Mare
Caldarola
Ripe San Ginesio
Fermo
San Ginesio
Montegiorgio
Servigliano
Monterubbiano
Pedaso
Sarnano
S239
Santa Vittoria in Matenano
S238
Cupra Marittima
S78
Ripatransone
Grottommare
Amandola
Comunanza
Cossignano
A14
San Benedetto del Tronto
Offida
Acquaviva Picena
Porto d'Ascoli
Montemonaco
ASCOLI PICENO
Martinsicuro
Roccafluvione
12
S235
S4
RA11
Alba Adriatica
Arquata del Tronto
Acquasanta Terme
ABRUZZO, MOLISE AND PUGLIA
p476
Giulianova
Ceppo
S81
Teramo
ABRUZZO

Croatia, Greece

The 15th-century Palazzo Ducale above the town of Urbino ↑

①

URBINO

🅰D3 🚌 *ℹ* Via Puccinotti; www.turismo.marche.it

Central Urbino is a wonderful tangle of steeply sloping medieval and Renaissance streets, dominated by the stunning Palazzo Ducale with its fairytale twin-towered façade. Italy's most beautiful Renaissance palace, it was built for Duke Federico da Montefeltro, ruler of Urbino (1444–82) and became a major centre for Renaissance development. The city was also home to one of history's most remarkable artists, Raphael.

Palazzo Ducale and Galleria Nazionale

🏛 Piazza Duca di Urbino
🕐 8:30am–7:15pm Tue–Sun
📅 1 Jan, 25 Dec 🌐 palazzo ducaleurbino.it

Federico da Montefeltro, Duke of Urbino (1422–82), was a soldier but also a patron of the arts, and his palace – with its library, paintings and refined architecture – is a tribute to courtly life and to the artistic and intellectual ideals of the Renaissance. Architect Luciano Laurana was responsible for much

of the design – including the courtyard – but it was Francesco di Giorgio Martini who completed the work in the mid-1470s with some additions, including a remarkably complex plumbing system.

> ### Did You Know?
>
> After losing an eye while jousting, Montefeltro had the bridge of his nose removed to help his vision.

The palazzo houses the Galleria Nazionale delle Marche, which has numerous masterpieces. The gallery's most famous works are Piero della Francesca's enigmatic *The Flagellation* (c 1460), often cited as the world's greatest small painting; *The Ideal City*, a perspective study attributed to Piero or his students; and the gorgeous portrait *La Muta* (1507) by Raphael.

②

Casa Natale di Raffaello

🏛 Via di Raffaello 57
📞 0722 32 01 05 🕐 9am–1pm & 3–7pm Mon–Sat, 10am–1pm & 3–6pm Sun & pub hols

Urbino's famous son, the painter Raphael (1483–1520), was born in the Casa Natale di Raffaello and received his early training here under his father, the artist Giovanni Santi. The house retains an evocative historic atmosphere. The stone on which father and son mixed their pigments is on display, alongside a sweet *Madonna and Child* by Raphael.

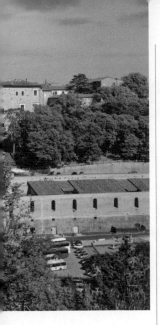

PIADINA

Central Italy's most loved speciality is this simple and delicious flatbread. Cold cuts of cured ham, rocket and soft cheese, particularly the tangy local kind called Squacquerone, make an ideal accompaniment to the bread. Try *piadina* and other local specialities at Piadineria L'Aquilone (*Via Cesare Battisti 23*).

③
Duomo and Museo Diocesano Albani

🏠 Piazza Pascoli 1 📞 0722 32 25 29 🔒 For renovation until 2021

The Neo-Classical Duomo, on Piazza Federico, was founded in 1062, but mostly built in 1789. Of interest here is the painting of *The Last Supper* by Federico Barocci (c 1535–1612). The Museo Diocesano contains a fine collection of ceramics, glass and religious artifacts ranging from the 13th century to the present.

EAT

Il Cortegiano
Located close to the Palazzo Ducale, this restaurant provides quick snacks or proper dining in a courtyard.

🏠 Via Pucinotti 13
📞 0722 373 07

€€€

④
Oratorio di San Giovanni Battista

🏠 Via Federico Barocci 31
📞 0722 91 02 59 🕐 10am–1pm & 3–6pm daily

The 14th-century Oratorio di San Giovanni Battista houses some minutely detailed frescoes from 1416 of the *Crucifixion* and the *Life of St John the Baptist* by Giacomo and Lorenzo Salimbeni.

⑤
Fortezza dell'Albornoz

🏠 Parco della Resistenza

There are magnificent views over the rooftops of Urbino and beyond from this 15th-century fortress, which is the defensive focus of the town's surviving 16th-century walls and bastions. The views are also excellent from the surrounding public park, located just a short walk above the town on Viale Bruno Buozzi.

EXPERIENCE MORE

2

San Marino

 D3 🚌 **San Marino Città (from Rimini)** 🛈 **Contrada Omagnano 20; www.visit sanmarino.com**

Europe's oldest republic, San Marino was reputedly founded by St Marinus, a 4th-century monk. On the slopes of Monte Titano, this tiny country has its own Mint, stamps, football team – even its own army.

There are no customs formalities in San Marino, whose borders are just 12 km (7 miles) apart at the widest point. The town of Borgomaggiore, at the foot of Monte Titano, has a cable car to the medieval citadel of San Marino, which is overrun with visitors and souvenir stalls.

3

Pèsaro

 D3 🚌 🛈 **Viale Trieste 164; www.turismo. pesarourbino.it**

One of the Adriatic's larger seaside resorts, Pèsaro has

managed to retain a stylish air. Behind the promenade and the wall of white stucco hotels is a lively, attractive medieval area.

The **Musei Civici** contains Giovanni Bellini's sumptuous *Coronation of the Virgin* (c 1470) polyptych and works from the Baroque era, including Guido Reni's *Fall of the Giants* and *St Joseph Penitent* by Cantarini. Many of the museum's impressive collection of Renaissance ceramics were donated by the Marchesa Vittoria Toschi Mosca.

The church of Sant'Agostino, on Corso XI Settembre, is known for its choir stalls, each a patchwork of inlaid landscapes and narrative scenes.

The composer Gioacchino Rossini was born in Pèsaro in 1792. His home, **Casa Rossini**, contains memorabilia, while his piano and some original manuscripts lie in the **Conservatorio Rossini**. His operas are performed in Teatro Rossini during the annual August music festival.

Gradara, about 13 km (8 miles) from Pesaro, is

a well-preserved hilltop village dominated by a majestic 14th-century castle, the Rocca, which was the scene of the tragic love story of Paolo and Francesca, mentioned by Dante in his *Divine Comedy*.

Musei Civici

⊘ 🏛 Piazza Mosca 29 🕐 Times vary, check website 🗓 1 Jan, 25 Dec 🌐 pesaromusei.it

Casa Rossini

⊘ 🏛 Via Rossini 34 📞 0721 38 73 57 🕐 Tue-Sun

Conservatorio Rossini

🏛 Piazza Olivieri 5 📞 0721 336 71 🕐 Mon-Fri, but phone first to arrange 🗓 Pub hols

Did You Know?

At 60 sq km (23 sq miles), San Marino is the world's smallest republic.

← Dusk falling over San Marino citadel

Fano

A D3 🚉 Pèsaro FS 🚍 🚌
ℹ️ Piazza XX Settembre 23;
www.turismofano.com

Named after Fanum Fortunae, a pagan temple to the goddess Fortuna, Fano became the terminus of the Via Flaminia (an important consular road from Rome) and the largest Roman colony on the Adriatic coast. The Arco d'Augusto (AD 2), on Via Arco d'Augusto, is Fano's most significant ancient monument. In 1463 Federico da Montefeltro destroyed its upper section while besieging the town as a papal *condottiere*.

The 16th-century Fontana della Fortuna, in Piazza XX Settembre, is dedicated to the goddess Fortuna. Also on the square, the imposing Palazzo Malatesta was built around 1420 and enlarged in 1544 for Fano's rulers, the Rimini-based Malatesta family. Inside is the small **Museo Civico** and the **Pinacoteca Malatestiana**, with works by Guercino and Guido Reni.

Museo Civico and Pinacoteca Malatestiana

⊛ 🏛 Piazza XX Settembre
📞 0721 88 78 45 🕐 Tue–Sun
📅 1 Jan, 25 Dec

Macerata

A D3 ℹ️ Corso della Repubblica 32; www.turismo.provinciamc.it

The elegant walled town of Macerata is best known for its Sferisterio, an open-air arena that hosts concerts and an annual opera festival.

Palazzo Buonaccorsi houses a museum of carriages and collections of modern and ancient art, including a *Madonna and Child* by Carlo Crivelli (1470). The **Basilica della Misericordia**, built by Luigi Vanvitelli (1736–41), is set over a votive chapel erected in 1447 to celebrate the end of the plague. It has a richly decorated interior.

Palazzo Buonaccorsi

⊛ 🏛 Via Don Minzoni 24
🕐 10am–7pm Fri–Sun
🌐 maceratamusei.it

Basilica della Misericordia

⊛ 🏛 Piazza San Vincenzo Strambi 🕐 8:30am–noon & 4–6pm daily 🌐 basilica misericordia.it

Urbania

A D3 🚉 Pèsaro 🚍 ℹ️ Corso Vittorio Emanuele 21; 0722 31 31 40

Urbania, with its elegant arcaded centre, takes its name from Pope Urban VIII (1623–44), who sought to convert an old medieval village into a model Renaissance town.

Its chief attraction is the huge **Palazzo Ducale**, built by the dukes of Montefeltro as a residential alternative to the Palazzo Ducale in nearby Urbino. It was begun in the 13th century, and then rebuilt in the 15th and 16th centuries. Situated alongside the River Metauro, it houses a small art gallery, a modest museum, old maps and globes, and

STAY

La Grotta
Cosy, contemporary rooms and a great position in San Marino's historic centre.

A D3 🏠 Contrada Santa Croce, San Marino 🌐 lagrottahotel sanmarino.com

€€€

Palazzo Guiderocchi
Stay in a prestigious 16th-century palazzo with original frescoes in Ascoli Piceno.

A E4 🏠 Via Cesare Battisti 3, Ascoli Piceno 🌐 hotelguiderocchi.it

€€€

the remnants of Duke Federico's famous library.

Palazzo Ducale
⊛ 📞 0722 31 31 51
🕐 Tue–Sun

Grotte di Frasassi

A D3 🏠 Ancona FS Genga San Vittore Terme 🕐 Daily 📅 10–30 Jan, 4 & 25 Dec 🌐 frasassi.com

Some of Europe's largest publicly accessible caverns lie in the cave network gouged out by the River Sentino southwest of Jesi. The colossal Grotta del Vento is large enough to contain Milan cathedral – its ceiling extends to a height of 240 m (787 ft). This cavern has been used for a range of experiments, from sensory deprivation to an exploration of the social consequences of leaving a group of people alone in its depths for long periods.

HILL-TOWNS IN LE MARCHE

Charming medieval towns and villages dot the hillsides of Le Marche. Sarnano, for one, is a medley of narrow lanes, steps and archways arranged in concentric circles; from the nearby ski area in the Monti Sibillini, you can see the coast on a clear day. A 14th-century castle with stunning views dominates Acquaviva Picena. Offida, famous both for lace and winemaking, is surrounded by vine-covered hills. Just inland from Senigallia, Corinaldo is centred on the striking Piaggia, a flight of 109 steps with a well halfway up, and has particularly well-preserved walls.

↑ The picturesque hilltop village of Acquaviva Picena

8

Senigallia

AD3 **A**Ancona **🚊**
ℹ Via Manni 7; www.
feelsenigallia.it

Famous for its sandy beach, Senigallia also has some fascinating sights. On pedestrianized Piazza del Duca are the imposing **Rocca Roveresca**, a 14th- and 15th-century castle, and **Palazzetto Baviera**, featuring some remarkable stucco decoration by Federico Brandani (16th century). Nearby, the Baroque **Chiesa della Croce** (1608) has a richly decorated interior, including an altarpiece with the *Entombment of Christ* by Federico Barocci (1592). The elegant Foro Annonario is a circular colonnaded piazza and marketplace.

Rocca Roveresca

⊗ **A** Piazza del Duca 2
🕒 Times vary, check website
w roccasenigallia.it/en

Palazzetto Baviera

⊗ **A** Piazza del Duca **☎** 071 662 93 48 **🕒** Wed–Sun

Chiesa della Croce

A Via Fagnani 1
🕒 9:30–11:30am Mon–Sat, 3:30–6:30pm Sun

9

Ancona

AD3 **✕**FS**🚌🚊** **ℹ** Banchina Nazario Sauro 50; www.
turismo.marche.it

The capital of Le Marche and its largest port, Ancona dates back to at least the 5th century BC, when it was settled by the Greeks. Its name derives from *ankon* (Greek for "elbow"), a reference to the rocky spur that juts into the sea to form the town's fine natural harbour.

Heavy bombing in World War II destroyed much of the medieval town, but the 15th-century Loggia dei Mercanti (Merchants' Exchange) on Via della Loggia survives.

Just north of the loggia is the **Pinacoteca Comunale F Podesti e Galleria d'Arte Moderna**, with canvases by Titian and Lorenzo Lotto. In the **Museo Archeologico Nazionale delle Marche** there are displays of Greek, Gallic and Roman art. The Arco di Traiano, on Lungomare Vanvitelli, by the harbour, was erected in AD 115 and is one of Italy's better-preserved Roman arches.

Pinacoteca Comunale F Podesti e Galleria d'Arte Moderna

⊗ **A** E Vicolo Foschi 4
☎ 071 222 50 47 **🕒** By appt only, Tue–Sun

Museo Archeologico Nazionale delle Marche

⊗ **A** Via Ferretti 6 **☎** 071 20 26 02 **🕒** Tue–Sun

10

Conero Peninsula

AD3 **A** Ancona **FS🚊** Ancona **🚌** From Ancona to Sirolo or Numana **ℹ** Via Peschiera 30/A, Sirolo; www.
parcodelconero.org

Easily accessible from Ancona to the north, the cliff-edged Conero peninsula is a semi-wild area known for its scenery, its wines (notably Rosso del Conero) and for a collection of coves, beaches and resorts.

The best of these resorts is Portonovo, above whose beach stands Santa Maria di Portonovo, a pretty 11th-century Romanesque church mentioned by Dante in Canto XXI of *Paradiso*. Sirolo and Numana are busier, but you can escape the crowds by hiking the flower-swathed slopes of Monte Conero, or by taking a boat trip to the smaller beaches.

Loreto

A D3 **A** Ancona **FS** **🚌**
i Corso Boccalini 67; www.loretoturismo.info

Legend has it that in 1294 the house of the Virgin Mary (Santa Casa) miraculously uprooted itself from the Holy Land and was brought by angels to a laurel grove (*loreto*) south of Ancona. Each year millions of pilgrims visit the **Santa Casa** in Loreto and its **Basilica**. Begun in 1468, the latter was designed by architects Bramante, Sansovino and Giuliano da Sangallo. Its paintings include works by Luca Signorelli. The **Museo Pontificio Santa Casa** has 16th-century art by Lorenzo Lotto.

Basilica and Santa Casa
A Piazza della Madonna 1
📞 071 974 71 55 **🕐** Daily

Museo Pontificio Santa Casa
♿ **A** Piazza della Madonna 1
📞 071 974 71 98 **🕐** 10am–1pm & 3:30–6:30pm Tue–Sun

Ascoli Piceno

A D4 **🚌** **i** Palazzo Comunale, Piazza Arringo; 0736 29 82 13

This alluring town takes its name from the Piceni, a tribe eventually conquered by the Romans in 89 BC. The gridiron plan of Roman Asculum Picenum is visible in the streets today, but it is the town's medieval heritage that attracts most visitors.

The enchanting Piazza del Popolo is dominated by the 13th-century Palazzo dei Capitani del Popolo and the church of San Francesco, a large and faintly austere Gothic ensemble built between 1262 and 1549.

Around Piazza dell'Arringo is the 12th-century Duomo. Its Cappella del Sacramento contains a polyptych by the 15th-century artist Carlo Crivelli. The **Pinacoteca Civica** has more works by Crivelli and by Guido Reni, Titian and Alemanno. Among the troves of precious pieces is the 13th-century Opus Anglicanum cope, a beautifully detailed tapestry that was bequeathed to the museum by Pope Nicholas IV in 1288.

Pinacoteca Civica
♿ **A** Palazzo Comunale, Piazza Arringo **📞** 0736 29 82 13 **🕐** Tue–Sun

↑ Dramatic coastline around the Conero peninsula

EMILIA-ROMAGNA

The heartland of central Italy, Emilia-Romagna has many attractive towns: the lively regional capital, Bologna, with its arcaded streets and delicious pasta; Ferrara, with its fantastic fortress; Parma, famed for its tasty cheese and ham; Ravenna, gleaming with Byzantine mosaics; and Rimini with its long sandy beaches.

Most of the major towns in Emilia-Romagna lie near the Via Aemilia, a Roman road built in 187 BC, which linked Rimini on the Adriatic coast with the garrison town of Piacenza. Prior to the Romans, the Etruscans ruled from their capital, Felsina, located on the site of present-day Bologna. After the fall of Rome, the region's focus moved to Ravenna, which became a principal part of the Byzantine Empire.

During the Middle Ages pilgrims heading for Rome continued to use the Via Aemilia. Political power, however, passed to influential noble families. Great courts grew up around them, attracting poets such as Dante and Ariosto, as well as painters, sculptors and architects.

Cobbled together from separate Papal States in 1860, modern Emilia-Romagna was given its present borders in 1947. Emilia, the western part of the region, is traditionally associated with a more northern outlook and a tendency towards the left in politics. Romagna, on the other hand, has witnessed an increase in the support for right-wing parties calling for political independence from Rome.

With its rich agricultural land, historic cities and thriving industry, Emilia-Romagna is now one of the most prosperous areas in Italy. The entire region has a reputation as a great gastronomic centre.

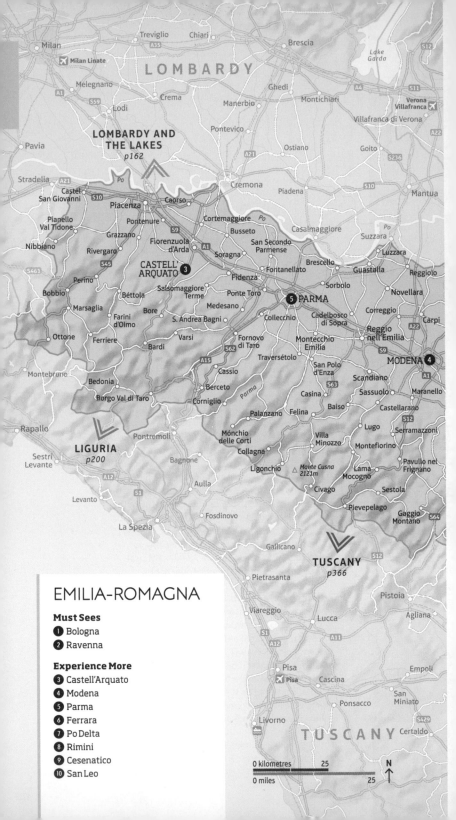

LOMBARDY

Lake Garda

✈ Milan Linate

LOMBARDY AND
THE LAKES
p162

Verona
Villafranca ✈

LIGURIA
p200

CASTELL'
ARQUATO ③

PARMA ⑤

MODENA ④

Monte Cusna
2121m △

TUSCANY
p366

✈ Pisa

EMILIA-ROMAGNA

Must Sees

❶ Bologna
❷ Ravenna

Experience More

❸ Castell'Arquato
❹ Modena
❺ Parma
❻ Ferrara
❼ Po Delta
❽ Rimini
❾ Cesenatico
❿ San Leo

TUSCANY

0 kilometres   25

0 miles   25

N ↑

↑ View of Bologna's rooftops from the top of Torre degli Asinelli

② San Giacomo Maggiore

⌂ **Piazza Rossini** ⏱ **Daily**

This Romanesque-Gothic church, begun in 1267 but altered substantially since, is visited mainly for the Cappella Bentivoglio, a superb family chapel founded by Annibale Bentivoglio in 1445 and consecrated in 1486. Pride of place naturally goes to a portrait with subtle characterization of the patrons by Lorenzo Costa (1460–1535), who was also responsible for the frescoes of the *Apocalypse*, the *Madonna Enthroned* and the *Triumph of Death*. The chapel's altarpiece, depicting the *Virgin and Saints with Two Angel Musicians* (1488), is the work of painter Francesco Francia. The Bentivoglio family is further glorified in

---

> 💬 **INSIDER TIP**
> **Dozza**
>
> Take a trip to the hilltop village of Dozza, 25 km (16 miles) from Bologna. The medieval buildings here are decorated with bright murals, thanks to a biennial art festival.

---

① BOLOGNA

⌂ C2 ✈ **Marconi 9 km (5 miles) NW** 🚊 **Piazza Medaglia d'Oro** 🚌 **Piazza XX Settembre** ℹ **Piazza Maggiore 1/e; www.bolognawelcome.com**

Widely recognized as Italy's gastronomic capital, Bologna is home to an almost overwhelming number of eateries and food markets. The city's historic core is a handsome ensemble of brick buildings and charming porticoed streets. Medieval palaces are clustered around the central Piazza Maggiore, which is dominated by the Basilica di San Petronio. The University of Bologna is the oldest in Europe and the venerable Archiginnasio was its first official building. The city's main landmark is its pair of medieval towers – the 97-m- (318-ft-) high Asinelli and the leaning Garisenda tower.

① Due Torri

 Piazza di Porta Ravegnana

Only 20 of the original 100 towers that shaped Bologna's skyline in medieval times are still standing today and this eye-catching pair is in prime position in the centre of town. At 97 m (318 ft), **Torre degli Asinelli** is Italy's fourth-tallest tower. The reward for climbing the 498 steps to the top is a fine view that stretches over the rooftops and hills. Torre della Garisenda, mentioned in Dante's *Inferno*, was reduced in height from 60 m (197 ft) to 48 m (157 ft) in the mid-14th century, when it was feared it would collapse due to its lean from the vertical of 3 m (10 ft). Torre degli Asinelli also has a lean of around 2 m (7 ft).

Torre degli Asinelli

⊗ ⏱ **10am–6pm daily**
🌐 **duetorribologna.com**

The famous Neptune Fountain (1566) was designed by painter Tommaso Laureti.

The 13th-century Palazzo del Podestà was remodelled in 1484.

⑤ ↗
Museo delle Cere Anatomiche (600 m/ 650 yds)

↖ ⑩
MAMbo (1.5 km/ 0.9 miles)

VIA UGO BASSI

VIA DELL'INDIPENDENZA

VIA RIZZOLI

VIA ZAMBONI

VIA BENEDETTO XIV

VIA SAN VITALE

VIA IV NOVEMBRE

VIA OREFICI   VIA CAPRARIE

PIAZZA MAGGIORE

VIA DAZEGLIO

VIA DELL'ARCHIGINNASIO

PIAZZA DI PORTA RAVEGNANA

STRADA MAGGIORE

VIA CASTIGLIONE

VIA SANTO STEFANO

The historic streets surrounding the Due Torri in Bologna ↑

⑧
Santuario di San Luca (5 km/ 3 miles) ↓

VIA FARINI

VIA DE' POET

VIA GARIBALDI

The flagged medieval streets and shady porticoed buildings in Piazza Cavour are typical of Bologna's elegant city centre.

Did You Know?

Bologna has 38 km (24 miles) of covered walkways – more than any other city in the world.

the tomb of Anton Galeazzo Bentivoglio (1435) opposite the chapel. It was among the last works of the noted Sienese sculptor Jacopo della Quercia. The Oratory of Santa Cecilia features frescoes on the lives of Santa Cecilia and San Valeriano by Costa and Francesco Francia (1504–6).

---

③
Basilica di Santo Stefano

⌂ Via Santo Stefano 24
☎ 051 498 34 23 ⌚ 9:30am–12:30pm & 2:30–6pm daily (summer: to 7:30pm)

Standing on central Bologna's prettiest piazza, this is a complex of ecclesiastical buildings also known as the

Sette Chiese, or the Seven Churches. It is a curious collection of four medieval churches (originally seven) jumbled together under one

↑ Light streaming into the Church of the Crucifix, Basilica di Santo Stefano

roof. The 11th-century church of the Crocifisso provides little more than a corridor leading to the polygonal San Sepolcro, the most appealing of the quartet. Also dating from the 11th century, its centrepiece is the tomb of St Petronius, a marvellously overstated affair that is modelled on the Holy Sepulchre of Jerusalem.

Parts of the church – those dedicated to saints Vitale and Agricola – date back to ancient times. To the rear of the complex is a courtyard with the Fontana di Pilata (a fountain incorporating an 8th-century marble basin), the Chiesa della Trinità, a 12th-century cloister with a Romanesque double-loggia, and a small museum featuring minor paintings and religious artifacts.

Pinacoteca Nazionale

🏛 Via delle Belle Arti 56
🕐 8:30am-7:30pm Tue-Sun & pub hols (last adm: 30 mins before closing)
🔒 1 Jan, 8 & 25 Dec
🌐 pinacoteca bologna.beniculturali.it

Bologna's principal art gallery, and one of the region's most important collections, stands on the edge of the city's university district, a bustling area of bars, bookshops and cheap restaurants. The gallery is mainly dedicated to work by Bolognese painters, notably Vitale da Bologna, Guido Reni, Guercino and the Carracci family. Members of the Ferrarese school are also represented, in particular Francesco del Cossa and Ercole de' Roberti. The two highlights are *Madonna in Glory* (c 1491) and *Ecstasy of St Cecilia* (c 1515) by Perugino and Raphael respectively, both artists who worked in Bologna.

Museo delle Cere Anatomiche

🏛 Via Irnerio 48
📞 051 209 1556
🕐 Summer: 10am-1pm Tue-Fri, 10am-6pm Sat, Sun & pub hols (winter: from 9am)
🔒 1 Jan, Easter, 1 May, 15 Aug, 24 & 25 Dec, pub hols

The Museum of Anatomical Waxworks is one of the more interesting and memorable of Bologna's smaller museums, featuring occasionally gruesome, visceral waxworks and numerous models of organs, limbs and flayed bodies. Sculpted rather than made from casts, the exhibits have an artistic as well as scientific appeal. The models were used as medical teaching aids until the 19th century. Exhibits from the 18th century are in Palazzo Poggi, which also contains the Geografia e Nautica collection.

FOOD MARKETS

Just off Piazza Maggiore, Mercato di Mezzo is great for a snack while Mercato delle Erbe has good restaurants. The weekly Mercato Ritrovato *(Via Azzo Gardino)* includes high-quality Slow Food produce. FICO Eataly World *(Via Paolo Canali)* is an agri-food theme park with a range of eateries, factories and activities.

San Domenico

🏛 Piazza di San Domenico 13
📞 051 640 04 11
🕐 8:30am-noon & 3:30-6pm Mon-Fri, 8:30am-5pm Sat, Sun & pub hols

Bologna's San Domenico can lay claim to being the most important of Italy's many Dominican churches. Begun in 1221, after St Dominic's death, it was built to house the body of the saint, who died here and lies buried in a tomb known as the Arca di San Domenico, a magnificent composite work. The tomb's statues were executed by Pisan sculptor Nicola Pisano; the reliefs of scenes from the *Life of St Dominic* were the work of Pisano and his assistants; the canopy (1473) is attributed to Nicola di Bari; while the figures of the angels

↑ The arcaded cloisters of San Domenico

and saints Proculus and Petronius are early works by Michelangelo. The reliquary (1383) behind the simple marble sarcophagus contains St Dominic's head.

San Petronio

🏛 Piazza Galvani 5
📞 051 23 14 15
🕐 8:30am-12:30pm & 2-6pm daily (to 6:30pm Sun & pub hols)

Dedicated to the city's 5th-century bishop, this church ranks among the greatest of Italy's brick-built medieval buildings. Founded in 1390, it was originally intended to be larger than St Peter's in Rome, but its size was scaled down when funds were diverted to the nearby Palazzo Archiginnasio. The resulting financial shortfall left the church decidedly lopsided, with a row of columns on its eastern flank that were meant to support an additional internal aisle. The project's financial recklessness, nonetheless, was said to have been instrumental in turning Martin Luther against Catholicism.

The airy Gothic interior features graceful pillars supporting the roof and a 67-m- (220-ft-) long meridian line on the floor which was traced in 1655 by the astronomer Gian Domenico Cassini. Twenty-two chapels, shielded by screens, open off the nave. In 1547 the Council of Trent was temporarily moved here due to the plague.

Santuario di San Luca

📍 Via San Luca 36 📞 051 614 23 39 🕐 7am-6:30pm daily (summer: to 7pm)

The longest uninterrupted section of the city's porticoes leads the 4 km (2.5 miles) from the Porta Saragozza city gate to this hilltop church, a familiar beacon to travellers.

The current church, built between 1723 and 1757, presents an elegant exterior, while the interior contains a Byzantine Madonna and Child, which is carried in procession to the city's San Pietro cathedral for a week each May. There are marvellous views out over the surrounding hills from the terraces.

Palazzo Pepoli

📍 Via Castiglione 8 🌐 genusbononiae.it

Built between 1276 and 1344, this palazzo houses a multi-media museum that takes visitors on a journey through 2,500 years of local history, from the Etruscan period to the present. The chronological displays are interspersed with thematic rooms, such as the City of Water room.

MAMbo

📍 Via Don Minzoni 14 🕐 2-6:30pm Tue-Fri (from 11am Sat & Sun) 🌐 mambo-bologna.org

The permanent collection at Bologna's modern art museum covers Italian art from the second half of the 20th century to today. Regular temporary exhibitions are also hosted in this former bakery.

The monumental façade of San Petronio; one of its stained-glass windows *(inset)*

EAT

Serghei
A traditional trattoria, Serghei serves tasty dishes like stuffed zucchini with meatballs.

📍 Via Piella 12 📞 051 23 35 33 🕐 Sun

€€€

E' Cucina
An unassuming looking place with a bright and modern interior, E'Cucina dishes up a selection of inspired dishes at low prices.

📍 Via Leopardi 4 📞 051 275 00 69

€€€

Caminetto d'Oro
This restaurant serves quality regional specialities in a refined environment.

📍 Via de' Falegnami 4 🕐 Sun 🌐 caminetto doro.it

€€€

Cesarina
Authentic Bolognese dishes are served here in the attractive environs of the Piazza Santo Stefano.

📍 Via Santo Stefano 19B 🌐 ristorantecesarina.it

€€€

Osteria Bartolini
Enjoy seafood, including mixed fried fish, in the courtyard garden here.

📍 Piazza Malpighi 16 🌐 osteriabartolini bologna.com

€€€

Saints Apollinare and Vitale atop their columns in Piazza del Popolo

2

RAVENNA

 D3 FS🚌 *i* Piazza San Francesco 7; www.turismo.ra.it
🅦 ravennamosaici.it (for combined tickets for all the mosaic sites)

Famed for its glittering Byzantine mosaics, Ravenna's centre is a pleasant medley of historic cobbled streets, fine shops and piazzas, and is close to some excellent beaches. The city rose to power in the 1st century BC under Emperor Augustus. As Rome's power declined, Ravenna was made capital of the Western Empire in AD 402, a role it had during the Ostrogoth and Byzantine rule in the 5th and 6th centuries, when many of the city's spectacular churches and basilicas were built.

①
Piazza del Popolo

This elegant square is famed for its two Venetian-style columns with saints Vitale and Apollinare perched on top. Behind is Palazzo Communale and Palazzo Veneziano, built when Ravenna was part of the Venetian Republic in the 15th century. The archway in Palazzo Veneziano leads to Via Cairoli, a narrow shopping street. Nearby is Piazza Andrea Costa, home to a covered market that sells all manner of fresh local produce every morning.

②
Basilica di San Vitale

🏛 Via San Vitale 17
🕐 9am-7pm daily (Nov-Feb: 10am-5pm) 🚫 1 Jan, 25 Dec

Finished in 548, this octagonal basilica is the only major church from the period of Emperor Justinian I to survive virtually intact. Its colourful mosaics are the height of Byzantine splendour. Look out for the emperor portrayed with court officials and, on the opposite wall, the Empress Theodora. The apse mosaics show Christ, San Vitale and Bishop Ecclesius, who began the church.

③
Tomba di Dante

🏛 Via Dante Alighieri
☎ 0544 21 56 76 🕐 10am-7pm daily (to 9pm Sun)
🚫 1 Jan, 25 Dec

The interior of Dante's tomb, built in the late 18th century, contains a bas-relief by Pietro Lombardo (1483) and a votive lamp that continually burns olive oil donated by Florence each year on the anniversary of Dante's death. The adjacent Dante museum includes paintings of the poet as well as research findings.

🔍 HIDDEN GEM
Ravenna's Beaches

Relaxed, surfer-style beach bars and restaurants abound at Marina di Ravenna and all its nearby resorts. To experience ultimate seaside refinement, head for Milano Marittima.

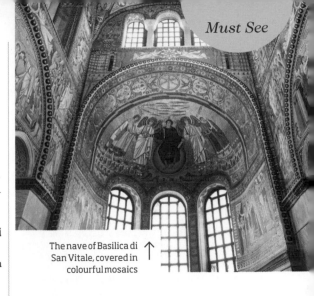

Must See

④ Basilica di San Francesco

⬛ Piazza San Francesco
📞 0544 332 56 🕐 7am–noon & 3–7pm daily

The main feature of interest in this church is the flooded crypt, which contains 10th-century mosaics and columns.

⑤ Battistero degli Ariani

⬛ Via degli Ariani 📞 0544 54 37 24 🕐 8:30am–4:30pm daily (summer: to 7:30pm) 🚫 1 Jan, 1 May

The cupola of this tiny late 5th-century baptistry has an impressive mosaic showing the 12 Apostles ringed around a scene depicting the baptism of Christ.

⑥ Basilica di Sant' Apollinare Nuovo

⬛ Via di Roma 53
🕐 Same as San Vitale

This glorious 6th-century church has a cylindrical bell tower and some of the largest Byzantine mosaics in the

↑ The nave of Basilica di San Vitale, covered in colourful mosaics

city. Look out for the two rows of mosaics showing processions of martyrs and virgins bearing gifts for Christ and the Virgin.

⑦ Domus dei Tappeti di Pietra

⬛ Via Gian Battista Barbiani 16 🕐 Times vary, check website 🌐 domus deitappetidipietra.it

A Byzantine house dating from the 5th and 6th centuries, Tappeti di Pietra was only

discovered in the 1990s and has beautiful mosaics on the floors of the 14 rooms.

⑧ Battistero Neoniano

⬛ Piazza Duomo 1
🕐 Same as San Vitale

The Neonian Baptistry dates from the 5th century and is named after the bishop who may have commissioned its decoration, which includes a mosaic of the baptism of Christ. It is Ravenna's oldest monument.

EXPERIENCE MORE

③ Castell'Arquato

🅰 B2 🏠 Piacenza 🚌
ℹ Piazza Municipio 1;
0523 80 32 15

Castell'Arquato is one of the prettiest villages in the countryside south of the Po. Day visitors come at the weekends, thronging the restaurants and bars around the beautiful Piazza Matteotti. The best building on the piazza is the 13th-century Palazzo Pretorio, a Romanesque basilica. The impressive Rocca Viscontea (14th century), a former fortress, is on Piazza del Municipio. The village's hilltop site offers good views, particularly over the verdant Arda Valley to the east.

④ Modena

🅰 C2 FS🚌 ℹ Piazza Grande 14; www.visit modena.it

To most Italians Modena means fast cars (both Ferrari and Maserati have factories in its industrial outskirts) and opera (this is the birthplace of Luciano Pavarotti). Monuments to an earlier age, however, make this one of Emilia's most enticing historic destinations. A thriving colony since Roman times, the city rose to medieval prominence with the arrival in 1598 of the d'Este nobles from Ferrara. This family continued to rule the city until the end of the 18th century.

Modena's Romanesque **Duomo** was founded by Countess Matilda of Tuscany, ruler of Modena in the 11th century. It was dedicated to San Geminiano, the city's patron saint, whose stone coffin lies under the choir. Its most noticeable feature is the Torre Ghirlandina, a leaning tower begun at the same time as the Duomo and completed two centuries later. It once housed the *Secchia*, a wooden bucket whose 1325 theft from Bologna allegedly sparked a war between the two cities. It also inspired Tassoni's 17th-century mock epic poem *La Secchia Rapita* (The Stolen Bucket).

The large reliefs on the Duomo's main (west) façade are the work of the 12th-century sculptor Wiligelmus. The highlight of the rather severe interior is a large carved *tribuna* (rood screen) decorated with 12th-century scenes from the Passion.

Formerly an arsenal and workhouse, the **Palazzo dei Musei** is now home to the city's best museums and galleries. Its finest section is the Galleria Estense, given over to the d'Este private art collection. Most of the paintings are by Emilian artists, but there are also works by Velázquez, Tintoretto, Bernini and Veronese.

Among the permanent displays in the Biblioteca Estense, the d'Este Library, are a 1481 edition of Dante's *Divine Comedy* and dozens of fascinating maps and diplomatic letters, many dating back centuries. The jewel of the collection is the illuminated Borso d'Este

←

Castell'Arquato's Rocca Viscontea, dominating the surrounding landscape

Bible, whose pages contain over 1,200 miniatures by 15th-century artists of the Ferrara school.

The Ferrari factory, 20 km (12 miles) south of Modena, was founded by Enzo Ferrari in 1945 and now produces around 2,500 cars annually. The **Museo Ferrari** has an excellent exhibition featuring memorabilia, classic engines and many vintage cars.

Duomo

⊗ 🏠 Corso Duomo 📞 059 21 60 78 🕒 7am-7pm Tue-Sun 🚫 Lunch Mon

Palazzo dei Musei

⊗⊗⊗ 🏠 Largo Porta Sant'Agostino 337 📞 059 203 31 25 🕒 8am-7:30pm Mon-Thu & Sat (to 11pm Fri), 9:45am-7:15pm Sun & pub hols

Museo Ferrari

⊗ 🏠 Via Dino Ferrari 43, Maranello 📞 053 694 97 13 🕒 9:30am-6pm daily (summer: to 7pm) 🚫 1 Jan, 1 Dec

---

TOP 3
CASTLES OF PIACENZA & PARMA

Castello di Bardi
🅰 B2 🏠 Bardi
🌐 castellodibardi.info
This castle dominates the surrounding area from a rocky spur.

Rocca Sanvitale
🅰 C2 🏠 Fontanellato
📞 0521 82 90 55
Surrounded by a moat, this fortress contains Parmigianino frescoes.

Grazzano Visconti
🅰 B2 🏠 Grazzano
📞 351 277 81 62
Rebuilt in the early 20th century around a 14th century castle, this village is filled with workshops and taverns.

PARMESAN CHEESE AND PARMA HAM

A visit to a Parmigiano Reggiano dairy, such as Giansanti Di Muzio *(Strada Traversetolo 228, Parma)* shows how this unique product is made, a method that has barely changed since the 12th century.

Prosciutto di Parma also involves a strictly regulated process - only salt may be added. Antica Salumeria Rastelli *(Strada della Repubblica 54A, Parma)* is a traditional deli.

Parma

🅰 C2 📷📧 ℹ️ **Piazza Garibaldi 1; www.turismo. comune.parma.it**

A byword for fine food and good living, Parma is also a treasure trove of superlative art and fine medieval buildings.

The Lombard-Romanesque Duomo on Piazza Duomo is renowned for the painting that fills its main cupola, the *Assumption* (1526–30) by Antonio da Correggio. The south transept features a carved frieze of *The Deposition* (1178) by Benedetto Antelami, who was also responsible for much of the Baptistry (1196) just south of the cathedral. The reliefs inside and outside the latter are among the most important of their age in Italy.

East of the Duomo is the church of San Giovanni Evangelista (rebuilt 1498–1510), whose dome features a fresco (c 1520) of the *Vision of St John at Patmos* by Correggio. If this wasn't enough, frescoes by Parmigianino can also be seen here.

Look out for the vast **Palazzo della Pilotta**, which was built for the Farnese family during the 1500s. It comprises several parts, including the Teatro Farnese (1628), a copy of Palladio's ravishing theatre in Vicenza, built entirely of wood.

Both Parmigianino and Correggio are represented in the palace's Galleria Nazionale, which also houses works by Fra Angelico, Bronzino and El Greco, and two by Ludovico Carracci: the *Apostles at the Sepulchre* and the *Funeral of the Virgin* (late 1500s).

The Museo Archeologico Nazionale, on the lower floor, has exhibits from Velleia, an Etruscan necropolis, and from prehistoric sites around Parma.

Originally the refectory of a Benedictine convent, the **Camera di Correggio** was frescoed by the local artist in 1518 with mythological scenes.

Palazzo della Pilotta
⊗ 🏠 Piazzale della Pilotta 15 📞 0521 22 04 00 🕒 8:30am-7pm Tue-Sat, 1-7pm Sun

Camera di Correggio
⊗ 🏠 Via Melloni 📞 0521 23 33 09 🕒 8:30am-2pm Tue-Sun

> **A byword for fine food and good living, Parma is also a treasure trove of superlative art and fine medieval buildings.**

Cycling past majestic Renaissance buildings in Ferrara

from Spina, a Greco-Etruscan trading post near Comacchio on the Po Delta.

Named after the diamond motifs on its façade, the **Palazzo dei Diamanti** houses a modern art gallery, a museum devoted to the Risorgimento (p44), and the Pinacoteca Nazionale, which contains works from leading exponents of the local Renaissance school.

Ferrara has been a major centre for Jewish communities since the 15th century, when the d'Este family guaranteed a safe welcome for Jews persecuted elsewhere. The **Museo Nazionale dell'Ebraismo Italiano e della Shoah** features multimedia displays and exhibits related to the history of Judaism in Italy.

Dating in parts from the 7th and 8th centuries, the **Abbazia di Pomposa** sits 42 km (26 miles) east of Ferrara. The abbey incorporates a fine Romanesque bell tower (1063) and the Basilica di Santa Maria, which has a mosaic floor with geometric designs and animal motifs, plus richly frescoed walls, including The Last Judgment.

6
Ferrara

C2 🚇🚌 ℹ️ Castello Estense, Largo Castello; www.ferrarainfo.com

The d'Este dynasty has left an indelible mark on the walled town of Ferrara. The noble family took control of the town in the late 13th century, holding power until 1598, when they were forced by the papacy to move to Modena.

The **Castello Estense**, the family's dynastic seat (begun 1385), looms over the town centre. Ferrante and Giulio d'Este were incarcerated in its dungeons for plotting to overthrow Alfonso I d'Este, and Parisina d'Este, wife of Nicolò III, was executed here for having an affair with Ugo, her illegitimate stepson.

Bronze statues of Nicolò III and Borso d'Este, one of Nicolò's reputed 27 children, adorn the medieval **Palazzo del Comune** (begun 1243).

Both are copies of the 15th-century originals by Leon Battista Alberti.

Ferrara's 12th-century Duomo was designed by Wiligelmus, widely regarded as the first great Italian sculptor. Fine reliefs on the façade depict scenes from the Last Judgment. The excellent **Museo della Cattedrale** contains a fine set of marble reliefs of the Labours of the Months (late 1100s), two painted organ shutters (1469) of St George and the Annunciation by Cosmè Tura, and the Madonna of the Pomegranate (1408) by Jacopo della Quercia.

The d'Este family's summer retreat, the **Museo Schifanoia** is famous for its Salone dei Mesi (Room of the Months), decorated with detailed 15th-century murals depicting the 12 months of the year.

The most interesting exhibits in the **Museo Archeologico Nazionale** are artifacts that were excavated

---

CERVIA SALT FLATS & FLAMINGOES

A particularly pure type of salt has been produced at the salt flats just outside the coastal town of Cervia, to the south of the Po Delta, since ancient times. The area, now a nature reserve, is year-round home to a community of flamingoes. Tours on foot, by bicycle or by boat are available March–November.

Castello Estense
⌖ 🏠 Largo Castello
📞 0532 29 92 33 🕐 Wed-Mon 🔒 Dec-Jun

Palazzo del Comune
🏠 Piazza Municipale

Museo della Cattedrale
⌖ 🏠 Via San Romano
📞 0532 24 49 49 🕐 Tue-Sun 🔒 1 & 6 Jan, 25 Dec

Museo Schifanoia
⌖ 🏠 Via Scandiana 23
📞 0532 24 49 49 🕐 10am-7pm Tue-Sun

Museo Archeologico Nazionale
⌖ 🏠 Palazzo di Ludovico il Moro, Via XX Settembre 122 📞 0532 662 99 🕐 Tue-Sun 🔒 1 Jan, 1 May, 25 Dec

Palazzo dei Diamanti
⌖⌖ 🏠 Corso Ercole d'Este 21 📞 0532 24 49 49 🕐 Daily

Museo Nazionale dell'Ebraismo Italiano e della Shoah
⌖ 🏠 Via Piangipane 79/83 🕐 Tue-Sun
🌐 meisweb.it

Abbazia di Pomposa
🏠 Via Pomposa Centro 1, Codigoro 🕐 8:30am-7:30pm Tue-Sun 🌐 ferrara terraeacqua.it

---

⑦
Po Delta

🗺 D2 🏠 Ferrara 🚆 Ferrara Ostellata 🚌 To Goro or Gorino ⛴ From Porto Garibaldi, Goro & Gorino ℹ Corso Mazzini 200, Comacchio; www.parcodeltapo.it

The Po is Italy's longest river. Although ravaged in many places by industrial pollution, at its finest it offers beautiful landscapes – rows of poplar trees across misty fields and vistas over the shifting sands of its vast island-dotted delta.

The immense Parco Delta del Po national park stretches all the way to the Veneto. Wetland areas such as the Valli di Comacchio (north of Ravenna) provide a winter home to breeding and migrating birds, from coots, bean geese and black terns, to rarer species such as the white egret, hen harrier and pygmy cormorant. Comacchio, the nearest town, comprises 13 tiny islands linked by bridges.

The Bosco della Mesola, a tract of ancient woodland, is home to large herds of deer.

It is possible to take a boat trip to some of the delta's more remote corners: key departure points include the villages of Ca' Tiepolo, Ca' Vernier and Taglio di Po. Most areas also offer the possibility of hiring bicycles. The 125-km (78-mile) ride along the right bank of the Po is very popular with cyclists.

EAT

La Sangiovesa
The wine and much of the produce used in the kitchen come from this restaurant's own estate. Find it 10 km (6 miles) from Rimini.

🗺 D3 🏠 Piazza Beato Simone Balacchi 14, Santarcangelo di Romagna 🕐 Lunch Sun & pub hols 🌐 sangiovesa.it

€€€

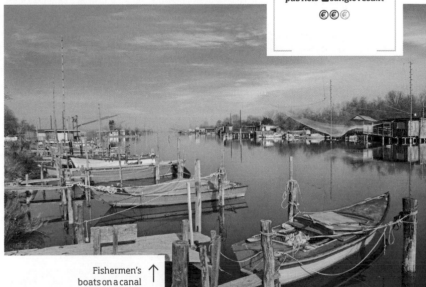

Fishermen's boats on a canal in the Po Delta ↑

8

Rimini

🅰D3 🚉 **ⓘPiazzale Fellini 3; www.rimini turismo.it**

Rimini was once a quaint seaside resort, whose relaxed charms were celebrated in the early films of Federico Fellini (1920–93), the director born and raised here. Today it is the largest beach resort in Europe. The seafront, which stretches unbroken for almost 15 km (9 miles), is lined with clubs, bars, cafés and restaurants. The crowded beaches are clean and well maintained, though entrance fees are charged at private beaches.

The town's old quarter, by contrast, is pleasantly quiet. Its charming cobbled streets gather around Piazza Cavour, dominated by the 14th-century Palazzo del Podestà. Rimini's finest building is its main cathedral, the **Tempio Malatestiano**. Built as a Franciscan church, it was converted in 1450 by Leon Battista Alberti, the great Florentine architect, into one of Italy's great Renaissance monuments. The work was commissioned by Sigismondo Malatesta (1417–68), a descendant of Rimini's ruling medieval family, and reputedly one of the most evil and debauched men of his time. Ostensibly designed as a chapel, the Tempio became little more than a monument to Malatesta. Inside are sculptures by Agostino di Duccio and a fresco (1451) by Piero della Francesca of Malatesta kneeling before St Sigismund (1451).

Did You Know?

San Leo has only been part of Emilia-Romagna since 2006, when the town voted to leave Le Marche in a referendum.

The entwined initials of Sigismondo Malatesta and his fourth wife, Isotta degli Atti, provide a recurring decorative motif, and there are reliefs depicting scenes of bacchanalian excess and oddities such as strangely posed elephants (a Malatesta family emblem). All this led Pope Pius II to condemn the building as "a temple of devil-worshippers", and to burn Malatesta's effigy for acts of "murder, violation, adultery, incest, sacrilege and perjury".

Tempio Malatestiano

🏛 Via IV Novembre 35
☎ 0541 511 30 🕐 8:30am-noon & 3:30-6:30pm Mon-Fri, 8:30am-7pm Sat, 9am-12:30pm & 3:30-6:30pm Sun)

9

Cesenatico

🅰D3 **ⓐForlì-Cesena** 🚉 **ⓘViale Roma 112; www.cesenatico.it**

The heart of Cesenatico, a city 18 km (11 miles) north of Rimini, lies around its attractive canal-port, which was designed by

Leonardo da Vinci in 1502. Today it hosts an open-air museum of historic boats with mustard-yellow sails decorated with deep-red designs. At Christmas, nativity figures positioned on the boats add to the atmosphere.

The town, one of the area's top fishing centres, has an important fish market and the canal-port is lined on both sides with an impressive selection of seafood eateries, including the Michelin-starred La Buca and the more low-key Osteria del Gran Fritto next door, both run by the same family. The sandy beach, popular with families, is well equipped for young children.

10

San Leo

🅰D3 **ⓐRimini** 🚌**From Rimini, change at Villanova** **ⓘPiazza Dante Alighieri 14; www.san-leo.it**

The captivating village of San Leo has a quaint cobbled square with a superb 9th-

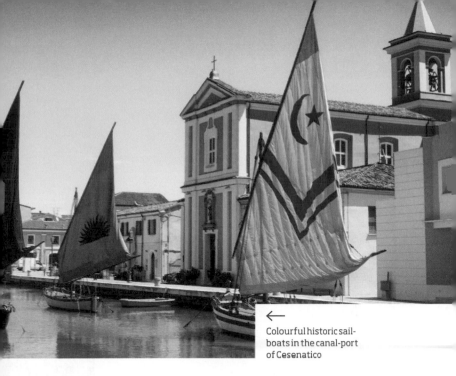

← Colourful historic sail-boats in the canal-port of Cesenatico

century Pieve (parish church). Built partly with stone collected from the ruined Mons Feretrius, the church was raised over the site of a 6th-century chapel.

Just behind the Pieve is the 12th-century Duomo, a fine Romanesque building with Corinthian capitals and Roman columns from the Mons Feretrius. The lid of St Leo's sarcophagus is in the crypt. Ancient pagan carvings can be seen on the wall behind the altar.

Few castles are as impressive as the great **Fortress** that towers over San Leo. Dante used this crag-top site as a model for the landscapes of *Purgatorio*, while Machiavelli considered the citadel to be the finest piece of military architecture in Italy. Its rocky ramparts once contained the Mons Feretrius, a Roman temple dedicated to Jupiter.

An earlier Roman fortress on the site became a papal prison in the 18th century. Its most famous inmate was the larger-than-life Conte di Cagliostro. A swindler, womanizer, necromancer, quack and alchemist, Cagliostro was imprisoned for heresy in the 1790s. His tiny cell – known as *pozzetto* (little well), because he had to be lowered into it from the ceiling – was specially built so that its window faced the village's two churches. The cell is still visible, together with a small picture gallery, state rooms and the majestic Renaissance ramparts, built by Francesco di Giorgio Martini for the dukes of Montefeltro in the 15th century.

Fortress
⊘ 🏛 Via Leopardi
📞 0541 92 69 67 🕐 Daily, by appt only

FAENZA CERAMICS

Located on the road between Rimini and Bologna, Faenza has been a major player in the world of ceramics since 16th-century crafts-men introduced white majolica and light blue painted designs. The town has a museum (*Museo Internazionale delle Ceramiche, Viale Baccarini 19, closed Mon*) displaying a collection of ancient and modern pieces, including works by Picasso and Matisse.

↑ Typical example of Faenza ceramics

SOUTHERN ITALY

La Corricella Harbour in Procida, an island in the Bay of Naples

EXPLORE SOUTHERN ITALY

This section divides southern Italy into six colour-coded sightseeing areas, as shown on the map below. Find out more about each area on the following pages.

TUSCANY

Arezzo

Perugia   Assisi

UMBRIA

Orvieto

Viterbo

Tarquinia   LAZIO

Cerveteri   Tivoli
Rome

Aprilia

Latina

Santa Teresa Gallura

Porto Torres   Olbia

Alghero

Bosa   Siniscola

Nuoro

Oristano   Tortoli

SARDINIA
p526

Carbonia

Cagliari

Pula

Tyrrhenian Sea

ITALY

Trapani   Palermo

GETTING TO KNOW
SOUTHERN ITALY

Rich in archaeological sites, as well as some extraordinarily varied landscapes and coasts, southern Italy is a fascinating region. Although the Roman site of Pompeii is high on everyone's list, there are also Greek ruins in Sicily and mysterious *nuraghi* (ancient structures) in Sardinia. The cuisine alone, with its eclectic heritage and diverse flavours, provides an excuse to dawdle on the coast or in pretty mountain villages.

NAPLES

PAGE 448

A chaotic yet spectacular metropolis, Naples sprawls noisily and dirtily around the edge of the magnificent Bay of Naples. To one side is Mount Vesuvius, to the other the smouldering sulphurous fields of the Campi Flegrei, while out at sea, across from the city, are the enticing islands of Capri, Ischia and Procida. Everything about Naples is exuberant, from its streetlife and traditional music to the lavish interiors of its many churches and two royal palaces. Naples is also home to what is reckoned to be the best pizza in Italy.

Best for
Full-on streetlife and lavish religious festivals

Home to
Museo Archeologico Nazionale

Experience
The original pizza Margherita

CAMPANIA

PAGE 462

To the north of Naples, fertile plains sweep down to the town of Santa Maria Capua Vetere, home to one of the largest remaining amphitheatres in Italy. The remote, mountainous and little-visited interior of Campania is overshadowed by the glories of the Amalfi Coast with its famous *cornice* road, and the astonishing Roman towns of Pompeii and Herculaneum, preserved under ash from the volcano that destroyed them in AD79. Before the Romans, the area was colonized by the Greeks, who left behind the ruins of a beautiful temple at Paestum.

Best for
Beautiful sunsets over the Tyrrenhian Sea

Home to
Pompeii, Herculaneum and the winding roads of the Amalfi Coast

Experience
Diving above the ruins of the sunken Roman city of Baiae

ABRUZZO, MOLISE AND PUGLIA

PAGE 476

Puglia is the "heel" of the Italian boot, the picturesque, serrated coastline of the Gargano peninsula is its "spur" and Abruzzo and Molise together form the "ankle". The mountainous regions of Abruzzo and Molise are wonderful for hiking and exploring rarely visited villages. Puglia is a wealthy, agricultural region with a beautiful coastline. Its jewel is Baroque Lecce, but the curious *trulli* houses around Alberobello, the labyrinthine centre of old Bari, and the Castel del Monte, are all worth visiting.

Best for
Eating sundried tomatoes and freshly picked produce

Home to
The florid Baroque buildings of Lecce and the Parco Nazionale d'Abruzzo, Lazio e Molise

Experience
Burrata from the region's cheese makers

→

PAGE 490

BASILICATA AND CALABRIA

Basilicata and Calabria receive relatively few tourists, except for the incredible cave-city of Matera and the fabulous coastline between Tropea and Maratea. Mostly upland country, Basilicata is peppered with Greek ruins, medieval abbeys and Norman castles. Calabria, bounded by the Ionian and Tyrrhenian seas, has many lovely beaches. Greek ruins can be found at Locri Epizephiri, while the slopes of the Aspromonte and Sila mountains are popular with walkers and skiers.

Best for
Getting off the beaten track

Home to
Matera, wild mountains and beautiful beaches

Experience
Sleeping in a cave hotel

SICILY

PAGE 500

Lying at the heart of the Mediterranean, the island of Sicily has been fought over and colonized by Greeks, Phoenicians, Romans, Arabs, Normans, Spanish, English and French, all of whom influenced the food and the language, as well as its art and architecture. Palermo, the busy capital, and Siracusa, with its historic centre, the island of Ortygia, are the most interesting cities. The island's coastline has sandy beaches, while the varied interior is characterized by remote hill-towns and plains punctuated by mountains. Among the most famous sights are the Mount Etna and Stromboli volcanoes.

Best for
Visiting ancient Greek temples and lazing on the beach

Home to
Palermo, the Valley of the Temples and Mount Etna

Experience
Island hopping around the Aeolian volcanic archipelago

SARDINIA

PAGE 526

With an interior of dramatic, soaring uplands and a coastline of beguiling sandy beaches and marine caves, Sardinia is extraordinarily beautiful – and in places still utterly wild. Cagliari, Alghero and Sassari are all worth visiting, but the true highlight of the island is its amazingly varied coastline, ranging from the white quartz beaches of the Sila peninsula to the exclusive resorts of the Costa Smeralda. Sardinia's ancient inhabitants are known as Nuragic after the strange truncated drystone structures with which they peppered the island.

Best for
Snorkelling in crystalline waters

Home to
Relics of the Nuragic civilization, the exclusive resorts of the Costa Smeralda

Experience
Flamingoes flying above Cagliari on their way to the salt flats on a spring evening

NAPLES

Naples is a vibrant cacophony of world-class museums, ancient ruins, crumbling churches and Baroque palaces blended into the fabric of a bustling modern city. Founded by the Greeks, it is one of only a few Italian cities that have remained continuously occupied from ancient times to the present day. The Romans enlarged and embellished it and in later centuries it was the much sought-after prize of foreign invaders and Imperialists – most notably the Normans, Hohenstaufen, French and Spanish.

Greek colonists founded a settlement overlooking the Bay of Naples as early as the 4th century BC, calling it Parthenope. As the settlement continued to expand, they established Neapolis (new city) next to the Palaeopolis, or old city. Neapolis was a leading commercial centre, and the Greek language and customs survived even during the Roman period, when this was a favourite area of the elite.

After the fall of the Roman Empire and a wave of invasions, the city came under Byzantine influence and went through a period of rebirth. In the 12th century, the invading Normans succeeded in conquering the whole of southern Italy. Naples itself became a capital, and the court began to attract famous artists. The 1400s were a golden era for Naples, but there followed two centuries of oppressive rule by Spain. In 1734 King Charles began the period of Bourbon hegemony. With the exception of the short-lived republican government in 1799 and the subsequent decade of French dominion, the Bourbons ruled Naples until 1860.

Since the unification of Italy, in the mid-19th century, the city's problems have become national issues – most notably the wealth gap between northern and southern Italy.

NAPLES

Must See

1. Museo Archeologico Nazionale

Experience More

2. MADRE
3. Castel Capuano and Porta Capuana
4. Duomo
5. Pio Monte della Misericordia
6. Cappella Sansevero
7. San Lorenzo Maggiore
8. San Gregorio Armeno
9. Sant'Angelo a Nilo
10. San Domenico Maggiore
11. Santa Chiara
12. Gesù Nuovo
13. Sant'Anna e San Bartolomeo dei Lombardi
14. Castel Nuovo
15. Museo Nazionale di San Martino
16. Galleria Umberto I
17. Palazzo Reale
18. Museo di Capodimonte
19. Catacombs of San Gennaro
20. Castel dell'Ovo

Eat

1. Da Michele
2. Sorbillo
3. Concettina ai Tre Santi

Stay

4. Constantinopoli 104
5. Hotel Romeo
6. Decumani

MUSEO ARCHEOLOGICO NAZIONALE

Q C1 **A** Piazza Museo **M** Piazza Cavour-Museo **⊞** 147, 168, 178, 182, 184, 604, C63
Ö 9am–7:30pm Wed–Mon; Farnese Collection: closed at the time of publication
∅ 1 Jan, 25 Dec **W** museoarcheologiconapoli.it/en

One of the world's top museums of ancient art, Naples' Archaeological Museum overwhelms with its wealth of beautiful objects. Among the many items on display are archaeological finds from excavations at Pompeii and Herculaneum.

Sculptures

The fine collection of Greco-Roman sculpture consists mostly of works found in excavations around Vesuvius and the Phlegraean Fields, as well as the treasures from the Farnese Collection (King Ferdinando IV's Roman antiquities, inherited from his grandmother Elisabetta Farnese). The sculptures – most of which are the only existing Roman copies of lost Greek originals – are displayed on the ground floor. Among the numerous fine works are the *Farnese Hercules*, an enlarged Roman copy of a sculpture by the Greek master Lysippus, and the *Farnese Bull*, the largest sculptural group to have survived from antiquity (end of 2nd century BC).

Frescoes

Most of the frescoes in the collection were removed from buildings in cities buried by the eruptions of Vesuvius, and assembled here from the mid-1700s onwards. The most important of these came from the Basilica in Herculaneum. Others were taken from the Villa di Fannio Sinistore at Boscoreale and from the extensive landed property of Julia Felix in Pompeii. The frieze from her house, with a still life of apples and grapes and scenes from the forum, gives a fascinating glimpse of everyday life in a 1st-century-AD city.

GALLERY GUIDE

The Farnese Collection (currently closed) and sculpture from Herculaneum, Pompeii and other Vesuvian cities can be seen on the ground floor, the mezzanine level and the first floor. Mosaics, on the mezzanine level, and domestic items, weapons and murals, on the first floor, show daily life in the ancient cities. A lower-ground-floor level houses the Egyptian Collection. The arrangement displays the exhibits in context.

←
Mosaic found at Pompeii depicting the Battle of Alexander

Timeline

1616
The building is adapted and becomes the seat of Naples university

1957
Museo Archeologico Nazionale is renamed after the picture collection moves

1980
▽ An earthquake causes serious damage to many of the exhibits

1500s
The structure that will house the museum is built as the home of the royal cavalry

1738
△ Excavations of Vesuvian towns begin. King Charles III collects finds

1860
The collection becomes public property and known as the Museo Nazionale

Mosaics

The majority of the mosaics on display in the museum come from Pompeii, Stabiae, Herculaneum and Boscoreale and date from the 2nd century BC to AD 79. The realistic images, such as the female portraits from Pompeii, are particularly fascinating. Among the highlights is a depiction of the Battle of Alexander, found at Pompeii. This large, detailed mosaic was based on a Hellenistic painting and depicts Alexander the Great leading his cavalry against Darius III of Persia.

Egyptian Collection

The museum is home to many valuable works of Egyptian art from the Ancient Kingdom (2700–2200 BC) to the Roman age. As well as human and animal mummies, the Egyptian section includes Canopic jars and containers for the internal organs of the deceased. The collection of *shabti* comprises wood, stone and faience statuettes representing workers for the deceased in the afterlife.

←

Elegant exterior of the Museo Archeologico Nazionale

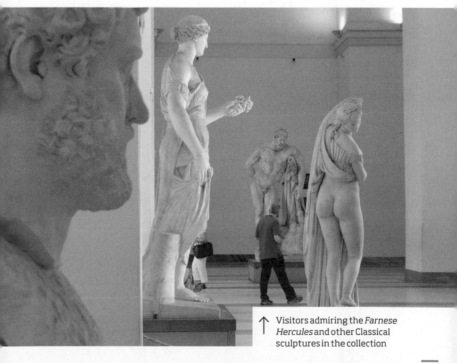

↑ Visitors admiring the *Farnese Hercules* and other Classical sculptures in the collection

EXPERIENCE MORE

2 MADRE

D1 **Via Settembrini 79**
**10am-7:30pm Mon &
Wed-Sat, 10am-8pm Sun**
madrenapoli.it

Opened in 2005, the Museo
d'Arte Contemporanea
Donna Regina Napoli
(MADRE) is located in the
Palazzo Donnaregina, from
which it gets its name.
The museum houses a
remarkable collection by
well-known artists, such
as Andy Warhol, Robert
Rauschenberg, Mimmo
Paladino, Claes Oldenburg,
Robert Mapplethorpe and
Roy Lichtenstein among
others. On the first floor
is a library and a children's
area, while the third floor
is used for temporary
exhibitions. The museum
often hosts special events
such as cinema screenings,
concerts and theatrical
performances. The church
of Santa Maria Donnaregina,
at the back of the museum,
provides additional
exhibition space in a
beautiful setting.

← Mimmo Paladino's
Cavallo, at MADRE

3 Castel Capuano and Porta Capuana

E1 **Piazza Enrico
de Nicola**

Begun in 1165 by Norman
King William I and completed
by Frederick II, Castel
Capuano was a royal palace
until 1540, when Don Pedro
de Toledo turned it into law
courts, a function it maintains
to the present day.

Nearby, between the
Aragonese towers of the
Capua Gate and facing a
market, is a rare sculpture in
the Florentine-Renaissance
style. Created by Giuliano
da Maiano (and finished in
1490 by Luca Fancelli) as
a defensive gate, Porta
Capuana is perhaps Italy's
finest Renaissance gateway.

4 Duomo

D1 **Via Duomo 147**
081 44 90 97 **8:30am-
1pm & 3-7pm daily**

Built between 1294 and
1323, the Cattedrale di
Santa Maria Assunta, or
Duomo, lies behind a
mostly 19th-century
façade. The nave is lined
with ancient columns,
and there is an array of
monuments to past rulers,
along with paintings by
Lanfranco and Domenichino.
The Duomo houses the
relics of San Gennaro, Naples'
patron saint (martyred
AD 305). The Cappella San
Gennaro, erected in the
1600s, holds phials of his
congealed blood, which
miraculously liquefies three

times a year (the Saturday
before the first Sunday
in May, 19 September and
16 December). The Cappella
Carafa, a Renaissance masterpiece built from 1497 to 1506,
contains the saint's tomb.
Accessible from the
Duomo's north aisle is the
Cappella di Santa Restituta,
founded in the 4th century
on the site of a former
Temple of Apollo, and
rebuilt in the 1300s. It has
ceiling paintings by Luca
Giordano (1634–1705) and
a 5th-century baptistry. The
nearby Museo del Tesoro
di San Gennaro requires an
entrance fee and exhibits
a range of gold, silverware,
jewels, statues and art.

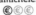

EAT

Da Michele
A pizzeria for purists:
only Margherita and
Marinara varieties
are on the menu.

E2 **Via Cesare
Sersale 1**
damichele.net
€€€

Sorbillo
The delicious pizza
served here is well
worth queueing up for.

C2 **Via dei
Tribunali 32** **sorbillo.it**
€€€

**Concettina
ai Tre Santi**
A superb fourth-
generation pizzaiolo.

C1 **Via Arena
alla Sanità 7 Bis**
pizzeriaoliva.it
€€€

↑ Via Nilo, just round the corner from Cappella Sansevero

5

Pio Monte della Misericordia

📍 D2 🏛 Via dei Tribunali 253 🕐 By appt only; Sep-Jun: 9am-6pm Mon-Sat (to 2:30pm Sun); Jul & Aug: 9am-1pm daily ❌ Easter, Christmas 🌐 piomonte dellamisericordia.it

Pio Monte is one of the most important charitable institutions in Naples. It was founded in 1602 to aid the poor and ill, and to free enslaved Christians in the Ottoman Empire. After passing through the five-arch loggia (where pilgrims could shelter), you enter the octagonal church. The eye is immediately drawn to the extraordinary altarpiece, Caravaggio's *Seven Acts of Mercy* (1607). The art gallery features paintings by Luca Giordano, Francesco de Mura and Mattia Preti.

6

Cappella Sansevero

📍 C2 🏛 Via Francesco de Sanctis 19 🕐 9am-7pm Wed-Sun 🌐 museo sansevero.it

This tiny 16th-century chapel is the burial sepulchre of Raimondo di Sangro, Prince of Sansevero. Featuring both Christian and Masonic symbolism, it has an unusual character.

The chapel is filled with remarkable 18th-century sculpture, including a *Pietà*, by an unknown artist, and Giuseppe Sammartino's *Veiled Christ*, an alabaster figure beneath a marble veil.

Prince Raimondo was an 18th-century alchemist who performed gruesome experiments on human bodies, for which he was excommunicated. The results of some of his experiments can be seen in the crypt.

THE STORY OF PIZZA

Deeply ingrained in Naples' gastronomic identity, pizza first emerged in southern Italy in the late 1700s, quickly becoming a working-class staple. In 1889, when touring the kingdom, Queen Margherita of Savoy developed a taste for this peasant delicacy. After she summoned chef Raffaele Esposito to the royal-palace ovens, pizza Margherita was born. In order to raise awareness of pizza-making's endangered status, in 2017 the culinary art was added to UNESCO's Intangible Cultural Heritage of Humanity list.

7

San Lorenzo Maggiore

📍D2 🏛Piazza San Gaetano 316 🕐9:30am–5:30pm daily 🌐laneapolis sotterrata.it

This Franciscan church is mainly 14th-century (with an 18th-century façade) and was built during the reign of Robert the Wise of Anjou. The storyteller Giovanni Boccaccio (1313–75) reputedly based the character Fiammetta on King Robert's daughter Maria, whom he saw here on Easter Eve in 1334. For Naples, San Lorenzo Maggiore is a rare Gothic edifice. Its nave and the apse ambulatory have a magnificent period simplicity. The church houses medieval tombs that include the Gothic tomb of Catherine of Austria, who died in 1323, by a pupil of Giovanni Pisano. Excavations in the monastic cloister, where the lyric poet and scholar Petrarch (p118) once stayed, have revealed the remains of a Roman basilica. There are also important Greek and medieval excavations, for which there is an admission fee.

← Sculpture in the church of San Lorenzo Maggiore

 ↑ Ceiling of San Lorenzo Maggiore

nuns, traditionally from noble families, were accustomed to lavish living. The Baroque interior of the church sports frescoes by Luca Giordano. There is a lovely fountain in the cloister with a statue of *Christ and the Samaritan*.

The church is located in a street known to locals as "Christmas Alley" because it is lined with workshops manufacturing and selling Nativity figures (*presepi*).

8

San Gregorio Armeno

📍D2 🏛Via San Gregorio Armeno 1 📞081 552 01 86 🕐9am–noon Mon–Fri

Benedictine nuns still preside over this church. The attached convent earned a reputation for luxury since the

---

9

Sant'Angelo a Nilo

📍D2 🏛Piazzetta Nilo 23 📞081 211 08 60 🕐1:30pm daily

This 14th-century church holds a fine Renaissance work: the Tomb of Cardinal Rinaldo Brancaccio. Designed by Michelozzo, the marble work was sculpted in Pisa, then shipped to Naples upon completion in 1428. Donatello reputedly carved the right-hand angel drawing back the curtain, the shallow-relief *Assumption* and the cardinal's head. From the church you can visit the courtyard of Palazzo Brancaccio, home to Naples' first public library (1690).

San Domenico Maggiore

📍 C2 🏛 Piazza San Domenico Maggiore 8A 🕐 10am–6pm daily 🌐 museosandomenico maggiore.it

In 1283 Charles II ordered the construction of a new church and monastery for the Dominican order. The Gothic three-nave building was built onto the pre-existing church of San Michele Arcangelo a Morfisa, which was the original seat of Naples' University of Theology, headed by St Thomas Aquinas. A relic of the saint's arm is said to be kept inside the monastery. In 1850–53 Federico Travaglini rebuilt the interior in Neo-Gothic style. The sacristy houses 42 ornate coffins arranged along the balcony. Some contain the corpses of the Aragonese kings, including Alphonse and Ferdinand I.

STAY

Constantinopoli 104
Impeccably appointed boutique hotel.

📍 C2 🏛 Via S Maria di Costantinopoli 104 🌐 costantinopoli104.it

€€€

Hotel Romeo
Rooms in the old town.

📍 C4 🏛 Via C Colombo 45 🌐 romeohotel.it

€€€

Decumani
Tasteful furnishings in a 20th-century palazzo.

📍 C3 🏛 Via S Giovanni Maggiore Pignatelli 15 🌐 decumani.com

€€€

↑ The cloister of San Gregorio Armeno, in a pretty garden setting

11

Santa Chiara

📍C3 🏛Via Santa Chiara 49C ⏰9:30am–5:30pm Mon–Sat, 10am–2:30pm Sun 🌐monasterodi santachiara.it

This 14th-century church was bombed in World War II, but a reconstruction uncovered the original Provençal-Gothic structure. The tombs of the Angevin monarchs are housed here. The tomb of Robert the Wise (died 1343) is by Giovanni and Pacio Bertini; that of his son, Charles of Calabria (died 1328), is by Tino da Camaino; and the tomb of Charles' wife, Mary of Valois (died 1331), is by da Camaino and his followers. Adjacent is a convent with a **cloister** designed by Vaccaro (1742). The cloister's perimeter is lined with octagonal pillars covered with majolica ceramic floral decorations. The pillars are connected by tiled benches. There is also a museum with ornaments and sculptures from Santa Chiara, as well as a Roman bathhouse (AD 1).

12

Gesù Nuovo

📍C2 🏛Piazza del Gesù Nuovo 2 ⏰7am–1pm & 4–8pm daily 🌐gesunuovo.it

This 16th-century Jesuit church was constructed by Valeriano (and later Fanzago and Fuga) from the Severini palace (15th century), of which only a façade survives. The interior decoration (1600s) is in accordance with the needs of the Jesuits, who used dramatic appeal to draw the faithful. It is resplendent with coloured marble and paintings, including works by Ribera and Solimena, such as the latter's *Expulsion of Heliodorus from the Temple* fresco. In 1688 an earthquake destroyed the dome – the present one is 18th century.

13

Sant'Anna e San Bartolomeo dei Lombardi

📍C3 🏛Piazza Monteoliveto 4 ⏰9:30am–1:30pm Tue–Thu (to 6pm Fri & Sat) 🌐santannadei lombardi.com

Also known as Santa Maria di Monteoliveto, this church – the favourite of the Aragonese kings – was built in 1411 and restored after World War II. It is a repository of Renaissance art. Entering, past the tomb (1627) of Domenico Fontana (who completed the dome of St Peter's in Rome after Michelangelo's death), the richness of the interior unfolds.

The Cappella Mastrogiudice contains an *Annunciation* panel by Florentine sculptor Benedetto da Maiano (1489). In the Cappella Piccolomini is Antonio Rossellino's monument (c 1475) to Maria d'Aragona (completed by da Maiano). The Cappella del Santo Sepolcro houses a *Pietà* by Guido Mazzoni (1492). Its eight terracotta figures are life-size portraits of the artist's contemporaries. The old Sacristy, frescoed by Vasari (1544), has inlaid stalls by Giovanni da Verona (1510).

14

Castel Nuovo

📍C4 🏛Piazza Municipio 📞081 795 77 22 ⏰8:30am–7pm daily 🚫Some pub hols

Also known as the Maschio Angioino, this Angevin fortress was built for Charles of Anjou in 1279–82 and given the *nuovo* ("new") part of its name to distinguish it from two earlier castles. Despite its origins, apart from the squat towers and the Cappella Palatina (which features Francesco Laurana's *Madonna* of 1474 above the portal), most of the structure is Aragonese.

TOP 3 **GREEN SPACES**

Giardini del Molosiglio
📍C5 🏛Via Ammiraglio Ferdinando Acton 9
A small park with palm trees and a view over a marina.

Parco Vergiliano a Piedigrotta
📍A2 🏛Salita della Grotta
This park is a tribute to the poet Virgil. He is said to have been buried here.

Parco Virgiliano a Posillipo
📍A2 🏛Viale Virgilio
On the hill of Posillipo, with impressive vistas over the Gulf of Naples.

The castle was the main royal residence. In the Sala dei Baroni (Hall of the Barons), Ferdinand I of Aragon brutally suppressed the ringleaders of the Barons' revolt of 1486. The Aragonese were capable of violence, but they were also patrons of the arts.

The triumphal arch of the castle's entrance (begun 1454) is theirs. Commemorating Alfonso of Aragon's entry to Naples in 1443, this ingenious application of the ancient triumphal arch design was worked on, in part, by Laurana. The original bronze doors by Guillaume le Moine (1468) are in the Palazzo Reale. Part of the castle houses the **Museo Civico**.

Museo Civico
⊗ 📞 081 795 77 22
🕐 8:30am–7pm daily

The castle was the main royal residence. In the Sala dei Baroni, Ferdinand I of Aragon brutally suppressed the ringleaders of the Barons' revolt of 1486.

15

Museo Nazionale di San Martino

📍 A3 🏛 Largo San Martino 8
📞 848 800 288 🕐 8:30am–7:30pm Thu–Tue

Standing high above Santa Lucia, the Baroque Certosa di San Martino, founded in the 1300s as a Carthusian monastery, offers great views out across the Bay of Naples. It contains a museum housing a variety of *presepi* – Christmas cribs of Neapolitan tradition, some featuring hundreds of figures. The cloister was completed in 1629 by Cosimo Fanzago (the creator of Neapolitan Baroque) to designs of Dosio. The church and choir are other examples of his virtuosity. Next to the Certosa is **Castel Sant'Elmo**, built between 1329 and 1343 and rebuilt in the 1500s, from where there are further stunning views.

Castel Sant'Elmo
🕐 8:30am–7:30pm daily

↓ Castel Nuovo, the medieval seat of Naples' kings

← The majestic arcades of Galleria Umberto I, with its handsome glass roof

16

Galleria Umberto I

 B4   Via Toledo Daily

The handsome arcades of the Galleria Umberto I were built in 1887 and rebuilt after World War II. They face Italy's largest and oldest opera house: the **Teatro San Carlo**, built for Charles III of Naples in 1737.

Teatro San Carlo

 10:30am-6pm daily teatrosancarlo.it

17

Palazzo Reale

 C5 Piazza del Plebiscito 1 081 580 82 55 9am-8pm Thu-Tue 1 Jan, 25 Dec

Begun by Domenico Fontana in 1600, and later expanded, Naples' royal palace is filled with furniture, tapestries, paintings and porcelain. The small private Teatro di Corte (1768) was built by Ferdinando Fuga. It contains 12 *papier-mâché* and plaster statues of Apollo, Minerva, Mercury and the nine Muses by Angelo Viva. The building also houses the **Biblioteca Nazionale** (library). The great colonnades in Piazza del Plebiscito sweep towards 19th-century San Francesco di Paola, modelled on Rome's Pantheon.

Biblioteca Nazionale

 By appt only; 8:30am-7pm Mon-Fri, 8:30am-1:30pm Sat; bring ID bnnonline.it

---

18

Museo di Capodimonte

 A1 Via Miano 2 8:30am-7:30pm Thu-Tue, check website for details 1 Jan, 25 Dec museocapodimonte.beniculturali.it

Begun in 1738 by King Charles VII of Naples and

> **INSIDER TIP**
> ## Street Food
>
> For great street food, head to Spaccanapoli – a street crisscrossing the old centre. Try a *pizza a portafoglio* (folded pizza) and deep-fried *palle 'e riso* (balls of rice). Don't miss a *babà* (rum-soaked dough) at Scaturchio (*www.scaturchio.it*).

Sicily (later Charles III, king of Spain) as a hunting lodge, the Palazzo Reale di Capodimonte houses this museum and its magnificent collections of Italian paintings. Included are works by Titian, Botticelli, Raphael and Perugino, much of it originating in the Farnese family collections. There is also a gallery of 19th-century art, largely from southern Italy.

19

Catacombs of San Gennaro

 A1 Via Tondo di Capodimonte 13 By appt only; 10am-5pm Mon-Sat (to 2pm Sun) catacombedinapoli.it

These catacombs – the original burial place of San Gennaro – are near the church of San Gennaro in Moenia. The small church was founded in the 8th century. Two tiers of catacombs dating from the 2nd century penetrate the tufa, and there are mosaics and early Christian frescoes. Further along the street, the Catacombs of San Gaudioso honour the 5th-century saint who founded a monastery on the spot. Above is the 17th-century church of Santa Maria della Sanità.

20

Castel dell'Ovo

 A2 Via Eldorado 3 081 795 45 93 9am-6:30pm Mon-Sat (to 1pm Sun & pub hols)

Begun in 1154, the Castel dell'Ovo is the oldest castle in Naples. It is set on a small island facing, and joining, the Santa Lucia district – once the site of the city's shellfish market. A royal residence under the Normans and Hohenstaufen, today it belongs to the army. It is now used for cultural events, and there are great views from the ramparts.

Beneath its ramparts, tiny Porto di Santa Lucia is filled with seafood restaurants. The Via Partenope, running past it, makes a really lovely promenade.

→

Statue of Frederick II in the Palazzo Reale

CAMPANIA

Set beneath the shadow of Mount Vesuvius, Campania is a region of dramatic contrasts. The hinterland, home to rich, well-cultivated plains, is eclipsed by the Amalfi coastline with its breathtaking views and the spectacular Cilento seaboard. The mountainous interior, remote and unvisited, contains small towns that were settled by the Greeks, developed by the Romans and often abandoned in the wake of malaria and Saracen attacks. Elsewhere, extraordinary Roman towns and Greek ruins, preserved by a blanket of volcanic ash, reveal the area's ancient history.

Campania was first settled by the Etruscans and the Greeks, whose massive ruins can be seen at Paestum. Next came a time of great prosperity under the Romans; archaeological evidence of which still exists at Benevento, Santa Maria Capua Vetere and, of course, Pompeii and Herculaneum.

Today, a visit to Pompeii is a high priority for tourists, but this was not always so. Travellers on the Grand Tour in the 1600s and early 1700s preferred the volcanic phenomena of the Solfatara crater and the Phlegraean Fields to the west of Naples. Only when the first archaeological digs unearthed the remains of Paestum and the buried cities around Mount Vesuvius did a tour of the ancient ruins become popular.

The beautiful colour, light and atmosphere found on the islands of Capri and Ischia, and on the Sorrento peninsula, began to interest landscape painters in the 19th century. The southern flank of the peninsula – the Amalfi coast – remained isolated until the mid-1960s, when it attracted visitors in search of an alternative, remote lifestyle. Ironically, the area has since become a popular holiday spot.

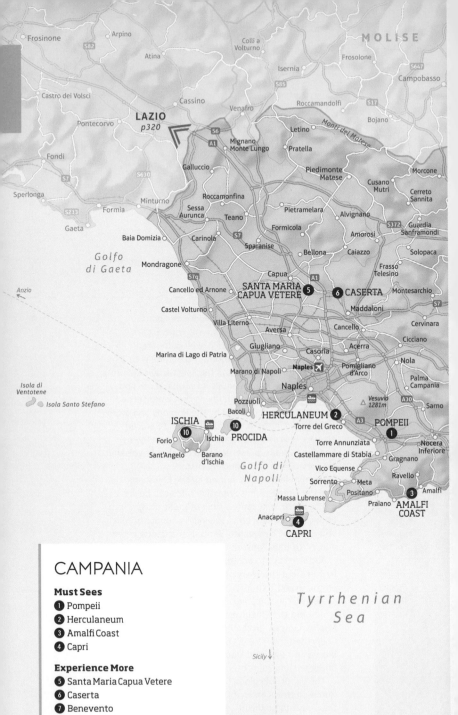

CAMPANIA

Must Sees

1. Pompeii
2. Herculaneum
3. Amalfi Coast
4. Capri

Experience More

5. Santa Maria Capua Vetere
6. Caserta
7. Benevento
8. Salerno
9. Paestum
10. Ischia and Procida

0 kilometres   20

0 miles   20

N

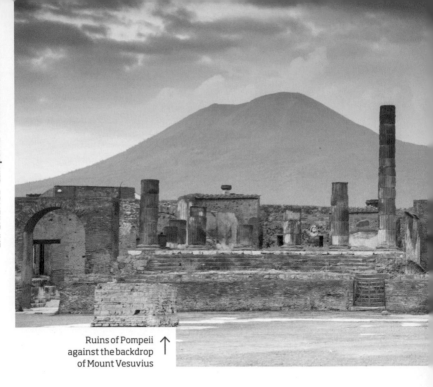

↑ Ruins of Pompeii against the backdrop of Mount Vesuvius

POMPEII

⚐E5 ⌂Piazza Esedra 5 ⌚Apr–Oct: 9am–7:30pm daily (last adm: 5:30pm); Nov–Mar: to 5pm, 9am–5pm daily (last adm: 3:30pm); online booking advised ⊘1 Jan, 1 May, 25 Dec ⊞pompeiisites.org

When Vesuvius erupted in AD 79 Pompeii and its 20,000 residents were frozen in time, preserved in ash. The city has transfixed visitors since its discovery in the 18th century.

↑ Plaster cast of one of Vesuvius's victims at Pompeii

Today, haunting plaster casts of Pompeii's inhabitants lie sprawled where they died, while exquisite mosaics and wall paintings – among the ruins of shops, homes and temples – offer total immersion into the Roman world.

Villas

Pompeii contains the remains of many large houses of great historical and architectural value. Highlights include the House of the Tragic Poet, with its *cave canem* ("beware of the dog") mosaic at the entrance, and the House of the Vettii, with its numerous frescoes depicting mythological scenes, such as the Punishment of Ixion.

The Forum

The Forum was the centre of public life. Set around it were important administrative and religious institutions, including the Basilica and the temples of Apollo, Jupiter and Vespasian.

MOUNT VESUVIUS

Nearly 2,000 years after the eruption that destroyed the port of Pompeii and Herculaneum, Vesuvius remains the most dangerous volcano in Europe, with an estimated 700,000 people living in the danger zone. The volcano, which last erupted in 1944, is constantly monitored. Scientists fear an eruption will put Naples in danger. If signs of activity increase to a potentially dangerous level, a 72-hour evacuation programme will be implemented.

To experience the volcano close-up take a minibus from Ercolano Scavi train station to the Mount Vesuvius car park, from where it's a half-hour climb to the steaming crater. For more volcanic experiences, head to the Solfatara, 30 minutes' drive west of Naples, where you can have the unforgettably bizarre experience of walking on the hot, spongy, stinking fields of sulphur in another volcanic crater. Visit www.vulcanosolfatara.it for more details.

The *cave canem* mosaic decorating the entrance to the House of the Tragic Poet

Perhaps the most impressive ruins in the forum are its public baths. Built after 80 BC, the baths would have been widely used for daily ablutions. They follow a sequence from dressing room to *frigidarium* (cold room), then on to *tepidarium* (warm room) and *calidarium* (hot room). Mythological figures decorate the vaults of the *tepidarium*, and the *calidarium* contains a mammoth marble basin.

Theatres

Performance spaces included the Odeon (a small theatre for 1,500 people), the Great Theatre (which held 5,000 people) and the Amphitheatre (for up to 20,000 spectators of gladiatorial combat). Beautifully preserved, the Great Theatre is still used for modern productions in the summer months.

Brothels

Numerous *lupanare* (brothels) have been discovered during excavation work. The most striking is on a street parallel to Via Stabiana. Here, erotic frescoes and ancient graffiti line the walls, indicating the services offered by prostitutes, including boys, to satisfy their clients and lovers.

↓ Ruins lining a cobbled street in Pompeii

2

HERCULANEUM

E5 ⌂ Ercolano Scavi, Corso Resina ⏱ Apr-Oct: 10:30am-7:30pm Wed-Mon; Nov-Mar: 8:30am-5pm daily 🖥 ercolano.beniculturali.it

Named after Hercules, this ancient Roman town was destroyed by Vesuvius in AD 79 – the same blast that engulfed Pompeii with rocks and ash. Herculaneum was entombed in superheated mud and ash, and is now the best-preserved ancient Roman city in Italy. Along with the town's buildings and decorations, wood, plants, textiles and other perishable materials have been uncovered in excavations.

Before the eruption of Vesuvius, Herculaneum fell under Greek influence around the 5th century BC and then under Samnite rule. In 89 BC the town became part of the Roman Empire, a residential *municipium* and resort.

Excavations began in the 18th century, and uncovered Roman houses built around a rectangular plan. Ancient Herculaneum is well below the level of the modern town, and the area is still being excavated. Highlights include the frescoes of the Villa dei Papiri (so-called because over 1,000 papyrus scrolls were discovered here), the frescoes in the College of the Augustales, the mosaics in the House of Neptune and Amphitrite, the changing rooms and mosaics of the City Baths, the two-storey Trellis House, and the replica sculptures in the courtyard of the House of the Stags. Look out for the remains of a wooden boat (complete with a coil of rope) in the Boat House, and for

↑ Visitors admiring the frescoes in the College of the Augustales

terracotta amphorae set into marble counters in the Thermopolia (the Roman answer to fast-food outlets). Many of the best-preserved sculptures and frescoes from Herculaneum are now on display in the Museo Archeologico Nazionale (*p452*).

← Mosaic in the summer dining room of the House of Neptune and Amphitrite

→ Stag and dog sculpture discovered in the courtyard of the House of the Stags

Ruined houses and
shops lining a street in ↑
Herculaneum

↑ Colourful villas spilling down the hillside to the sea in Positano

 3

AMALFI COAST

A E5 **Amalfi** **i** Corso delle Repubbliche Marinare, Amalfi; www.amalfitouristoffice.it

Suspended between sea, sky and earth, state road 163, which twists and turns along the full length of the Amalfi coast, offers stunning views at every corner. Until the 19th century, this stretch of the "divine coast" was isolated but by the early 1900s it had began to attract travellers, artists and writers. Today, popular pleasures here include beach-hopping and taking trips to coastal summits to admire the breathtaking views.

① Sorrento

i Azienda Autonoma di Soggiorno Sorrento-Sant'Agnello, Via Luigi de Maio 35; www.sorrentotourism.com

On the cliffs at the southern end of the Bay of Naples, Sorrento has ancient origins, seen in the original Greek town plan in the centre. In the summer the town fills with tourists taking in the views or relaxing at cafés. Both Marina Grande and Marina Piccola have small beaches.

② Positano

 i AAST, Via G Marconi 288; www.azienda turismopositano.it

Pastel-coloured houses here clamber down a vertiginous slope into the sea, with the oldest houses in the upper part of Positano decorated with pretty Baroque stuccoes. The traffic-free street going down to the sea, Via Pasitea, penetrates the heart of town with its narrow-stepped alleys, houses with vaulted roofs, terraces and tiny gardens that defy the rock. Near the beach is the small church of Santa Maria Assunta, whose cupola is covered with yellow, blue and green majolica tiles. The descent ends at Marina Grande, lined with high-end bars and restaurants.

③ Amalfi

 i AAST, Corso delle Repubbliche Marinare 27; www.amalfi.it

Tucked in between mountains and sea, Amalfi is a perennial favourite with visitors for its scenic beauty and original architecture. It also has a glorious history as a powerful maritime republic. Amalfi's cathedral, the **Duomo di**

> HIDDEN GEM
> **Nocelle**
>
> Positano can get very busy with day-trippers. To escape the crowds, make the steep ascent to Montepertuso, from where a splendid scenic path leads to the quiet mountain village of Nocelle, a pleasant place to pause for lunch.

Sant'Andrea, founded in the 9th century, was rebuilt in Romanesque style in the 11th century and altered several times. Heading inland from Amalfi, you can visit the Valle dei Mulini (Valley of the Mills), known for its traditional paper production, and the **Museo della Carta** or Paper Museum.

Duomo di Sant'Andrea

⊕ ◘ Piazza Duomo
◷ Mar-Oct: 9am-6:45pm daily; Nov-Feb: 10am-1pm & 2:30-4:30pm daily ⊠ museo diocesanoamalfi.it

Museo della Carta

⊕ ◘ Via delle Cartiere 23
◷ Mar-Oct: 10am-6:30pm daily (Nov-Feb: to 4pm Tue-Sun) ⊠ museodellacarta.it

④
Ravello

⊠ ⓘ AAST, Piazza Fontana Moresca 10; www.ravello time.com

A little off the beaten track, Ravello is for those who love peace and quiet – though it does liven up for the Ravello Festival in July and August. The town's architectural highlights include the **Duomo**, dedicated to San Pantaleone; **Villa Rufolo**, famed for its tropical gardens; and **Villa Cimbrone**, now a small luxury hotel (see box) with coastal views.

Duomo

◘ Piazza Duomo ◷ Daily ⊠ chiesaravello.com

Villa Rufolo

⊕ ◘ Piazza Duomo ◷ 9am-8pm daily ⊠ villarufolo.it

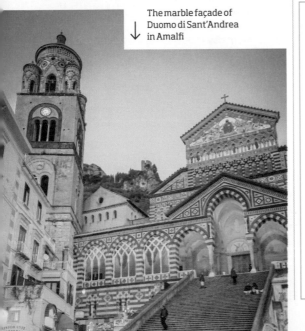

↓ The marble façade of Duomo di Sant'Andrea in Amalfi

STAY

Hotel Villa Cimbrone
Perched high atop the town of Ravello, this graceful hotel has memorable gardens with idyllic views along the coast to Punta Licosa, two restaurants, a pool, and delicately frescoed rooms that once hosted Greta Garbo, D H Lawrence and Gore Vidal.

◘ Via Santa Chiara 26 ⊠ hotelvilla cimbrone.com

€€€

↑ View of Capri Town and I Faraglioni from Mount Solaro

CAPRI

A E5 **🚢** Capri **ℹ** Piazza Umberto I, Capri; www.capritourism.com

Nestled at the southern end of the Bay of Naples, this small, rugged island has a long history of attracting well-heeled visitors. Roman emperors Augustus and Tiberius enjoyed lengthy stays here, the latter spending his last years ruling from his luxurious Capri villa. In the 19th century, the island ushered in the arrival of foreign artists, politicians and intellectuals. It remains a tourist mecca and, while it can swell with crowds of day-trippers, its charm and beauty make it well worth a visit.

① Capri Town

Straddling the eastern part of the island, the town of Capri is from where most excursions around the island begin. Visitors usually arrive by ferry into the main harbour, Marina Grande, a colourful village of seafood restaurants, bars and shops. From here, a ride on the funicular leads straight to the heart of the old town within a few minutes. Stroll along Via Camerelle, Capri's answer to New York's Fifth Avenue, for luxury brand shopping. The picturesque dome of Baroque church Santo Stefano overlooks the bustling scene.

② Piazza Umberto I

The famous "Piazzetta" in Capri Town is an outdoor living room, crowded day and night. A prime people-watching and celebrity-spotting venue, it is packed with café tables buzzing with gossip and animated discussion. The narrow alleys surrounding the piazza are also a delight to explore.

③ Anacapri

ℹ AAST, Via G Orlandi 59; 081 837 15 24

On the slopes of Monte Solaro is the second town on the island, Anacapri. A refreshing contrast to the pomp of Capri Town, its relatively quiet lanes and piazzas feature churches, museums and artisanal shops. Here you can visit the church of San Michele, the Villa San Michele (former home of the Swedish physician Axel Munthe) and the excavations at Emperor Tiberius's imperial

---

EAT

L'Olivo
One of two Michelin-starred restaurants at the luxurious Capri Palace Hotel, L'Olivo is a study in masterful Mediterranean cuisine.

A Via Capodimonte 14, Anacapri **⏱** Mid-Oct–mid-Apr **W** capri palace.com

€€€

→ Fishing vessels moored in Marina Grande, Capri Town

Villa Damecuta and, of course, appreciate the magnificent view from the top of the hill.

④ Grotta Azzurra

🚤 **Boat tours from the Marina Grande, Capri Town**

One of the island's most popular sights, this large sea cave is illuminated by an incredible, otherworldly blue light, created by the sunlight that streams through the small entrance and is then reflected from the bottom of the sea. Trips are often cancelled during high tide or in rough seas.

⑤ Villa Jovis

🏛 **Via Tiberio** ⏱ **10am–1 hr before sunset daily** 🚫 **Jan & Feb**

The retreat built by Emperor Tiberius stands proudly on the mountain named after him, the dramatic setting chosen for its seclusion. Excavations

of the site have unearthed baths, apartments and the infamous "Tiberius's drop", from which the emperor's victims were said to be thrown into the sea. The ruins also include the remains of a tower once used to communicate with the mainland.

⑥ Marina Piccola

Occupying a picturesque bay dotted with yachts, the laid-back Marina Piccola has bars and restaurants pressed along the water and a few spits of sand wedged between rocky outcrops. It is a great spot for

Did You Know?

Emperor Augustus decided to build villas on Capri after he saw a dead tree miraculously sprout leaves on the island.

swimming and sunbathing, with views of I Faraglioni, the rock formations soaring up to 109 m (360 ft) out of the sea. Commissioned by the German industrialist Alfred Krupp, the famous Via Krupp (often closed due to renovations) makes a vertiginous descent towards the marina from Capri Town in a series of striking hairpin bends. A quicker, more reliable route is to follow Via Roma and Via Mulo.

EXPERIENCE MORE

EXPERIENCE Campania

⑤

Santa Maria Capua Vetere

🅰E5 🚌 Caserta 🇫🇸🚍
ⓘ Palazzo Reale, Caserta;
0823 55 00 11

This town's 1st-century-AD Roman **amphitheatre** used to be Italy's largest after the Colosseum. There are well-preserved tunnels beneath it. The town occupies the site of ancient Capua, the scene of the revolt of the gladiators led by Spartacus in 73 BC. The on-site Gladiator Museum recreates their history. Nearby is a Mithraeum (2nd–3rd century) with well-preserved frescoes. Finds from the sites are shown in the **Museo Archeologico dell'Antica Capua** in Capua.

Amphitheatre

 🚩 Piazza 1 Ottobre 1860
📞 0823 84 42 06 🕒 9am–1 hr before sunset Tue–Sun

Museo Archeologico dell'Antica Capua

 🚩 Via Roberto d'Angiò 48, Capua 📞 0823 84 42 06
🕒 9am–6:30pm Tue–Sun

---

⑥

Caserta

🅰E5 🇫🇸🚍 ⓘ Palazzo Reale;
www.eptcasert.it

The magnificently opulent **Palazzo Reale** dominates Caserta. Built for the Bourbon King Charles III, Italy's largest royal palace boasts over 1,000 rooms, grand staircases and richly adorned apartments.

It was designed by Luigi Vanvitelli, and construction started in 1752. The surrounding park is dotted with fountains, ornamental waterworks and statuary.

San Leucio, 3 km (2 miles) northwest of Caserta, is a model town built by Ferdinand IV, who also founded its silk industry.

Palazzo Reale

 🚩 Viale Douhet 2a
📞 0823 44 80 84 🕒 By appt only; 8:30am–7:30pm Wed–Mon 🚫 Pub hols 🌐 reggiadi caserta.beniculturali.it

---

⑦

Benevento

🅰E5 🇫🇸🚍 ⓘ Via N Sala 31;
www.eptbenevento.it

The Roman city Beneventum was an important centre at the end of the first extension of the Via Appia from Capua. The well-preserved Arch of Trajan on Via Traiano was built of marble in AD 114–166. The relief sculpture adorning it – scenes from the life of Trajan and mythological subjects – is in excellent condition.

Evidence of the Romans is also found in the ruined **Roman theatre**, built during Hadrian's reign, and in the **Museo del Sannio**, which has regional artifacts, from ancient Greek finds to modern art.

During World War II, the city stood directly in the way of the Allied advance from the south. It was heavily bombed, hence its largely modern appearance. Benevento has centuries-old associations with pagan worship, and a liqueur called Strega (witch) is made here.

←

A marble-covered hall in the Palazzo Reale of Caserta, Italy's largest royal palace

↑ Corricella, a colourful village on the island of Procida

Roman Theatre

🏛 Piazza C Ponzio Telesino ☎ 0824 31 09 45 ⏰ 9am–7pm daily ⛔ Pub hols

Museo del Sannio

🏛 Piazza Santa Sofia ⏰ 9am–7pm Tue–Sun 🌐 museodelsannio.it

 8

Salerno

🗺 E5 🚆 Salerno 🛈 Via Lungomare Trieste 7/9; www.eptsalerno.it

The big, busy port of Salerno is visited today for its 11th-century Duomo. Its best feature is the Atrium, whose columns came from Paestum. In the crypt is the Tomb of St Matthew, which was brought here in 954.

The **Museo Diocesano** is home to most of the cathedral treasures, while local archaeological finds are in the **Museo Archeologico Provinciale**.

South of Salerno, the Cilento is a mountainous region with a lovely coastline. Outside Castellammare di Velia, 70 km (43 miles) south of Salerno, are the ruins of the Greek town of Elea (founded 6th century BC). Excavations have revealed a magnificent 4th-century Roman gateway, Roman baths and the remains of the acropolis.

Museo Diocesano

🏛 Largo Plebiscito 12 ⏰ 9am–1pm Thu–Tue 🌐 museodiocesano disalerno.it

Museo Archeologico Provinciale

🏛 Via San Benedetto 28 ⏰ 9am–7:30pm Tue–Sun 🌐 museoarcheologico salerno.it

---

9

Paestum

🗺 E6 🚆 From Salerno 🚉 Paestum ⏰ 9am–7:30pm daily 🛈 Via Magna Grecia 919; www.museopaestum. beniculturali.it

The Greeks founded this city in the 6th century BC and called it Poseidonia, City of Poseidon. In 273 BC, the Romans renamed it Paestum. Abandoned in the 9th century, the city was rediscovered in the 1700s.

Paestum has three massive Doric temples in an excellent state of repair: the Basilica or Temple of Hera I (mid-6th century BC); the Temple of Neptune (5th century BC), the largest and most complete at Paestum; and the Temple of Ceres, thought to date between its two neighbours.

Excavations have revealed the remains of the ancient city, its public and religious buildings, roads and protective walls. A **museum** contains the finds from the site, including terracotta votive offerings, architectural fragments and sculpture.

Museum

⏰ 9am–7:30pm Tue–Sun

 10

Ischia and Procida

🗺 E5 🛫 Napoli 🚢 Ischia & Procida 🛈 Via Iasolino 7, Ischia; www.infoischia procida.it

The biggest island in the Bay of Naples, Ischia is known for its beach resorts, thermal springs and therapeutic mudbaths. The northern and western shores are developed; the southern flank of the island is the quietest. Here, the village of Sant'Angelo is dominated by a long-extinct volcano, Monte Epomeo, whose summit offers views across the bay. Also worth a visit are the gardens of **La Mortella** in Forio.

The tiny, picturesque island of Procida is less visited and very tranquil, with good swimming at Chiaiolella.

La Mortella

🏛 Apr–Oct: 9am–7pm Tue, Thu, Sat & Sun 🌐 lamortella.org

Trulli in Alberobello

ABRUZZO, MOLISE AND PUGLIA

Hugging the southeastern seaboard of Italy and looking towards the Balkans, the mountainous regions of Abruzzo and Molise, separated in 1963, are sparsely populated, quiet places where the wild landscape exerts a strong influence. Settled by various Apennine tribes in the Middle Bronze Age, Abruzzo and Molise were later subdued by the Romans, united under the Normans in the 12th century and, thereafter, ruled by a succession of dynasties based in Naples. Abruzzo, dominated by the Apennines, is a brooding region characterized by tracts of forest, sandy shores and breathtaking mountain scenery. Vertiginous drops preface the ascent to ramshackle hill-towns clinging to the sides of mountains. Molise's landscape is less dramatic, featuring high plains, gentle valleys and lonely peaks.

Bathed in ivory light, Puglia radiates warmth all year round. Phoenicians, Greeks and Romans, medieval Crusaders and pilgrims have all been drawn here by its fertile lands and easy access to the East. Its lively commercial centres – Lecce, Bari and Taranto – continue to draw visitors to the area. Puglia has glorious architecture, particularly in the churches and castles of the north. The curious *trulli* houses in central Puglia, the florid Baroque of Lecce and the Levantine atmosphere of its merchant cities complete the picture of an ancient land subject to more influences from outside the Italian peninsula than from within it.

ABRUZZO, MOLISE AND PUGLIA

Must Sees

1 Lecce

2 Parco Nazionale d'Abruzzo, Lazio e Molise

Experience More

3 Atri

4 Sulmona

5 Scanno

6 Lanciano

7 Isole Tremiti

8 Gargano

9 Lucera

10 Troia

11 Trani

12 Castel del Monte

13 Ruvo di Puglia

14 Alberobello

15 Bari

16 Ostuni

17 Taranto

18 Galatina

19 Otranto

Adriatic Sea

Isola Pianosa

Rodi Gargánico
Péschici
Vieste
GARGANO
8
Pugnochiuso
Mattinata
Manfredonia
Golfo di Manfredonia
Lupara
Margherita di Savoia
Barletta
Cerignola
11 TRANI
Molfetta
Andria
Canosa di Puglia
Corato
Bari
15 BARI
CASTEL DEL MONTE 12
Bitonto
Mola di Bari
13 RUVO DI PUGLIA
Modugno
Spinazzola
Rutigliano
Polignano a Mare
PUGLIA
Turi
Monopoli
Gravina in Puglia
Altamura
Putignano
Fasano
ALBEROBELLO 14
Torre Santa Sabina
Martina Franca
16 OSTUNI
Matera
Mottola
Salento
BASILICATA AND CALABRIA
p490
Ginosa
Massafra
Ceglie Messapica
Mesagne
Brindisi
Torre Mattarelle
Palagiano
BASILICATA
TARANTO 17
Francavilla Fontana
San Pietro Vernotico
Bernalda
Pulsano
Manduria
San Pancrazio Salentino
San Cataldo
Librari
Veglie
1 LECCE
Montemurro
Torre Lapillo
Lequile
Melendugno
GALATINA 18
Policoro
19
Maglie
OTRANTO
Latronico
Gallipoli
Rocca Imperiale
Golfo di Taranto
Taurisano
Posto Racale
Tricase
Amendolara
Torre Pali
Trebisacce
Santa Maria di Leuca
Castrovillari
San Sosti
CALABRIA
Rossano
Cetraro
Acri
Cariati

Greece, Albania, Croatia

Greece

0 kilometres 40
0 miles 40

N ↑

↑ The 1st-century-BC Roman amphitheatre on Piazza Sant'Oronzo

❶ LECCE

G6 **FS** Viale Oronzo Quarta 🚌 Viale Porta d'Europa
i Piazza Sant'Oronzo; www.ilecce.it

With scores of Baroque churches and palazzi, their golden façades a frolic of scrolls, curlicues, flowers, foliage, monsters, dragons, cherubs and angels, Lecce is a lively provincial capital and university town. It has always been beautiful, but in recent years, this part of Puglia has become fashionable. Churches and palaces have been restored, much of its historic centre has been pedestrianized, and its cobbled streets are full of stylish bars, restaurants and hip hotels.

① Piazza del Duomo

This elegant square is home to the Bishop's Palace (rebuilt 1632), the grand Duomo and the Seminary. Originally built around 1100, the present Duomo dates from the middle of the 17th century and was designed by Giuseppe Zimbalo, who also designed the five-storey bell tower. The Seminary once supplied the Vatican with *castrato* singers – eunuchs noted for their high voices.

② Chiesa di San Giovanni Battista

Via Giuseppe Libertini 5
☎ 0832 30 85 40 **Times vary, call ahead**

Arguably Zimbalo's finest work (begun 1691), the exterior of this church is wonderfully ornate. Set on a Greek-cross plan, the church was due to be topped by a dome, but the plans were abandoned in favour of a simple wooden roof after Zimbalo's death in 1710.

③ Basilica di Santa Croce

Via Umberto I 1 **9am-6pm daily** **chieselecce.it**

Built 1549–1679, this is perhaps Lecce's most famous Baroque building. The extravagantly

LECCESE BAROQUE

Lecce's architecture is mostly in the highly decorative Baroque style, which flourished in the 1600s and earned the city the nickname "Florence of the South". This style was possible due to the pietra di Lecce, an easily carved golden sandstone used by the city's architects. Giuseppe Zimbalo (1620-1710) was the greatest exponent of the style.

decorated façade is a riot of grotesque beasts, animals and allegorical figures set around a large rose window by Giuseppe Zimbalo. The slightly more subdued interior features 17 altars.

Museo Provinciale Sigismondo Castromediano

🏛 Viale Gallipoli 28
📞 0832 37 35 72 🕐 9am-8pm Tue-Sat

This fascinating museum contains objects dating from the Bronze Age and an excellent collection of Attic vases. The exhibit labels are mainly in Italian, but the staff speak good English and are generally eager to help.

Castello di Lecce

🏛 Viale XXV Luglio
🕐 9am-9pm Mon-Fri, 9:30am-9pm Sat & Sun (Jul & Aug: to 11pm daily)
🌐 castellocarlov.it

A Norman castle expanded by Charles V, the Castello di Lecce is Puglia's biggest fortress. Part of the building is now home to the Museo della Cartapesta, a museum of papier-mâché sculptures.

Piazza Sant'Oronzo

In this square is a 1739 bronze statue of St Oronzo, who was appointed Bishop of Lecce by St Paul in AD 57, and later martyred by Roman emperor Nero. The statue was erected as thanks for deliverance from a plague in 1656, attributed to St Oronzo. Next to the column is a Roman amphitheatre, from Emperor Hadrian's time.

PARCO NAZIONALE D'ABRUZZO, LAZIO E MOLISE

🅰 E5 🚆 Avezzano or Castel di Sangro 🚌 To Pescasseroli 🕐 10am–5:30pm daily (Jul & Aug: to 6:30pm) 🛈 Via Colli dell'Oro, Pescasseroli; www.parcoabruzzo.it

This vast park, inaugurated in 1922, has a rich landscape of high peaks, rivers, lakes and forests, and is one of Europe's most important nature reserves. Part of a royal hunting reserve until 1877, today it provides refuge for 60 species of mammal, 40 types of reptile, amphibian and fish, and 300 species of bird, including the golden eagle and white-backed woodpecker, as well as over 2,000 varieties of flora.

Exploring the Park

The park has an extensive network of paths, and there are opportunities for horse riding, trekking and climbing. Pescasseroli is a great base from which to explore – the town has a visitor centre, good tourist facilities and a small zoological garden with animals living in the region. Other highlights of the park include Lake Barrea, a spectacular artificial lake surrounded by valleys and forests offering walking and pony trekking, and the Camosciara, a dramatic region of mountains, valleys, waterfalls and streams. The park is famous for its many dense forests – of maple, hornbeam, ash, hawthorn, cherry, wild apple and pear – which protect the once persecuted Marsican brown bears and Apennine wolves that roam the area.

WILDLIFE IN THE PARK

This great expanse of protected land offers an array of different habitats, home to an abundance of flora and fauna. The park's biodiversity is testament to careful conservation work by the Park Authority.

Apennine Chamois
This species of goat-antelope can be seen hiding in dense forests of beech and maple.

Apennine Wolves
The park guarantees protection for the Apennine wolf, and about 60 wolves survive here. The chances of seeing one, however, are fairly remote.

Marsican Brown Bear
Once hunted almost to extinction, between 45 and 69 brown bears now prowl the park. Shy and solitary, the bears tend to roam at night.

Golden Eagles
These spectacular predators may be seen near the Sangro River, and can often be observed flying over mountain peaks and ridges as they hunt for prey.

↑ Hikers taking a break to enjoy views of Pescasseroli from Mancino Castle ruins

←

Peaceful valley of the Camosciara mountain range

EXPERIENCE MORE

③

Atri

Ⓐ E4 **Ⓣ Teramo** 🚌
Ⓦ comune.atri.te.it

The prettiest in a series of small hill-towns in Abruzzo, Atri is a warren of stepped streets, alleys and passages bound by mostly brick-and-stone churches and houses. The 13th-century Duomo occupies the site of a Roman bath; the crypt was once a swimming pool, and fragments of the original mosaic floor are visible in the apse. Also in the apse is Andrea Delitio's beautiful 15th-century fresco cycle, in which he combined landscape and architecture in a variety of religious scenes from the Old and New Testaments. The cloister has views of the 15th-century brick campanile.

South of Atri is the picturesque hill-town of Penne, with its homogeneous buildings of reddish brick, which give it a wonderful, warm glow. East of Atri, Loreto Aprutino is known for *The Last Judgment* fresco (15th century) in Santa Maria in Piano.

④

Sulmona

Ⓐ E4 **Ⓛ L'Aquila** 🚊🚌
ⓘ Piazza SS Annunziata 3;
www.visit-sulmona.it

Famous as the home of Ovid, Sulmona is filled with ancient buildings, especially along medieval Via dell'Ospedale. The Palazzo dell'Annunziata, founded in 1320, combines Gothic and Renaissance styles. The church of the Annunziata, with a Baroque façade, was rebuilt in the 18th century. Behind the church are 1 BC–AD 2 ruins of a Roman house.

At the end of Viale Matteotti is the cathedral of San Panfilo, built over a Roman temple. San Francesco della Scarpa, in Piazza del Carmine, has a 13th-century portal. Winding past it to the Fontana del Vecchio (1474) is an aqueduct that once fuelled local industry.

To the north of Sulmona is the Hermitage of Sant'Onofrio. It was founded in 1293 by Fra' Pietro Angelerio, the future Pope Celestine V, who dedicated it to the saint. Though located on a 600-m- (1,970-ft-) high rock face overlooking the Peligna valley, the hermitage is accessible via a short path.

East of Sulmona is the Maiella National Park, a massif of 61 peaks and forested valleys offering walking, birdwatching, climbing and skiing.

To the west, Cocullo hosts the May Processione dei Serpari (Procession of Snakes) in which a statue of Domenico Abate, the patron saint, is draped with serpents and carried through the town. In the 11th century he is said to have rid the area of venomous snakes.

---

⑤

Scanno

Ⓐ E4 **Ⓛ L'Aquila** 🚌 **ⓘ Piazza S Maria della Valle 12; www.comune.scanno.aq.it**

Wonderfully well preserved, this medieval hill-town features alleys and narrow flights of steps, oddly shaped courtyards with small churches, and ancient mansions in whose windows women can be seen making lace or embroidering.

In the shadow of Apennine peaks and beside lovely Lago di Scanno, the town is also a favoured stop on the way to the Parco Nazionale d'Abruzzo (p482).

OVID, THE LATIN POET

Born in 43 BC, Ovid was Sulmona's most illustrious inhabitant. Not much survives here to remind you of his presence, apart from at Corso Ovidio, a 20th-century statue of him in Piazza XX Settembre and, just outside the town, a ruin traditionally known as Ovid's Villa. Ovid's subjects included love (*Ars Amatoria*) and mythology (*Metamorphoses*). In AD 8 he was banished into exile on the Black Sea, the far edge of the Roman Empire, after being implicated in a scandal of adultery with Julia, the granddaughter of Emperor Augustus. Ovid died in exile in AD 17.

↑ Peaceful stretch of the mountain-fringed Lago di Scanno

6

Lanciano

 E4 Chieti
Piazza Plebiscito 51;
www.lanciano.eu

Large parts of Lanciano's old nucleus remain from the Middle Ages. In the crumbling Civitanova quarter is the 13th-century church of Santa Maria Maggiore, with a magnificent 14th-century portal and a silver processional cross (1422). The Duomo stands on the remains of a Roman bridge. An underground passage links the latter to the Sanctuary of the Eucharistic Miracle, where a host and wine that turned into live flesh and blood in the 8th century are kept.

7

Isole Tremiti

 F4 Foggia San Nicola Via Emilio Perrone 17, Foggia; www.lecinqueisole.it

The Tremiti are the Italian islands least visited by foreigners. San Domino is the largest, with a sandy beach and coves. Julia, granddaughter

of Augustus, was exiled here for adultery from AD 8 until her death in AD 28. The poet Ovid was allegedly involved.

Santa Maria a Mare, in San Nicola, is an abbey fortress founded in the 8th century. It was turned into a prison in the late 1700s, a role it maintained until 1945.

The Islands of San Domino and San Nicola are popular with Italians. The swimming is good, though the coastline of San Nicola is rocky.

8

Gargano

 F5 Foggia
Strada Provinciale 159, Manfredonia; www. parcogargano.gov.it

A rocky spur jutting into the Adriatic Sea, the Gargano is dotted with coves and cliffs. Its coastal towns – Peschici, Vieste, Manfredonia and Rodi Garganico – are popular with holiday-makers. To the east lies the Foresta Umbra, a woodland of beech, oak, yew and pine, and to the north the salt lakes of Lesina and Varano, havens for waterfowl. Plunging through the Gargano is an old pilgrim route (SS272) from

 HIDDEN GEM
The Grottoes of Isole Tremiti

A designated marine reserve, this group of islands is rife with grottoes, including del Bue Marino, del Sale, delle Rondinelle, delle Murene and delle Viole. The caves offer a glimpse into the benthic ecosystem under the deep blue Adriatic Sea. Boats can be taken from Vasto, Ortona, Vieste, Capoiale and Termoli.

San Severo in the west to the shrine at Monte Sant'Angelo in the east. The first stop is San Marco in Lamis, dominated by a huge 16th-century convent. Further along, San Giovanni Rotondo is a focus for pilgrims visiting the tomb of Padre Pio (1887–1968), a beatified miracle worker. The last stop is Monte Sant'Angelo, with its grotto where the Archangel Michael is said to have appeared to the Bishop of Sipontum in 493. To the south of Manfredonia is the oriental-inspired 12th-century church of Santa Maria di Siponto.

Lucera

E5 **Foggia** **Piazza Nocelli 6; www.comune. lucera.fg.it**

On the northeast edge of town, once a prosperous Roman colony, are the ruins of a Roman amphitheatre. Lucera was rebuilt in the 13th century by Frederick II, who peopled it with 20,000 Sicilian Muslims. It became one of the strongest fortresses in southern Italy. Built in 1233, its magnificent castle features a fortified wall interspersed with 15 towers.

In 1300, Charles II, who killed most of Lucera's Muslim population, began the Duomo on the site of their main mosque. The soaring nave is filled with 15th- and 16th-century frescoes and carvings.

The **Museo Civico Fiorelli** has displays of episodes from throughout Lucera's history.

Museo Civico Fiorelli
Via Famiglia de Nicastri 74 0881 54 70 41 9:30am–1:30pm & 3:30–7:30pm Tue–Sun

Troia

E5 **Foggia** **comune.troia.fg.it**

Founded in 1017 as a Byzantine fortress against the Lombards, Troia fell to the Normans in 1066. Until Frederick II destroyed it in 1229, the town had been ruled by a succession of powerful bishops who were responsible for producing many remarkable buildings, including Troia's Duomo.

Constructed over 30 years from 1093, it blends elements of Lombard, Saracenic and Byzantine style with that of the Pisan-Romanesque. Elegant blind arcading distinguishes the Duomo's lower storey. The upper sections are characterized by powerfully carved sculpture – projecting lions and bulls. The upper façade displays a rose window with Saracenic-style detailing.

The main entrance, with bronze doors by Oderisio da Beneventano (1119), is dominated by carved Byzantine-style capitals.

Trani

F5 **Bari** **Piazza Trieste 8; www.comune. trani.bt.it**

In the Middle Ages, this small, whitewashed port bustled with mercantile activity and was filled with merchants and traders from Genoa, Amalfi and Pisa. It reached its peak of prosperity under Frederick II.

Today it is visited for its Norman Duomo, built mainly

 The magnificent bell tower of Trani's Duomo

from 1159 to 1186. It is dedicated to St Nicholas the Pilgrim, a little-remembered miracle worker (died 1094) who was canonized as an act of rivalry against the town of Bari, which possessed the bones of another, more memorable St Nicholas. The Duomo's most notable external features are its sculptures, particularly surrounding the rose window and the arched window below it, and the entrance portal with bronze doors (1175–9) by Barisano da Trani.

Next to the Duomo is the castle (1233–49) founded by Frederick II. Rebuilt in the 14th and 15th centuries, it is a well-preserved edifice with one wall dropping sheer into the sea.

On Via Ognissanti is the Chiesa di Ognissanti, a reportedly 12th-century Templar church that was built as part of a hospital. Note the sculpture of the Annunciation in the lunette above the door.

Castel del Monte

F5 **Località Andria, Bari** **By appt only; 10am-6:45pm daily** **1 Jan, 25 Dec** **casteldelmonte. beniculturali.it**

This UNESCO World Heritage Site built in the mid-13th century, outclasses every other castle associated with Frederick II. The emperor had broad intellectual interests, and he used his castles as hunting lodges where he could retire from court life with his falcons and books. Inside there are two floors, each with eight rooms, some still lined with marble. This, and the marble mouldings on the entrance and the upper floor, as well as sophisticated

lavatory arrangements, mark the castle as a palace.

Ruvo di Puglia

F5 **Bari** **FS** **Via Vittorio Veneto 48; 080 362 84 28**

Once celebrated for its vases, Ruvo di Puglia's ceramics industry flourished until the 2nd century BC. The style was inspired by the striking red and black colours of Attic and Corinthian models.

The imposing 13th-century Cattedrale is a bold example of the Apulian-Romanesque style with a portal that blends Byzantine, Saracenic and Classical motifs.

The 16th-century **Chiesa del Purgatorio** was built over Grotta di San Cleto, a Roman cistern. It contains a magnificent papier-mâché Pietà.

Chiesa del Purgatorio
Via Cattedrale 103 **9am-10pm daily** **confraternita purgatorio.it**

Alberobello

G5 **Bari** **To Alberobello & Ostuni** **Via Monte Nero 1; 080 432 28 22**

Alberobello is a UNESCO World Heritage Site and the *trulli* capital. It is known for its strange whitewashed buildings, with conical roofs, crowding the narrow streets. *Trulli* are built from limestone stacked without using mortar. Many of the stone roof tiles have mysterious symbols painted on them. The origins of *trulli* are obscure, though the name is traditionally applied to round Roman tombs. Most of Alberobello's *trulli* are now souvenir shops or tiny cafés, though the Parrocchia Sant'Antonio di Padova, a diminutive church, is inspired by *trulli* architecture.

Did You Know?

Some say that *trulli* were built to be easily demolished to evade property taxes in the 14th century.

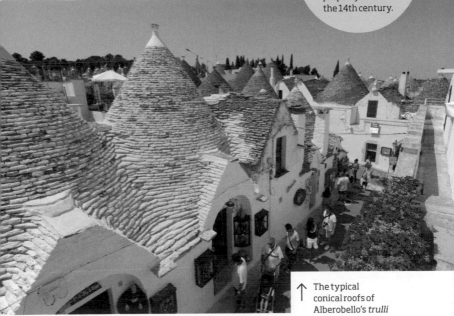

↑ The typical conical roofs of Alberobello's *trulli*

15

Bari

 F5 **i** Piazza del Ferrarese 29; www.comune.bari.it

Roman Barium was simply a commercial centre, but the city became the regional capital under the Saracens in 847, and was later the seat of the *catapan*, the Byzantine governor of southern Italy. Under the Normans, to whom it fell in 1071, Bari became a centre of maritime significance. Today it is Puglia's lively capital and an important port with ferries to and from Croatia and Greece.

The Basilica di San Nicola, one of Puglia's first great Norman churches (begun 1087), has a plain exterior with a tall gabled section flanked by towers. The Apulian-Romanesque portal has carving on the door jambs and arch in Arabic, Byzantine and Classical styles. Beyond the choir screen is a fine 12th-century altar canopy and an episcopal throne (c 11th century). The relics of St Nicholas – patron saint of the city – are buried in the crypt.

The late 12th-century Apulian-Romanesque Cattedrale is based on San Nicola, with a dome and one

surviving tower (the other one collapsed in 1613). The Baroque portals on the façade incorporate 12th-century doorways. The interior has been restored to its medieval simplicity. The sacristy, built as a baptistry, is known as the *Trulla*. The crypt houses the remains of San Sabino, Bari's original patron saint.

The city's castle, founded by Roger II, was adapted by Frederick II in 1233–9. In the vaulted hall is a collection of plaster casts of sculpture and architectural fragments from various Romanesque monuments in the region.

___

16

Ostuni

 G5 Brindisi FS **i** Corso Mazzini 8; www.borgostuni.it

Known as the *Città Bianca* (white city), the hill-town of Ostuni is a beguiling tangle of whitewashed houses, cobbled streets and arched alleyways. The white citadel is traffic-free, but there are well-signposted car parks in the newer, lower town.

There are some lovely palaces and churches – as well as cafés and restaurants – along Via della Cattedrale,

leading up to the cathedral. Highlights include the former Carmelite monastery of Santa Maria Maddalena dei Pazzi and the adjoining church of San Vito Martire, which now houses the **Museo di Civiltà Preclassiche della Murgia Meridionale**. The star exhibit of this museum is Delia, the 28,000-year-old skeleton of a pregnant woman – and her foetus – discovered in a nearby cave. The burial has been laid out as it was found, along with an eerie wax reconstruction of Delia, who is thought to have died in childbirth.

At the foot of the citadel, Piazza della Libertà is the focus of modern life, its bars and cafés overlooked by a column with Ostuni's patron, St Oronzo, at its pinnacle.

Museo di Civiltà Preclassiche della Murgia Meridionale
  Via Cattedrale 15 10am–1pm Sat & Sun, 5–9pm daily ostuni museo.it/museo-civico

___

17

Taranto

 G6 FS **i** Corso Umberto I 121; www.comune.taranto.it

Little remains of the old city of Taras, founded by Spartans in 708 BC. The **Museo Archeologico Nazionale** has artifacts that shed light on the region's history.

The run-down but picturesque Città Vecchia, an island dividing the Mare Grande from the Mare Piccolo, was the site of the Roman citadel of Tarentum. The city is famous for its shellfish, which can be bought fresh from the lively fish market, housed in an Art Nouveau building. Here, too, is the Duomo, founded in 1071 and subsequently rebuilt. The most interesting features include the catacomb-like crypt, with its sarcophagi and fragments of frescoes, and

THE TARANTELLA

Italy's folk dance, the tarantella grew out of tarantism - a dancing hysteria that appeared in 15th- to 17th-century Italy - and was prevalent in Galatina *(opposite)*. Victims of the tarantula spider's bite could supposedly cure themselves through frenzied dancing. The strange ritual takes place annually on 29 June at celebrations in Galatina, the only place on the Salentine peninsula where tarantism has survived.

Alfresco dining tables overlooking Otranto's seafront →

the antique marble columns of the nave. Behind it is the 11th-century San Domenico Maggiore, which later gained a high double-approach Baroque staircase. The huge castle built by Frederick of Aragon (15th century) covers the eastern corner of the Città Vecchia. Now a military area, the castle can be seen on daily guided tours (free of charge).

Museo Archeologico Nazionale

⊘ 🏠 Via Cavour 10 🕐 By appt only; 8:30am-7:30pm Tue-Sat (from 3:30pm Sun), 9am-1pm Sun 🌐 museo taranto.beniculturali.it

---

18

Galatina

🏠 Lecce 🚈🚌
ℹ Via Umberto I 36; www.visitgalatina.it

An important Greek colony in the Middle Ages, this *città d'arte* (city of art) retains its Greek flavour. It is the centre of one of Puglia's chief wine-producing regions, although it is more famous for the ritual of tarantism *(see box)*. The Gothic

church of Santa Caterina d'Alessandria (begun in 1383) on Piazza Orsini contains early 15th-century frescoes with scenes from the Old and New Testaments that glorify the Orsini, who were feudal lords.

19

Otranto

🏠 Lecce 🚈🚌⛴
ℹ Piazza Castello 1; www. comune.otranto.le.it

Otranto was one of Republican Rome's leading ports for trade with Asia Minor and Greece, and under the Byzantines was an important toehold of the Eastern Empire in Italy. In 1068 it fell to the Normans. Turks attacked in 1480, asking its 800 inhabitants to renounce Christianity. All refused and were subsequently slaughtered. The Norman Duomo (founded 1080) on Via Duomo houses the bones of these martyrs. There is a 12th-century mosaic floor and a fine crypt.

A castle (1485–98) built by the Aragonese adds to Otranto's charm, and there are some fine beaches close by.

BASILICATA AND CALABRIA

Remote and wild, Basilicata is one of the poorest regions in Italy. It is underdeveloped and its rural areas remain largely unspoiled. Neighbouring Calabria has been immortalized in drawings by Edward Lear, who, travelling through on a donkey in 1847, was transfixed by the "horror and magnificence" of its savage landscape.

Today, these regions are distinctly separate but they share a common history and, along with Sicily and Puglia, were part of Magna Graecia. Ancient Metaponto in Basilicata was an important centre, as was Locri Epizefiri in Calabria.

After the Greeks came the Romans, followed by Basilian monks. These were members of the Greek-Byzantine church who were fleeing their territories, which had been invaded by Muslims. Their religious establishments make up a core of interesting monuments, such as the Cattolica at Stilo and Matera, where monks took refuge in caves.

Many of the historic remains are Norman, but sporadic evidence of the Swabian, Aragonese, Angevin and Spanish occupation still exists.

Nowadays, Calabria has an infamous reputation due to the 'Ndrangheta, the ferocious first cousin to the Mafia. Concerned mainly with drug trafficking, this criminal gang presents little threat to tourists.

Owing to emigration, Basilicata and Calabria are sparsely populated and have as much to offer in unspoiled countryside as in historic centres. The coastline has fine beaches, while inland are the Aspromonte and Sila mountain ranges. The remote landscape has kept change at bay. Isolated Pentedattilo, for example, preserves customs of Byzantine origin, while around San Giorgio Albanese there live close-knit communities of Albanians, descended from 15th-century refugees.

Fondi
Terracina
S7 · S630 · A1
Teano
Gaeta
Mondragone
S7
CAMPANIA
SS7
Capua · A1 · Benevento
Castel Volturno · Maddaloni
Giugliano · Pratola Serra
Naples · Avellino · A30 · RA2
Isola d'Ischia · Ischia
Castellammare di Stabia
Golfo di Napoli · Sorrento · Salerno
Isola di Capri · Amalfi · Battipaglia
Capri
Golfo di Salerno
Agropoli
Castellabate

Tyrrhenian Sea

Aeolian Islands
Santa Marina Salina
Lipari

Capo d'Orlando · Brolo
Cefalu · Patti
Caronia
A20
Castelbuono · SICILY · Randazzo
Cerda
A19
Gangi · Bronte
Valledolmo · Nicosia

BASILICATA AND CALABRIA

Must See

Experience More

①

MATERA

A F5 **FS** **i** Via De Viti De Marco 9; www.sassiweb.it

Fused to a cave-ridden outcrop above a deep ravine, Matera is one of the most extraordinary cities in the Italian south. Cave dwellings, churches, houses, stepped streets and twisting pavements form an astonishing maze of limestone. Declared a UNESCO World Heritage Site in 1993, Matera is now a thriving destination dotted with many boutique cave hotels and excellent restaurants.

spacious square at its liveliest in the early evenings, when traffic is banned. Stroll along Via del Corso to see some lovely palazzi and churches. At the far end is the elliptical façade of Chiesa del Purgatorio, a ghoulishly decorated 17th-century church with a chequerboard of Edvard-Munch-style screaming skull and skeleton sculptures.

The Sassi

The Sassi district is made up of a labyrinth of cave dwellings on the eastern slope of Matera (the literal translation of *sassi* is "stones"). It is divided into two quarters: Sasso Caveoso, to the south, and Sasso Barisano, to the north. The *sassi* are reached by winding downhill through steep twisting alleyways. From outside the Hotel Sassi, you can wander through a series of unrestored *sassi*, many of which retain stoves carved into the stone, staircases and courtyards overgrown with brambles and prickly pears.

The Upper Town

The centre of the historic town, perched on the higher slopes of Matera above the *sassi*, is Piazza Vittorio Veneto, a

③

Convicinio S Antonio

A Rione Casalnuovo
C 393 957 5031 **⊙** May-Sep: 9am-8pm daily **⊙** Oct-Apr

These four interlinked churches were used as wine cellars in the 18th century and feature wine spouts emerging from the altar. There are great views from outside the church right over the ravine.

←

Ancient cave dwelling in Sasso Caveoso

The spectacular city of Matera, a UNESCO World Heritage Site

(5)

Parco delle Chiese Rupestri

🏛 CEA, Contrada Murgia Timone 🌐 ceamatera.it

Pack a picnic and plenty of water, and explore the caves and *chiese rupestri* (rock-hewn churches) across the river on the far side of the ravine. Alternatively take one of the two daily guided hikes (the best leaves around sunset).

(6)

Casa Grotta di Vico Solitario

🏛 Vicinato di Vico Solitario 11 🕒 9:30am–dusk daily 🌐 casagrotta.it

This traditional cave dwelling has been reconstructed with the help of a family who lived here until the 1950s.

Madonna de Idris

🏛 Via Madonna dell'Idris 🕒 9am–6pm daily (Apr–Nov: to 7pm) 🌐 oltrelartematera.it

Soaring above the *sassi*, this church is carved right into the rock of conical Monte Errone. Inside are the evocative traces of medieval frescoes.

EAT

Alle Fornaci

Fish are brought in daily from the Ionian and Tyrrhenian seas to create local culinary specialities in an elegant and classy atmosphere. Try the grilled swordfish steak.

🏛 Piazza Cesare Firrao 7 🕒 Mon 🌐 ristorante allefornaci.it

La Grotta nei Sassi

Eat in the intimate, vaulted stone dining room or, in warmer months, on the rooftop terrace and feast on regional recipes such as ricotta with honey-toasted almonds.

🏛 Via Rosario 73 🕒 Mon 🌐 ristorante sassidimatera.com

Melfi's forbidding medieval castle, set on a mound ↑

EXPERIENCE MORE

② Melfi

F5 **Potenza** FS⊟
ℹ️ Via del Gallitello 89;
www.basilicataturistica.it

A brooding medieval town, Melfi is crowned by the castle where in 1059 Pope Nicholas II conducted Robert Guiscard's investiture, thus legitimizing the Normans in the south. Melfi later became the Norman capital. Here Frederick II proclaimed his *Constitutiones Augustales* (1231), which unified his kingdom as a state. In the castle is the **Museo Archeologico Nazionale del Vulture Melfese**, with its collection of Byzantine jewellery. The Duomo, off Via Vittorio Emanuele, was begun in 1155 but rebuilt in the 18th century.

Museo Archeologico Nazionale del Vulture Melfese

 Castello di Melfi, Via Normanni ☎ 0972 23 87 26 🕐 2–8pm Mon (from 9am Tue–Sun) 🚫 1 Jan, 25 Dec

③ Venosa

F5 **Potenza** FS⊟
ℹ️ Via Roma 24; www.comune.venosa.pz.it

Venosa was an important Roman colony around 290 BC, and remains of baths and an amphitheatre survive in the archaeological zone along Via Vittorio Emanuele. It was also the birthplace of the Latin poet Horace (65–8 BC) and the site where the Roman general Marcellus died at the hands of Hannibal in 208 BC. Marcellus's reputed tomb is in Via Melfi. For more ancient treasures, visit the **Museo Archeologico Nazionale**.

The Duomo, also on Via Vittorio Emanuele, and the huge castle in Piazza Umberto I, date from the 16th century.

An abbey complex formed by an older, possibly early Christian church (5th–6th century), La Trinità is backed by an unfinished 11th-century construction, in which five members of the Norman Hauteville family were buried. Only the tomb of Alberada, the first wife of Robert Guiscard, has survived.

Museo Archeologico Nazionale

 Piazza Umberto I
☎ 0972 360 95 🕐 9am-8pm Wed-Mon (from 2pm Tue)

④

Lagopesole

F5 **Potenza** FS To Castel Lagopesole, then bus to town 🕐 Apr-Oct: 9:30am-1pm & 4-7pm daily; Nov-Mar: 9:30am-1pm & 3-5pm 🚫 24 Dec-2 Jan
🌐 castellodilagopesole.com

Rising dramatically on a hill, Lagopesole's castle (1242–50) was the last castle built by Frederick II. The interesting carved heads above the portal of the keep are generally said to represent Frederick Barbarossa (grandfather of Frederick II) and Barbarossa's wife, Beatrice. Inside, the royal apartments and chapel can be visited.

Museo Archeologico Nazionale di Metaponto

 🏛 Via D Adamesteanu 21, Metaponto 📞 0835 74 53 27 ⏰ 2-8pm Mon, 9am-8pm Tue-Sun

Museo Archeologico Nazionale della Siritide

 🏛 Via C Colombo 8, Policoro 📞 0835 97 21 54 ⏰ 9am-8pm Mon, Wed & Sun, 2pm-8pm Tue 🚫 1 Jan, 1 May, 25 Dec

---

⑥

Maratea

🅰 F6 🚉 Potenza 🚉🚌
ℹ Via Santavenere 144; www.marateaproloco.it

Basilicata's tiny stretch of coast is home to Maratea. Its tiny port (Maratea Inferiore) is beneath the old town (Maratea Superiore), which straddles the flank of a hill. From here the road climbs Monte San Biagio to a summit with great views and a 1960s statue of the Christ the Redeemer.

Rivello, 23 km (14 miles) to the north, once had a largely Greek population. Byzantine influences can still be seen in its churches.

⑤

Parco Archeologico di Metaponto

🅰 F6 🚉 Matera 🚌🚉 To Metaponto ⏰ 9am-30 mins before sunset daily 🚫 Mon am, 1 Jan, 1 May, 25 Dec
ℹ Via Apollo Licio; www. beniculturali.it

Founded in the 7th century BC, ancient Metaponto was once the centre of a wealthy city-state with a philosophical tradition expounded by Pythagoras, who settled here after his expulsion from Croton. Its sights include the Tavole Palatine, the ruins of a 6th-century-BC Doric temple that was probably dedicated to the goddess Hera, which is located near the Bradano River bridge. The **Museo Archeologico Nazionale di Metaponto** displays artifacts from the site. The remains of a theatre and a Doric Temple of Apollo Lycius (6th century BC) are in the Archaeological Zone.

Further south, modern Policoro occupies what was ancient Heracleia (founded 7th–5th century BC). Its **Museo Archeologico Nazionale della Siritide** has finds from this and other sites.

⑦

Rossano

🅰 F6 🚉 Cosenza 🚉🚌
ℹ Via Plebiscito 1; www. rossanoturismo.it

This pretty hill-town was one of the main centres of Byzantine civilization in Calabria. The **Museo Diocesano** houses the *Codex Purpureus Rossanensis*, a rare 6th-century Greek Gospel with silver lettering and intricate miniatures.

The Baroque cathedral contains the *Madonna Achiropita* fresco, a much-venerated Byzantine relic of the 6th to 8th century.

On a hilltop to the southeast is the five-domed Greek church of San Marco (10th century). The 10th or 11th-century Panaghia, another Greek church, lies on Via S Giovanni di Dio.

Santa Maria del Patire, 15 km (9 miles) to the west, is adorned with coloured brickwork, tile and stone.

Museo Diocesano

 🏛 Via Arcivescovado 5 ⏰ 9:30am-12:30pm & 3-6pm Tue-Sun 🌐 museocodex rossano.it

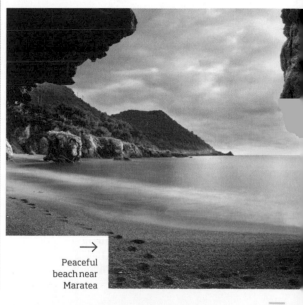

→ Peaceful beach near Maratea

8

Tropea

🅰F7 🚇Vibo Valentia 🄵🄢🚌
**🄵 Piazza Ercole; www.
prolocotropea.eu**

One of the most picturesque towns on Calabria's largely built-up Tyrrhenian coast, Tropea offers superb views of the sea and beaches. The old town hangs on to a cliffside facing a large rock, formerly an island. The rock is topped by Santa Maria dell'Isola, a former medieval Benedictine sanctuary. The cathedral at the end of Via Roma is of Norman origin, although it has been rebuilt several times. Inside is a 14th-century painting, the *Madonna di Romania*, by an unknown artist. Casa Trampo (14th century) and Palazzo Cesareo (early 20th century) in Vicolo Manco are the most interesting of the mansions in Tropea. The latter has a splendid balcony adorned with carvings.

Below the town are pretty beaches and a good choice of places to eat. Other seaside towns to visit are Scilla to the south and Pizzo to the north.

 9

Stilo

🅰F7 🚇Reggio di Calabria
🚌 **🄵 Town hall, Viale Roma
34; www.comune.stilo.rc.it**

A short distance from the coast, Stilo is an earthquake-damaged town clamped to the side of Monte Consolino. On a ledge looking out over the olive trees is the **Cattolica di Stilo**, which has made the town a focus of pilgrimage for lovers of Byzantine architecture. Built in the 10th century by Basilian monks, the brick building with its terracotta-

↑ The church of Santa Maria dell'Isola, on a rocky spur in Tropea

tiled roof is based on a Greek cross-in-a-square plan. Four antique, mismatched marble columns divide the interior into nine sections. The capitals are placed at the base of the columns, instead of on top, to indicate the triumph of Christianity over paganism. The frescoes within, discovered in 1927, date from the 11th century.

The Cattolica dominates the town, but on Via Tommaso Campanella there is a medieval Duomo as well as the 17th-century ruins of the Convent of San Domenico, where the philosopher and Dominican friar Tommaso Campanella (1568–1639) lived. The church of San Francesco, built around 1400, has an ornate carved wooden altar and a lovely 16th-century painting of the *Madonna del Borgo* (unknown origin).

Bivongi, northwest of Stilo, is home to the Byzantine and Norman monastery of San Giovanni Theristis and its stunning frescoes. The monastery is still used by Greek Orthodox monks.

> **The capitals are placed at the base of the columns, instead of on top, to indicate the triumph of Christianity over paganism.**

SHOP

Here are some of the best shops in Reggio di Calabria.

Archaeological Museum Shop

Lovely bookstore and souvenir shop.

🏠 Piazza G de Nava 26

Oro Argento e Mirra

Artisan goldsmiths since 1975.

🏠 Corso Garibaldi 277

La Libreria Nuova Ave

The oldest independent bookstore in the city.

🏠 Corso Garibaldi 206

Cattolica di Stilo

 🏠 2 km (1 mile) above Stilo on Via Cattolica ⏰ 8am-2pm Tue-Thu, 2-8pm Fri-Sun 🌐 cattolicadistilo.it

---

⑩ Reggio di Calabria

🗺 F7 🚇🚌🚏🚢 *i* Stazione Lido; www.turismo. reggiocal.it

One reason to visit Reggio di Calabria, which was heavily rebuilt after a devastating earthquake almost destroyed the area in 1908, is the **Museo Archeologico Nazionale di Reggio Calabria**. It houses an important collection of artifacts from ancient Rhegion – a Greek city on the site of the present town – and from other ancient Greek sites.

Chief among its treasures are two larger-than-life Greek bronze statues of warriors dredged from the sea off the coast of Riace Marina in 1972, and known as statues A (460 BC) and B (430 BC). It is possible that the statues originated from an Athenian shrine at Delphi built to celebrate the victory of Marathon. The sculptors are not known, though some have attributed Statue A to Phidias, the Athenian sculptor and chief exponent of the idealizing, Classical style. If true, it is a rare survivor, because his works were hitherto only known to us from Roman copies.

Museo Archeologico Nazionale di Reggio Calabria

🎦 🕐 🏠 Piazza G de Nava 26 🔒 By appt only; 9am-8pm Tue-Sun 🌐 museo archeologicoreggiocalabria.it

---

⑪ Gerace

🗺 F7 🏠 Reggio di Calabria 🚌 *i* Town hall, Piazza del Tocco; www.comune. gerace.rc.it

Occupying a crag on the northeastern flank of the Aspromonte, Gerace was founded by refugees from Locri Epizefiri who fled in the 9th century to escape Saracen attack. Its defensive character is reinforced by the medieval town walls and the remains of the castle.

Apart from the slow pace of life here – where you are as likely to meet a flock of sheep in an alley as a Fiat 500 – the main attraction is the magnificent Duomo. This large structure indicates the significance of Gerace at least up to the time of the Normans. Constructed around the early 12th century, rebuilt in the 13th century and restored in the 18th century, the crypt takes pride of place as its chief treasure. Both crypt and church are simple, adorned by a series of antique coloured marble-and-granite columns probably stolen from the site of ancient Locri Epizefiri. At the end of Via Cavour is 10th-century San Giovannello, part Byzantine and part Norman. Nearby is the Gothic church of San Francesco d'Assisi, which contains a Baroque marble altar (1615) and the Pisan-style tomb of Niccolò Ruffo (died 1372), a member of a prominent Calabrian family.

The vast site of **Locri Epizefiri**, the first Greek city to have a written code of law (660 BC), was a famous centre of the cult of Persephone. There are remains of temples, a theatre and Greek and Roman tombs. The **Museo Nazionale** displays a ground plan of the site, as well as Greek and Roman votive statues, coins and sculptural fragments.

Locri Epizefiri

🏠 Southwest of Locri on the SS 106, Contrada Marasà ⏰ 9am-1 hr before sunset Tue-Sun 🌐 locriantica.it

Museo Nazionale

🏠 Piazza Tribuna 1 🔒 For restoration 🌐 locriantica.it/ sito/museo

→

Bronze statue at Museo Archeologico Nazionale di Reggio Calabria

SICILY

On a crossroads in the Mediterranean, part of Europe and Africa, yet belonging to neither, Sicily was tramped across by half the ancient civilized world. As conquerors came and went, they left behind elements of their culture, resulting in the rich and varied mixture that typifies every aspect of Sicilian life, from language, customs and cooking to art and, most notably, architecture.

During the 6th and 5th centuries BC, there cannot have been much difference between Athens and the Greek cities of Sicily. Their ruins are among the most spectacular of the ancient Greek world. The Romans took over in the 3rd century BC, followed by the Vandals, Ostrogoths and Byzantines. Not much that is tangible is left from the days of Arab rule in the 9th to 11th centuries. Their influence is most visible in the Arab-Norman architecture of Palermo, the Kasbah in Mazara del Vallo and the groves of citrus fruits they introduced. The Norman era, beginning in 1061, spawned achievements such as the Arab-Norman cathedrals of Monreale and Cefalù.

The Sicilian Baroque of the 17th and 18th centuries is just as distinctive. The palaces and churches of Palermo, reflecting the elaborate ritual of the Spanish Viceregal court, tend towards extravagant display. At Noto, Ragusa, Modica, Scicli and Catania the buildings are wonderfully flamboyant sporting exaggerated concave and convex curves, twisting columns, highly decorative flourishes and gorgeous *putti*. The distinctive gargoyles on churches and palazzi balconies recall those found on ancient Greek temples on the island.

Naples, Salerno,
Genoa, Cagliari ↑

Isola
di Ustica

T y r r h e n i a n
S e a

← *Cagliari*

Capo
Gallo

Punta
Raisi

✈ **Palermo**

Carini

PALERMO

1 ⛴

Capo Zafferano

Bagheria

SAN VITO LO CAPO **7**

Zingaro
Nature Reserve

MONREALE 2

S113

Termini
Imerese

ERICE

8

Castellammare
del Golfo

Partinico

Misilmeri

A19

*Isola
Marettimo*

TRAPANI **6** ⛴

Paceco

Alcamo

S121

*Isola
di Levanzo*

SEGESTA

Camporeale

Villafrati

Ciminna

*Isola
Favignana*

Trapani ✈

10

Calatafimi

Torto

*Egadi
Islands*

*Isole dello
Stagnone*

S115

Salemi

Roccamena

Corleone

Alia

Tabaccaro

Val di Mazara

*Pizzo Cangialoso
1457m* △

Prizzi

Lercara Friddi

MARSALA 9

A29

Partanna

Bisacquino

S188

Vallelunga
Pratameno

Castelvetrano

S115

*Pizzo Stagnataro
1346m* △

Mazara del Vallo

S188

Menfi

Burgio

Mussomeli

Campobello di Mazara

Belice

Caltabellotta

Cianciana

Gallo d'Oro

Capo Granitola

SELINUNTE

11

Sciacca

Ribera

Verdura

S118

S189

Milena

Platani

Aragona

Capo Bianco

Raffadali

S115

↓ Pantelleria

AGRIGENTO 13

Porto Empedocle

5 ⛴ **VALLEY OF
THE TEMPLES**

Favara

Palma di
Montechiaro S115

SICILY

Must Sees

1 Palermo

2 Monreale

3 Siracusa

4 Ortygia

5 Valley of the Temples

Experience More

6 Trapani

7 San Vito Lo Capo

8 Erice

9 Marsala

10 Segesta

11 Selinunte

12 Cefalù

13 Agrigento

14 Piazza Armerina

15 Enna

16 Messina

17 Taormina

18 Mount Etna

19 Pantalica

20 Catania

21 Scicli

22 Sampieri

23 Ragusa

24 Modica

25 Noto

*Pelagie
Islands ↓*

Naples

Isola Stromboli

Isola Panarea

Isola Salina

Isola Filicudi

Santa Marina Salina

Isola Alicudi

Aeolian Islands

Isola Lipari

Lipari

Isola Vulcano

Capo di Milazzo

Milazzo

MESSINA **16**

12 **CEFALÙ**

Capo d'Orlando

S113

Tindari

Barcellona Pozza di Gotto

A20

Monti Peloritani

A18

Reggio di Calabria

S106

Sant'Agata di Militello

Naso Patti

Pizzo di Vernà 1287m

Ali Terme

Torremuzza

A20

San Fratello

Floresta

Mandanici

San Francesco di Paola

Collesano

Castelbuono

Nebrodi

Monti

Randazzo

Alcántara

Gole dell'Alcántara

Pizzo Carbonara 1979m

Mistretta

Monte Soro 1847m

Linguaglossa

17 **TAORMINA**

Monte Castelli 1566m

Capizzi

Troina

Bronte

Naxos

Petralia

S120

Madonie

Gangi

Nicosia

MOUNT ETNA **18**

Riposto

Giarre

S114

Alimena

S117

Agira

S121

Adrano

Aci Castello

A18

Leonforte

Paternò

Belpasso

Aci Castello

S I C I L Y

15 **ENNA**

A19

Dittaino

Misterbianco

20 **CATANIA**

Ionian Sea

Santa Caterina Villarmosa

Valguarnera Caropepe

Catania Fontanarossa

Caltanissetta

Pietraperzia

Gornalunga

Piana di Catania

Golfo di Catania

Barrafranca

14 **PIAZZA ARMERINA**

S640

S626

Villa Romana del Casale

S417

Palagonia

S114

Sommatino

Mazzarino

Mineo

Lentini

Capo Campolato

Ravanusa

Gela

Caltagirone

Monti Iblei

S194

Francofonte

Melilli

Capo Santa Croce

Augusta

Butera

S117

Grammichele

Sortino

A18

Golfo di Augusta

Niscemi

Vizzini

PANTALICA **19**

Anapo

Castello Eurialo

Licata

S514

Floridia

3 **SIRACUSA**

Gela

Chiaramonte Gulfi

Palazzolo Acreide

4 **ORTYGIA**

Golfo di Gela

Comiso Airport "Pio La Torre"

S115

S164

Canicattini Bagni

Capo Murro di Porco

Vittoria

Irminio

23 **RAGUSA**

NOTO **25**

Avola

Scoglitti

Comiso

Val di Noto

24 **MODICA**

Golfo di Noto

Marina di Ragusa

21 **SCICLI**

Rosolini

Ispica

SAMPIERI **22**

Pozzallo

Pachino

Mediterranean Sea

Punta delle Formiche

0 kilometres 25

0 miles 25

N

↑ Palermo's bustling port surrounded by an impressive landscape

PALERMO

F1 ✈ Falcone Borsellino 35 km (22 miles) W **FS** Palermo Centrale 🚌 Piazza Cairoli ⛴ Molo Vittorio Veneto al Porto
🛈 Via Maqueda 189; www.turismo.comune.palermo.it

Vibrant, scruffy and very, very noisy, Palermo sprawls chaotically around a sweeping natural harbour, dominated by the limestone bulk of Monte Pellegrino. The city was the seat of the Arab Emirate in the 10th century, and Middle Eastern influences can still be seen in the architecture of the churches and in the narrow streets and alleys of the old Arab quarter between Palazzo dei Normanni and the sea.

① Piazza Bellini and Piazza Pretoria

Tucked behind the Quattro Canti intersection (*p507*), Piazza Bellini is home to three engaging churches. With its red domes, **San Cataldo** is a two-storey cuboid perched on a bank overlooking the square. **Santa Caterina** is Palermitan Baroque at its most exuberant, every inch of the interior is encrusted with coloured marble and stucco. Nearby **La Martorana**'s Baroque façade conceals an Arab-Norman core featuring a beautiful medieval mosaic. Adjoining

Piazza Pretoria has the 16th-century Fontana della Vergogna (Fountain of Shame), named after the immodesty of its nudes.

San Cataldo

◈ ⏰ 9:30am–12:30pm & 3–6pm daily 🌐 santo sepolcrosicilia.it

Santa Caterina

◈ ⏰ 9:30am–1:30pm & 3–7pm daily 🌐 monasterosanta caterina.com

La Martorana

◈ ⏰ 9:30am–1pm & 3:30–5:30pm Mon-Sat, 9am–10:30pm Sun & pub hols

② Palazzo dei Normanni and Cappella Palatina

🏛 Piazza Indipendenza
📞 091 705 56 11 ⏰ 8:30am–2:30pm Mon-Thu, 9am–4pm Fri, 8:30am–4:30pm Sat, 8:30am–9:30am & 11:30am–2:30pm Sun
🌐 federicosecondo.org

Dominating the high ground on the western edge of the old centre, the nucleus of the present palace was built by the Arabs and enlarged for the Norman court after they conquered the city in 1072. The jewel is the Cappella Palatina, a cocktail of Byzantine, Islamic and Norman influences built by Roger II (1132–40).

↑ Pretty Cappella Palatina in Palazzo dei Normanni

Ballarò Market

📍 Via Ballarò 1 🕐 7:30am-8pm daily (to noon Sun)

Nowhere captures the spirit of Palermo better than this fresh produce market, overlooked by the gorgeous majolica-tiled dome of Santa Maria del Carmine.

Piazza Marina

Now a busy traffic junction, Piazza Marina occupies land reclaimed from the sea in the 10th century. Nearby **Palazzo Mirto** gives a glimpse of 18th-century aristocratic life, as well as servants' experiences.

Palazzo Mirto

♿ 📍 Via Merlo 2 ☎ 091 616 4751 🕐 9am-6pm Tue-Sat, 9am-1pm Sun

Palazzo Abatellis

📍 Via Alloro 4 ☎ 091 623 00 47 🕐 9am-7pm Tue-Fri, 9am-1:30pm Sat, Sun & pub hols

This 15th-century palazzo makes an atmospheric home for Sicily's best collection of medieval and Renaissance art. Exhibits include a collection of works by 15th-century artist Antonello da Messina.

San Giovanni degli Eremiti

📍 Via dei Benedettini 20 🕐 9am-7pm Mon-Sat, 9am-1:30pm Sun & pub hols

With its Islamic-style onion domes and filigreed windows, this deconsecrated Norman church (1130–48) was built in the grounds of a mosque.

EAT

I Cuochini

A tiny *friggitoria* founded in 1826, I Cuochini produces traditional pastries and *arancini*.

📍 Via Ruggero Settimo 68 🌐 icuochini.com

€€€

Spinnato

This *pasticceria*, with tables outside on a quiet street, is perfect for a lazy breakfast or an evening cocktail.

📍 Via Principe di Belmonte 107-115 🌐 spinnato.it

€€€

⑦
Duomo

 Via Vittorio Emanuele
🕐 7am–7pm Mon–Sat, 8am–1pm & 4–7pm Sun
🕐 For Mass 🌐 cattedrale.palermo.it

Palermo's cathedral stands on the site of an Early Christian basilica, later a mosque. Despite frequent rebuildings and alterations, elements of the original Norman building have survived, notably the arched crenellations along the walls and the beautiful interlaced arches and small columns that decorate the exterior of the apse.

⑧
Oratorio del SS Rosario in San Domenico

 Via dei Bambinai 2
☎ 091 33 27 79 🕐 Apr–Oct: 9am–6pm Mon–Sat (Nov–Mar: to 2pm)

The Oratory of San Domenico was founded at the end of the 16th century by the Society of the Holy Rosary, whose members included the artist Pietro Novelli and sculptor Giacomo Serpotta. A tumult of figures of great ladies, knights and playful *putti* form a kind of frame for statues of Christian virtues by Giacomo Serpotta and paintings representing the mysteries of the Rosary by Pietro Novelli. The altarpiece was painted by Anthony Van Dyck in 1628.

⑨
Vucciria

 Piazza Caracciolo

Nowhere is Palermo's Arabic past more apparent than in this medieval kasbah-style market, which burrows through the ruinous Loggia district below Via Roma. The alleys are named after their professions, such as silversmiths, dyers and key-makers. Immortalized by Renato Guttuso in his painting *La Vucciria*, this is an atmospheric place to wander in the early mornings, when the fishmongers set up shop.

 HIDDEN GEM
Castello della Zisa

Beyond the centre, this country retreat *(Piazza Zisa)* was built by Arab craftsmen for Norman kings William I and William II.

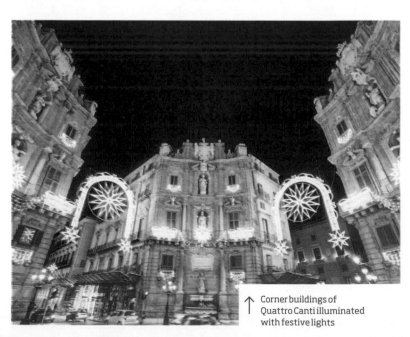
↑ Corner buildings of Quattro Canti illuminated with festive lights

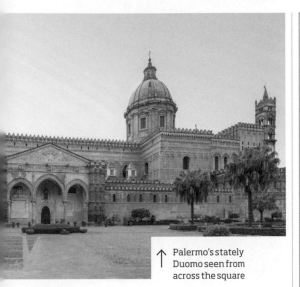

↑ Palermo's stately Duomo seen from across the square

Oratorio del Rosario di Santa Zita

⌂ Via Valverde 3 ☎ 091 33 27 79 🕔 Apr-Oct: 9am-6pm Mon-Sat (Nov-Mar: to 2pm)

Founded in 1590, this was one of the city's richest oratories, and it is sumptuously decorated by Giacomo Serpotta. The panel on the rear wall depicts the Battle of Lepante, and other reliefs show scenes from the New Testament. The neighbouring 16th-century church of Santa Zita, from which the oratory takes its name, is filled with sculptures (1517–27) by Antonello Gagini.

Museo Archeologico Regionale

⌂ Piazza Olivella 24 ☎ 091 611 68 05 🕔 9am-6pm Tue-Sat (to 1:30pm Sun & pub hols)

This fascinating museum has treasures from excavations across the west of the island, ranging from Phoenician sarcophagi (6th–5th centuries BC) to a fine 3rd-century-BC ram's head. There are also marvellous pieces from the temples at Selinunte, including a leonine head from the Temple of Victory and reliefs of mythological scenes, for example one showing Actaeon being attacked by dogs and Athena slaying a giant.

Catacombe dei Cappuccini

⌂ Via Cappuccini 1 ☎ 329 415 04 62 🕔 9am-12:30pm & 3-5:30pm Mon-Sat, 9am-12:30pm Sun (Apr-Sep: 9am-1pm & 3-6pm daily)

In Palermo's scruffy residential western suburbs are these fascinating – at least for the non-squeamish – catacombs. Over several hundred years monks here mummified the bodies of some 8,000 priests and wealthy Palermitani.

Quattro Canti

⌂ Via Vittorio Emanuele

The busy intersection of Corso Vittorio Emanuele and Via Maqueda is marked by the Quattro Canti, or "Four Corners", an elaborate Baroque crossroads shaped by the concave façades of the four corner buildings. It dates from 1600, when the new town plan that split the old city into four quadrants was put into effect. Each façade is decorated with a fountain and statues of saints, the seasons and Spanish kings.

Did You Know?

The cathedral contains around 6,500 sq m (70,000 sq ft) of brilliant mosaics.

The enormous apse mosaic of Christ Pantocrator (12th to 13th century) ↑

② ⊘ Ⓜ

DUOMO DI MONREALE

🅰 F1 🅐 Piazza Guglielmo II 1 🚌 389 from Piazza Indipendenza 🕐 9am–1pm
& 1:30–5:30pm Mon–Sat, 2:15–5:15pm Sun & pub hols 🌐 monrealeduomo.it

The cathedral at Monreale sits high above the Conca d'Oro, a fertile plain overlooking
Palermo. Despite its rather austere exterior, the cathedral's interior is embellished
with the most extensive and significant mosaic cycle of its kind in Sicily.

Magnificently adorned, and with a splendid
view of the Conca d'Oro, the Duomo at
Monreale is one of the greatest sights of
Norman Sicily. Founded in 1172 by the Norman
King William II, it flanks a monastery of the
Benedictine Order. The interior of the cathedral
glitters with mosaics carried out by Sicilian
and Byzantine artists – commissioned by a
king who wanted to rival the power of the
Archbishop of Palermo. Like Cefalù, and later
Palermo, it was to serve as a royal sepulchre,
housing the tombs of William I and William II.

↑ Intricately carved Norman-era
columns in the cloisters

This section of the
apse exterior is
richly ornamented
in tufa and marble.

An imposing
mosaic of Christ
Pantocrator is at
the heart of the
cathedral's
Latin-cross plan.

Completed in
1182, the stunning
mosaic cycle
depicts scenes
from the Bible.

The elaborately
decorated cloister
columns support
Saracenic-style
arches.

The royal tombs of
William I and William II
are in the corner of
the transept.

Portico designed by
Gian Domenico and
Fazio Gagini (1547–69)

Bonanno da Pisa's
fine bronze door
panel (1185)

The cathedral at ↑
Monreale, a triumph of
Norman architecture

③

SIRACUSA

🅰 G2 🚆🚌⛴ 🛈 Via della Maestranza 33, Ortygia;
www.comune.siracusa.it

For three centuries, from around 500 BC, Siracusa was the most powerful city in the Mediterranean, birthplace of Archimedes and home to Plato and Sappho. The city's history, from prehistoric populations through to the introduction of Baroque architecture, is still clearly visible. This bustling city is home to Greek and Roman amphitheatres, the archaeological museum and the Roman catacombs.

The Neapolis Archaeological Zone

🅰 Greek Theatre and Neapolis Archaeological Zone: Via del Teatro Greco 🕐 By appt only; times vary, check website 🔗 aditusculture.com

The Neapolis Archaeological Zone was established in 1955 with the aim of grouping the antiquities of Siracusa within one site.

Roman Amphitheatre and Altar of Hieron II

Built during the early years of the Roman Empire, the amphitheatre, with an outer diameter of 140 by 119 m (459 by 390 ft), is only slightly smaller than the Arena in Verona (p108). Beneath the tiers were corridors through which the gladiators and wild beasts entered the arena.

Beyond are the massive foundations of the Altar of Hieron II. Dedicated to Zeus, it was used for public sacrifices in which as many as 400 bulls were put to death at one time.

The Greek Theatre

Built in the 5th century BC, this is one of the most important examples of ancient theatre architecture anywhere. From May to July, the theatre still hosts an annual festival of Greek drama.

Latomie

A huge hollow separates the theatre area and the southern section of the site. This is the area of the Latomie – stone quarries – from which the architects of ancient Siracusa extracted millions of cubic metres of stone for building. The enormous caves carved out by the quarries were used as prisons. The Ear of Dionysius (Orecchio di Dioniso) is one of the most impressive. The artist Caravaggio – who had himself recently escaped from prison in Malta – reputedly coined the cave's nickname when taken to see the quarries here.

← Demeter and seated Kore statue, Museo Archeologico Regionale

← View from the top of the vast Greek Amphitheatre of Siracusa

Greek colonies of Sicily's southeast. Highlights include reconstructions of ancient Greek temples, the fossilized skeletons of two indigenous Sicilian dwarf elephants and various sculptures, including the *Venus Landolina*, a Roman copy of a Greek statue showing Venus emerging from the sea.

↑ Church above the Catacombs of San Giovanni Evangelista

Museo Archeologico Regionale Paolo Orsi

🅰 Via Teocrito 66 🕙 By appt only; 9am–7pm Tue–Sat, 9am–2pm Sun & pub hols 🆆 aditusculture.com

Sicily's finest archaeological collection is a fabulous showcase of antiquities from Greek and Roman Siracusa, Megara Hyblaea, Thapsos and the

Catacombs of San Giovanni Evangelista

🅰 Via San Giovanni alle Catacombe 🕻 0931 64 694 🕙 9:30am–12:30pm, 2:30–5:30pm daily (winter: to 4:30pm)

This underground complex, dating to the 4th century AD, housed hundreds of *loculi*, or rooms, used to bury the followers of the new Christian religion during Roman times. The main gallery of the catacombs leads to a series of chapels.

Castello Eurialo

🅰 Piazza Eurialo 1, Belvedere, 8 km (5 miles) from Siracusa 🕻 0931 71 17 73 🕙 9am–12:30pm daily

Standing on a hill overlooking the city, this castle is an impressive work of ancient Greek military architecture. It was built by Dionysius the Elder in 402 BC to defend Siracusa against attack. The fortress was protected by two rock-cut moats, a tower and a keep.

↑ The Piazza del Duomo and Duomo illuminated in the evening

ORTYGIA

 G2   *i* Via della Maestranza 33; www.comune.siracusa.it

Traces of Siracusa's glorious past are everywhere in its historic centre, Ortygia, an offshore island where Baroque buildings of mellow golden sandstone twist and turn along a labyrinth of narrow medieval streets lined with pavement cafés, restaurants and stylish little shops. Intersperse sightseeing with lunch in the market, take a swim in one of the miniature lidos along Lungomare Levante, or enjoy a predinner drink while watching the sun set over the Porto Grande.

①
Duomo

⌂ Piazza del Duomo 5
☏ 0931 65 328 ⊙ 7:15am–7:30pm daily ⊗ For Mass

Siracusa's Duomo is an ancient Greek temple that was converted into a church sometime during the 6th century. Twelve of the Doric temple's fluted columns are embedded in the Duomo's battlemented Norman wall, while inside, the nave was formed by hacking eight arches in the cellar walls. The Norman façade was destroyed in the earthquake of 1693 and replaced with the flamboyant Baroque edifice that now dominates the piazza.

②
Piazza del Duomo

Piazza Duomo is Sicily's most magnificent piazza, an immense theatrical space free of traffic, except for the occasional wedding car. It is gorgeous at any time of day, but perhaps most magical at night when its pavement gleams like silk and the Baroque façades that surround it are illuminated.

③
Santa Lucia alla Badia

⌂ Via Santa Lucia alla Badia 2 ⊙ 11am–4pm Tue–Sun

The façade of Santa Lucia alla Badia, with its barley-sugar twist columns and intricate stonework, is one of Ortygia's prettiest. The church houses one of Siracusa's most prized works of art, *The Burial of Santa Lucia* by Caravaggio (removed for restoration at the time of going to press). The canvas was not designed for this church but for the Church of Santa Lucia across in the Borgata, the location of the saint's martyrdom. Bathed in sunlight, dwarfed by stark, bare plaster walls, two gravediggers brace themselves to lower the corpse of the saint into her tomb, watched by a bishop and a group of mourners.

④
Temple of Apollo

⌂ Largo XXV Luglio

The ruins of the oldest temple in Magna Graecia were discovered in 1860 inside an old Spanish barracks. Built in the early 6th century BC,

EAT

Fratelli Burgio

Siracusa's best delicatessen has a simple outdoor restaurant among the bustle of the market, where guests can feast on platters of gourmet cheeses, hams and salamis sourced from all over Italy, along with their own cured olives, *caponata*, sun-dried tomatoes and other delectable conserves.

🏠 Piazza Cesare Battisti 4 🕐 Sun
🌐 fratelliburgio.com

€€€

the temple is huge and over the centuries has served as a Byzantine church, a mosque and a military stronghold. Visiting in the 18th century, the French writer Vivant Denon reported finding one of the columns embedded in the wall of a bedroom of a house on the adjacent Via Resalibera. To make more room, the owner had hacked away part of the stone.

⑤
Fonte Aretusa

🏠 Largo Aretusa

Surrounded by papyrus plants and inhabited by a colony of ducks and bream, this fountain is fed by a freshwater spring that bubbles up under the

SWIMMING SPOTS IN ORTYGIA

The most popular place to swim in Ortygia is the big rock at Forte Vigliena (commonly known as "Lo Scoglio", or "the rock") – during the summer the local council "extends" it by erecting a platform. There is also a small beach at Cala Rossa (the foot of Via Roma). There are two lidos in Ortygia, one on the Lungomare Levante (at the foot of Via Maestranze), the other below the Fonte Aretusa.

sea. It is the origin of the myth of the nymph Arethusa, who escaped the advances of the river god Alpheios by turning into the spring, which disappeared beneath the Ionian sea and re-emerged here.

⑥
Palazzo Bellomo: Galleria d'Arte Regionale

🏠 Via Capodieci 14-16
📞 0931 69511 🕐 9am-7pm Tue-Sat, 9am-1pm Sun & pub hols

Palazzo Bellomo is a sprawling 13th-century building, whose austere façade dates from a time when Sicily was part of the Holy Roman Empire. The palace now houses a regional art museum. A highlight of the collection is Antonello da Messina's *Annunciation*, painted for a church in Palazzolo Acreide, with the Hyblaean mountains visible through the windows behind the angel.

Well-preserved ruins of the 5th century BC Temple of Concordia ↑

5

VALLEY OF THE TEMPLES

F2 **Agrigento** **Ruins: 8:30am–8pm daily; Museo Archeologico: 9am–7:30pm daily**
parcodeitempli.net

Straddling a low ridge to the south of Agrigento, the Valley of the Temples (Valle dei Templi) is one of the most impressive complexes of ancient Greek buildings outside Greece and a prime example of the magnificence of Magna Graecia.

The Valley of the Temples was once at the heart of the ancient city of Akragas. Founded in 581 BC by colonists from Gela, Akragas was one of Sicily's richest and most powerful cities – visitors reported that its citizens had ivory furniture, abundant silver and gold, and even made elaborate tombs for their pets. The city was well known for breeding horses, which consistently won in the Olympic Games. After being besieged by the Carthaginians in 406 BC, Akragas was taken by the Romans in 261 BC, renamed Agrigentum, and remained in Roman control until the fall of the Empire. Today, you can explore the ruins of nine major temples, a series of minor shrines and an archaeology museum nearby, at Contrada San Nicola.

Must See

Museo Archeologico Pietro Griffo

◀ The archaeological museum has objects ranging from prehistoric times to the early Christian period, but the emphasis is on Greek and Roman finds such as vases, statues and sarcophagi. There is also a Telamon (pillar in the form of a male statue) from the Temple of Olympian Zeus.

Temple of Olympian Zeus

Only fragmentary ruins remain of this 5th-century-BC temple – the largest Doric temple ever built. It was once supported by 38 giant Telamons, one of which is now on display in the Museo Archeologico.

Temple of Concordia

This is one of the world's best-preserved Doric temples. After becoming a Christian basilica in the 4th century, it was restored to its original Classical form in 1748.

Temple of Hera

▶ Relatively well-preserved, this 5th-century-BC temple was restored in Roman times. There are 25 of the original 34 columns still standing. Steps lead up to an altar where animals were sacrificed to the goddess Hera, known by the Romans as Juno.

Temple of Heracles

◀ These eight columns belonged to the oldest temple dedicated to Heracles, worshipped by both the Greeks and the Romans (as Hercules). The archaic 6th-century-BC Doric structure has an elongated rectangular plan.

EKKLESIASTERION

In ancient Greece, the *ekklesiasterion* was the meeting place of the *ekklesia* (popular assembly) in a democratic city-state. In Agrigento, one is located next to Museo Archeologico. The building would have originally been circular. The section of the *cavea* that remains is semi-circular in shape with extended ends and 19 concentric rows of steps on a slope to the south. Next to it, set on a podium, is a temple – the Oratory of Phalaris.

Temple of Castor and Pollux

▶ This temple's four surviving columns, a symbol of the Valley of the Temples, were restored in the 19th century.

Kolymbetra

From the Greek for "pool", this sunken garden with a stream running through it formed part of the city's irrigation system.

EXPERIENCE MORE

6

Trapani

E1 🚩FS🚌⛴ *i*Piazza Umberto I 15; www.distretto siciliaoccidentale.it

Old Trapani occupies a narrow peninsula. The best buildings in this lively quarter are the Cathedral of San Lorenzo (1635) and the Chiesa del Collegio dei Gesuiti (c 1614–40). The façades of both churches reflect the ebullience of west Sicilian Baroque architecture.

The 17th-century Purgatorio on Via San Francesco d'Assisi contains 18th-century *Misteri* – realistic, life-sized wooden statues used in the annual Good Friday procession. Santa Maria del Gesù on Via Sant'Elisabetta houses the *Madonna col Bambino* by Andrea della Robbia (1435–1525) and Antonello Gagini's marble baldachin (1521).

The **Museo Agostino Pepoli** displays local antiquities such as coral objects and Christmas crib figures (*presepi*). Next to the museum, the Santuario di Maria Santissima Annunziata contains the *Madonna di Trapani*, a statue revered by fishermen and sailors for its legendary miraculous powers.

Museo Agostino Pepoli

⊛ ⬛Via Conte Agostino Pepoli 180 📞0923 55 32 69 🕒9am–5:30pm Tue–Sun

7

San Vito Lo Capo

E1 ⬛Trapani 🚌 🌐sanvitolocapoweb.co.uk

A popular holiday resort set on the magnificent Golfo di Castellammare, San Vito Lo Capo is a lively place with one of the finest sandy beaches in Sicily. The focus of life is pedestrianized Via Savoia,

lined with shops and restaurants and the main scene of the evening *passeggiata*. Another highlight is the promenade backing the sweeping crescent of white sand that stretches east of town. A 10-minute walk beyond the harbour is a lighthouse perched on a windswept cape. Beyond there are great views across the entire gulf from the cliffs, although in hot weather you may prefer to take in the coast from one of the many boat trips operating from the harbour.

Just 12 km (7 miles) south of San Vito, the **Zingaro Nature Reserve** is a pristine 7-km (4-mile) stretch of coastline with tiny white pebble bays backed by steep mountains. Home to the rare Bonelli's eagle and some 600 species of plant, it is a fantastic place for a day's hiking. There are two main paths, the upper Sentiero Alto and the lower Sentiero Basso, which keeps close to the shore, with access to little coves. There are no shops or facilities here, so bring food and plenty of water.

Zingaro Nature Reserve

⊛ 🕒 ⬛ San Vito Lo Capo 🚌From Castellammare del Golfo 🌐lnx.riservazingaro.it

↑ Coastline of the Zingaro Nature Reserve

ZINGARO RESERVE DIVES

TOP 3

Capua Wreck, Coast of Scopello

F1

During WWII, a British cargo ship carrying arms for Italian troops sank. Mysteries still linger, making this 38-m (125-ft) dive extra intriguing.

Grotta dell'Acqua Dolce, Uzzo Bay

E1

For more experienced divers, this 60-m- (197-ft-) deep chamber of glassy, fresh water is alive with marine life.

Grotta del Camino, Park Entrance

F1

The cave has two accesses: one at 18 m (59 ft) and the other at 35 m (115 ft). A rock wall partitions the cavity, home to a troupe of fascinating red- and white-striped shrimp.

⑧ Erice

ⒶE1 **Ⓠ**Trapani
𝒊 Via Castello di Venere;
www.prolocoerice.it

Poised on a crag overlooking Trapani, the town of Erice was once the seat of the cult of the fertility goddess Venus Erycina. Her temple stood on the present site of the Norman castle (Castello di Venere), beyond the public gardens. On a clear day, you can see all the way to Tunisia from the castle. The ancient town of Eryx was renamed Gebel-Hamed by the Arabs, Monte San Giuliano by the Normans and, finally, Erice in 1934 by Mussolini.

The Duomo (14th century) has a battlemented campanile and a 15th-century porch. Inside is a *Madonna and Child* (c 1469), attributed to either Francesco Laurana or Domenico Gagini. The view from outside the decon-secrated 13th-century church of San Giovanni Battista on Via San Giovanni is a good place to enjoy the fabulous views across central Sicily. In the **Polo Museale A Cordici** is Antonello Gagini's *Annunciation* (1525).

Polo Museale A Cordici
Ⓐ Vico San Rocco 1
☎ 388 097 2089
🕑 10am-6:30pm daily

⑨ Marsala

ⒶE2 **Ⓠ**Trapani 🚆🚌🚢
𝒊 Via XI Maggio 100;
www.turismocomune
marsala.com

The port of Marsala is the home of a strong, sweet wine that has been in production here since the 18th century. **Cantine Florio** offers popular guided tours of the wine cellars, followed by a tasting. Be sure to book in advance.

A former wine warehouse is now the **Museo Archeologico Baglio Anselmi**, housing Phoenician artifacts.

The ruins of Lilybaeum are another attraction. Founded in 397 BC, this outpost of the Phoenician Empire was peopled by the survivors of the massacre by Dionysius I of Siracusa at Mozia (ancient Motya). Best of all are the reconstructed remains of a Punic ship thought to have been active in the First Punic War (263–241 BC). The **Museo Whitaker**, on the tiny island of Mozia, contains a remarkable early 5th-century-BC statue of a Greek youth.

The Duomo, begun in the 17th century, is full of sculptural works by members of the Gagini family.

Cantine Florio
♿🚭 **Ⓐ** Via Florio 1
🕑 Apr-Oct **ⓦ** duca.it/florio

Museo Archeologico Baglio Anselmi
♿ **Ⓐ** Lungomare Boeo 30
☎ 0923 95 25 35 **🕑** 9am-6:30pm Tue-Sat (to 1:30pm Sun)

Museo Whitaker
♿ **Ⓐ** Isola di Mozia (San Pantaleo) **🕑** 10am-2pm daily **ⓦ** museodimozia.it

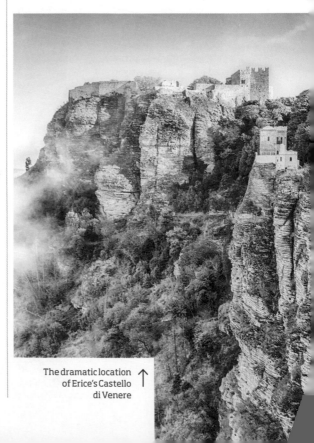

The dramatic location of Erice's Castello di Venere ↑

SICILIAN ISLANDS

From the dramatic volcanic islands of the Aeolian archipelago to the divers' paradise of Ustica, each of the minor islands surrounding Sicily has its own distinctive character. The best times to visit are spring and autumn, when you can experience island life without the summer hordes, yet with warm seas, balmy evenings and hotels, bars and restaurants still open.

Aeolian Islands

Climb Stromboli and see it erupting at night, take a boat trip around the islets off Panarea, or wallow in the sulphurous mudbaths of Vulcano. You can follow the old mule tracks of Filicudi, or laze on the beach at Alicudi, where donkeys are the only form of transport.

Ustica

Dive or snorkel in Ustica's pristine waters, protected by a marine reserve, or follow the coastal footpath that circles the entire island. In the evening, sample local fish and locally grown lentils in one of the port's trattorias.

Egadi Islands

Cycle Favignana's network of unpaved roads, stopping for swims at Cala Azzurra and Cala Rossa. Take a boat trip to see prehistoric cave engravings on the island of Levanzo, or hike the solitary paths of spectacular Marettimo.

Pantelleria

Swim in the volcanic lake known as Specchio di Venere, and discover the rocky bays and hot springs along the coast. Follow the walking trail from the crumbling village of Siba to a natural outdoor sauna, or sample local dessert wines in the island's vineyards.

Pelagie Islands

Laze on the gorgeous sandy beach of the Isola dei Conigli, off Lampedusa, or opt for the brightly coloured houses, little black beaches and silence of remote Linosa.

1 Dramatic eruption of the Stromboli volcano.

2 Diving amid shoals of fish in the waters around Ustica.

3 The marina at Favignana.

4 Picking grapes in Pantelleria for the island's sweet wine.

5 Craggy Isola dei Conigli.

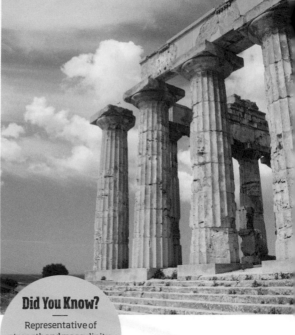

→ Monumental Doric columns at a Greek temple in Selinunte

 10

Segesta

AF1 **A**Trapani **From Trapani & Palermo** **By appt only; 9am-7:30pm daily (Mar & Oct: to 6:30pm; Nov-Feb: to 5pm)** **W**parco disegesta.com; youline.eu/laculturariparte.html

According to legend, the town of Segesta – still largely unexcavated – was founded by Trojan followers of Aeneas. It presents one of the island's most spectacular sights: a massive unfinished temple on a remote hillside. Its construction started between 426 and 416 BC, and it was left incomplete after the devastation of Selinunte by the Carthaginians in 409 BC. Nearby, close to the summit of Monte Barbaro, the ruins of a theatre (3rd century BC) can be visited. Summer concerts are held here.

 11

Selinunte

AF2 **A**Trapani **Castelvetrano then bus** **9am-8pm daily** **W**selinunte.gov.it

Founded in 651 BC, Selinunte became one of the great cities of Magna Graecia – the part of southern Italy that was colonized by ancient Greece – and its toppled ruins are among Sicily's most important historic sites. Its ancient name, Selinus, comes from the wild celery that still grows here. The city was an important port, and its wall defences can still be seen around the Acropolis. The Carthaginians, under Hannibal, destroyed the city in 409 BC in a battle famous for its epic and savage proportions.

While the city itself has virtually disappeared, eight of its temples (each named after a letter of the alphabet) are distinguishable, particularly the so-called Eastern Temples (E, F and G). Of these, the columns of huge Doric Temple E (490–480 BC) have been partially re-erected. Temple F (c 560–540 BC) is in ruins. Temple G (late 6th century BC), which had 17 massive side columns, was one of the greatest Greek temples ever built.

Higher on the Acropolis lie the remains of Temples A, B, C, D and O. Metope sculptures from Temple C (early 6th century), originally located on the frieze between the triglyphs, can be seen in the Museo Archeologico Regionale in Palermo (p507), along with other artifacts excavated here. A small museum on site houses less important finds, as does one in Castelvetrano, 14 km (9 miles) north of Selinunte. The city is still being excavated; its North Gate entrance is well preserved, and further north there is also a necropolis.

> ## Did You Know?
> ——
> Representative of strength and masculinity, Doric columns were thicker than both Corinthian and Ionic columns.

12

Cefalù

AF1 **A**Palermo **** **Corso Ruggero 139; www.visitcefalu.com**

This pretty seaside town is dominated by a huge rock known as La Rocca – once the site of a Temple of Diana – and by one of the finest Norman cathedrals in Sicily. Begun in 1131 by Roger II, the Duomo was intended as the main religious seat in Sicily. Though it failed to fulfil this function, the building's magnificence has never been eclipsed. Its splendid mosaics (1148), which feature an image of Christ Pantocrator in the apse, are remarkable and often celebrated as purely Byzantine works of art on Sicilian soil.

The **Museo Mandralisca** houses a fine *Portrait of a Man* (c 1465) by Antonello da Messina and a collection of coins, ceramics, vases and minerals.

Museo Mandralisca
Via Mandralisca 21 **9am-7pm daily (Jul & Aug: to 11pm)** **W**fondazione mandralisca.it

Girls in bikinis mosaic at the Villa Romana del Casale

⑬ Agrigento

🚗F2 🚉🚌🚌 𝒊 Via Empedocle 73 & Piazzale Aldo Moro; www.living agrigento.it

Modern Agrigento occupies the site of Akragas, an important city of the ancient Greek world. Founded by Daedalus, according to legend, it was famed for the luxurious lifestyle of its inhabitants, and was a great power and rival to Siracusa. In 406 BC it fell to the Carthaginians, who sacked and burned it.

The historic core of the city, with its medieval streets, focuses on the Via Atenea. Santo Spirito (13th century) houses stuccoes by Giacomo Serpotta (1695). Santa Maria dei Greci was built on the remains of a 5th-century-BC temple – see the flattened columns in the nave. The Duomo, founded in the 14th century and altered in the 16th and 17th centuries, exhibits a unique mixture of Arab, Norman and Catalan detailing.

The chief reason to visit Agrigento is to see the archaeological zone known as the Valley of the Temples (p514). The **Museo Regionale Archeologico Pietro Griffo** houses an interesting display of artifacts from the temples and the city, including a collection of vases, coins and Greek and Roman sculpture.

Museo Regionale Archeologico Pietro Griffo

⊗ 🏛 Contrada San Nicola 🕘 9am–7:30pm daily 🌐 parcovalledeitempli.it

⑭ Piazza Armerina

🚗F2 🚉Enna 🚌 𝒊 Via Gen.le Muscarà; www.piazzaarmerina.org

This active town is half medieval and half Baroque. The 17th-century Duomo, at its highest point, is the most interesting of the Baroque buildings.

↑ Greek vase in the Museo Regionale Archeologico in Agrigento

---

⛰ GREAT VIEW
Scala dei Turchi

Named one of the Seven Wonders of Italy, these white marl cliffs are the result of centuries of erosion. Folklore tells of marauding Saracens and the healing powers of the staircase's marl – a chalk-like mixture of mud and silt.

In August, the lively Palio dei Normanni festival attracts many visitors, but the star sights are the mosaics in the UNESCO-listed **Villa Romana del Casale**, 5 km (3 miles) southwest of the town.

It is thought that this huge villa, with its public halls, private quarters, baths and courtyards, once belonged to Maximianus Herculeus, Diocletian's co-emperor, from AD 286 to 305. His son and successor, Maxentius, probably carried on its decoration, with Constantine taking over on Maxentius's death in 312.

Although little remains of the building fabric, the floors have some of the finest

→

Impressive white cliffs of the Scala dei Turchi, near Agrigento surviving mosaics from Roman antiquity. Highlights include a circus scene showing a chariot race, ten female athletes dressed in bikinis and a 60-m- (197-ft-) long hunting scene featuring tigers, ostriches, elephants and a rhino being trapped and transported to games at the Colosseum.

Villa Romana del Casale

♿ 🏠 Contrada Casale ⏰ By appt only; 9am–11pm daily (Nov–Mar: to 5pm) 🌐 villa romanadelcasale.it; youline. eu/laculturariparte.html

---

Enna

🅰 F2 🚉🚌 ℹ Via Roma 413; www.provincia.enna.it

Impregnable on a crag above a fertile landscape where Persephone, mythological daughter of Demeter, once played, Sicily's highest town (942 m/3,090 ft) has always been coveted by successive invaders. The seat of the Cult of Demeter (goddess of fertility) was at Enna. Her temple stood on the Rocca Cerere, not far from the huge Castello di Lombardia (13th century) built by Frederick II.

Most sights are clustered in the old town, among the ancient streets that open out of the Via Roma. The church of San Francesco has a 16th-century tower. Piazza Crispi offers stunning views of the mountains of the Madonie and Nebrodi, and Mount Etna. The 14th-century Duomo, altered in later centuries, contains parts of Demeter's temple, an arch of which is still visible in the exterior of the apse. Its façade is rich in Gothic decorations. Inside, don't miss the original wooden ceiling.

The **Museo Archeologico di Palazzo Varisano** has exhibits on the area's history, from the Neolithic to Roman periods. Standing outside the centre, the octagonal Torre di Federico II (13th century) is a former watchtower.

The ancient hill-town of Nicosia, northeast of Enna,

> **Founded by Daedalus, according to legend, Agrigento was famed for the luxurious lifestyle of its inhabitants, and was a great power and rival to Siracusa.**

was damaged in the 1967 earthquake, but still contains a smattering of churches. San Nicolò, built in the 14th century, has a magnificent, carved entrance portal. Inside there is a much-venerated wooden crucifix (17th century) by Fra Umile di Petralia. Santa Maria Maggiore houses a 16th-century marble polyptych by Antonello Gagini and a throne reputedly used by Charles V in 1535. Further east is Troina, with the Norman Cathedral of Maria Santissima Assunta.

Museo Archeologico di Palazzo Varisano

♿ 🏠 Piazza Mazzini 8 📞 0935 50 76 304 ⏰ 9am–7pm daily

Did You Know?

Many scenes from the three *Godfather* movies were filmed in the hill-towns of Savoca and Forza d'Agrò.

16
Messina

🅰 G1 FS 🚌🚃 ℹ️ Via Consolato del Mare; www. turismoecultura.citta metropolitana.me.it

Messina has been the victim of earthquakes and World War II bombing. The **Museo Regionale** houses treasures including works by Antonello da Messina and Caravaggio.

The cathedral's bell tower on Piazza Duomo features a large astronomical clock, with mechanically animated statues illustrating events from the city's history every day at noon.

In front of the cathedral, G A Montorsoli's Fontana di Orione (1547) is the finest fountain of its kind from 16th-century Sicily. His Fontana di Nettuno (1557), on Via Garibaldi, celebrates Messina's foundation and status as a principal commercial port.

Museo Regionale
👁 ♿ 🏛 Viale della Libertà 465 📞 090 36 12 92/93 🕐 9:30am–7:45pm Tue–Fri (to 3pm Sat, to 2pm Sun)

17
Taormina

🅰 G2 🚉 Messina FS 🚌 ℹ️ Palazzo Corvaja; 0942 232 43

Splendidly situated, Taormina is Sicily's best-known resort. It retains an air of exclusivity while being on the tourist trail, with sandy beaches and a wide range of restaurants and hotels.

The most illustrious relic of the past is the theatre. Begun in the 3rd century BC by the Greeks, it was subsequently rebuilt by the Romans. Among other Classical remains are the ruins of the odeon (for musical performances) and the *naumachia* (an artificial lake for mock-battles). On Piazza Vittorio Emanuele II (site of the Roman Forum), Palazzo Corvaja (14th century) was built using stone from a temple that once stood here. The 13th-century Duomo (renovated in 1636) is a fortress-like building.

Taormina's main beach, Mazzarò, boasts crystal-clear waters and is easily reached from the town by cable car. South of Taormina at Capo Schisò are the ruins of ancient Naxos. To the west is the Gole dell'Alcantara, a 20-m- (66-ft-) deep gorge of basalt rock, a river and waterfalls.

18
Mount Etna

🅰 G2 🚉 Catania FS Linguaglossa or Randazzo; Circumetnea railway from Catania to Riposto 🚌 To Nicolosi ℹ️ Via del Convento 45, Nicolosi; www.parco etna.it 🖥 etnaguide.eu (to hire a guide)

At 3,320 m (10,822 ft), Mount Etna is Europe's highest and most active volcano. It was thought by the Romans to have been the forge of Vulcan, the god of fire. The climb to the summit should be tackled only with an experienced guide. The Circumetnea railway runs around the base of the volcano, offering a good alternative to hiking and fantastic views.

The city of Messina and the cathedral bell tower ↓

← The desert-like landscape on Mount Etna, the most active volcano in Europe

19

Pantalica

 G2 🚉**Siracusa** 🚌**From Siracusa to Sortino, then 5-km (3-mile) walk to entrance (partial access), or bus from Siracusa to Ferla, then 10-km (6-mile) walk to entrance** ℹ️ **Via Gramsci 13, Ferla** 🌐**comune.ferla.sr.it**

In the desolate Monti Iblei, the vast prehistoric necropolis of Pantalica is a pleasant place to walk and picnic. Those wishing to explore should contact the tourist council for a list of licensed guides. The dead of a large, unexcavated village (occupied from the 13th to 8th centuries BC) were buried here in cave-like tombs cut into the rock. More than 5,000 of these tombs were arranged in tiers with a single flat stone sealing each opening.

The inhabitants of Pantalica are thought to have come from coastal Thapsos, which was abandoned after raids by tribes from mainland Italy. The site was re-inhabited during the Byzantine period, when some of the tombs were made into cave dwellings. Artifacts from the necropolis are in Siracusa's Museo Archeologico Regionale Paolo Orsi (*p511*).

20

Catania

G2 🚆🚌 ℹ️ **Via Etnea 63/65; www.citta metropolitana.ct.it**

Mount Etna looms high over Catania. A volcanic eruption in 1693 completely destroyed the city, and its centre was entirely reconstructed from Etna lava – even the streets and piazzas are paved with lava. The 18th-century rebuilding created imposing Baroque edifices, set on broad, straight streets and unevenly shaped squares, a precaution for earthquakes. Today it is a big, bustling city, with a compact historic centre.

Via Etnea slices through Catania, with Etna rising at one end. At the other end stands Piazza Duomo, a large pedestrianized space with a lava monument of an elephant (Catania's emblem) in its centre. Black lava buildings trimmed with white limestone dominate: the Duomo's façade incorporates columns filched from the city's Roman amphitheatre (still visible 500 m/500 yd away on Piazza Stesicoro), while inside is the elaborately decorated chapel of the city's patron saint, Agatha, whose statue and relics are paraded through the city during the Festa di Sant'Agata (3–5 February). At the far end of the piazza, steps lead down to the Pescheria, where Catania's exuberant morning fish, fruit and vegetable market is held.

From Piazza dei Duomo, bus line 2–5 goes to the train station, beyond which, in the former sulphur works of Le Ciminiere, is a superb arts complex. Also here is the Museo dello Sbarco in Sicilia 1943, housing a modern, moving exhibition that documents the Allied landings of World War II.

↑ Market stalls in front of a Baroque church in Catania

Scicli

 Ragusa
 Via Francesco Mormino
Penna; www.proloco
scicli.it

Many of Scicli's exuberant
churches and palaces appear
in the *Inspector Montalbano* TV
series. Fans of the programme
can visit the Municipio, or town
hall (filmed as Montalbano's
police station). The church
of San Bartolomeo has a
Baroque façade framed by a
backdrop of limestone crags.
Other must sees are Palazzo
Beneventano, its balconies
supported by snarling Baroque
monsters, and the church of
San Giovanni. The latter is
home to the *Cristo di Burgos*,
a 17th-century Spanish
portrait of Christ wearing
what appears to be a dirndl
skirt (it is, in fact, his shroud).

Sampieri

G2 Ragusa

Sampieri is a diminutive
summer resort at the head
of a 3-km (2-mile) sweep of
fine sandy dunes. Unlike many
coastal villages, it retains a
grid of simple, cubic fishermen's houses built of the
same vanilla-hued limestone
as the cobbles of its narrow
streets. There are two lidos
and, in the summer, Sampieri
beach becomes a nightclub
that goes on until dawn.

BAROQUE TOWNS OF THE VAL DI NOTO

In 1693 a devastating earthquake destroyed the entire
southeast corner of Sicily. At the time, Sicily was under
the rule of the Spanish Bourbons, and the architecture
favoured was flamboyant, bold and extravagant. Many
of the towns were rebuilt in this style and, as a result,
this beautiful region of dramatic limestone gorges,
flower-filled meadows and long sandy beaches is
peppered with glorious Baroque towns. Now designated
World Heritage Sites by UNESCO, Noto, Ragusa, Modica
and Scicli are the most famous, but there are also some
wonderful smaller towns to discover, such as Ispica,
Chiaramonte Gulfi and Militello Val di Catania.

Ragusa

G2 Piazza
Repubblica, Ragusa Ibla;
www.comune.ragusa.gov.it

A UNESCO World Heritage Site,
Ragusa is divided into two by
a dramatic gorge. Ibla, the
original settlement on a rocky
crest, was rebuilt in Baroque
style after the 1693 earthquake
but retains its medieval street
plan. The upper town, Ragusa
Superiore, was founded on
the plain above the gorge
after the earthquake.
  In Ibla, the three-tiered
Baroque façade of the Duomo
di San Giorgio, designed by
Rosario Gagliardi, stands atop
a voluptuous flight of steps.
On Via Orfanotrofio, to the
left of San Giuseppe, is the
exquisite church of San
Francesco all'Immacolata,
which incorporates the Gothic
portal of Palazzo Chiaramonte,
a nobleman's palace destroyed
in the earthquake. From here

zigzag back through Ibla to the
church of Santa Maria della
Scala, which presides over the
steps linking Ibla with Ragusa
Superiore. The main target in
the newer town is the **Museo
Archeologico Ibleo**, which has
a collection of prehistoric,
Greek and Roman artifacts
unearthed in the region.

Museo Archeologico Ibleo
  Via Natalelli 11 0932
62 29 63 Times vary, call
ahead to check

Modica

G2 Ragusa
 Corso Umberto I 141;
346 65 58 227

The historic centre of
Modica – a town famous for
its chocolate – spills down the
opposing slopes of a ravine.
Sweeping between the ornate
façades of Baroque palazzi,
Corso Umberto is the focus of
local life, full of restaurants,
shops, delicatessens and cafés.
  If you want to find out about
Modica's chocolate, which is
made to an Aztec recipe
brought to Sicily by Spanish
conquistadores, head to the
historic chocolatier Bonajuto.
It offers free tastings, but

←

Ragusa Ibla, the town's
original core, situated on
a rocky crag

EAT

Locanda Don Serafino

Set in a cave-cum-wine cellar in Ragusa, this restaurant offers traditional dishes.

 G2 Via Avv. Giovanni Ottaviano 13, Ragusa Ibla locanda donserafino.it

€€€

Ristorante Duomo

One of the best restaurants in Ragusa, if not Sicily. The menu here is tirelessly innovative.

 G2 Via Capitano Bocchieri 31, Ragusa Ibla cicciosultano.it

€€€

I Banchi

This Ragusa restaurant, café and deli is perfect for lunch.

 G2 Via Orfanotrofio 39, Ragusa Ibla ibanchiragusa.it

€€€

Trattoria la Bettola

Try the braised pork at this family-run trattoria in Ragusa.

 G2 Largo Camerina, Ragusa Ibla trattoria labettola.it

€€€

---

it's also worth trying a hot chocolate spiked with chilli, or even a savoury meat-and-chocolate pastry (*mpanatigghi*) at the Caffè dell'Arte.

The real pleasure of Modica lies in exploring the steep labyrinth of streets on either side of the ravine, while the architectural jewel of the town is the Duomo di San Giorgio, spectacularly sited at the head of a theatrical 250-step Baroque stairway.

Modica once had more churches per square metre than anywhere else in the world. Many still remain – from San Pietro in Modica Bassa (Lower Modica) to San Giorgio, halfway up the hill, and San Giovanni in Modica Alta (Upper Modica).

25
Noto

G2 Siracusa FS 🚌 Corso Vittorio Emanuele 135; www.comune.noto.sr.it

All that was left of Noto following the 1693 earthquake was "a mountain of abandoned rocks", according to Giuseppe Lanza, who was given the job of rebuilding it. He decided to create a new town from scratch, 16 km (10 miles) away, and the people of Noto were

---

↑ Modica's church of San Pietro, a splendid example of Sicilian Baroque

furious – they had begun to rebuild the old town (Noto Antica) among the ruins. Rebuilt in Baroque style out of apricot-hued limestone, the new Noto was revolutionary, divided into an upper town for the people, and a monumental lower town, its broad avenues lined with political and religious buildings.

To see the best of the town, walk along the main street, Corso Vittorio Emanuele, passing through the imposing Porta Reale. On the left is the church of Santa Chiara, built on an unusual elliptical plan, and beyond, the theatrical central square, Piazza Municipio, where a magnificent flight of steps rises to the muscular Baroque Duomo, its interior flooded with light from the rebuilt dome. Opposite the Duomo is the elegant Palazzo Ducezio, Noto's town hall. Walk alongside the Duomo to Palazzo Trigona, with its curvaceous balconies, where steps lead up past more fine Baroque buildings to Noto Alta, the upper town, from where there are views of the surrounding countryside.

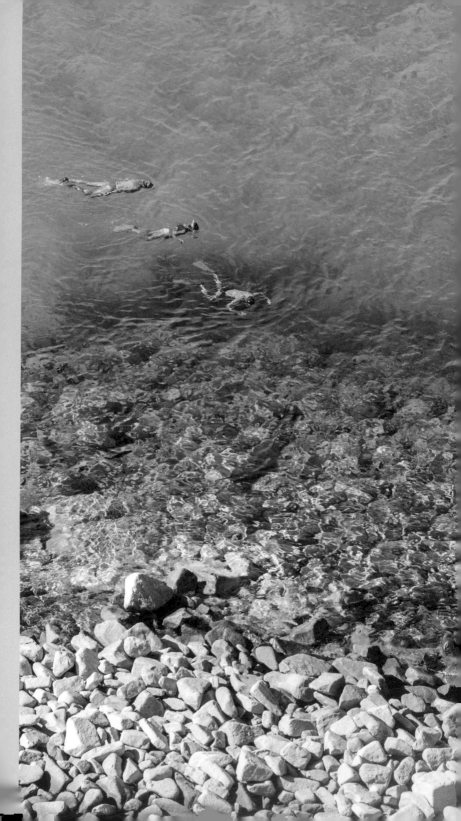

SARDINIA

In his travelogue *Sea and Sardinia*, D H Lawrence wrote that Sardinia was "left outside of time and history". Indeed, the march of time has been slow here, and traditions from ancient Europe have survived – the legacy of invasion by Phoenicians, Carthaginians, Romans, Arabs, Byzantines, Spaniards and Savoyards. These traditions are displayed in Sardinia's many festivals – some soberly Christian, others with pagan roots. Several different dialects and languages are spoken in Sardinia. Catalan can be heard in Alghero, and on the island of San Pietro there is a Ligurian dialect. In the south, the traditional influences are Spanish, while conservative native strains of people and language survive in the Gennargentu mountains. Peopled by shepherds in isolated communities, this region is so impenetrable that invaders have never bothered it.

Of particular interest are the prehistoric nuraghic castles, villages, temples and tombs dotted around the countryside – most notably around Barumini, north of Cagliari, and in the Valle dei Nuraghi, south of Sassari. The *nuraghi* were built by a people whose origins constitute one of the Mediterranean's great mysteries.

Sassari, Oristano, Alghero and Olbia are all centres of areas marked by their individuality. Some remarkable Pisan-Romanesque churches are located around Sassari and here, too, dialects reveal close links with the languages of Tuscany. Olbia is a boom town made rich by tourism and the proximity of the jet-setting Costa Smeralda. Sober Nuoro with its province in the shadow of the Gennargentu mountains, by contrast, offers dramatic scenery and a rich literary heritage.

Genoa,
Marseille, Barcelona ↑

Isola Asinara

Golfo
dell' Asinara

Fornelli

Stintino

Castelsardo

S200

Porto Torres

Sorso

Palmadula

La Nurra

S131

SASSARI 2

Osilo

Capo dell'
Argentiera

S291

Olmedo

Ploaghe

Alghero-
Fertilia

Mannu

Ardara

Grotta di
Nettuno

Ittiri

S131

3

Torralba

ALGHERO

S292

Valle dei
Nuraghe

Monteleone Rocca Doria

Montresta

Bonorva

Capo Marargiu

4 BOSA

S129b

Bosa Marina

Macomer

Mediterranean
Sea

Cuglieri

Monte Ferru
1050m

Ghilarza

Capo Mannu

S292

Riola Sardo

Fordongianus

Stagno di Cabras

Crabas

Simaxis

ORISTANO 7

Santa Giusta

Usellus

Arborea

S131

Ales

Capo della
Frasca

Terralba

Uras

S126

Pardu Atzei

Sardara

Campidano

Guspini

Capo Pecora

Villacidro

Monte Linas
1236m

Buggerru

Vallermosa

Masua

S126

Iglesias

S130

Siliqua

Gonnesa

Narcao

Portoscuso

Carbonia

Monte Caravius
1116m

Isola di
San Pietro

Calasetta

Santadi

Sant'Antioco

S195

Porto Botte

SANT'ANTIOCO 8

Golfo di
Palmas

Teulada

Capo Teulada

SARDINIA

Experience

1 The Maddalena Archipelago and
Costa Smeralda

2 Sassari

3 Alghero

4 Bosa

5 Nuoro

6 Cala Gonone

7 Oristano

8 Sant'Antioco

9 Cagliari

EXPERIENCE

❶ The Maddalena Archipelago and Costa Smeralda

 B5 Sassari Olbia Porto Cervo Via XX Settembre, La Maddalena & AAST Palau, Via Nazionale 94; www.comunela maddalena.gov.it

The islands of the Maddalena Archipelago have white sandy beaches and turquoise waters. Linked with Palau, on the mainland, by ferry, the only settlement of any size is La Maddalena, on the Isola Maddalena island. A causeway runs across the sea to the island of Caprera, the home and final resting place of revolutionary hero Giuseppe Garibaldi (1807–82). The **Compendio Garibaldino** is a small museum in his former home. The archipelago's smaller islands can be accessed only by boat.

Southeast of Palau, stretching from the Golfo di Arzachena to the Golfo di Cugnana, the Costa Smeralda was developed in the 1950s by a consortium of magnates headed by the Aga Khan. One of the world's most exclusive holiday playgrounds, it is kept immaculate by strict controls. Its boutiques, restaurants, clubs and luxury hotels cater for the seriously rich, like billionaires, crowned heads and pop stars.

Compendio Garibaldino
Isola Caprera 8:30am–2pm Tue–Sun compendio garibaldino.it

❷ Sassari

A5 *Palazzo di Città, Via Sebastiano Satta 13; www.turismosassari.it

Founded by Genoese and Pisan merchants in the 13th century, Sassari has a tight, church-filled medieval quarter around the Duomo (11th-century, with later additions). To the north is the huge Fontana del Rosello, a late Renaissance fountain. The **Museo Archeologico Nazionale G A Sanna** is a good starting point for investigating the region's nuraghic history.

To the southeast along the SS131 is the Pisan-Romanesque church of Santissima Trinità di Saccargia (1116), with the only extant 13th-century fresco cycle in Sardinia. Further on is the 12th-century church of San Michele di Salvenero, and at Ardara the basalt-built Romanesque Santa Maria del Regno, or "Black Cathedral".

↑ Pristine landscape and turquoise waters along the Costa Smeralda

Museo Archeologico Nazionale G A Sanna
Via Roma 64 079 27 22 03 For renovations

❸ Alghero

A5 Sassari Ex Casa del Caffè, Via Cagliari 2; www. algheroturismo.eu

Founded in the 12th century, and taken from the Genoese Dorias by the Aragonese in 1353, Alghero was peopled by settlers from Barcelona and Valencia. Its original occupants – Ligurians and Sardinians – were expelled with such thoroughness that today the Catalan language and culture is enjoying a revival and the look of the old town is consistently Spanish.

The lively port of old Alghero is flanked by battlemented walls and defensive towers. Facing the Giardino Pubblico is the massive 16th-century Torre Porta a Terra, also known as the Jewish Tower after its builders.

The 16th-century Duomo at the bottom of Via Umberto is predominantly Catalan-Gothic with an Aragonese portal. Off Via Carlo Alberto,

---

NURAGHI IN SARDINIA

There are 7,000 or so *nuraghi* dotted around Sardinia. Dating from 1800 to 300 BC, these truncated cone structures were built from huge basalt blocks without any bonding. Little is known about the identity of the nuraghic people. They must have possessed remarkable engineering skills, but appear to have left no written record.

San Francesco (14th century) has a pretty cloister and octagonal campanile towering over Alghero, and Baroque San Michele has a bright tiled dome. The **Museo del Corallo**, housed in an elegant Art Nouveau villa, tells the story of the town's relationship to the "red gold" of *Corallium rubrum*.

Take a boat trip to the spectacular Grotta di Nettuno, a deep natural cave round the point of Capo Caccia, or the nearby Grotta Verde.

Museo del Corallo
 Via XX Settembre 8 5:30–8pm Mon, Wed, Thu, Fri, Sat & Sun, 10:30am–1pm Tue, Thu, Sat & Sun museialghero.it

---

❹
Bosa

A5 Nuoro

Bosa is a small seaside town at the mouth of Sardinia's only navigable river, the Temo. The historic Sa Costa district struggles up the side of a low hill capped by the Castello di Serravalle, built in 1122 by the Malaspina family. The narrow passages and alleys here have changed little since the Middle Ages. By the Temo are Sa Costa, the former tanneries, dyers' houses and workshops.

Languishing on the riverside, the cosmopolitan Sa Piatta district houses the Baroque-Neo-Classical Duomo (19th century) and Romanesque San Pietro (11th century), with a Gothic façade added in the 13th century.

---

❺
Nuoro

B5 FS Piazza Mameli 1; www.provincia.nuoro.it

This town, in a spectacular setting beneath Monte Ortobene and the dramatic Supramonte, was the home of Grazia Deledda, who won the Nobel Prize for Literature in 1926 for her portrayal of the communities around her. A collection of ethnic items, such as traditional Sardinian costumes and jewellery, can be seen in the excellent **Museo Etnografico Sardo**.

Nuoro is on the edge of the Barbagia region, which has isolated villages of shepherds who have never experienced the hand of any overlord, so impenetrable are the Gennargentu mountains. This region was known to the Romans as Barbaria, an area they were never able to subdue. In Orgosolo, you may see wall murals calling for Sardinia's independence.

Museo Etnografico Sardo
Via Antonio Mereu 56 10am–1pm & 3–7pm Tue–Sun (Mar–Sep: to 8pm) isresardegna.it

---

STAY

Villas Las Tronas
This palatial Alghero hotel has scenic views, gardens, indoor and outdoor pools, and a Turkish bath. Offering genteel, old-style elegance, it is open all year round.

A5 Lungomare Valencia 1, Alghero hotelvillalastronas.it

€€€

Hotel Cala Di Volpe
This tranquil resort overlooks the turquoise waters of the Costa Smeralda. The hotel's design is inspired by traditional Sardinian craftsmanship.

B5 Cala di Volpe, Porto Cervo caladivolpe.com

€€€

Valle dell'Erica Resort Thalasso & Spa
Looking on to the Maddalena archipelago, this family-friendly resort has four swimming pools and a spa with a hammam.

B5 Valle dell'Erica, Santa Teresa Gallura hotelvalle dellerica.com

€€€

TOP 5 BEACHES IN SARDINIA

Cala Granara, Isole della Maddalena
 B5

A crescent of silvery sand in a sheltered turquoise cove backed by maquis.

Cala Goloritzé, nr Baunei, Orosei
B6

At the foot of a ravine, This tiny white-sand beach is a great place for snorkelling.

Cala Gonone, Orosei
B6

This picturesque bay includes several gorgeous beaches reached by footpath.

Sinis Peninsula, Oristano
A6

A series of exquisite beaches of glistening white quartz sand.

Costa Rei, Sarrabus
B6

The beaches of Costa Rei have fabulous turquoise waters and soft, white-gold sands.

 6

Cala Gonone

B6 Nuoro from Dorgali to grottoes Viale Umberto 37, Dorgali; www.enjoydorgali.it

East of Nuoro, between the sea and the mountains, is the hamlet of Cala Gonone – a bustling seaside resort and fishing port, with magnificent beaches. Along the unspoiled coast are the isolated coves of Cala Luna, linked with Cala Gonone by a well-marked 2-hour trail, and Cala Sisine. The famous Grotta del Bue Marino, adorned with weird rock formations, can only be reached by boat.

7

Oristano

A6 Cagliari FS Piazza Eleonora 18; www.gooristano.com

The province of Oristano corresponds roughly with historical Arborea, over which Eleonora of Arborea ruled in the late 14th century. She is commemorated by a 19th-century statue in Piazza Eleonora. On Corso Vittorio Emanuele is the 16th-century Casa di Eleonora, and nearby the **Antiquarium Arborense**, which has Neolithic, nuraghic, Punic and Roman artifacts. The Torre di San Cristoforo (1291) in Piazza Roma once formed part of Oristano's fortifications. The Duomo (13th century) was later rebuilt in the Baroque style. More interesting are the churches of Santa Chiara (1343) on Via Santa Chiara and 14th-century San Martino on Piazza San Martino.

The 12th-century Pisan-Romanesque Cathedral at Santa Giusta has columns probably taken from Tharros, an 8th-century-BC Punic settlement, 20 km (12 miles) west of Oristano on the Sinis Peninsula.

Antiquarium Arborense
Piazza Corrias 9am–8pm Mon–Fri, 9am–2pm & 3–8pm Sat & Sun antiquariumarborense.it

↑ The island of Sant'Antioco, seen from the lagoon

8

Sant'Antioco

AA6 **C**Cagliari **FS** **i**Pro Loco, Piazza Repubblica 41; 0781 84 05 92

The main town on this tiny island is Sant'Antioco, once a Phoenician port and an important Roman base. Proof of almost continuous occupation is clear from the **catacombs**, a Phoenician burial place later used by Christians, under the basilica of Sant'Antioco Martire (12th century). The **Museo**

Archeologico Ferruccio Barreca has Phoenician artifacts. The Punic Tophet (sanctuary of the goddess Tanit) and the necropolis are located nearby.

Catacombs

⊛⊛ **C**Piazza Parrocchia 22 **C**0781 92 18 87 **O**9am-noon & 3:30-5pm Mon-Sat (to 5:30pm Sat), 11am-noon & 3:30-6:30pm Sun & pub hols

Museo Archeologico Ferruccio Barreca

⊛⊛⊜ **C**Via Sabatino Moscati **O**9am-7pm daily **w**mabsantantioco.it

9

Cagliari

AB6 **✈FS** **i**Via Roma 145; www.cagliari turismo.it

The capital of Sardinia, Cagliari was occupied by the Phoenicians, Carthaginians and Romans, and extensive ruins of the Phoenician city of Nora lie to the southwest. A 2nd-century amphitheatre survives from the Roman era, cut from rock. Discover the town's earlier history in the **Cittadella dei Musei**, which houses several museums, including the Museo Archeologico Nazionale. The nuraghic items are the most interesting in the collection. Also in the Cittadella dei Musei is the Pinacoteca, an art gallery.

The old core of Cagliari has an appealing North African character. In the high Castello district, the Romans and, later, Pisans built defences. The gracious Bastione di Saint Remy on Piazza Costituzione offers magnificent views over the city and surrounding countryside. The Duomo is a 20th-century rehash of a

←

Pastel-coloured buildings in Cagliari's old town

Romanesque building. Flanking the entrance are two 12th-century pulpits originally destined for Pisa's cathedral.

Nearby is the Pisan tower Torre San Pancrazio (14th century). Down in Stampace quarter, Piazza Yenne is the lively centre of old Cagliari. In Piazza San Cosimo, the 5th-century church of San Saturnino is a rare monument to Byzantine occupation.

Cittadella dei Musei

⊛ **C**Piazza Arsenale 1 **C**070 675 76 27 **O**9am-8pm Tue-Sun

EAT

Antico Caffè
Landmark bistro with a terrace over the square.

AB6 **C**Piazza Costituzione 10/11, Cagliari **w**anticocaffe1855.it

---

Dal Corsaro
Classic cooking by an expert chef.

AB6 **C**Viale Regina Margherita 28, Cagliari **w**stefanodeidda.it

---

Stella Marina di Montecristo
Simple seafood osteria.

AB6 **C**Via Sardegna 140, Cagliari **C**347 578 89 64

Su Cumbidu
A range of traditional Sardinian dishes.

AB6 **C**Via Napoli 13, Cagliari **w**sucumbidu.com

NEED TO KNOW

Manarola station on the Riviera di Levante

BEFORE
YOU GO

Things change, so plan ahead to make the most of your trip. Be prepared for all eventualities by considering the following points before you travel.

AT A GLANCE

CURRENCY
Euro (EUR)

AVERAGE DAILY SPEND

SAVE	SPEND	SPLURGE
€50	**€100**	**€200+**

BOTTLED WATER	COFFEE	BEER	DINNER FOR TWO
€1.30	**€1**	**€5**	**€60**

ESSENTIAL PHRASES

Hello	Buongiorno
Goodbye	Arrivederci
Please	Per favore
Thank you	Grazie
Do you speak English?	Parla inglese?
I don't understand	Non capisco

ELECTRICITY SUPPLY

Power sockets are type F and L, fitting two- and three-pronged plugs. Standard voltage is 220–230v.

Passports and Visas

For entry requirements, including visas, consult your nearest Italian embassy or check the **Polizia di Stato** website. EU nationals and citizens of the UK, US, Canada, Australia and New Zealand do not need visas for stays of up to three months.
Polizia di Stato
🅦 poliziadistato.it

Government Advice

Now more than ever, it is important to consult both your and the Italian government's advice before travelling. The **UK Foreign and Commonwealth Office**, the **US State Department**, the **Australian Department of Foreign Affairs and Trade** and the Italian **Ministero della Salute** offer the latest information on security, health and local regulations.
Australian Department of Foreign Affairs and Trade
🅦 smartraveller.gov.au
Ministero della Salute
🅦 salute.gov.it
UK Foreign and Commonwealth Office
🅦 gov.uk/foreign-travel-advice
US State Department
🅦 travel.state.gov

Customs Information

You can find information on the laws relating to goods and currency taken in or out of Italy on the ENIT (Italy's national tourist board) website (*p542*).

Insurance

We recommend that you take out a comprehensive insurance policy covering theft, loss of belongings, medical care, cancellation and delays, and read the small print carefully.

EU and Australian citizens are eligible for free emergency medical care in Italy provided they have a valid **EHIC** (European Health Insurance Card) or are registered to **Medicare**.
EHIC
🅦 ec.europa.eu

Medicare
 humanservices.gov.au/individuals/medicare

Vaccinations

No inoculations are needed for Italy.

Booking Accommodation

Italy offers a huge variety of accommodation and the ENIT website (p542) provides an extensive list of options. To avoid disappointment, and inflated prices, book well in advance.

In some cities you will be charged a city tax on top of the price for the room (usually a few euro per person per night).

Under Italian law, hotels are required to register guests at police headquarters and issue a receipt of payment (ricevuta fiscale), which you must keep until you leave Italy.

Money

Most establishments accept major credit, debit and pre-paid currency cards. Contactless payments are becoming increasingly common in Italy, but it's always a good idea to carry some cash for smaller items such as coffee, gelato and pizza-by-the-slice, and when visiting markets or more remote areas. Cash is also needed for ticket machines at stations. Wait staff should be tipped €1–2 and hotel porters and house-keeping will expect €1 per bag or day.

Travellers with Specific Requirements

Italy's historic towns and cities are ill-equipped for disabled access. Many buildings do not have wheelchair access or lifts. Always call ahead to ensure that your needs will be met.

AIAS and **Rome and Italy**, in addition to **MilanoPerTutti** in Milan, provide information and general assistance for disabled travellers. Trenitalia (p538) can arrange special reservations and assistance at stations.

AIAS
 aiasnazionale.it
Rome and Italy
 romeanditaly.com
MilanoPerTutti
 milanopertutti.it

Language

Italian is the official language, but there are also many regional languages spoken, such as Friulian, Piedmontese, Sardinian and Sicilian.

The level of English and other foreign languages spoken can be limited, particularly in rural areas, and locals appreciate visitors' efforts to speak Italian, even if only a few words.

Opening Hours

> **COVID-19** The pandemic continues to affect Italy. Some museums, tourist attractions and hospitality venues are operating on reduced or temporary opening hours, and require visitors to make advance bookings for a specific date and time. Always check ahead before visiting.

Lunchtime Most churches and small businesses close for a few hours in the afternoon.
Monday Museums and some restaurants and cafés close for the day.
Sunday Restaurants usually close for lunch. Churches and cathedrals forbid tourists from visiting during Mass, and public transport runs a reduced service.
Public holidays Shops, churches and museums either close early or for the entire day.

PUBLIC HOLIDAYS 2021	
1 Jan	New Year's Day
6 Jan	Epiphany
4 Apr	Easter Sunday
5 Apr	Easter Monday
25 Apr	Liberation Day
1 May	Labour Day
2 Jun	Republic Day
15 Aug	Ferragosto
1 Nov	All Saints' Day
8 Dec	Feast of the Immaculate Conception
25 Dec	Christmas Day
26 Dec	St Stephen's Day

GETTING AROUND

Whether you are visiting for a short city break or rural country retreat, discover how best to reach your destination and travel like a pro.

PUBLIC TRANSPORT COSTS

MILAN

€2

One-way
Bus, tram & metro

ROME

€1.50

One-way
Bus, tram & metro

FLORENCE

€1.50

One-way
Bus & tram

SPEED LIMIT

MOTORWAY

130 km/h
(80 mph)

DUAL CARRIAGEWAY

110 km/h
(65 mph)

NATIONAL ROADS

90 km/h
(55 mph)

URBAN AREAS

50 km/h
(30 mph)

Arriving by Air

Rome's Leonardo da Vinci (Fiumicino) and Milan's Malpensa are Italy's main airports.

European budget airlines fly to cities across Italy year round at very reasonable prices. They also offer very good rates on internal flights within the country – ideal if you want to cover multiple destinations in one trip.

For information on getting to and from Italy's main airports, see the table opposite.

Train Travel

International Train Travel

Regular high-speed international trains connect Italy to the main towns and cities in Austria, Germany, France and Eastern Europe. Reservations for these services are essential and tickets are booked up quickly.

You can buy tickets and passes for multiple international journeys via **Eurail** or **Interrail**, however you may still need to pay an additional reservation fee depending on which rail service you travel with. Always check that your pass is valid before boarding.

Eurail
W eurail.com
Interrail
W interrail.eu

Domestic Train Travel

Trenitalia is the main operator in Italy. Safety and hygiene measures, timetables, ticket information, transport maps and more can be obtained from the Trenitalia website.

Italo Treno (NTV) and Trenitalia (FS) offer a high-speed service between major train stations throughout Italy. Book in advance to ensure a good price; reservations are essential.

Train tickets must be validated before boarding by stamping them in machines at the entrance to platforms. Heavy fines are levied if you are caught with an unvalidated ticket.

Italo Treno
W italotreno.it
Trenitalia
W trenitalia.com

GETTING TO AND FROM THE AIRPORT

Airport	Distance to City	Taxi Fare	Public Transport	Journey Time
Bergamo (Orio al Serio)	6 km (4 miles)	€34	bus	15 mins
Florence (Amerigo Vespucci)	8 km (5 miles)	€22	bus	20 mins
Milan (Linate)	8 km (5 miles)	€40	bus	25 mins
Milan (Malpensa)	50 km (31 miles)	€80	train (FS)	50 mins
Naples (Capodichino)	13 km (8 miles)	€25	bus	30 mins
Palermo (Falcone-Borsellino)	35 km (22 miles)	€45	bus	50 mins
Pisa (Galileo Galilei)	2 km (1 mile)	€10	train (FS)	5 mins
Rome (Fiumicino)	32 km (20 miles)	€48	train (FS)	30 mins
Rome (Ciampino)	15 km (9 miles)	€30	bus	45 mins
Turin (Torino-Caselle)	16 km (10 miles)	€30	train (GTT)	45 mins
Venice (Marco Polo)	10 km (6 miles)	€35	bus	20 mins
Venice (Treviso)	40 km (25 miles)	€80	bus	1 hour
Verona (Villafranca)	10 km (6 miles)	€25	bus	15 mins

This map is a handy reference for intercity travel on Italy's major train routes. Journey times given below are for the fastest available service on each route.

••• Direct train routes

Milan to Bologna	1 hr
Milan to Florence	2 hrs
Milan to Rome	3 hrs
Milan to Turin	1 hr
Naples to Bari	4 hrs
Naples to Palermo	9 hrs
Pisa to Florence	1 hr
Rome to Florence	1.5 hrs
Rome to Naples	1 hr
Venice to Bologna	1.5 hrs
Venice to Milan	2.5 hrs

Public Transport

Most cities operate multiple public transport services comprising buses, trams, metro and, in the case of Venice, boats. Safety and hygiene measures, timetables, ticket information, transport maps and more can be obtained from individual operators' websites. Florence's public transport operator is **ATAF**, Milan's is **ATM**, Rome's is **ATAC** and Venice's is **Venezia Unica**.

ATAF
ⓦ ataf.net
ATAC
ⓦ atac.roma.it
ATM
ⓦ atm.it
Venezia Unica
ⓦ veneziaunica.it

Tickets

Tickets (*biglietti*) are available from kiosks, stations, bars and newsstands. A single ticket is normally valid on all modes of public transport and transfers for a designated amount of time (usually around one hour).

Some operators accept contactless payments or smart cards rather than traditional paper tickets. It is always best to check the website of the local transport company before travelling.

Discounted tickets bought in bulk (*un blocchetto* or *un carnet*), or day- or week-long visitor's tickets and passes, are usually better value than paying as you go.

Tickets for public transport must be validated at the time of boarding. Validation machines are usually placed in the entrance hall at metro stations and on board buses and trams.

Long Distance Bus Travel

Flixbus offers a variety of coach routes to various destinations in Italy from other European cities. Fares are very reasonable, with discounts available for students, children and seniors.

SITA offer reasonably priced coach travel throughout Italy. You can usually buy tickets on board for long-haul buses (*pullman* or *corriera*) between towns and cities.

Services often depart from outside main railway stations or from a town's main piazza. In rural areas, check bus stops for timetables and the details of local transport companies.

Flixbus
ⓦ flixbus.it
SITA
ⓦ sitabus.it

Metro

Italy's major cities have a metro system (*la metropolitana*, or *la metro* for short), with the exception of Florence and other historic cities. Milan, Naples and Rome are the largest with multiple lines, while Brescia, Catania, Genoa and Turin have only one line.

For transport information about a specific town or city, consult the relevant public transport operator.

Taxis

Taxis are not hailed; take one at an official taxi stand (usually found at the station, main piazza or close to key sights), or reserve one by phone.

Only accept rides in licensed, metered taxis. In Rome, official taxis are white, have a "taxi" sign on the roof and an official taxi licence number on the doors.

Extra charges are added for each piece of luggage placed in the boot, for rides between 10pm and 7am, on Sundays and public holidays, and for journeys to and from airports.

Taxi apps such as Uber (Uber Black service only in Rome, Milan and Turin), MyTaxi and AppTaxi also operate in cities.

Driving

One of the best ways to explore Italy is by car. However, it can also be a hair-raising experience. Italians have a reputation for driving erratically; this is particularly true in the south. Make sure you are familiar with the rules of the road and have all the necessary documentation, as traffic police (*carabinieri*) carry out routine checks.

Driving to Italy

Italy is easily reachable from other European countries via E-roads, the International European Road Network connecting major roads across national borders within Europe, or by national (N) and secondary (SS) roads from neighbouring France, Switzerland, Austria and Slovenia.

Vehicles may also be transported into the country by ferry or rail.

Car Rental

To rent a car in Italy you must be over 21 and have held a valid driver's licence for at least a year. Some companies will rent cars to drivers as young as 18.

Driving licences issued by any of the EU member states are valid throughout the European Union, including Italy. If visiting from outside the EU, you may need to apply for an International Driving Permit (IDP). Check with your local automobile association.

Driving in Italy

If you bring your own foreign-registered car into the country, you must carry a Green Card, the vehicle's registration documents, proof of car insurance, V5C registration certificate and a valid driver's licence. All non-EU-registered vehicles must also display a nationality sticker at the rear.

Main towns and cities often enforce a Limited Traffic Zone (ZTL). To avoid fines, consult the **Urban Access Regulations in Europe** website.

Tolls are payable on most motorways (*autostrade*), and payment is made at the end of the journey in either cash, credit card or pre-paid VIA cards, available from tobacconists and the **ACI** (Automobile Club d'Italia). Avoid tolls by using the national roads (*strade nazionali*), or secondary state roads (*strade statali*). Although less direct, they are often more scenic, allowing you to stop at viewpoints and towns.

ACI
W aci.it
Urban Access Regulations in Europe
W urbanaccessregulations.eu

Rules of the Road

Drive on the right, use the left lane only for passing, and yield to traffic from the right.

Seat belts are required for all passengers in the front and back, and heavy fines are levied for using a mobile phone while driving. A strict drink-drive limit (*p543*) is enforced.

During the day dipped headlights are compulsory when you are driving on motorways, dual carriageways and on all out-of-town roads.

A red warning triangle, spare tyre and fluorescent vests must be carried at all times, for use in the event of an emergency.

In the event of an accident or breakdown switch on your hazard warning lights and place a warning triangle 50 m (55 yd) behind your vehicle. For breakdowns call the ACI emergency number (803 116 from an Italian phone or 800 116 800 from a foreign mobile) or the emergency services (112 or 113). The ACI will tow any foreign-registered vehicle to the nearest ACI-affiliated garage free of charge.

Hitchhiking

Hitchhiking, or *autostop*, is illegal on motorways. While it is permitted in rural areas, always consider your own safety before entering an unknown vehicle.

Bicycle and Scooter Hire

Bicycle sharing systems are available in most major cities, such as **BikeMi** in Milan and **[TO] BIKE** in Turin. You can rent bicycles, motorcycles and scooters hourly or by the day. You may have to leave your passport with the rental shop as a deposit, and you must have a valid licence to hire a scooter or motorcycle. By law, motorcycle and moped riders must wear a helmet.

BikeMi
W bikemi.com
[TO]BIKE
W tobike.it

Walking

From long-distance hikes to city strolls, Italy rewards exploration on foot. Many towns and cities are made up of narrow lanes and alleys, which are impenetrable to buses, and many streets are pedestrianized. By exploring on foot, you can take in the architectural details, absorb the streetlife and peek into any church, shop or bar that catches your interest. In the country-side, trails are well signposted and offer everything from mountain scenery to coastal views.

Boats and Ferries

The Italian islands are linked by sea to the mainland by regular ferry services including car ferries and hydrofoils. The main Italian ports that serve the large islands of Sicily and Sardinia in the south are Genoa, Livorno, Civitavecchia, Fiumicino, Naples and Villa San Giovanni. Ferry services are more frequent and reliable in summer, but it is best to book in advance.

GNV, **Grimaldi Lines** and **Snav** run regular services to Italy's main ports from Spain, France, Corsica, Malta, Tunisia, Morocco, Slovenia, Croatia and Greece.

GNV
W gnv.it
Grimaldi Lines
W grimaldi-lines.com
Snav
W snav.it

TRAVEL IN VENICE

Venice has a unique transport network made up of the following vehicles:

Gondolas
A luxury form of transport. Before boarding, check the official tariffs and agree a price with the gondolier.

Traghetti
These gondola ferries cross the Grand Canal at seven different points. To find traghetti stops, look out for yellow street signs featuring a gondola.

Vaporetti
These large boats connect numerous ports across Venice and are the cheapest and most efficient way to travel. Smaller boats called Motoscafi and larger boats called Motonave also service the Vaporetti route.

Watertaxis
The fastest and most practical means of getting around in Venice. Beware of extra charges for transporting luggage, waiting, night service and call-out fees.

PRACTICAL
INFORMATION

A little local know-how goes a long way in Italy. Here you will find all the essential advice and information you will need during your stay.

EMERGENCY NUMBERS

GENERAL EMERGENCY

112

POLICE

113

AMBULANCE

118

FIRE SERVICE

115

TIME ZONE
CET/CEST
Central European
Summer Time
(CEST) runs
28 Mar–31 Oct 2021

TAP WATER
Unless stated
otherwise, tap
water in Italy
is safe to drink.

WEBSITES AND APPS

ENIT
Check out Itay's national tourist board website at www.italia.it

ProntoTreno
A useful app for buying tickets and checking journey times.

Navigazione Laghi
This app displays ferry times and routes for lakes Como, Garda and Maggiore.

WiFi Italia
This app allows you to connect to free Wi-Fi hotspots throughout Italy.

Personal Security

Italy is a relatively safe place to visit, but you should still take precautions to avoid incidences. Bag-snatching scooter drivers are a problem in some Italian cities, so hold bags on the inside of the pavement where possible, especially in crowded tourist areas. Pickpockets are common on public transport and in crowded city centres, so keep your belongings in a safe place and with you at all times.

If you have anything stolen, report the crime within 24 hours to the nearest police station and take ID with you. If you need to make an insurance claim, get a copy of the crime report (*denuncia*). Contact your embassy if you have your passport stolen, or in the event of a serious crime or accident.

As a rule, Italians are very accepting of all people, regardless of their race, gender or sexuality. Homosexuality was legalized in 1887 and in 1982, Italy became the third country to recognize the right to legally change your gender. If you do feel unsafe, the **Safe Space Alliance** pinpoints your nearest place of refuge.

Women may receive unwanted and unwelcome attention, especially around tourist areas. If you feel threatened, head straight for the nearest police station.
Safe Space Alliance
w safespacealliance.com

Health

Italy has a world-class healthcare system. Emergency medical care in Italy is free for all EU and Australian citizens (*p537*). If you have an EHIC, be sure to present this as soon as possible. You may have to pay after treatment and reclaim the money later.

For visitors from outside the EU and Australia, payment of medical expenses is the patient's responsibility. As such it is important to arrange comprehensive medical insurance.

Seek medicinal supplies and advice for minor ailments from pharmacies (*farmacia*). You can find details of the nearest 24-hour service on all pharmacy doors.

Smoking, Alcohol and Drugs

Smoking is banned in enclosed public places. and the possession of illegal drugs is prohibited and could result in a prison sentence.

Italy has a strict limit of 0.05 per cent BAC (blood alcohol content) for drivers. This means that you cannot drink more than a small beer or a small glass of wine if you plan to drive. For drivers with less than three years' driving experience, and those under 21, the limit is 0.

ID

By law you must carry identification at all times in Italy. A photocopy of your passport photo page (and visa if applicable) should suffice. If you are stopped by the police you may be asked to present the original document within 12 hours.

Local Customs

Italians are relatively relaxed when it comes to etiquette. Strangers usually shake hands, while friends and family greet each other with a kiss on each cheek. But there are some strict rules. In some cities you can be fined for dropping litter, sitting on monument steps, or eating or drinking outside churches and monuments. It is an offence to bathe in public fountains. You can also be fined for buying something from illegal traders operating on the streets.

Visiting Churches and Cathedrals

Entrance to churches is free, but you may be charged a small fee to see a certain area, such as a chapel, cloister or underground ruins. Visiting may be prohibited during Mass.

Strict dress codes apply: cover your torso and upper arms, and ensure shorts and skirts cover your knees. Shoes must be worn. In some places of worship photography is banned.

Mobile Phones and Wi-Fi

Wi-Fi is generally widely available throughout Italy, and cafés and restaurants will usually give you the password for their Wi-Fi on the condition that you make a purchase.

EU visitors to Italy can use their devices without being affected by roaming charges. Users will be charged the same rates for data, SMS and voice calls as they would pay at home.

Post

Stamps (*francobolli*) are sold in kiosks and tobacconists (*tabacchi*). The Vatican City and San Marino have their own post systems and stamps. Only letters bearing San Marino or Vatican stamps can be posted in San Marino and Vatican postboxes.

Italian post is notorious for its unreliability. Letters and postcards can take anything between four days and two weeks to arrive, depending on the destination.

Taxes and Refunds

VAT (called IVA in Italy) is usually 22 per cent, with a reduced rate of 4 to 10 per cent on some items. Non-EU citizens can claim an IVA rebate subject to certain conditions.

It is easier to claim before you buy (you will need to show your passport to the shop assistant and complete a form). If claiming retrospectively, at the airport, present a customs officer with your purchases and a *fattura* receipt, with your name and the amount of IVA on the item purchased. Receipts will be stamped and sent back to the vendor to issue a refund.

Discount Cards

Many cities offer a visitor's pass or discount card for exhibitions, events and museum entry. Some even cover the cost of public transport for the duration of your stay. These are not free, so consider carefully how many of the offers you are likely to take advantage of before purchasing a card.

For a full list of the discount cards available across Italy, visit the ENIT website (*p542*). **Campania Artecard**, **Firenze Card** and **Roma Pass** offer some of the best deals.

Campania Artecard
🔲 campaniartecard.it
Firenze Card
🔲 firenzecard.it
Roma Pass
🔲 romapass.it

INDEX

Page numbers in **bold** type
refer to main entries

Index

PHRASE BOOK

IN EMERGENCY

Help!	Aiuto!	eye-yoo-toh
Stop!	Ferma!	fair-mah
Call a doctor	Chiama un medico	kee-ah-mah oon meh-dee-koh
Call an ambulance	Chiama un' ambulanza	kee-ah-mah oon am-boo-lan-tsa
Call the police	Chiama la polizia	kee-ah-mah lah pol-ee-tsee-ah
Call the fire brigade	Chiama i pompieri	kee-ah-mah ee pom-pee-air-ee
Where is the telephone?	Dov'è il telefono?	dov-eheel teh-leh-foh-noh?
The nearest hospital?	L'ospedale più vicino?	loss-peh-dah-leh pee-oovee-chee-noh?

COMMUNICATION ESSENTIALS

Yes/No	Sì/No	see/noh
Please	Per favore	pair fah-vor-eh
Thank you	Grazie	grah-tsee-eh
Excuse me	Mi scusi	mee skoo-zee
Hello/good morning	Buon giorno	bwon jor-noh
Goodbye	Arrivederci	ah-ree-veh-dair-chee
Good evening	Buona sera	bwon-ah sair-ah
morning	la mattina	lah mah-tee-nah
afternoon	il pomeriggio	eel pom-meh-ree-joh
evening	la sera	lah sair-ah
yesterday	ieri	ee-air-ee
today	oggi	oh-jee
tomorrow	domani	doh-mah-nee
here	qui	kwee
there	la	lah
What?	Quale?	kwah-leh?
When?	Quando?	kwan-doh?
Why?	Perchè?	pair-keh?
Where?	Dove?	doh-veh

USEFUL PHRASES

How are you?	Come sta?	koh-meh stah?
Very well, thank you.	Molto bene, grazie	moll-toh beh-neh grah-tsee-eh
Pleased to meet you.	Piacere di conoscerla.	pee-ah-chair-eh dee coh-noh-shair-lah
See you soon.	A più tardi.	ah pee-oo tar-dee
That's fine.	Va bene.	va beh-neh
Where is/are ...?	Dov'è/Dove sono...?	dov-eh/doveh sohnoh?
How long does it take to get to ...?	Quanto tempo ci vuole per andare a ...?	kwan-toh tem-poh chee voo-oh-leh pair an-dar-eh ah...?
How do I get to ...?	Come faccio per arrivare a ...?	koh-meh fah-choh pair arri-var-eh ah...?
Do you speak English?	Parla inglese?	par-lah een-gleh-zeh?
I don't understand.	Non capisco.	non ka-pee-skoh
Could you speak more slowly, please?	Può parlare più lentamente, per favore?	pwoh par-lah-reh pee-oo len-ta-men-teh pair fah-vor-eh?
I'm sorry.	Mi dispiace.	mee dee-spee-ah-cheh

USEFUL WORDS

big	grande	gran-deh
small	piccolo	pee-koh-loh
hot	caldo	kal-doh
cold	freddo	fred-doh
good	buono	bwoh-noh
bad	male	mal-eh
enough	basta	bas-tah
well	bene	beh-neh
open	aperto	ah-pair-toh
closed	chiuso	kee-oo-zoh
left	a sinistra	ah see-nee-strah
right	a destra	ah dess-trah
straight on	sempre dritto	sem-preh dree-toh
near	vicino	vee-chee-noh
far	lontano	lon-tah-noh
up	su	soo
down	giù	joo
early	presto	press-toh
late	tardi	tar-dee
entrance	entrata	en-trah-tah
exit	uscita	oo-shee-ta
toilet	il bagno	eel ban-yo
free, unoccupied	libero	lee-bair-oh
free, no charge	gratuito	grah-too-ee-toh

MAKING A TELEPHONE CALL

I'd like to place a long-distance call.	Vorrei fare una interurbana.	vor-ray far-eh oona in-tair-oor-bah-nah.
I'd like to make a reverse-charge call.	Vorrei fare una telefonata a carico del destinatario.	vor-ray far-eh oona teh-leh-fon-ah-tah ah kar-ee-koh dell dess-tee-nah-tar-ree-oh.
I'll try again later.	Ritelefono più tardi.	ree-teh-teh-foh-noh pee-oo tar-dee.
Can I leave a message?	Posso lasciare un messaggio?	poss-oh lash-ah-reh oon mess-sah-joh?
Hold on	Un attimo, per favore	oon ah-tee-moh, pair fah-vor-eh
Could you speak up a little please?	Può parlare più forte, per favore?	pwoh par-lah-reh pee-oo for-teh, pair fah-vor-eh?
local call	la telefonata locale	lah teh-leh-fon-ta loh-kah-leh

SHOPPING

How much does this cost?	Quanto costa questo?	kwan-toh cos-stah kweh-stoh?
I would like ...	Vorrei ...	vor-ray...
Do you have ...?	Avete ...?	ah-veh-teh...?
I'm just looking.	Sto soltanto guardando	stoh sol-tan-toh gwar-dan-doh
Do you take credit cards?	Accettate carte di credito?	ah-chet-tah-teh kar-teh dee creh-dee-toh?
What time do you open/close?	A che ora apre/ chiude?	ah keh or-ah ah-preh/kee-oo-deh?
this one	questo	kweh-stoh
that one	quello	kwell-oh
expensive	caro	kar-oh
cheap	a buon prezzo	ah bwon pret-soh
size, clothes	la taglia	lah tah-lee-ah
size, shoes	il numero	eel noo-mair-oh
white	bianco	bee-ang-koh
black	nero	neh-roh
red	rosso	ross-oh
yellow	giallo	jal-loh
green	verde	vair-deh
blue	blu	bloo
brown	marrone	mar-roh-neh

TYPES OF SHOP

antique dealer	l'antiquario	lan-tee-kwah-ree-oh
bakery	la panetteria	lah pah-net-tair-ree-ah
bank	la banca	lah bang-kah
bookshop	la libreria	lah lee-breh-ree-ah
butcher's	la macelleria	lah mah-chell-eh-ree-ah
cake shop	la pasticceria	lah pas-tee-chair-ee-ah
chemist's	la farmacia	lah far-mah-chee-ah
department store	il grande magazzino	eel gran-deh mag-gad-zee-noh
delicatessen	la salumeria	lah sah-loo-meh-ree-ah
fishmonger's	la pescheria	lah pess-keh-ree-ah
florist	il fioraio	eel fee-or-eye-oh
greengrocer	il fruttivendolo	eel froo-tee-ven-doh-loh
grocery	alimentari	ah-lee-men-tah-ree
hairdresser	il parrucchiere	eel par-oo-kee-air-eh
ice cream parlour	la gelateria	lah jel-lah-tair-ree-ah
market	il mercato	eel mair-kah-toh
news-stand	l'edicola	leh-dee-koh-lah
post office	l'ufficio postale	loo-fee-choh pos-tah-leh
shoe shop	il negozio di scarpe	eel neh-goh-tsioh dee skar-peh
supermarket	il supermercato	eel su-pair-mair-kah-toh
tobacconist	il tabaccaio	eel tah-bak-eye-oh
travel agency	l'agenzia di viaggi	lah-jen-tsee-ah dee vee-ad-jee

SIGHTSEEING

art gallery	la pinacoteca	lah peena-koh-teh-kah
bus stop	la fermata dell'autobus	lah fair-mah-tah dell ow-toh-booss
church	la chiesa la basilica	lah kee-eh-zah lah bah-seel-i-kah
garden	il giardino	eel jar-dee-no
library	la biblioteca	lah beeb-lee-oh-teh-kah
museum	il museo	eel moo-zeh-oh
railway station	la stazione	lah stah-tsee-oh-neh

| tourist information | l'ufficio turistico | loo-*fee*-choh too-ree-*stee*-koh |
| closed for the public holiday | chiuso per la festa | kee-*oo*-zoh pair lah *fess*-tah |

STAYING IN A HOTEL

Do you have any vacant rooms?	Avete camere libere?	ah-*veh*-teh *kah*-mair -eh *lee*-bair-eh?
double room	una camera doppia	oona *kah*-mair-ah *doh*-pee-ah
with double bed	con letto matrimoniale	kon *let*-toh mah-tree-moh-nee-*ah*-leh
twin room	una camera con due letti	oona *kah*-mair-ah kon *doo*-eh *let*-tee
single room	una camera singola	oona *kah*-mair-ah *sing*-goh-lah
room with a bath, shower	una camera con bagno, con doccia	oona *kah*-mair-ah kon *ban*-yoh, kon *dot*-chah
porter	il facchino	eel fah-*kee*-noh
key	la chiave	lah kee-*ah*-veh
I have a reservation.	Ho fatto una prenotazione.	oh *fat*-toh oona preh-noh-tah-tsee-*oh*-neh

EATING OUT

Have you got a table for …?	Avete un tavolo per … ?	ah-*veh*-teh oon *tah*-voh-loh pair …?
I'd like to reserve a table.	Vorrei riservare un tavolo.	vor-*ray* ree-sair-*vah*-reh oon *tah*-voh-loh
breakfast	colazione	koh-lah-tsee-*oh*-neh
lunch	pranzo	*pran*-tsoh
dinner	cena	*cheh*-nah
The bill, please.	Il conto, per favore.	eel *kon*-toh pair fah-*vor*-eh
I am a vegetarian.	Sono vegetariano/a.	*soh*-noh veh-jeh-tar ee-*ah*-noh/nah
waitress	cameriera	kah-mair-ee-*air*-ah
waiter	cameriere	kah-mair-ee-*air*-eh
fixed price menu	il menù a prezzo fisso	eel meh-*noo* ah *pret*-soh *fee*-soh
dish of the day	piatto del giorno	pee-*ah*-toh dell *jor*-no
starter	antipasto	an-tee-*pass*-toh
first course	il primo	eel *pree*-moh
main course	il secondo	eel seh-*kon*-doh
vegetables	il contorno	eel kon-*tor*-noh
dessert	il dolce	eel *doll*-che
cover charge	il coperto	eel koh-*pair*-toh
wine list	la lista dei vini	lah *lee*-stah day *vee*-nee
rare	al sangue	al *sang*-gweh
medium	a puntino	a poon-*tee*-noh
well done	ben cotto	ben *kot*-toh
glass	il bicchiere	eel bee-kee-*air*-eh
bottle	la bottiglia	lah bot-*teel*-yah
knife	il coltello	eel kol-*tell*-oh
fork	la forchetta	lah for-*ket*-tah
spoon	il cucchiaio	eel koo-kee-*eye*-oh

MENU DECODER

apple	la mela	lah *meh*-lah
artichoke	il carciofo	eel kar-*choff*-oh
aubergine	la melanzana	lah meh-lan-*tsah*-nah
baked	al forno	al *for*-noh
beans	i fagioli	ee fah-*joh*-lee
beef	il manzo	eel *man*-tsoh
beer	la birra	lah *beer*-rah
boiled	lesso	*less*-oh
bread	il pane	eel *pah*-neh
broth	il brodo	eel *broh*-doh
butter	il burro	eel *boor*-oh
cake	la torta	lah *tor*-tah
cheese	il formaggio	eel for-*mad*-joh
chicken	il pollo	eel *poll*-oh
chips	patatine fritte	pah-tah-*teen*-eh *free*-teh
baby clams	le vongole	leh *von*-goh-leh
coffee	il caffè	eel kah-*feh*
courgettes	gli zucchini	lyee dzoo-*kee*-nee
dry	secco	*sek*-koh
duck	l'anatra	*lah*-nah-trah
egg	l'uovo	loo-*oh*-voh
fish	il pesce	eel *pesh*-eh
fresh fruit	frutta fresca	*froo*-tah *fress*-kah
garlic	l'aglio	*lahl*-yoh
grapes	l'uva	*loo*-vah
grilled	alla griglia	ah-lah *greel*-yah
ham cooked/cured	il prosciutto cotto/crudo	eel pro-*shoo*-toh *kot*-toh/*kroo*-doh
ice cream	il gelato	eel *jel*-lah-toh
lamb	agnello	la-*gnel*-lo

lobster	l'aragosta	lah-rah-*goss*-tah
meat	la carne	la *kar*-neh
milk	il latte	eel *laht*-teh
mineral water sparkling/still	l'acqua minerale gassata/naturale	*lah*-kwah mee-nair-*ah*-leh gah-*zah*-tah/ nah-too-*rah*-leh
mushrooms	i funghi	ee *foon*-gee
oil	l'olio	*loll*-yoh
olive	l'oliva	loh-*lee*-vah
onion	la cipolla	lah chee-*poll*-ah
orange	l'arancia	lah-*ran*-chah
orange/lemon juice	succo d'arancia/ di limone	*soo*-kohdah-*ran*-chah/ dee lee-*moh*-neh
peach	la pesca	lah *pess*-kah
pepper	il pepe	eel *peh*-peh
pork	carne di maiale	*kar*-neh dee mah-*yah*-leh
potatoes	le patate	leh pah-*tah*-teh
prawns	i gamberi	ee *gam*-bair-ee
rice	il riso	eel *ree*-zoh
roast	arrosto	ar-*ross*-toh
roll	il panino	eel pah-*nee*-noh
salad	l'insalata	leen-sah-*lah*-tah
salt	il sale	eel *sah*-leh
sausage	la salsiccia	lah sal-*see*-chah
seafood	frutti di mare	*froo*-tee dee *mah*-reh
soup	la zuppa, la minestra	lah *tsoo*-pah, lah mee-*ness*-trah
steak	la bistecca	lah bee-*stek*-kah
strawberries	le fragole	leh *frah*-goh-leh
sugar	lo zucchero	loh *zoo*-kair-oh
tea	il tè	eel *teh*
herb tea	la tisana	lah tee-*zah*-nah
tomato	il pomodoro	eel poh-moh-*dor*-oh
tuna	il tonno	eel *ton*-noh
veal	il vitello	ecl vee-*tell*-oh
vegetables	le verdure	leh vair-*du*-rah
vinegar	l'aceto	lah-*cheh*-toh
water	l'acqua	*lah*-kwah
red wine	vino rosso	*vee*-noh *ross*-oh
white wine	vino bianco	*vee*-noh bee-*ang*-koh

NUMBERS

1	uno	*oo*-noh
2	due	*doo*-eh
3	tre	treh
4	quattro	*kwat*-roh
5	cinque	*ching*-kweh
6	sei	*say*-ee
7	sette	*set*-teh
8	otto	*ot*-toh
9	nove	*noh*-veh
10	dieci	dee-*eh*-chee
11	undici	*oon*-dee-chee
12	dodici	*doh*-dee-chee
13	tredici	*treh*-dee-chee
14	quattordici	kwat-*tor*-dee-chee
15	quindici	*kwin*-dee-chee
16	sedici	*say*-dee-chee
17	diciassette	dee-chah-*set*-teh
18	diciotto	dee-*chot*-toh
19	diciannove	dee-chah-*noh*-veh
20	venti	*ven*-tee
30	trenta	*tren*-tah
40	quaranta	kwah-*ran*-tah
50	cinquanta	ching-*kwan*-tah
60	sessanta	sess-*an*-tah
70	settanta	set-*tan*-tah
80	ottanta	ot-*tan*-tah
90	novanta	noh-*van*-tah
100	cento	*chen*-toh
1,000	mille	*mee*-leh
2,000	duemila	*doo*-eh *mee*-lah
5,000	cinquemila	*ching*-kweh *mee*-lah
1,000,000	un milione	oon meel-*yoh*-neh

TIME

one minute	un minuto	oon mee-*noo*-toh
one hour	un'ora	oon *or*-ah
half an hour	mezz'ora	medz-*or*-ah
a day	un giorno	oon *jor*-noh
a week	una settimana	oona set-tee-*mah*-nah
Monday	lunedì	loo-neh-*dee*
Tuesday	martedì	mar-teh-*dee*
Wednesday	mercoledì	mair-koh-leh-*dee*
Thursday	giovedì	joh-veh-*dee*
Friday	venerdì	ven-air-*dee*
Saturday	sabato	*sah*-bah-toh
Sunday	domenica	doh-*meh*-nee-kah

ACKNOWLEDGMENTS

DK would like to thank the following for their contribution to the previous edition:
Ros Belford, Paul Duncan, Tim Jepson, Andrew Gumbel, Christopher Catling, Sam Cole, Zoe Ross

The publisher would like to thank the following for their kind permission to reproduce their photographs:

Key: a-above; b-below/bottom; c-centre; f-far; l-left; r-right; t-top

123RF.com: Boris Breytman 307t; gonewiththewind 138-9b, 140bl; Yulia Grogoryeva 64tl; itsajoop 328tc; Valerio Mei 29br; Yana Menshchikova 274cra; Christian Mueller 336cl; Davide Ferdinando Precone 193tl; manjik 288t; mikolaj64 473tr; Roman Smirnov 126tl; Ekaterina Spirina 486tr; Vaclav Volrab 137bl; Valentyn Volkov 67cl;.

4Corners: Marco Arduino 6-7b; SIME / Paolo Giocoso 504br.

500px: David Juan 12-3b; Carlo Murenu 447bl, 526-7; Gabi Rusu 250bl.

Alamy Stock Photo: Adam Eastland Art + Architecture 237cl, 324b; AF archive 275tl; age fotostock 64-5b, 365br; AGF Srl 150br, 152-3t, 188-9t, 430bc, / Algol 397b / Hermes Images 186-7b; Ambrosiniv 347c; Alessandro Avondo 39bl; Awakening / Xianpix / Massimiliano Donati 67br; Azoor Photo 305tl; Paul Springett B 243t, 274-5b; Bailey-Cooper Photography 11br; Riccardo Bianchini 63br; Stuart Black 11t; Ceri Breeze / Stockimo 34t; Michael Brooks 235br; Angelo Fausto Lo Buglio 188bl; Nattee Chalermtiragool 276t; Chromorange / Lynne Otter 111tl; Classic Image 40bc, 242cl; Sorin Colac 346t; Roy Conchie 25bl; Davide D'Amico 521b; Luis Dafos 259bc; Ian G Dagnall 174t, 348-9, 356t; De Agostini / M. Leigheb 518br; Danita Delimont / Jaynes Gallery 338-9t; DGB 118-9b; Martin A. Doe 515cb; saturno dona' 336cr; dpa picture alliance / Runway Manhattan / Valentina Ranieri 147bl; Adam Eastland 281tr, 290bl; edpics 233br; Elbardamu 339b; FC_Italy 109cra; Findlay 235tr; Kirk Fisher 347crb; Florilegius 43bc; Nicola Forenza 273; Funky Stock - Paul Williams 381t; Jeff Gilbert 160bl; GL Archive 258cb; Susana Guzman 277br; Dennis Hallinan 294tl; Andrew Hasson 354t; Gary Hebding Jr. 291t; Hemis 152br, 430tc, / Jean-Pierre Degas 19cla, / Lionel Montico 186tl, / Francis Leroy 456t, / Bertrand Rieger 11cr, / Jacques Sierpinski 518crb; Peter Horree 289clb; Jiri Hubatka 179tl, 179br; Ian Dagnall Commercial Collection 349cra; imageBROKER 20-1b, 187br, 259bl, 447t, 500-1, / Katja Kreder 530b,/ Martin Moxter 458-9b; Ilpo Musto 233clb; Image Source / Sofie Delauw 340bl; Interfoto 41bc; ITPhoto 406b; Brian Jannsen 220tl, 366-7; Alexander Karelin 272cla; John Kellerman 272cl, 343ca; Kiefer 352br; Art Kowalski 63tr, 351tr; Raimund Kutter 328bl; Julian Money-Kyrle 520t; Lanmas 261tl; Brian Lawrence 339cla; Lebrecht Music & Arts / Lebrecht Authors 35cla; Lefrancq / Andia 314-5b; Lifestyle pictures 242clb; Enzo Lisi 235clb; Melvyn Longhurst 445bl, 476-7; Luca Antonio Lorenzelli 141t; Lphoto 351cr; Cedric Maes 453tc; angel manzano 435tr; Marka 452-3b; Andrea Palma 237br; Panther Media GmbH / beatrice preve

233tl; Stefano Politi Markovina 134bc; Martin Thomas Photography 114; mauritius images GmbH 289fcrb; Valerio Mei 18cla; Andrew Michael 295; Mikel Bilbao Gorostiaga- Travels 288br; Hercules Milas 81tr, 86-7t, 230br; MuseoPics - Paul Williams 342crb, 499br; National Geographic Creative 405; Olivia Nitaji 161t; North Wind Picture Archives 43cr; B.O'Kane 75cr; Panther Media GmbH 20tl; Photononstop 483cr; J. Pie 244cra; Prisma Archivo 72fcrb; QEDimages 136tl; Andrea Raffin 148crb; M Ramìrez 315cr; Realy Easy Star / Luca Scamporlino 13t,/Toni Spagone 34br, 518cr; REDA &CO srl 35br, 157c, / Gimmi 384cr; John Rees 248clb; robertharding 304clb, / Nico Tondini 340-1t; Giorgio Rossi 68-9t; Scenics & Science 109cr; Peter Scholey 515ca; Andrea Spinelli 66b; Kumar Sriskandan 32bl; Stockimo / Keri Billen 72cl; Krystyna Szulecka 248br; Domenico Tondini 341bl; Travelwide 12t; Trigger Image 25cla; Viennaslide 81tr; Antonio Violi 28-29t; WaterFrame 518cra; WENN UK 154bl; Wojciech Stróżyk 385.

Armani/Silos Museum/Giorgio Armani: Davide Lovatti 159bl.

AWL Images: Marco Bottigelli 219t, 320-1; ClickAlps 371tl, 445tl, 462-3; Matteo Colombo 2-3, 37clb; Christian Handl 308t; Francesco Iacobelli 221tl, 414-5, 446, 490-1, Maurizio Rellini 4, 46-7, 258t; Mark Sykes 336br.

Bridgeman Images: Basilica San Francesco, Arezzo / Piero della Francesca *The Verification of the True Cross, The Victory of Heraclius and the Execution of Chosroes in 628 AD* (c1415-92) 384bc; Gabinetto Comunale delle Stampe, Rome, Italy / De Agostini Picture Library / A. Dagli Orti 258clb.

Cortina Adrenalin Center: 133crb.

Depositphotos Inc: Bertl123 94t; borisb17 305cra; diabolique04 408tl; Ody1988 109tr; scorton 220cb, 400-1; scrisman 212t; siculodoc 116br.

Dorling Kindersley: Nigel Hicks 327tr; Mockford and Bonetti 280b, / MAXXI 316t;.

Dreamstime.com: Adrea 522-3t; Akulamatiau 209b; Alfiofer 455br; Amoklv 470t; Giuseppe Anello 523br; Antonel 65br; Anyaivanova 81tl, 317b; Areinwald 16-7t; Stefano Armaroli 433tr; Roberto Atzeni 21br; Kushnirov Avraham 166br; Frank Bach 41tl; Barmalini 331tr; Bbeckprano 25cr; Gordon Bell 363; Yulia Belousova 467b; Alexey Belyaev 290tr; Benkrut 310bl; Alexander Bezmolitvennyy 13cr; Blitzkoenig 357bl, 381br, 515cr; Bographics 468clb; Boris Breytman 252bl; Theodor Bunica 309br; Duncan Campbell 407cla; Marco Dal Canto 398b; Francesco Carniani 191cra; Stefano Carocci 311tl; Joaquin Ossorio Castillo 171tl; Ekaterina Chernenko 68br; Galina Chet 30-31t; Christophefaugere 101tl; Claudiodivizia 25tr, 151tl, 187clb, 191tr; Sorin Colac 307bc; Claudio Giovanni Colombo 394b; Andrea Comari 48-9; Copora 60cr; Cosmin - Constantin Sava 22-3t; Alessandro Cristiano 191cr, 197cra; Daliu80 389t; Dogofg 147crb; Sergey Dzyuba 158t, 211t; Eddygaleotti 513bl; Emicristea 74-5b, 279bl, 296-7b; Enzodebe 115cl, 422cla; Ermess 390tl, 409bl, 411b, 412t, 437bl; F11photo 60t; Giovanni Gagliardi 498t; Veronika Galkina 355b; Gianluigibec 532-3b; Ruslan Gilmanshin 242cla; Giuseppemasci 436tl, 481tr; Viktor Gladkov

161bc; Rostislav Glinsky 198b; Golasza 489t; Kaspars Grinvalds 65cl; Marco Guidi 388bl; Zbigniew Guzowski 66-7t; Sven Hansche 112t; Eliane Haykal 87br; Francesco Riccardo Iacomino 8cl; Ilongplay 392bl; Inavanhateren 133cla; InesPorada 31ca; Gabriela Insuratelu 474bl; Mihail Ivanov 98b; Ivansmuk 120bl; Ixuskmitl 374t; Wieslaw Jarek 112bc, 298br; Javarman 94bl; Jorisvo 431clb; Thomas Jurkowski 154-155; Kasto80 127crb, 191br; Nikolai Korzhov 134t; Krivinis 512t; Fabio Lamanna 24b; Laudibi 457r; Iuliia Lavrinenko 534-5; Ethan Le 19tr; Lejoch 391tr; Lindom 98tr; Loren Image 135tc; Luca Lorenzelli 32-3t, 140tc, 194t, 195tc; Lorenzobovi 370tl; Anna Lurye 514-5t; Luxerendering 306b; Mirko Macari 191crb; Madrabothair 370tr; Marcorubino 517br; Marinv 227t, 254-5; Alberto Masnovo 37tr; Ewa Mazur 138tl; Aliaksandr Mazurkevich 8clb; Antony Mcaulay 242c; Mfron 522bl; Mikolaj64 475t; Milacroft 511tr; Hercules Milas 75bl; Mineria6 338bc; Minnystock 10-1b, 70b, 176-177b, 213b, 370-1c, 404cra; Martin Molcan 372-3t, 524bl, 530-1t; Sergey Mostovoy 172-3t; Nejron 261tr; Neneo 32tc, 45br; Andrey Omelyanchuk 77t, 77cra, 244-5b; Dmitry Ometsinsky 92tl; Michelangelo Oprandi 36tl; Anna Pakutina 376cra; Ralph Paprzycki 109tl; Pavlinec 519tr; Roberto Pecci 533tl; William Perry 72crb, 78cla, 247tr, 286bl; Perseomedusa 193br; Sergey Peterman 37br; Photogolfer 22bl, 289bl, 292-3, 361b, 456bl; Enrico Della Pietra 318, 466bl, 468cra, 496-7t; Progosu81 483tr; Dzianis Rabtsevich 466-7t; Rigmanyi 382t; Fabrizio Robba 24tr; M. Rohana 375br; Valerio Rosati 264bl, 319br; Rosshelen 221bl, 424-5; Rudi1976 53t, 102-3, 420-1t; Rusel1981 252t; Koba Samurkasov 360-1t; Marco Saracco 166-7t, 190-1t, 407t; Sborisov 372bl, 396t; Scaliger 78-9b, 84b, 93cl, 93b, 148bl, 150-1t, 246-7t, 251tl, 308br; Schlenger86 132b; Eleonora Scordo 187tr; Jozef Sedmak 81cr, 97t, 253br, 278bc, 304b; Olena Serditova 108t; Sikeyplus 189cr; Serghei Starus 169br; Stefanocar75 198tc; Stevanzz 377, 391b, 393tr, 399t; Alessandro Antonio Storniolo 17cla; Kanokrat Tawokhat 452cra; Tcantlon 471bl; Theripper 483cra; Thevirex 525t; Timedreamer 353tl; Toldiu74 31br; Alexander Tolstykh 418-9t; Tomas1111 8-9b; Anibal Trejo 347br; Lev Tsimbler 276crb; Tupungato 262tl; Gian Marco Valente 434bl; Stefano Valeri 299t, 330tl; Vdvtut 266bc; Alvaro German Vilela 461br; Volodymyr Vyshnivetskyy 378t; Wallaceweeks 350-1; Hilda Weges 60cl; Xantana 196-7b; Xbrchx 168t; Natalia Zakharova 111bl; Andreas Zerndl 504t, 508; Znm 291cr; Zoom-zoom 17tr.

Enoteca Pinchiorri: Gianni Ugolini 341cr

Fondazione Musei Civici di Venezia: 70clb, 79tr.

Getty Images: AFP / Alberto Pizzoli 45tr, 344bl; AGF / Contributor 206-7b; Alinari Archives 315tc; Ayhan Altun 365tl; alxpin 431bl; Rob Atkins 42tl; Atlantide Phototravel 71cra; Andrew Bain 483crb; Salvator Barki 429bc; Bloomberg / Chris Warde Jones 236br; Lutz Bongarts 45bl; Marco Bottigelli 52c, 54cb, 56-7, 162-3; De Agostini 21cl, 72cb; DEA / Biblioteca Ambrosiana 62tr, 261ca, / G. Cigolini 439br, / G. Nimatallah 23b, 520bl, / G. Dagli Orti 510br, / L. Romano 488bl,/ V. Prozzi 315br; Sofie Delauw 26-7t; DigitalVision / Kathrin Ziegler 232tl; Dosfotos 242bl; EyeEm / Jerry Hoekstra 515br, / Devis Marchetto 516tr, / Antonio Sangermano 428t; Fine Art 345bl; Mark Harris 23cla; Norbert Eisele-Hein 133br; Heritage Images 43tr, 153cr,

297tc; Francesco Riccardo Iacomino 440-1; Italian School 42bc; Omar Kamel 484-5t; Dmitri Kessel 289crb; Keystone-France 44br, 45cra; Leemage / Contributor 159tc; Moment / Valentino Grieco 82-3t, / Harald Nachtmann 226c, 238-9, / visionandimagination.com 99t; Mondadori Portfolio 95br, 345cr, / Contributor 151br; NurPhoto / Oscar Gonzalez 146bl; Photo Josse / Leemage 44-5t; Popperfoto / Bob Thomas 44bl; Andrea Pucci 326tl; Vittoriano Rastelli 293br; REDA&CO 106crb; Roberto Serra - Iguana Press 38bl; Slow Images 230cl; Ekaterina Smirnova 88bc; soblue.weina@gmail. com 344-5t; Sylvain Sonnet 69cla; Laszlo Szirtesi 261cr; ullstein bild Dtl. 44tl, 453cra; Universal Images Group 72clb, 294br, / Jumping Rocks 299bl; Guy Vanderelst 518tr; Eric Vandeville 248cr.

iStockphoto.com: agustavop 73; aizram18 331br; AlexPro9500 26tl; Alfaproxima 124b; alle12 184crb; Alphotographic 72cra; alxpin 218c, 222; Anna Kolesnikova 536bl; ArtMarie 444c, 448-9, 455t; bdsklo 207tr; belenox 230t; benedek 266-7t; bennymarty 222-3; bernotto 432t; binabina 171cla; Javier GarcÂa Blanco 60br; bluejayphoto 2 8bl, 62-3b, 116t; boggy22 41cla; borchee 342-3t, chang 10clb; Charles03 178b; ChiccoDodiFC 125tr; Creativaimage 30bl; dade80 419tr; deimagine 148br; edella 469; Ekspansio 395tr; eugenesergeev 33b; EunikaSopotnicka 480t; Fabrizio_Esposito 26cra; fazon1 227bl, 268-9; Flory 41br; FooTToo 438-9t; Francesco Cantone 263br; frankix 383t; gaffera 397cr; gameover2012 127b; Garsya 204-5t; georgeclerk 10ca, 287cla; Giacomomo 122-3b; Gim42 12clb; GitoTrevisan 39br, 106t, 120-1t; Givaga 89b; holgs 18tl; InnaFelker 371tr; ipag 54tl, 142-3; izanbar 467cla; KavalenkavaVolha 259clb; kenex 539tl; kurmyshov 244cr; Ladiras 175br; LightFieldStudios 234b; lillisphotography 275cr; Marcus Lindstrom 63cl; lkonya 18-9t; Mableen 184t; Marco Saracco 199t; MasterLu 236-7t; MatteoCozzi 460; mikolajn 472t; miralex 148-9; mrtom-uk 29cb; Nastasic 277bc; nejdetduzen 260cla; nicolamargaret 16-7cra; NiseriN 214-5; outcast85 487b; pabloborca 276bl; peeterv 506b; piola666 39c, 327b; Poike 494-5t; QQ7 55bl, 200-201; rararororo 234tr; Remedios 53bl, 128-129; rez-art 27crb; RolfSt 119cr; RomanBabakin 18-9cra; Romaoslo 228cb, 248cra, 278t, 300-1, 506-7t; RossHelen 16tl, 26b; sandrixroma 265tr; Massimo Santi 36b; SerrNovik 336t; sphraner 123tr; spooh 325tr; StevanZZ 208t; taratata 386-7t; TatyanaGl 287cr; tomazl 13br; TommasoT 106bl; TommL 146-7t; treeffe 422-3b; ultramarinfoto 132-3t; undefined undefined 27cl; ValerioMei 482-3b; ventdusud 21tr; WEKWEK 246br; Wicki58 106cr; Zolga_F 65tr; ZU_09 277clb, 287tc.

La Biennale di Venezia: Giorgio Zucchiatti 38br

Museo MADRE, Naples: 454bl.

Museo Poldi Pezzoli, Milan: Walter Gumiero 156br; / Piero del Pollaiolo *Portrait of a Young Woman*, 56tl.

Museo Teatrale alla Scala: 157t.

Picfair.com: Turzo Almerindo 494bc.

Robert Harding Picture Library: Neale Clark 228tl, 282-3; Marco Cristofori 229, 312-3; Christian Goupi 468br; Ingolf Pompe 184cl, 184cr; Matthew Williarns-Ellis 509cla, 510-1t; Walter Zerla 55t, 180-1.

Photo Scala, Florence: courtesy of the Ministero Beni e Att. Culturali e del Turismo 384cl, 384clb, 384cb, 384bl; DeAgostini Picture Library 155cr; Mauro Ranzani 155clb, 171br.

SuperStock: 4X5 Collection 115cb, 115br; age fotostock / Marco Brivio 90cl, 171cra, / Funkystock 230cr, 452bl, / Phil Robinson 40bl, / Ivan Vdovin 192bl; AGF / Smith Mark Edward 90-1b; The Art Archive 44cr; Peter Barritt 88tr; ClickAlps / Mauritius 497br; DeAgostini 40t, 41tr, 43cra, 349br; Hemis / Bertrand Rieger 210bl; Iberfoto 42-3t, 43br; imageBROKER / Barbara Boensch 379bl, / Christian Handl 484bl, / Raimund Kutter 329t, / Michael Nitzschke 358-9b; Prisma / van der Meer Rene 399br; Quint & Lox Limited 42br.

Unsplash: Heidi Kaden / @infinitexplorer 219bl, 332-3.

Front flap images:
500px: Carlo Murenu cra; **AWL Images:** ClickAlps cla; Francesco Iacobelli bl; **Dreamstime.com** Tomas1111 cb; **Getty Images:** Marco Bottigelli t; **Picfair.com:** monti br.

Cover images:
Front & Spine: **Dreamstime.com:** Minnystock.
Back: **Dreamstime.com:** Francesco Riccardo Iacomino cl; Minnystock b; **iStockphoto.com:** ipag c, QQ7 tr.

For further information see: www.dkimages.com

Cartographic Data:
Lovell Johns Ltd.

Illustrators Stephen Conlin, Donati Giudici Associati srl, Stephen Gyapay, Roger Hutchins, Maltings Partnership, Simon Roulstone, Paul Weston, John Woodcock, Andrea Corbella, Richard Draper, Kevin Jones Associates, Chris Orr and Associates, Robbie Polley, Simon Roulstone, Martin Woodward

This edition updated by
Contributors Cristina Dainotto, Toni DeBella, Carol King, Daniel Mosseri
Senior Editor Alison McGill
Senior Designer Vinita Venugopal
Project Editors Dipika Dasgupta, Rebecca Flynn
Project Art Editor Bharti Karakoti
Editor Kanika Praharaj
Picture Research Coordinator Sumita Khatwani
Assistant Picture Research Administrator Vagisha Pushp
Jacket Coordinator Bella Talbot
Jacket Designers Bess Daly, Ben Hinks
Senior Cartographic Editor Mohammad Hassan
Cartography Manager Suresh Kumar
DTP Designers Rohit Rojal, Tanveer Abbas Zaidi
Senior Production Editor Jason Little
Production Controller Rebecca Parton
Deputy Managing Editor Beverly Smart
Managing Editors Shikha Kulkarni, Hollie Teague
Managing Art Editors Bess Daly, Priyanka Thakur
Art Director Maxine Pedliham
Publishing Director Georgina Dee

First edition 1996
Published in Great Britain by Dorling Kindersley Limited, DK, One Embassy Gardens, 8 Viaduct Gardens, London SW11 7BW

Published in the United States by DK Publishing, 1450 Broadway, Suite 801, New York, NY 10018

Copyright © 1996, 2021 Dorling Kindersley Limited
A Penguin Random House Company
21 22 23 24 10 9 8 7 6 5 4 3 2 1

A CIP catalogue record for this book is available from the British Library.

A catalogue record for this book is available from the Library of Congress.

ISSN: 1542-1554

ISBN: 978-0-2415-0978-4

Printed and bound in China.

www.dk.com

A NOTE FROM DK EYEWITNESS

The rapid rate at which the world is changing is constantly keeping the DK Eyewitness team on our toes. While we've worked hard to ensure that this edition of Italy is accurate and up-to-date, we know that opening hours alter, standards shift, prices fluctuate, places close and new ones pop up in their stead. So, if you notice we've got something wrong or left something out, we want to hear about it. Please get in touch at travelguides@dk.com